Maths
The Basics
3rd Edition

June Haighton
Deborah Holder
Veronica Thomas

OXFORD
UNIVERSITY PRESS

Great Clarendon Street, Oxford, OX2 6DP, United Kingdom

Oxford University Press is a department of the University of Oxford. It furthers the University's objective of excellence in research, scholarship, and education by publishing worldwide. Oxford is a registered trade mark of Oxford University Press in the UK and in certain other countries

© Oxford University Press 2020

The moral rights of the authors have been asserted

First published in 2020

All rights reserved. No part of this publication may be reproduced, stored in a retrieval system, or transmitted, in any form or by any means, without the prior permission in writing of Oxford University Press, or as expressly permitted by law, by licence or under terms agreed with the appropriate reprographics rights organization. Enquiries concerning reproduction outside the scope of the above should be sent to the Rights Department, Oxford University Press, at the address above.

You must not circulate this work in any other form and you must impose this same condition on any acquirer

British Library Cataloguing in Publication Data
Data available

978-1-38-2005067

10 9 8 7 6 5 4 3 2 1

Paper used in the production of this book is a natural, recyclable product made from wood grown in sustainable forests.
The manufacturing process conforms to the environmental regulations of the country of origin.

Printed in India by Repro India Ltd.

Acknowledgements

The publisher and authors would like to thank the following for permission to use photographs and other copyright material:

Cover illustration by Daniel Frost

All photos © Shutterstock, except: p67: Anatoliy Kosolapov/Alamy Stock Photo; p250(br): Sasa Peric/123RF; p271: Oxford University Press.

p342, Google and the Google logo are registered trademarks of Google LLC, used with permission.

Every effort has been made to contact copyright holders of material reproduced in this book. Any omissions will be rectified in subsequent printings if notice is given to the publisher.

Links to third party websites are provided by Oxford in good faith and for information only. Oxford disclaims any responsibility for the materials contained in any third party website referenced in this work.

Contents

About this book ix

Number

1 Number Value

Numbers up to 1000	1	EL3.N1
Large numbers	4	L1.N1
Positive and negative numbers in practical contexts	6	L1.N2
Compare numbers of any size	7	L2.N1
Chapter Summary	9	

2 Addition and Subtraction

Add and subtract 3-digit numbers	10	EL3.N2
Add and subtract large numbers	16	L1.N1
Add and subtract positive and negative numbers	17	L2.N1, L2.N2
Add and subtract numbers of any size	19	L2.N2
Chapter Summary	20	

3 Multiplication and Division

Multiplication	21	EL3.N4
Multiplication methods	22	EL3.N4
Division	24	EL3.N3
Multiply and divide whole numbers by 10, 100 and 1000	28	L1.N3
Use multiplication and division	32	EL3.N3, EL3.N4, L1.N4
Recognise numerical relationships	33	EL3.N6, L1.N4
Square numbers and indices	34	L1.N6
Multiply and divide large numbers	37	L1.N4
Efficient methods of calculating with numbers of any size	39	L1.N4, L2.N2
Chapter Summary	42	

4 Rounding and Estimation

Approximate and estimate with numbers up to 1000	43	EL3.N5
Approximate and estimate with large numbers	48	L1.N12
Strategies for checking calculations with numbers of any size	52	L2.N2
Chapter Summary	54	

5 Ratio and Proportion

Work with ratio and proportion	55	L1.N17
Calculate with ratios	58	L1.N17, L2.N11
Inverse proportion	65	L2.N11
Chapter Summary	68	

6 Using Algebra

Number patterns and formulae	69	EL3.N6
Use simple formulae	71	L1.N5
Order of operations (BIDMAS)	72	L1.N7, L2.N12
Evaluate algebraic expressions and make substitutions in formulae	73	L2.N3
Chapter Summary	76	

7 Mixed Operations and Calculator Practice

Solve problems	77	EL3.N2, EL3.N3, EL3.N4, EL3.M10
Calculate efficiently	81	EL3.M10
Calculate efficiently with numbers of any size	82	L2.N1, L2.N2
Chapter Summary	84	

8 Fractions

Understand fractions	85	EL3.N7
Equivalent fractions	87	EL3.N7
Compare fractions	91	L1.N8, L2.N7
Mixed numbers and improper fractions	94	L1.N8
Find or estimate fractions	96	EL3.N7
Calculate a fraction of something	97	EL3.N7, L1.N9, L1.N15
One number as a fraction of another	102	L2.N8
Add and subtract fractions	107	L2.N7
Multiply fractions	112	Non-specification content
Divide fractions	113	Non-specification content
Fractions on a calculator	115	L1.N9, L2.N7, L2.N8
Chapter Summary	117	

9 Decimals

Understand decimals in context (up to 2 decimal places)	118	EL3.N8
Write and compare decimals up to 3 decimal places	121	L1.N10
Use a calculator to solve problems	124	EL3.N8
Multiply and divide decimals by 10, 100 and 1000	126	L1.N3
Round decimal numbers and approximate	128	L1.N12, L2.N9

Add and subtract decimals	131	EL3.N8, L1.N11, L1.N15, L2.N10
Decimal sequences	132	EL3.N9
Multiply decimals	134	L1.N11, L2.N10
Divide decimals	135	L1.N11, L2.N10
Chapter Summary	138	

10 Percentages

Understand percentages	139	L1.N13
Find percentages of quantities	140	L1.N14, L2.N5
Equivalent fractions, decimals and percentages	145	L1.N16, L2.N4
Percentage increase and decrease	150	L1.N14, L2.N6
Use a calculator to find percentages	152	L1.N14, L2.N5
Write one number as a percentage of another	155	L2.N5
Calculate the original value after a percentage change	158	L2.N6
Chapter Summary	160	

Measures, Shape and Space

11 Money

Write in pounds (£) and pence	161	EL3.M10
Calculate with money	162	EL3.M10
Round money to the nearest 10p or £1	165	EL3.M11
Discounts in multiples of 5%	167	L1.M19
Simple interest	169	L1.M18
Compound interest	170	L2.M13
Budget with money	173	L2.M13
Calculate using rates of pay	177	L2.M15
Value Added Tax (VAT)	180	L2.M13
Taxes on income	184	L2.M13
Convert between currencies	188	L2.M13
Chapter Summary	191	

12 Time

Read, measure and record time	192	EL3.M12
Use the 12 and 24 hour clock	194	EL3.M13
Units of time	198	L1.M20
Calculate time	199	L1.M20
Use timers	203	EL3.M13, L1.M20
Chapter Summary	206	

13 Length

Understand distance: miles and kilometres	207	EL3.M14, EL3.M15
Measure length in metric units	209	EL3.M14, EL3.M15, L1.M20
Estimate and measure lengths	214	EL3.M14, EL3.M18, L1.M20
Convert between metric lengths	217	EL3.M15, L1.M20
Calculate with metric lengths	219	L1.M20
Use a scale on a plan or map	222	L1.M21, L2.M18
Use ratios on scale drawings	225	L1.M21, L2.M18
Measure length in imperial units	228	EL3.M14, EL3.M18
Convert between imperial lengths	229	L1.M20
Convert between metric and imperial lengths	231	L2.M14
Chapter Summary	234	

14 Weight

Measure weight in metric units	235	EL3.M14, EL3.M16, L1.M20
Choose units and instruments	240	EL3.M18, L1.M20
Convert between metric weights	240	L1.M20
Calculate using metric weights	242	L1.M20
Weigh with metric and imperial units	244	EL3.M14, EL3.M18
Convert between imperial weights	245	L1.M20
Calculate using imperial weights	246	L1.M20
Convert between metric and imperial weights	247	L2.M14
Chapter Summary	249	

15 Capacity

Measure capacity and volume	250	EL3.M14, EL3.M17
Choose units and instruments	254	EL3.M17
Convert between millilitres, litres and centilitres	255	L1.M20
Calculate using metric units of capacity	257	L1.M20
Measure with metric and imperial units of capacity	259	EL3.M14, L1.M20
Convert between imperial units of capacity	260	L1.M20
Calculate capacity and volume using imperial units	261	L1.M20
Convert between metric and imperial measures	262	L2.M14
Chapter Summary	264	

16 Temperature

Measure temperature on the Celsius scale	265	EL3.M14
Temperatures below freezing point	266	L1.N2, L2.N1
Celsius and Fahrenheit	268	EL3.M14
Use formulae to convert temperatures	269	L2.N3
Chapter Summary	270	

17 Shape

Angles	271	EL3.M19, L1.M24, L1.M26
Horizontal, vertical and parallel lines	273	EL3.M20, L2.M22
Two-dimensional (2-D) shapes	275	EL3.M19, L1.M24
Triangles	277	EL3.M19, L1.M24, L1.M26, L2.22
Symmetry	280	EL3.M19, L1.M24
Tessellations	283	L1.M24
Three-dimensional (3-D) shapes	284	EL3.M19
Plans and elevations	285	L1.M25, L2.M18, L2.M20, L2.M21
Chapter Summary	294	

18 Position and Direction

Compass points	295	EL3.M20, L1.M26
Describe positions and give directions	296	EL3.M20, L1.M25
Bearings	298	L1.M26
Positions on maps	300	EL3.M20
Coordinates	301	L2.M19, L2.M22
3-D coordinates	305	L2.M22
Chapter Summary	308	

19 Perimeter, Area and Volume

Perimeter	309	L1.M22, L2.N3, L2.M16
Area	312	L1.M22, L2.N3, L2.M16
Circles	315	L2.M16
Use formulae to find areas of triangles and other shapes	317	L2.M16
Perimeters and areas of composite shapes	318	L2.M16
Nets	321	L1.M25
Surface area	323	L2.M17
Volume of a cuboid	325	L1.M23
Volume of a cylinder	327	L2.M17
Use other formulae to find volumes	328	L2.M17
Solve problems involving 2-D and 3-D shapes	330	L1.M20, L1.M25, L2.M16, L2.M17, L2.M20
Chapter Summary	333	

20 Compound Measures

Calculate using compound measures	334	L2.M15
Chapter Summary	340	

Contents

Handling Information and Data

21 Extracting and Interpreting Information

Information from lists, tables and pictograms	341	EL3.H21
Information from bar charts and line graphs	347	EL3.H21, EL3.H22, L1.H27
Information from pie charts	358	L1.H27
Information from conversion graphs	362	L2.M14
Chapter Summary	364	

22 Collecting and Illustrating Data

Create frequency tables	365	EL3.H21, L1.H28
Represent data in pictograms	367	EL3.H23, L1.H27
Represent data in bar charts and line graphs	368	EL3.H23, L1.H27, L1.H28
Illustrate data using a pie chart	376	L1.H27
Draw and use conversion graphs	378	L2.M14
Choosing a statistical diagram	380	L1.H27, L1.H28
Chapter Summary	383	

23 Averages and Range

Find the mean	384	L1.H29, L2.H24, L2.H25
Find the mode and the median	389	L2.H23, L2.H25
Find the range	393	L1.H29, L2.H25
Compare data sets	397	L2.H25
Chapter Summary	400	

24 Scatter Diagrams

Scatter diagrams and correlation	401	L2.H28
Chapter Summary	407	

25 Probability

Compare the likelihood of events	408	L1.H30, L1.H31
Use fractions to measure probability	409	L1.H30, L1.H31, L2.H27
Write probabilities as decimals and percentages	411	L2.H27
Combined events	413	L2.H26
Chapter Summary	417	

Answers 418
Index 470

About this book

This book is divided into the three main sections of the functional skills curriculum:

- Number
- Measures, Shape and Space
- Handling Information and Data

The content covers everything you need to know for the Functional Skills Mathematics qualification at Entry Level 3 (EL3), Level 1 (L1), and Level 2 (L2). The book can be used with any exam board, including Pearson Edexcel and City & Guilds.

All content in this book is clearly labelled with the icons below to show the level of difficulty. Some topics include more than one level of work. These topics begin with work at the lowest level (usually EL3) and progress to the higher levels.

The curriculum elements covered in each topic are given in the contents list and at the beginning of each topic.

Step-by-step solutions are available online at
http://www.oxfordsecondary.com/maths-the-basics

How to use this book

This depends on what you are aiming for, but in all cases it is recommended that you work through the levels you need, starting with Entry Level 3. If you already have some knowledge of a topic you may be able to miss out some parts, but always look through the work to make sure.

Is your main aim to improve your understanding of a particular mathematical topic?

If so, look for the topic in the contents list and work through from Entry Level 3 to the level you need.

Is your main aim to prepare for a Functional Mathematics qualification?

Functional Mathematics can be taken at all of the levels included in this book – the higher the level, the more difficult the real-life problems that you will be asked to solve.

If you are preparing for a qualification at Entry Level 3, work through all the topics labelled EL3. For Level 1 work through all the topics labelled EL3 and L1. For Level 2 work through all of the topics in this book.

MyMaths.co.uk

Throughout the book four-digit MyMaths codes are provided allowing you to link directly to related lessons and homeworks on the www.mymaths.co.uk website. Just log into MyMaths and type the four digit code into the search bar. MyMaths provides extra practice and support and may help you see the topic from a different perspective. Your institution will need to have an active subscription in order for you to log in. If you are unsure, ask your teacher.

Number 1 Number Value

Numbers up to 1000
Specification reference: EL3.N1

A. Place value

There are three hundred and sixty-five days in a year.

The number 365 has   3   **H**undreds
                     6   **T**ens
                     5   **U**nits

```
H T U
3 0 0
  6 0
    5
-----
3 6 5
```
→ 3 Hundreds, 6 Tens and 5 Units

The 3, 6 and 5 are called digits.

Practice

1. Write the following numbers in figures.

   Example: Six hundred and seventy

   ```
   H T U
   6 7 0
   ```

   Use columns like this on squared paper.

   a. One hundred and sixty-five
   b. Fifty-three
   c. Two hundred and twelve
   d. Four hundred and three
   e. Nine hundred and ninety
   f. Sixty-eight
   g. Eight hundred and twenty
   h. Seven
   i. Two hundred and seventeen
   j. Nine hundred and two

2. Write the following numbers in words. Then write the value of each digit.

   Example: 245 is **two hundred and forty-five**
              245 has **2 hundreds, 4 tens, 5 units**.

   a. H T U 2 3 6
   b. H T U 1 0 5
   c. H T U 6 1 7
   d. H T U   8 2
   e. H T U 7 5 0
   f. H T U 5 0 0
   g. H T U 1 2 3
   h. H T U   9 0
   i. H T U 9 3 8
   j. H T U 3 4 4

3. Copy this table.

Planet	Number of days to go round the sun	Planet	Approximate number of years to go round the sun
Earth		Jupiter	
Mercury		Neptune	
Mars		Saturn	
Venus		Uranus	

MyMaths 1216 SEARCH

Number

Read the information below.

Write the coloured numbers as figures in your table.

> It takes the **Earth** three hundred and sixty-five **days** to go round the sun.
>
> It takes **Mercury** just eighty-eight days, **Mars** six hundred and eighty-seven days and **Venus** nearly two hundred and twenty-five days.
>
> The other planets take much longer.
>
> **Jupiter** takes nearly twelve years.
>
> **Neptune** takes nearly one hundred and sixty-five years, **Saturn** nearly thirty years and **Uranus** eighty-four years.

4. List the planets in order according to how long they take to go round the sun. Start with the planet that takes the **least** time.

5. This table shows the times for five dwarf planets to go around the sun.

Ceres	Eris	Haumea	Makemake	Pluto
5 years	557 years	285 years	310 years	248 years

Write each time in words.

 Activity

Pick three **different** digits. (Choose from 0, 1, 2, 3, 4, 5, 6, 7, 8, 9.)
See how many different numbers you can make from them.

Put the numbers you have made in order, starting with the **smallest**.

Try this again but with two digits the same and the other one different.

What happens if all of the digits are the same?

Write a rule for making the **largest** possible number with three digits.

Write a rule for making the **smallest** possible number with three digits.

B. Count in 10s

If you add or subtract 10, the Tens digit changes. The Units digit doesn't change.

```
Adding:    9      19     119        Subtracting:  18      58     158
         +10    +10    + 10                      −10     −10    − 10
         ———    ———    ———                      ———     ———    ———
          19     29     129                       8      48     148
```

The Hundreds digit may change.

Number Value

It changes if adding 10 takes you up into the **H**undred above.

$$\begin{array}{r}91\\+\ 10\\\hline 101\end{array}\qquad\begin{array}{r}99\\+\ 10\\\hline 109\end{array}\qquad\begin{array}{r}191\\+\ 10\\\hline 201\end{array}\qquad\begin{array}{r}399\\+\ 10\\\hline 409\end{array}$$

It changes if subtracting 10 takes you down into the **H**undred below.

$$\begin{array}{r}106\\-\ 10\\\hline 96\end{array}\qquad\begin{array}{r}103\\-\ 10\\\hline 93\end{array}\qquad\begin{array}{r}206\\-\ 10\\\hline 196\end{array}\qquad\begin{array}{r}503\\-\ 10\\\hline 493\end{array}$$

Practice

1. Copy each list. Fill in the missing numbers by adding 10

a. | 11 | 21 | 31 | | 51 | 61 | 71 | 81 | | 101 | 111 | | 131 | 141 |

b. | 441 | 451 | | 471 | 481 | 491 | | 511 | 521 | | 541 | 551 | 561 | |

c. | 383 | 393 | | 413 | 423 | 433 | | 453 | 463 | 473 | | 493 | 503 | |

2. Copy each list. Fill in the missing numbers by subtracting 10

a. | 195 | 185 | 175 | | 155 | 145 | 135 | | 115 | 105 | 95 | | 75 | 65 |

b. | 596 | 586 | | 566 | 556 | | 536 | 526 | 516 | | 496 | 486 | 476 | |

c. | 139 | 129 | | 109 | | 89 | 79 | 69 | 59 | | 39 | 29 | 19 | |

C. Count in 100s

If you add or subtract 100, the **H**undreds digit changes. The **T**ens and **U**nits digits don't change.

Adding: $\begin{array}{r}234\\+100\\\hline 334\end{array}$ Subtracting: $\begin{array}{r}586\\-100\\\hline 486\end{array}$

Practice

1. Copy each list. Fill in the missing numbers by adding 100

a. | 25 | 125 | | 325 | 425 | | 625 | | 825 | |

b. | 63 | | 263 | | 463 | 563 | | 763 | | 963 |

2. Copy each list. Fill in the missing numbers by subtracting 100

a. | 982 | 882 | | 682 | | 482 | 382 | | 182 | 82 |

b. | 907 | | 707 | | 507 | 407 | | 207 | 107 | |

Number

Large numbers

Specification reference **L1.N1**

A. Place value

In 1851 the population of London was about two million, six hundred and eighty-five thousand.

population 2 685 000

The number 2 685 000 has:

2	**M**illions	2 000 000
6	**Hund**red **Th**ousands	600 000
8	**Ten Th**ousands	80 000
5	**Th**ousands	5 000
0	**H**undreds	000
0	**T**ens	00
0	**U**nits	0
		2 685 000

To read large numbers split the digits into groups of three (starting at the end).

> **Example**   7 302 064 is:
>
>   7   302   064
> seven million,   three hundred and two thousand   and sixty-four
> and
>
> **3 020 500 is:**
> three million, twenty thousand, five hundred.

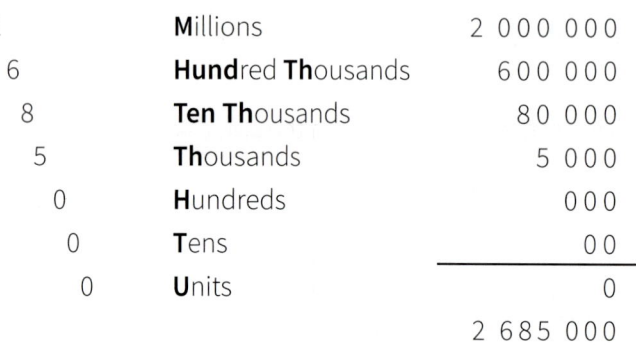

Practice

1. Copy the headings onto squared paper.

   Write these numbers as figures in the correct columns.

   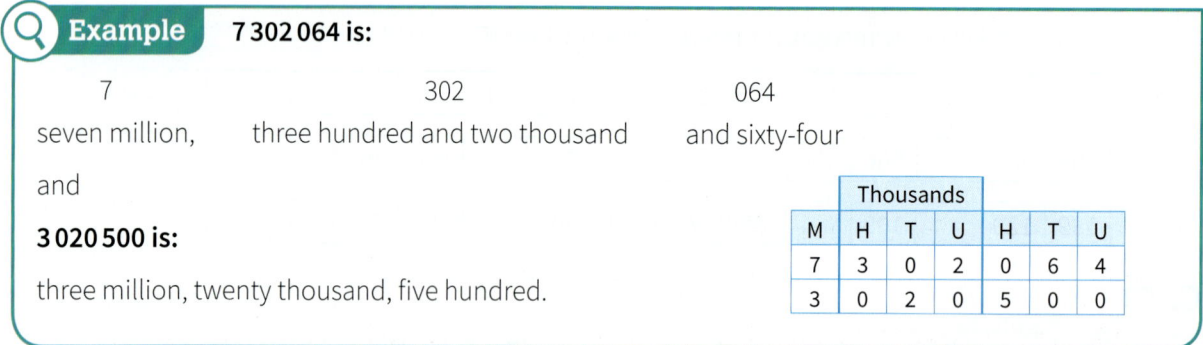

   a. Two thousand
   b. Thirty-two thousand
   c. One hundred and sixty-five thousand, two hundred
   d. One hundred and nine thousand, eight hundred and seventy
   e. Four million, two hundred thousand
   f. Ninety thousand, seven hundred and fifty
   g. Eight thousand and twenty-five
   h. One hundred and nineteen thousand
   i. Six million, two hundred and ninety-nine thousand
   j. Nine million, three hundred and six

2. Write each number in words.

	M	H	T	U	H	T	U
			Thousands				
a.			4	5	0	0	0
b.		3	7	5	0	0	0
c.	6	7	0	0	0	0	0
d.		2	0	5	0	0	0
e.			7	0	7	5	0
f.	1	2	0	0	0	0	0

	M	H	T	U	H	T	U
			Thousands				
g.				5	0	6	5
h.			2	0	3	0	6
i.			4	0	3	5	2
j.	9	6	7	0	0	8	0
k.	5	0	9	0	4	0	0
l.	3	5	0	3	2	4	1

3. List the numbers in question **2** in order of size, starting with the **smallest**.

4. a. Copy the table.
   b. Read the information below.
      Write the coloured numbers as figures in your table.

Year	Estimated population of London
1100	
1300	
1500	
1600	
1801	
1851	
1939	
2000	

In the year **1100** the population of London was about twenty-five thousand.

By **2000** it was about seven million, six hundred and forty thousand.

Between these two dates the population both increased and decreased.

By **1300** the population could have been as large as one hundred thousand.

Due to the black death it fell to about fifty thousand by **1500**.

Research shows that by **1600** the population had reached two hundred thousand.

The first census in **1801** recorded a population of one million, one hundred and seventeen thousand.

The population more than doubled by **1851** reaching two million, six hundred and eighty-five thousand.

At the beginning of the Second World War in **1939** London's population reached eight million, seven hundred thousand.

   c. Use your table to answer the following questions.
      i. Between which years did the population fall?
      ii. In which year was the population the highest?

Number

B. Greater than > and less than <

Symbols can be used to show that one number is greater (larger) than or less (smaller) than another.

> means **greater than**   < means **less than**

5 is greater than 4   This can be written as 5 > 4

100 is greater than 50   This can be written as 100 > 50

6 is less than 9   This can be written as 6 < 9

25 is less than 50   This can be written as 25 < 50

 **Key point**
The larger number always goes at the open end of the symbol.

Practice

1. Rewrite each of these using < or >
   a. 1 is less than 3
   b. 7 is greater than 5
   c. 9 is greater than 4
   d. 0 is less than 1

2. Copy these. Write < or > between each pair of numbers.
   a. 2   8
   b. 6   1
   c. 18   13
   d. 19   23
   e. 99   101
   f. 170   159

3. Rewrite each of these using < or >
   a. 269 is less than 270
   b. 15 000 is greater than 2500
   c. 9900 is greater than 7500
   d. 50 000 is less than 75 000
   e. 9 is less than 900
   f. 10 500 is greater than 10 499
   g. 99 900 is less than 100 000
   h. 4 010 000 is greater than 4 009 999

Positive and negative numbers in practical contexts

Specification reference L1.N2

 Level 1

Positive numbers are **greater than 0**

Negative numbers are **less than 0**

Negative numbers are sometimes used to describe temperature.

For example, −2 °C is 2 degrees **colder** than 0 °C.

Note that −6 °C is **colder** than −2 °C.

Negative numbers are also used to describe overdrawn bank accounts.

For example, a balance of −£25 means that £25 is **owed** to the bank.

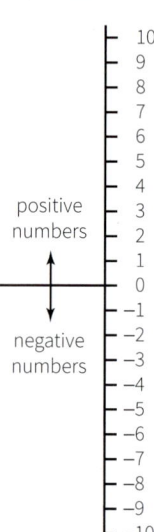

MyMaths 1776 SEARCH

Practice

1. In each part, put the temperatures in order.
   Start with the **coldest**.
   a. −5°C   8°C   4°C   0°C   −2°C   1°C
   b. 10°C   −8°C   −10°C   9°C   −7°C   6°C
   c. 0°C   12°C   −15°C   20°C   −18°C   −10°C

2. A supermarket chain needs to store food at the following temperatures to meet health and safety regulations:

Chilled food	Between 0°C and 8°C
Frozen vegetables	−18°C or lower
Ice cream	−20°C or lower

   The temperatures below were recorded at different supermarkets.
   Write the temperatures that do not meet health and safety regulations.
   a. Chilled food   5°C   9°C   7°C   −1°C   3°C   2°C
   b. Frozen vegetables   −20°C   −16°C   −19°C   −17°C   −21°C   −14°C
   c. Ice cream   −18°C   −21°C   −19°C   −23°C   −17°C   −24°C

3. Four bank accounts have these balances:

Account name	M Patel	J Robinson	R Dale	C Yeung
Balance (£)	225	−365	−50	75

   a. Which account has the most money in it?
   b. Which account is the most overdrawn?

4. An account holder has arranged an overdraft of £200 with his bank. If he owes any more than this he has to pay a fee. When the balance of the account is zero the account holder makes two payments with his debit card for £125 and £100
   Will he have to pay a fee?

Compare numbers of any size

Specification reference **L2.N1**

One **billion** is one thousand million.
In figures **1 billion = 1 000 000 000**

The distance from the Earth to the sun is about 150 billion metres (150 000 000 000 m).

Four billion, five hundred and thirty million is written like this:

B	Millions			Thousands					
	H	T	U	H	T	U	H	T	U
4	5	3	0	0	0	0	0	0	0

Number

Very large numbers can be written neatly using decimals.

> ### Example
> 1 500 000 (one million, five hundred thousand) is **1.5 million**.
>
> 3 450 000 000 (three billion, four hundred and fifty million) is **3.45 billion**.
>
> (Put the decimal point after the whole millions or billions.)

Practice

1. Use the headings of the table from the previous page to write these numbers in full.
   - **a.** 2.5 million
   - **b.** 2.56 million
   - **c.** 1.7 billion
   - **d.** 1.85 billion
   - **e.** 30 million
   - **f.** 300 million
   - **g.** 1.3 billion
   - **h.** 0.5 billion
   - **i.** 0.25 million

2. Write these numbers in millions or billions, using decimals where necessary.
   - **a.** 2 500 000
   - **b.** 5 600 000
   - **c.** 4 750 000
   - **d.** 3 800 000 000
   - **e.** 2 950 000 000
   - **f.** 1 050 000 000
   - **g.** 20 000 000
   - **h.** 600 000 000
   - **i.** 34 500 000

3. The table gives the biggest UK EuroMillions Lottery wins from the start up to the year 2018.

   Write each amount in full and put them in order of size, starting with the **largest**.

Year	Largest win
2010	£113 million
2011	£161.7 million
2012	£148.7 million
2018	£121.3 million

   Data source: euro-millions.com

4. A company's turnover (the amount of business it does) and profit (the amount of money it makes) are often large numbers.

   A **negative profit** means the company made a **loss**.

   Use the table to answer the questions.
   - **a.** Which company had:
     - **i.** the greatest turnover
     - **ii.** the smallest turnover
     - **iii.** the greatest profit?
   - **b. i.** Which companies made a loss?
     - **ii.** Which company made the greatest loss?

Company	Turnover (£)	Profit (£)
A	2.6 billion	1.5 million
B	12 billion	45.6 million
C	20 million	−99 000
D	45 million	60 000
E	8 billion	−1.5 million
F	1.2 billion	125 000
G	0.9 billion	−25 000

Chapter Summary
1 Number Value

- Numbers with three digits have three columns: **H**undreds, **T**ens, **U**nits.
- Adding 10 to a number changes the tens column.
- Adding 100 to a number changes the hundreds column.

- Numbers with more than three digits have additional place names. For a seven-digit number, there are seven columns:
  Millions, **H**undred **Th**ousands, **T**en **Th**ousands, **Th**ousands, **H**undreds, **T**ens, **U**nits.
- > is used to show a number is larger (or more than) another number.
- < is used to show a number is smaller (or less than) another number.
- Larger numbers are always at the open end of the inequality symbols (<, >).
- Positive numbers are greater than 0 (> 0).
- Negative numbers are smaller than 0 (< 0).
- Negative numbers can be used for temperature or bank accounts that are overdrawn.

- 1 billion is one thousand million (1 000 000 000).
- You can write large numbers (such as millions or billions) using decimals, for example 1 500 000 = 1.5 million.

Number 2 Addition and Subtraction

Add and subtract 3-digit numbers

Specification reference **EL3.N2**

A. Add in columns

Line up the numbers in columns to add **U**nits to **U**nits, **T**ens to **T**ens, etc.

Example 332 + 265

```
  H T U
  3 3 2
+ 2 6 5
  5 9 7
```

Add the **U**nits, then the **T**ens, then the **H**undreds.

Key point
Words for adding: total, altogether, sum, plus

If the **U**nits total is 10 or more, carry **10** to the **T**ens column as **1 Ten** to be added to the other **T**ens.

Example 336 + 45

```
  H T U
  3 3 6
+   4 5
  3 8 1
    1
```

6 + 5 = 11
so 1 **T**en is carried over to the **T**ens column.
Then 3 + 4 + 1 makes a total of 8 in the **T**ens column.

Key point
It doesn't matter where you put the number you carry. Some people write it at the top and some at the bottom. Take care to add it to the correct column.

If the total of the **T**ens column is 10 or more, carry **10 Tens** to the Hundreds column as **1 Hundred**.

Example 765 + 165

```
  H T U
  7 6 5
+ 1 6 5
  9 3 0
  1 1
```

5 + 5 = 10 so 1 **T**en is carried over to the **T**ens column

Then 6 + 6 + 1 makes a total of 13 in the **T**ens column.

3 **T**ens go in the **T**ens column and 1 **H**undred (10 **T**ens) is carried over to the **H**undreds column and added to the 7 and 1

10

MyMaths 1020, 1028, 1986 SEARCH

Addition and Subtraction

Practice

1. Copy and complete these.

a. 234 + 145		**b.** 530 + 249		**c.** 403 + 93		**d.** 188 + 301	
e. 415 + 365		**f.** 528 + 144		**g.** 269 + 125		**h.** 458 + 329	
i. 160 + 340		**j.** 193 + 125		**k.** 675 + 271		**l.** 194 + 111	
m. 199 + 201		**n.** 834 + 97		**o.** 363 + 258		**p.** 255 + 355	

You can add more than two numbers. Line them all up in columns.

Example

476 men, 195 women and 72 children attend a football match.

How many people is this altogether?

In the **T**ens column:

7 + 9 + 7 + 1 = 24

Put 4 in the **T**ens column

Carry the 2

Add 4 + 1 + 2 in the **H**undreds column.

```
    4 7 6
    1 9 5
  +   7 2
  -------
    7 4 3
    2 1
```

In the **U**nits column:

6 + 5 + 2 = 13

Put 3 here.

Carry 1 **T**en.

Total

= **743 people**

2. Line up the **H**undreds, **T**ens and **U**nits in columns, then add the numbers.

    a. 890 + 76 + 23   **b.** 99 + 109 + 264   **c.** 189 + 7 + 45

3. An insurance company has 258 full-time employees and 83 part-time employees. How many employees does it have altogether?

4. A school office manager photocopies a letter for every child. There are 208 boys and 232 girls in the school. How many photocopies are needed?

5. A lorry travels 162 miles from Dover to Peterborough, then 188 miles from Peterborough to Liverpool. How far does the lorry travel altogether?

6. In a stocktake, shop staff count 42 phone cases on display and 440 in the stock room. How many phone cases are there altogether?

Number

7. A customer buys a computer for £699, a scanner for £89 and a dust cover for £7
   How much does the customer pay altogether?

8. A holiday company charges £879 for a flight and accommodation, plus a £9 booking fee and £38 for insurance. What is the total cost of the holiday?

9. A swimming pool sells 45 adult tickets, 162 child tickets and 8 senior tickets in an afternoon. How many tickets is this altogether?

Now use a calculator to check your answers.

B. Add in your head

Examples

63 + 24 — Add the **T**ens and **U**nits separately in your head.
6 + 2 = **8**, 3 + 4 = **7** giving **87**

253 + 145 — Add the **H**undreds, **T**ens and **U**nits separately.
2 + 1 = **3**, 5 + 4 = **9**, 3 + 5 = **8**, giving **398**

Try different methods.

71 + 27 — Count on in **T**ens, then add the **U**nits:

71 → 81 → 91 → 98
+10 +10 +7

27 = 10 + 10 + 7

234 + 45 — 234 → 244 → 254 → 264 → 274 → 279
+10 +10 +10 +10 +5

45 = 10 + 10 + 10 + 10 + 5

156 + 45 — Break up the number to be added. Here break 45 into **40**, **4** and **1**:
156 + **40** = 196   + **4** = 200   + **1** = **201**

199 + 76 — Round to a near number (here 200) then adjust the answer:
200 + 76 = 276 then subtract 1 = **275**

Practice

Try different methods to add these.

1. a. 35 + 22   b. 41 + 16   c. 32 + 37   d. 29 + 14
    e. 57 + 15   f. 38 + 25   g. 49 + 36   h. 19 + 79

2. a. 216 + 25   b. 159 + 22   c. 199 + 199   d. 154 + 233
    e. 145 + 63   f. 129 + 56   g. 250 + 156   h. 123 + 123
    i. 206 + 156   j. 149 + 152   k. 312 + 256   l. 209 + 329
    m. 515 + 59   n. 267 + 104   o. 311 + 190   p. 297 + 196

C. Subtract in columns

Line up the numbers so **U**nits are subtracted from **U**nits, **T**ens from **T**ens, etc.

Example 365 − 45

```
  H T U
  3 6 5
−   4 5
  ─────
  3 2 0
```

Subtract the **U**nits, then the **T**ens and then the **H**undreds.

 Key point

Words for subtracting: take away, difference, minus

Sometimes changes are needed to make subtracting possible.

Method 1

Example 382 − 165

```
  H T U
    7 1
  3 8̷ 2̷
− 1 6 5
  ─────
  2 1 7
```

Look at the **U**nits. You cannot subtract 5 from 2

So take one 10 from the **T**ens column and put it with the 2 to make 12 **U**nits. This leaves 7 **T**ens.

(The 382 was changed into 3 **H**undreds, 7 **T**ens and 12 **U**nits.)

Example 512 − 291

```
  H T U
  4 1
  5̷ 1 2
− 2 9 1
  ─────
  2 2 1
```

Start with the **U**nits.

Now look at the **T**ens. You cannot subtract 9 from 1

So take a **H**undred and put it in the **T**ens column as 10 **T**ens.

You can now subtract the 9 **T**ens from 11 **T**ens.

(The 512 was changed into 4 **H**undreds, 11 **T**ens and 2 **U**nits.)

Example 306 − 159

```
  H T U
  2 9 1
  3̷ 0̷ 6
− 1 5 9
  ─────
  1 4 7
```

Start with the **U**nits. You cannot subtract 9 from 6

You cannot take a **T**en because there aren't any!

Take a **H**undred. Put it in the **T**ens column as 10 **T**ens.

Now take a **T**en and put it with the 6 to make 16 **U**nits.

This leaves 9 **T**ens.

(The 306 was changed into 2 **H**undreds, 9 **T**ens and 16 **U**nits.)

Number

You can check your answer by adding. This is called using a reverse calculation.

For example if   403   then   226
                − 177   + 177
                  226   403

> **Key point**
> **Adding takes you back to the number you started with.** Adding is the **inverse** of subtracting.

Practice

1. Copy and complete these, then check the answers.

   a.   465   b.   927   c.   763   d.   670
      − 254   − 606   − 563   − 155

   e.   832   f.   276   g.   300   h.   201
      − 523   − 49   − 230   − 170

   i.   518   j.   330   k.   523   l.   721
      − 365   − 131   − 344   − 654

   m.   500   n.   206   o.   901   p.   700
      − 255   − 137   − 602   − 199

   q.   404   r.   600
      − 75   − 301

   > **Hint** Not all of these subtractions need changes.

2. Line up the **H**undreds, **T**ens and **U**nits in columns, then do the subtractions.

   a. 465 − 78   b. 503 − 406   c. 783 − 85

   > **Key point**
   > When subtracting remember to put the larger number at the top.

3. 175 envelopes are used from a box of 500. How many are left in the box?

4. A TV costing £399 is reduced by £75 in a sale. What is the sale price?

5. A company employs 412 office staff and 285 drivers. How many more office staff than drivers does it employ?

6. A travel company charges £529 for a holiday in April and £635 for the same holiday in July. What is the difference in price?

7. The journey by road from London to Edinburgh is 413 miles. I have already driven 250 miles of this journey. How far have I left to go?

£399 reduced by £75

D. Subtract in your head

Examples

Start with the smaller number. *Try different methods.*

53 − 29   Count on to the next **T**en, then count on in **T**ens:

29 + 1 = 30   + 20 = 50   + 3 = 53   **Answer 24**

230 − 175   175 + 5 = 180   + 10 = 190   + 10 = 200   + 30 = 230   **Answer 55**

Subtract a near number, then adjust:

71 − 19   71 − 20 = 51   + 1 = **52**

234 − 45   234 − 44 = 190   − 1 = **189**

199 − 172   Break the number up: 199 − 100 = 99   − 70 = 29   − 2 = **27**

Practice

Try different methods to subtract these.

1. a. 42 − 19   b. 54 − 38   c. 75 − 47   d. 81 − 25
   e. 56 − 37   f. 89 − 47   g. 90 − 53   h. 63 − 29

2. a. 200 − 51   b. 249 − 50   c. 183 − 34   d. 832 − 210
   e. 600 − 199 f. 350 − 145 g. 460 − 254 h. 321 − 122
   i. 459 − 133 j. 650 − 160 k. 679 − 522 l. 880 − 181
   m. 301 − 102 n. 479 − 180 o. 900 − 191 p. 786 − 492

E. Use addition and subtraction

Try these questions. You will need to decide whether to add or subtract.

Look out for words like 'total' and 'altogether'. They usually mean that you need to add.

Words like 'difference' and 'how many more' usually mean that you need to subtract.

Practice

1. Paul spends £56 on a jacket and £38 on trousers. How much does he spend altogether?
2. A pencil costs 29p. A pen costs 82p. What is the difference in price?
3. There are fifty-four people on a coach trip. Thirty-eight of these are children. How many are adults?
4. An estate agent sells forty-three houses and eighteen flats in one month. How many is this in total?
5. Meera earns £576 basic pay and £165 commission. What is her total pay?

Number

6. A laptop costing £430 is reduced by £45 in a sale. What is the sale price?

7. Ahmed uses 148 sheets of paper from a pack of 500. How many sheets of paper are left?

8. A company employs 362 women and 178 men.
   a. Find the total number of employees.
   b. How many more women than men are there?

9. In one day a card shop sells 357 birthday cards, 109 anniversary cards and 216 other cards. How many cards do they sell altogether?

10. Sally has £175 to spend. She buys a dress for £39, a bag for £24 and shoes for £35. How much does she have left?

£45 off!
Usual Price
£430

Now use a calculator to check your answers.

Add and subtract large numbers

Specification reference **L1.N1**

 Level 1

With large numbers take even more care to line up the digits in columns.

Leave a space between the **T**housands and **H**undreds.

Examples

Add 12 535 and 8 036.

```
   1 2  5 3 5
+     8  0 3 6
   ─────────
   2 0  5 7 1
     1    1
```

Subtract 1 659 from 75 000.

```
        4  9 9 1
   7 5̷  0̷ 0̷ 0
 −      1  6 5 9
   ─────────
   7 3  3 4 1
```

Key point

You can check using the inverse operation (that is, doing the reverse), see page 14, or by using a calculator.

Practice

1. Write the numbers in columns before adding or subtracting them. Check each answer.
   a. 50 360 + 1 999
   b. 2 652 + 36 853
   c. 945 + 27 650
   d. 136 500 + 23 999
   e. 3 565 000 + 175 000
   f. 6 500 000 + 27 500
   g. 325 156 − 13 067
   h. 250 000 − 37 525
   i. 1 675 000 − 149 500
   j. 902 856 − 7 580
   k. 500 000 − 136 750
   l. 301 000 − 4 650

2. It is 11 934 miles from London to Melbourne by air. How many miles will you travel if you fly there and back?

3. A couple earn £28 000 and £19 762. What is their joint income?

4. A live concert is also shown on TV. There are 12 000 people at the concert and 1 320 000 people watch it on TV. How many people watch the concert altogether?

MyMaths 1908 SEARCH

Addition and Subtraction

5. The diagram shows the mileage of a car at the start and end of a journey. How far has the car travelled?

   Start: 4 8 5 7 6 End: 5 0 3 1 0

6. In its first year of trading, a company has a turnover of £78 600. In the second year, its turnover is £1 265 000. By how much has the turnover increased?

7. A charity is trying to raise £1 000 000. The charity shop raises £45 650 and donations raise £19 500
   a. Altogether how much money has the charity raised so far?
   b. How much more does the charity need to raise?

8. In an election 659 208 people voted for Party A, 330 629 for Party B and 78 344 for Party C.
   a. How many people voted altogether?
   b. How many more people voted for Party A than either of the other parties?

9. A couple buy a house for £372 900 and sell it for £449 500. They say the difference between the buying and selling price is £77 400. Are they correct?

10. The estimated population of Scotland was 5 062 940 in the year 2000 and 5 438 100 in 2018. What is the increase in the estimated population between the years 2000 and 2018? Check your answer using a reverse calculation.

Add and subtract positive and negative numbers

Specification reference: L2.N1, L2.N2

Level 2

You may have to do calculations with negative numbers.

Examples

1. The temperature is 6 °C. The temperature falls by 9 °C. What is the new temperature?

   Starting from 6 and counting down 9 gives −3

   This is written as $6 - 9 = -3$

   The new temperature is **−3 °C**.

2. The temperature is −4 °C. It rises by 10 °C. What is the new temperature?

   Starting from −4 and counting up 10 gives 6

   $-4 + 10 = 6$

   The new temperature is **6 °C**.

3. The temperature is −4 °C. It falls by 5 °C. What is the new temperature?

   Starting from −4 and counting down 5 gives −9

   $-4 - 5 = -9$

   The new temperature is **−9 °C**.

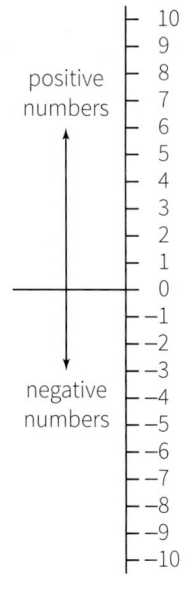

17

Number

Example

The table gives the temperature at midnight in some European cities.

How much warmer is it in London than in Berlin?

City	Temperature (°C)
Berlin	−7.2
Brussels	−2.5
Dublin	2.3
London	−1.8
Paris	3.1

The difference in temperature is

   7.2
− 1.8
   5.4

London is 5.4 °C warmer than Berlin.

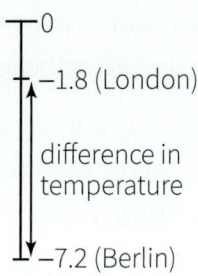

Practice

For each of these questions write the calculation that you do.

1. Copy and complete this table.

Temperature now	Temperature change	New temperature
−3 °C	rises by 8 °C	
−3 °C	falls by 8 °C	
7 °C	falls by 10 °C	
−1 °C	rises by 6 °C	
−2 °C	falls by 7 °C	

2. **a.** A bank account has a balance of £35. £50 is paid from the account. What is the new balance?
   b. A bank account has a balance of −£20. £45 is paid into the account. What is the new balance?
   c. A bank account has a balance of −£5. £35 is paid from the account. What is the new balance?

3. Use the city temperatures given in the second Example above.
   Find the difference in temperature between:

   a. London and Paris
   b. Berlin and Brussels
   c. Dublin and Brussels
   d. London and Brussels.

4. This table shows the highest and lowest recorded temperatures, rounded to the nearest whole number, for England, Northern Ireland, Scotland and Wales (up to the year 2019). Find the difference between the highest and the lowest temperatures for each country and complete the third column of the table.

UK Countries	Highest recorded temperature (°C)	Lowest recorded temperature (°C)	Difference between highest and lowest recorded temperatures (°C)
England	39	−26	
Northern Ireland	31	−19	
Scotland	33	−27	
Wales	35	−23	

Add and subtract numbers of any size

Specification reference L2.N2

You may have to work with very large numbers, both positive and negative.

Example

Two National Lottery prizes were not claimed in one month. One prize was £700 000 and the other was £1.04 million. What was the total?

Work in millions   or   write the numbers in full.

```
    0.7                           700 000
+   1.04                      + 1 040 000
   ─────                        ─────────
   £1.74 million                1 740 000 = £1.74 million
```

Example

In its first year of trading a company makes a profit of £50 000

In its second year the company makes a profit of –£25 000 (a loss of £25 000). By how much has the profit fallen in the second year?

The answer is **£75 000**.

(£50 000 down to 0 and then a further £25 000 down to –£25 000)

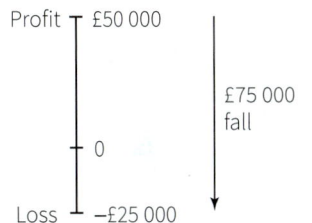

Practice

1. Calculate the following. You may need to write some numbers in full first.

   a. 3 million + 0.5 million
   b. 6.5 million − 3.9 million
   c. £1.2 million − £86 500
   d. £15 billion − £8.5 billion
   e. £2 billion + £250 million
   f. £3.2 billion − £790 million

2. In a lottery game the prize for 6 balls was £2.35 million and the prize for 5 balls and the bonus ball was £160 000. What is the difference between these prizes?

3. The table below shows the profits made by a company's outlets.

Outlet	Profit for year (£ millions)				Total
	2016	2017	2018	2019	
A	0.5	1.2	1.3	1.7	
B	0.9	0.1	−0.7	−1.1	
C	2.6	2.4	2.8	2.9	
D	−2.5	−1.7	−0.7	0.5	
Total	1.5	2	2.7	4	

Remember:
positive means **profit**,
negative means **loss**.

   a. Calculate the total profit for each outlet over the four years. Check your answer by adding the totals for each year together. The result should agree with your total for the four outlets.

b. Use the table to answer the following questions.
  i. What is the difference between Outlet A's profits in 2018 and 2019?
  ii. By how much did Outlet B's profits fall between 2017 and 2018?
  iii. By how much did Outlet D's profits increase between 2018 and 2019?
  iv. What is the difference between Outlet A's and Outlet B's total profit for the four years?
  v. What is the difference between Outlet C's and Outlet D's total profit for the four years?
  vi. What is the difference between Outlet B's and Outlet D's total profit for the four years? Explain your answer.

Chapter Summary
2 Addition and Subtraction

- Words that usually mean you need to add include: total, altogether, sum, plus.
- Words that usually mean you need to subtract include: take away, difference, minus.
- When adding and subtracting, make sure that numbers are lined up in **H**undreds, **T**ens and **U**nits columns.
- For addition start with the digits in the **U**nits column, then move to the **T**ens and **H**undreds. If the digits in a column add to 10 or more then carry the **T**ens digits to the next column.
- When subtracting, always write the larger number at the top of the calculation.
- For subtraction, start with the digits in the **U**nits column. If the digit being subtracted is bigger than the digit above, take a 10 from the column to the left. If there is a 0 in the column to the left then take 100 from the next column and then take 10 from this.
- Answers to additions and subtractions can be checked using the **inverse calculation**. For addition, this means subtracting one of the original numbers in the question from the answer. For subtraction, this means adding the subtracted number from the question to the answer.
- You can use different methods for addition and subtraction: splitting the numbers into **H**undreds, **T**ens and **U**nits and counting in your head, or rounding the numbers then adjusting.

- Large numbers need to be lined up in columns (**H**undred **Th**ousands, **T**en **Th**ousands, **Th**ousands, **H**undreds, **T**ens, **U**nits) for addition and subtraction.
- Subtraction using large numbers may require a series of adjustments. If there are multiple zeros in the columns to the left then keep taking 10 from the next column until you get to a useful value.
- Draw a number line to help when working with positive and negative numbers.

- When adding or subtracting with large numbers written in decimal form, take care to line the numbers up correctly in columns. It may be easier to first write them out in full.
- With money problems a **profit** will be a positive number and a **loss** will be a negative number.

Number 3 Multiplication and Division

Multiplication
Specification reference **EL3.N4**

Do you know the answers to the following?
If not, revise your times tables before moving on to the next exercise.

5 × 5 =   4 × 6 =   7 × 3 =   9 × 8 =
0 × 10 =   6 × 7 =   12 × 8 =   11 × 11 =

Use a calculator to check your answers, or look at the answers at the back of the book.

You can use your times tables to help you multiply larger numbers.
When you multiply by 10, the numbers move one column to the left.
This is because each column is worth 10 times more than the last.

Key point
Words for multiplying: times, product, lots of.

H T U   H T U
   3 × 10 =   3 0
 1 2 × 10 = 1 2 0
 5 0 × 10 = 5 0 0

When a whole number moves left, it leaves a space in the **U**nits column.
Fill this with a 0

Example Calculate 4 × 30

Multiplying 4 × 30 is the same as multiplying   4 × 3 × 10
                                                 4 × 3 = 12 × 10 = **120**

Example Calculate 30 × 30

Multiplying 30 × 30 is the same as multiplying   3 × 3 × 10 × 10
                                                 3 × 3 = 9 × 10 = 90 × 10 = **900**

Practice

1. Multiply these.

   a. 3 × 20   b. 4 × 50   c. 6 × 60   d. 5 × 70
   e. 3 × 90   f. 4 × 70   g. 6 × 90   h. 8 × 90
   i. 8 × 80   j. 9 × 70   k. 8 × 60   l. 9 × 90
   m. 30 × 20   n. 20 × 20   o. 20 × 40   p. 20 × 50

MyMaths   1024, 1367   SEARCH

Number

Multiplication methods

Specification reference: **EL3.N4**

A. Multiply 1-digit with 2-digit numbers

Example 21 × 3

You can break up the 21 into 20 + 1, then multiply each of these by 3

There is more than one way to write this out.

Like this in columns:

```
   2 1
 ×   3
   6 3
```

- 3 × 1 = 3 (or 1 × 3 = 3) Put 3 in the **U**nits column
- 3 × 2 = 6 (or 2 × 3 = 6) Put 6 in the **T**ens column

or like this using a grid:

×	20	1
3	60	3

= 63

- 3 × 20 = 60 and 3 × 1 = 3 Add the 60 and the 3 = 63
- Note: 3 × 2 = 6 so 3 × 20 = 60 (10 times as big)

If neither method is familiar to you, try using the column method first. If you find this difficult you may prefer the grid method.

Example 45 × 7

```
   4 5
 ×   7
   3 1 5
     3
```

- 7 × 5 = 35 (or 5 × 7 = 35) Put 5 in the **U**nits column Carry the 3
- 7 × 4 = 28 (or 4 × 7 = 28) Add the 3 making 31

or

×	40	5
7	280	35

= 315

- 7 × 40 = 280 and 7 × 5 = 35 Add the 280 and the 35 = 315

Practice

1. Multiply these.

   a. 24 × 2   b. 31 × 3   c. 44 × 2   d. 42 × 3
   e. 35 × 3   f. 43 × 4   g. 65 × 4   h. 75 × 6
   i. 39 × 6   j. 56 × 8   k. 76 × 4   l. 89 × 6
   m. 88 × 7   n. 49 × 9   o. 97 × 5   p. 93 × 9

2. There are 12 curtain rings in each pack. How many are there in 5 packs?

3. There are 25 paper plates in each pack. How many are there in 3 packs?

4. A film lasts for 3 hours. How many minutes in this? (1 hour = 60 minutes)

5. A worker earns £9 an hour. How much does the worker earn for a 37-hour week?

MyMaths — 1024, 1025, 1914

6. A hotel has 7 floors. Each floor has 23 bedrooms.
   How many bedrooms does the hotel have altogether?

7. An office intern makes 9 photocopies of a 42-page report.
   How many pages is this altogether?

8. A commuter travels 85 miles each day to get to work and back.
   Altogether how many miles does the commuter travel in 5 days?

9. The instructions on a packet of rice say,
   'Allow 75 grams per person.'
   How many grams do you need for 8 people?

Now use a calculator to check your answers.

B. Multiply 2-digit with 2-digit numbers

Break down the numbers so that the **T**ens and **U**nits of each number are multiplied together. Use your preferred method, either the column or grid method.

Example 35 × 24

Column method This works out 35 × 4 then 35 × 20, then adds them.

```
    3 5
  × 2 4
  1 4 0
    2
  7 0 0
  1
  8 4 0
```

Multiply 5 × 4 = 20   Put the 0 in the **U**nits column and carry the 2 to the **T**ens.

Multiply 3 × 4 = 12
add the 2 = 14   Put the 4 in the **T**ens column and the 1 in the **H**undreds.

(You have now multiplied 35 × 4)

Put a zero in the **U**nits first (because you are now multiplying **T**ens.)

Multiply 5 × 2 = 10   Put the 0 in the **T**ens column and carry the 1 to the **H**undreds column.

Multiply 3 × 2 = 6
add the 1 = 7   Put the 1 in the **H**undreds column.

(You have now multiplied 35 × 20)

Add together the 140 and the 700 = **840**

If you prefer, you can start by multiplying 35 × 20

The first line in the answer would be 700 with the 140 underneath.

Grid method This works out the **T**ens and **U**nits separately.

×	30	5
20	600	100
4	120	20

  700
+ 140
  ———
  840

Separate the **T**ens and **U**nits.

Multiply 20 × 30 and 20 × 5

Multiply 4 × 30 and 4 × 5

Add the answers across then down.

Number

Practice

1. Multiply these.
   a. 23×25
   b. 22×34
   c. 46×19
   d. 33×30
   e. 72×11
   f. 24×41
   g. 13×56
   h. 29×33

2. A caterer charges £16 per head.
   How much is the charge for 45 people?

3. There are 48 tins in each tray.
   How many tins are there in 20 trays?

4. A hotel has 15 floors. Each floor has 18 bedrooms.
   How many bedrooms does the hotel have?

5. Araf's phone contract costs £28 a month.
   How much is this for a year (12 months)?

6. A weekly bus pass costs £17. How much is this for a year (52 weeks)?

7. A swimming pool is 25 metres long. How many metres is 30 lengths?

Now use a calculator to check your answers.

Division

Specification reference EL3.N3

You can think of division in different ways:
- the reverse (or inverse) of multiplication
- how many times a number goes into another
- how many times you can take one number away from another.

Key point
Words for dividing: share, goes into

Division Using Times Tables Check

Do you know the answers to the following? If not, it may help if you write down the times tables before moving on. (Note: some of these have remainders.)

$25 \div 5 =$	$33 \div 3 =$	$36 \div 6 =$	$42 \div 7 =$
$32 \div 5 =$	$30 \div 4 =$	$50 \div 9 =$	$65 \div 8 =$

Use a calculator to check your answers, or look at the answers at the back of the book.

A. Use standard method to divide 2-digit numbers

When the number is too large to use times tables, use this written method that breaks the number into **T**ens and **U**nits.

Multiplication and Division

Example: 96 ÷ 3

Rewrite the calculation 3)96

Divide 3 into 9 first: 9 ÷ 3 = 3
Put the 3 above the 9

```
  3
3)96
```

Then divide 3 into 6: 6 ÷ 3 = 2
Put the 2 above the 6

```
  32
3)96
```

96 ÷ 3 = **32**

Sometimes the numbers do not divide exactly.

Example: 57 ÷ 2

2)57   5 ÷ 2 = 2 remainder 1

```
  2
2)5 ¹7
```
Put the 2 above the 5 and the 1 in front of the 7
The 1 is 1 **T**en so this makes 17
Divide 2 into 17
17 ÷ 2 = 8 remainder 1

```
  2 8 r1
2)5 ¹7
```
Put the 8 above the 17 then write down the remainder.
57 ÷ 2 = **28 r 1**

Practice

1. Copy and complete these divisions.
   - **a.** 2)48
   - **b.** 3)99
   - **c.** 2)80
   - **d.** 5)60
   - **e.** 5)75
   - **f.** 4)92
   - **g.** 6)78
   - **h.** 4)76
   - **i.** 3)87
   - **j.** 3)88
   - **k.** 5)92
   - **l.** 7)86
   - **m.** 8)99
   - **n.** 4)70
   - **o.** 3)95
   - **p.** 6)89

2. How many 5-millilitre doses of medicine can be taken from a 90-millilitre bottle?

3. Four people divide a £68 restaurant bill equally. How much does each person pay?

4. 75 plants are packed into trays of 6
   - **a.** How many trays are filled?
   - **b.** How many plants are left over?

Key point

Multiplication and division are **inverse** operations. (Inverse means opposite.)

You can check the result of a multiplication by dividing. If the result of a division is exact, you can check it by multiplying.

Number

In the first example in this section we found that 96 ÷ 3 = 32

To check this, work out 32 × 3. The answer is 96

Note that if there is a remainder, you multiply then add the remainder.

The second example showed that 57 ÷ 2 = 28 r 1

The check for the second example is 28 × 2 = 56 + 1 = 57

Check your answers to question **1** by multiplying. This is called using a reverse calculation.

B. Divide 3-digit numbers

The standard written method for division can be used for numbers of any size.

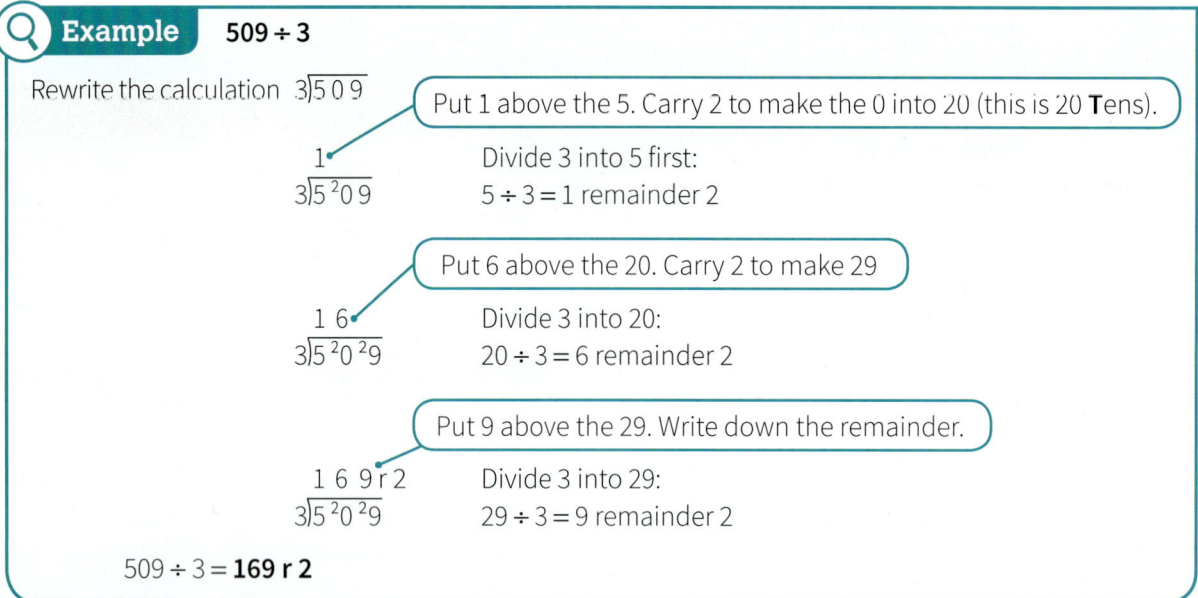

Example 509 ÷ 3

Rewrite the calculation 3)509

Put 1 above the 5. Carry 2 to make the 0 into 20 (this is 20 **T**ens).

Divide 3 into 5 first:
5 ÷ 3 = 1 remainder 2

Put 6 above the 20. Carry 2 to make 29

Divide 3 into 20:
20 ÷ 3 = 6 remainder 2

Put 9 above the 29. Write down the remainder.

Divide 3 into 29:
29 ÷ 3 = 9 remainder 2

509 ÷ 3 = **169 r 2**

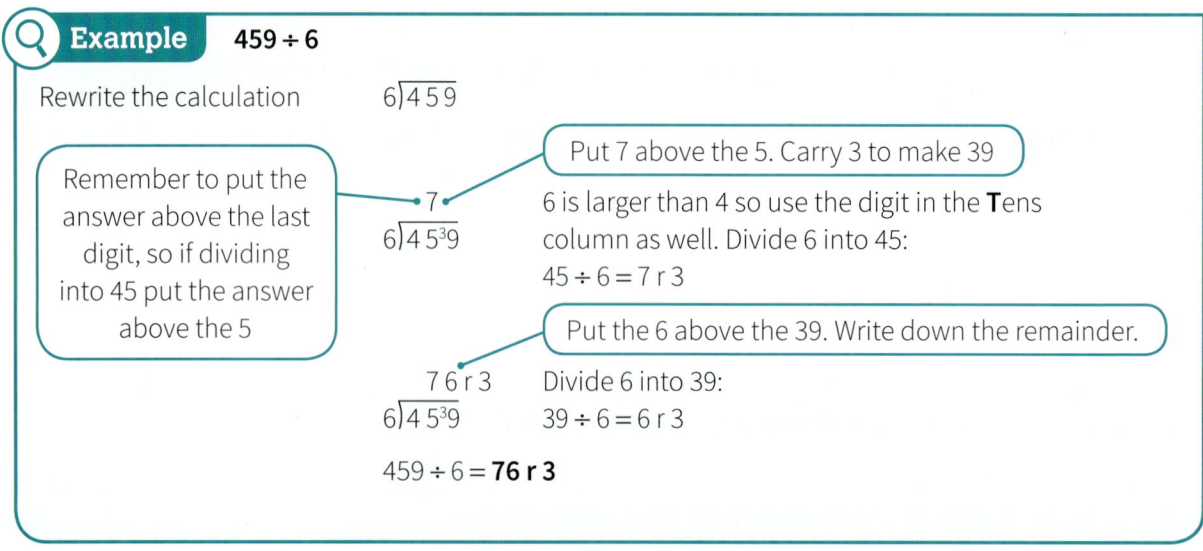

Example 459 ÷ 6

Rewrite the calculation 6)459

Put 7 above the 5. Carry 3 to make 39

6 is larger than 4 so use the digit in the **T**ens column as well. Divide 6 into 45:
45 ÷ 6 = 7 r 3

Remember to put the answer above the last digit, so if dividing into 45 put the answer above the 5

Put the 6 above the 39. Write down the remainder.

Divide 6 into 39:
39 ÷ 6 = 6 r 3

459 ÷ 6 = **76 r 3**

Multiplication and Division

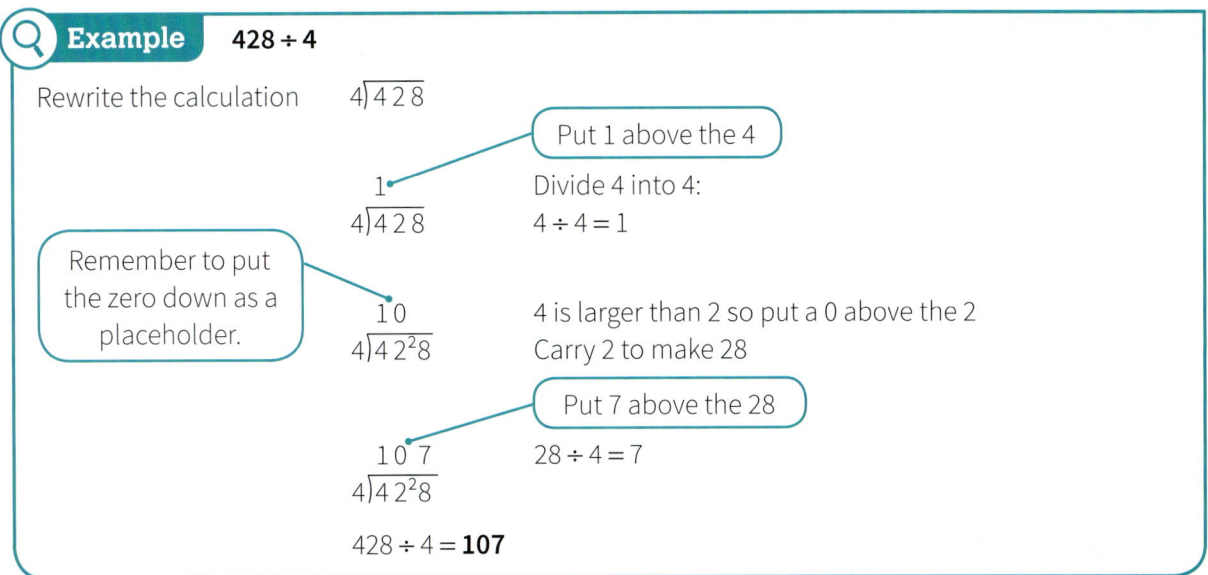

Practice

1. Calculate these.

   a. 640 ÷ 5   b. 928 ÷ 4   c. 828 ÷ 6   d. 702 ÷ 9

   e. 384 ÷ 6   f. 512 ÷ 7   g. 499 ÷ 5   h. 197 ÷ 4

   i. 123 ÷ 3   j. 614 ÷ 6   k. 907 ÷ 3   l. 799 ÷ 8

2. A 180 metre length of tape is cut into 6 equal pieces. How long is each piece?

3. 400 cookies are packed into boxes of 8. How many boxes are filled?

4. The cost of a holiday is shared equally between 4 people. If the holiday costs £984 how much does each person pay?

5. 175 plants are packed into trays of 6
   a. How many trays are filled?
   b. How many plants are left over?

6. 214 students on a trip are split into 7 groups. Can each group be the same size?
   Give reasons for your answer.

7. The cost of a yearly train ticket is £900
   How much is this per month?

   Hint there are 12 months in a year.

8. A television costing £960 is paid for in 30 equal monthly payments. How much is each payment?

It is more difficult to divide by a large number. You may need to try out estimates at each stage.
Set the working out in either of the ways shown on the following page.

Number

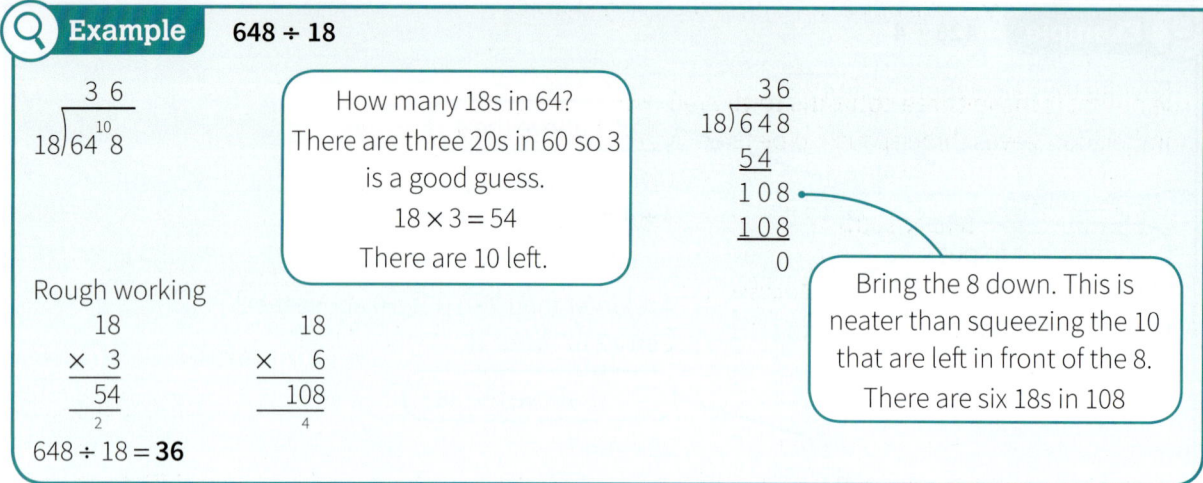

9. Work these out. Check your answers on a calculator.

   a. 882 ÷ 21
   b. 988 ÷ 19
   c. 675 ÷ 15
   d. 925 ÷ 25
   e. 377 ÷ 29
   f. 800 ÷ 32

10. A new sofa costs £864. It can be paid for in 18 equal monthly payments. Calculate the monthly payment.

11. One box holds 24 cans. How many boxes will be needed for 600 cans?

Multiply and divide whole numbers by 10, 100 and 1000

Specification reference L1.N3

A. Multiply by 10, 100 and 1000 in your head

Multiplying (and dividing) by 10, 100 and 1000 in your head is useful when you need to estimate answers or work with large numbers.

Example 36 × 10

When you **multiply by 10** the numbers move **one column to the left**. The gap is filled with a 0

Th	H	T	U
		3	6

×10 =

Th	H	T	U
	3	6	0

36 × 10 = 360

Multiplying by 100 is the same as multiplying by 10, then 10 again.

The numbers move **two columns to the left**. With a whole number this leaves two spaces to be filled by zeros.

Example 75 × 100

Th	H	T	U
		7	5

×100 =

Th	H	T	U
	7	5	0	0

75 × 100 = 7500

Multiplication and Division

Multiplying by 1000 is the same as multiplying by 10, then 10, then 10 again.

The numbers move **three columns to the left**. With a whole number, this leaves three spaces to be filled by zero.

Example 540 × 1000

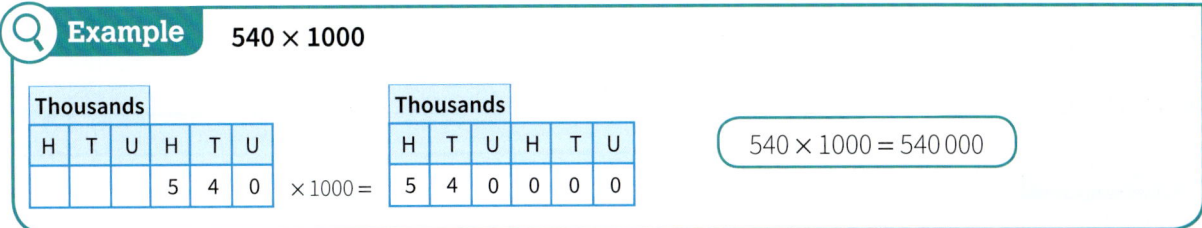

540 × 1000 = 540 000

Practice

1. Calculate these in your head.

   a. 13 × 10
   b. 75 × 10
   c. 136 × 10
   d. 202 × 10
   e. 90 × 10
   f. 190 × 10
   g. 12 × 100
   h. 37 × 100
   i. 129 × 100
   j. 120 × 100
   k. 303 × 100
   l. 23 × 1000
   m. 70 × 1000
   n. 904 × 1000
   o. 750 × 1000
   p. 3581 × 1000

2. How many pence would you get for a £5 note? (£1 = 100p)

3. How many 10p coins would you get for a £20 note? (£1 = 10 × 10p)

4. There are 10 millimetres in 1 centimetre.
   How many millimetres are there in 66 centimetres?

5. There are 100 centimetres in 1 metre. How many are there in 15 metres?

6. There are 100 envelopes in one box. How many are there in 25 boxes?

7. A cashier has forty-five £10 notes in the till. How much is this?

8. There are 10 cards in one box. How many cards are there in 50 boxes?

9. 100 people each donate £25 to charity. How much money is this altogether?

10. There are 1000 millimetres in 1 metre. How many are there in 12 metres?

11. There are 1000 leaflets in one pack. How many leaflets are there in 250 packs?

12. One kilogram equals 1000 grams. How many grams are equal to 78 kilograms?

13. 3000 concert tickets are sold at £100 each. How much money is taken for the tickets in total?

14. There are 1000 grams in a kilogram and 1000 kilograms in a metric ton. How many grams are there in a metric ton?

B. Divide by 10, 100 and 1000 in your head

When you divide by 10, 100 or 1000 the numbers move to the right.

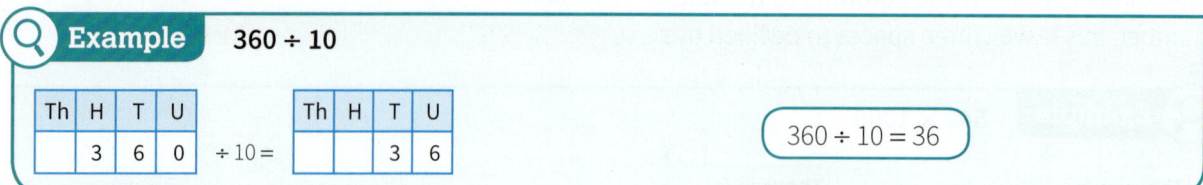

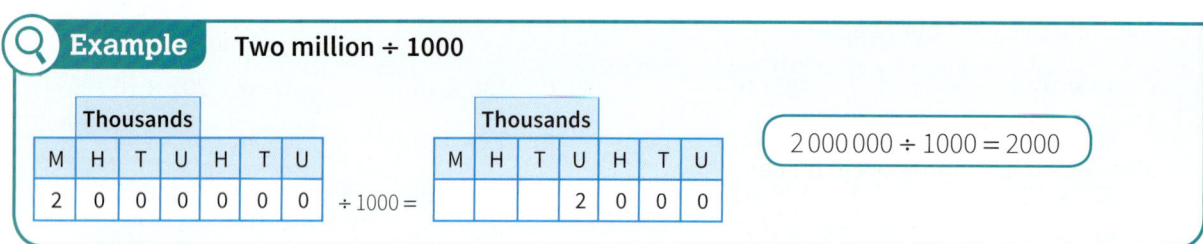

If the number to be divided does not end in zero, the answer is a decimal.

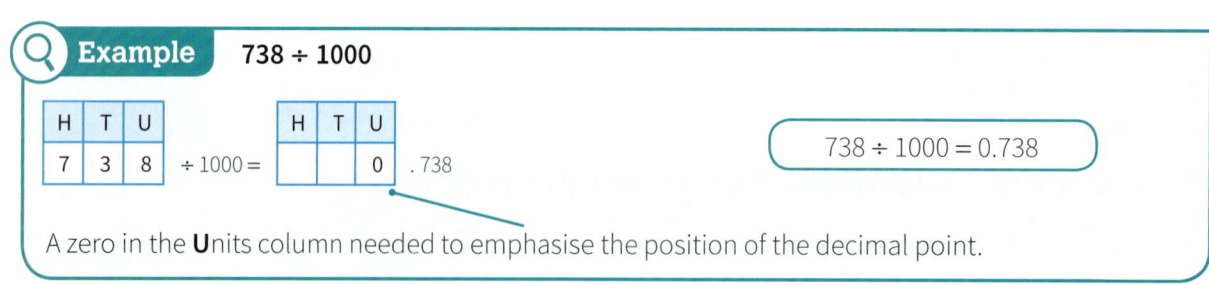

A zero in the **U**nits column needed to emphasise the position of the decimal point.

If you need an exact answer, give the decimal form (see page 126).

If you do not need an exact answer, you can round the number (see page 128).

Multiplication and Division

Practice

1. Calculate these.
   a. 460 ÷ 10
   b. 4600 ÷ 10
   c. 4600 ÷ 100
   d. 46 000 ÷ 1000
   e. 530 ÷ 10
   f. 5300 ÷ 10
   g. 5300 ÷ 100
   h. 53 000 ÷ 100
   i. 9900 ÷ 10
   j. 750 ÷ 10
   k. 57 000 ÷ 1000
   l. 3800 ÷ 100
   m. 64 000 ÷ 1000
   n. 2300 ÷ 1000
   o. 96 200 ÷ 1000
   p. 275 ÷ 100

2. A lottery win of £12 000 is shared between 100 people.
   How much does each person get?

3. A printing company charges £15 for 100 colour copies.
   What is the cost per copy? (£1 = 100p)

4. There are 10 millimetres in 1 centimetre.
   What is 720 millimetres in centimetres?

5. There are 100 centimetres in 1 metre.
   What is 24 000 centimetres in metres?

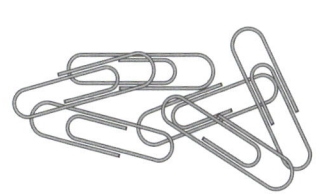

6. Paperclips are packed in boxes of 100
   How many boxes would 275 000 paperclips fill?

7. Candles are sold in boxes of 10
   How many boxes will 3500 candles fill?

8. 100 workers in a call centre each answer the same number of calls.
   How many does each worker answer out of a total of 17 600 calls?

9. About one out of ten people are left-handed.
   How many people out of 150 are likely to be left-handed?

10. There are 1000 metres in 1 kilometre.
    a. What is 18 000 metres in kilometres?
    b. What is 3500 metres in kilometres?
    c. What is 675 metres in kilometres?

11. A box of 100 pens costs £15
    What is the cost per pen?

12. A minibus costs £325 to hire. 10 friends share the cost equally.
    How much do they each pay?

Number

Use multiplication and division
Specification reference EL3.N3, EL3.N4, L1.N4

Entry Level 3

Try to do these in your head.

In some questions you will need to decide whether to multiply or divide.

⚙ Practice

1. Copy and complete these by putting the missing number in each box.

    a. 4 × 7 = ☐
    b. 4 × ☐ = 280
    c. 5 × ☐ = 50
    d. 6 × ☐ = 36
    e. ☐ × 8 = 320
    f. 9 × 7 = ☐
    g. 9 × ☐ = 810
    h. 7 × ☐ = 42
    i. ☐ × 7 = 56
    j. ☐ × 8 = 64
    k. 20 × 20 = ☐
    l. 30 × ☐ = 600

2. How many 2 pence coins make 20p?

3. There are 6 eggs in a box.
   How many boxes do you need to get 54 eggs?

4. A £72 bill is shared equally between 8 people.
   How much does each person pay?

5. One book costs £9. How much do 7 of these books cost?

6. One box holds 3 light bulbs. How many boxes do I need to buy to get 27 light bulbs?

7. I save £30 each month. How many months will it take me to save £120?

8. I work 40 hours a week for 5 weeks. How many hours is this altogether?

9. I sell raffle tickets for £5 each. How many raffle tickets do I need to sell to raise £100?

Level 1

The following questions involve larger numbers but can still be done in your head.
Using multiples of 10 (numbers that end in zero) can be useful when estimating.

10. a. 60 × 60 = ☐
    b. 40 × ☐ = 2000
    c. ☐ × 80 = 5600
    d. 30 × 30 = ☐
    e. 30 × ☐ = 9000
    f. 50 × 500 = ☐
    g. 40 × 600 = ☐
    h. 200 × ☐ = 8000
    i. 400 × 300 = ☐

11. It takes 30 payments of £40 each to repay a loan. How much is paid altogether?

12. Tickets for a concert cost £40. Altogether £8000 is taken in ticket sales. How many tickets are sold?

13. How many seconds are in 1 hour? (1 minute = 60 seconds, 1 hour = 60 minutes)

14. 1000 kg of potatoes are put into 20-kg bags. How many bags are filled?

Recognise numerical relationships

Specification reference: **EL3.N6, L1.N4**

A. Number sequences

A **number sequence** is a list of numbers which all follow a particular pattern or rule.

Example

The three times table is a sequence.

3   6   9   12   15   18   ...

The first term of the sequence is 3. The rule for finding the next term is 'add 3'.

The sixth term in this sequence is 18

The sequence carries on unless a limit is given.

Example

4   7   10   13   16   19   ...

The rule for this sequence is also 'add 3'.
However, this time the first term is 4 and this gives a different sequence.

The sixth term in this sequence is 19

Not all sequences are based on addition.

Example

50   45   40   35   30   25   ...

The first term of this sequence is 50 and the rule is 'subtract 5'.

Practice

1. Write down the rule for these sequences and find the next three terms.

a.	4	8	12	16	20	☐	☐	☐
b.	5	9	13	17	21	☐	☐	☐
c.	20	18	16	14	12	☐	☐	☐
d.	2	7	12	17	22	☐	☐	☐
e.	3	9	15	21	27	☐	☐	☐
f.	70	65	60	55	50	☐	☐	☐
g.	51	48	45	42	39	☐	☐	☐
h.	60	56	52	48	44	☐	☐	☐
i.	97	87	77	67	57	☐	☐	☐
j.	140	120	100	80	60	☐	☐	☐

2. A family are going on holiday for a month. They ask neighbours to take turns to feed their cat while they are away.

Mr Dvorak agrees to feed the cat every 4 days, starting on 3rd April.

   a. What are the next two dates when Mr Dvorak will feed the cat?

   b. Will Mr Dvorak feed the cat on 27th April? Give a reason for your answer.

3. A woman has to take 4 tablets (of the same type) each day.

On Monday she starts taking tablets from a packet of 30 tablets.

Assuming she takes the correct amount, how many tablets will there be in the packet by the end of Thursday? Show your working.

B. Multiples

A **multiple** of a number can be divided **exactly** by that number.

Example: 18 is a multiple of 2, 3, 6 and 9 because 2 × 9 = 18 and 3 × 6 = 18

Practice

1. a. Which of these are multiples of 4?   7   12   23   32   37   40

   b. Which of these are multiples of 7?   21   29   36   42   64   70

   c. Which of these are multiples of both 3 **and** 4?

       6   12   17   20   21   24

   d. Which of these are multiples of both 2 **and** 5?

       4   10   15   18   25   30

2. Write down all the multiples below 100 of:

   a. 6   b. 8   c. 9   d. 11   e. 20

3. Write down all the multiples below 1000 of:

   a. 50   b. 200   c. 250

4 Write down five multiples of 1000

Square numbers and indices   Specification reference L1.N6

A. Square numbers

A **square number** is made when you multiply any whole number by itself.

Example: 25 is a square number, because 5 × 5 = 25

5 × 5 can also be written as 5^2. This reads as '5 **squared**'.

The small ^{2} is called a **power** or **index number**. 5^2 can also be read as '5 to the power 2'.

Example: $20^2 = 20 \times 20 = 400$

Multiplication and Division

Practice

1. Calculate the first 12 square numbers.

   Hint Multiply $1 \times 1, 2 \times 2, 3 \times 3$, etc.

2. Calculate the following.

   a. 30^2 b. 50^2 c. 60^2 d. 90^2

   Hint Use your answers to question **1** to help you.

For harder numbers a calculator can be used. Depending on the type of calculator you have, there are different ways of doing this.

> **Example** 25^2
>
> With any calculator press [25] [×] [25] [=]
>
> With most scientific calculators you can press [25] [x^2] [=]
>
> Answer **625**

3. Use a calculator for the following.

   a. 28^2 b. 42^2 c. 63^2 d. 99^2

Reversing the process of squaring a number is called finding the **square root**.

The symbol for square root is $\sqrt{\ }$. Most calculators have a key with this symbol on for finding a square root.

> **Example**
>
> $5^2 = 25$ so the square root of $25 = 5$. Show this by evaluating $\sqrt{25}$ on a calculator.
>
> Press [$\sqrt{\ }$] [25] [=]
>
> Answer **5**

4. Use a calculator to work out the following.

   a. $\sqrt{256}$ b. $\sqrt{1024}$ c. $\sqrt{14\,400}$ d. $\sqrt{62\,500}$

B. Calculating with indices

An index such as ^{2} is used to show how many times a number should be multiplied by itself.

Key point The plural of index is indices.

Indices can take any value. (index number 3) (index number 4)

5^3 means $5 \times 5 \times 5 = 125$ 5^4 means $5 \times 5 \times 5 \times 5 = 625$

5^3 can be read as '5 to the power 3' or as '5 **cubed**'.

Number

The **cube root** or 'third root' of 125 is 5

The symbol for cube root is $\sqrt[3]{}$

The fourth root of 625 is 5

The symbol for the fourth root is $\sqrt[4]{}$

Example

1. 9^3

With any calculator press 9 × 9 × 9 =

With most scientific calculators you can press 9 x^3 =

Or press 9 x^y 3 =

Answer **729**

2. 3^4

With any calculator press 3 × 3 × 3 × 3 =

With most scientific calculators you can press 3 x^y 4 =

Answer **81**

Practice

1. Use a calculator for the following.

   a. 8^3 b. 9^3 c. 12^3 d. 2^4 e. 2^5 f. 6^4 g. 10^6

2. Check your answers to question **1** by finding the roots.

3. Match the equal pairs. The first one has been done for you.

   5 × 5 × 5 —————— 3^2
   3 × 3 81
   2 × 2 × 2 ———————— 5^3
   9 × 9 3^3
   3 × 3 × 3 16
   2 × 2 × 2 × 2 2^3

Key point

To find the cube root on most scientific calculators press 'shift' and use the key with $\sqrt[3]{}$ above it.

To find any other root press 'shift' and use the key with $\sqrt[\square]{}$ or $\sqrt[x]{}$ above it.

For further practice with use of indices see page 34–36.

Multiply and divide large numbers

Specification reference L1.N4

A. Multiply large numbers

Example 245 × 63

Column method This works out 245 × 3 then 245 × 60, then adds them.

```
    2 4 5
  ×   6 3
    7 3 5
    1 1
  1 4 7 0 0
      2 3
  1 5 4 3 5
          1
```

Carry numbers

Multiply 3 × 5 = 15   Put down 5, carry 1
Multiply 3 × 4 = 12   Add the carried 1 = 13. Put down 3, carry 1
Multiply 3 × 2 = 6   Add the carried 1 = 7. Put down 7
                      (You have now multiplied 245 × 3)

Put 0 in the **U**nits column. (To multiply by 60, multiply by 10 then 6)

Multiply 6 × 5 = 30   Put down 0 and carry 3
Multiply 6 × 4 = 24   Add the carried 3 = 27
                      Put down 7, carry 2
Multiply 6 × 2 = 12   Add the 2 carried = 14
                      Put down 14
                      (You have now multiplied 245 × 60)

Add together the 735 and 14 700 = **15 435**

Some people put carried numbers at the top. Wherever you put them, take care not to get carried numbers muddled. You can cross them out when you have finished with them.

Grid method

×	200	40	5
60	12 000	2400	300
3	600	120	15

```
  14 700
+    735
  15 435
     1
```

Separate the **H**undreds, **T**ens and **U**nits.

Multiply 60 × 200, 60 × 40 and 60 × 5

Multiply 3 × 200, 3 × 40 and 3 × 5

Add the answers across then down.

Practice

1. Work these out without a calculator, then use a calculator to check.

   a. 123 × 35   b. 632 × 47   c. 225 × 57   d. 342 × 80
   e. 512 × 63   f. 309 × 42   g. 708 × 96   h. 573 × 48

2. A lorry driver travels about 350 miles a day. Approximately how many miles does he travel in 20 days?

3. Jade makes a New Year's resolution to cycle 25 kilometres every day. If she keeps to her resolution, how many kilometres will she cycle in the year (365 days)?

4. Roughly how many days old is a man on his 85th birthday? Assume that there are 365 days in every year.

Number

B. Divide large numbers

You can use the standard method to divide large numbers as well as small numbers.

 See page 4.

Example 18 053 ÷ 9

$$\begin{array}{r}2\,0\,0\,5\,r\,8\\ 9\overline{)1^18\,0\,5^5\,3}\end{array}$$

Cannot do 1 ÷ 9 so carry the 1 to make the 8 into 18
18 ÷ 9 = 2   Put the 2 above the 8
0 ÷ 9 = 0   Put the 0 above the 0
Cannot do 5 ÷ 9 so put 0 above the 5 and carry the 5 to make 3 into 53
53 ÷ 9 = 5 rem 8   Put the 5 above the 3
Write down the remainder.

18 053 ÷ 9 = **2005 r 8**

Example 12 876 ÷ 37

$$37\overline{)1\,2\,8\,^{17}7\,^{29}6}$$

Rough working:

37 is approximately 40

| $3 \times 40 = 120$ so 3 is a good guess | $\begin{array}{r}3\,7\\ \times\ 3\\ \hline 1\,1\,1\end{array}$ |

128 − 111 = 17

111 + 37 = 148 so 4 × 37 = 148

177 − 148 = 29

| $8 \times 40 = 320$ so 8 is a good guess | $\begin{array}{r}3\,7\\ \times\ 8\\ \hline 2\,9\,6\\ _5\end{array}$ |

Answer 12 876 ÷ 37 = **348**

$$\begin{array}{r}3\,4\,8\\ 37\overline{)1\,2\,8\,^{17}7\,^{29}6}\\ -1\,1\,1\downarrow\\ \hline 1\,7\,7\\ -1\,4\,8\\ \hline 2\,9\,6\end{array}$$

37 × 3 = 111
Subtract from 128 = 17
Drop the next digit down.

37 × 4 = 148
Subtract from 177 = 29

Drop the next digit down.

Check: $\begin{array}{r}3\,4\,8\\ \times\ \ 3\,7\\ \hline 2\,4_3\,3_5\,6\\ 10_1\,4_2\,4\,0\\ \hline 1\,2\,8\,7\,6\end{array}$

Multiplication and Division

Practice

1. Work these out without a calculator.

   a. 5910 ÷ 6   b. 3240 ÷ 8   c. 7929 ÷ 9
   d. 14 608 ÷ 4   e. 29 470 ÷ 7   f. 34 125 ÷ 5
   g. 14 508 ÷ 8   h. 62 500 ÷ 6   i. 25 127 ÷ 3
   j. 48 950 ÷ 6   k. 50 000 ÷ 9   l. 80 225 ÷ 4

2. A market research company employs 8 people to carry out 2000 interviews.
   How many people will they each interview if they share the 2000 equally?

3. A bill for £2025 is paid in 9 equal payments.
   How much is each payment?

4. Tickets for an outdoor event cost £6 each. Altogether £19 326
   is taken in ticket sales. How many tickets are sold?

5. At a factory 34 000 ice lollies are packed into boxes of 8
   How many boxes are filled?

6. 26 000 millilitres of perfume is packed as 5 millilitre samples.
   How many samples are there?

7. Six people inherit £135 000 to be shared equally between them.
   How much does each person inherit?

8. £250 000 is divided equally between 4 charities.
   How much does each charity get?

9. Work these out. Check your answers by using a reverse calculation (multiplication).

   a. 10 266 ÷ 29   b. 22 008 ÷ 42   c. 17 408 ÷ 34   d. 44 255 ÷ 53

10. A loan for £16 200 is to be paid back in 36 equal payments. How much is each payment?

Efficient methods of calculating with numbers of any size

Specification reference L1.N4, L2.N2

A. Multiples, factors and prime numbers

A multiple of a number can be divided **exactly** by that number.
For example, 6, 21 and 30 are all multiples of 3

A **factor** of a number is something that **divides exactly into it**.
For example, 2, 3, 4 and 6 are all factors of 12

A **prime** number has **two factors** — itself and 1
For example, 2, 5, 7 and 11 are all prime numbers.

There are some quick ways of checking for factors and multiples.

> **Key point**
> 1 is not a prime number. It has only one factor — itself

Number

To check whether 2 is a factor of a number, look at the last digit.
If it is **even**, then **2 is a factor** (that is, the number is a multiple of 2).
So 2 is a factor of numbers like 74, 348, 74 256, etc.

To check whether 5 is a factor of a number, look at the last digit.
If it is **0 or 5**, then **5 is a factor** (that is, the number is a multiple of 5).
So 5 is a factor of numbers like 70, 345, 74 250, etc.

To check whether 3 is a factor of a number, add all the digits.

If the total is **divisible by 3**, then **3 is a factor**

(that is, the number is a multiple of 3).

> **Example**   12 345
>
> $1 + 2 + 3 + 4 + 5 = 15$ then $1 + 5 = 6$
>
> 6 is divisible by 3 so 3 is a factor of 12 345
>
> (and 12 345 is a multiple of 3).
>
> *Keep adding the digits together.*

This method also works for 9 (but not other numbers).

> **Example**   13 860
>
> $1 + 3 + 8 + 6 + 0 = 18$ then $1 + 8 = 9$
>
> so 9 is a factor of 13 860 (and 13 860 is a multiple of 9).

Practice

1. Which of the numbers listed below are multiples of:

   a. 2   **b.** 5   **c.** 3   **d.** 9?

   98   127   165   243   364   539   720   945   1603   25 245

2. **a.** What is the smallest number that is a multiple of both 3 **and** 5?

   b. Find the smallest number that is a multiple of both 4 **and** 6

   c. What is the largest number that is a factor of both 18 **and** 30?

   d. Find the largest number that is a factor of both 21 **and** 70

3. **a.** Find the numbers that are factors of 12 and also multiples of 3

   b. Find two factors of 18 that are also factors of 81

4. **a.** Find a prime number greater than 3 that is a factor of 30

   b. What is the next prime number after 23?

5. Find a number that is a factor of 15, 171 and 411

B. Calculations with numbers of any size

Level 2

The standard methods for multiplying and dividing are given earlier. For large numbers it is often quicker to use a calculator, but it is useful to be able to do a rough check to make sure the calculator is giving the right answer. Try to use mental arithmetic whenever you can. Everything gets easier with practice! Look out for short-cuts.

Example

A £1 500 000 lottery win is shared equally between 30 people. How much does each person get?

1 500 000 ÷ 10 = 150 000

15 ÷ 3 = 5   So the answer is **£50 000**

To divide by 30, divide by 10 then by 3

Example

Four charities each receive £125 000. How much is this in total?

2 × 125 = 250   250 × 2 = 500

so   4 × 125   = 500

and   4 × £125 000 = **£500 000**

To multiply by 4, double then double again.

Practice

Work these out. Use mental arithmetic when the numbers are easy enough.

1. How much is each payment if a debt of £3600 is paid off in:
   a. 12 equal payments
   b. 40 equal payments
   c. 100 equal payments?

2. Each month a company sends out 3500 customer account statements. How many statements does it send out in a year (12 months)?

3. A mortgage is paid off at £5000 a year for 30 years. How much is paid in total?

4. A local paper sells an estimated 32 000 papers. On average four people read each paper. How many people read the paper altogether?

5. A company doubles its original advertising budget of £750 000. What is its budget now?

6. The total salary bill for 8 company directors is £2.4 million. Each director earns the same amount. What is each salary?

7. A builder sells 20 flats for £145 000 each. How much is this in total?

8. Approximately 1.3 million tourists visit a country each year. Estimate how many tourists will visit the country during the next 5 years?

9. A company announces spending of £1.5 million over the next 4 years. How much is this per year?

10. The table shows the profits made by the three sections of a company. The total profit is shared equally between two partners. How much do they each receive?

Section	Profits
A	£2.46 million
B	−£3.28 million
C	£5.14 million

Chapter Summary
3 Multiplication and Division

- Words that usually mean you need to multiply include: times, product, lots of.
- Words that usually mean you need to divide include: share, goes into.
- Use times tables to help you when multiplying and dividing larger numbers.
- When you multiply by 10, the digits move one column to the left.
- To multiply any 2 digit numbers, multiply the tens and units separately, then combine the answers. You can use the column method or the grid method.
- To use short or long division, rewrite the calculation so the number being divided is in the box. Start with the digit in the column on the left. Remember to use a zero, 0, as a place holder if there are no factors for a digit.
- Sometimes numbers do not divide exactly and the final answer will have a remainder.
- Answers to multiplication and division calculations can be checked using the **inverse calculation**. For multiplication, this means dividing the answer by one of the original numbers in the question. For division, this means multiplying the answer by the divisor in the question.
- A **number sequence** is a list of numbers, created using a first term and a rule.

- When multiplying by 100, you move the digits two place values to the left. Multiplying by 1000 moves the digits three place values to the left, and so on. Fill the resultant empty places to the right with zeros.
- When dividing by 100, you move the digits two place values to the right. Dividing by 1000 moves the digits three place values to the right, and so on. Fill the resultant empty places to the left with zeros.
- Written methods for multiplication can be extended for large numbers by multiplying all the place values together separately and then adding the answers.
- Written methods for division can be extended for large numbers but a different layout can be used if preferred. Estimation and rough working are also needed at each stage.
- A **square number** is made when a whole number x is multiplied by itself and can be written x^2 where the small ^{2} is called a **power** or **index number**.
- The reverse process of squaring a number is called finding a **square root** ($\sqrt{\ }$).
- If the index is 3, x^3, then it is read as x **cubed** and the third root is read as the **cube root** ($\sqrt[3]{\ }$).
- Indices (plural of index) and square roots can take any value and can be calculated using your calculator.
- Values in the times table of a number are **multiples** of that number, a **factor** of a number divides exactly into it, and a **prime number** only has two factors, 1 and itself.
- 2 is a factor of all even numbers, 5 is a factor of all numbers ending in 5 or 0
- If the sum of a number's digits is a multiple of 3 then 3 is a factor of that number. If the sum of a number's digits is a multiple of 9 then 3 and 9 are factors of that number.

- Use multiples, factors and prime numbers to help simplify problems with large numbers.

Number 4 Rounding and Estimation

Approximate and estimate with numbers up to 1000

Specification reference **EL3.N5**

A. When to estimate

Estimation is used to work out an **approximate** answer.

This is useful if you want to:

- do a quick rough calculation
- check that an answer to a calculation is sensible
- find an approximate figure when you cannot calculate something exactly.

Estimation is **not** used to find an accurate answer.

> **Example**
>
> A child has 95p left in his purse.
> Is this enough cash to buy 3 pencils costing 28p each?
>
> 28p is nearly 30p. 3 × 30p = 90p
> **Yes, this is enough cash for the 3 pencils.**

> **Example**
>
> A shopper buys 3 items costing £49 each. The shop charges £196
> Is this approximately correct?
>
> £49 is nearly £50   3 × £50 = £150
> **No, the shop has charged too much.**

> **Example**
>
> A businessman needs to arrive at an airport **at least** 2 hours before his flight departs at 11:30 am.
> He has to drive 50 miles to the airport.
> What time should he leave home?
>
> There is no single correct answer to this problem.
>
> The businessman needs to use his knowledge and experience to work it out.
>
> He might estimate that the journey will take about **2 hours** due to traffic.
>
> He might also allow **another hour** to park and find the check in.
>
> If so, he will estimate that he needs to leave home at **6:30 am** to arrive at 9:30 am.

MyMaths 1003 SEARCH

Number

Practice

1. In which of these situations would you use estimation?

    a. To work out how much food to buy for a party.
    b. To calculate an employee's pay.
    c. To work out how much spending money to take on holiday.
    d. To measure a dose of medicine.
    e. To measure a piece of glass to fit a frame.
    f. To work out how far it is from London to Edinburgh.
    g. To work out how long it will take to get to the cinema.
    h. To count the number of children on a school trip.
    i. To work out how much paint to buy to decorate a room.
    j. To calculate how much change to give.

B. Round to the nearest 10 and 100

Rounding numbers to the **nearest 10** gives whole numbers that end in **zero** (for example, **10**, **20**, **30**). This is useful because numbers like 50 and 90 are much easier to work with than numbers like 49 or 93

> ### Example
>
> Round 74 to the nearest 10
>
>
>
> 74 lies between 70 and 80. It is nearer to 70, so it is rounded down to **70**
>
> Round 238 to the nearest 10
>
>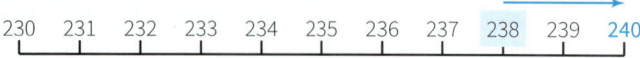
>
> 238 lies between 230 and 240. It is nearer to 240, so it is rounded up to **240**
>
> Round 196 to the nearest 10
>
> 190 191 192 193 194 195 **196** 197 198 199 **200**
>
> 196 is between 190 and 200. It is nearer to 200, so it is rounded up to **200**
>
> Round 485 to the nearest 10
>
>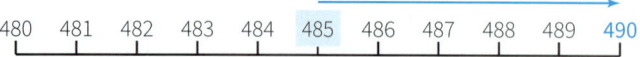
>
> 485 lies between 480 and 490. It is in the middle.
>
> In maths we use the rule:
>
> **If it is in the middle**, you should **round up**, in this case to **490**

Rounding and Estimation

💡 Key point

To round to the nearest 10:

If the **Units** digit is **less than 5, round down**   (for example, 28**3** = 280 to the nearest 10)

If the **Units** digit is **5 or more, round up**   (for example, 28**7** = 290 to the nearest 10)

The answers always end in 0

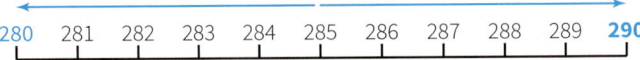

280 281 282 283 284 285 286 287 288 289 **290**

⚙ Practice

1. Round each number to the nearest 10

   a. 37   b. 15   c. 22   d. 92
   e. 137   f. 215   g. 422   h. 992
   i. 412   j. 99   k. 699   l. 313
   m. 242   n. 175   o. 368   p. 707
   q. 365   r. 811   s. 901   t. 275

Large numbers are often rounded to the nearest 100

Deciding whether to round to the nearest 10 or 100 depends on the size of the number and how accurate you want the answer to be.

🔍 Example

Round 370 to the nearest 100

300 310 320 330 340 350 360 **370** 380 390 **400**

370 lies between 300 and 400. It is nearer to 400 so it is rounded up to **400**

Any whole number from 350 to 399 would be rounded up to 400.
So numbers like 351, 365, 382 and 399 are all 400 to the nearest 100

🔍 Example

Round 720 to the nearest 100

700 710 720 730 740 750 760 770 780 790 800

720 lies between 700 and 800. It is nearer to 700 so it is rounded down to **700**

Number

Any whole number from 700 to 749 would be rounded down to 700
So numbers like 706, 721, 736 and 749 are all 700 to the nearest 100

> **Example**
>
> Round 550 to the nearest 100
>
> 500 510 520 530 540 **550** 560 570 580 590 **600**
>
> 550 lies between 500 and 600. It is in the middle.
>
> Remember the rule in maths is: **if it is in the middle, round up**; here to **600**

> **Key point**
>
> **To round to the nearest 100:**
>
> If the **Tens** digit is **less than 5, round down**. (for example, 4**2**7 = 400 to the nearest 100)
>
> If the **Tens** digit is **5 or more, round up**. (for example, 4**8**3 = 500 to the nearest 100)
>
> The answers always end in two zeros.
>
> 400 410 420 430 440 450 460 470 480 490 500
>   ↑   ↑
>   427   483

2. Round each number to the nearest 100

   a. 170   b. 350   c. 620   d. 880
   e. 175   f. 357   g. 629   h. 851
   i. 383   j. 199   k. 750   l. 749
   m. 851   n. 999   o. 235   p. 428
   q. 857   r. 810   s. 250   t. 59

3. A local newspaper has the following headline.

   > New shopping centre to open, creating 500 new jobs!

   The newspaper has rounded the actual number of jobs to the nearest 100

   a. What is the minimum number of actual jobs there could be?
   b. What is the maximum number of actual jobs there could be?

Rounding and Estimation

C. Use estimates to check calculations

You can check whether the answer to a calculation is sensible by rounding the numbers and estimating the answer.

Example

A student calculates that if one train ticket costs £18 then three tickets will cost £34.

A rough check shows this cannot be correct:

£18 rounded to the nearest £10 is £20. 3 × £20 = £60
Therefore the student's answer is not sensible. (The correct answer is £54.)

Example

A saver has £912 in her account.
She thinks that if she takes out £285 there will be £773 left in the account.

A rough check shows this cannot be correct:

£912 rounded to the nearest £100 is £900 and £285 rounded to the nearest £100 is £300

£900 − £300 = £600 (The correct answer is £627)

Practice

1. Use an estimate to check whether each statement is correct.

   Menswear – Price list

Jumpers	£25	Jackets	£67
Shirts	£20	Coats	£85
Ties	£8	Suits	£159
Trousers	£29		

   Hint Round to numbers you can work out easily.

   a. The total cost of a jacket and trousers is £136
   b. A suit costs £92 more than a jacket.
   c. A jacket and two pairs of trousers cost £125 altogether.
   d. A shopper spends £87 on trousers. He has bought 2 pairs.
   e. Coats are reduced by £27 in a sale. The sale price is £58
   f. A shopper buys 9 jumpers. The total cost is £225   **Hint** Work out £25 × 10
   g. A man buys 3 suits. Altogether they cost £577   **Hint** Work out £160 × 3
   h. Last year suits cost £115. The price has increased by £64

Number

2. The table shows the number of pairs of gloves of different sizes sold in a shop.

Size	Number sold
Small	191
Medium	412
Large	286

   a. Find the total number sold.

   b. How many more medium than large pairs were sold?

   Check each answer by rounding the numbers to the nearest hundred.

3. Use the information in the table below to answer the questions. In each part you will need to carry out a series of calculations. Use estimates to check each calculation you do.

	Hotel price list		
	Cost per person, per night (£)	English breakfast per person (£)	Continental breakfast per person (£)
Adult	55	8	6
Child	38	5	3

   Find the cost for:

   a. 2 adults and 1 child, staying 2 nights with English breakfast

   Hint Work out the cost for 1 night with breakfast, then double it.

   b. 1 adult and 3 children, staying 4 nights with Continental breakfast

   c. 2 adults and 4 children, staying 3 nights with Continental breakfast.

4. Use estimation to check which of these answers must be wrong.

   a. $512 + 287 = 799$

   b. $888 - 57 = 310$

   c. $29 \times 7 = 77$

   d. $321 \div 3 = 107$

Approximate and estimate with large numbers

Specification reference **L1.N12**

A. Round to the nearest 1000, 10 000, 100 000, 1 000 000

The method for rounding larger numbers is similar to that for smaller numbers. For example:

To round a number to the nearest thousand:

- Identify which digit is in the **Th**ousands column.
- Look at the **H**undreds digit to the right. This is the 'deciding digit'. If it is **below 5, round down** so the **Th**ousands digit stays the same.
- If the **H**undreds digit is **5 or above, round up** so the **Th**ousands digit increases by 1
- After the **Th**ousands digit write 000 (because a number rounded to the nearest **Th**ousand will have no **H**undreds, **T**ens or **U**nits).

Rounding and Estimation

Examples

1. To round 3 257 432 to the nearest 1000

   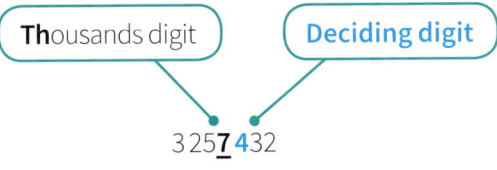

   3 25**7** 432

   4 is **less than 5**, so **round down**.
   The **Th**ousands digit, 7, stays the same.

   3 257 432 to the nearest thousand is **3 257 000**

   To the nearest **Th**ousand means there are no **H**undreds, **T**ens or **U**nits. The number must end in 000

2. To round 3 257 432 to the nearest 10 000

   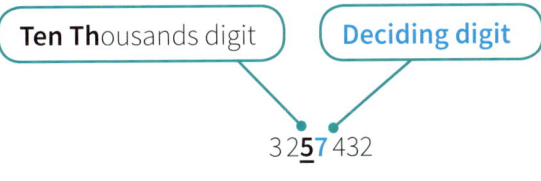

   3 2**5**7 432

   7 is **more than 5**, so **round up**
   The **T**en **Th**ousands digit increases by 1

   3 257 432 to the nearest ten thousand is **3 260 000**

   To the nearest **T**en **Th**ousand means there are no **T**housands, **H**undreds, **T**ens or **U**nits. The number must end in 0 000

3. To round 3 257 432 to the nearest 100 000

   3 **2**57 432

   When the deciding digit is **5**, **round up**.
   The **H**undred **Th**ousands digit increases by 1

   3 257 432 to the nearest hundred thousand is **3 300 000**

   A number rounded to the nearest **H**undred **Th**ousand ends in 00 000

4. To round 3 257 432 to the nearest 1 000 000 (million)

   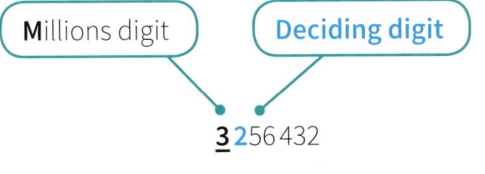

   3 256 432

   2 is **less than 5**, so **round down**.

   3 256 432 to the nearest million is **3 000 000**

   A number rounded to the nearest **M**illion ends in 000 000

Number

Practice

1. Round each number to the nearest 1000
   a. 4562
   b. 6500
   c. 27 421
   d. 30 950
   e. 255 756
   f. 105 220
   g. 951 021
   h. 1 365 500

2. Round each number to the nearest 10 000
   a. 29 000
   b. 52 000
   c. 145 000
   d. 209 000
   e. 765 900
   f. 231 900
   g. 684 625
   h. 1 909 000

3. Round each number to the nearest 100 000
   a. 480 000
   b. 320 000
   c. 1 450 000
   d. 4 608 000
   e. 1 659 000
   f. 2 783 540
   g. 1 999 000
   h. 12 832 359

4. Round the following numbers to the nearest 1 000 000
   a. 2 990 000
   b. 3 050 000
   c. 6 500 000
   d. 15 650 000
   e. 4 459 999
   f. 1 755 000

Newspapers often use numbers that have been rounded.

They are easier to read and have more impact.

> **Example**
>
> 24 989 fans attend football match!   or   25 000 fans attend football match!
>
> The second headline is more likely to grab the reader's attention.

5. Round the numbers in the following headlines.
   a. 2 987 000 unemployed
   b. Company announces 7018 job losses
   c. 12 756 people attend charity event
   d. £1 987 649 lottery win
   e. 4721 new jobs created
   f. 3 005 021 copies of record sold
   g. £21 095 000 profits for company
   h. 278 650 people to benefit from new laser treatment

Rounding and Estimation

 Activity

See how many numbers you can find, in newspapers, that have been rounded.

B. Use estimates to check calculations

You can use an estimate to check whether the answer to a calculation is about the right size (sometimes said to be 'of the **correct order**').

 Example

	Year 1	Year 2
Company profits	£145 270	£277 650

The chairman of the company says,

'In the second year company profits rose by over £132 000'

Is this likely to be true?

To the nearest £10 000:   £145 270 is approximately £150 000

£277 600 is approximately £280 000

280 − 150 = 130 so £280 000 − £150 000 = £130 000

The answer is about the right size and the statement is **likely to be true**.

 Practice

1. The table below gives the number of employees in the four main sectors of industry in the North East and South East regions of England in one year.

	Number of people employed			
	Manufacturing	Wholesale and retail	Construction	Health and social work
North East	117 995	117 216	91 300	170 555
South East	306 391	662 860	339 761	495 212

Data source: 2011 Census, Office for National Statistics

Use estimates to decide whether each statement is true or false.

   a. Just under 200 000 more people were employed in manufacturing in the South East than in the North East. True or False?

   b. Approximately twice as many people were employed in construction in the South East as in the North East. True or False?

   c. Approximately three times as many people were employed in health and social work in the South East as in the North East. True or False?

51

Number

d. Approximately three times as many people were employed in wholesale and retail in the South East than in the North East. True or False?

e. Approximately 300 000 people were employed in either manufacturing or construction in the North East. True or False?

f. Nearly half a million people were employed in health and social work in the South East. True or False?

g. Approximately one million people were employed in either manufacturing or wholesale and retail in the South East. True or False?

You will need to carry out a series of calculations with large numbers to solve the following problem. Use estimation to check your answers at each stage.

2. The money taken at a charity concert is listed below in the income table. The expenditure table shows the costs of putting on the concert.

Income	Total (£)
2976 tickets @ £25 each	
2204 tickets @ £12 each	
1008 programmes @ £3 each	
592 souvenir mugs @ £8 each	
Total	

Expenditure	Total (£)
Hire of venue and insurance	17 750
Publicity and printing	4 899
8 technicians @ £489 each	
50 security staff @ £175 each	
Performers (donated time)	0
Total	

a. Copy and complete the tables to find the total income and total expenditure.

b. Calculate the difference between the values in part **a** to find out how much money was raised.

Strategies for checking calculations with numbers of any size

Specification reference L2.N2

A. Use estimates to check answers are of the correct order

Example

The table gives UK cinema admissions (no. of tickets sold).
How many more admissions were there in 2010 than 2000?

169.2 − 142.5 = 26.7 million = **26 700 000**

```
  169.2
− 142.5
  ─────
   26.7
```

| 2000 | 142.5 million |
| 2010 | 169.2 million |

Data source: Cinema Exhibitors Association (EDI Rentrak)

Check: 170 million − 140 million = 30 million

This agrees as 26 700 000 rounded to the nearest ten million is 30 million.

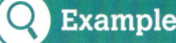 1002 SEARCH

Rounding and Estimation

Practice

1. Use estimation to identify which of the following have answers of the wrong order and must therefore be incorrect. Write down your estimations.
   a. 285 × 79 = 222 515
   b. 1 242 800 − 39 700 = 1 203 100
   c. 288 760 ÷ 120 = 23.98
   d. 375 472 + 412 299 + 1 200 000 = 1 987 771

2. The table gives the number of people who went to a cinema in each year shown.
   a. Use a calculator to find the increase or decrease in cinema admissions between consecutive years shown in the table. Give your answers in full.
   b. Use estimation to check that your answers are of the right order.

Year	Cinema admissions (millions)
1935	912.3
1945	1585.0
1955	1181.8
1965	326.8
1975	116.3
1985	72.0
1995	114.6
2005	164.6
2015	171.5

Data source: www.cinemauk.org.uk

B. Use reverse calculations to check answers are accurate

Example

Profits of £2 540 000 million are shared equally between 8 company directors. How much does each director get?

£2 542 000 ÷ 8 = **£317 750**

Check: £317 750 × 8 = £2 542 000

Reverse the division by multiplying.

Example

A bank account is overdrawn with a balance of −£148

£167 is paid into the account. What is the balance of the account now?

−£148 + £167 = **£19**

Check: £19 − £167 = −£148

Reverse the addition by subtracting.

Practice

Use a calculator for the following questions and check your answers using reverse calculations.

1. a. 199 × 256
   b. 597 622 + 32 546 + 188 995
   c. 119 472 ÷ 152
   d. 10 000 000 − 192 856 − 28 732

2. A £1 329 000 lottery win is shared between three people. How much do they each get?

3. A bank account has a balance of £312. Two amounts of £189 and £176 are paid out of the account and £41 is paid into the account. What is the balance of the account now?

For more practice see 'Calculate efficiently' page 81.

Chapter Summary
4 Rounding and Estimation

- Estimation uses rounded numbers that are easy to calculate with to give an approximate answer to a complicated calculation. Estimation can be used when an exact answer is not needed. It can also be used to check whether the answer to an exact calculation is sensible.
- Rounding to the nearest 10 gives whole numbers that end in 0. If the **U**nits digit is less than 5 then the **T**ens digit stays the same, if it is 5 or above the **T**ens digit goes up.
- Rounding to the nearest 100 gives whole numbers with 0 in the **T**ens and **U**nits places. If the **T**ens digit is less than 5 then the **H**undreds digit stays the same, if it is 5 or above the **H**undreds digit goes up.
- Whether you round to 10 or 100 depends on the size of the number and how accurate the answer needs to be.

- Rounding to the nearest 1000, 10 000, 100 000, 1 000 000 is similar to rounding to 10 or 100. Look at the **deciding digit** (the digit to the right of the column the number is being rounded to). If the deciding digit is below 5 then the digit to its left will stay the same, if it is 5 or above the digit to the left will go up.
- Rounded numbers and estimation can be used to check whether answers are of **the correct order** (about the right size).

- **Reverse calculations** can be used to check that answers to calculations are accurate (subtraction is the reverse of addition, division is the reverse of multiplication).

Number — 5 Ratio and Proportion

Work with ratio and proportion

Specification reference: **L1.N17**

A. Ratios

When you dilute drinks or chemicals or follow a recipe you need to mix ingredients in the correct **ratio** to get the right result. The ratio is often given in terms of 'parts'. The size of a 'part' depends on how much of the mixture you need.

Example

The instructions on a bottle of plant food say, 'Dilute 1 part plant food to 3 parts water'.

This means you need to use **3 times as much water as plant food** to get the correct strength.

You can mix up a large amount

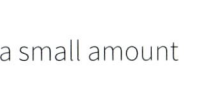 + [3 parts water (1 × 3)] = [4 parts of diluted plant food (1 × 4)]

1 part plant food

or a small amount

[1 part plant food (250 mℓ)] + [3 parts water (250 × 3 = 750 mℓ)] = [4 parts of diluted plant food (250 × 4 = 1000 mℓ)]

depending on how much you need.

As long as the ratio of plant food to water stays the same, the mixture will have the same strength or dilution.

Example

Instructions for mixing pink paint say, 'Mix 1 part red with 4 parts white.'

a. How much white paint should you mix with 500 mℓ of red paint?
b. How much red paint should you mix with 500 mℓ of white paint?

a. Red paint   1 part = 500 mℓ
   White paint   4 parts = 500 × 4 = **2000 mℓ** or **2 litres**

                                                                                               1 litre = 1000 mℓ

b. White paint   4 parts = 500 mℓ
   Red paint   1 part = 500 ÷ 4 = **125 mℓ**

$$4\overline{)5^{1}0^{2}0} = 125$$

MyMaths   1036, 1037   SEARCH

Number

Practice

1. a. How much water should you mix with 50 mℓ of orange squash?
   b. How much water should you mix with 100 mℓ of orange squash?
   c. If you mix the correct amount of water with 200 mℓ of orange squash, how much diluted squash will you have?

2. a. How much water should you mix with 250 mℓ of shampoo?
   b. How much water should you mix with 500 mℓ of shampoo?
   c. If the correct amount of water is mixed with 800 mℓ of shampoo, will it fit into a 5 litre (5000 mℓ) bucket?

Dilute 1 part orange squash with 4 parts water

Mix one part shampoo with six parts warm water

Carpet Shampoo

3. For **standard** mortar mix 1 part cement with 5 parts sand.
   For **strong** mortar mix 1 part cement with 3 parts sand

	Cement	Sand
Standard mortar	5 kg	
		50 kg
	15 kg	
Strong mortar	3 kg	
	12 kg	
		60 kg

Hint
For sand **multiply** by 5 (or 3).
For cement **divide** by 5 (or 3).

Copy and complete the table by giving the missing quantities for sand and cement.

B. Direct proportion

Sometimes instructions give the amount of each ingredient rather than using 'parts'. If you need more (or less) of the mixture then you need to increase (or decrease) the quantity of each ingredient **in proportion**.

For example: to **double** the amount, **multiply everything by 2**
to make **five** times as much, **multiply everything by 5**
to make **half** the amount, **divide everything by 2**
to make a **third** of the amount, **divide everything by 3**

Example

Mushroom Soup (serves 4)

225 g mushrooms	1 onion	1 potato
710 mℓ milk	50 g butter	5 mℓ thyme
sprig of parsley	salt & pepper to taste	

How much of each ingredient do you need to make mushroom soup for 8 people?

For twice as many people, you need double the amount of soup. Therefore, you need to double the amount of each ingredient.

| 450 g mushrooms | 2 onions | 2 potatoes | 1420 mℓ milk |
| 100 g butter | 10 mℓ thyme | 2 sprigs of parsley | salt & pepper to taste |

Ratio and Proportion

Example

The instructions on a bottle of floor cleaner say:
'Pour 2 capfuls (30 mℓ) into a bucket with 6 litres of water.'

1. How much floor cleaner should you use with 3 litres of water?
2. How much floor cleaner should you use with 1 litre of water?

1. The amount of water has been halved (divided by 2), so the amount of floor cleaner should be halved. This means you need **1 capful (15 mℓ)** of floor cleaner.

2. This is a third of the amount of water in part **1**.

   You should use a third of the amount of floor cleaner. $15 \div 3 = 5$

   This means you need **5 mℓ (a third of a capful)** of floor cleaner.

Practice

1. a. Rewrite the naan bread recipe to make:
      i. 12 naan breads
      ii. 3 naan breads.
   b. How much milk, flour and yoghurt do you need to make 2 naan breads?

   Naan Bread Ingredients
150 mℓ milk	2 teaspoons caster sugar
450 g plain flour	2 teaspoons dried yeast
150 mℓ plain yoghurt	$\frac{1}{2}$ teaspoon salt
1 egg	1 teaspoon baking powder
	2 tablespoons vegetable oil

   Makes 6 breads

2. Look at the instructions on the jar of gravy granules.
   How many teaspoons of gravy granules do you need to make:
   a. 560 mℓ (1 pint) of gravy
   b. 140 mℓ ($\frac{1}{4}$ pint) of gravy
   c. 70 mℓ ($\frac{1}{8}$ pint) of gravy?

Gravy granules
Mix 4 teaspoons of granules with 280 mℓ ($\frac{1}{2}$ pint) of water

3. Look at the instructions on the box of plaster.
   a. How much water should you mix with these amounts of plaster?
      i. 1250 g
      ii. 500 g
      iii. 250 g
   b. How much water and plaster should you mix together to cover:
      i. 2 square metres
      ii. 4 square metres?

Note: 1 litre = 1000 mℓ

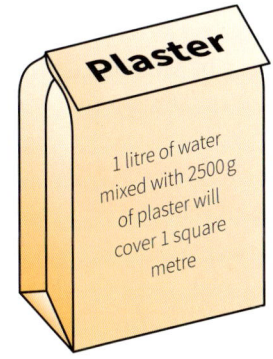

Plaster
1 litre of water mixed with 2500 g of plaster will cover 1 square metre

Number

Calculate with ratios

Specification reference: **L1.N17, L2.N11**

Level 1

A. Simplify ratios and find amounts

The ratio '1 part plant food to 3 parts water' can be written as 1:3

This form is useful for simplifying ratios with large numbers and units of measurement.

> 💡 **Key point**
> To simplify a ratio, divide both sides by the same number.

 This is like simplifying fractions. See pages 107–108.

Suppose a recipe for pastry uses 100 g of butter and 200 g flour.

The ratio of butter to flour is 100:200

In this case, you can divide by 100 (or by 10 then 10 again, or by 5 then 20).

The ratio of butter to flour is 1:2

This means there is twice as much flour as butter.

When the units are the same, you do not need to write them in the ratio.

1:2

This ratio can be applied to any quantity.

The table shows some possibilities.

Butter (g)	Flour (g)
50	100
75	150
200	400

🔍 Example

A builder mixes 150 kg of sand with 50 kg of cement to make concrete.

1. Write the ratio of sand to cement in its simplest form.
2. The builder needs more concrete.
   a. How much sand should he mix with 600 kg of cement?
   b. How much cement should he mix with 750 kg of sand?

1. The ratio of sand to cement is 150:50

   To simplify this, divide each number by 50 (or divide by 10, then by 5).

   The ratio of sand to cement is **3:1**

2. Use the ratio of sand to cement 3:1
   a. If 1 part cement = 600 kg
      then 3 parts sand = 600 × 3 = **1800 kg**
   b. If 3 parts sand = 750 kg
      then 1 part cement = 750 ÷ 3 = **250 kg**

> 💡 **Key point**
> 3:1 means the builder uses 3 times as much sand as cement.
> The order is very important. 1:3 would mean 3 times as much cement as sand.

58   MyMaths   1039, 1052, 1243   SEARCH

Ratio and Proportion

Practice

1. Simplify the ratio in each statement.
   a. The ratio of tennis players to badminton players in a sports club is 80 : 40
   b. The ratio of management to staff in a factory is 30 : 150
   c. In a batch of light bulbs the ratio of good to faulty is 7000 : 500
   d. The ratio of adults to children is 15 : 75
   e. The ratio of home to away supporters at a match is 24 000 : 8000

   Hint Keep dividing until you have the smallest possible numbers.

2. A painter mixes 2 litres of red paint with 8 litres of yellow paint to make orange.
   a. Write the ratio of red paint to yellow paint in its simplest form.
   b. The painter needs more of the same shade of orange paint.
      i. How much yellow paint should she mix with 3 litres of red?
      ii. How much red paint should she mix with 400 millilitres of yellow?

3. A gardener makes potting compost by mixing 100 litres of soil with 20 litres of peat.
   a. Write the ratio of soil to peat in its simplest form.
   b. The gardener needs more compost.
      i. How much soil should he mix with 50 litres of peat?
      ii. How much peat should he mix with 300 litres of soil?

Sometimes ratios are more difficult.

Example

The recipe for a mocktail says:
'Mix 75 mℓ of strawberry syrup with 100 mℓ of mango juice and 150 mℓ of apple juice.'

1. Write this as a ratio in its simplest form.
2. How much mango juice and apple juice should you mix with 120 mℓ of strawberry syrup?

1. The ratio of the ingredients is   75 : 100 : 150

   To simplify this, divide each number by 25 (or 5 then 5 again).

   The ratio of strawberry syrup to mango juice to apple juice is **3 : 4 : 6**

2. Using the ratio 3 : 4 : 6   if 3 parts strawberry syrup = 120 mℓ

   then 1 part = 120 ÷ 3 = 40 mℓ

   4 parts mango juice = 4 × 40 = **160 mℓ**

   6 parts apple juice = 6 × 40 = **240 mℓ**

   Find one part first, then multiply to find each amount.

4. Simplify the ratio in each statement.
   a. The ratio of boys to girls at a party is 20 : 30
   b. The ratio of helpers to children is 12 : 54
   c. The ratio of games won, drawn and lost is 12 : 3 : 18
   d. The ratio of A, B and C exam grades is 30 : 45 : 75
   e. The ratio of votes for 3 candidates is 132 000 : 72 000 : 40 000

5. a. Look at the descaler instructions for coffee machines.
      i. Write the ratio of descaler to water in its simplest form.
      ii. How much water should you mix with 100 mℓ of descaler?
   b. Look at the descaler instructions for kettles.
      i. Write the ratio of descaler to water in its simplest form.
      ii. How much water should you mix with 400 mℓ of descaler?

Descaler instructions

For coffee machines mix 125 mℓ of descaler with 500 mℓ of water.

For kettles mix 500 mℓ of descaler with 750 mℓ of water.

6. a. Use the 'Mix and Match' information for velvet green paint.
      i. Write the quantities of white, moss and leaf green paint as a ratio in its simplest form.
      ii. How much moss and leaf green paint should you mix with 80 mℓ of white paint?
      iii. How much white and leaf green paint should you mix with 1800 mℓ of moss paint?
   b. Use the 'Mix and Match' information for Sepia Tint paint.
      i. Write the quantities of white, beige and chocolate brown paint as a ratio in its simplest form.
      ii. How much beige and chocolate brown paint should you mix with 80 mℓ of white paint?
      iii. How much white and chocolate brown paint should you mix with 180 mℓ of beige paint?
      iv. How much white and beige paint should you mix with 750 mℓ of chocolate brown paint?

Mix and Match Paints

Velvet Green
To make 1 litre (1000 mℓ) mix:
  50 mℓ white
  450 mℓ moss
  500 mℓ leaf green

Sepia Tint
To make 1 litre (1000 mℓ) mix:
  200 mℓ white
  300 mℓ beige
  500 mℓ chocolate brown

 Key point

Quantities must be in the **same units** before you can simplify the ratio.

Ratio and Proportion

Example

The instructions on a bottle of cleaning fluid say:
'Mix 50 mℓ of cleaning fluid with 1 litre of water.'

How much water should you mix with 80 mℓ of cleaning fluid?

> 1 litre = 1000 mℓ

The ratio of cleaning fluid to water is 50 mℓ : 1 litre.

It is easier to convert the larger units into the smaller ones.

The ratio of cleaning fluid to water = 50 : 1000 = 1 : 20

> Divide both sides by 50, or by 10 then 5

The amount of cleaning fluid = 1 part = 80 mℓ.

The amount of water = 20 parts = 80 mℓ × 20 = **1 600 mℓ (or 1.6 litres)**.

7. Write each ratio in its simplest form.
   a. cream : milk = 40 mℓ : 1 litre
   b. biscuits : butter = 1 kg : 250 g
   c. gate : fence = 90 cm : 18 m
   d. present : postage = £12 : £1.50
   e. plan : actual distance = 6 cm : 3 m
   f. cost : VAT = £4 : 80p

Conversions

1 litre = 1000 mℓ	1 m = 100 cm
1 kg = 1000 g	1 m = 1000 mm
1 tonne = 1000 kg	1 km = 1000 m
1 lb = 16 oz	

8. Look at the bottle of dye.
   a. Write the ratio of dye to water in its simplest form.
   b. How much dye do you need to mix with 5 litres of water?
   c. How much water do you need to mix with 50 mℓ of dye?

DYE
Mix 200 mℓ with 1 litre of water

9. A food shop sells different sized packs of fruit and nuts (in the same proportions).
   A medium pack contains 500 g of fruit and 1 kg of nuts.
   a. Write the ratio of fruit to nuts in its simplest form.
   b. A small pack contains 200 g of fruit. What weight of nuts does it contain?
   c. A giant pack contains $2\frac{1}{2}$ kg of nuts. What weight of fruit does it contain?

Example

Level 2

The scale of a map is 4 cm : 1 km.

Write this as a ratio in the form 1 : n.

We need to convert 1 km to cm.

1 km = 1000 m and 1 m = 100 cm so 1 km = 1000 × 100 = 100 000 cm

The ratio = 4 : 100 000

Divide both sides by 4:   Ratio = **1 : 25 000**

10. A plan of a kitchen has a scale of 20 mm : 1 m.
    a. Write this ratio in the form $1:n$.
    b. A kitchen unit is 600 mm wide. What is its width on the plan?
    c. The length of the kitchen is 90 mm on the plan.
    What is the actual length of the kitchen?

11. Write each ratio in its simplest form.
    a. lawn food : water = 30 mℓ : 1 litre
    b. chocolate : toffee = 1 kg : 800 g
    c. lace trim : ribbon = 25 cm : 3.5 m
    d. card : stamp = £1.95 : 60p
    e. map : actual distance = 6 cm : 3 km
    f. cost : VAT = £42 : £8.40
    g. cement : lime : sand = 500 kg : 1 tonne : 4.5 tonnes
    h. flour : butter : sugar : dried fruit = 1 lb : 8 oz : 8 oz : 12 oz   **Hint** 1 lb = 16 oz

12. Look at the bottle of weedkiller.
    a. Write the ratio of weedkiller and water in its simplest form.
    b. How much water is needed with 40 mℓ of weedkiller?
    c. How much weedkiller is needed with 2400 mℓ of water?

13. A pet shop makes 'Small Pet Food Mix' by mixing
    $1\frac{1}{2}$ kg cereal, 400 g nuts and 200 g seeds.
    a. Write these quantities in the same units as a ratio, then simplify it.
       (Note: 1 kg = 1000 g)
    b. The mixture is always made with the ingredients in the same proportion.
        i. What quantities of cereal and nuts are mixed with 20 g of seeds?
        ii. What quantities of nuts and seeds are mixed with 600 g of cereal?

14. The scale on a map is 1 : 50 000
    a. What does 1 cm on the map represent?
       Give your answer in metres.

    For more practice with scale diagrams and maps, see pages 222–228.

    b. What does 2 cm on the map represent?
       Give your answer in kilometres.
    c. What measurement on the map would represent the following distances?
        i. 5 km
        ii. 2.5 km
        iii. 1.5 km
        iv. 0.75 km

B. Make a total amount

Sometimes you need to find the quantity of each ingredient to make a particular total amount.

Example

How much anti-freeze and how much water do you need to make 1 litre (1000 mℓ) of diluted anti-freeze?

The ratio 1 : 3 means
1 part anti-freeze + 3 parts water
= 4 parts diluted anti-freeze.

Add the parts to find the total number of parts.

These 4 parts need to make 1000 mℓ so 1 part = 1000 ÷ 4 = 250 mℓ.

Divide to find one part.

Amount of anti-freeze = 1 part = **250 mℓ**.
Amount of water = 3 parts = 3 × 250 = **750 mℓ**.

Check your answer by adding:
250 mℓ anti-freeze + 750 mℓ water
= 1000 mℓ diluted anti-freeze.

The ratio 1:3 means that $\frac{1}{4}$ of the diluted anti-freeze will be anti-freeze and $\frac{3}{4}$ will be water.

Anti-Freeze
Dilute with water in ratio 1 : 3

Practice

1. Stacey makes necklaces using black and white beads in the ratio 1 : 2
   She wants to make a necklace with a total of 45 beads.
   How many black and how many white beads does she need?

2. A food company mixes oats and fruit in the ratio 3 : 1 to make breakfast cereal.
   Work out the weight of oats and the weight of the fruit in:
   a. 400 g of breakfast cereal
   b. 1 kg of breakfast cereal. (Remember 1 kg = 1000 g)

3. Rowan mixes white and brown flour in the ratio 4 : 1 to make bread.
   How much white flour and how much brown flour does he mix to make a total of:
   a. 750 g of flour
   b. 1 kg of flour? (Remember 1 kg = 1000 g)

4. The instructions on a bottle of squash say, 'Dilute one part orange squash with four parts water.'
   How much squash and how much water do you need to make:
   a. 1 litre of diluted squash (Remember 1 litre = 1000 mℓ)
   b. $1\frac{1}{2}$ litres of diluted squash?

5. Look at the information for Sunny Day paint.
   How much of each colour of paint do I need to make:
   a. 5 litres of Sunny Day paint
   b. 1 litre of Sunny Day paint?

Mix and Match Paints
To make Sunny Day, mix
1 part tangerine paint,
1 part white paint and
3 parts buttercup paint

Number

6. A health shop mixes ingredients to make bags of muesli.

   The amounts for a 1 kg bag are: 600 g cereal, 250 g fruit, 150 g nuts.

   a. Write this as a ratio in its simplest form.
   b. Calculate how much of each ingredient is needed to make:
      i. 800 g of muesli
      ii. 1800 g of muesli.

7. The population of a town consists of 15 000 red-haired people, 45 000 blonde-haired people and 150 000 dark-haired people.

   a. Write this information as a ratio and simplify it.
   b. A new company in the town plans to employ 420 people. If the new employees are representative of the population of the town, state how many of each hair colour there are likely to be.

8. Ahmed, Ben and Cilla invest £4000, £10 000 and £16 000 in a new business.

   They agree to share any profits in the ratio of their investments.

   a. Write the investments as a ratio in its simplest form.
   b. In its first year the company makes a profit of £45 000

      How much does each person get?
   c. Ben gets £25 000 from the second year's profits.

      What was the total profit for the second year?
   d. Cilla gets £100 000 from the third year's profits.

      What was the total profit for the third year?
   e. Find the total amount received by each person during these 3 years.

C. Use ratios to compare prices

You can compare prices by finding the value of a 'part'.

> **Example**
>
> The 200 g jar of coffee costs £5.50
> The 300 g jar costs £6.99
> Which is better value?
>
> The ratio of the weights of the jars is 200 : 300 = 2 : 3
>
> The smaller jar has 2 parts and the larger jar has 3 parts.
>
> For the smaller jar: cost of 1 part = £5.50 ÷ 2 = £2.75
>
> For the larger jar: cost of 1 part = £6.99 ÷ 3 = £2.33
>
> The **larger** jar is the better value.
>
>
>
> Find the cost of 1 part for each jar.
> (This is the cost per 100 g in this case.)

There are other ways to work out the best value. In the Example above you could find the cost per 100 g for the smaller jar, then multiply by 3 and compare the result with the cost of the larger jar. You could use this way as a check.

Ratio and Proportion

Practice

1. In each case find which is the better value.

a.
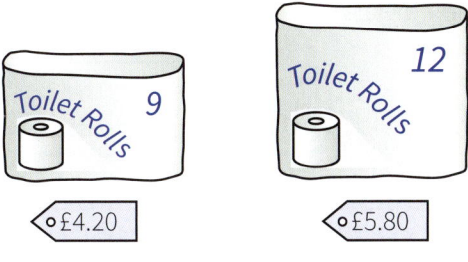
£4.20   £5.80

b.

£3.40   £4.80

c.

Corn Flakes 375 g — £2.85
Corn Flakes 500 g — £3.90

d.

Envelopes 100 — £1.25
Envelopes 200 — £4.50
Envelopes 500 — £9.99

e.
 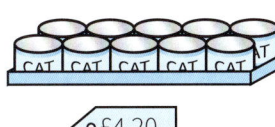 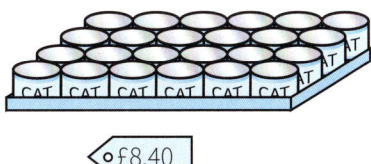
£1.90   £4.20   £8.40

2. A builders' merchant delivers loose sand at £27.50 for 0.5 tonnes, £52.50 for 1 tonne or £240 for 5 tonnes.

The builders' merchant also sells bags of sand at £2.75 for a 25-kg bag and £4.50 for a 40-kg bag.

A local store charges £2.50 for a 5-kg bag of sand.

a. Calculate the price per tonne in each case. (Remember 1 tonne = 1000 kg)

b. A builder buys 0.5 tonnes of loose sand from the builders' merchant but only uses 0.3 tonnes. He sells the rest at the same rate as he paid for it. How much money does he get from the sale?

c. What would a 5-kg bag cost if it was charged at the same rate as 5 tonnes of loose sand?

Inverse proportion

Specification reference **L2.N11**

Level 2

Sometimes an increase in one quantity leads to a proportionate decrease in another quantity. This is called **inverse proportion.**

Example

A packet of biscuits is shared between 6 people. They get 4 biscuits each.

If the same packet was shared between 3 people, how many biscuits would each person get?

The number of people has halved.

The number of biscuits for each person will double.

4 biscuits × 2 = **8 biscuits**

MyMaths   1038, 1052   SEARCH

Example

A machine fills 6000 jam jars in an hour.

How long would it take 5 machines to fill the same number of jars?

The number of machines has been multiplied by 5

The time taken will be divided by 5

> This assumes the machines are identical.

60 minutes ÷ 5 = **12 minutes**

Example

It takes 3 people 2 hours to paint a wall.

Estimate how long it would take if there were 4 people.

First estimate how long it would take **1 person**.

> This is called the **unitary** method.

Assuming that 1 person takes 3 times as long as 3 people:

1 person would take 2 hours × 3 = 6 hours.

4 people would take $\frac{1}{4}$ of this time so 6 hours ÷ 4 = $1\frac{1}{2}$ **hours**.

> This assumes that all the people, however many there are, work at the same rate. Although this may not be true, $1\frac{1}{2}$ hours is the best estimate that can be found.

The unitary method in the last Example, of reducing the quantity that changes to 1, is useful when there is no obvious connection between the numbers.

Example

A ship with 450 passengers has enough food for 21 days.
60 of the passengers leave the ship at this point.

Estimate how much longer the food will last now. State any assumptions.

Assume each passenger needs the same amount of daily food.

Number of days the food would last 1 passenger = 450 × 21 days.

Number of days the food will last 390 passengers = $\frac{450 \times 21}{390}$ = 24.23… days

The food is likely to last **3 days longer**.

> When an estimate is asked for, round the answer sensibly. It is not exact.

Ratio and Proportion

Practice

1. A bunch of grapes is shared equally between 8 children. Each child gets 5 grapes. If the same bunch were shared equally between 4 children, how many grapes would each child get?

2. Ten 25-kg sacks of potatoes are re-packed into 5-kg bags. How many 5-kg bags will there be?

3. Eight people share the cost of hiring a minibus. They each pay £30.
   How much would it cost each person if:
   a. 6 people shared the cost
   b. 12 people shared the cost?

4. One filling machine can fill 5000 cans in an hour.
   a. How long would it take 3 filling machines?
   b. How long would it take 6 filling machines?

5. A journey takes 45 minutes travelling at an average speed of 40 miles an hour. How long would the journey take travelling at an average speed of:
   a. 20 miles an hour
   b. 60 miles an hour?

   Hint Use your answer to part **a** to help in **b**.

6. Three printing machines can print 300 sheets in a minute. How long would it take:
   a. 2 machines
   b. 4 machines?

In questions **7–12** state any assumptions you make.

7. Two pumps fill a swimming pool in $3\frac{1}{2}$ hours. Estimate how long this would take with three pumps.

8. Last year a fruit farm employed 8 workers who picked a crop in 9 days.
   This year only 6 workers have applied for the job.
   How many days is it likely to take to pick the crop this year?

9. A builder has employed 5 labourers to clear a site in 12 days. The owner says the site needs to be cleared in 10 days. How many extra labourers are needed?

10. Five friends each agree to invest £3000 to set up a business. One of the friends drops out.
    How much more does each of the other people need to invest?

11. A supplier says a consignment of rice will give 16 meals for each of 200 people.
    A charity buys the rice to feed a camp of 440 people.
    Estimate how many meals each person will get.

12. Instructions on a ready meal say:

    > **Microwave:** Cook for 6 minutes at 850 watts.
    > For lower wattage microwaves, increase the cooking time.

    The power of Oliver's microwave is only 600 watts.
    Suggest how much longer he should give the meal to cook.

Chapter Summary
5 Ratio and Proportion

- Ratios can be expressed as parts e.g. 1 part to 4 parts, or in the form 1 : 4. The order in which the parts are written is important.
- **Direct proportion** means that as one quantity increases the other quantities increase by the same factor. If one quantity is multiplied or divided, the other quantities are multiplied or divided by the same amount.
- Ratios can be simplified by dividing both sides by the same number.
- If each part of the ratio has the same units e.g. 1 km : 4 km, then you do not need to include the units.

- Ratios can have any number of parts e.g. 1 : 2 : 5 includes 8 parts.
- To find the value of one part, divide the total amount by the total number of parts.
- Quantities must be in the same units before the ratio can be simplified.
- Ratios can be used to find the best value by finding the cost of equal parts and comparing them.
- **Inverse proportion** means that as one part increases, the other decreases by the same factor. If one quantity is multiplied, the other quantity is divided by the same amount.
- The **unitary method** finds the value of one part to calculate others.

Number — 6 Using Algebra

Number patterns and formulae

Specification reference **EL3.N6**

Look at the table. It shows the cost of hiring a boat for different lengths of time.

Number of hours	1	2	3	4
Cost (£)	7	14	21	28

You may recognise the number pattern in the bottom row.
These numbers are **multiples** of 7.
This is because the boat costs £7 per hour to hire.

The number pattern can be described as a **sequence** where the rule for finding the next term is 'add 7'.

> See page 33 for Number Sequences

The sequence can also be written as a **formula** which can be used to work out the cost for any number of hours:

Cost = £7 × number of hours

Example: use the formula to find the cost for 10 hours:

Cost = £7 × 10 = £70

> **Key point**
> A formula gives a relationship between quantities.

You can check this by continuing the number pattern:

7   14   21   28   35   42   49   56   63   70

Example

A kayak can be hired for £8 an hour. There is also a £5 fixed fee for hiring a waterproof container.

The table shows the cost per hour.

The rule for this pattern or sequence is 'add 8' because the kayak costs £8 an hour to hire.

Number of hours	1	2	3	4
Cost (£)	13	21	29	37

The first term is 8 + 5 because it costs £5 to hire the container for any number of hours.

The formula is:

Cost = £8 × number of hours + £5

Calculate the cost for 7 hours:

Cost = £8 × 7 + £5 = **£61**

To check the answer continue the sequence in the table, adding 8 to each term.

Number of hours	1	2	3	4	5	6	7
Cost (£)	13	21	29	37	45	53	61

Practice

1. The table shows how much it costs to buy different numbers of coffee mugs.

   a. Describe the pattern in numbers in the bottom row of the table.

Number of mugs	1	2	3	4
Cost (£)	4	8	12	16

   b. Write down a formula that works out the cost for any number of mugs.

   c. Use your formula to find the cost of 6 mugs.

   d. Use a different method to check your answer to part **c**.

2. A company charges £15 an hour for a cleaning machine plus £10 for the cleaning fluid.

   a. Copy and complete the table.

Number of hours	1	2	3	4	5
Cost (£)	25				

   b. Write a formula that works out the cost for any number of hours.

   c. Use your formula to find the cost for 8 hours.

   d. Use a different method to check your answer to part **c**.

3. A garden centre charges £12 per metre for fencing and £30 for a gate.

   a. Copy and complete the table to show the total cost for different lengths of fencing and a gate.

Length of fencing (m)	3	4	5	6
Total cost of the fencing and gate (£)	66			

   b. Write a formula that works out the total cost for different lengths of fencing.

   c. Use your formula to find the total cost of 10 metres of fencing and a gate.

   d. Use a different method to check your answer to part **c**.

4. Ian is saving £40 per week for a weekend away that will cost £280.

   The formula that works out how much Ian still needs to save is:

   Amount Ian still needs to save = £280 − £40 × number of weeks that Ian has been saving

   a. Copy and complete the table.

   Hint You will need to multiply before subtracting.

Number of weeks that Ian has been saving	1	2	3	4
Amount still to be saved (£)	240			

   b. Describe the pattern in the numbers in the bottom row of the table.

   c. Use the formula to find how much Ian still needs to save after 7 weeks. Explain what your answer means.

   d. Use a different method to check your answer to part **c**.

5. An electrician charges £42 for a call-out plus £25 for each hour he works on the job.

   a. Draw a table that shows how much it costs for jobs that take 1 hour, 2 hours, 3 hours and 4 hours.
   b. Describe the rule for this sequence.
   c. Write down a formula that works out the total cost for jobs that take different amounts of time.
   d. Use your formula to find the total cost for a job that takes 8 hours.
   e. Use a different method to check your answer to part **d**.

Use simple formulae

Specification reference **L1.N5**

For 2 hours the total charge is 2 × £20 + £10 = £50
For 5 hours the total charge is 5 × £20 + £10 = £110
The formula in words for the total charge is:

Total charge = number of hours × £20 + £10

Hiring the church hall costs £20 an hour plus a fixed administration fee of £10

This formula can be written as a flow chart to make it easier to follow. A flow chart shows the order of the operations.

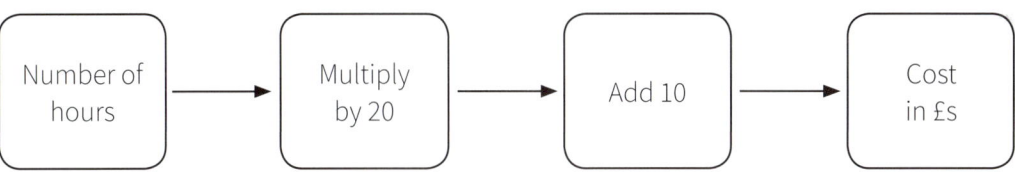

Practice

1. Hiring a hotel conference room for a day costs £15 per delegate plus a fixed charge of £75

   a. Write a flow chart that shows how to calculate the cost of hiring the conference room for a day.
   b. Use your flow chart to calculate the cost of a day's hire for:
      i. 10 delegates   ii. 20 delegates   iii. 50 delegates.

2. A cookery book gives this formula for the time to roast a joint of meat:
   Time in minutes = number of kilograms × 50 minutes + 25 minutes extra

   a. Write this as a flow chart.
   b. Use your flow chart to find the cooking time for a joint of meat weighing:
      i. 2 kg   ii. 2.5 kg   iii. 0.8 kg.

3. A taxi company charges £1.60 a mile plus an £8 call-out fee.

   a. Write a flow chart to calculate the total fare.
   b. Use your flow chart to calculate the total fare for a journey of:
      i. 5 miles   ii. 12 miles   iii. 17.5 miles.

Number

4. Each week a sales assistant earns £7.50 for each customer account he opens, plus his basic pay of £340.

   a. Write a flow chart to calculate his weekly earnings.

   b. Use your flow chart to find how much he earns in a week when he opens:

      i. 4 accounts   ii. 10 accounts   iii. 15 accounts.

5. A builder uses this flow chart to calculate how many bricks are needed.

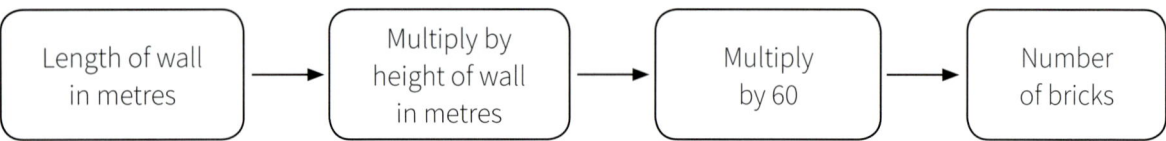

   a. How many bricks are needed for a wall that is:

      i. 3 m long, 0.5 m high   ii. 2.5 m long, 2.5 m high?

   b. Would 300 bricks be enough for a wall that is 6 m long and 0.8 m high? Show how you got your answer.

Order of operations (BIDMAS)

Specification reference L1.N7, L2.N12

A church charges £20 an hour for the hire of its hall, £5 an hour for the hire of its kitchen plus a fixed administration charge of £10. What is the total charge for hiring the hall and kitchen for 3 hours?

The correct answer is £85. Did you get this? How did you work it out?
One way is to add the two charges per hour together first: £20 + £5 = £25
Then multiply by 3 to find the charge for 3 hours: £25 × 3 = £75
Then add the £10 administration charge: £75 + £10 = £85
This arithmetic can be written as one expression: 3 × (£20 + £5) + £10

The brackets show the part that is worked out first.

When you do arithmetic it is essential to add, subtract, multiply or divide the numbers in the correct order. The mathematical convention that you must follow is often called BIDMAS:

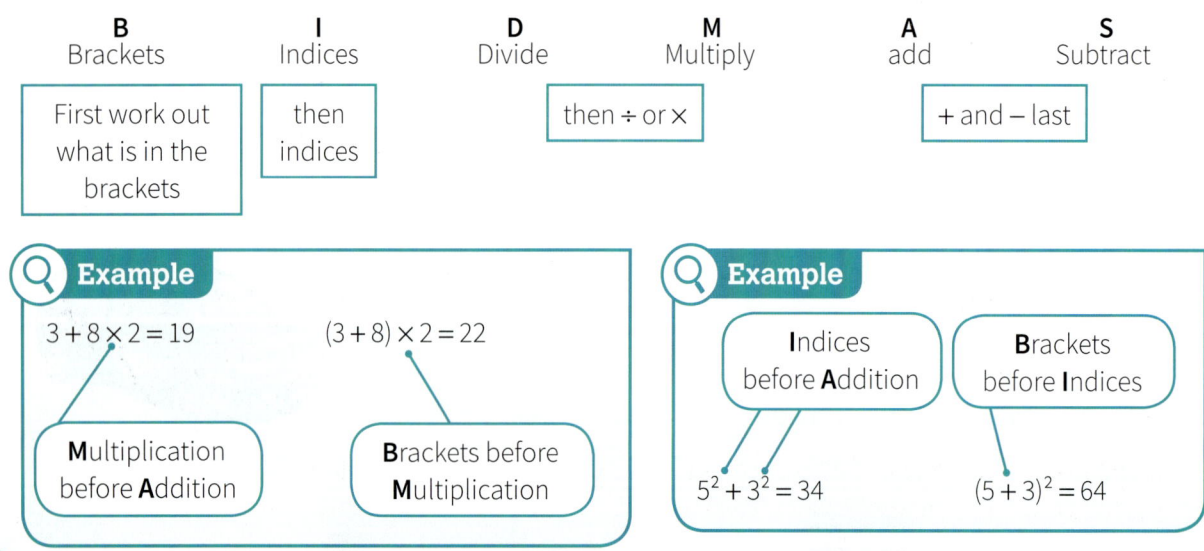

All scientific calculators are programmed to do calculations in the right order.
Many phone calculators also follow BIDMAS.

Check your calculator using the examples on the previous page.

Practice

1. Calculate these without a calculator. Take care to use the right order.

   a. $4 + 8 \div 2$
   b. $(4 + 8) \div 2$
   c. $4 + 8^2$
   d. $(4 + 8)^2$
   e. $11 - 2 \times 3$
   f. $(11 - 2) \times 3$
   g. $11 - 2 \times 3 + 5$
   h. $(11 - 2) \times (3 + 5)$
   i. $20 + 4 \div 2$
   j. $4^2 + 6^2$
   k. $(4 + 6)^2$
   l. $5 - 12 \div 3 - 5$
   m. $20 \div 2 - 3 \times 3$
   n. $6 \times 2 + 3^2$
   o. $6 \times (2 + 3)^2$

2. Write each of these with brackets so that the answer is correct.

   a. $12 - 4 \times 2 = 16$
   b. $20 \div 5 - 3 = 10$
   c. $15 \times 8 - 6 = 30$
   d. $6 + 6 \div 7 - 3 = 3$
   e. $4 + 1^2 = 25$
   f. $2 \times 5^2 = 100$

3.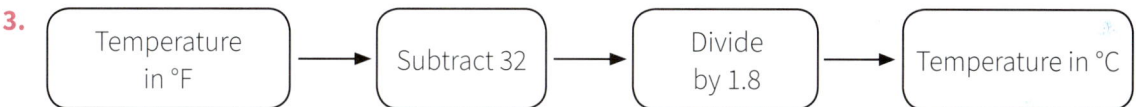

   Use the flow chart to convert these temperatures to °C.

   a. 212 °F
   b. 68 °F
   c. 176 °F
   d. 32 °F

   Hint If you are using a calculator, use brackets to make sure the subtraction comes before the division.

Evaluate algebraic expressions and make substitutions in formulae

Specification reference **L2.N3**

A formula, as well as being written in words or as a flow chart, can be written as an **algebraic** expression using letters. Algebraic formulae are used in many areas such as science, engineering and finance and also for working things out on a spreadsheet.

In the example on page 71 hiring a church hall costs £20 an hour plus a fixed administration fee of £10

Total charge = number of hours × £20 + £10

This can be written as

$C = 20n + 10$

where C = total charge and n = number of hours.

Key point

$20n$ means $20 \times n$

In algebra, the × for multiplication is left out to avoid confusion with the letter x.

Practice

1 a. A plumber charges £50 an hour plus a call out fee of £25

Write this as an algebraic formula. Use C to represent the total cost in £s and n to represent the number of hours.

b. Use your formula to calculate the cost for a plumbing job that takes:

   i. 2 hours   **ii.** 4 hours   **iii.** 6 hours.

2. A demonstrator earns £11 an hour plus £5 for every sewing machine she sells.

a. Write this as a formula. Use P to represent the total pay in £s, t to represent the number of hours worked and n to represent the number of machines sold.

b. Use your formula to calculate her total pay if she:

   i. works 8 hours and sells 3 machines

   ii. works 15 hours and sells 5 machines

   iii. works 40 hours and sells 12 machines.

When using algebraic expressions BIDMAS must be applied.

Example

When a car accelerates smoothly the distance in metres it travels is given by

$$d = \frac{t(u+v)}{2}$$

where u metres per second is its starting speed, v metres per second is its finishing speed and t seconds is the time taken.

The brackets mean you should add u and v first. Then multiply by t because this is next to the brackets (remember this means multiply). Finally divide by 2.

If a car accelerates from 8 metres per second to 12 metres per second in 5 seconds, the distance it travels is:

$$d = \frac{5(8+12)}{2} = \frac{5 \times 20}{2} = \frac{100}{2} = 50 \text{ metres}$$

This means ÷ 2 after working out the top.

3. Use the formula in the above example to calculate the distance d when:

a. $t = 10$, $u = 0$ and $v = 10$ **b.** $t = 3$, $u = 7$ and $v = 11$

4. A building society uses this formula to calculate the maximum loan it allows a couple to have:
$M = 3(A + B)$

M is the maximum loan and A and B are the couple's annual incomes in £s.
Calculate the maximum loan the couple can have when:

a. $A = £20\,000$ and $B = £18\,000$ **b.** $A = £28\,000$ and $B = £25\,000$

c. $A = £35\,000$ and $B = £30\,000$ **d.** $A = £54\,700$ and $B = £38\,250$

5. Use the formula $V = IR$, where V = voltage in volts, I = current in amps and R = resistance in ohms, to find V when $I = 2.4$ and $R = 50$

6. Use the formula $s = \dfrac{d}{t}$, where s = average speed, d = distance and t = time, to find s when:

  a. $d = 150$ miles and $t = 2.5$ hours   **b.** $d = 6$ km and $t = 15$ minutes.

7. Skiing tuition costs a fixed charge of £10 for insurance plus £28 per hour for the instructor and £E per hour for equipment hire (depends on the equipment).

  a. Write this as a formula, using C to represent the total cost in £s and n to represent the number of hours.

  b. Use your formula to calculate the cost for:

    i. 3 hours when $E = 5$ **ii.** 5 hours when $E = 7$ **iii.** $7\tfrac{1}{2}$ hours when $E = 10.50$

8. The formula for calculating the area of a trapezium is:

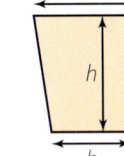

$A = \dfrac{h(a+b)}{2}$ (Assume all the lengths are in cm.)

Find the area of a trapezium when:

For more area and volume formulae, see pages 325–329.

  a. $a = 6, b = 3$ and $h = 4$ **b.** $a = 10, b = 7$ and $h = 8$

  c. $a = 4.5, b = 2.5$ and $h = 3$ **d.** $a = 25, b = 13$ and $h = 15$

9. Use the formula $C = \dfrac{5(F - 32)}{9}$, where C = temperature in °Celsius and F = temperature in °Fahrenheit, to find C when:

  a. $F = 212$ **b.** $F = 77$

10. The area of a circle can be estimated using the formula:

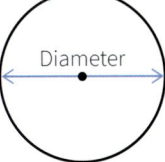

$A = 3\left(\dfrac{d}{2}\right)^2$

The diameter is the distance across the centre of the circle.

where A = area in units squared (cm²) and d = diameter in units (cm).

Estimate the area of a circle with a diameter of:

  a. 2 cm   **b.** 6 cm   **c.** 10 cm.   **Hint** **B**rackets before **I**ndices

11. The formula for calculating Body Mass Index (BMI) is

$$\text{BMI} = \dfrac{w}{h^2}$$

where w = weight in kilograms and h = height in metres.

Use a calculator to find the BMI from the following measurements:

  a. $w = 54$ kg, $h = 1.5$ m   **b.** $w = 64$ kg, $h = 1.6$ m   **c.** $w = 81$ kg, $h = 1.8$ m.

Hint **I**ndices before **D**ivision

Chapter Summary
6 Using Algebra

- A **sequence** is a number pattern created using a rule.
- A **formula** gives a relationship between quantities, such as numbers in a sequence.
- When completing a calculation remember to multiply or divide before you add or subtract.

- Remember **BIDMAS (Brackets, Indices, Division, Multiplication, Addition, Subtraction)** and use the order of the words to help with the order of operations.
- Use **brackets** to show which part of an expression needs to be worked out first.
- Write out a formula using a **flow chart** to make sure that you follow the correct order of operations.
- Remember to use brackets with your calculator so that it performs the calculations in the correct order.

- A formula can be written as an **algebraic expression** using letters, words or a flow chart.
- The multiplication sign (×) isn't used in algebraic expressions, if a letter is multiplied by a number then they are just written next to each other.
- Remember to use BIDMAS for algebraic expressions.
- A straight horizontal line with an expression above and an expression below is a divisor line. The expression on top of the **divisor line** needs to be calculated before the expression below.

Number

7 Mixed Operations and Calculator Practice

Solve problems
Specification reference EL3.N2, EL3.N3, EL3.N4, EL3.M10

When you use maths to solve real-life problems, take care to choose the correct operators (+, −, × or ÷). Always **check that your answer is sensible**, especially if you use a calculator, as it is easy to press the wrong button.

If you do enter a wrong number, you may be able to correct it by pressing a CE (Clear Entry) button. This deletes the last number you entered, without clearing the whole calculation. (Mobile phone calculators may use a different symbol, for example ⟨X.) A C (Clear) button, often in red, clears everything. However, calculators vary and often use other notation such as DEL or AC. Check how your calculator works.

Example

A householder buys a new table for £499

She pays £280 deposit. How much is left to pay?

She pays the rest in 6 equal instalments. How much is each instalment?

Work it out on paper

For the amount left to pay work out 499 − 280

```
  499
− 280
─────
 £219
```

To find the cost of one instalment work out 219 ÷ 6

This means **£36.50**

then check on your calculator

Press

4 9 9 − 2 8 0 =

The calculator will give **219**

See page 119 for money in decimals.

Carry on the calculation

÷ 6 =

The calculator will give 36.5

To show the pence add a zero at the end.

Number

🔍 Example

300 football fans want to go to an away match.

1. One coach can carry 48 fans. How many coaches will be needed?
2. Could one of the 48 seat coaches be replaced by a smaller coach? If so how many seats would it need to have?

Use a calculator.

1. Divide the number of fans by the number of seats on a coach.

   6.25 means 6 whole coaches and part of a coach.

   So **7 coaches** will be needed.

2. 6 coaches could carry 6 lots of 48 people.

   The difference between the number of fans and number of seats in 6 coaches is

   300 − 288 = 12

   A smaller coach could be used to carry **12 fans**.

   Using a written method:

   ```
         6 r 12
   48) 300
       288
       ———
        12
   ```

⚙ Practice

Work these out on paper, then check with a calculator.

1. Jars of jam are packed in boxes of 72. How many jars of jam are there in 8 boxes?
2. A prize of £936 is shared equally between six people. How much do they get each?
3. There are 196 Japanese, 218 Americans and 372 Europeans staying in a hotel.
   a. How many people is this altogether?
   b. How many more Americans than Japanese are there?
4. A householder pays £65 deposit plus 6 instalments of £78 for a new cooker.
   a. What is the total of the instalments?
   b. How much does he pay altogether?
5. Two friends book a holiday. The total cost is £994
   a. They pay a deposit of £99. How much is left to pay altogether?
   b. How much has each friend left to pay? Assume they split the cost equally.

Mixed Operations and Calculator Practice

6. A worker earns £17 per hour overtime.
   a. How much does she earn for 9 hours overtime?
   b. Her basic wage is £418 per week.
   How much does she earn altogether in a week when she does 9 hours overtime?

7. A new car has a mileage of 278 at the beginning of June and 548 at the end of June.
   a. How many miles has the car travelled in June?
   b. How many miles is this per day? (There are 30 days in June.)

8. Tickets for a charity concert cost £16
   a. The organisers sell 62 tickets. What is the total amount of money taken for tickets?
   b. £175 of the money taken for tickets is used to pay for expenses. How much is left for the charity?

9. 500 tulip bulbs are packed in boxes of 15   *(This means use a calculator.)*
   a. How many boxes are filled?
   b. How many bulbs are left over?

Sometimes working things out without a calculator is easier, especially with small numbers.

Example

Paint is sold in 5-litre, 2-litre and 1-litre tins.
The bigger the tin, the better the value, that is,
the bigger the tin, the cheaper the price per litre.

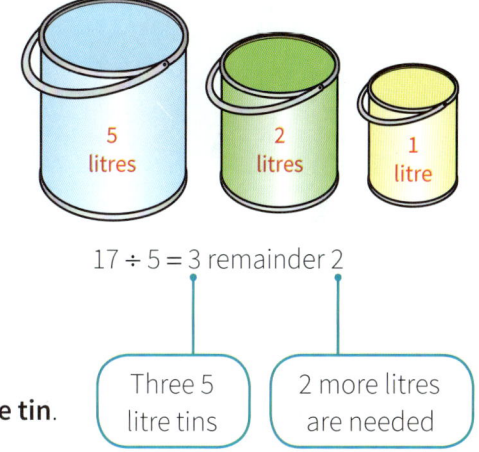

A decorator needs 17 litres of red paint.
Which tins should she buy?

The 5 litre tins are the best value, so the decorator
should buy most of the paint in these.

$17 ÷ 5 = 3$ remainder 2 — Three 5 litre tins — 2 more litres are needed

The decorator should buy **three 5-litre tins and one 2-litre tin**.

Working out $17 ÷ 5$ on a calculator gives 3.4 (5 goes into 17 'three and a bit times'). This means you need 3 whole 5 litre tins and 0.4 (just under half) of the next 5 litre tin. If you decide to buy just three 5 litre tins, you must calculate further to see how much more paint you need:

$3 × 5 = 15$ $17 − 15 = 2$ that is, you need another 2-litre tin (as above).

10. Use the information about paint tins in the example above. Find the cheapest combination of tins for:
   a. 27 litres   **b.** 39 litres   **c.** 128 litres.

11. Paper plates can be bought in packs of 10, 25 or 50
   What combination of packs gives **exactly**:
   a. 40 plates   **b.** 75 plates   **c.** 275 plates   **d.** 360 plates?

Number

> **Example**
>
> A sofa costs £785 when paid for in one go. You can also buy it on credit with a deposit of £50 and 9 monthly payments of £90. How much extra is this?
>
> 9 monthly payments of £90 costs   9 × £90 = £810
>
> To find the total cost, add the £50 deposit   £810 + £50 = £860
>
> Extra cost = difference between the 2 amounts   £860 − £785 = **£75**
>
> You can do these calculations on any calculator as follows: See page 124–125 for the use of calculators with mixed operations.
>
> 9 × 90 = 810   + 50 = 860   − 785 = 75

12.

Pay £399 now or £60 deposit and 6 payments of £65

Pay £995 today or £90 deposit and 9 payments of £120

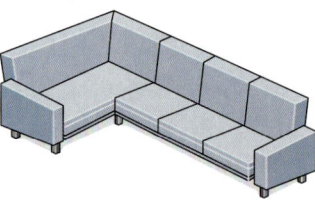

 a. How much more does it cost to buy the armchair on credit?

b. How much more does it cost to buy the sofa on credit?

13.

The pack of 2 batteries is on special offer.

If you buy 2 packs you get one pack free (so a total of 6 batteries costs £6).

Find the cheapest combination of packs to get:

a. 6 batteries   **b.** 8 batteries   **c.** 10 batteries   **d.** 12 batteries.

14.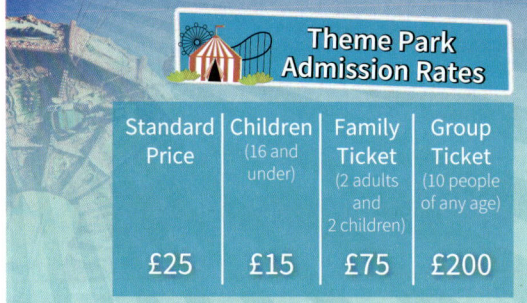

Find the cheapest combination of tickets for

a. 2 adults and 1 child
b. 1 adult and 5 children
c. 2 adults and 3 children
d. 8 adults
e. 4 adults and 6 children
f. 5 adults and 5 children.

Calculate efficiently

Specification reference EL3.M10

Calculators are useful for working with large or difficult numbers and problems that involve several stages. It is very easy to enter a number incorrectly, so it is important to check that the answer you get is sensible. You can check your answer using estimation or by reversing the process to take you back to the number you started with.

Example

Two jobs are advertised in a newspaper:

Which job pays the higher **annual** salary and by how much?

Administration clerk's annual salary
= £1580 × 12 = £18 960

Office assistant's annual salary
= £369 × 52 = £19 188

Checks:

18 960 ÷ 12 = 1580

19 188 ÷ 52 = 369

The **office assistant** has the higher annual salary.

Difference between salaries = £19 188 − £18 960

= **£228**

Check: 228 + 18 960 = 19 188

If your calculator has a memory, you can store the answer 18 960 so you don't need to enter it again. On some calculators pressing M+ stores the number. When you want to use it again, press MR (Memory Recall).

However, calculators vary. Find out how yours works.

Number

Practice

1. Which job pays the higher **annual** salary and by how much?

   a. Sales assistant: £9.50 an hour 20 hours a week **or** Part-time receptionist: £860 a month

   b. Warehouse supervisor: £435 a week **or** Delivery worker: £1795 a month

   Check your working using division (as in the Example).

2. Use the information in the table.

   a. Calculate the cost for:
      i. 2 people spending 3 nights in the Hotel Grand
      ii. 4 people spending 4 nights in the Hotel Splendid
      iii. 4 people spending 5 nights in the Hotel Magnificent.

Hotel	Cost per person for 2 nights (£)	Cost per person for extra night (£)
Grand	199	45
Splendid	227	52
Magnificent	255	63
Supremo	312	71

   b. How much more expensive is it for 4 people to spend 4 nights in the Hotel Supremo than in the Hotel Magnificent?

   c. How much more expensive is it for 4 people to spend 7 nights in the Hotel Supremo than in the Hotel Grand?

   Check your working by rounding the numbers and estimating.

   d. A tourist has a budget of £650 for hotel accommodation. How many nights can she stay at:
      i. the Hotel Grand
      ii. the Hotel Supremo?

Calculate efficiently with numbers of any size

Specification reference **L2.N1, L2.N2**

Negative numbers can be entered into most calculators using the +/− button. This changes positive numbers into negative numbers. Some calculators have a (−) button instead.

Example

A company has two factories. One makes a profit of £0.8 million, the other a loss of £1.5 million. What is the overall profit?

$$0.8 \text{ million} + -1.5 \text{ million} = -0.7 \text{ million}$$

There should be a minus sign before the 0.7 showing it is a negative number.
The company has made an overall profit of **−£0.7 million**. This means a loss of £0.7 million.

Find out how to enter negative numbers on your calculator.
You may need to use a (−) or +/− button.

MyMaths   1932   SEARCH

Mixed Operations and Calculator Practice

Practice

1. The highest recorded temperature at a weather station was 28.7 °C.
   The lowest recorded temperature was −26.9 °C.
   What is the difference between these temperatures?

2. The table shows the profit made by a company in three consecutive years.
   Calculate the total profit.

Year	Profit (£)
Year 1	£0.25 million
Year 2	−£0.76 million
Year 3	£1.42 million

3. The table gives the balance in a bank account at the beginning of each day at the end of February.
   Calculate the total amount paid into or drawn out of the account each day.

Date	Balance (£)
25th Feb	564.32
26th Feb	−18.49
27th Feb	−835.60
28th Feb	1943.26
1st Mar	−154.42

4. a. In 2018 Mr Woods paid £88.60 a month for gas and electricity.
      At the end of the year his total bill for gas and electricity was £1158.30

      i. Was Mr Woods in debit or in credit?

      ii. By how much was he in debit or credit?

   In debit means he owes money.
   In credit means he is owed money.

   b. In 2018 Mr Bennet paid £97.80 a month for gas and electricity.
      At the end of the year the total bill for gas and electricity was £1099.60

      i. Was Mr Bennet in debit or in credit?

      ii. By how much was he in debit or credit?

5. a. Copy the table.
      Use the information below to write the profits for each year in your table.
      Write the numbers in full (in figures but not in decimal form) and show whether they are positive or negative.

   In its first year of trading in 2010 MT Productions made a profit of £1.2 million. Profits fell by £500 000 in the second year, a further £1 million in the third year and £250 000 in 2013. In 2014 profits rose by £450 000, but 2015 brought about fresh disasters with profits falling again by £0.9 million. Profits then increased steadily by £500 000 per year, reaching £500 000 in 2018.

Year	Profit (£)
2010	
2011	
2012	
2013	
2014	
2015	
2016	
2017	
2018	500 000

   b. Use your table to find:

      i. the difference between the highest and lowest years' profits

      ii. the total profit made by MT Productions from 2010 to 2018.

Scientific calculators and some phone calculators have other useful buttons, for example, brackets.
If you have a scientific calculator, use the brackets buttons to calculate the answers to questions 3, 4, 7, 8 and 9 on pages 74–75.

83

Chapter Summary
7 Mixed Operations and Calculator Practice

- There are four basic operations: ÷, ×, +, −
  Check that your answer is sensible and that you have used the correct operation.
- Calculators have a button to clear everything you have entered, usually C (often in red) or AC. They should also have a button to delete only your last entry, usually CE or X.
  Check how your calculator works.
- Sometimes it might be easier not to use a calculator, especially if working with small numbers.
- If one number does not divide exactly into another number, the **remainder** is the amount left over following division. A calculator does not usually display the remainder; it shows the whole and partial (or fractional) number of times the denominator goes into the numerator.
- To find the remainder of a division using a calculator, multiply the whole number part of the answer by the number you are dividing by. Then take this answer away from the number being divided.

- Use **estimation** to check whether you have entered a calculation into the calculator correctly by rounding the numbers in the calculation. You can also **reverse the process** to check an answer: remember addition and subtraction are the reverse of each other, and multiplication and division are the reverse of each other.
- Use your **calculator's memory** to store an answer so that you do not need to enter it again. Typically, the **M+** button stores the number and you can use the **MR** button when you want to use it again. You can also use the **Ans** button to recall your previous answer.

- To change positive numbers into negative numbers on your calculator, you can use the +/− button or (−) button. Check which button your calculator has.
- If someone is in **debit** then they owe money.
- If someone is in **credit** then they are owed money.
- Learn how to use some of the other buttons on your calculator (such as brackets or the x^2 button).

Number — 8 Fractions

Understand fractions
Specification reference **EL3.N7**

A. Fractions in words, numbers and sketches

Each fraction has a top called the **numerator** and a bottom called the **denominator**.

These numbers are fractions: $\frac{3}{4}, \frac{1}{3}, \frac{2}{5}, \frac{6}{10}$ — numerator / denominator

You can show fractions by shading.

Examples

three quarters

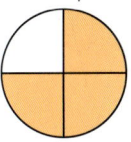

3 out of 4 **equal** parts = $\frac{3}{4}$

one third

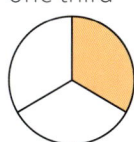

1 out of 3 **equal** parts = $\frac{1}{3}$

This is a **unit** fraction. It has 1 on the top.

two fifths

2 out of 5 **equal** parts = $\frac{2}{5}$

six tenths

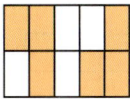

6 out 10 **equal** parts = $\frac{6}{10}$

Practice

1. Write these fractions as numbers.
   a. two thirds
   b. one fifth
   c. three eighths
   d. five twelfths

2. Write these fractions in words.
   a. $\frac{1}{2}$
   b. $\frac{1}{4}$
   c. $\frac{3}{5}$
   d. $\frac{5}{6}$
   e. $\frac{5}{8}$
   f. $\frac{7}{9}$

3. What fraction is shaded? Write your answers in words and numbers.

   a.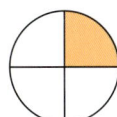
   b.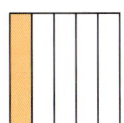
   c.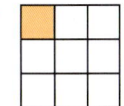

   d.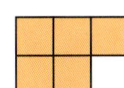
   e.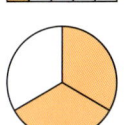
   f.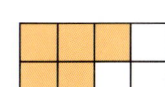

   g.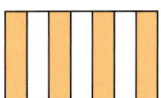
   h.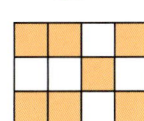
   i.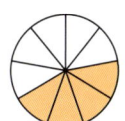

Number

B. Shade fractions

Practice

1. In which of these is two thirds shaded?

   A 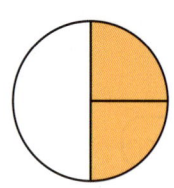 B 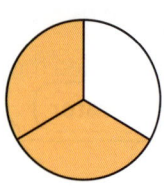 C 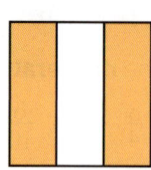 D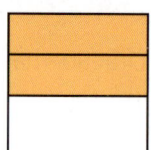

2. In which of these is $\frac{3}{4}$ shaded?

   A 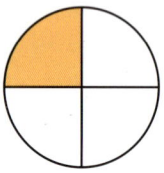 B 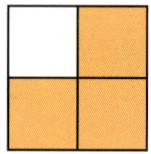 C 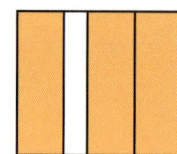 D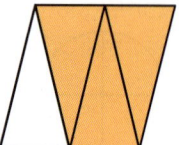

3. Copy each sketch. Shade the fraction.

   a. $\frac{2}{5}$
   b. $\frac{3}{10}$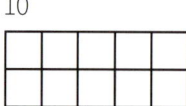
   c. $\frac{7}{8}$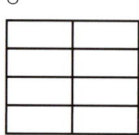

   d. three sevenths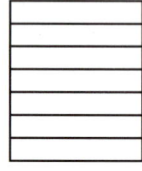
   e. five eighths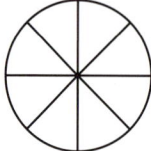
   f. eleven twelfths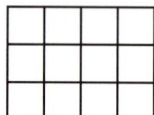

4. Draw a sketch to show each fraction.

   a. $\frac{1}{2}$ b. $\frac{1}{3}$ c. $\frac{1}{4}$ d. $\frac{1}{8}$ e. $\frac{1}{10}$ f. $\frac{4}{5}$
   g. $\frac{3}{8}$ h. $\frac{2}{9}$ i. $\frac{6}{7}$ j. $\frac{9}{10}$ k. $\frac{5}{12}$ l. $\frac{11}{15}$

5. A student says that all of these shapes are $\frac{3}{5}$ shaded. Why are they wrong?

   A 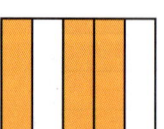 B 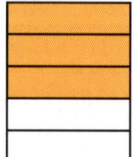 C 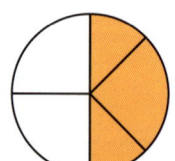 D

Fractions

C. Read about fractions

Common fractions like one half (or 'a half'), one third (or 'a third') and three quarters are used in many ways. For example, adverts often use fractions to describe special offers. Government reports and the media sometimes give survey results as fractions. Recipes in cookery books give some amounts in fractions.

Practice

Write down each fraction in words and in numbers.

1.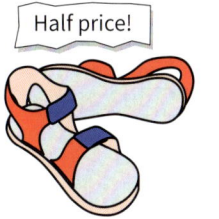

   Half price!

   One third off!

2.

Lentil Patties	
1 cup lentils	1 pint stock
$\frac{1}{4}$ cup peas	1 onion
$\frac{3}{4}$ cup potato	1 clove garlic
$1\frac{1}{2}$ tablespoons oil	$\frac{1}{2}$ tablespoon thyme
1 egg	salt & pepper

3. **Christmas Reductions**

   Shops are reducing prices by as much as two thirds in post-Christmas sales.

   Almost half of the shops started reducing prices before December 25.

4. **Community Life Survey 2016–2017**

   In 2016–17, around a fifth of adults said they had taken part in formal volunteering at least once a month. When looking at all volunteering (formal and informal), nearly two thirds of adults had engaged at least once a year. Three quarters of adults said they had given to charity in the four weeks prior to completing the survey. The average amount given was £22

   Data source: www.statistics.gov.uk

Activity

Collect other examples where fractions are used.

Equivalent fractions

Specification reference **EL3.N7**

A. Use sketches

Look at these sketches of pizzas.

 $\frac{1}{3}$ 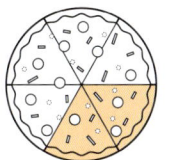 $\frac{2}{6}$ 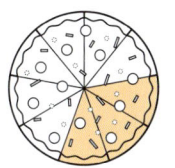 $\frac{3}{9}$

The same amount is shaded in each pizza. This shows that $\frac{1}{3} = \frac{2}{6} = \frac{3}{9}$

Using the whole circles gives $\frac{3}{3} = \frac{6}{6} = \frac{9}{9} = 1$

Number

Practice

1. These sketches show that some fractions are equal. Write down the fractions that are equal.

   a.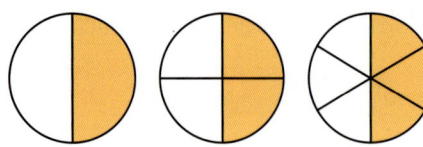

   b.

   c.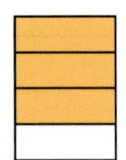

   d.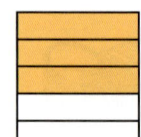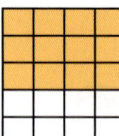

2. Draw sketches to show that:

   a. $\dfrac{1}{2} = \dfrac{4}{8}$
   b. $\dfrac{1}{2} = \dfrac{5}{10}$
   c. $\dfrac{1}{4} = \dfrac{3}{12}$

   d. $\dfrac{3}{5} = \dfrac{6}{10}$
   e. $\dfrac{2}{3} = \dfrac{6}{9}$
   f. $\dfrac{2}{5} = \dfrac{6}{15}$

   g. $\dfrac{3}{4} = \dfrac{6}{8}$
   h. $\dfrac{5}{6} = \dfrac{10}{12}$
   i. $\dfrac{4}{5} = \dfrac{16}{20}$

B. Use numerators and denominators

The sketches of pizzas on page 87 showed that $\dfrac{1}{3} = \dfrac{2}{6} = \dfrac{3}{9}$

Although these fractions look different, they are the same size. They are called **equivalent** fractions.

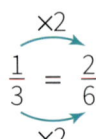 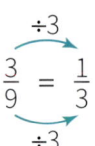

You can find a missing numerator or denominator.

> **Key point**
>
> The size of a fraction is not altered when you multiply or divide the numerator (top) and denominator (bottom) by the **same number**.

> **Examples**
>
> $\dfrac{3}{5} = \dfrac{?}{10}$ $\qquad\qquad$ $\dfrac{12}{20} = \dfrac{3}{?}$
>
> The bottom has been multiplied by 2 $\qquad$ The top has been divided by 4
>
> Do the same to the top: $\qquad\qquad$ Do the same to the bottom:
>
> $\dfrac{3}{5} = \dfrac{\mathbf{6}}{10}$ $\qquad\qquad$ $\dfrac{12}{20} = \dfrac{3}{\mathbf{5}}$

Fractions

Example

In a survey, 40 out of 100 people said they like cats more than dogs.

The report says that this is two fifths of the people. Is this correct?

$$\frac{40}{100} \underset{\div 20}{\overset{\div 20}{=}} \frac{2}{5}$$

Write 40 out of 100 as a fraction. Then divide the top and bottom of the fraction by 20

The report is **correct**. 40 out of 100 is equivalent to 2 out of every 5 people.

Practice

1. For each part, write 'True' or 'False'.
   a. $\frac{1}{2} = \frac{5}{10}$
   b. $\frac{2}{6} = \frac{4}{12}$
   c. $\frac{3}{4} = \frac{9}{10}$
   d. $\frac{2}{5} = \frac{6}{15}$
   e. $\frac{14}{21} = \frac{2}{3}$
   f. $\frac{12}{20} = \frac{3}{4}$
   g. $\frac{8}{10} = \frac{3}{5}$
   h. $\frac{16}{24} = \frac{4}{6}$

2. Find the missing numbers.
   a. $\frac{3}{5} = \frac{9}{?}$
   b. $\frac{1}{4} = \frac{6}{?}$
   c. $\frac{1}{2} = \frac{?}{8}$
   d. $\frac{2}{5} = \frac{?}{20}$
   e. $\frac{6}{20} = \frac{3}{?}$
   f. $\frac{20}{30} = \frac{2}{?}$
   g. $\frac{14}{35} = \frac{?}{5}$
   h. $\frac{20}{25} = \frac{?}{5}$

3. a. 50 out of 100 students travel to college on a bus.
      Sam says this is half of the students. Is Sam correct?
   b. 20 out of 100 students cycle to college.
      Tara says this is a quarter of the students. Is Tara correct?

4. The fractions $\frac{2}{4}$ and $\frac{3}{6}$ are both equivalent to $\frac{1}{2}$
   Write down six more fractions that are all equivalent to $\frac{1}{2}$

5. Find three other fractions that are equivalent to:
   a. $\frac{2}{8}$
   b. $\frac{2}{5}$
   c. $\frac{2}{6}$
   d. $\frac{4}{10}$

6. Twelve out of thirty students in a language class are beginners.
   Ian says that two fifths of the class are beginners. Is he correct?

7. The following fractions are all equal to 1. What are the missing numbers?
   $\frac{?}{2}$ $\frac{?}{4}$ $\frac{5}{?}$ $\frac{7}{?}$ $\frac{?}{11}$ $\frac{15}{?}$ $\frac{20}{?}$ $\frac{?}{100}$

8. a. List the fractions below that are equivalent to $\frac{1}{3}$
   b. List those that are equivalent to $\frac{2}{3}$

   $\frac{6}{9}$ $\frac{6}{18}$ $\frac{4}{12}$ $\frac{5}{15}$ $\frac{8}{12}$ $\frac{2}{6}$ $\frac{4}{6}$ $\frac{12}{18}$ $\frac{3}{9}$ $\frac{10}{15}$

9. Fifteen out of twenty people pass a fitness test.
   Lily says three fifths of the people have passed. Is she correct?

10. Copy each diagram. Draw arrows between equivalent fractions.
One arrow has been drawn on the first diagram.

a.
$\frac{1}{5}$ $\frac{9}{15}$
$\frac{3}{4}$ $\frac{15}{18}$
$\frac{2}{5}$ $\frac{15}{20}$
$\frac{5}{6}$ $\frac{2}{10}$
$\frac{1}{3}$ $\frac{5}{15}$
$\frac{3}{5}$ $\frac{6}{15}$

b.
$\frac{3}{4}$ $\frac{6}{24}$
$\frac{2}{3}$ $\frac{4}{24}$
$\frac{1}{3}$ $\frac{9}{24}$
$\frac{1}{4}$ $\frac{9}{12}$
$\frac{3}{8}$ $\frac{8}{12}$
$\frac{1}{6}$ $\frac{8}{24}$

C. Write quantities as fractions

Here are some important facts about length, capacity and weight.

1 cm = 10 mm	1 m = 100 cm	1 m = 1000 mm	1 km = 1000 m
1 cℓ = 10 mℓ	1 ℓ = 100 cℓ	1 ℓ = 1000 mℓ	1 kg = 1000 g

You can use these facts to write some quantities as fractions.

Example

$8 \text{ mm} = \frac{8}{10}$ cm (8 out of 10)

$= \frac{4}{5}$ cm

(by dividing top and bottom by 2)

$250 \text{ g} = \frac{250}{1000}$ kg   (250 out of 1000)

$= \frac{25}{100}$ kg   (dividing by 10)

$= \frac{1}{4}$ kg   (dividing by 25 or 5 then 5 again)

Practice

1. Write these lengths as fractions of a centimetre.
   a. 5 mm   **b.** 4 mm   **c.** 6 mm

2. Write these weights as fractions of a kilogram.
   a. 500 g   **b.** 750 g   **c.** 100 g   **d.** 200 g   **e.** 600 g

3. Write these lengths as fractions of a kilometre.
   a. 5 m   **b.** 50 m   **c.** 500 m   **d.** 100 m   **e.** 150 m

4. Write these volumes as fractions of a litre.
   a. 20 mℓ   **b.** 50 mℓ   **c.** 200 mℓ   **d.** 500 mℓ   **e.** 400 mℓ

5. Write these lengths as fractions of a metre.
   - **a.** 20 cm
   - **b.** 50 cm
   - **c.** 90 cm
   - **d.** 80 cm
   - **e.** 5 cm
   - **f.** 100 mm
   - **g.** 200 mm
   - **h.** 400 mm
   - **i.** 600 mm
   - **j.** 20 mm

Compare fractions

Specification reference L1.N8, L2.N7

A. Compare unit fractions

These fractions are all **unit fractions** because they all have 1 in the numerator.

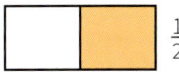

In unit fractions, the larger the denominator, the smaller the fraction.

For example, $\frac{1}{15}$ is smaller than $\frac{1}{10}$

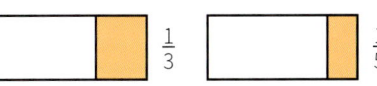

Practice

1. Which is **smaller**?
   - **a.** $\frac{1}{7}$ or $\frac{1}{8}$
   - **b.** $\frac{1}{10}$ or $\frac{1}{6}$
   - **c.** $\frac{1}{20}$ or $\frac{1}{19}$
   - **d.** $\frac{1}{12}$ or $\frac{1}{3}$

2. Which is **larger**?
   - **a.** $\frac{1}{20}$ or $\frac{1}{25}$
   - **b.** $\frac{1}{19}$ or $\frac{1}{17}$
   - **c.** $\frac{1}{5}$ or $\frac{1}{50}$
   - **d.** $\frac{1}{13}$ or $\frac{1}{11}$

3. Write these fractions in order of size. Start with the **smallest**.

$\frac{1}{4}$ $\frac{1}{12}$ $\frac{1}{2}$ $\frac{1}{5}$ $\frac{1}{10}$ $\frac{1}{15}$ $\frac{1}{3}$ $\frac{1}{6}$ $\frac{1}{20}$

4. Write these fractions in order of size. Start with the **largest**.

$\frac{1}{8}$ $\frac{1}{11}$ $\frac{1}{21}$ $\frac{1}{14}$ $\frac{1}{9}$ $\frac{1}{16}$ $\frac{1}{13}$ $\frac{1}{7}$ $\frac{1}{17}$

B. Use fraction walls

Example

The fraction wall shows:

$1 = \frac{2}{2} = \frac{4}{4} = \frac{8}{8} = \frac{16}{16}$

The shaded part shows:

$\frac{1}{4} = \frac{2}{8} = \frac{4}{16}$

The diagram also shows that $\frac{3}{8}$ is bigger than $\frac{1}{4}$ and $\frac{3}{8}$ is less than $\frac{1}{2}$

Number

Practice

1. Use the fraction wall in the example to find the missing numbers.
   - a. $\frac{1}{2} = \frac{?}{4}$
   - b. $\frac{1}{2} = \frac{?}{8}$
   - c. $\frac{1}{2} = \frac{?}{16}$
   - d. $\frac{3}{4} = \frac{?}{8}$
   - e. $\frac{3}{4} = \frac{?}{16}$
   - f. $\frac{3}{8} = \frac{?}{16}$
   - g. $\frac{5}{8} = \frac{?}{16}$
   - h. $\frac{2}{8} = \frac{?}{4}$

2. Use the fraction wall on the previous page to put each set of fractions in order of size. Start with the **smallest**.
   - a. $\frac{3}{8}, \frac{7}{16}, \frac{5}{16}$
   - b. $\frac{5}{8}, \frac{9}{16}, \frac{1}{2}$
   - c. $\frac{13}{16}, \frac{7}{8}, \frac{3}{4}$

3. This fraction wall shows halves, fifths and tenths. Find the missing numbers.
   - a. $1 = \frac{?}{5} = \frac{?}{10}$
   - b. $\frac{1}{2} = \frac{?}{10}$
   - c. $\frac{1}{5} = \frac{?}{10}$
   - d. $\frac{2}{5} = \frac{?}{10}$
   - e. $\frac{3}{5} = \frac{?}{10}$
   - f. $\frac{5}{5} = \frac{?}{10}$

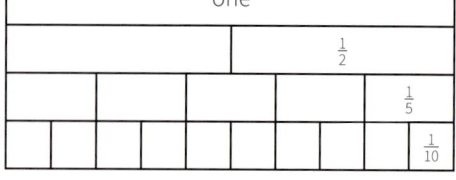

4. Use the fraction wall shown in question **3** to put these fractions in order of size. Start with the **largest**.

   $\frac{2}{5} \quad \frac{7}{10} \quad \frac{1}{2} \quad \frac{1}{10} \quad \frac{9}{10} \quad \frac{3}{5} \quad \frac{3}{10} \quad \frac{1}{5} \quad \frac{4}{5}$

It can be more difficult to compare some other fractions.

Shading parts of equal rectangles helps.

The sketch shows that $\frac{4}{5}$ is larger than $\frac{2}{3}$

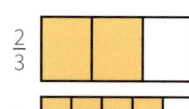

Draw sketches to illustrate your answers to questions **5** to **7**.

5. Which is **larger**?
   - a. $\frac{3}{4}$ or $\frac{2}{3}$
   - b. $\frac{1}{2}$ or $\frac{2}{5}$
   - c. $\frac{1}{3}$ or $\frac{2}{5}$

6. Which is **smaller**?
   - a. $\frac{1}{2}$ or $\frac{4}{7}$
   - b. $\frac{3}{5}$ or $\frac{7}{9}$
   - c. $\frac{5}{6}$ or $\frac{3}{4}$

7. Emma says that $\frac{3}{7}$ is bigger than a half. Is she correct? Explain your answer.

C. Put fractions in order using a common denominator

Comparing fractions is easy if they have the same denominator.

For example, 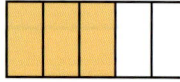 $\frac{3}{5}$ is more than $\frac{2}{5}$

Fractions

 Practice

1. Which is **larger**?

   a. $\frac{1}{3}$ or $\frac{2}{3}$ b. $\frac{7}{9}$ or $\frac{5}{9}$ c. $\frac{7}{10}$ or $\frac{9}{10}$

2. Put each set of fractions in order. Start with the **smallest**.

   a. $\frac{3}{5}, \frac{2}{5}, \frac{4}{5}$ b. $\frac{5}{7}, \frac{1}{7}, \frac{2}{7}, \frac{4}{7}$ c. $\frac{4}{9}, \frac{5}{9}, \frac{2}{9}, \frac{8}{9}, \frac{1}{9}$

 Comparing fractions with different denominators is harder. You can do this by making the denominators the same.

Example

To compare $\frac{2}{3}$ with $\frac{7}{12}$, write $\frac{2}{3}$ as an equivalent fraction in twelfths:

$$\frac{2}{3} \xrightarrow{\times 4} = \frac{8}{12} \xleftarrow{\times 4}$$

Because 3 divides into 12, you can change the denominator from 3 to 12

To change the bottom to 12, multiply 3 by 4 Then do the same to the top.

$\frac{8}{12}$ is bigger than $\frac{7}{12}$ so $\frac{2}{3}$ is bigger than $\frac{7}{12}$

The denominator, 12, is the **common denominator** for these fractions.

Example

Write $\frac{5}{8}, \frac{7}{10}$ and $\frac{3}{5}$, in order of size, starting with the **smallest**.

Look for a common denominator — a number that 8, 5 and 10 all divide into.
The best common denominator for these numbers is 40

Now write all the fractions with 40 as the denominator:

$$\frac{5}{8} \xrightarrow{\times 5} = \frac{25}{40} \xleftarrow{\times 5} \quad \frac{7}{10} \xrightarrow{\times 4} = \frac{28}{40} \xleftarrow{\times 4} \quad \frac{3}{5} \xrightarrow{\times 8} = \frac{24}{40} \xleftarrow{\times 8}$$

Other common denominators (for example, 80) could be used. 40 is the **best** because it is the **smallest**.

In order of size the fractions are: $\frac{3}{5} \quad \frac{5}{8} \quad \frac{7}{10}$

3. Write each pair with the same denominator, then say which is the **larger**.

  a. $\frac{1}{4}$ or $\frac{1}{5}$
  b. $\frac{3}{5}$ or $\frac{3}{10}$
  c. $\frac{2}{3}$ or $\frac{3}{4}$
  d. $\frac{1}{2}$ or $\frac{4}{7}$

4. Write each group in order of size, starting with the **smallest**.

  a. $\frac{1}{2}, \frac{5}{8}, \frac{3}{8}$
  b. $\frac{2}{5}, \frac{3}{10}, \frac{1}{4}$
  c. $\frac{5}{16}, \frac{3}{4}, \frac{7}{8}, \frac{1}{2}$
  d. $\frac{5}{6}, \frac{3}{4}, \frac{2}{3}, \frac{11}{12}$
  e. $\frac{3}{4}, \frac{1}{2}, \frac{5}{7}, \frac{3}{7}$
  f. $\frac{1}{3}, \frac{5}{12}, \frac{1}{4}, \frac{1}{2}, \frac{3}{8}$

5. Write each group in order of size, starting with the **largest**.

  a. $\frac{1}{2}, \frac{4}{7}, \frac{2}{7}$
  b. $\frac{5}{9}, \frac{2}{3}, \frac{5}{6}$
  c. $\frac{1}{2}, \frac{4}{9}, \frac{3}{4}, \frac{2}{3}$
  d. $\frac{4}{5}, \frac{2}{3}, \frac{9}{10}, \frac{13}{15}$
  e. $\frac{5}{9}, \frac{5}{8}, \frac{4}{9}, \frac{7}{12}$
  f. $\frac{3}{5}, \frac{2}{3}, \frac{7}{10}, \frac{13}{15}, \frac{2}{9}, \frac{11}{15}$

Mixed numbers and improper fractions

Specification reference **L1.N8**

Level 1

A **mixed number** is a mixture of a whole number and a fraction, for example, $1\frac{1}{4}$

The diagram shows $1\frac{1}{4} = \frac{5}{4}$

whole one + 1 quarter = one and a quarter

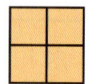

$\frac{3}{4}$ is less than $1\frac{1}{4}$

A fraction with a bigger numerator than denominator, for example, $\frac{5}{4}$, is called an **improper** fraction.

4 quarters + 1 quarter = 5 quarters

3 quarters

Practice

1. What do these diagrams show?
For each part give a mixed number and an improper fraction.

  a.
  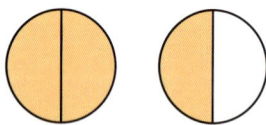

  b.

  c.
  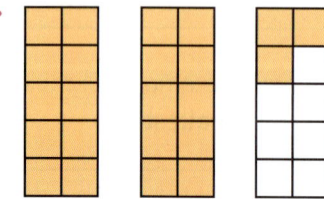

  d.
  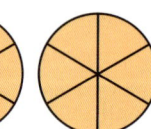  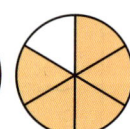

e. 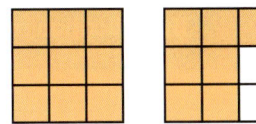   f.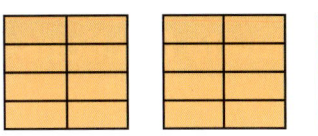

2. Draw diagrams to show that:

   a. $1\frac{3}{4} = \frac{7}{4}$ b. $2\frac{1}{2} = \frac{5}{2}$

   c. $1\frac{2}{3} = \frac{5}{3}$ d. $3\frac{4}{5} = \frac{19}{5}$

   > Can you see a quick way to write mixed numbers as improper fractions?

3. a. Draw diagrams to show each of these numbers in eighths.

   $\frac{7}{8}$ $1\frac{3}{8}$ $\frac{5}{8}$ $2\frac{1}{8}$ $1\frac{1}{4}$ $\frac{3}{4}$ $1\frac{1}{2}$

   b. List the original numbers in order of size, starting with the **smallest**.

To put a mixture of fractions and mixed numbers in order, you can consider them in groups.

Example

To put $\frac{2}{3}$ $1\frac{3}{4}$ $1\frac{2}{3}$ $2\frac{1}{3}$ $\frac{5}{6}$ in order:

Under 1: $\frac{2}{3}$ and $\frac{5}{6}$ common denominator 6 $\frac{2}{3} = \frac{4}{6}$ is smaller than $\frac{5}{6}$

Between 1 and 2: $1\frac{3}{4}$ and $1\frac{2}{3}$ common denominator 12 $1\frac{3}{4} = 1\frac{9}{12}$ $1\frac{2}{3} = 1\frac{8}{12}$

Above 2: $2\frac{1}{3}$ only

In order, starting with the smallest: $\frac{2}{3}$ $\frac{5}{6}$ $1\frac{2}{3}$ $1\frac{3}{4}$ $2\frac{1}{3}$

4. Write each group in order of size, starting with the **smallest**.

   a. $1\frac{3}{5}$ $\frac{3}{4}$ $2\frac{2}{5}$ $1\frac{1}{2}$ $2\frac{1}{3}$

   b. $\frac{5}{8}$ $1\frac{3}{4}$ $\frac{4}{7}$ $1\frac{7}{12}$ $1\frac{5}{6}$

   c. $\frac{4}{9}$ $2\frac{2}{3}$ $\frac{5}{7}$ $2\frac{3}{7}$ $1\frac{3}{4}$ $2\frac{1}{2}$

   d. $1\frac{2}{3}$ $1\frac{5}{8}$ $\frac{1}{4}$ $1\frac{11}{12}$ $2\frac{1}{8}$ $1\frac{5}{6}$

Number

Find or estimate fractions

Specification reference **EL3.N7**

The first sketch shows a chocolate bar.
The second shows it again after some has been eaten.
What fraction is left?

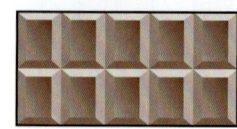 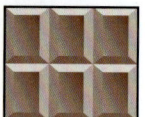

6 out of 10 chunks are left. $\dfrac{6}{10} = \dfrac{3}{5}$ (dividing by 2)

You can also imagine the bar divided into 5 parts, as in this sketch.
This also shows that $\dfrac{3}{5}$ is left and $\dfrac{2}{5}$ was eaten.

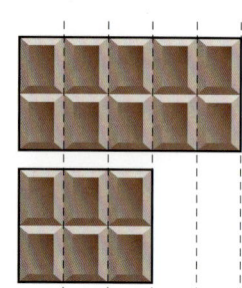

Use your ruler to measure the lengths of the bars in the diagram:
Length of original bar = 30 mm. Length after some was eaten = 18 mm.
The fraction that is left is $\dfrac{18}{30} = \dfrac{3}{5}$ (dividing top and bottom by 6).

Practice

1. Here are some more chocolate bars. In each case estimate:

   i. the fraction that is left   **ii.** the fraction that was eaten.

   a.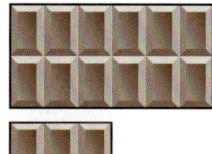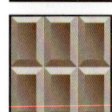
   b.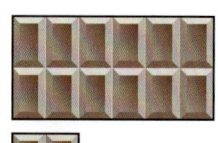
   c.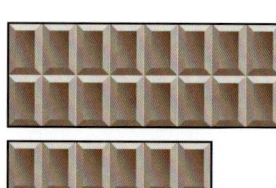

   Use your ruler to check your answers.

2. Use a fraction to describe how much is in each jug.

   Hint You can use a ruler to measure the height of the jug and the height of the liquid.

   a.
   b.
   c.

3. Here is a water tank. Use a fraction to describe how full it is in each sketch.

   a.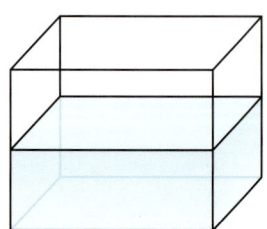
   b.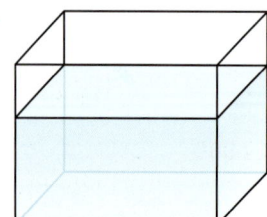
   c.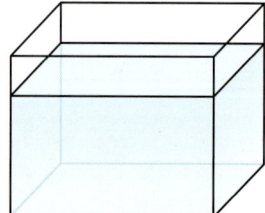

4. Estimate what fraction of the drink is left in each sketch.

a. 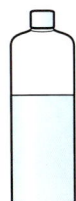 b. 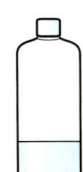 c.

5. The sketch shows a pie.
   For each part:
   i. estimate what fraction of the pie has been eaten
   ii. estimate what fraction of the pie is left.

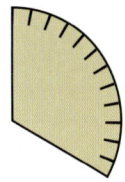

a. 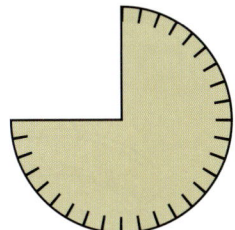 b. 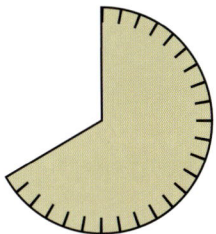 c.

Calculate a fraction of something

Specification reference: EL3.N7, L1.N9, L1.N15

A. By dividing when the numerator is 1

Entry Level 3

To find $\frac{1}{2}$ of something, divide it by 2

To find $\frac{1}{3}$ of something, divide it by 3

To find $\frac{1}{4}$ of something, divide it by 4, and so on.

Key point
When the numerator is 1, divide by the denominator.

Example for E3

$\frac{1}{3}$ of 84 kg = 84 kg ÷ 3 = **28 kg**

$$3\overline{)8^24}$$
   28

Example for L1

Five partners in a company each get a fifth of the profits of £64 500

They each get $\frac{1}{5}$ of £64 500

$$5\overline{)6^14^45\,0\,0}$$
   1 2 900

£64 500 ÷ 5 = £12 900 so they each get **£12 900**

Number

Practice

1. Find:

   a. $\frac{1}{2}$ of £56
   b. $\frac{1}{3}$ of 72 cm
   c. $\frac{1}{5}$ of £780
   d. $\frac{1}{10}$ of £990

   e. $\frac{1}{4}$ of £816
   f. $\frac{1}{6}$ of £546
   g. $\frac{1}{8}$ of 576 m
   h. $\frac{1}{9}$ of 423

2. There are 24 students in a class. Half of them are women. How many are women?

3. A jacket costs £45. This price is reduced by a third in a sale.

   a. How much is saved?
   b. What is the sale price?

4. Seventy people take a driving test. A fifth of them fail.

   a. How many people fail?
   b. How many people pass?

5. A petrol tank holds 60 litres when full. It is a quarter full. How many litres of petrol are in the tank?

   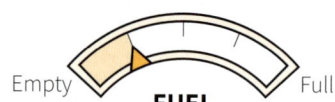

6. Four friends share a prize of £340 equally between them. How much do they get each?

7. A sixth of the adults in a town did not vote. There are altogether 21 000 adults. How many adults: a. did not vote   b. voted?

8. A chef uses one eighth of a kilogram bag of flour to thicken a sauce.

   a. How many grams of flour does he use? (1 kg = 1000 g)
   b. How many grams are left in the bag?

B. Find more than one part

When the numerator is not 1, divide by the denominator, then multiply by the numerator.

Example

Find $\frac{3}{4}$ of £540.

To find $\frac{3}{4}$ of £540, divide it by 4, then multiply by 3

£540 ÷ 4 = £135

Then £135 × 3 = **£405**

```
    1 3 5
4 ) 5¹4²0
```

```
  1 3 5
×     3
  4 0 5
  1 1
```

> Divide by the denominator.
> Then multiply by the numerator.

Key point

To find a fraction of an amount, divide by the denominator and then multiply by the numerator.

Fractions

Practice

1. Find:
   a. $\frac{3}{4}$ of £840
   b. $\frac{2}{3}$ of £156
   c. $\frac{2}{5}$ of 75 m
   d. $\frac{3}{5}$ of 250 g
   e. $\frac{5}{6}$ of 420 cm
   f. $\frac{2}{7}$ of £1610
   g. $\frac{5}{8}$ of £2880
   h. $\frac{4}{9}$ of 3285 kg.

2. An IT company has 360 employees.
   Two thirds of these are salespeople.
   How many are salespeople?

3. A box contains 45 chocolates.
   Two-fifths of these are dark chocolates.
   How many dark chocolates are there?

4. A firm makes £45 000 profit.
   The firm spends three quarters of the profit on new equipment.
   How much does the firm spend on new equipment?

5. There are 34 500 spectators at a football match. Nine tenths of these support the home team.
   How many spectators support the home team?

6. Two hundred and seventy-five people go to a Christmas pantomime.
   Three fifths of them are children.
   How many children go to the pantomime?

7. A car costs £6900. The buyer gets a loan for five sixths of the price.
   How much is the loan?

8. A holiday company sells 480 000 holidays during a year.
   Three quarters of these are holidays abroad.
   How many of the holidays are abroad?

C. Estimate to check answers

Examples

A student says $\frac{1}{9}$ of 243 is 17. Is this correct?

$\frac{1}{10}$ of 243 is approximately 24. One ninth is larger than one tenth so the answer is **wrong**.

A student says $\frac{4}{7}$ of 392 is 164. Is this correct?

$\frac{4}{7}$ is greater than $\frac{1}{2}$
Half of 392 is 196. So the answer is **wrong**.

Number

Practice

1. Use estimation to check which of these answers must be wrong.

   A $\frac{1}{3}$ of 57 = 34
   B $\frac{1}{11}$ of 836 = 121
   C $\frac{2}{5}$ of 90 = 36
   D $\frac{4}{9}$ of 450 = 200

   E $\frac{9}{11}$ of 363 = 185
   F $\frac{6}{8}$ of 600 = 540
   G $\frac{2}{5}$ of 750 = 300
   H $\frac{3}{10}$ of 640 = 122

2. Find the correct answers for the parts of question **1** that are wrong.

D. Other methods

Links between some fractions give other methods for calculating a fraction. For example, to find a quarter of something you can halve it, then halve again.

Also, the sketch shows $\frac{3}{4} = \frac{2}{4} + \frac{1}{4} = \frac{1}{2} + \frac{1}{4}$

So, to find $\frac{3}{4}$ of something, you can add $\frac{1}{2}$ and $\frac{1}{4}$

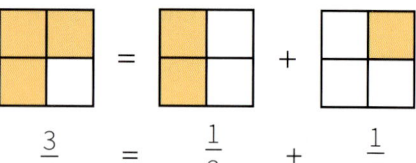

$$\frac{3}{4} = \frac{1}{2} + \frac{1}{4}$$

Example

$\frac{1}{2}$ of £540 = £270

270
$2\overline{)5^14 0}$

$\frac{1}{4}$ of £540 = £135

135
$2\overline{)27^10}$

So $\frac{3}{4}$ of £540 = £270 + £135

270
$+135$
$\overline{405}$
_1

= **£405**

You can check this by multiplying £135 by 3

You can also check the answer by adding the amounts for $\frac{1}{4}$ and $\frac{3}{4}$

You should get back to the whole amount (because $\frac{4}{4}$ = 1).

405
$+135$
$\overline{540}$
_1

Practice

1. Find these and check each answer.

   a. $\frac{3}{4}$ of £1520
   b. $\frac{3}{4}$ of 56 kg
   c. $\frac{3}{4}$ of 432 m

Fractions

2. a. Draw a sketch to show that $\frac{5}{8} = \frac{4}{8} + \frac{1}{8} = \frac{1}{2} + \frac{1}{8}$

   b. Find: **i.** $\frac{1}{2}$ of £960   **ii.** $\frac{1}{8}$ of £960   **iii.** $\frac{5}{8}$ of £960

   c. Check **biii** by multiplying your answer to **bii** by 5

3. a. Draw a sketch to show that $\frac{3}{8} = \frac{2}{8} + \frac{1}{8} = \frac{1}{4} + \frac{1}{8}$

   b. Find: **i.** $\frac{1}{4}$ of 256 m   **ii.** $\frac{1}{8}$ of 256 m   **iii.** $\frac{3}{8}$ of 256 m

   c. Check **biii** by multiplying your answer to **bii** by 3

4. a. Draw a sketch to show that $\frac{5}{6} = \frac{3}{6} + \frac{2}{6} = \frac{1}{2} + \frac{1}{3}$

   b. Find: **i.** $\frac{1}{2}$ of £7200   **ii.** $\frac{1}{3}$ of £7200   **iii.** $\frac{5}{6}$ of £7200

   c. Find $\frac{1}{6}$ of £7200 and use your answer to check **biii**.

E. Scale up and down

> ### Example
>
> A recipe for macaroni cheese for 6 people includes these ingredients:
> 300 g cheese   120 g butter   240 g macaroni.
>
> Suppose there are only 4 people. You need $\frac{4}{6} = \frac{2}{3}$ of the quantities.
>
> To find what you need, divide each quantity by 3, then multiply by 2:
>
> Cheese: 300 g ÷ 3 = 100 g   100 g × 2 = **200 g**
> Butter: 120 g ÷ 3 = 40 g   40 g × 2 = **80 g**
> Macaroni: 240 g ÷ 3 = 80 g   80 g × 2 = **160 g**
>
> Note that there is twice as much macaroni as butter in both sets of ingredients.
>
> If there were 9 people, you would need $\frac{9}{6} = \frac{3}{2}$ of the quantities.
>
> In this case you would need to divide each quantity by 2, then multiply by 3
> Check that this gives 450 g of cheese, 180 g of butter and 360 g of macaroni.

Practice

1. The recipe gives the ingredients for leek and potato soup for 6 people.
Find the quantities you need for:

   a. 4 people   **b.** 8 people.

Leek & Potato Soup (for 6 people)
270 g potatoes   450 g leeks
750 mℓ milk   150 mℓ stock

2. The main ingredients for a nut loaf for 8 people are:
   400 g nuts   200 g breadcrumbs   240 g tomatoes   4 onions
   a. What fraction of the quantities do you need for 6 people?
   b. Find the quantities for 6 people.

3. These are the ingredients for 20 almond biscuits:
   300 g flour   160 g sugar   140 g butter   60 g ground almonds
   a. What fraction of the quantities do you need for 16 biscuits?
   b. Find the quantities for 16 biscuits.

4. For sandwiches for 20 people a caterer uses:
   4 loaves of bread   800 g butter   8 tomatoes   2 cucumbers
   400 g pâté   300 g chicken   500 g cheese   1 lettuce
   Find the quantities for sandwiches for:
   a. 15 people   b. 25 people.

One number as a fraction of another

Specification reference L2.N8

A. Simplest form

The fractions $\frac{8}{12}, \frac{2}{3}, \frac{4}{6}, \frac{10}{15}$ and $\frac{6}{9}$ are all equal to each other.

See Equivalent fractions, pages 87–90.

$\frac{2}{3}$ is the **simplest form**. Its numerator and denominator are the smallest.

Example

Write $\frac{240}{320}$ in its simplest form.

Look for numbers that divide into the top and bottom.

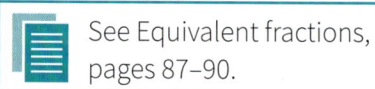

There is more than one way of doing this. Here is another way:

$$\frac{240}{320} \xrightarrow{\div 2} \frac{120}{160} \xrightarrow{\div 2} \frac{60}{80} \xrightarrow{\div 20} \frac{3}{4}$$

Finding the simplest form is sometimes called **cancelling**.

If you divide by large numbers it is quicker, but it is sometimes easier to divide by small numbers. Keep going until you are sure there is nothing else you can divide by.

Fractions

Key point
To find the simplest form of a fraction, divide the top and bottom by the same number. Repeat this as far as you can.

Practice

Write each fraction in its simplest form.

1. $\dfrac{20}{50}$
2. $\dfrac{12}{16}$
3. $\dfrac{9}{27}$
4. $\dfrac{12}{30}$
5. $\dfrac{80}{100}$
6. $\dfrac{32}{48}$
7. $\dfrac{200}{400}$
8. $\dfrac{150}{200}$
9. $\dfrac{25}{75}$
10. $\dfrac{72}{96}$
11. $\dfrac{140}{700}$
12. $\dfrac{81}{270}$
13. $\dfrac{560}{840}$
14. $\dfrac{1500}{3500}$
15. $\dfrac{1320}{2200}$

B. Write one quantity as a fraction of another

Example
Write 60 cm as a fraction of a metre.

1 m = 100 cm, so the fraction is $\dfrac{60}{100} = \dfrac{6}{10} = \dfrac{\mathbf{3}}{\mathbf{5}}$ (dividing by 10, then 2).

> Both parts of the fraction must be written in the same units.

Example
Seventy students and fifty-six full-time workers work in a call centre. What fraction of the workers are full-time?

The total number of workers = 70 + 56 = 126

The fraction that are full-time = $\dfrac{56}{126} = \dfrac{28}{63} = \dfrac{\mathbf{4}}{\mathbf{9}}$ (dividing by 2, then 7).

> Always write the answer as a fraction in its simplest form.

Example
A survey of 20 000 households shows that 8800 of them own more than one car. What fraction of the households own more than one car?

$\dfrac{8800}{20\,000} = \dfrac{88}{200} = \dfrac{44}{100} = \dfrac{\mathbf{11}}{\mathbf{25}}$

> Dividing by 100, then 2, then 4

Number

Practice

1. What fraction of an hour is:
   a. 15 minutes   b. 20 minutes   c. 48 minutes?

   Remember metric units:
   1 kg = 1000 g
   1 g = 1000 mg
   1 cℓ = 10 mℓ
   See pages 235 and 250.

2. What fraction of a kilogram is:
   a. 100 g   b. 750 g   c. 400 g   d. 640 g?

3. Write each of these volumes as a fraction of a centilitre.
   a. 3 mℓ   b. 5 mℓ   c. 2 mℓ   d. 4 mℓ   e. 6 mℓ

4. Find the equivalent weight for each of these weights.
   a. 50 g   b. 500 mg   c. 250 g   d. 250 mg   e. 200 g

   Choose from $\frac{1}{4}$g, $\frac{1}{2}$kg, $\frac{1}{5}$g, $\frac{1}{50}$kg, $\frac{1}{2}$g, $\frac{1}{4}$kg, $\frac{1}{5}$kg, $\frac{1}{20}$kg

5. One pound is equal to 16 ounces. What fraction of a pound is:
   a. 8 ounces   b. 4 ounces   c. 12 ounces   d. 6 ounces?

6. A caterer buys 36 eggs. She finds that 24 of the eggs are broken. What fraction of the eggs are broken?

7. Neil earns £2100 per month. His rent costs £420 per month. What fraction of Neil's earnings does he spend on rent?

8. During one day at a driving test centre, 18 people pass their driving test and 12 people fail. What fraction of the drivers pass?

9. A car costs £14 400 when it is new. It is sold later for £8800 What fraction is this of its original value?

10. The table shows the results of a survey at an office about how employees travel to work.

    a. Copy and complete the table.
    b. Find the fraction of
       i. men
       ii. women who travel by each method.

    Hint use the total of the column for the denominator.

    c. What fraction of the total workforce are:
       i. men   ii. women?

	Men	Women	Total
Car	240	300	
Bus	120	270	
Train	80	100	
Cycle	15	10	
Walk	25	40	
Total			

C. Estimate one quantity as a fraction of another

Example

The table gives the number of employees in different departments of a company.

Department	Men	Women	Total
Haulage	1347	707	2054
Finance	59	20	79
Administration	48	196	244
Advertising	29	13	42
Total	1483	936	2419

1347 out of the 2054 haulage workers are men.

As a fraction this is $\frac{1347}{2054}$ — not a very easy or convenient fraction!

There are several ways of giving a simpler estimate. The best way depends on the numbers in the fraction. In this fraction:

Rounding both numbers to the nearest 1000 gives $\frac{1000}{2000} = \frac{1}{2}$

This is a much simpler fraction, but not very accurate.

Rounding both numbers to the nearest 100 gives $\frac{1300}{2100} = \frac{13}{21}$

This is more accurate than $\frac{1}{2}$, but not very simple.

As 1347 is very close to 1400 (which is an easy multiple of 7), you could round it up to 1400, and round 2054 up to 2100

$\frac{1400}{2100} = \frac{14}{21} = \frac{2}{3}$ About two thirds of the haulage workers are men.

This fraction is simpler than $\frac{13}{21}$ and is actually more accurate as well.

When estimating fractions, **try to find near numbers that will cancel**.

Practice

Use the table in the Example above to answer questions **1–4**.

1. By rounding the numbers to the nearest 10, estimate the fraction of the people in Finance who are:

    a. women   b. men.

2. a. Estimate the fraction of the people in Administration who are women by rounding the numbers:

    i. to the nearest 10

    ii. to the nearest 50

    b. What happens if you round the numbers to the nearest 100?

3. a. Use these methods to estimate the fraction of people in Advertising who are men.

    i. Round 29 and 42 to the nearest 10

    ii. Round 29 to 28, but leave the total as 42

    b. Which answer do you think gives the most accurate fraction? Why?

Number

4. **a.** Estimate the fraction of the total workforce who work in:

   i. administration **ii.** advertising

   iii. finance **iv.** haulage.

   b. Estimate the fraction of the total workforce who are:

   i. men **ii.** women.

5. The number of kilometres travelled by passengers on the railway in one year was 10.1 billion. Of these, 7.4 billion kilometres were on ordinary tickets and the rest were on season tickets.

   a. Which of these fractions is the best estimate of the fraction of the distance that was on ordinary tickets?

   i. $\frac{7}{10}$ **ii.** $\frac{3}{4}$

   b. Estimate the fraction of kilometres that were travelled on season tickets.

6. The table shows the amount of different types of energy consumed in the UK in 2017.

   a. Find the total consumption.

   b. Estimate the fraction of energy that was:

   i. Natural gas

   ii. Electricity

   iii. Petroleum

   iv. Other

Energy type	Amount (tonnes of oil equivalent)
Natural gas	42 200 000
Electricity	25 900 000
Petroleum	63 900 000
Other	9 200 000

Data source: www.gov.uk/government/statistics/energy-consumption-in-the-uk

7. The table shows the amount of packaging waste recycled in the UK in 2018. Estimate the fraction of the total that is of each type.

Waste type	Amount (thousand tonnes)
Paper and cardboard	3754
Glass	1623
Metal	736
Plastic	1044
Wood	411

Data source: https://www.gov.uk/government/statistics/uk-waste-data

Fractions

Activity

Go to government or other websites to find some interesting statistics.

Write the information you find in terms of fractions.

Some suggestions are given below.

- Data for employment, industry, population, leisure and tourism etc. from the Office for National Statistics website (www.ons.gov.uk)
- Transport figures from the Department for Transport (www.gov.uk/government/organisations/department-for-transport)
- Information from the Department of Health and Social Care (www.gov.uk/government/organisations/department-of-health-and-social-care)
- Crime figures from the Home Office website (www.gov.uk/government/organisations/home-office)

Add and subtract fractions

Specification reference **L2.N7**

A. Add and subtract fractions with the same denominator

Look at the diagrams.

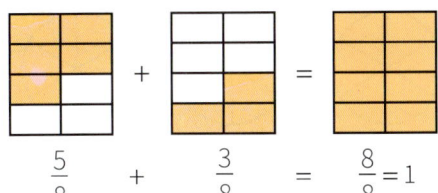

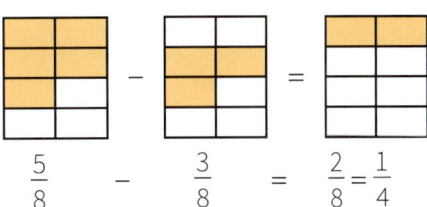

When two fractions have the same denominator:

To add them, add the numerators. The denominator stays the same.

To subtract them, subtract the numerators. Simplify the answer if possible.

> **Example**
>
> $\frac{7}{12} + \frac{1}{12} = \frac{8}{12} = \frac{2}{3}$ (cancelling by 4) $\frac{9}{10} - \frac{3}{10} = \frac{6}{10} = \frac{3}{5}$ (cancelling by 2)

Practice

Work these out. Write each answer in its simplest form.

1. $\frac{3}{5} + \frac{1}{5}$
2. $\frac{3}{5} - \frac{1}{5}$
3. $\frac{5}{6} + \frac{1}{6}$
4. $\frac{5}{6} - \frac{1}{6}$
5. $\frac{2}{7} + \frac{3}{7}$
6. $\frac{5}{7} - \frac{2}{7}$
7. $\frac{5}{8} - \frac{1}{8}$
8. $\frac{4}{9} + \frac{2}{9}$
9. $\frac{9}{10} - \frac{1}{10}$
10. $\frac{2}{5} + \frac{3}{5}$
11. $\frac{4}{15} + \frac{2}{15}$
12. $\frac{7}{8} - \frac{3}{8}$

MyMaths 1017, 5033 SEARCH

13. A café sells drinks, meals and snacks.

It makes $\frac{1}{5}$ of its profits on meals and $\frac{2}{5}$ of its profits on snacks.

   a. What is the total fraction of its profits that it makes on meals and snacks?

   b. What fraction of its profits does it make on drinks?

14. The audience at a pantomime is made up of children, their parents and grandparents. Five eighths of the audience are children.

   a. What fraction of the audience are adults?

   One eighth of the audience are grandparents of the children.

   b. What fraction of the audience are parents of the children?

B. Add and subtract fractions with different denominators

If two fractions have different denominators, you cannot add or subtract them immediately. You must change the fractions into equivalent fractions with the same denominator.

Look for the **smallest** number that all the denominators divide into exactly.

In the diagram, 2 and 3 both divide into 6

6 is the **common denominator**.

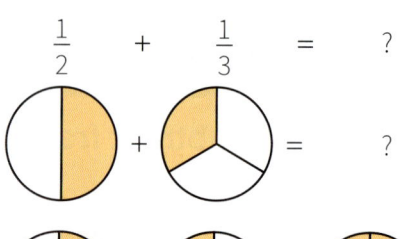

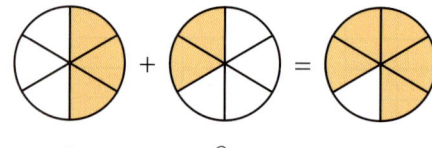

Examples

$\frac{1}{6} + \frac{3}{8} + \frac{1}{3}$

6, 8 and 3 all divide into 24

so make 24 the common denominator.

$\frac{1^{\times 4}}{6_{\times 4}} + \frac{3^{\times 3}}{8_{\times 3}} + \frac{1^{\times 8}}{3_{\times 8}}$

$= \frac{4}{24} + \frac{9}{24} + \frac{8}{24}$

$= \frac{21}{24} = \frac{7}{8}$

$\frac{5}{7} - \frac{3}{8}$

7 and 8 both divide into 56

so make 56 the common denominator.

$\frac{5^{\times 8}}{7_{\times 8}} - \frac{3^{\times 7}}{8_{\times 7}}$

$= \frac{40}{56} - \frac{21}{56}$

$= \frac{19}{56}$

Key point

Before adding or subtracting fractions, you must change them into fractions with a common denominator.

Practice

Work these out. Write each answer in its simplest form.

1. $\dfrac{3}{5} + \dfrac{1}{10}$
2. $\dfrac{4}{5} - \dfrac{3}{10}$
3. $\dfrac{2}{3} + \dfrac{1}{6}$
4. $\dfrac{1}{2} - \dfrac{1}{6}$
5. $\dfrac{2}{3} + \dfrac{1}{4}$
6. $\dfrac{3}{4} - \dfrac{2}{5}$
7. $\dfrac{3}{4} - \dfrac{5}{8}$
8. $\dfrac{5}{9} + \dfrac{1}{3}$
9. $\dfrac{2}{3} - \dfrac{2}{5}$
10. $\dfrac{4}{7} + \dfrac{1}{3}$
11. $\dfrac{2}{5} + \dfrac{1}{3}$
12. $\dfrac{9}{10} - \dfrac{3}{5}$
13. $\dfrac{1}{4} + \dfrac{1}{3} + \dfrac{1}{6}$
14. $\dfrac{5}{8} - \dfrac{2}{5}$
15. $\dfrac{1}{2} + \dfrac{2}{15} + \dfrac{1}{3}$
16. $\dfrac{8}{9} - \dfrac{5}{6}$
17. $\dfrac{8}{9} + \dfrac{1}{3} - \dfrac{3}{4}$
18. $\dfrac{9}{10} - \dfrac{3}{4}$
19. $\dfrac{9}{10} - \dfrac{2}{5} - \dfrac{1}{2}$
20. $\dfrac{3}{4} + \dfrac{1}{2} - \dfrac{3}{8}$

21. A woman spends a quarter of her income on rent, a third on clothes and a sixth on food.
    a. What is the total fraction that she spends?
    b. What fraction does she have left?

C. Improper fractions and mixed numbers

Sometimes adding gives an **improper** fraction, that is, a 'top-heavy' fraction.

For example, $\dfrac{9}{10} + \dfrac{3}{10} = \dfrac{12}{10} = \dfrac{6}{5}$

As a mixed number, $\dfrac{6}{5} = \mathbf{1\dfrac{1}{5}}$

> A **mixed number** has a whole number and a fraction part. See page 94.

Examples

$\dfrac{17}{5} = \mathbf{3\dfrac{2}{5}}$ $\left(\dfrac{15}{5} \text{ equals 3, } \dfrac{2}{5} \text{ left over}\right)$

$\dfrac{19}{7} = \mathbf{2\dfrac{5}{7}}$ $\left(\dfrac{14}{7} \text{ equals 2, } \dfrac{5}{7} \text{ left over}\right)$

$\dfrac{35}{4} = \mathbf{8\dfrac{3}{4}}$ $\left(\dfrac{32}{4} \text{ equals 8, } \dfrac{3}{4} \text{ left over}\right)$

How many 4s in 35? (8)
How many are left? (3)

Key point

To change an improper fraction to a mixed number:

Make as many whole numbers as possible.
The rest is the fraction part.

Number

Practice

Write these improper fractions as mixed numbers.

1. $\frac{9}{5}$
2. $\frac{13}{5}$
3. $\frac{13}{3}$
4. $\frac{17}{3}$
5. $\frac{15}{4}$
6. $\frac{9}{2}$
7. $\frac{13}{2}$
8. $\frac{10}{7}$
9. $\frac{21}{4}$
10. $\frac{17}{6}$
11. $\frac{19}{3}$
12. $\frac{33}{5}$
13. $\frac{23}{8}$
14. $\frac{37}{10}$
15. $\frac{40}{9}$

If an answer to a calculation is an improper fraction, change it to a mixed number.

Examples

$$\frac{5}{8}+\frac{7}{8}=\frac{12}{8}=1\frac{4}{8}=1\frac{1}{2}$$

$$\frac{1}{2}+\frac{3}{8}+\frac{1}{3}=\frac{12}{24}+\frac{9}{24}+\frac{8}{24}=\frac{29}{24}=1\frac{5}{24}$$

Add these fractions. Give your answers as mixed numbers and cancel where possible.

16. $\frac{7}{9}+\frac{5}{9}$
17. $\frac{11}{14}+\frac{5}{14}$
18. $\frac{7}{8}+\frac{3}{4}$
19. $\frac{1}{2}+\frac{2}{3}$
20. $\frac{4}{5}+\frac{7}{10}$
21. $\frac{4}{7}+\frac{3}{4}$
22. $\frac{3}{10}+\frac{2}{5}+\frac{1}{2}$
23. $\frac{5}{6}+\frac{3}{4}+\frac{5}{8}$

D. Add and subtract mixed numbers

When adding and subtracting, it is sometimes useful to change mixed numbers into improper fractions.

Example

$1\frac{3}{4}=\frac{7}{4}$ $2\frac{1}{4}=\frac{9}{4}$ $2\frac{3}{5}=\frac{13}{5}$ $4\frac{1}{5}=\frac{21}{5}$

(1 is 4 quarters
+ 3 quarters
= 7 quarters)

(2 is 8 quarters
+ 1 quarter
= 9 quarters)

(2 is 10 fifths
+ 3 fifths
= 13 fifths)

(4 is 20 fifths
+ 1 fifth
= 21 fifths)

Numerator = $4 \times 5 + 1 = 21$

Denominator stays the same

Key point

To change a mixed number to an improper fraction:
change the whole number, then add the other part.

Fractions

Practice

Write these mixed numbers as improper fractions.

1. $1\frac{1}{2}$
2. $2\frac{1}{2}$
3. $3\frac{1}{2}$
4. $1\frac{2}{3}$
5. $2\frac{2}{3}$
6. $2\frac{1}{5}$
7. $3\frac{4}{5}$
8. $2\frac{1}{6}$
9. $1\frac{5}{6}$
10. $2\frac{3}{8}$
11. $2\frac{3}{7}$
12. $5\frac{7}{8}$
13. $4\frac{9}{10}$
14. $3\frac{4}{9}$
15. $6\frac{2}{7}$

To add or subtract mixed numbers:
either
- work with the whole numbers and fractions separately

or
- change them into improper fractions.

Choose the method you prefer.

Example

$$2\frac{1}{4} + 1\frac{2}{3}$$

$$2\frac{1}{4} + 1\frac{2}{3} = 3\frac{1}{4} + \frac{2}{3}$$ or $$2\frac{1}{4} + 1\frac{2}{3} = \frac{9}{4} + \frac{5}{3}$$ ($2 \times 4 + 1 = 9$)

The common denominator is 12 (3 and 4 both divide into 12).

$$3\frac{3}{12} + \frac{8}{12} = 3\frac{11}{12}$$ $$\frac{27}{12} + \frac{20}{12} = \frac{47}{12} = 3\frac{11}{12}$$

Example

$$4\frac{2}{5} - 2\frac{7}{10}$$

$$4\frac{2}{5} - 2\frac{7}{10} = 2\frac{2}{5} - \frac{7}{10}$$ or $$4\frac{2}{5} - 2\frac{7}{10} = \frac{22}{5} - \frac{27}{10}$$ ($4 \times 5 + 2 = 22$)

The common denominator is 10 (5 divides into 10).

$$2\frac{4}{10} - \frac{7}{10} = 1\frac{14}{10} - \frac{7}{10} = 1\frac{7}{10}$$ $$\frac{44}{10} - \frac{27}{10} = \frac{17}{10} = 1\frac{7}{10}$$

Work these out. Write each answer in its simplest form.

16. $1\frac{1}{4} + 1\frac{1}{2}$
17. $2\frac{3}{5} - 1\frac{3}{4}$
18. $3\frac{1}{2} + 1\frac{5}{6}$
19. $3\frac{3}{4} - 2\frac{1}{3}$
20. $5\frac{1}{2} + 2\frac{5}{8}$
21. $4\frac{1}{3} - 1\frac{1}{2}$
22. $2\frac{3}{4} - 1\frac{4}{5}$
23. $3\frac{7}{10} + 2\frac{2}{5}$
24. $5\frac{2}{3} - 1\frac{4}{5}$
25. $3\frac{4}{7} + 2\frac{1}{2}$
26. $4\frac{1}{2} + 2\frac{3}{4}$
27. $2\frac{1}{2} - 1\frac{3}{8}$

Number

28. The preparation of food for a meal takes $1\frac{1}{4}$ hours and it takes $1\frac{3}{4}$ hours to cook it. How long does it take altogether?

29. A piece of cheese weighing $1\frac{1}{2}$ pounds is cut from a cheese that weighs $5\frac{3}{4}$ pounds. What weight of cheese is left?

30. The table shows the hours worked by a part-time hairdresser.
    a. Find the total time she worked.
    b. How much longer did she work on Friday than on Saturday?
    c. How much longer did she work on Friday than on Thursday?

Day	Time worked
Thurs	$3\frac{3}{4}$ hours
Fri	$6\frac{1}{2}$ hours
Sat	$5\frac{1}{4}$ hours

Multiply fractions   Non-specification content

$\frac{1}{2} \times \frac{1}{3}$ means $\frac{1}{2}$ of $\frac{1}{3}$

Think of × as meaning 'of'.

The sketch shows a rectangle split into 3 thirds.
Half of one of these thirds equals one sixth.

$\frac{1}{2} \times \frac{1}{3} = \frac{1}{6}$

This content is beyond the specification but you may find it useful for your studies.

Example

Find: 1. $\frac{3}{4}$ of $\frac{2}{5}$ 2. $\frac{2}{3} \times 1\frac{1}{2}$

1. $\frac{3}{4} \times \frac{2}{5} = \frac{6}{20} = \frac{3}{10}$ (÷2)

   Always simplify your answer where possible.

2. $\frac{2}{3} \times 1\frac{1}{2} = \frac{2}{3} \times \frac{3}{2}$

   $= \frac{6}{6}$

   $= 1$

   Change mixed numbers to improper fractions first.

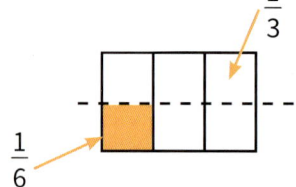

The sketch shows that $\frac{2}{3}$ of $1\frac{1}{2} = 1$

Key point

To multiply fractions, multiply the numerators, then multiply the denominators. Change mixed numbers to improper fractions first.

MyMaths 1047 SEARCH

Fractions

Practice

Work these out. Write each answer in its simplest form.

1. $\frac{1}{2} \times \frac{1}{5}$
2. $\frac{1}{3} \times \frac{1}{7}$
3. $\frac{1}{2} \times \frac{4}{9}$
4. $\frac{2}{3} \times \frac{6}{7}$
5. $\frac{3}{4} \times \frac{8}{11}$
6. $\frac{2}{5} \times \frac{1}{4}$
7. $\frac{3}{4} \times \frac{2}{3}$
8. $\frac{7}{8} \times \frac{4}{5}$

9. Kelly says that a half of a quarter is one eighth. Is she correct?

10. Show that a third of a quarter is the same as a half of one sixth.

Work these out.
Cancel and write the answers as mixed numbers where possible.

11. $\frac{1}{2} \times 3\frac{1}{3}$
12. $\frac{3}{4} \times 2\frac{2}{5}$
13. $\frac{5}{6} \times 1\frac{1}{2}$
14. $1\frac{1}{2} \times \frac{4}{9}$
15. $2\frac{1}{4} \times 1\frac{1}{3}$
16. $3\frac{3}{5} \times 1\frac{1}{4}$
17. $2\frac{1}{3} \times 4\frac{1}{2}$
18. $3\frac{4}{7} \times 1\frac{3}{5}$

19. A chef uses two thirds of a $2\frac{1}{2}$ kilogram bag of potatoes to make chips.
    Find the weight of the potatoes used to make the chips.

20. A roll of fabric is $4\frac{4}{5}$ metres long.
    Half of the roll is used to make a jacket and a third of the roll to make a skirt.
    Work out:
    a. the length of fabric used for the jacket
    b. the length of fabric used for the skirt
    c. the length of fabric that is left on the roll.
    Show that the length left on the roll is one sixth of the original length.

Divide fractions   Non-specification content

To answer $\frac{1}{2} \div \frac{1}{4}$, you need to find how many quarters there are in a half.

The answer is 2

To divide one fraction by another, turn the fraction you are dividing by upside down, then multiply:

This content is beyond the specification but you may find it useful for your studies.

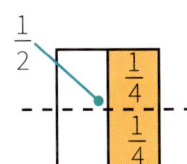

$$\frac{1}{2} \div \frac{1}{4} = \frac{1}{2} \times \frac{4}{1} = \frac{4}{2} = \frac{2}{1} = 2$$
(÷2)

Number

🔍 Example

Find: **1.** $\dfrac{2}{5} \div \dfrac{3}{10}$ **2.** $5\dfrac{1}{4} \div 1\dfrac{1}{2}$

1. $\dfrac{2}{5} \div \dfrac{3}{10} = \dfrac{2}{5} \times \dfrac{10}{3}$ *Turn the second fraction upside down and multiply.*

$= \dfrac{20}{15} = \dfrac{4}{3} = 1\dfrac{1}{3}$ (÷5 top and bottom)   *If possible, simplify your answer and change to mixed numbers.*

2. $5\dfrac{1}{4} \div 1\dfrac{1}{2} = \dfrac{21}{4} \div \dfrac{3}{2}$ *Change mixed numbers to improper fractions first.*

$= \dfrac{21}{4} \times \dfrac{2}{3}$

$= \dfrac{42}{12} = \dfrac{7}{2} = 3\dfrac{1}{2}$ (÷6)   or $= \dfrac{42}{12} = \dfrac{21}{6} = \dfrac{7}{2} = 3\dfrac{1}{2}$ (÷2 then ÷3)

💡 Key point

To divide fractions, turn the fraction you are dividing by upside down, then multiply.
Change mixed numbers to improper fractions first.

The answer to **2** means that there are $3\dfrac{1}{2}$ lots of $1\dfrac{1}{2}$ in $5\dfrac{1}{4}$.
The sketch below shows that this is true.

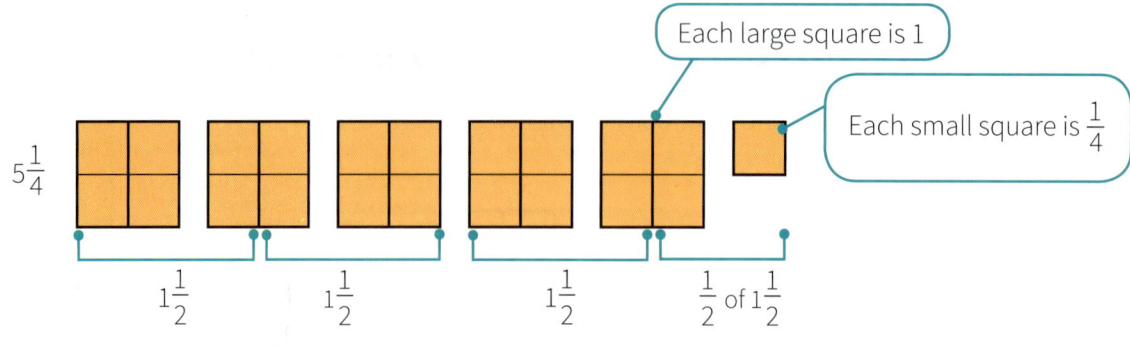

Each large square is 1
Each small square is $\dfrac{1}{4}$

Fractions

 Practice

Work these out. Write each answer in its simplest form.

1. $\dfrac{1}{2} \div \dfrac{1}{6}$
2. $\dfrac{1}{6} \div \dfrac{1}{3}$
3. $\dfrac{2}{5} \div \dfrac{1}{10}$
4. $\dfrac{3}{4} \div \dfrac{3}{8}$
5. $\dfrac{2}{3} \div \dfrac{8}{9}$
6. $\dfrac{3}{5} \div \dfrac{6}{7}$
7. $\dfrac{5}{9} \div \dfrac{2}{3}$
8. $\dfrac{7}{8} \div \dfrac{3}{5}$

9. A bag contains $\dfrac{4}{5}$ kg of icing sugar.

   Jan divides this into smaller bags, each containing $\dfrac{1}{10}$ kg.

   How many smaller bags does she use?

10. Show that there are six ninths in two thirds.

    Do this in **two different ways**.

Work these out.

Cancel and write the answers as mixed numbers where possible.

11. $1\dfrac{2}{3} \div \dfrac{1}{6}$
12. $\dfrac{3}{4} \div 1\dfrac{1}{2}$
13. $2\dfrac{1}{4} \div \dfrac{3}{5}$
14. $\dfrac{5}{6} \div 1\dfrac{1}{3}$
15. $3\dfrac{1}{2} \div 1\dfrac{4}{5}$
16. $2\dfrac{1}{7} \div 1\dfrac{1}{4}$
17. $2\dfrac{4}{9} \div 3\dfrac{2}{3}$
18. $3\dfrac{4}{7} \div 1\dfrac{1}{3}$

19. Katie cuts ribbons to decorate her kite. Each ribbon is $1\dfrac{1}{4}$ metres long.

    How many ribbons does she cut from a roll that is $7\dfrac{1}{2}$ metres long?

20. It takes three quarters of an hour to hand-paint a plate.

    Use fractions to work out how many plates can be hand-painted in 6 hours.

    Hint Write 6 as $\dfrac{6}{1}$

Fractions on a calculator

Specification reference: L1.N9, L2.N7, L2.N8

 Level 1

Scientific calculators have a key for fractions.

The key usually looks like this:

Number

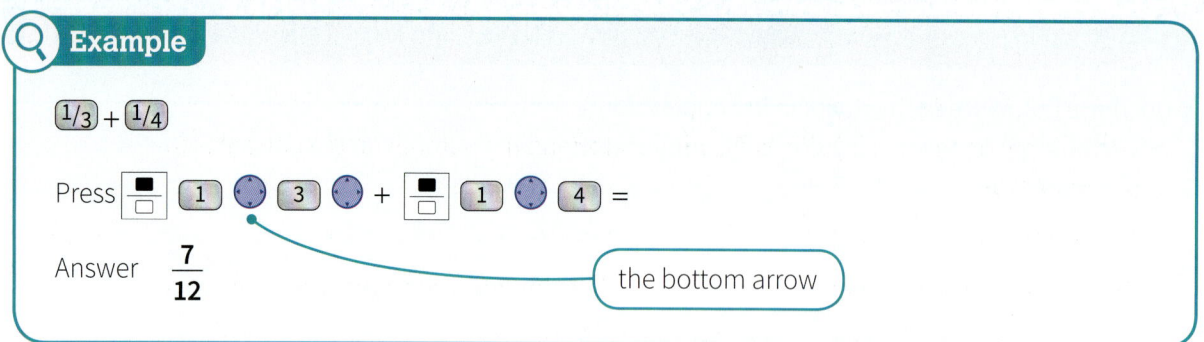

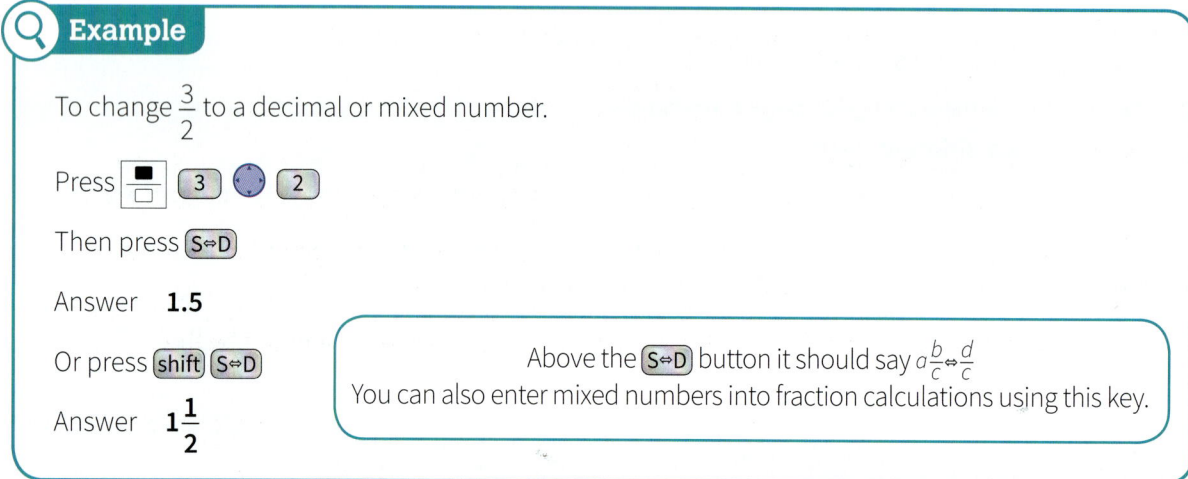

Experiment with your calculator and refer to the manufacturer's instructions if necessary.

Practice

Try the questions in the earlier fractions exercises again, this time using a calculator.

Chapter Summary
8 Fractions

- The number on top of a fraction is the **numerator** and the number on the bottom is the **denominator**.
- A **unit fraction** has a numerator of 1
- Equivalent fractions are equal in size but have different numerators and denominators.
- To find an **equivalent fraction**, multiply or divide the numerator and denominator by the same number.
- To find the **unit fraction** (1 part) of an amount, divide by the denominator.

- In **unit fractions**, the larger the denominator, the smaller the fraction.
- You can use a **fraction wall** to help visualise equivalent fractions. If the denominators aren't multiples of each other, then divide equal rectangles into the correct number of equal parts.
- A **mixed number** is a mixture of a whole number and a fraction. An **improper** fraction has a larger numerator than denominator, and can be made into a mixed number.
- To find a fraction of an amount when the numerator is not 1, divide the amount by the denominator and then multiply by the numerator.
- You can check your answers using **estimation**.
- Make sure you know how to use the fraction button on your calculator.

- To compare fractions with different denominators, use a common multiple to create equivalent fractions with the same denominator. The new denominator of the fractions is called the **common denominator** (try to find the smallest possible).
- A fraction in its **simplest form** means that it has the smallest numerator and denominator of all the equivalent fractions. Write all answers in their simplest form.
- **Cancel** (find the simplest form) by dividing the numerator and denominator by the same number as far as you can.
- When estimating fractions, try to find near numbers that will cancel.
- If an answer is an improper fraction, then change it into a mixed number by making as many whole numbers as possible and writing the remainder as a fraction.
- When you add and subtract fractions the denominators must be the same (use equivalent fractions with a common denominator). Only add the numerators.
- When multiplying and dividing fractions, change mixed numbers into improper fractions first.
- To multiply, think of the multiplication (×) sign as meaning 'of' and multiply the numerators, then the denominators. To divide, flip the fraction you are dividing by and then multiply.

Number — 9 Decimals

Understand decimals in context (up to 2 decimal places)

Specification reference: **EL3.N8**

Decimal numbers have a whole number part and a fraction part.

The **decimal point** separates the two parts.

Read 7.3 as '**seven point three**.'

We often use decimals to give lengths.

Look at a ruler or tape measure.

Each centimetre (cm) is divided into 10 equal divisions. Each division is $\frac{1}{10}$ cm.
As a decimal this is 0.1 cm.

2 divisions = $\frac{2}{10}$ cm or 0.2 cm, 3 divisions = $\frac{3}{10}$ cm or 0.3 cm and so on.

Example

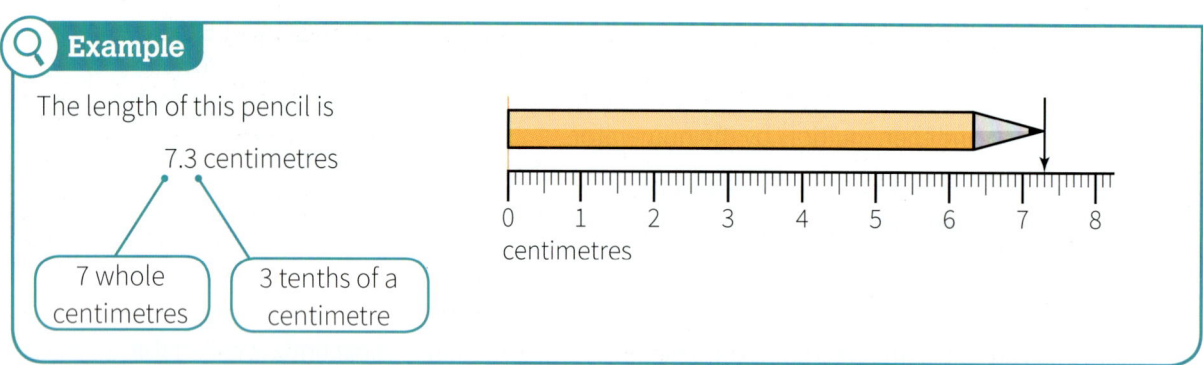

The length of this pencil is 7.3 centimetres
- 7 whole centimetres
- 3 tenths of a centimetre

Practice

1. Write down the length in centimetres marked by each arrow.

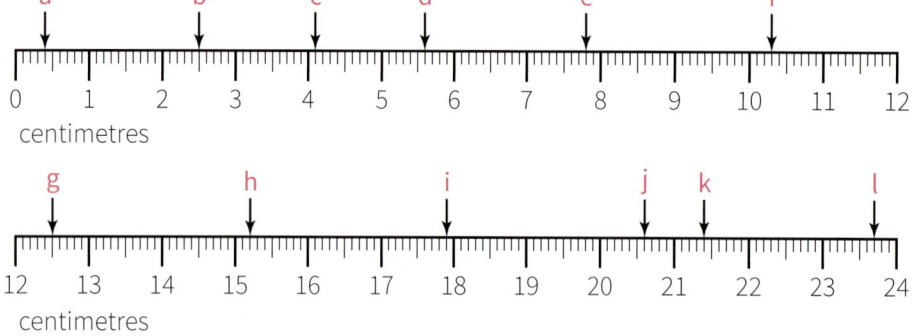

MyMaths — 1014, 1146, 1379

Decimals

To put lengths in order, compare the whole number part then the fraction part.

Example

The lengths of 5 pencils are: 7.6 cm, 8.1 cm, 6.9 cm, 7.3 cm, 7.9 cm.

Look at the **whole numbers first**.

8 is the largest so the longest pencil is 8.1 cm.

There are three lengths starting with 7   (7.6 cm, 7.3 cm and 7.9 cm).

To put them in order **compare the Tenths**:   7.9 cm then 7.6 cm then 7.3 cm.

The shortest pencil is 6.9 cm long.

The answer is: **8.1 cm, 7.9 cm, 7.6 cm, 7.3 cm, 6.9 cm**

Whole numbers	tenths
7 .	6
8 .	1
6 .	9
7 .	3
7 .	9

2. Put each group in order, starting with the **longest**.
   a. Caterpillars: 1.9 cm, 2.4 cm, 1.8 cm, 2.5 cm, 2.1 cm
   b. Leaves: 4.5 cm, 3.8 cm, 3.9 cm, 3.4 cm, 4.1 cm, 4.3 cm
   c. Twigs: 10.6 cm, 9.9 cm, 11.1 cm, 10.5 cm, 9.6 cm, 10.7 cm
   d. Tree heights: 5.3 m, 6.1 m, 5.8 m, 5.5 m, 6.4 m, 5.7 m, 6.2 m, 5.1 m
   e. Road lengths: 1.8 km, 2.9 km, 2.3 km, 1.2 km, 0.9 km, 1.7 km, 1.4 km, 2.1 km

Each length in the last section had **1 decimal place** (1 dp), that is, each length had 1 digit after the decimal point.

7.3 cm — 1 decimal place

For money we often use **2 decimal places** (2 dp).

£2.31 is 2 pounds, 31 pence — 2 decimal places

There are **100 pence in each pound**

so   £2.31 = 231p

Each penny is one hundredth of a pound.   31p = £$\frac{31}{100}$ (31 **hundredths** of a £)

3. Write each amount in pence.
   a. £1.00   b. £2.18   c. £1.09   d. £4.07   e. £0.62
   f. £8.24   g. £5.70   h. £9.04   i. £10.17   j. £16.40

4. Write each amount in £ using decimals.
   a. 213p   b. 402p   c. 85p   d. 350p   e. 103p
   f. 600p   g. 725p   h. 937p   i. 1000p   j. 2409p

Number

To put prices in order, **compare the £ first then the pence**.

> **Example**
>
> Put these prices in order, starting with the **cheapest**.
> £3.45 £2.98 £3.06 £2.80 £2.77
>
> Look at the whole £s first: 2 is less than 3
>
> The prices starting with 2 are £2.98, £2.80 and £2.77
>
> Now compare the pence. The correct order is £2.77, £2.80, £2.98
>
> The prices starting with 3 are £3.45 and £3.06
>
> Now compare the pence. The correct order is £3.06, £3.45
>
> The answer is: **£2.77 £2.80 £2.98 £3.06 £3.45**
>
> | £ | pence |
> |---|---|
> | 3 . | 45 |
> | 2 . | 98 |
> | 3 . | 06 |
> | 2 . | 80 |
> | 2 . | 77 |

5. Put each group of prices in order from cheapest to most expensive.

    a. £1.21   £1.37   £1.02   £2.07   £1.46   £1.19   £1.87

    b. £74.02   £47.20   £56.78   £66.18   £63.21   £63.02

    c. £11.17   £10.08   £11.91   £10.07   £11.01   £10.70

---

100 centimetres = 1 metre

Each centimetre (cm) is **one hundredth** of a metre (m). (2 metres) (34 centimetres)

15 cm = 0.15 m (just like 15p = £0.15)   and   234 cm = 2.34 m

(Read 0.15 as 'zero point one five' and 2.34 as 'two point three four'.)

Working with m and cm is like working with £ and pence, but with measurements we usually leave off any zero at the end of the decimal part.

> **Example**
>
> In measurements: 30 cm = **0.3 m**   and   750 cm = **7.5 m**   (zero not needed)
>
> In money: 30p = **£0.30**   and   750p = **£7.50**   (zero needed)

6. How many centimetres are there in each of these measurements?

    a. 0.22 m   **b.** 1.07 m   **c.** 1.73 m   **d.** 0.74 m   **e.** 1.33 m

    f. 1.12 m   **g.** 1.15 m   **h.** 0.67 m   **i.** 2.6 m   **j.** 5.4 m

7. Write each measurement in metres using decimals.

    a. 154 cm   **b.** 315 cm   **c.** 94 cm   **d.** 120 cm   **e.** 762 cm

    f. 402 cm   **g.** 70 cm   **h.** 250 cm   **i.** 1134 cm   **j.** 2230 cm

Decimals

8. The heights of some groups of children are given below.
   Put each group in order starting with the **shortest**.

a. 1.5 m	1.67 m	1.72 m	1.8 m	1.55 m	1.63 m	1.74 m
b. 1.32 m	1.26 m	1.39 m	1.28 m	1.31 m	1.3 m	1.4 m
c. 0.72 m	0.99 m	1.02 m	0.88 m	1.01 m	0.84 m	1.03 m

In fractions, 50 out of 100 = $\frac{50}{100} = \frac{1}{2}$

Half of £1 = 50 pence, that is, £0.50

Half of a metre = 50 cm = 0.5 m

and $3\frac{1}{2}$ m = 3.5 m

> **Key point**
> 0.5 in decimals = $\frac{1}{2}$ in fractions

Learn this.

9. a. Write these as decimals.   i. $1\frac{1}{2}$ m   ii. $7\frac{1}{2}$ m   iii. $10\frac{1}{2}$ m

   b. Write these as mixed numbers.   i. 2.5 m   ii. 6.5 m   iii. 15.5 m

> **Activities**
> 1. Read prices from adverts, price lists, etc. Select coins and/or notes to match.
> 2. Measure some items in cm then write the measurements in m using decimals.

Write and compare decimals up to 3 decimal places

Specification reference **L1.N10**

A. Place value

Look at the decimal numbers below. The table headings show the **place value** of each digit.

	Hundreds 100s	Tens 10s	Units 1s	.	Tenths 10ths	Hundredths 100ths	Thousandths 1000ths
14.13		1	4	.	1	3	
7.509			7	.	5	0	9
0.173			0	.	1	7	3

Look at the first decimal 14.13 (fourteen point one three).
It has no **H**undreds, 1 **T**en, 4 **U**nits, 1 **T**enth, 3 **H**undredths and no **Th**ousandths.

In money, £14.13 can be made up from 1 ten-pound note, 4 pound coins, 1 ten-pence coin and 3 one-penny coins. (10 pence is $\frac{1}{10}$ of a £ and 3 pence is $\frac{3}{100}$ of a £.)

ten = 10

tenth = $\frac{1}{10}$

Number

There is more than one way of writing the decimal part in fractions.

$$14.13 = 14 + \frac{1}{10} + \frac{3}{100}$$ (as separate fractions) or $$14\frac{13}{100}$$ (in a single fraction)

This is like having 1 ten-pence coin and 3 one-pence coins, or 13 one-pence coins.

Now look at the second decimal in the place value table (on page 121), 7.509

The **place value** of the **digit** 5 is $\frac{5}{10}$ and the place value of the 9 is $\frac{9}{1000}$

There are no **H**undredths, but the zero is important as it keeps the 9 in the **Th**ousandths column.

In fractions $7.509 = 7 + \frac{5}{10} + \frac{9}{1000}$ or $7\frac{509}{1000}$ (decimal digits / heading for last digit)

The last decimal, 0.173, has no whole number part.

In fractions $0.173 = \frac{1}{10} + \frac{7}{100} + \frac{3}{1000}$ or $\frac{173}{1000}$

⚙ Practice

1. **a.** Draw a place value table. Write the following numbers in it.

    i. 116.7**4** **ii.** 37.5**4** **iii.** 12.0**6** **iv.** 4.**5**2

    v. **5**36.09 **vi.** 506.92**6** **vii.** 67.3**5**4 **viii.** 127.06**3**

    ix. 107.**4**01 **x.** 231.0**7**9 **xi.** 6**1**9.102 **xii.** 4**2**3.073

    b. Write down the place value of each digit that is coloured blue.

2. Draw a place value table. Write the following numbers in it.

    a. Fifty-seven point three two
    b. Six point nine
    c. Twelve point four one
    d. One hundred point three five
    e. Ninety-six point nought seven
    f. Twelve point five nought six
    g. Four hundred and ninety-seven point six four three

3. Write these as fractions or mixed numbers using tenths, hundredths or thousandths.

    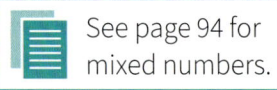
    See page 94 for mixed numbers.

    a. 0.7 **b.** 0.06 **c.** 0.003 **d.** 0.04 **e.** 3.05

    f. 6.4 **g.** 15.007 **h.** 8.02 **i.** 10.6 **j.** 240.009

4. Write each of these numbers in terms of fractions in **two different ways** (that is, as separate fractions and as a single fraction).

    a. 0.17 **b.** 0.49 **c.** 0.031 **d.** 0.357 **e.** 6.23

    f. 8.043 **g.** 42.107 **h.** 1.241 **i.** 502.69 **j.** 17.653

Decimals

B. Write decimals as common fractions

You can simplify fractions by dividing the top and bottom by the same number.

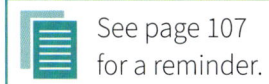 See page 107 for a reminder.

 Example

Write 0.75 as a fraction.

$0.75 = \dfrac{75}{100} = \dfrac{15}{20} = \dfrac{3}{4}$

Dividing top and bottom by 5 then 5 again

 Practice

Write these decimals as simple fractions.

1. 0.5
2. 0.2
3. 0.4
4. 0.6
5. 0.8
6. 0.15
7. 0.35
8. 0.55
9. 0.25
10. 0.45

C. Put decimals in order of size

When comparing decimals: first compare the whole number part and then compare the digits after the decimal point, starting from the left.

Example

Put 2.97, 3.081, 2.963, 2.79, 2.805, 2.965 in order, starting with the largest.

3.081
2.97
2.965
2.963
2.805
2.79

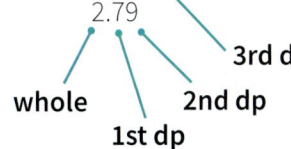
whole 1st dp 2nd dp 3rd dp

First look at the whole numbers.
3 is bigger than 2 so 3.081 is the largest.
All the other numbers start with 2

Look at the 1st decimal place.
9 is the largest, but there are 3 numbers.
To compare 2.97, 2.963 and 2.965:

Look at the 2nd decimal place.
7 is larger than 6 so 2.97 is the largest.
Now to compare 2.963 and 2.965:

Look at the 3rd decimal place.
5 is larger so 2.965 is next, then 2.963
The remaining numbers are 2.79 and 2.805. To compare these:

Go back to the 2nd decimal place.
8 is larger than 7, so 2.805 is next.

The answer is: 3.081   2.97   2.965   2.963   2.805   2.79

Number

Alternative method

You may find it easier to write all the original numbers to 3 decimal places (by adding zeros to the end where necessary): 2.97**0**, 3.081, 2.963, 2.79**0**, 2.805, 2.965
Then compare the whole numbers and decimal parts in two stages.
Try this and see which method you prefer.

Practice

1. Put each group in order of size, starting with the **largest**.
   a. 5.02   7.21   6.76   4.32   6.12   5.98   5.03   4.68   7.11
   b. 13.1   14.21   12.97   14.26   12.5   13.03   12.43   12.07
   c. 26.42   21.5   25.06   26.11   21.8   25.17   21.43   26.47
   d. 3.19   7.21   3.5   6.48   3.21   7.84   6.96   4.06   5.74

2. Put each group in order of size, starting with the **smallest**.
   a. 1.075   0.307   0.003   1.11   1.05   1.761   0.23
   b. 12.05   12.502   12.429   12.5   12.121   12.005
   c. 20.095   19.16   21.35   19.006   21.101   19.375
   d. 604.002 483.562 581.879 581.098 428.003 412.438

3. Put each group of weights in order, **largest** (heaviest) first.
   a. 2.009 kg   1.045 kg   1.762 kg   2.032 kg   1.104 kg
   b. 1.7 kg   1.07 kg   1.707 kg   1.007 kg   1.077 kg
   c. 0.041 kg   0.405 kg   0.318 kg   0.058 kg   0.201 kg

4. The following times (in seconds) are recorded at a race day.
   Write each group in order, starting with the **shortest** (quickest) time.
   a. 12.056   12.009   11.909   11.099   12.201   12.037
   b. 18.567   19.002   18.411   18.591   18.302   19.041
   c. 26.057   25.503   25.601   25.072   26.001   25.021

Use a calculator to solve problems

Specification reference EL3.N8

A calculator is useful for working with decimals, but it is easy to press the wrong key. It is important that you always check the answer.

When using a calculator:

- Take care to press the numbers and the decimal point correctly.
- Include a zero before the decimal point in the answer if there is no whole number.
- Write down a sensible number of decimal places. For money, use 2 decimal places to give the nearest whole pence and add a zero if necessary (for example, 3.5 means £3.50).

Decimals

- Write down the units if there are any (for example, £, m, kg).
- Think about whether the answer is sensible.
- Use estimation, inverse calculations or a different method to check the answer.

Example

Three presents cost £5.99, £2.45 and £3.95

Using a calculator gives the total: 5.99 + 2.45 + 3.95 = 12.39   Answer = **£12.39**

Check by estimating (to the nearest £): £6 + £2 + £4 = £12

or

Check using inverse calculations: 12.39 − 3.95 − 2.45 = 5.99

or

Check by adding in a different order: 3.95 + 2.45 + 5.99 = 12.39

There is a choice of ways to check. Just use one way.

Practice

Use a calculator to work these out. Check each answer.

1.
   a. 13 + 1.05
   b. £1.02 + £3.74
   c. 1.5 m + 0.5 m
   d. 5.75 + 3.05 + 1.9
   e. £4.57 − £0.86
   f. £11.00 − £2.19
   g. 9 m − 4.5 m
   h. 23 − 1.14
   i. 5.03 × 3
   j. £3.07 × 0.5
   k. 5 × 0.2 kg
   l. £7.15 × 4
   m. 6.45 ÷ 3
   n. £3.13 ÷ 4
   o. 6 m ÷ 0.3 m
   p. 1.35 ÷ 0.2

2. Four friends share the cost of a meal, £46.80. How much do they pay each?

3. A girl spends £1.17 on sweets and her brother spends £4.20. How much do they spend altogether?

4. A boy saves £3.50 each week. How much does he save in 8 weeks?

5. a. A dress designer has 14.75 metres of material. She only uses 9.5 metres. How much material does she have left?
   b. The dress designer cuts 1.5 metres of ribbon into 5 equal lengths. How long is each length?

6. A teenager spends £4.85 on her favourite magazine each week. How much does she spend during 6 weeks?

7. In a charity shop, a customer spends £4.07, £1.99 and £2.70 How much is this altogether?

8. Omar wins £20. He spends £15.74 of his winnings. How much does he have left?

Number

Multiply and divide decimals by 10, 100 and 1000

Specification reference **L1.N3**

To multiply by 10, 100 or 1000, move the numbers to the **left** so they become **larger**.

Move the numbers as many times as there are zeros in 10, 100 or 1000:

one column for 10 (as it has 1 zero); two columns for 100 (2 zeros); three columns for 1000 (3 zeros).

To divide by 10, 100 or 1000, move the numbers to the **right** so they become **smaller**.

Example 4.1×100

$4.1 \times 100 = $ **410**

The 4 moves 2 places. It is now 4 hundreds instead of 4 units.

The 1 is now worth ten instead of a tenth. Put zero in the **U**nits column to keep the numbers in place.

Hundreds 100	Tens 10s	Units 1s	.	Tenths 10ths
		4	.	1
4	1	0	.	

 Compare this with page 7 (whole numbers).

Example $32 \div 10$

$32 \div 10 = $ **3.2**

The 3 and 2 both move 1 place to the right.
The 3 is now 3 **U**nits.
The 2 is now 2 **T**enths.

Tens 10s	Units 1s	.	Tenths 10ths
3	2	.	0
	3	.	2

Example $970 \div 1000$

$970 \div 1000 = $ **0.97**

Hundreds 100	Tens 10s	Units 1s	.	Tenths 10ths	Hundreds 100ths	Thousands 1000ths
9	7	0	.	0		
		0	.	9	7	0

This is needed to emphasise the position of the decimal point.

Not needed as there are no thousandths.

Decimals

Practice

Use a place value table to help you work these out.

1. a. 17.4 × 10
    b. 5.63 × 100
    c. 17.2 × 1000
    d. 11.743 × 10
    e. 16.01 × 1000
    f. 112.2 × 100

2. a. 56.22 ÷ 10
    b. 63.04 ÷ 100
    c. 1.44 ÷ 100
    d. 102.01 ÷ 10
    e. 57.4 ÷ 1000
    f. 106 ÷ 1000

3. a. 26.11 × 10
    b. 5.77 ÷ 10
    c. 1.04 × 100
    d. 121 ÷ 100
    e. 47.2 × 1000
    f. 566.02 ÷ 1000

The metric system is based on tens, hundreds and thousands.

£1 = 100p   1 cm = 10 mm   1 m = 100 cm = 1000 mm   1 km = 1000 m

1 kg = 1000 g   1 cℓ = 10 mℓ   1 ℓ = 100 cℓ = 1000 mℓ

To convert from one unit to another, you need to multiply or divide by 10, 100 or 1000

To convert from **large** units **to small** units, **multiply**.

To convert from **small** units **to large** units, **divide**.

Example

4.6 m to cm

4.6 m × 100 = **460 cm**

1679 g to kg

1679 g ÷ 1000 = **1.679 kg**

 Key point
There are 100 cm in a metre. To convert metres to centimetres multiply by 100

 Key point
There are 1000 g in a kilogram. To convert grams to kilograms divide by 1000

---

4. Convert these.
   a. 30 cm to mm
   b. 3.7 m to cm
   c. 145 cm to m
   d. 45 mm to cm
   e. £3.45 to pence
   f. 789p to £
   g. 0.66 m to cm
   h. 65 cℓ to litres
   i. 1567 g to kg
   j. 18 mm to cm
   k. 0.6 km to m
   l. 7580 m to km

5. Copy the amounts below. Draw lines between the equivalent amounts.

   a. 7500 g   2.3 m
      230 cm   0.75 ℓ
      2300 g   7.5 kg
      75 cℓ   1.25 ℓ
      125 cℓ   2.3 kg

   b. 0.5 m   750 g
      1.2 ℓ   5 mℓ
      0.75 kg   50 cm
      1.2 cm   120 cℓ
      0.5 cℓ   12 mm

 For more conversions see pages 217, 240 and 255.

127

Number

Round decimal numbers and approximate

Specification reference: **L1.N12, L2.N9**

Level 1

To round decimal numbers to whole numbers:
- Look at the **first decimal place** (1st dp).
- If it is **below 5, leave the whole number as it is**.
- If it is **5 or above, round the whole number up by 1**

 Key point
Rounding is used to estimate or check calculations.

Example

Round 2.47 to the nearest whole number.

Units 1s	.	Tenths 10ths	Hundreds 100ths
2	.	4	7

↑ 1st dp — This is the 'deciding digit'.

4 is **below 5**
so 2.**4**7 = **2** to the nearest whole number.

Example

Round 9.8 to the nearest whole number.

Whole number — 9.**8** — Deciding digit (1st dp)

8 is above **5**
so 9.**8** = **10**
to the nearest whole number.

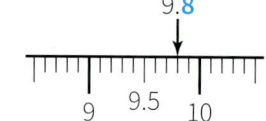

9.**8** is more than 9.5 — nearer to 10 than 9

Practice

1. Round each of these to the nearest whole number.
   - a. 14.7
   - b. 13.1
   - c. 7.4
   - d. 3.8
   - e. 9.7
   - f. 6.21
   - g. 16.31
   - h. 11.81
   - i. 9.84
   - j. 11.71
   - k. 15.07
   - l. 0.71
   - m. 4.315
   - n. 5.572
   - o. 0.469
   - p. 26.98
   - q. 249.5
   - r. 99.67

In these questions round values to whole numbers then estimate the answers.

2. Three friends spend £4.96 each. Estimate how much they spend altogether.

3. A fabric artist buys 1.8 m of blue silk, 1.2 m of red silk and 2.9 m of green silk. Estimate how much material is bought altogether.

4. A traveller buys items costing £4.21, £0.91 and £1.21 in airport shops before a flight. Estimate the total cost.

 1001, 1004

Decimals

5. Estimate the total weight of the parcels shown here.

6. Rita says she has £15, to the nearest £.
   What is the least amount of money she can have?

To round a decimal to **one decimal place, look at the second decimal place**.
If this is **5 or above, round the first decimal place up**.

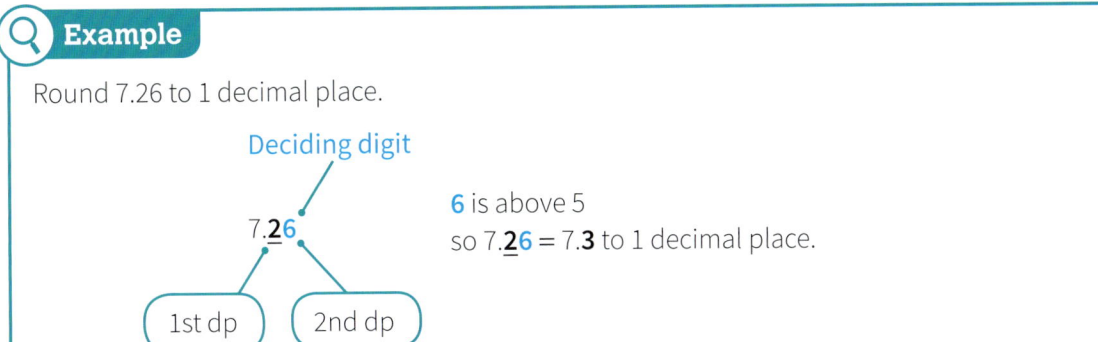

To round to **two** decimal places, look at the **third** decimal place.
If this **is 5 or above, round the second decimal place up** (otherwise leave it as it is).

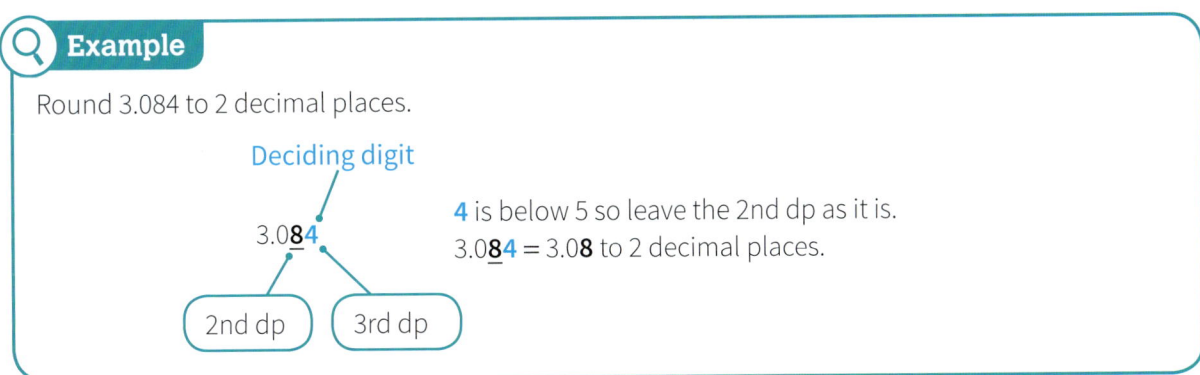

Sometimes you may need to choose an appropriate level of accuracy.
For money written in £, this is usually 2 decimal places (nearest pence).

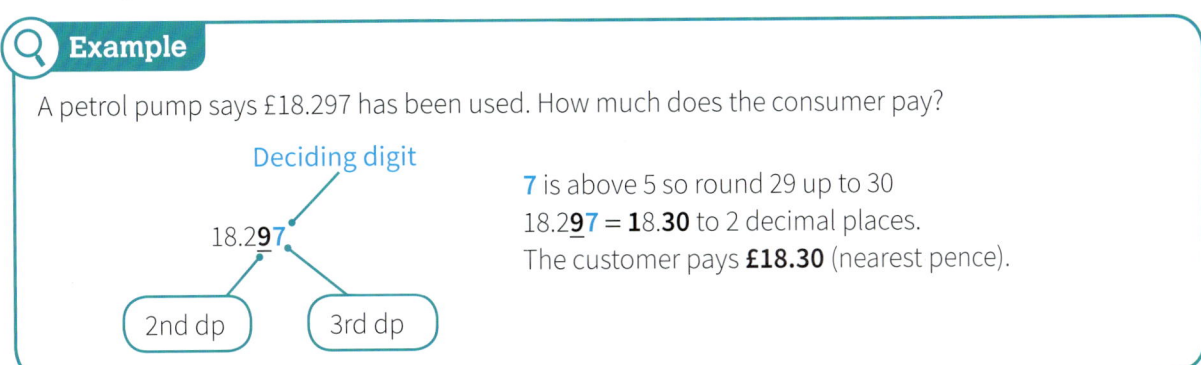

To round to **three** decimal places, look at the **fourth** decimal place and so on.

Number

7. Round these numbers to 2 decimal places.
   - a. 5.678
   - b. 16.591
   - c. 11.325
   - d. 21.898
   - e. 155.793
   - f. 16.224
   - g. 131.076
   - h. 6.749
   - i. 121.903
   - j. 1.891
   - k. 2.396
   - l. 16.7081
   - m. 15.9152
   - n. 13.5618
   - o. 1.0065

8. Round these amounts to 2 decimal places.
   - a. £1.273
   - b. 2.726 kg
   - c. £12.158
   - d. 17.415 m
   - e. 22.567 km
   - f. 14.725 g
   - g. 16.194 cm
   - h. £9.6439
   - i. 0.473 ℓ
   - j. 15.098 km

9. Round these.
   - a. £15.39 to the nearest pound
   - b. 13.606 kg to the nearest kg
   - c. 5.1128 litres to 2 dp
   - d. £31.566666 to 2 dp
   - e. £7.165431 to the nearest pence
   - f. 6.597 m to 2 dp

10. A student is asked to give answers correct to 1 dp. Round these to 1 dp.
    - a. 9.533333
    - b. 12.3567
    - c. 13.17098
    - d. 6.6974
    - e. 121.79311
    - f. 5.7217
    - g. 91.7508
    - h. 151.90854
    - i. 65.0911
    - j. 73.64842

11. Round these amounts to the appropriate accuracy suggested.

	Quantity	Amount
a.	Interest on savings to the nearest pence	£7.362
b.	Weight of raspberries to the nearest tenth of a kilogram	6.184 kg
c.	Width of a kitchen to the nearest hundredth of a metre	4.753 m
d.	Cost of electricity to the nearest pence	£123.685
e.	Capacity of a watering can to the nearest tenth of a litre	9.17 litres

12. Round the following numbers to 3 decimal places.
    - a. 5.79241
    - b. 16.9376
    - c. 3.74912
    - d. 0.97386
    - e. 4.03189
    - f. 16.7701
    - g. 12.08051
    - h. 27.90109
    - i. 1.54973
    - j. 17.6999

13. 1 mile equals 1.609344 kilometres. Round this to the nearest metre.

    Hint 1 kilometre = 1000 metres.

14. 1 pint = 0.56826125 litres. Round this to the nearest millilitre.

    Hint 1 litre = 1000 millilitres.

Activity

Find out how to round decimals on your calculator or on a spreadsheet.

Use this method to check your answers to the questions above.

Add and subtract decimals

Specification reference EL3.N8, L1.N11, L1.N15, L2.N10

You can check your answer by:
- rounding to the nearest whole numbers and estimating
- using inverse (opposite) calculations (see page 14)
- using a calculator.

See pages 10 and 13 for a reminder of addition and subtraction methods.

Example

One package weighs 15.07 kilograms. Another weighs 3.1 kilograms. What is the total weight?

15.07 kg + 3.1 kg

```
  15.07
+  3.10
  18.17
```

Check (estimating)
```
  15
+  3
  18
```

Check (inverse)
```
  18.17
−  3.10
  15.07
```

The total weight is **18.17 kg**.

Example

An upholsterer has 24.3 metres of fabric. He uses 3.75 metres to make some cushions. How much fabric is left?

24.3 m − 3.75 m

```
  2³4.¹²3̶10
−    3. 7 5
  20. 5 5
```
← Fill gaps with zeros.

Check (estimating)
```
  24
−  4
  20
```

Check (inverse)
```
  20.55
+  3.75
  24.30
    1 1
```

There is **20.55 m** of fabric left.

Key point
To add or subtract decimals, line up the decimal points.

Practice

1. Calculate and check these without a calculator.

a. 5.2 kg + 3.9 kg
b. 4.9 m − 2.1 m
c. 10.4 cm + 12.96 cm
d. £72.34 − £49.67
e. £204.07 − £196.30
f. £137.60 − £107.06
g. £18.99 + £108.17
h. 2.1 m − 0.75 m
i. 57.06 km + 106.1 km
j. £13.12 − £12.07
k. 105.17 kg + 22.4 kg
l. £49.35 + £107.19

Number

Work these out, then check with a calculator.

2. A saver has £354.60 in the bank. She withdraws £217.74
   What is her new balance?

3. A family book a holiday costing £980.89. They pay a deposit of £98.08
   How much is left to pay?

4. A shopper receives £13.49 change from a twenty pound note.
   How much has he spent?

5. A student buys three books costing £55.44, £13.62 and £17.29
   What is the total cost?

6. A workshop has 476.5 m of wire in stock. It uses 326.25 m.
   How much is left?

7. A householder receives bills for £372.15, £32.07 and £11.19
   How much is this altogether?

8. A farmer wants to fence some land. The lengths of the sides are 65.8 m, 67.75 m, 78.95 m and 96.5 m.
   Add these lengths to find the perimeter.

9. The table shows the time in seconds taken by each swimmer in two relay teams.
   a. Find the total time taken by each team.
   b. Which team won and by how many seconds?

	Team A	Team B
1st swimmer	21.42	22.56
2nd swimmer	25.58	23.10
3rd swimmer	24.17	24.78
4th swimmer	19.96	20.34

10. A worker earns £1120.09. He spends £875.42.
    How much does he have left?

11. The interest on a loan of £1500 is £427.61. What is the total amount owed?

Work these out without a calculator, then use rounding to check.

12. a. 2.396 + 5.274 + 2.821   b. 9.08 − 2.765   c. 3.24 + 6.382 − 5.493

13. In a race the fastest time is 43.456 seconds and the slowest time is 59.572 seconds.
    What is the difference between these times?

Decimal sequences

Specification reference **EL3.N9**

Number sequences may involve decimal numbers.

> **Examples**
>
> 0.8   0.9   1.0   1.1   1.2   1.3   ...
>
> The first term of this sequence is **0.8** and the rule is **add 0.1**
>
> 0.15   0.14   0.13   0.12   0.11   0.1   ...
>
> The first term of this sequence is **0.15** and the rule is **subtract 0.01**

Decimals

Practice

1. For each sequence, write the rule and find the next 3 terms.

   a. 1.2   1.4   1.6   1.8   2.0   ☐ ☐ ☐
   b. 2.7   2.9   3.1   3.3   3.5   ☐ ☐ ☐
   c. 1.55 1.6   1.65 1.7   1.75 ☐ ☐ ☐
   d. 1.1   2.2   3.3   4.4   5.5   ☐ ☐ ☐
   e. 0.2   0.5   0.8   1.1   1.4   ☐ ☐ ☐
   f. 0.05 0.1   0.15 0.2   0.25 ☐ ☐ ☐
   g. 10   9.5   9   8.5   8   ☐ ☐ ☐
   h. 4   3.8   3.6   3.4   3.2   ☐ ☐ ☐
   i. 1.96 1.95 1.94 1.93 1.92 ☐ ☐ ☐
   j. 10.6 10.5 10.4 10.3 10.2 ☐ ☐ ☐

2. A carpenter wants to mark where holes in a wall are needed for a set of shelves. The first hole must be 0.65 m above the ground.
   The next 4 holes must be at intervals of 0.3 m. What will be the height above the ground of:

   a. the second hole
   b. the fifth hole?

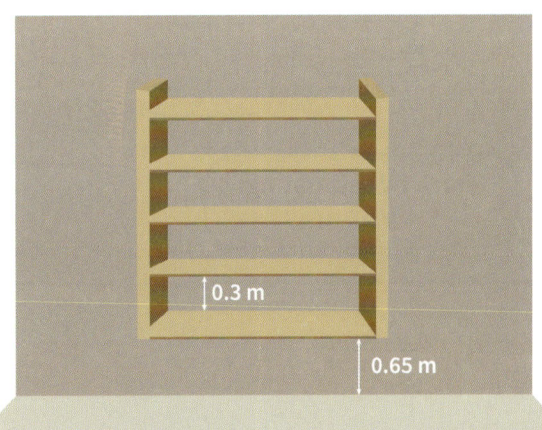

3. A wedding cake maker has a 5-m roll of ribbon. She ties ribbon around cakes that she has made.
   Each cake takes 0.6 m of ribbon.

   a. Copy and continue this table to show how much ribbon is left after each cake.
   b. How many cakes can the baker tie with ribbon?
   c. How much ribbon is left?

Number of cakes tied with ribbon	Length of remaining ribbon (m)
0	5
1	4.4
2	

4. Glasses are filled from a 2-litre bottle of lemonade. Each glass holds 0.3 litres.

   a. Copy and continue this table to show how much lemonade is left after each glass.
   b. How many glasses can be filled?
   c. How much lemonade is left?

Number of Glasses	Amount of remaining lemonade (ℓ)
0	2

Number

Multiply decimals

Specification reference **L1.N11, L2.N10**

To multiply decimals:

- Ignore the decimal points and use your usual method to multiply the figures.

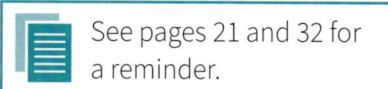

See pages 21 and 32 for a reminder.

- Count the total number of decimal places (dp) in **both** numbers being multiplied. Starting at the end of the answer, count the same number of decimal places and insert the decimal point. (Add zeros if needed, for example, $0.3 \times 0.2 = 0.06$)
- Round the answer to a sensible number of figures (for example, money to the nearest £ or pence).
- Check the answer.

Example

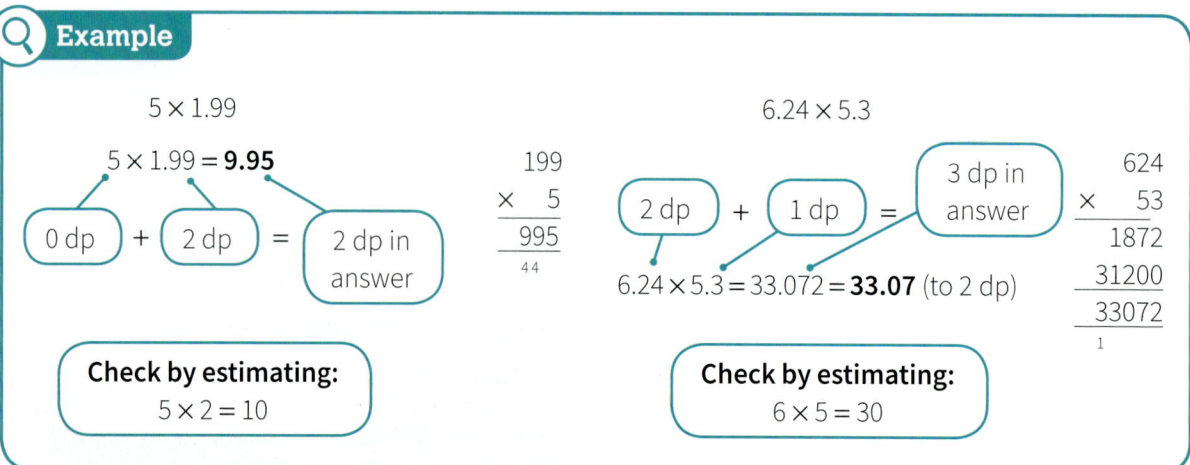

Practice

1. Calculate these without a calculator. Round answers to 2 dp where necessary. Use estimation to check each answer.

   a. 0.6×4 b. 0.2×0.1 c. 7×0.05 d. 0.3×0.4

   e. 3.65×4 f. 19.7×3 g. 11.22×0.5 h. 165×0.09

   i. 40.7×0.8 j. 85.7×0.06 k. 5.01×2.1 l. 1.8×0.69

   m. 5.19×7.3 n. 7.43×1.08 o. 18.1×3.66 p. 4.25×3.07

Work these out, then check with a calculator.

2. A tailor needs to make 4 suits. Each suit uses 3.75 m of material. How much material is needed altogether?

3. James buys 6 bottles of wine containing 0.75 litres each. How many litres of wine is this altogether?

4. A shop cashier's hourly wage is £8.95 How much does he earn for 37.5 hours?

5. An office puts in an order for stationery.
Copy and complete the table by working out the prices and total cost.

Order No	Item description	Price of item	Quantity	Price
PHF/1357	A4 paper	£4.99	5	
PHF/1359	A3 paper	£8.75	3	
ZL/129	Box black pens	£3.59	8	
FL/376	White board pens	£3.02	6	
GH/76P	Chrome stapler	£6.50	3	
GH/76L	Staples	£1.49	12	
		Total cost of all items		

6. A rectangular lawn is 43.6 m long and 28.4 m wide. What is its area to the nearest square metre?

See 'Area of a rectangle' page 312.

7. Calculate these without a calculator. Use estimation to check each answer.

   a. 3.725×8
   b. 1.864×0.9
   c. 5.209×4.3

8. A tourist is going to Japan. She changes £800 to yen.
The exchange rate is £1 = 134.894 yen. How many yen does she get?

9. A cuboid is 3.6 m × 1.7 m × 5.8 m. Multiply these lengths to work out its volume to 1 dp.

10. A circular fish pond has a diameter of 3.2 m.
Find its circumference and area to 1 dp. Use π = 3.142

See page 319 for the formulae.

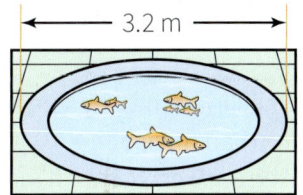

Divide decimals

Specification reference L1.N11, L2.N10

To divide a decimal by a whole number:

- Divide the figures as usual.
- Keep the decimal points in line.
- Round the answer to a sensible number of figures (where necessary).
- Check the answer.

See page 24 for a reminder.

Example 172.6 ÷ 4

```
    4 3 . 1 5
4 )1 7 ¹2 . 6² 0
```

Keep the decimal points in line.

Add zeros to the end if necessary.

Check using inverse:
```
    43.15
    ×  4
   172.60
      1 2
```

MyMaths 1008, 1923 SEARCH

135

Number

Practice

1. Do these without a calculator. Check each answer.

   a. 49.2 ÷ 4   b. 33.78 ÷ 3   c. 79.9 ÷ 5   d. 232.47 ÷ 7

   e. 137.88 ÷ 9   f. 67.08 ÷ 6   g. 423.06 ÷ 3   h. 301.14 ÷ 8

To divide a decimal by a decimal:

- Change the number you are dividing by into a whole number.
  Do this by multiplying by 10 or 100 or 1000
- Do exactly the same to the number you are dividing.
- Divide to find the answer.

Example

7.4 ÷ 0.05

7.4 ÷ 0.05 = 740 ÷ 5

> Multiply 0.05 by 100 to make it into the whole number 5
> Also multiply 7.4 by 100

```
     1 4 8
5 ) 7 ²4 ⁴0
```

Answer = 148

> Check by doing the inverse on a calculator:
> 148 × 0.05 = 7.4

Thinking of money sometimes helps to make sense of the answer.
You can think of 7.4 ÷ 0.05 as 'How many 5p coins make £7.40?'
The answer, 148, then makes sense.

Example

Find 31.52 ÷ 2.4 to 2 decimal places.

31.52 ÷ 2.4 = 315.2 ÷ 24

```
      1 3. 1 3
24 ) 3 1 ⁷5. ³2 ⁸0
```

> Multiply 2.4 by 10 to make it into the whole number 24
> Also multiply 31.52 by 10

This is difficult!

- Try out some values in rough when you need to or write down
  the multiples of 24 that you need:
  24, 48, 72, 96, …

- For the last figure, you need to decide which is nearer to 80:
  24 × 3 = 72 or 24 × 4 = 96   3 is nearer
  (Alternatively you could work it out to
  3 dp then round your answer.)

for example
```
    2 4
  × 3
  ─────
    7 2
      ¹
```

> Check by estimating:
> 30 ÷ 2 = 15

Answer = **13.13**

2. Calculate these without a calculator. Give the answer to 2 dp when not exact.
   Check each answer.

   a. 0.8 ÷ 0.2
   b. 1.5 ÷ 0.5
   c. 0.4 ÷ 0.02
   d. 1.8 ÷ 0.9
   e. 3.9 ÷ 0.03
   f. 6.8 ÷ 0.2
   g. 13.25 ÷ 0.5
   h. 10.8 ÷ 0.03
   i. 2.5 ÷ 0.04
   j. 34 ÷ 0.7
   k. 74.16 ÷ 0.06
   l. 43.2 ÷ 1.2
   m. 56.9 ÷ 3.1
   n. 90.1 ÷ 5.3
   o. 115.2 ÷ 0.12
   p. 35 ÷ 0.25
   q. 5.75 ÷ 1.1
   r. 120 ÷ 7.9
   s. 14.3 ÷ 4.6
   t. 101.52 ÷ 2.16

3. A total of 8.4 mm of rain fell in a week. What was the average rainfall per day?

4. Three friends share the cost of a taxi between them as equally as they can.
   The taxi cost £16.50. How much do they each pay?

5. A reel of cable is 20 metres long. How many pieces of length 0.4 metres can be cut from the reel?

6. A drinks company sells cola in 0.33 litre cans. How many cans can be filled from 2000 litres of cola?

Level 2

7. Calculate these without a calculator (note: You will need to multiply by 1000 this time).
   Check each answer.

   a. 9.7 ÷ 0.005
   b. 0.378 ÷ 0.012
   c. 0.48 ÷ 0.025
   d. 14.2 ÷ 0.125

8. A holidaymaker buys a present costing 18 euros. The exchange rate is 1.173 euros = £1
   How much does the present cost in pounds, to the nearest pound?

9. A tourist returns from America with $200 and wants to change the dollars to pounds. The exchange rate is $1.301 = £1
   What will she receive? Give your answer to the nearest pound (£).

 For more practice on exchanging currency, see pages 188–190.

10. Estimate the answers to these calculations, then work them out accurately to 2 decimal places.

    a. 15.435 + 16.586
    b. 3.791 × 1.9
    c. 21.452 − 7.693
    d. 11.924 ÷ 2.1
    e. 5.798 × 7.1
    f. 19.687 − 7.132
    g. 9.687 + 2.763
    h. 9.782 ÷ 2.5
    i. 5.7 × 3.793

11. The table shows a caterer's vegetable order.

    a. Find the total cost.
    b. The caterer is given a discount of a third of the price.
       How much does she pay?

Item	Weight (kg)	Price per kg (£)
Potatoes	50	0.64
Carrots	25	0.86
Sprouts	12.5	1.32
Mushrooms	6.4	4.35

12. It takes 25 lengths of wallpaper, each 3.2 m long, to paper a room.
    The decorator allows an extra 0.25 m per length for matching the pattern.
    Rolls of wallpaper are 10.05 m long.
    How many rolls does the decorator need to cover the room?

Chapter Summary
9 Decimals

- **Decimal numbers** have a whole number part and a fraction part separated by a **decimal point**.
- The first decimal place is the **tenths** and the second decimal place is the **hundredths**.
- A centimetre on a ruler is divided into 10 equal divisions (millimetres).
- A metre is divided into 100 equal divisions (centimetres), each cm is one hundredth of a m.
- Money is usually written using 2 decimal places. Add a zero in the second decimal place if there are no hundredths.
- When putting lengths (or money) in order, compare the whole number part first (the £ part) and then the fraction part (the pence part).
- 0.5 in decimals is equal to $\frac{1}{2}$ in fractions.
- Remember to include units in the answer and use rounding and estimation or inverse calculations (or another method) to check that the answer is sensible.
- Line up the decimal points to add or subtract decimals.
- Number sequences may involve decimal numbers.

- The names of the place values after the decimal point are: tenths, hundredths, thousandths.
- Remember ten = 10 and a tenth = $\frac{1}{10}$
- You can write the decimal parts as one fraction with the smallest place value as the denominator, or as a sum of fractions for each place value.
- You can simplify fractions by dividing the numerator and denominator by the same number.
- 0.75 is equal to $\frac{3}{4}$ in fractions.
- Put decimals in order by comparing the whole number part and then the decimal digits, beginning with the first decimal place.
- When multiplying or dividing by 10, 100, 1000, always keep the decimal point in the same place and move the digits by the number of zeroes in 10, 100 or 1000. For multiplication, move the numbers left (becoming larger) and move them right for division (becoming smaller).
- The metric system is based on tens, hundreds and thousands and to convert between units, you need to multiply/ divide by 10, 100 or 1000. Multiply to convert from large units to small units and divide to convert from small units to large units.
- The **deciding digit** is the digit to the right of the decimal place you need to round to. Only round up if the deciding digit is 5 or above, otherwise, leave it alone.
- To multiply decimals, ignore the decimal points and multiply as usual. Then count the total number of decimal places in the numbers being multiplied in the question and insert the decimal point so that the final answer has this many decimal places.
- To divide a decimal by another decimal, multiply both numbers by 10, 100 or 1000 to get whole numbers and then carry out the division.

Number 10 Percentages

Understand percentages
Specification reference L1.N13

Per cent means 'out of 100'. It is also written using the sign %.

100% of something = the whole amount

This grid has been split into 100 squares:

30 out of 100 are white.   30% are white.
37 out of 100 are grey.   37% are grey.
18 out 100 are orange.   18% are orange.
15 out of 100 are black.   15% are black.
                The total % = 100%

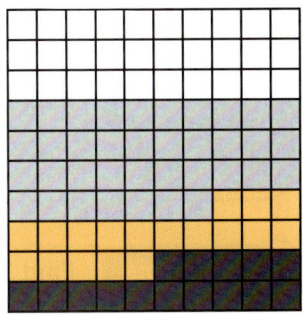

Practice

1. Look at the coloured squares in this grid.
   a. Write down the percentage for each colour.
   b. Check that the total % is 100%.

2. Draw a grid of 100 squares.
   a. Colour in these percentages:
      34% red, 16% green, 21% blue, 19% black.
   b. What % of the squares are not coloured?

There are 100 pence in a pound.
10 pence out of a pound = 10% of £1   90 pence out of a pound = 90% of £1

3. Write these amounts as percentages of £1
   a. 20 pence   b. 45 pence   c. 16 pence   d. 85 pence

4. The following are percentages of £1. Write each amount in pence.
   a. 17%   b. 99%   c. 22%   d. 51%

5. If 10% of £1 = 10p, calculate the following.
   a. 10% of £2   b. 10% of £3   c. 10% of £5   d. 10% of £10

6. Use your answer to question **3a** to calculate the following.
   a. 20% of £2   b. 20% of £3   c. 20% of £5   d. 20% of £10

Number

Find percentages of quantities

Specification reference L1.N14, L2.N5

A. Find 50%, 25% and 75%

50 out of 100 squares on this grid are **orange**.

This is half of the grid.

$50\% = 50 \text{ out of } 100 = \frac{50}{100} = \frac{1}{2}$

Learn $50\% = \frac{1}{2}$

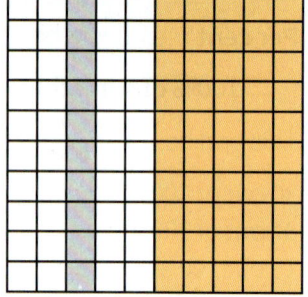

 Example Find 50% of 8 m.

$8 \div 2 = 4$ so 50% of 8 m = **4 m**

 Example Find 50% of £15

$15 \div 2 = 7.5$ so 50% of £15 = **£7.50**

$$2 \overline{)15.^10} \quad 7.5$$

💡 **Key point**

To find 50% of something, divide it by 2 (halve it).

$25\% = 25 \text{ out of } 100$
$= \frac{25}{100} = \frac{1}{4}$

Learn $25\% = \frac{1}{4}$

$75\% = 75 \text{ out of } 100$
$= \frac{75}{100} = \frac{3}{4}$

Learn $75\% = \frac{3}{4}$

To find 25% of something, divide it by 4.
One way to divide something by 4 is to halve it (to find 50%), then halve again.

 Examples

Find 25% of £80

50% of £80 = £40
so 25% of £80 = **£20**

Find 25% of 8.4 m.

50% of 8.4 m = 4.2 m
so 25% of 8.4 m = **2.1 m**

You can use the other method to check:

25% of £80 = 80 ÷ 4 = £20

25% of 8.4 m = 8.4 ÷ 4 = 2.1 m

$$4 \overline{)8.4} \quad 2.1$$

 Examples

Find 25% of £9

50% of £9 = £4.50
25% of £9 = **£2.25**

Find 25% of 1.4 m.

50% of 1.4 m = 0.7 m
25% of 1.4 m = **0.35 m**

You can use another method to check:

25% of £9 = 9 ÷ 4 = £2.25

25% of 1.4 m = 1.4 ÷ 4 = 0.35 m

Percentages

To find 75% of something, divide by 4 (to find 25%) then multiply by 3.
One way to do this is to halve it to find 50%, halve again to find 25%, then add the two values together.

75% = 50% + 25%

> **Example** Find 75% of 240 m.
>
> 50% of 240 m = 240 ÷ 2 = 120 m
> 25% of 240 m = 120 ÷ 2 = 60 m
> (50% + 25%)   **75% of 240 m = 180 m**
>
> Using the other method to check:
> 25% of 240 m = 240 ÷ 4 = 60 m
> 75% of 240 m = 60 × 3 = **180 m**

Practice

Work these out without using a calculator.

Fruit Crumble
250 g plain flour
120 g butter
90 g sugar
280 g blackberries
200 g redcurrants
150 g strawberries

1. This recipe is for fruit crumble for four people.
   a. Find 50% of each ingredient.
   b. How many people would the new amount of crumble feed?

2. Find 50% of these.
   a. £160
   b. 50 m
   c. 96 km
   d. £45
   e. 780 kg
   f. 900 g

3. A coat priced at £120 is reduced by 50% in a sale. How much is the reduction?

4. A carpenter has 90 metres of skirting board. He needs 50% more. What extra length does he need?

5. Find 25% of these by halving (÷ 2), then halving (÷ 2) again.
   a. £60
   b. 92 m
   c. 12.8 m
   d. £24.80
   e. 768 m
   f. 196 cm
   g. £150
   h. £27.40
   i. 15.4 kg
   j. 99 m
   k. 45 km
   l. £6.60

   Check your answers by dividing each quantity by 4

6. Find 75% of these using the two different ways shown in the Example on page 140.
   a. £180
   b. 96 m
   c. 360°
   d. 520 m
   e. 176 kg
   f. £36.40
   g. £12.80
   h. 124 cm
   i. 4.8 m
   j. 18.48 kg
   k. 20.6 g
   l. £74.20

7. A teacher says that you can find 75% by finding 25% first, then taking the answer away from the original amount. To show how to find 75% of 240 m he writes:

    25% of 240 m = 240 ÷ 4 = 60 m

    75% = 100% − 25%

    75% of 240 m = 240 − 60 = 180 m

    Use this method to check three of your answers in question **6**.

Use two different methods to answer questions **8–14**.

8. Last year 300 people came to the school play.
   This year they have sold 25% more tickets.
   How many more tickets have they sold?

9. There are 60 seats on a coach. 75% of these are taken. How many seats are taken?

10. A social club has 320 members. 25% of the members are over 80 years.
    a. How many members are over 80?   b. How many members are 80 or younger?

11. Jamal buys 480 tiles. 75% of these are blue. How many blue tiles are there?

12. A holiday costs £1870. The travel company asks for a 25% deposit.
    a. How much is the deposit?   b. How much is left to pay?

13. The items in a shopper's basket cost £4.99, £17.98 and £19.99.
    The shop gives a 25% discount on the total bill. What is the discount?

14. A company has a budget of £3.2 million to spend on a new factory.
    The company spends 75% of this on the building and the rest on equipment.
    How much does the building cost?

B. Use 10%

Look at the grid on page 140 again. 10 of the 100 squares are grey.

This is one tenth of the grid.

10% = 10 out of 100 = $\frac{10}{100}$ = $\frac{1}{10}$

> Learn 10% = $\frac{1}{10}$

> **Examples**
>
> 10% of 150 km = **15 km**
>
> 10% of £3.50 = **£0.35** or **35p**

 See page 126 for help with dividing by 10

> 💡 **Key point**
>
> To find 10% of something, divide it by 10

Often you can use links between 10% and other percentages.

To find 20%, find 10% then double it (multiply by 2)
To find 30%, find 10% then multiply by 3
To find 40%, find 10% then multiply by 4
You can use a similar method for other multiples of 10% (for example, 60%, 70%, etc.)

> **Key point**
> To find 5% of something, find 10% then halve it (divide by 2).

Example Find 30% of 80 kg.

10% of 80 kg = 8 kg   (because 80 ÷ 10 = 8)
30% of 80 kg = 8 × 3 = **24 kg**

(30% = 10% × 3)

Example

A TV costs £470 without Value Added Tax (VAT).
VAT is charged at a rate of 20%. Find the amount of VAT.
10% of £470 = £47   (because £470 ÷ 10 = £47)

```
    £47
  ×  2
20% of £470 = £94
```

(20% = 10% × 2)

Example

VAT is charged at a rate of 5% on electricity bills.
Find the VAT charged on an electricity bill of £275

10% of £275 = £27.50
5% of £275 = **£13.75**

```
      13. 7 5
    2)27.¹5¹0
```

(5% = 10% ÷ 2)

Practice

Work these out without using a calculator.

1. Find 10% of these.
   a. £450
   b. 90 m
   c. £2400
   d. 54 cm
   e. 62 kg
   f. 325 m
   g. £4.20
   h. £8
   i. £23.70
   j. £105
   k. 2.8 tonnes
   l. 0.7 km

2. Work these out.
   a. 20% of £120
   b. 30% of 170 kg
   c. 60% of 560 g
   d. 40% of 960 m
   e. 20% of 54 kg
   f. 40% of £15
   g. 30% of £12
   h. 20% of £574
   i. 70% of £63.20
   j. 80% of 91 m
   k. 90% of 14.2 kg
   l. 60% of 18.5 km

3. Find 5% of these.
   a. 80 kg
   b. £12 800
   c. £45
   d. £62.40
   e. 436 m
   f. 72.8 litres
   g. £129.60
   h. 9.5 km

4. A couple pay a 10% deposit on a house costing £329 900. How much is the deposit?

5. 30% of the proceeds from ticket sales for a concert go to charity. Ticket sales total £4300. How much of this goes to the charity?

6. A trainee earns £1575 per month. She gets a 5% pay rise. How much extra does she earn per month?

7. An insurance agent sells a policy for £449. His commission is 15%. How much commission does he make?

   Hint 15% = 10% + 5%

8. A salesman gets 35% commission on any furniture he sells. How much does he get for selling a table costing £590?

9. A bakery makes 540 rolls. 65% are sold to a cafe. How many rolls is this?

10. 85% of charity card sales is given to a charity. Card sales total £976. How much of this goes to the charity?

11. A teacher asks how you can find $12\frac{1}{2}\%$ of £640

    Thea says 'Find 25% of £640, then halve it.'

    Jack says 'Find 10%, then 5%, halve that to find $2\frac{1}{2}\%$ then add the 10% and $2\frac{1}{2}\%$ together.'

    Show that both of these methods give the correct answer of £80

C. Use 1%

1 square out of the 100 in this grid is black.

$1\% = 1$ out of $100 = \frac{1}{100}$

> **Key point**
>
> To find 1% of something, divide it by 100

Example 1% of £750 = £7.50

Note also that 1% is 1p in each pound (£).
So 1% of £750 = 750 pence = £7.50

Example 1% of 20 m = 0.20 m = 0.2 m

 See page 126 for help with dividing by 100

Percentages

Practice

1. Find 1% of these.
   a. 500
   b. 630 km
   c. 894 g
   d. £30
   e. £480
   f. £26

 To find other percentages, find 1%, then multiply.

> **Example** Find 3% of 250 kg
>
> 1% of 250 kg = 2.5 kg   (dividing by 100)
>
>   2.5 kg
>   × 3   (multiplying by 3)
>
> 3% of 250 kg = 7.5 kg

2. Find 3% of these.
   a. 400
   b. £540
   c. 80 km
   d. £50
   e. 35 kg
   f. £17

3. Find 4% of these.
   a. 7000
   b. 450 m
   c. 750 g
   d. 95 km
   e. £360
   f. £32

4. Find 7% of these.
   a. 500
   b. 1600 kg
   c. 90 litres
   d. £25
   e. 405 cm
   f. £89

5. Find 9% of these.
   a. 2000
   b. £730
   c. 120 m
   d. 70 kg
   e. 75 litres
   f. £62

Equivalent fractions, decimals and percentages

Specification reference L1.N16, L2.N4

 Fractions, decimals and percentages all represent parts of something. (Fractions and decimals are parts of 1, percentages are parts of 100.) You can convert each form to the others. For example, 9% means 9 out of 100

As a fraction this is $\frac{9}{100}$ and as a decimal it is 0.09

Number

A. Convert between percentages and decimals

3% = 0.03 and 67% = 0.67 because the value of the second decimal place is hundredths.

> **Examples**
>
> 75% = **0.75**   70% = 0.70 = **0.7**   7% = **0.07**
> 23% = **0.23**   12.5% = **0.125**   7.5% = **0.075**
> 0.2 = **20%**   0.45 = **45%**   0.02 = **2%**
> 0.87 = **87%**   1.2 = **120%**   0.175 = **17.5%**

 See page 126 for a reminder of how to × and ÷ by 100

> **Key point**
>
> To change a percentage to a decimal, divide the percentage by 100
> To change a decimal to a percentage, multiply the decimal by 100

Practice

1. Change these percentages to decimals.
   a. 25%   b. 35%   c. 40%   d. 30%
   e. 80%   f. 5%   g. 10%   h. 15%
   i. 4%   j. 8%   k. 55%   l. 85%

2. Write these percentages as decimals.
   a. 16%   b. 32%   c. 49%   d. 95%
   e. 64%   f. 52%   g. 17.5% h. 62.5%
   i. 37.8% j. 3.6%   k. 2.5%   l. 1.25%

3. Change these decimals to percentages.
   a. 0.75   b. 0.25   c. 0.65   d. 0.6
   e. 0.06   f. 0.1   g. 0.01   h. 0.5
   i. 0.05   j. 0.9   k. 0.09   l. 0.99

4. Write these decimal numbers as percentages.
   a. 0.29   b. 0.57   c. 0.43   d. 1.5
   e. 2.5   f. 0.875 g. 0.325 h. 0.065
   i. 0.005 j. 0.205 k. 0.168 l. 2.45

5. Put these in order of size, smallest to largest.
   a. 15%   0.045   12.5%   0.013   0.9
   b. 75%   0.098   0.1   11%   0.65
   c. 0.018 33.3%   0.4   0.202   22%
   d. 0.5%   0.3   17%   0.006   0.52
   e. 16%   0.017   31%   1.2%   0.2%

B. Write percentages as fractions

53% = 53 out of 100 = $\frac{53}{100}$. This fraction does not cancel, but some others do.

Examples

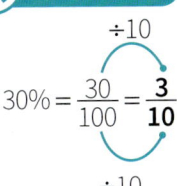

$30\% = \frac{30}{100} = \frac{3}{10}$ (÷10)

$75\% = \frac{75}{100} = \frac{3}{4}$ (÷25)

$7\% = \frac{7}{100}$ (doesn't cancel)

Key point

To write a percentage as a fraction, write it over 100, then cancel if possible.

 For a reminder of cancelling see page 102.

Practice

Write each percentage as a fraction in its simplest form.

1. a. 10%   b. 20%   c. 40%   d. 80%
    e. 70%   f. 90%   g. 50%   h. 25%
    i. 5%   j. 15%   k. 45%   l. 3%

2. a. 19%   b. 64%   c. 95%   d. 8%
    e. 86%   f. 72%   g. 41%   h. 96%

Level 2

Sometimes you need to multiply the top and bottom to give whole numbers.

Examples

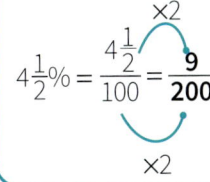

$4\frac{1}{2}\% = \frac{4\frac{1}{2}}{100} = \frac{9}{200}$ (×2)

$33\frac{1}{3}\% = \frac{33\frac{1}{3}}{100} = \frac{100}{300} = \frac{1}{3}$ (×3)

Remember this one. It is used a lot in sales.

Examples

$7.5\% = \frac{7.5}{100} = \frac{15}{200} = \frac{3}{40}$ (×2, ÷5)

$1.25\% = \frac{1.25}{100} = \frac{5}{400} = \frac{1}{80}$ (×4, ÷5)

There is often more than one way to do this.

or $7.5\% = \frac{7.5}{100} = \frac{75}{1000} = \frac{3}{40}$ (×10, ÷25)

or $1.25\% = \frac{1.25}{100} = \frac{125}{10000} = \frac{5}{400} = \frac{1}{80}$ (×100, ÷25, ÷5)

Number

3. Write each percentage as a fraction in its simplest form.

   a. $1\frac{1}{2}\%$
   b. 2.5%
   c. 6.4%
   d. $12\frac{1}{2}\%$

   e. 8.5%
   f. 62.5%
   g. 37.5%
   h. 10.5%

   i. 8.75%
   j. $66\frac{2}{3}\%$
   k. 12.8%
   l. $3\frac{3}{4}\%$

C. Write fractions as decimals and percentages

There are quick ways to write some fractions as decimals and percentages.

For example, $\frac{9}{10} = 0.9$ because the value of the first decimal place is in tenths.

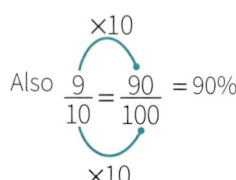

Also $\frac{9}{10} = \frac{90}{100} = 90\%$

> 💡 **Key point**
> Changing the denominator to 100 is a quick way to find the percentage.

When it is not easy to see how to change the denominator to 100, there is another method that **always** works:

🔍 Example

$\frac{3}{4} = 3 \div 4 = \mathbf{0.75}$ as a decimal

$= \mathbf{75\%}$ as a percentage

$\begin{array}{r} 0.75 \\ 4\overline{)3.^30^20} \end{array}$

— Add zeros if needed.

— For difficult divisions, use a calculator.

The quick method is  $\frac{3}{4} = \frac{75}{100}$ (×25 / ×25)

📄 To change decimals to fractions see page 123.

> 💡 **Key point**
> Write a fraction as a decimal by dividing the top by the bottom.
> Then change the decimal to a percentage by multiplying by 100

🔍 Example

$\frac{2}{5} = 2 \div 5 = \mathbf{0.4}$ as a decimal

$= \mathbf{40\%}$ as a percentage

The quick method is $\frac{2}{5} = \frac{40}{100}$ (×20 / ×20)

Percentages

Practice

1. Write each fraction as a percentage by changing the denominator to 100
   a. $\frac{1}{2}$ b. $\frac{3}{10}$ c. $\frac{1}{4}$ d. $\frac{9}{20}$
   e. $\frac{4}{5}$ f. $\frac{7}{25}$ g. $\frac{17}{50}$ h. $\frac{18}{25}$

   Use a different method to check each answer.

2. Write these fractions as decimals and then as percentages.
   a. $\frac{1}{10}$ b. $\frac{1}{5}$ c. $\frac{2}{5}$ d. $\frac{1}{20}$
   e. $\frac{3}{50}$ f. $\frac{1}{25}$ g. $\frac{7}{20}$ h. $\frac{4}{25}$

   Use a calculator to check your answers.

3. Copy and complete these tables.

Fraction	Decimal	%
$\frac{1}{2}$		
$\frac{1}{4}$		
$\frac{3}{4}$		
$\frac{1}{10}$		
$\frac{1}{5}$		
$\frac{1}{3}$		$33\frac{1}{3}$%

Fraction	Decimal	%
	0.4	
	0.7	
	0.35	
		60%
		90%
		15%

(Learn those in the first table.)

4. Write these fractions as decimals and then as percentages.
   a. $\frac{11}{20}$ b. $\frac{5}{8}$ c. $\frac{7}{8}$ d. $\frac{7}{25}$
   e. $\frac{27}{40}$ f. $\frac{2}{3}$ (to 3 dp)   g. $\frac{1}{16}$ h. $\frac{2}{15}$ (to 4 dp)

   Use a calculator to check your answers.

5. Put each group in order of size, starting with the **smallest**.

   a. 0.76   78% $\frac{3}{4}$ b. $\frac{1}{2}$ 0.49   51%   **Hint** Change them to the same type.
   c. 24% $\frac{1}{4}$ 0.22   d. 0.21   19% $\frac{1}{5}$
   e. $\frac{5}{9}$ 50%   0.58   f. $\frac{8}{9}$ 88%   0.9
   g. 59%   0.56 $\frac{7}{12}$ h. $\frac{7}{16}$ 0.49   45%

Number

Percentage increase and decrease

Specification reference: **L1.N14, L2.N6**

Wage and price rises are often given as percentages.

In a sale, shops often advertise price reductions as percentages.

20 % Reduction on all prices

A. Find the change first

Example

An employee who earns £11 per hour gets a 5% increase.
What is his new rate of pay?

1% of £11 = £11 ÷ 100 = 11p
5% of £11 = 11p × 5 = 55p

New rate of pay = £11 + 55p = **£11.55** per hour

Check (by a different method):

10% of £11 = £11 ÷ 10 = £1.10
5% of £11 = 110p ÷ 2 = 55p

Key point

To find the new amount after a % change, add the increase or subtract the reduction.

Example

A coat that costs £89.90 is reduced by 30% in a sale.
Find the sale price.

Find the reduction:

10% of £89.90 = £8.99

           £8.99
           × 3

30% of £89.90 = £26.97

then take it away:

    £89.90
 − £26.97

Sale price = **£62.93**

Check (by rounding): 9 × 3 = 27   **Check:** 90 − 30 = 60

Practice

1. A hotel charges the following prices:

   The manager increases these prices by 5%.
   Find the new prices.

   PRICE LIST

Breakfast	£8
Lunch	£16
Evening meal	£24
Single room	£70 per night
Double room	£120 per night

MyMaths   1060   SEARCH

Percentages

2. For each price, find the new price after an increase of:

   a. 10%   **b.** 30%.

   i. £80   **ii.** £120   **iii.** £780

   iv. £64   **v.** £10.70   **vi.** £64.40

3. A saver puts £600 into a savings account. The interest rate is 5% per year.
How much will the saver have after one year?

4. An upholsterer needs 25 m of material. She decides to buy 10% extra in case of mistakes.
How much material does she buy altogether?

5. The number of tickets available for a play is 900. Only 75% of these tickets are sold.

   a. How many tickets are sold?   **b.** How many tickets are left?

6. A market stall holder has 120 potatoes in a sack. 40% have gone green. How many potatoes are not green, and so good to sell?

7. A deposit of 25% has been paid on a holiday costing £1040.
How much is there left to pay?

8. The old design of a greenhouse costs £920. A new design costs 35% more. How much is the new design?

9. The table shows the weekly wage of each assistant in a shop before they all get a pay rise of 4%.

Find each worker's new weekly wage.

Worker	Weekly wage
Jess	£350
Kate	£325
Luke	£320
Wes	£295

10. A stationery shop gives a 9% discount to employees.
How much does an employee pay for goods priced at £20?

11. For each price, find the sale price after a reduction of 7%.

   a. £12   **b.** £89   **c.** £592
   d. £1460   **e.** £15 300

12. For each price, find the new price after an increase of 8%.

   a. £780   **b.** £1920   **c.** £84.50
   d. £21.25   **e.** £16.75

B. Find the new amount directly

As an alternative method, you can add or subtract the % from 100% first.

Example

A worker who earns £12 an hour gets a 4% wage rise.
The new wage is 100% + 4% = 104% of the old wage.
   1% of the old wage = £12 ÷ 100 = 12p
   New wage = 104% = 104 × 12p = 1248p = **£12.48**

Add the % increase to 100%.

151

Number

Example

A coat costing £85 is reduced by 20% in a sale.
The sale price is 100% − 20% = 80% of the original price.
10% of the original price = £85 ÷ 10 = £8.50

$$\begin{array}{r} £8.50 \\ \times\ 8 \\ \hline \end{array}$$

Sale price = 80% of the original price = **£68.00**

> Subtract the % decrease from 100%.

Practice

Use the method shown in the examples above.

1. A worker who earns £10 an hour gets a 3% wage rise.
   What is his new wage rate?

2. A shop makes 10% profit on confectionery. The cost prices of some items are shown.
   Find how much the shop sells each of these items for.

 80p
 50p (PASTILLES)
 £1.20 (TOFFEE)
 £7.50 (CHOCOLATE TRUFFLES)

3. A jacket costing £56 is reduced by 30% in a sale.
   What is the sale price?

4. A car bought for £13 500 loses 20% of its value in a year.
   How much is it worth at the end of the year?

> Now check your answers to some of the Practice questions on pages 150–151 using this method.

Use a calculator to find percentages

Specification reference **L1.N14, L2.N5**

Two methods of using a calculator to work out percentages are given below.

Method A

- Divide the amount by 100 to find 1%.
- Multiply by the required percentage.
- Add or subtract the result if you need to give the final amount.

Method B

- Divide the % by 100 to write it as a decimal.
- Multiply the decimal by the amount.
- Add or subtract the result if you need to give the final amount.

> Your calculator may have a % key. The way this works varies from one calculator to another. Consult your instruction booklet to find out how yours works and use it if you wish.

Percentages

Example

VAT is charged at 5% on a gas bill for £249.32
Find: **1.** the VAT charged **2.** the total amount charged.

1.

Method A
1% of £249.32 = £249.32 ÷ 100
          = £2.4932
5% of £249.32 = £2.4932 × 5
          = £12.466 = **£12.47** (to 2 dp)

Method B
5% = 5 ÷ 100 = 0.05
0.05 × £249.32 = £12.466
          = **£12.47** (to 2 dp)

For part **2**, carry on the working on your calculator.

2. Total amount = VAT + original amount = £12.466 + £249.32
          = £261.786 = **£261.79** (to 2 dp)

See pages 128–130 for help with rounding

Whichever method you use:
- Think about whether the answer is sensible.
- Carry out a check. You could use the other method or find an estimate.

Practice

Use a calculator to work these out.
Use one method to work out the answer, then another method to check.

1. Calculate these.
   a. 5% of £65
   b. 35% of £170
   c. 80% of 12 m
   d. 85% of £520
   e. 15% of 25 kg
   f. 45% of 920 g
   g. 25% of 94 euros
   h. 30% of 46 cm
   i. 5% of 16 litres
   j. 60% of 154 m
   k. 75% of £672
   l. 55% of £178
   m. 65% of 74 km
   n. 15% of £45
   o. 40% of £85
   p. 70% of 120 cm

2. The prices shown below do not include VAT. Find each price including VAT at 20%.

Number

3. Two websites sell the same digital camera. Work out the prices to find out which is the best buy.

   Website A Original price £259 now reduced by **30%**

   Website B Original price £249 and now $\frac{1}{4}$ off

4. A car costs £14 800 when new. It is resold later for 65% of this price.
   How much is it sold for?

Level 2

5. This table shows the annual percentage interest rate for loans from four different lenders.

Lender	Bayleys	Anchor	Rock Solid	Direct
Interest rate	6.6%	6.5%	6.3%	6.7%

   Work out the interest charges from each lender for one year on loans of:

   a. £1000
   b. £2500
   c. £1750
   d. £3225
   e. £12 500
   f. £0.8 million.

6. A photocopier can enlarge or reduce the dimensions of anything it copies. Find the new length and width of this image when the photocopier is set at:

   a. 75%
   b. 125%
   c. 133%
   d. 141%.

Remember you can increase or decrease the % first to find the final amount.

> **Example**
>
> VAT is charged at 5% on a gas bill for £249.32
> Find the total amount charged.
>
> 100% plus 5% VAT = 105%
> Total amount = 105% of £249.32 = £2.4932 × 105 = **£261.79** (to 2 dp) (method A)
> or 1.05 × £249.32 = **£261.79** (to 2 dp) (method B)

7. Find the final amounts.

   a. A 22% discount on £42
   b. 105 g plus an extra 8%
   c. 600 m plus an extra 15%
   d. 42 cm minus 19%
   e. 24 km increased by 32%
   f. 106 kg minus 12%
   g. 57 m plus 15%
   h. 25 litres minus 35%
   i. £14 increased by 60%
   j. A 25% wage rise on £9 an hour

8. Someone buys the following goods:
   a radio for £21.99   3 DVDs at £14.99 each   a book for £14.95.
   These prices do not include VAT. What is the total price of the goods including VAT at 20%?

Percentages

Write one number as a percentage of another

Specification reference L2.N5

- Write the information as a **fraction**.
- If possible, **make the denominator 100**. The numerator then gives the percentage.
- If this is not possible, **simplify** the fraction then **divide the top by the bottom** to write the fraction as a **decimal**. Finally, **multiply by 100** to change into a percentage.

Example

A student gets 32 out of 40 in a test. What percentage is this?

32 out of 40 = $\dfrac{32}{40} = \dfrac{16}{20} = \dfrac{80}{100}$. The percentage is **80%**.

(÷2, ×5 / ÷2, ×5)

Example

9 students out of a class of 24 have fair hair.

The fraction having fair hair is $\dfrac{9}{24} = \dfrac{3}{8}$. (÷3)

$8 \overline{)3.\,{}^{3}0\,{}^{6}0\,{}^{4}0} = 0.375$

As a decimal this is 0.375

The % who have fair hair = $0.375 \times 100 = $ **37.5%**

Check on a calculator:
$9 \div 24 = 0.375$
$0.375 \times 100 = 37.5$

Practice

1. In an evening class of 20 men and women, 12 are men.
   What percentage of the students are:

   a. men   b. women?

2. Ten chocolates in a box of twenty five are soft centred. What percentage is this?

3. The table shows the marks a student gets in his course assignments.
   Find his percentage mark for each assignment.

Assignment	1	2	3	4
Student's marks	18	56	52	66
Marks available	30	70	80	120

155

For a percentage change, write the change as a percentage of the **original amount**.

> **Example**
>
> A fare costing £2.50 goes up by 75p to £3.25
>
> What is the percentage increase?
>
> Write 75p as a fraction of 250p: $\frac{75}{250} = \frac{3}{10} = \frac{30}{100}$
>
> The original price £2.50 = 250 pence
>
> The percentage increase is **30%**.

> **Key point**
>
> Quantities must be in the **same units**.

4. **a.** What is 450 g as a % of 900 g?
   b. What % of £60 is £20?
   c. What % of £6 is 30 p?
   d. What % of 1 kg is 250 g?
   e. What is 50 mm as a % of 1 m?
   f. What is 33 cℓ as a % of 1 litre?

   1 kg = 1000 g
   1 m = 1000 mm
   1 litre = 100 cℓ
   1 km = 1000 m

5. A water company is laying 2 km of pipe. In the first week it lays 160 m of pipe. What % of the total length is this?

6. A bank loan of £5000 is repaid, with interest, over 3 years at £150 a month.
   Write the total interest as a % of the original amount.

7. £1000 is invested in a savings account and receives interest of £3.75 each month.
   a. How much money is there after a year?
   b. What is the annual % interest rate?

8. Out of 75 people who take a driving test, 45 pass. What percentage is this?

9. A car is bought for £16 000 and sold one year later for £14 000 What is the % loss?

10. There is £600 in a bank account before a withdrawal of £168 is made. What percentage is withdrawn?

Percentages

 Use a calculator for the next questions. Give your answers to 1 dp when they don't work out exactly.

11. There are 150 houses on Sherbourne Close.

   a. 102 houses are lived in by families with children. In what % of the houses are there no children?

   b. A survey carried out in Sherbourne Close shows that in 21 of the households everyone is vegetarian. What percentage of households is this?

   c. 86 of the houses on Sherbourne Close have a front lawn. What % is this?

12. In one month a travel company sells 780 holidays. 520 of these are in Europe.

   a. What % of the holidays are: **i.** in Europe **ii.** outside Europe?

   b. Check your answers to part **a** by adding the percentages. The total should be 100%.

13. A school has 378 pupils. 203 of these speak a different language at home. What percentage do not speak a different language at home?

14. In a college with 1254 students, 358 students are part-time.

   a. What percentage are part-time?

   b. 25 of the 358 part-time students study maths. What percentage is this?

15. Look at the menu.

If you order this meal between 6pm and 7pm, it costs £19.00
What percentage do you save?

Set meal	
Onion Bhajee	£2.20
Chicken Chat	£2.45
Balti Chicken	£6.45
Chicken Tikka Masala	£5.99
Aloo Gobi	£1.95
Pilau Rice	£1.80
Keema Nan	£1.30

Sometimes you may just want a rough percentage or you may want to estimate a percentage to check an answer from a calculator.

Example

1546 out of 6012 students in a college are full-time.

This gives the fraction $\frac{1546}{6012}$

Rounding to the nearest 100 gives $\frac{1500}{6000} = \frac{1}{4}$

The % of students who are full-time is approximately **25%**.

Note: rounding to the nearest 1000 gives $33\frac{1}{3}\%$. This is not as accurate.

16. Estimate these.

  a. What percentage of 587 is 294?
  b. What percentage of 1960 is 978?
  c. What percentage of 987 is 254?
  d. What percentage of £124 is £27?

17. In the crowd of 20 162 who watch a football match, there are 4213 women and 4936 children. The rest of the crowd are men.

  a. Estimate the % of the crowd who are:

  i. women   **ii.** children   **iii.** men.

  b. Check your answers by adding these percentages together.

18. The table shows a householder's gas bills during a year.

  a. What is the total for the year?

  b. Approximately what percentage of this total was for:

Season	Bill (£)
Spring	122.88
Summer	57.26
Autumn	176.60
Winter	236.52

  i. spring   **ii.** summer   **iii.** autumn   **iv.** winter?

  c. Check your answers to part **b** by adding the percentages together.

Calculate the original value after a percentage change

Specification reference **L2.N6**

When an amount has been increased or decreased by a %, the original value can be found using the method below. This is called a **reverse percentage**.

> **Key point**
>
> A reverse percentage gives the original amount, before an increase or decrease.

Example

The price of a smart speaker is reduced by 30% in the sale.
It now costs £105. What was the original price?

The original price represents 100%.
100% − 30% = 70%
The sale price is 70% of the original price.
70% of the original price = £105
1% of the original price = £105 ÷ 70 = £1.50
The original price = £1.50 × 100 = **£150**

Step 1: Find what percentage of the original amount is given.
Step 2: Divide by this to find 1%.
Step 3: Multiply by 100 to find the original amount.

> **Check:** 10% of £150 = £15
> 30% of £150 = £45
> Sale price = £150 − £45 = £105

Percentages

Example

The price of a laptop is £312. This includes VAT at 20%.
What was the price of the laptop before VAT was added?

100% + 20% = 120% of original price = £312 **(Step 1)**

1% of original price = £312 ÷ 120 = £2.60 **(Step 2)**

Original price = £2.60 × 100 = **£260 (Step 3)**

Check:
10% of £260 = £26
20% of £260 = £52
£260 + £52 = £312

Key point

Take care with VAT calculations. Subtracting 20% from the price including VAT is **wrong** because 20% of the final price is **not the same** as 20% of the original price.

Practice

1. How much did this camera cost before the price reduction?

   Special Offer
   15% off
   Now £170

   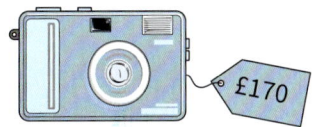

2. A plumber charges for parts and labour.
   The total bill is £252 including VAT at 20%.
   What is the cost for the parts and labour?

3. A bill is £247.80 including VAT at 5%.
   How much is the bill without the VAT?

4. In a local election 16 380 people voted for one candidate.
   This is 60% of the people who voted.
   How many people voted altogether?

5. A restaurant bill comes to £76.50 including a $12\frac{1}{2}$% service charge.
   How much was the bill without the service charge?

6. 51 students passed an exam. This is 85% of the students on the course.
   How many students didn't pass the exam?

7. A company pays for stationery costing £2920.80 including VAT at 20%.
   The company is able to claim back the VAT. How much can it claim back?

8. A shopper buys some furniture in a sale for £600. The price of the furniture has been reduced by 40%. The shopper incorrectly thinks she has saved £240
   a. How much has the shopper actually saved?
   b. What mistake has she made?

9. How much of the washing-up liquid, shown to the right, do you get for free?

Chapter Summary
10 Percentages

Level 1

- **Per cent** means out of 100 and can be written using the sign **%**, **100%** = the whole amount.
- Since there are 100p in a £, the amount of pennies can be written as a percentage of a pound.
- $50\% = \frac{50}{100} = \frac{1}{2}$ so to find 50% of something, divide it by 2 or halve it.
  $25\% = \frac{25}{100} = \frac{1}{4}$ so to find 25% of something, divide it by 4 or halve it twice.
- Check answers by checking percentage values add up to 100%.
- Remember $10\% = \frac{10}{100} = \frac{1}{10}$ so to find 10% of something, divide it by 10. You can use this to find other percentages such as 20% (multiply value by 2), 5% (halve the value) and so on.
- Remember $1\% = \frac{1}{100}$ so to find 1% of something, divide it by 100. You can find any percentage by finding 1% and then multiplying the value by the percentage you are trying to find.
- Fractions, decimals and percentages all represent parts of something: fractions and decimals are parts of 1 and percentages are parts of 100
- To convert between percentages and decimals, divide the percentage by 100 or multiply the decimal by 100
- To convert percentages to fractions, write them as a fraction over 100 and then simplify.
- To convert fractions to percentages, if possible make an equivalent fraction with 100 as the denominator. You can also divide the numerator by the denominator and then multiply by 100.
- To convert fractions to decimals, divide the numerator by the denominator.
- To work out percentages using a calculator, you can either divide the amount by 100 to find 1% and multiply by the required percentage OR divide the percentage by 100 and write as a decimal and then multiply the decimal by the amount.

Level 2

- Sometimes, when you write a percentage over 100 to convert it into a fraction, you will need to multiply the top and the bottom of the new fraction.
- $33\frac{1}{3}\% = \frac{1}{3}$ so to find $33\frac{1}{3}\%$ of something divide it by 3.
- To write one number as a percentage of another, write the information as a fraction then convert this to a percentage.
- For a percentage change, first make sure the amounts are in the same units, then write the change as a percentage of the original amount.
- A **reverse** percentage gives the original value after a percentage change. Use the percent of the amount given to find 1% and then multiply by 100 to find the original amount.
- Take care with VAT calculations. Subtracting 20% from the price including VAT is incorrect because 20% of the final price is not the same as 20% of the original price.

Measures, Shape and Space

11 Money

Write in pounds (£) and pence

Specification reference **EL3.M10**

Two hundred and forty-six pounds, thirty-five pence is written in numbers as £246.35

The 2 represents £200

The 4 represents £40

The 6 represents £6

The 3 represents 30p

The 5 represents 5p

WHOLE POUNDS				PARTS OF A £	
£			•	PENCE	
Hundreds of £s	Tens of £s	Single £s	DECIMAL POINT	Tenths of a £ 10p	Hundredths of a £ 1p
2	4	6	.	3	5

For writing money as decimals, see page 121.

Note that this notation also works for other currencies, for example for dollars ($) and cents, and for euros (€) and eurocents (also usually just known as cents).

Practice

1. What does the 3 represent in each amount?
   a. £531.42   b. £26.43   c. £143.15   d. £84.32   e. £306

2. What does the 9 represent in each amount?
   a. £92.12   b. £20.96   c. £119.20   d. £45.59   e. £931.45

3. Write these amounts in numbers.
   a. One hundred and ten pounds
   b. Twenty-five pounds, twenty pence
   c. Twelve pounds and fifty pence
   d. Thirty pounds, five pence
   e. Two hundred and thirty pounds, fifteen pence
   f. Four hundred and thirteen pounds, twenty-five pence
   g. Three hundred and three pounds, three pence
   h. Three hundred and twenty-five pounds

4. List these amounts in numbers, starting with the **smallest**.
   seven hundred and thirty-two pounds, sixty-one pence
   seven hundred and forty-one pounds, twelve pence
   seven hundred and thirty-six pounds, two pence
   seven hundred and thirty-one pounds, thirty-four pence

MyMaths 1014 SEARCH

Measures, Shape and Space

5. Write these amounts in words.
    a. £10.50
    b. £5.99
    c. £12.50
    d. £505.00
    e. £2.15
    f. £410.04
    g. £45.49
    h. £209.09

6. Put these amounts in order, starting with the **largest**.
    £324.14   £234.41   £324.41   £342.14   £234.14   £342.41

Calculate with money
Specification reference EL3.M10

A. Add and subtract money

To add or subtract money, use the methods given on page 131

Key point
To add or subtract, line up the decimal points.

Examples

£2 + £1.20 + 5p

```
  £   p
  2 . 00
  1 . 20
+ 0 . 05
 £3 . 25
```

£5 − 75p

```
  £   p
  5 . 00
− 0 . 75
 £4 . 25
```

Fill the gaps with zeros.

Write money correctly: £4.25, **not** £4.25p

If less than 10p, put a zero here.

Practice

1. Write these in columns, lining up the decimal points. Work out the answers.
    a. £5.80 + 45p + 6p
    b. £16.50 + 25p + 5p
    c. £2 + 60p + 7p
    d. £5 + 5p + 35p
    e. 75p + £2 + 50p + £1.10
    f. £3.99 − 54p
    g. £5.50 − 45p
    h. £5 − £2.40
    i. £5 − £3.99
    j. £5 − £1.49
    k. £2.76 + £5.80 + £17
    l. £80.05 − £15.99

2. A boy has £5 in his pocket. He finds 50p, then meets a friend who gives him £2.50. What is the total amount of money he has now?

3. A girl has £5. She spends £2.35 on a bus ticket. How much does she have left?

4. a. A lorry driver buys a beefburger, chips and a cup of coffee at the burger bar. The prices are in the list. What is the total cost?
   b. He pays with a £20 note. How much change should he get?

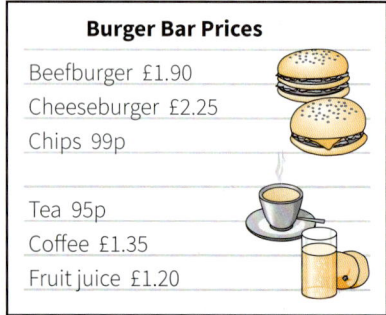

Burger Bar Prices
Beefburger £1.90
Cheeseburger £2.25
Chips 99p
Tea 95p
Coffee £1.35
Fruit juice £1.20

Money

B. Use a calculator to add and subtract money

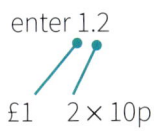
Parts of a £

Before the point	After the point
£	• 10p 1p

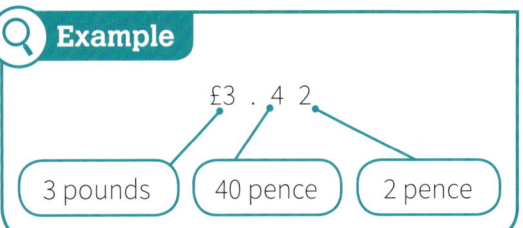
Example

£3 . 4 2

3 pounds | 40 pence | 2 pence

Either work in £s using decimals:

£1.20 + 60p − 5p   enter 1.2 [+] 0.6 [−] 0.05 [=]   answer 1.75

£1   2 × 10p   £0 6 × 10p   £0 0 × 10p 5 × 1p

Remember to include the £ sign.   **£1.75**

or work in pence (using £1 = 100p):

£1.20 + 60p − 5p   enter 120 [+] 60 [−] 5 [=]   answer 175

Remember to include the pence sign.   **175p**

Do not use both the £ and p signs. Your answer is in £ or p. It cannot be in both.

£1.75 ✓   175p ✓   £1.75p ✗

Practice

1. Add these amounts together using a calculator.
   Give the answer in pounds (£) if it is 100p or more.
   Check your answers using another method.

   a. £1.50 + 50p + 5p
   b. £2.25 + 35p − 10p
   c. £2.54 + 42p + 2p
   d. 60p + 42p + £2
   e. £3.13 + 35p − 9p
   f. 50p + 3p + 4p + 40p
   g. £3.30 + 3p − 50p
   h. 5p + 90p + £2 + £1.50
   i. £1.10 − 8p − 40p − 3p
   j. £3 + 65p + £2.50 + 10p
   k. £18.37 − 90p − £4.49
   l. £7.48 − £3.96 + £9

Activities

Use a catalogue to find the total cost for a list of goods, or work out what you can buy for £100.

Fill in an expenses claim form.

Check bills or wage slips.

Key point

Add a zero to the end if the calculator gives just 1 decimal place when you work in £.

For example, 4.5 means £4.50

For more money calculations, see pages 131–132.

163

C. Multiply and divide money

To multiply or divide money, use the methods given on pages 134–137.

> **Key point**
>
> To multiply decimals, multiply the numbers, then count the decimal places.
>
> To divide a decimal by a whole number, divide as usual, keeping the decimal points in line.

Examples

£4.15 × 3

```
  £4.15
×     3
 £12.45
```
— 2 decimal places in the question.
— 2 decimal places in the answer.

£14.46 ÷ 2

```
     7.23
2)£14.46    = £7.23
```
Divide as usual, keeping the decimal points in line.

Practice

1. Work these out without a calculator, then use a calculator to check.

   a. £6.95 × 4   b. £14.99 × 6   c. £18 ÷ 4   d. £25.80 ÷ 5

   e. 7 × £15.40 + £8.75   f. £7.80 ÷ 3 − 50p   g. 57p × 9 − £4.30

2. a. A student's course costs £84.50 for one term. How much does it cost for three terms?

   b. The exam fee is £28.60
   What is the total cost of the three-term course and the exam?

   > Remember that if the answer has one decimal place (for example, £4.2) add a zero to show the pence (£4.20).

3. A student pays £411.60 for a course for the full year. There are three equal terms. How much is the course per term?

4. A man pays £42.97 for 2 identical shirts and a tie. He returns the tie and gets a refund of £10.99

   a. How much did the 2 shirts cost?

   b. How much did each shirt cost?

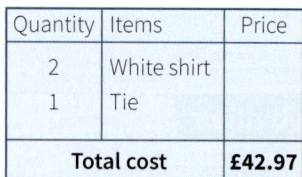

Quantity	Items	Price
2	White shirt	
1	Tie	
	Total cost	£42.97

5. An Assistance dog will attend three college sites. Three beds and three bowls are required. The college will pay half of the cost. How much does the student have to pay?

   Bed £22.99   Bowl £5.49

Money

Round money to the nearest 10p or £1

Specification reference EL3.M11

A. Round to the nearest 10p

The rounding rule is:

> **Key point**
>
> If the **amount ends in 5p or more, round up** to the next 10p above.
>
> If the **amount ends in less than 5p, round down** to the 10p below.

Examples

Look at the grid below.

54p ends in **4**, which is **less than 5**. **Round down** to **50p**

68p ends in **8** which is **more than 5**. **Round up** to **70p**

Round amounts in the **unshaded** area **down**. Round amounts in the **shaded** area **up**.

	1p	2p	3p	4p	5p	6p	7p	8p	9p	
0										10p
10p										20p
20p										30p
30p										40p
40p										50p
50p				54						60p
60p								68		70p
70p										80p
80p										90p
90p										£1.00

Practice

1. Find where each amount is on the grid, then round it to the nearest 10p
   - a. 12p
   - b. 27p
   - c. 34p
   - d. 41p
   - e. 85p
   - f. 59p
   - g. 25p
   - h. 62p
   - i. 46p
   - j. 77p
   - k. 90p
   - l. 3p

2. Round these to the nearest 10p.
   - a. £2.13
   - b. £4.43
   - c. £5.71
   - d. £7.24
   - e. £6.93
   - f. £9.11
   - g. £5.69
   - h. £4.18
   - i. £3.33
   - j. £8.85
   - k. £18.04
   - l. £27.97

Measures, Shape and Space

3. Round the cost of each item to the nearest 10p
   Then add to find the approximate total cost for each person.

   a. **Val**

pen	43p
ruler	27p
pencil	38p

   b. **Yui**

pen	29p
ruler	33p
pencil	54p

   c. **Carl**

pen	39p
ruler	28p
pencil	45p

B. Round to the nearest £1

The rounding rule is:

Key point

If the **amount ends in 50p or more, round up** to the pound above.

If the **amount ends in less than 50p, round down** to the pound below.

Examples

£5.42 = **£5** to the nearest £1   (because **42p** is less than 50p)

£62.59 = **£63** to the nearest £1   (because **59p** is more than 50p)

Practice

1. Round each amount to the nearest £1

   a. £2.60   b. £3.10   c. £4.80   d. £5.20   e. £6.90   f. £7.30

   g. £8.20   h. £9.40   i. £1.70   j. £0.50   k. £10.00   l. £19.70

2. Round these prices to the nearest £1.

   a. £12.13   b. £34.43   c. £15.71   d. £27.24   e. £336.93   f. £9.11

   g. £25.69   h. £24.18   i. £13.33   j. £228.85   k. £76.50   l. £76.49

3. a. Round the cost of each item to the nearest pound, then add to estimate the total cost.

i. Veg	£1.99	ii. Cake	£2.49	iii. Files	£4.10
Cheese	£2.27	Coffee	£3.05	Paper	£3.89
Meat	£5.90	Milk	99p	Calculator	£5.10

   b. Use a calculator to find the exact totals.

Activity

Round each amount on a shopping receipt (or bank statement, payslip, etc.) to the nearest £1 and find the total. Use a calculator to add the exact amounts and compare the results.

For more work on rounding decimals, see pages 128–129.

Discounts in multiples of 5%

Specification reference L1.M19

In a sale, shops frequently advertise price reductions as percentage discounts.

A. Find the discount

Key point

To find 5% without a calculator,
find 10% of the amount (by dividing by 10)
then halve the result.

$10\% = 100\% \div 10$
then $5\% = 10\% \div 2$

To find multiples of 5% without a calculator, use methods from Section 1 Number, Chapter 10 Percentages.

 See pages 143–144.

Examples

15%	Find 10%, then find 5%. Add 10% + 5%.
20%	Find 10%, then double it (or divide by 5).
50%	Divide by 2.
25%	Find 50%, then halve it (or divide by 4).
30%	Find 10%, then multiply by 3.
40%	Find 10%, then multiply by 4.
65%	Find 10%, multiply by 6, then add 5%.

$20\% = \dfrac{20}{100} = \dfrac{1}{5}$

$50\% = \dfrac{50}{100} = \dfrac{1}{2}$

$25\% = \dfrac{25}{100} = \dfrac{1}{4}$

Key point

To find 5% (or 15%) with a calculator,
divide by 100 to give 1%, then multiply by 5 (or 15).
Or multiply by 0.05 (or 0.15).

$5\% = \dfrac{5}{100} = 0.05$

$15\% = \dfrac{15}{100} = 0.15$

Note that this method works for any %.

Example

Find a 5% discount on £30

Without a calculator:

10% of £30 = £3
5% of £30 = **£1.50**

With a calculator:

5% of £30 = 30 ÷ 100 × 5 = £1.50
or 5% of £30 = 0.05 × £30 = **£1.50**

Measures, Shape and Space

Practice

In these questions use one method to find the answer and a different method to check.

1. A shop has a '5% off' sale. How much does the customer save by the discount on these items?
   a. drill £60
   b. hammer £24
   c. bag £56
   d. shelf £35
   e. book £7.80
   f. pack of screws £5.70

2. Find the amount saved by the discounts on these items:

a. £42 15% off
b. £75 25% off
c. £27.50 30% off
d. £84.90 20% off
e. £24.99 70% off
f. £42.95 40% off
g. £164.99 65% off
h. £7.99 35% off

3. Two holidays are advertised with discounts.
   Ruby thinks she will save more money on the hotel break.
   Is she correct? Explain your answer.

   River cruise
   £769 per person,
   with a flash '**35%** discount'

   Hotel break
   £860 per person,
   with a flash '**30%** discount'

B. Find the price after the discount

Example

A sofa that cost £639 is reduced by 15% in a sale.

Find the sale price.

There are a variety of methods you can use.

Without a calculator:

Find the discount:

10% of £639 = £63.90

5% of £639 = £31.95 (by ÷ 2)

15% of £639 = £95.85 (adding)

Sale price = £639.00
            − £95.85
          = **£543.15**

With a calculator:

Sale price = 100% (sofa) − 15% (discount)

= 85% of £639

Sale price = £639 ÷ 100 × 85 = £543.15

Or:

Sale price = 0.85 × £639
           = **£543.15**

Subtract the % discount from 100%.

$85\% = \dfrac{85}{100} = 0.85$

Money

Practice

In these questions use one method to find the answer and a different method to check.

1. For each price, find the sale price after a discount of:
   a. 5%   b. 20%   c. 25%   d. 15%
   i. £160   ii. £500   iii. £1500   iv. £1840   v. £10.60   vi. £892.

2. A shop is having a sale.
   a. A dress priced at £65 is reduced by 35%. What is the sale price?
   b. A tunic priced at £39 is reduced by 30%. What is the sale price?

3. A second-hand motorbike is advertised at £950. The seller offers a 10% discount for cash. What is the discounted price?

Simple interest

Specification reference L1.M18

Money kept in a savings account or in some bank accounts earns **interest**. The amount of interest depends on the **balance** of the account and the **percentage rate** of interest on the account.

Example

A saver has £2000 pounds in an account for a year.
The account pays 5% interest per annum.

How much interest does the saver receive after 1 year?

Per annum or **p.a.** means 'per year'.

Non-calculator method
1% of £2000 = £20
5% of £2000 = £100

Interest received = **£100**

Calculator method
5% of £2000 = £2000 ÷ 100 × 5 = £100
or 0.05 × £2000 = **£100**

For these and other percentage methods see pages 143–144.

Often people leave money in accounts for more than one year.
When a saver takes the interest out of the account at the end of each year, the interest is called **simple interest**.

Example

Calculate the simple interest on £86 for 3 years at an interest rate of 5% p.a.

Interest for 1 year = 5% of £86
$\qquad\qquad\qquad$ = £86 ÷ 100 × 5 ⟵ or 0.05 × £86
$\qquad\qquad\qquad$ = £4.30

Interest for 3 years = £4.30 × 3
$\qquad\qquad\qquad\quad$ = **£12.90**

MyMaths 1237 SEARCH

169

Measures, Shape and Space

Interest is usually added to money borrowed from lenders.
This increases the amount that needs to be paid back.

Example

Interest of 10% per annum is charged on a loan of £5000.
How much is owed at the end of a year?

Interest = 10% of £5000 = £500

Amount owed = £5000 + £500 = **£5500**

or amount owed
= 110% of the amount borrowed
= £5000 × 1.1

Practice

1. How much interest is earned in 1 year by these amounts in this Super Saver Account?

   a. £400   b. £3500   c. £50 000

   Super Saver Account
   Pays 5% interest p.a.

2. A saver has £965.72 in a savings account. The interest rate is 5% per year.
   How much interest does she earn in a year?

3. A saver has £1200 in an account for 3 months. The interest rate is 5% per annum.
   How much is the interest at the end of 3 months?

   Hint: what fraction of a year is 3 months?

4. Calculate the simple interest on:
   a. £450 for 2 years at an interest rate of 5%
   b. £1325 for 3 years at an interest rate of 10%
   c. £8250 for 4 years at an interest rate of 15%.

5. A borrower has a loan of £8500 for a year. She is charged interest at 15% per annum.
   How much does she owe at the end of the year?

6. A man borrows £10 000 for a year. He is charged interest at 20% per annum.
   The man says 'At the end of the year I will owe an extra £200.'
   Is the man correct? Give a reason for your answer.

Compound interest

Specification reference **L2.M13**

The interest on a savings account (or on a loan) may be added to the original amount. The interest for the following year is then calculated using the original amount plus the interest for the first year.
This is called **compound interest**.

Key point

When interest is **taken out** of an account each year it is called **simple interest**.
When interest is **left in** an account it is called **compound interest**.

Money

🔍 Example

A saver has £1000 in an account. Compound interest is paid at 4% per annum.

The saver takes no money out.

How much will be in the account at the end of 3 years?

Method A

Interest earned in 1st year = 4% of £1000 = £40
Amount at the end of 1st year = £1000 + £40 = £1040

Interest earned in the 2nd year = 4% of £1040
= £1040 ÷ 100 × 4 = £41.60

> or 4% of £1040
> = 0.04 × £1040

Amount at the end of 2nd year = £1040 + £41.60 = £1081.60

Interest earned in the 3rd year = 4% of £1081.60
= £1081.60 ÷ 100 × 4 = £43.26 (nearest pence)
Amount at the end of 3rd year = £1081.60 + £43.26 = **£1124.86**

Method B (more efficient)

Amount at the end of each year = amount at the beginning of the year × 1.04

Amount at the end of 1st year = £1000 × 1.04 = £1040

Amount at the end of 2nd year = £1040 × 1.04 = £1081.60

> This works out 104% of the balance at the beginning of the year.

Amount at the end of 3rd year = £1081.60 × 1.04 = **£1124.86** (nearest pence)

> 1.04 is called a **multiplier**.
> Multiplying by 1.04 gives the amount in the account at the end of each successive year.

104% = 1.04

⚙ Practice

1. Three accounts are opened with amounts:
   a. £500
   b. £4200
   c. £7600.

   Compound interest is paid at 3% per annum.
   How much is in each account after 2 years?

2. A loan of £6000 is taken out for 2 years. Compound interest is charged at 8%.
   How much is owed at the end of:
   a. 2 years
   b. 3 years?

3. A savings account is opened with £2000. Compound interest is paid at 5%.
   How much is in the account after:
   a. 3 years
   b. 4 years?

Compound Interest Formula

The working in the last example can be written as follows:

Amount at the end of 1st year = £1000 × 1.04

Amount at the end of 2nd year = £1000 × 1.04 × 1.04 = £1000 × 1.04^2

Amount at the end of 3rd year = £1000 × 1.04 × 1.04 × 1.04 = £1000 × 1.04^3

Repeatedly multiplying by 1.04 can give the amount in the account after any number of years.

For long periods of time it is quicker to use the formula:

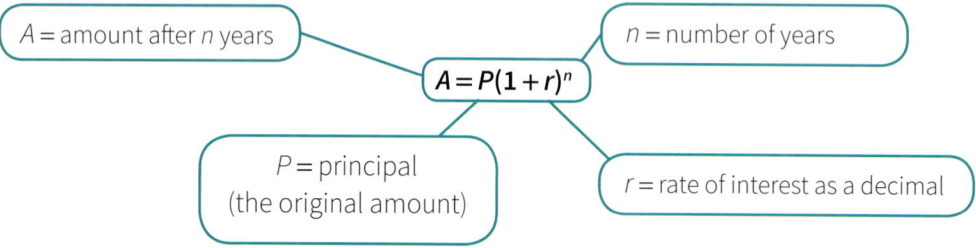

- A = amount after n years
- n = number of years
- P = principal (the original amount)
- r = rate of interest as a decimal

$$A = P(1+r)^n$$

In the Example on the previous page, $P = £1000$, $r = 0.04$, $n = 3$.

Using the formula gives:

amount after 3 years = $1000 × 1.04^3$ = £1124.86

For more work on formulae see pages 73–75.

Example

£6000 is borrowed for 5 years. Compound interest is charged at 4.5%. What is the total amount owed after 5 years?

$P = £6000$ $r = 0.045$ $n = 5$

Amount owed = $6000 × 1.045^5$ = **£7477.09** (nearest pence)

Round answers to the nearest pence.

4. Calculate the final amount for each of these investments.
   a. £500 for 4 years with compound interest at 3%
   b. £2760 for 6 years with compound interest at 4%
   c. £6700 for 5 years with compound interest at 4.5%

5. Calculate the final amount owed for each of these loans.
   a. £2000 for 3 years with compound interest at 6%
   b. £7500 for 5 years with compound interest at 7.2%
   c. £15 000 for 4 years with compound interest at 8.5%

6. A saver thinks that if he invests £12 500 in this account he will earn more than £3000 in interest. Is he correct? Give a reason for your answer.

5 Year Account

4.5% p.a.

Compound Interest

Money

Activities

1. Collect information from banks and building societies about savings accounts. Find out the meaning of the term Annual Equivalent Rate (AER). Imagine you had £5000 to invest for 4 years. Which account would you use? Work out how much interest you would earn from this account.

2. Look for loan adverts on TV or in newspapers or magazines. Write down the APR (Annual Percentage Rate) given in each advert. Find out the meaning of the term Annual Percentage Rate. Compare how much interest you would pay on a loan from each advert.

Budget with money

Specification reference L2.M13

A. Simple budgeting

A budget is a plan showing how much money you have and how it might be spent.

Planning a budget helps you check if you can afford to buy something.

Example

Tim has a £550 budget for a 4-day holiday.

    Travel costs are £90

    Hotel costs are £360

    He thinks he will spend £20 each day on food and drink.

Can he afford this? Explain your reasoning.

Total cost of food and drink = £20 × 4 (days) = £80

Total expenses = £80 + £360 (hotel) + £90 (travel) = £530

Yes, Tim can afford the holiday because he has £550 which is more than £530 (or £550 − £530 = £20 so Tim has £20 spare).

> Remember to answer the question. There are different ways to explain.

Practice

1. Yasmin has a budget of £3500 for a new bathroom.
   A plumber gives a quote for the work.
   He says it will take 7 days to do all the work and he charges £310 per day.
   The bathroom fittings cost £1395.
   Can Yasmin afford the new bathroom? Explain your reasoning.

2. Nathan has a budget of £450 to attend a Charity Run weekend.
   Travel costs are £120.
   Hotel and breakfast costs £214.
   Nathan's estimate for other food and drink is £30.
   He would like to take part in as many runs as possible.
   Which do you suggest? Explain your reasoning.

Charity Run weekend	
Entry costs	
5 km run	£28
10 km run	£37
Half marathon	£52

Measures, Shape and Space

3. Parveen has a budget of £55 for an artificial flower display.
   She buys 2 greenery stems, 3 small flower stems and 2 large flower stems.
   Can she afford to buy vase B as well?
   Explain your reasoning.

Item	Cost
Greenery stems	£4.95
Small flower stems	£6.99
Large flower stems	£8.59
Vase A	£5.50
Vase B	£8.50

4. Lu wants to start keeping hens. She has a budget of £250. She wants to buy two hens, a hen house, fencing, a feeding trough and a drinking tray. The table gives the costs.

   a. Calculate the total cost if Lu chooses:
      i. a mansion house and extra-safe fencing
      ii. a mansion house and basic fencing
      iii. a basic house and extra-safe fencing
      iv. a basic house and basic fencing.

   b. Which option do you think Lu should choose? Explain your choice.

Item	Cost
Hens	£28 each
Hen house	Basic £123 Mansion £149
Fencing	Basic £48.99 Extra-safe £63.99
Feeding trough	£3.95
Drinking tray	£2.95

5. There is a budget of £560 to buy furniture for a student's bedroom. The table shows the items needed and their cost.
   Which items do you suggest?
   Explain your reasoning.

Item	Cost
Bed	£319.99
Wardrobe	medium £164.99 or small £149.49
Desk	£49.49
Chair	swivel £39.49 or standard £34.99

6. Last year a company spent:
   £7 222 000 on wages
   £3 984 000 on other items.

   The manager wants to spend £2 million less next year.

   In her budget she plans to:
   - reduce the money spent on wages by $\frac{1}{4}$
   - reduce the money spent on other items by $\frac{1}{6}$

   Will the reductions save at least £2 million?

7. Pete starts a small pizza business. He expects to sell approximately 120 pizzas each Saturday.
   He thinks $\frac{2}{3}$ will be cheese and tomato only, and that $\frac{1}{3}$ will have cheese and tomato with both extra pepper and extra mushroom toppings.
   What is the material cost of producing:
   a. the cheese and tomato pizzas
   b. the pizzas with extra mushroom and pepper.

Item	Cost
Pizza bases	38p each
Tomato paste	50p per tube (enough for 5 pizzas)
Cheese	£3 (enough for 20 pizzas)
Bag of mushrooms	£1 (enough for 10 pizzas)
Bag of peppers	£1.20 (enough for 10 pizzas)

B. Household budgeting

Household bills can be **weekly**, **monthly**, **quarterly** (once every 3 months) or **annually** (once a year).

When budgeting, you need to be careful to include all costs on the same basis, usually per month or per week.

Example

Nafisha is buying a flat. Her take-home pay is £1524.15 per month.

She lists essential bills then plans a monthly budget to find how much she will have left each month for food, purchases, repairs, travel and leisure.

Bill	Cost	Monthly cost
Mortgage	£512 per month	£512
Council Tax	£114 per month	£114
Gas & Electric	£312 quarterly	312 ÷ 3 = £104
Internet & TV	£48 per month	£48
Mobile	£9 per month	£9
Insurance	£246 annually	246 ÷ 12 = £20.50
Water rates	£138 every 6 months	138 ÷ 6 = £23

Total monthly cost = 512 + 114 + 104 + 48 + 9 + 20.50 + 23 = £830.50

£1524.15 − £830.50 = £693.65

Nafisha has **£693.65** left each month for food, purchases, etc.

Practice

1. A driver has a budget of £360 per month to pay for a car. He considers the offer shown on the right:
   a. How much money would he have left each month for petrol and any repairs?
   b. Would you advise taking up this offer? Why?

2. Mike has a weekly take-home pay of £206.20
   He writes a list of his expenses:

   > £45 for household bills and food each week
   > £29 per month for gym membership
   > £62.60 travel pass for a month
   > about £30 on a night out each week

   a. Calculate the weekly cost of Mike's:
      i. gym membership
      ii. travel pass.

CAR OFFER

Monthly payment £185
Insurance £1324.80 annually
Tax £140 annually

b. Mike wants to save money. He thinks he can save at least £50 a week and have £50 a week left over.

Is this possible? Explain your reasoning.

3. Sameena's monthly take-home pay is £1722

She decides to rent a flat that costs £650 per month.

She lists her other household expenses:

council tax	£103.86 per month
gas & electric	£225 quarterly (approx.)
water	£126 every 6 months
contents insurance	£84 annually
internet & TV	£48 per month

a. Calculate the monthly cost of Sameena's:

i. gas and electric bill **ii.** water bill **iii.** contents insurance.

b. How much will Sameena have left each month?

c. Sameena likes holidays and spends about £1500 each year.

Do you think Sameena will be able to continue spending this on holidays? Explain your reasoning.

4. A married couple has an annual take home pay of £26 940

Their essential household bills are:

Mortgage	£456.14 per month
Council Tax	£124 per month
Gas & Electric	£225 quarterly
Water	£120.60 every 6 months
Insurance	£192 annually
Internet & TV	£56 per month

a. Calculate the monthly cost of the above household bills.

b. How much is left each month for other expenses?

c. Plan a budget each month to cover costs for the following:

food
travel
purchases and repairs
leisure activities and holidays
saving for unexpected events.

5. Lesley has an annual take-home pay of £14 880. She pays £120 per week for rent, which includes electricity and water. Her phone costs £16.99 each month. She pays £120 monthly for her car. Each week she budgets £90 for food, petrol and going out.

Lesley says she will be able to save £2000 in a year. Do you agree with her? Explain your answer.

Calculate using rates of pay

Specification reference L2.M15

Level 2

Some people get a fixed pay or wage per hour (or per week) plus sometimes a bonus for any sales. When they work extra hours they may get overtime pay at 'time and a half', or 'double time'.

Example 1 — Pay plus a bonus

A double-glazing salesperson earns £320 per week plus £50 for each sale.

In one week he sells windows to 5 customers. How much does he earn?

Pay for window sales = 5 × £50 = £250
Total pay = £320 + £250 = **£570**

> On a scientific calculator, you can check this in one calculation:
> 320 + 5 × 50 =

Example 2 — Pay plus overtime

A receptionist's basic hourly rate is £9.40
Work after 6pm is paid at time and a half. Saturday work is paid at double time.

Each week the receptionist works these hours:

Mon – Fri (each day)	3:30 pm – 8 pm
Saturday	8:30 am – 1 pm

What is the receptionist's weekly pay?

Time worked at £9.40 per hour = 5 × 2.5 = 12.5 hours *(5 days)*
Pay for this time = 12.5 × £9.40 = £117.50
Time worked at time and a half = 5 × 2 = 10 hours
Pay for this time = 10 × £9.40 × 1.5 = £141
Time worked at double time = 4.5 hours
Pay for Saturday = 4.5 × £9.40 × 2 = £84.60
Weekly pay = £117.50 + £141 + £84.60
         = **£343.10**

> 3:30 pm – 6 pm is $2\frac{1}{2}$ hours.
> 6 pm – 8 pm is 2 hours.
> 8:30 am – 1 pm is $4\frac{1}{2}$ hours.

> For time and a half, multiply the hourly rate by 1.5
> For double time, multiply it by 2

> There are other methods you can use to check (for example, work out the total for each day, then add)
> On a scientific calculator, you could do:
> 5 × 2.5 × 9.4 + 5 × 2 × 9.4 × 1.5 + 4.5 × 9.4 × 2 = £343.10

MyMaths 1240 SEARCH

Measures, Shape and Space

Practice

1. An electrician charges a £25 call-out fee plus £48 per hour.
   Calculate the pay she gets for a day when she has:

   a. 2 call-outs, taking 3 hours and 2 hours

   b. 4 call-outs for $1\frac{1}{2}$ hours, 2 hours, $\frac{1}{2}$ hour and $\frac{1}{4}$ hour

   c. 3 call-outs for $\frac{3}{4}$ hour, $1\frac{1}{2}$ hours, 1 hour and 2 hours.

   d. 4 call-outs, taking $\frac{1}{2}$ hour, $1\frac{1}{4}$ hours, 2 hours and $1\frac{1}{2}$ hours.

2. Yusuf and Nev are both TV sales staff but in different stores.

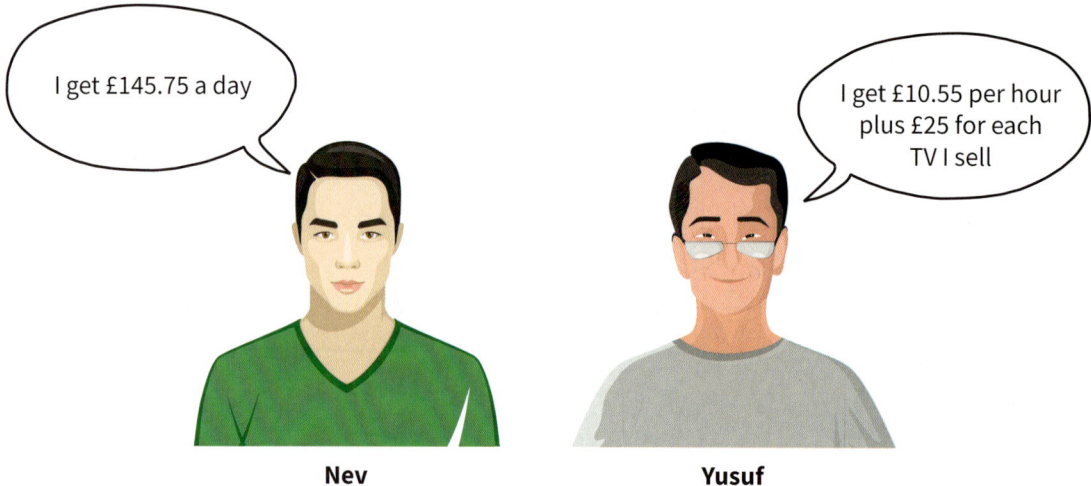

Nev: I get £145.75 a day

Yusuf: I get £10.55 per hour plus £25 for each TV I sell

   They each work 3 days a week, for 11 hours a day.
   Yusuf is paid per day.
   Nev is paid per hour with a bonus for each TV he sells.
   How many TVs must Nev sell in a week to earn as much as Yusuf?

3. Poppy earns £149.12 for a 16-hour week.
   Priya earns £209.76 for a 23-hour week.

   a. Who has the higher rate of pay?

   b. What is the difference in their hourly rates?

4. Jasmine sees two job offers.

Bees' Academy	Alpha College
Tutor support vacancy	Tutor assistant needed
22 hours per week	22 hours per week
42 weeks per year	42 weeks per year
£13.56 per hour	Annual salary £12 355

   Which offer is better financially? Explain your reasoning.

5. A tutor is paid £21 per hour until 8 pm.
   Teaching after 8 pm is paid at double time.
   The table shows the times that the tutor works in one week.
   Calculate the tutor's total pay for the week.

Day	Teaching times
Monday	9:30 am – 12 noon 6 pm – 9 pm
Tuesday	9:30 am – 12 noon
Wednesday	12:30 pm – 3 pm 6 pm – 9 pm
Friday	9:30 am – 12 noon

6. A checkout assistant's basic rate of pay is £9.24 per hour.
   Evenings after 6 pm and Saturday work are paid at time and a half.

   The table shows the hours that he worked in three weeks.

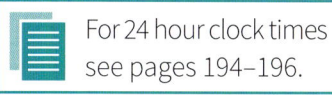

For 24 hour clock times see pages 194–196.

Week beginning	Monday	Tuesday	Wednesday	Thursday	Friday	Saturday
4th March	09:00–16:00	08:00–14:30	08:00–14:00	–	08:00–14:00	09:00–16:00
11th March	15:00–21:00	15:00–21:00	13:00–19:00	13:00–19:00	13:00–21:00	–
18th March	13:00–18:00	13:00–19:00	15:00–21:00	16:00–21:00	–	09:00–18:00

   a. In which week did he work most hours?
   b. How many more hours did he work in the week named in part **a** than in the next highest week?
   c. In which week did he earn most money?
   d. How much more was earned in the week from part **c** than in other weeks?

   Remember to write amounts of money to 2 decimal places (unless the answer is a whole number of pounds).

7. The table shows different shift patterns at a company.

	Shift A	Shift B	Shift C
Monday	10:30–18:00	13:00–20:00	07:00–12:30
Tuesday	10:30–18:00	13:00–20:00	07:00–12:30
Wednesday	10:30–18:00	13:00–20:00	07:00–12:30
Thursday	10:30–18:00	13:00–20:00	07:00–12:30
Friday	10:30–18:00	13:00–20:00	
Saturday			08:00–17:00

   a. Josie works Shift A. Her hourly rate is £10.15. What is her weekly pay?
   b. Liu works Shift B. Her weekly pay is £359.80. What is her hourly rate?
   c. Saj works part-time on Shift C.
      i. He usually gets £224.84 for working Monday to Thursday 07:00–12:30. What is his hourly rate?
      ii. Saj has agreed to work overtime on Saturday for time and a half. How much will Saj get in total for this week?
   d. Who has the best hourly rate of pay?

8. Carl works 5 days a week. He earns £11.20 per hour.
   Carl starts work each day at 8:30 am.
   He stops for an unpaid 45 minute lunch break at 12:00 and then carries on working until 4:30 pm.

   a. How many hours does Carl work each week?

   b. How much does Carl earn each week?

   c. Carl plans a holiday costing £360.
      He works 4 hours overtime each week at time and a half to save for this holiday.
      How many weeks will it take him to save enough money for the holiday?

Activity

You can use formulae in a spreadsheet program to carry out calculations.

If you have access to a computer with spreadsheet software, try this example, then experiment with other numbers and situations.

Example An employee's time sheet shows the hours she has worked:

   Monday: 6   Tuesday: 7   Wednesday: 8   Thursday: 7   Friday: 5

She earns £**9** an hour. Follow the instructions to find her wage for the week.

- Enter the days of the week in cells A1 to E1.
- Enter the number of hours in cells A2 to E2.
- In cell F2 enter: =**9***SUM(A2:E2) and press enter.

(Note that the symbol * means multiply, so this formula means **9** × the sum of the amounts in cells A2 to E2.)

Cell F2 should show £**297**, the amount the employee has earned.

Value Added Tax (VAT) Specification reference L2.M13

A. Calculate VAT

Value Added Tax (VAT) is added to the price of most goods and services. The government sometimes changes the percentage that is used for VAT.

For this section, assume that it is 20% of the value for most goods and services, but 5% for some special cases such as gas and electricity.

There are a variety of methods you can use to work out VAT.

You can use one way to work out the answer and a different way to check.

See page 143.

Money

 Key point

To find 20% without a calculator:

Find 10% of the amount (by dividing by 10), **then double** the result.

$10\% = 100\% \div 10$
then $20\% = 10\% \times 2$

Or:

Divide the amount by 5

$20\% = 100\% \div 5$

 Key point

To find 5% without a calculator:

Find 10% of the amount, **then halve** the result.

$5\% = 10\% \div 2$

 Key point

To find 20% (or 5%) with a calculator:

Divide by 100 to find 1%, then multiply by 20 (or 5).

Or:

Multiply by 0.2 (or 0.05).

$20\% = \dfrac{20}{100} = \dfrac{2}{10} = 0.2$ and $5\% = \dfrac{5}{100} = 0.05$

Example

Without a calculator, find the VAT on an item valued at £40, at a rate of 20%.

10% of £40 = £4   or $20\% = \dfrac{20}{100} = \dfrac{1}{5}$

20% of £40 = **£8**   20% of £40 = £40 ÷ 5 = **£8**

You can use a calculator to check the answer.

Practice

1. Work out the VAT on these values, at a rate of 20%.
   a. £900
   b. £2400
   c. £180
   d. £360
   e. £98
   f. £46
   g. £25.80
   h. £9.60
   i. £22.40
   j. £96.80
   k. £120.80
   l. £27.50

2. Work out the VAT on these values, at a rate of 5%.
   a. £400
   b. £300
   c. £760
   d. £70
   e. £128
   f. £24.40
   g. £30.36
   h. £19.30

Measures, Shape and Space

3. A decorator charges £480 plus VAT at 20%.
   Work out the VAT.
4. An electricity bill is £274.80 plus 5% VAT.
   Find the amount of VAT.
5. Work out the VAT at 20% on these items.

 **Key point**
Round answers to the nearest pence where necessary.

a.  £980

b.  £249

c.  £59.90

d.  £69.50

e.  £14.95

f.  £59.99

See pages 139–145 for more practice on percentages.

B. Calculate total cost including VAT

Example

A bike is advertised for sale for £540 + 20% VAT. Find the total cost.

There are several methods you can use.

Without a calculator:
Find VAT 10% of £540 = £54
           20% of £540 = £108
Total cost = £108 + £540
           = **£648**

With a calculator:
Total % = 100% (bike) + 20% (VAT)
Total cost = 120% of £540
           = £540 ÷ 100 × 120
           = **£648**

Or: Total cost = 1.2 × £540
              = **£648**

$120\% = \dfrac{120}{100} = 1.2$

Money

Practice

In these questions use one method to work out the answer and a different method to check.

1. Find the total cost of each item when 20% VAT is added to these prices.
   - **a.** rabbit hutch £120
   - **b.** vacuum cleaner £210
   - **c.** coat £72
   - **d.** lamp £48
   - **e.** fridge-freezer £299
   - **f.** houseplant £32.50

2. A builder calculates the cost for a new drive as £7400 + 20% VAT.
   What is the total cost?

3. An electricity bill is £152.60 + 5% VAT.
   What is the total bill?

4. A child car seat is sold for £85 + 5% VAT.
   What is the total cost?

5. The prices of some items before VAT are shown below.
   Find the prices including VAT at 20%.

See pages 139–145 for more practice on percentages.

C. Calculate original price and VAT

Some prices are **inclusive** of VAT. This means VAT has already been added.

Example

A gaming computer is advertised for £864 inclusive of VAT at 20%.

Find the original cost of the computer and the amount of VAT.

Original cost of computer (100%) + VAT (20%) = £864

120% of original cost = £864

1% of original cost = £864 ÷ 120 = £7.20

Original cost of computer = 100 × £7.20 = **£720**

VAT = 20 × £7.20 = **£144**

Check: Total cost = £720 + £144 = £864

Or: $120\% = \dfrac{120}{100} = 1.2$

1.2 × original cost = £864
so original cost = £864 ÷ 1.2
             = £720

VAT = 20% of £720
    = 0.2 × £720 = £144

Measures, Shape and Space

Practice

1. The following are prices inclusive of VAT at 20%.
   Find the original cost price and the VAT for each item.
   a. electric hob £186
   b. rug £72
   c. kettle £24
   d. flowers £12
   e. armchair £366
   f. bag £54
   g. laptop £238.80
   h. wok £25.80
   i. stool £46.80

2. What was the price of this bike before VAT?

3. These gas bills are inclusive of 5% VAT.
   How much was each bill before VAT was added?
   a. Total bill £129.36
   b. Total bill £164.64
   c. Total bill £213.36
   d. Total bill £418.53

4. A plumber charges £5874 for fitting a new bathroom.
   This price includes VAT at 20%.
   a. How much was the cost before VAT?
   b. How much is the VAT?

£276 including 20% VAT

Taxes on income

Specification reference L2.M13

Level 2

The amount of money you earn is called your **gross pay**.

Your employer deducts money for income tax, National Insurance (NI) and often for a pension.

Your pay after all the deductions have been made is called your **net pay**.

A. Income tax

Your **personal tax allowance** is the amount you can earn in one year before paying any income tax. Any remaining income is called your **taxable income**.

The rate of income tax depends on how much you earn. Most people pay the basic rate, but high earners pay higher rates on earnings over a threshold.

The Government announces the personal allowance and the tax bands each year in the Budget.

In this section use:

Personal tax allowance = £11 850 per annum

Income tax basic rate = 20%

Example

Sandra earns £32 500 per annum. Find how much income tax she pays in a year.

Sandra's taxable income = £32 500 − £11 850 = £20 650

Income tax = 20% of £20 650 = **£4130**   £20 650 ÷ 100 × 20 or £20 650 × 0.2

Practice

1. Find the income tax paid on the following annual incomes.
   a. £18 000
   b. £19 600
   c. £24 700
   d. £30 200
   e. £14 840
   f. £26 400
   g. £37 350
   h. £42 920

B. National Insurance (NI)

There is an earnings allowance on which you pay no National Insurance.

The NI that you pay on the rest of your earnings depends on how much you earn and on whether you are employed or self-employed.

The Government decides what the allowance and NI rates will be and usually announces any changes in the Budget.

In this section use:

NI allowance = £162 per week

NI rate for employees = 12%

Example

Sandra earns £32 500 per annum. Find how much National Insurance she pays in a year.

Annual NI allowance = £162 × 52 = £8424

Income after NI allowance = £32 500 − £8424 = £24 076

National Insurance = 12% of £24 076

= **£2889.12** per year

The NI allowance is per week. Multiply by 52 to find the allowance for a year.

£24 076 ÷ 100 × 12
or £24 076 × 0.12

Practice

1. Find the National Insurance paid on the following weekly wages.
   a. £200
   b. £350
   c. £240
   d. £432
   e. £520
   f. £618.50
   g. £725.60
   h. £890.25

2. Find the National Insurance paid on the following annual incomes.
   a. £18 000
   b. £19 600
   c. £24 700
   d. £30 200
   e. £14 840
   f. £26 400
   g. £37 350
   h. £42 920

C. Net pay

To find net pay, employers subtract tax and NI from gross pay.
Employers also deduct any contributions that their employees make for their pensions. Pension contributions are deducted from gross pay **before income tax** is calculated.

Measures, Shape and Space

In this section use:

NI allowance = £162 per week   NI rate = 12%

Tax allowance = £11 850 per annum   Income tax basic rate = 20%

 **Key point**
Take care to use consistent time periods. It is usually easier to work with yearly amounts.

Example

Leo has a gross pay of £15 000 per annum.

Leo's employer pays into a pension fund for Leo, but Leo makes no contribution.

Find Leo's net pay per annum.

1 Calculate NI to be paid

Income liable for NI = gross pay − NI allowance
= £15 000 − £8424
= £6576

Annual NI allowance = 52 × weekly allowance = 52 × £162 = £8424

NI = 12% of £6576 = £6576 ÷ 100 × 12 = **£789.12**

or £6576 × 0.12

2 Calculate income tax to be paid

Taxable income = gross pay − tax allowance
= £15 000 − £11 850 = £3150

Income tax = 20% of £3150 = £3150 ÷ 100 × 20 = **£630**

or £3150 × 0.2

3 Subtract total deductions from gross pay

Total deductions = NI + tax
= £789.12 + £630 = £1419.12

Net pay = gross pay − total deductions
= £15 000 − £1419.12 = **£13 580.88**

Example

Hameeda has a gross pay of £31 400 per annum.

She pays 6% of her earnings into her pension.

Find her net pay each month.

1 Calculate NI to be paid

Income liable for NI = Gross pay − NI allowance
= £31 400 − £8424
= £22 976

Annual NI allowance = 52 × weekly allowance = 52 × £162 = £8424

NI = 12% of £22 976 = **£2757.12**

£22 976 ÷ 100 × 12 or £22 976 × 0.12

Example

2 Calculate pension contribution

Pension contribution = 6% of gross pay

= **£1884** ← £31 400 ÷ 100 × 6 or £31 400 × 0.06

3 Calculate income tax to be paid

Pay after pension deduction = £31 400 − £1884 = £29 516

Taxable income = pay after pension deduction − tax allowance

= £29 516 − £11 850 = £17 666

Tax = 20% of £17 666 = **£3533.20** ← £17 666 ÷ 100 × 20 or £17 666 × 0.2

4 Subtract total deductions from gross pay

Total deductions = NI + pension + tax

= £2757.12 + £1884 + £3533.20 = £8174.32

Net annual pay = gross pay − total deductions

= £31 400 − £8174.32 = £23 225.68

Net monthly pay = £23 225.68 ÷ 12 = **£1935.47** (nearest pence)

> **Key point**
> Remember that pension contributions are deducted from gross pay before income tax is calculated (but not before NI is calculated).

> Note the question asks for the net pay **each month**.

Practice

Use the allowances and rates given above.

1. Find the NI contribution, income tax and net pay per year for these incomes.
   a. £27 000
   b. £32 500
   c. £18 450
   d. £24 700
   e. £31 800
   f. £41 980
   g. £23 475
   h. £43 658

2. Find the net pay for these incomes. Assume a pension contribution of 6%.
   a. £22 400
   b. £24 300
   c. £28 500
   d. £18 600
   e. £21 900
   f. £30 460
   g. £37 440
   h. £43 650

3. A man currently has a gross pay of £23 800 (after pension contribution).
   He sees a job advertised with a gross pay of £24 650 (after pension contribution).
   How much more money would there be in his net pay?

4. An employee has a gross pay of £21 640. She is given a pay rise of 4%.
   a. What is her new gross pay?
   b. How much more money will she have in her take-home pay each month?

5. Copy and complete these pay slips:

a. for one week

Payment for week		Deductions for week	
Hours worked	35	National Insurance	
Wage per hour	£18	Income tax	
Total pay		Total deductions	
		Take-home pay	

b. for one month

Earnings		Monthly deductions	
Annual gross earnings	£28 500	NI	
Monthly gross earnings		Pension (6%)	
		Income tax	
		Total	
		Net monthly earnings	

Activities

1. Use the internet to find the current allowances and rates for income tax and National Insurance.
2. Find a job advert for a career you are interested in. Work out what your take-home pay would be after income tax and National Insurance are deducted.
3. Investigate the amount earned by a footballer or pop star.

   Try to work out the total amount they should pay in income tax and National Insurance.
4. Find out about other taxes that are important to you. Possible examples are: vehicle tax, council tax, excise duties, inheritance tax, stamp duty.

   Write a report on your findings. Include worked examples.

Convert between currencies

Specification reference **L2.M13**

To find exchange rates, look on the internet, or in the daily papers.
The exchange rates change daily. The table shows some examples.

Country/area	Currency name	Bank SELLING rate £1 =	Bank BUYING rate £1 =
Europe	Euro (€)	€1.10	€1.15
India	Rupee	87.52 rupees	89.61 rupees
Japan	Yen	132.96 yen	139.34 yen
Poland	Zloty	4.67 zloty	4.90 zloty
South Africa	Rand	17.82 rand	18.69 rand
USA	Dollar ($)	$1.24	$1.30

If you want foreign currency, the bank SELLS it to you at the SELLING rate.

Example

For each £ you get €1.10 (euros) or 132.96 Japanese yen.

£ — **MULTIPLY by selling rate** (using a calculator) → Foreign currency

If you exchange £500: for euros you get   500 × 1.10 = **€550**

for Japanese yen you get 500 × 132.96 = **66 480 yen**

You can check these by dividing (the inverse) or rounding.

Practice

1. The table shows a bank's customers for foreign currency exchange on one day.
   Copy and complete the table using the rates given on the previous page.

Customer	Amount in £ to exchange	Currency type	Currency amount
Mr Black	£900	US dollars	
Mrs Smith	£750	Polish zloty	
Miss Patten	£1200	South African rand	
Ms Chang	£2000	Japanese yen	
Mr Davies	£150	Indian rupees	
Ms Bailey	£87 500	Euro	

If you want to change foreign currency back to £, the bank BUYS it from you at the BUYING rate.

Example

Foreign currency — **DIVIDE by buying rate** (using a calculator) → £

$300 (USA)   buying rate £1 = $1.30   You get   300 ÷ 1.30 = £230.77 = **£231**   (nearest £)

10 000 rupees buying rate £1 = 89.61 rupees You get 10 000 ÷ 89.61 = £111.59 = **£112** (nearest £)

2. Use the buying rates on p188 to find the value to the nearest £ for the following foreign currencies.

   a. 1200 Polish zloty   b. 550 South African rand   c. 290 euros
   d. 750 rupees   e. 15 000 Yen   f. 2000 US dollars

Measures, Shape and Space

3. A bank has customers returning from holiday who want to convert their foreign currency back into £. Copy and complete the following table to show to the nearest £ what they should receive.

Customer	Amount	Currency type	£
Mr Wragg	720	US dollars	
Miss Yen	950	Polish zloty	
Mr Ennis	3400	Japanese yen	
Ms Masters	5600	Indian rupees	
Miss Sharif	1200	Euro	
Mr Caine	256 000	Japanese yen	
Ms Wright	350	South African rand	

4. A family used 500 litres of petrol at 1.59 euros per litre whilst touring France.
   The exchange rate they received was 1.13 euros to the pound.
   How much did the petrol cost them to the nearest pound?

Travel agents and banks often charge a commission for changing currency.

For the following questions, assume that the commission charged is £10 for exchanges up to £1000 and $1\frac{1}{2}$% on amounts over £1000.

For exchanges from pounds to other currencies, the commission is taken **before** the conversion is calculated.
For exchanges from other currencies to pounds the commission is taken **after** the conversion is calculated.
Assume that the customers only receive the whole units of currency (for example, they would only get €642 of €642.73).

5. a. A businessman changes £950 into US dollars for a trip to America.
      How many dollars does he receive? (Use the rates given on page 189.)
   b. The businessman is ill, and has to cancel his trip. He changes the dollars back into pounds.
      How much does he get?
   c. Altogether how much does he lose because of the cancellation?

6. a. A couple changed £1200 into Polish zloty at 4.97 zloty to the £ when they booked a flight to Poland. How many zloty did they get?
   b. The exchange rate later rose to 5.06 zloty to the pound.
      How much extra, in zloty, would they have gained if they had waited to exchange their money?
   c. The couple returns from Poland with 750 zloty.
      How much do they receive after paying commission when they exchange these zloty for pounds at a rate of 5.24 zloty to the £?

Activity

Use information from the internet or holiday brochures to cost a holiday abroad.

Decide how much money you would take and estimate the amount of foreign currency you would receive.

Chapter Summary
11 Money

- The decimal point separates pounds (£) and pence (p) and there should always be two digits after the decimal point to represent the number of pence. Add a zero in the first decimal place if the number of pence is less than 10 pence.
- Always write money using a £ or a p, not both, and work in either pounds or pence, not both.
- Adding, subtracting, multiplying and dividing is the same with money as it is with other decimals.
- When rounding to the nearest 10p, if the amount ends in 5p or more then round up to the 10p above and if the amount ends in less than 5p then round down to the 10p below.
- When rounding to the nearest pound, if the amount ends in 50p or more then round up to the £ above, and if the amount ends in less than 50p then round down to the £ below.

- To find a 5% discount without a calculator, find 10% (by dividing by 10) and then divide by 2.
- Use 10% and 5% to find other % values.
- Money in bank accounts sometimes earns **interest** which depends on the **balance** (how much money is in the account) and the **percentage rate** of interest on the account.
- **Per annum** or **p.a.** means 'per year'.
- **Simple interest** is the interest taken out of an account at the end of each year.

- **Compound interest** is the interest left in an account at the end of each year.
- Compound interest formula: $A = P(1 + r)^n$ where A = amount after n years, P = principal amount (the initial amount), r = rate of interest and n = number of years.
- A **budget** is a plan to show how a limited amount of money might be spent.
- Costs need to be on the same basis, for example, all monthly, all weekly etc.
- Rates of pay may include **bonuses** such as working 'double time' or 'time and a half'
- You may need to add **VAT** (Value Added Tax) to a price. Assume VAT is usually 20% but 5% for special cases like gas or electricity.
- Goods inclusive of VAT = 100% original price + 20% VAT = 120%
- Round answers to the nearest penny to ensure there are always 2 decimal places.
- **Gross pay** is the amount you earn and **net pay** is the pay you take home.
- **Personal tax allowance** is the amount you can earn before paying any income tax.
- Net pay = gross pay − National Insurance (NI) − pension − **income tax** (taxable income)
- **Pension contributions** are deducted from gross pay before income tax is calculated, but not before NI is calculated.
- To convert currency from £s to another currency, multiply by the **selling rate**. Divide by the **buying rate** to convert a foreign currency back into £.

Measures, Shape and Space

12 Time

Read, measure and record time
Specification reference: **EL3.M12**

A. am and pm

8:30 could be when you get up in the morning, or when you watch TV in the evening. To tell us which it is, the day is split into two halves: **am** and **pm**.

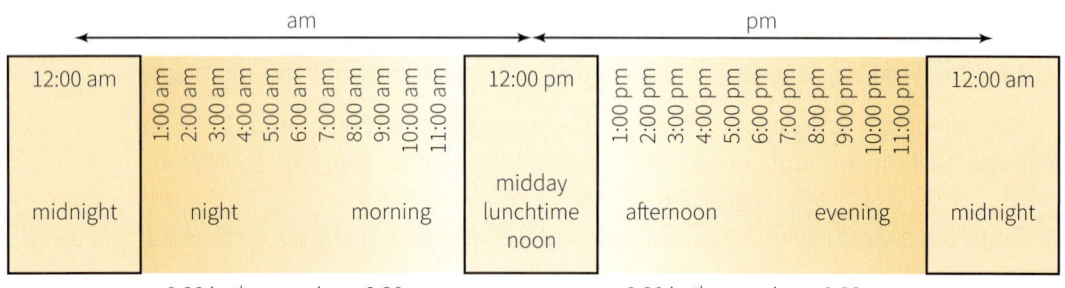

9:30 in the morning = 9:30 am   9:30 in the evening = 9:30 pm

Practice

1. Write these times in numbers using am or pm.
   a. 7:00 in the morning
   b. 4:00 in the afternoon
   c. 11:30 before lunch
   d. 5:00 when the shops are closing
   e. 1:00 when most people are asleep
   f. 8:45 the morning rush hour

2. Match the times to the events.
   a. Waking up with a bad dream
   b. Football kick-off time
   c. Coffee break
   i. 7:45 pm
   ii. 11:00 am
   iii. 1:00 am

3. Suggest activities for the following times.
   a. 9:00 am   b. 12:00 pm   c. 5:30 pm   d. 7:45 am

4. How many hours are there from:
   a. 3:00 am to 3:00 pm
   b. 5:30 am to 6:30 pm
   c. 4:15 am to 9:15 pm
   d. 10:00 am to 7:30 pm
   e. 8:00 pm Monday to 7:00 am Tuesday
   f. 7:00 pm Tuesday to 6:30 am Wednesday?

B. Read and record time to the nearest 5 minutes

There are **60 minutes** in **an hour**.

There are **30 minutes** in **half an hour**.

There are **15 minutes** in a **quarter of an hour**.

Time

Look at these clocks. The times are given underneath.

Example

10 minutes past 7
or
7:10

30 minutes past 9
or
9:30
or half past nine

40 minutes past 3
or
3:40

Practice

1. Write each time in two different ways.

   a.   b.   c.   d.

When the minute hand of a clock has gone past 30 minutes, we can count minutes **to the next hour**.

We often read the time to the nearest 5 minute mark.

To the nearest 5 minutes, this clock says **20 minutes to 10**.

Key point

To the nearest 5 minutes means to the nearest number marked on the clock.

Look at these clocks.

They both say 50 minutes past 1

or

10 minutes to 2.

193

Measures, Shape and Space

2. Write the time to the nearest 5 minutes in three ways.

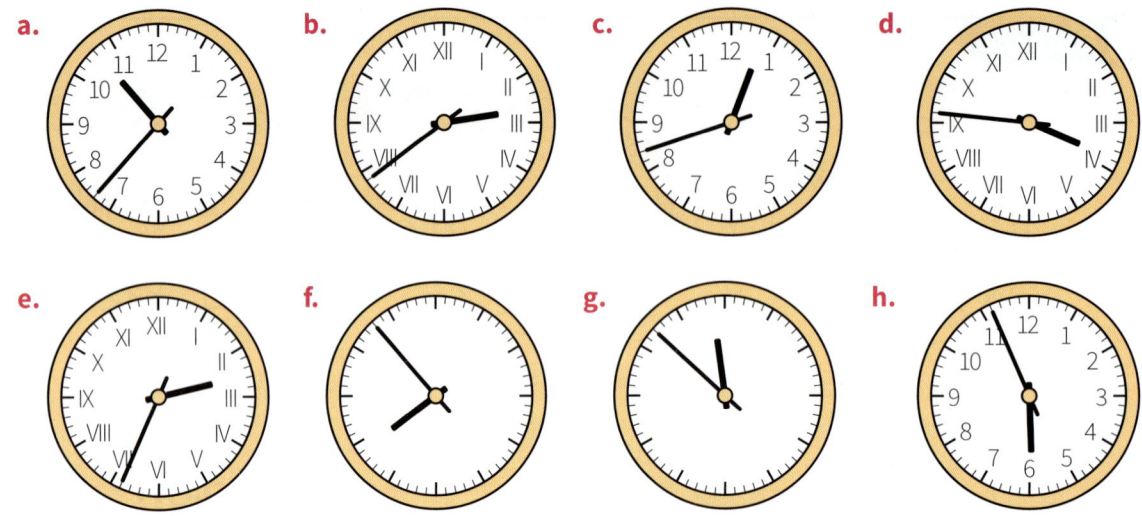

Use the 12 and 24 hour clock

Specification reference **EL3.M13**

A. 12 hour and 24 hour clock times

The 24 hour clock is used on timetables, digital clocks and other electronic timers.

The hours are numbered up to 24 instead of using am and pm.

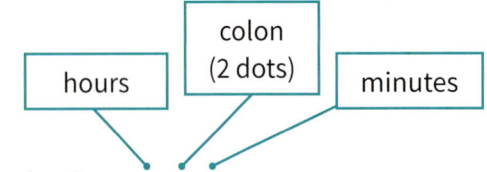

4 digits are used to give times _ _ : _ _

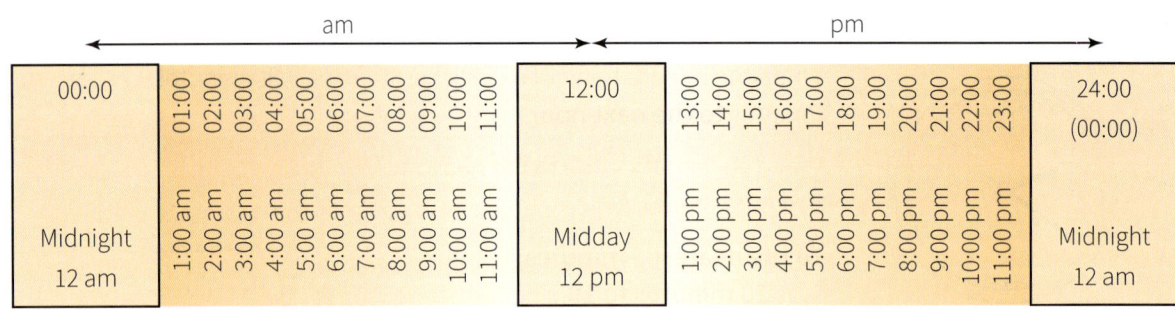

It is easy to write am times as 24 hour clock times:

Example

6:20 am = **06:20**   10:35 am = **10:35**

Timetables often omit the colon.

It is more difficult with pm times. Usually you need to add 12 hours.

 Example

Write 4:36 pm in 24 hour time.
               hours:minutes
                4:36 (remove the pm)
add 12 hours   +12:00
4:36 pm   is   **16:36**

 Key point

Add 12 hours to pm times to find the 24 hour clock time.

 Example

Write quarter to seven in the morning and in the evening as 24 hour clock times.
quarter to 7 in the morning: 15 minutes before 7 = 45 minutes past 6 = **06:45**
quarter to seven in the evening: add 12 hours to give **18:45**

 Key point

Take care near midnight and midday: 12:15 am = 00:15
                                                   12:15 pm = 12:15

 **Practice**

1. Write these as 24 hour clock times.
   - a. 3:50 pm
   - b. 7:00 am
   - c. 9:15 am
   - d. 10:26 pm
   - e. 3:42 pm
   - f. 1:30 pm
   - g. 6:45 am
   - h. 12:05 am
   - i. 7:40 pm
   - j. 6:59 pm
   - k. 6:42 am
   - l. 8.25 pm

2. Write these as 24 hour clock times.
   - a. Quarter past 3 in the morning
   - b. Quarter to 5 in the evening
   - c. Half past 7 in the morning
   - d. 10 to 9 in the morning
   - e. 10 past 11 at night
   - f. Midday
   - g. 5 to 4 in the afternoon
   - h. Quarter to 8 in the morning
   - i. 25 to 6 in the evening
   - j. 10 to 3 in the afternoon
   - k. 5 past 4 in the afternoon
   - l. 10 past 11 in the morning

3. Write these times in figures as 24 hour clock times.
   - a. Six minutes past four in the afternoon
   - b. Fifteen minutes past three in the afternoon
   - c. Eleven minutes past eight in the morning
   - d. Fifteen minutes to ten in the morning
   - e. Ten minutes to seven in the evening
   - f. Twenty-five minutes to midnight
   - g. Five minutes to eleven in the morning
   - h. Twelve minutes past midday
   - i. Twenty minutes past nine in the evening
   - j. Half past six in the evening

Measures, Shape and Space

 Example

Write 07:15 as a 12 hour clock time.

Remove the 0 and write am (morning time)   **7:15 am**

 Example

Write 23:50 in 12 hour clock time.

```
                     23:50
subtract 12 hours  − 12:00
              2350 = 11:50 pm   (evening time, so write pm)
```

 Key point

Subtract 12 hours to find the pm time.

---

4. Write these 24 hour clock times using am or pm.

   a. 23:30   b. 06:45   c. 07:12   d. 16:45   e. 12:10   f. 01:10

   g. 12:16   h. 14:10   i. 00:00   j. 06:05   k. 13:46   l. 09:15

5. Match the times.

   a. 15:52   14 minutes to 4 in the morning   5:05 pm
   b. 03:46   9 minutes past 7 in the evening   11:54 pm
   c. 17:05   28 minutes to 5 in the afternoon   3:46 am
   d. 23:54   8 minutes to 4 in the afternoon   4:32 pm
   e. 19:09   6 minutes to midnight   3:52 pm
   f. 16:32   5 minutes past 5 in the afternoon   7:09 pm

B. Use timetables

Most timetables are in 24 hour clock time. The colon is often omitted.

 Example

Find the first train leaving Bournville for Birmingham.

Extract from the Redditch – Birmingham timetable

1 Look down the first column. Find Bournville.

Redditch	d				0628			0658
Longbridge	d	0615	0623	0633	0644	0654	0702	0713
Kings Norton	d	0620	0627	0637	0649	0658	0707	0719
Bournville	2—d→ 0622	0630	0640	0651	0701	0710	0721
Five Ways	d	0629	0638	0648	0659	0708	0718	0729
Birmingham	a	0633	0642	0652	0703	0713	0722	0733

2 Read along the row. The first train leaves Bournville at 0622.

3 Check for any further information, for example, a = arrival (the train arrives at 0633), d = departure.

   With some timetables, trains only run on certain days.

Time

Practice

1. Use the timetable in the Example on the previous page to answer these questions.
   Give answers as 24 hour clock times.

   a. i. When is the first train from Redditch to Birmingham?

      ii. When does this train arrive in Birmingham?

   b. When is the first train after 7 o'clock in the morning to leave from Longbridge?

   c. i. When does the first train leave from Kings Norton?

      ii. At what time does this train arrive in Birmingham?

   d. Which is the latest train from Bournville that you can catch if you want to be in Birmingham by 7 o'clock in the morning?

   e. Which is the latest train you can catch from Kings Norton if you want to be in Birmingham by half past 7 in the morning?

   f. A commuter arrives at Kings Norton at half past six in the morning.

      i. Which is the next train she can catch?

      ii. When does this train depart from Five Ways?

2. This timetable gives the bus times going in both directions.
   It uses 12 hour clock time.
   Give your answers as am or pm times.

EASY RIDER 629		Woodgate Valley North – Selly Oak			
From **Woodgate** ↓ to ↓ **Selly Oak**	Woodgate Valley North	8:45	10:10	1:55	3:15
	Moat Meadow	8:53	10:18	2:03	3:23
	Quinbourne Centre	9:00	10:25	2:10	3:30
	Onneley House	9:15	10:40	2:25	3:45
	Harborne, High Street	9:25	10:50	2:35	3:55
	Old Tokengate	9:39	10:55	2:40	4:00
	Queen Elizabeth Hospital	9:40	—	2:45	4:05
	Selly Oak	9:50	—	3:00	4:10
From **Selly Oak** ↓ to ↓ **Woodgate**	Selly Oak	—	12:20	4:10	
	Queen Elizabeth Hospital	—	12:30	4:20	
	Old Tokengate	—	12:40	4:25	
	Harborne, High Street	11:25	12:45	4:30	
	Onneley House	11:35	12:55	4:40	
	Quinbourne Centre	11:50	1:10	4:50	
	Moat Meadow	11:57	1:17	4:55	
	Woodgate Valley North	12:05	1:25	5:00	

   a. When does the first bus leave Woodgate Valley North?

   b. When does the first bus return from Selly Oak to Woodgate Valley North?

   c. i. Which is the first bus from Quinbourne Centre after 10 am to go to Selly Oak?

      ii. When does this bus arrive at Selly Oak?

   d. Which is the first bus from Moat Meadow to go to Queen Elizabeth Hospital?

   e. You are at Queen Elizabeth Hospital at midday.
      What is the earliest time you could get to Harbourne High Street by bus?

   f. i. You are at Onneley House. Which bus should you catch to be at Queen Elizabeth Hospital by ten thirty in the morning?

      ii. If you leave the hospital at quarter to twelve, when will you catch your bus back to Onneley House?

      iii. When would you get back to Onneley House?

   g. You are at Moat Meadow. You are due to meet friends at Old Tokengate at 3 pm.
      What is the latest bus you could catch?

Measures, Shape and Space

Units of time

Specification reference **L1.M20**

60 seconds = 1 minute
60 minutes = 1 hour
24 hours = 1 day
7 days = 1 week
12 months = 1 year

52 weeks = 1 year
365 days = 1 year
366 days = 1 leap year (a leap year has an extra day)
100 years = 1 century
1000 years = 1 millennium

Practice

1. Copy and complete these.

   a. $\frac{1}{2}$ minute = _____ seconds
   b. $\frac{1}{4}$ year = _____ months
   c. $\frac{1}{2}$ hour = _____ minutes
   d. 2 centuries = _____ years
   e. $\frac{1}{4}$ hour = _____ minutes
   f. 1 millennium = _____ years
   g. $\frac{1}{2}$ year = _____ months
   h. 2 years = _____ weeks
   i. 2 weeks = _____ days
   j. $\frac{1}{2}$ year = _____ weeks

2. Do you know this poem?

   > 30 days have September, April, June and November
   >
   > All the rest have 31
   >
   > Except February alone, which has 28 days clear and 29 each leap year.

   a. How many days are there in: i. June   ii. November   iii. February in a leap year?
   b. How many days are there altogether in: i. July and August   ii. March and April?

3. Which unit of time would you use to measure the following events? Choose from the box.

   a. Boiling an egg
   b. Running a 100 metre sprint
   c. The time taken for 2nd class mail delivery
   d. A holiday abroad
   e. Flying from the UK to Europe
   f. Travelling by boat from the UK to Australia
   g. The natural age of an oak tree

seconds	minutes
hours	days
weeks	months
years	centuries

4. Copy and complete these.

   a. $3\frac{1}{2}$ minutes = _____ seconds
   b. 180 seconds = _____ minutes
   c. $4\frac{1}{2}$ hours = _____ minutes
   d. 300 minutes = _____ hours
   e. 3 years = _____ months
   f. 30 months = _____ years
   g. 7 weeks = _____ days
   h. 35 days = _____ weeks

i. $4\frac{1}{2}$ centuries = _____ years

j. 500 years = _____ centuries

k. 3 millennia = _____ years

l. 10 000 years = _____ millennia

5. A worker's wage is £15 000 per annum. How much is this each month?

> **Key point**
>
> **In finance:**
> per annum means per year
> a quarter means $\frac{1}{4}$ of a year

6. A hospital patient has to wait 28 days to hear the results of a test. How many weeks is this?

7. The instructions say, 'Cook the food in a microwave for $2\frac{1}{2}$ minutes', but the microwave timer is in seconds. Write the cooking time in seconds.

8. It takes $1\frac{3}{4}$ hours to cook a chicken in the oven. What is this in minutes?

9. Many bills come every quarter. How many weeks are there in one quarter?

10. A student's phone bill is £26 per month. What is the phone bill for:
    a. a quarter of the year   b. a full year?

11. a. A family go on a 7 night holiday on 28th July. On what date do they return?

    b. A couple go on holiday on 19th April and return on 3rd May. How many nights are they away?

Calculate time

Specification reference L1.M20

Level 1

A. Add and subtract time in hours, minutes and seconds

> **Key point**
>
> Remember   60 seconds = 1 minute   60 minutes = 1 hour

Example

1 minute + 40 seconds + $1\frac{1}{2}$ minutes

min	sec	
1	00	1 minute
	40	40 seconds
+1	30	1 minute 30 seconds
2	70	70 seconds = 1 minute + 10 seconds

2 min + 1 min + 10 sec = **3 minutes 10 seconds**

> Write $\frac{1}{2}$ minute as 30 seconds.

> Change 70 seconds to minutes and seconds.

> **Key point**
>
> Write fractions of a minute as seconds.

Measures, Shape and Space

Example

4 hours 36 minutes – 49 minutes

h	min
4	36
–	49

You can't take 49 from 36 so change an hour to minutes.

4 h 36 min = 3h 36 min + 1 hour = 3h 36 min + 60 min

h	min
3	96
–	49
3	47

3 hours 47 minutes

Key point

Subtracting minutes
Change an hour into minutes when necessary.

Practice

1. Add these times together.
   a. 3 hours 20 minutes + $1\frac{3}{4}$ hours + 15 minutes
   b. $6\frac{1}{2}$ minutes + $2\frac{1}{4}$ minutes + 12 seconds
   c. $2\frac{1}{2}$ minutes + 40 seconds + 25 seconds
   d. $3\frac{3}{4}$ minutes + 30 seconds + 2 minutes
   e. 7 hours 40 minutes + 35 minutes + $1\frac{1}{2}$ hours
   f. $1\frac{1}{2}$ hours + 40 minutes + 1 hour 55 minutes

2. Subtract these times.
   a. $3\frac{1}{4}$ hours – 55 minutes
   b. $2\frac{1}{4}$ hours – 35 minutes
   c. $2\frac{1}{4}$ minutes – 55 seconds
   d. $1\frac{1}{2}$ minutes – 38 seconds
   e. $4\frac{1}{4}$ hours – 40 minutes
   f. 2 minutes 10 seconds – 49 seconds

3. a. Cooking instructions for a curry in the microwave say, 'Cook for $6\frac{1}{2}$ minutes, stand for 3 minutes, then cook for a further $1\frac{1}{2}$ minutes.' What is the total time?
   b. For rice, the cooking time is $4\frac{1}{2}$ minutes, followed by 2 minutes standing, then another 45 seconds cooking. Altogether how long does it take to cook the rice?

4. A decorator takes altogether $1\frac{1}{2}$ hours to paint a window. He spends 35 minutes preparing the wood and the rest of the time painting. How long does he spend painting?

5. A dog trainer's working day is $7\frac{1}{4}$ hours. This includes a 1-hour lunch break away from the client and travel time to and from the client. The journey takes $\frac{3}{4}$ hour in each direction. How long does the dog trainer spend with the client?

B. Find the difference between times by adding on

Example

How long is it from 09:45 to 11:30?

Start time	09:45	
Number of minutes to the next hour	09:45 ⟶ 10:00 =	15 minutes
Number of hours	10:00 ⟶ 11:00 =	1 hour
Number of minutes after the hour	11:00 ⟶ 11:30 =	30 minutes
	Time from 09:45 to 11:30 =	**1 hour 45 minutes**

Add

To check this, round to the nearest hour: 10:00 to 12:00 is 2 hours.

Practice

1. Find the time from:
   a. 04:55 to 07:36
   b. 06:42 to 09:24
   c. 09:45 to 12:30
   d. 08:42 to 10:15
   e. 07:26 to 11:14
   f. 06:35 to 10:25
   g. 09:34 to 12:45
   h. 11:15 to 14:36
   i. 9:55 am to 2:10 pm
   j. 7:50 am to 4:26 pm
   k. 8:35 am to 12:16 pm
   l. Midday to 17:50
   m. 10:14 am to 3:20 pm
   n. 11:45 am to 7:15 pm
   o. 2:15 pm to midnight
   p. 2:15 am to midnight.

Hint Check your answers by rounding the times.

Example

A part-time worker starts work at 11:15 am and finishes at 3:45 pm.
For how long does he work?

Start time	11:15	
Number of minutes to the next hour	11:15 ⟶ 12:00 =	45 minutes
Number of hours	12:00 ⟶ 3:00 =	3 hours
Number of minutes after the hour	3:00 ⟶ 3:45 =	45 minutes
	Time between 11:15 and 15:45 (or 3.45) =	**3 hours 90 minutes**

Add

3 hours + 1 hour 30 minutes
He works 4 hours 30 minutes.

Key point
Remember 60 minutes = 1 hour

Measures, Shape and Space

2. Find the time worked by each worker.

	Started	Finished		Started	Finished		Started	Finished
a.	9 am	12:30 pm	b.	10:15	16:30	c.	12:10 pm	5:40 pm
d.	14:30	18:45	e.	7:30 pm	1 am	f.	22:45	06:30

3. Find each journey time.

	Departure	Arrival		Departure	Arrival		Departure	Arrival
a.	0615	1136	b.	1305	1723	c.	1910	2316
d.	1024	1436	e.	0816	1251	f.	1513	1726
g.	0822	1054	h.	1212	1436	i.	1806	2131
j.	1825	2134	k.	0628	1042	l.	2102	2314

4. A driver records when he starts and ends each journey in a day.

Journey 1   6:42 am–10:36 am

Journey 2   11:22 am–3.27 pm

Find the total driving time.

C. Find the difference between times by subtracting

Example

A journey starts at 10:15 am and ends at 1:46 pm. How long does it take?

Put the times into 24 hour clock time (if necessary)   10:15 to 13:46

Start with the final time   13:46

Subtract the start time   − 10:15   (Subtract)

Time for the journey =   3:31   = **3 hours 31 minutes**

Example

How long is it from 7:55 am to 2:10 pm?

In 24 hour clock time this is 07:55 to 14:10

Start with the final time   14:10   13:10 + 1 hour

Subtract the start time   − 07:55

You can't take 55 from 10, so change an hour into 60 minutes.

13:10 + 60 =   13:70

          − 07:55

Time between =   6:15   = **6 hours 15 minutes**

Practice

1. Find the time taken for these journeys.

- **a.** 1:15 pm to 3:42 pm
- **b.** 11:26 am to 1:55 pm
- **c.** 2:36 pm to 3:49 pm
- **d.** 1:26 pm to 2:59 pm
- **e.** 7:24 am to 2:50 pm
- **f.** 6:54 am to 1:05 pm
- **g.** 11:43 am to 1:32 pm
- **h.** 9:43 am to 1:28 pm
- **i.** 7:49 pm to 9:16 pm
- **j.** 11:56 am to 4:13 pm
- **k.** 3:33 pm to 5:13 pm
- **l.** 10:44 am to 9:13 pm

Time

2. The timetable below is for Eurostar.

London	Brussels
0609	1001
0653	1037
0822	1210
0827	1210
1022	1405

London	Calais
0614	0856
0619	0856
1148	1431
1153	1431
1518	1756

London	Paris
0922	1329
0927	1329

a. How long do these journeys take?

   i. 0822 from London to Brussels
   ii. 1022 from London to Brussels
   iii. 1153 from London to Calais
   iv. 0922 from London to Paris

b. What is the difference in journey time between the 0614 and the 0619 from London to Calais?

Activity

Plan a journey, a concert or an evening watching TV.

Write down the times for the start and end of each part/programme.

Work out how long each part takes.

Use timers

Specification reference EL3.M13, L1.M20

Alarm clocks can be set for any time. They use 12 or 24 hour clock time, with an analogue or digital display. **Analogue** means on a clock face or a scale.

These clocks have all been set to ring at 7 pm (to wake a nightshift worker).

The alarm hand on an analogue clock is usually a different colour.

(12 hour)

(24 hour)

Ovens often have timers — generally in 24 hour clock time. The diagram shows one type.

The oven will automatically turn on at 16:00 (4 pm).

The oven will stay on for $2\frac{1}{2}$ hours.

The meal will be cooked by 18:30, that is, 6:30 pm.

Measures, Shape and Space

Example

A meal takes 1 hour 20 minutes to cook. It must be ready by 18:00 (6 pm).

To find the time it needs to start cooking:

```
  18:00
-  1:20
-------
  16:40
```

The cooker times are as shown.

Meal ready for 18:00 (6 pm)

Practice

1. For each part sketch three clocks like the one on the right.
   Show the alarm time on each clock.

   a. 10:30 pm   b. 6 am
   c. 11:15 pm   d. 8:30 am

   (12 hour)   (24 hour)

   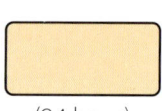

2. Copy the cooker display for each part. Fill in the times needed.

   a. You want a meal to be ready for 19:00.
      It takes $1\frac{1}{2}$ hours to cook.

   b. You want a meal to be ready at 17:30.
      It takes $2\frac{1}{4}$ hours to cook.

   c. A meal takes 1 hour 40 minutes to cook. You want it to be ready at 20:15.

   d. A meal takes $1\frac{3}{4}$ hours to cook. You want it to be ready at 7 pm.

Websites for different transport information have journey planners in which you need to enter where you want to travel from and to, the date, and either when you want to leave, or when you want to arrive.

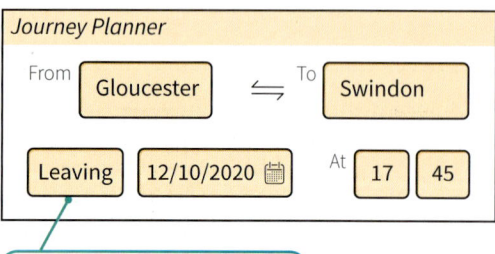

Activity

Investigate some train journey options using the National Rail website:
https://www.nationalrail.co.uk

Time

Some digital timers (such as stopwatches) show minutes, seconds and also tenths and hundredths of a second.

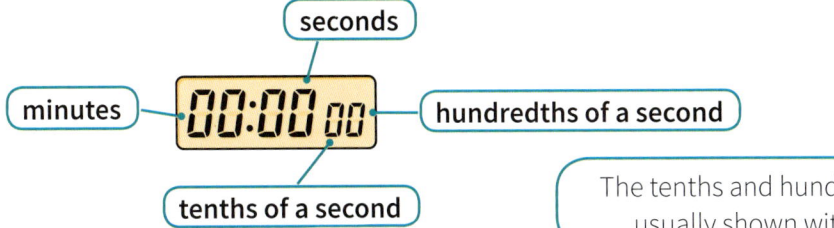

For example, these show the times for runners in a race:

1st **01:05 20** 1 minute, 5 seconds and 2 tenths of a second (1 min 5.20 s)

2nd **01:15 32** 1 minute, 15 seconds and 32 hundredths of a second (1 min 15.32 s)

3rd **01:16 02** 1 minute, 16 seconds and 2 hundredths of a second (1 min 16.02 s)

Example

The times of the first and second runners in a race are as shown.
How much quicker is the winner?

Put the longer time first.
```
minutes   seconds
4       : 02.38
3       : 56.23
```
You can't take 56.23 from 2.38, so change a minute to seconds.
```
minutes   seconds
3       : 62.38
3       : − 56.23    subtract
0         6.15
```

The winner is **6.15 seconds** quicker.

3. The race times of some runners are given below. Write them in words and figures.

   a. **01:16 47**   b. **01:21 05**   c. **01:16 59**
   d. **01:22 20**   e. **01:17 08**   f. **01:22 40**

4. Find the difference between each pair of times.

   a. **01:25 31** **01:27 52**   b. **02:43 03** **02:42 47**   c. **01:58 23** **02:00 38**
   d. **05:10 24** **04:59 56**   e. **04:36 01** **04:22 49**   f. **13:57 30** **14:22 32**

5. The times for the swimmers in the six swimming lanes in a race are given below.

   02:34 05 **02:49 30** **02:16 43** **03:01 09** **03:00 24** **02:44 51**

   Put the times in order, then find the difference between each time and the next.

Chapter Summary
12 Time

- 12:00 **am** – 11:59 **am** is morning time — from midnight to midday.
- 12:00 **pm** – 11:59 **pm** is afternoon and evening time — from midday/noon to midnight.
- There are 60 minutes in an hour, 30 minutes in half an hour, 15 minutes in a quarter of an hour.
- **Analogue clocks** have a clock face, with the short hand showing the hour and the longer hand showing the minutes past the hour, or to the next hour.
- Times can be written as minutes past the hour, like digital clocks. If the minute hand has gone past the 30 minutes, then you can write how many minutes there are to the next hour.
- On the analogue clock, to the nearest 5 minutes means to the nearest number marked on the clock.
- Time is written using a colon to separate hours and minutes, which should both be 2 digits (before 10 am, add a leading zero for the 1st digit and similarly for single digit minutes).
- **24-hour clock time** is used for digital clocks or timetables and numbers each hour from 00 to 23 instead of using am or pm.
- Add 12 hours to pm times to find the 24-hour clock time. This excludes 12 which is never written as 24:00, 12pm (midday) is written using 12 and 12am (midnight) is written using 00 instead.
- To read timetables, read down the 1st column to find the place you are looking for. Then read along the row to find the time you need.
- Timetables often omit the colon in a time.

- 60 seconds = 1 minute, 60 minutes = 1 hour, 24 hours = 1 day
- 7 days = 1 week, 52 weeks = 1 year, 12 months = 1 year
- There are 365 days in a year, or 366 days in a **leap year**.
- 100 years = 1 century, 1000 years = 1 millennium
- 30 days have September, April, June and November. All the rest have 31, except February alone which has 28 days clear and 29 each leap year.
- In finance, **per annum** means per year and **a quarter** = $\frac{1}{4}$ of a year = 3 months
- To help with some calculations, convert values from minutes to seconds or hours, or vice versa.
- To give an answer, convert values back into minutes and seconds or hours and minutes, when possible.
- Check answers by rounding the times to find an estimate.
- Some digital timers, such as stopwatches, show minutes, seconds and tenths and hundredths of a second. The tenths and hundredths of a second are usually shown with smaller font size.

Measures, Shape and Space

13 Length

Understand distance: miles and kilometres

Specification reference EL3.M14, EL3.M15

In Britain, we use **miles** to measure long distances on the roads.

In the rest of Europe, long distances are measured in **kilometres**.

>  **Key point**
>
> | | |
> |---|---|
> | km stands for kilometres | 1 km = 1000 m (metres) |
> | 1 mile is longer than 1 km | 1 km is about $\frac{2}{3}$ of a mile |

It takes about 20 minutes to walk 1 mile. It takes about 15 minutes to walk 1 km.

A. Use distances marked on a map

This is a sketch map of part of the county of Somerset. The towns are shown with dots.

The numbers give the distances in miles between the towns by road.

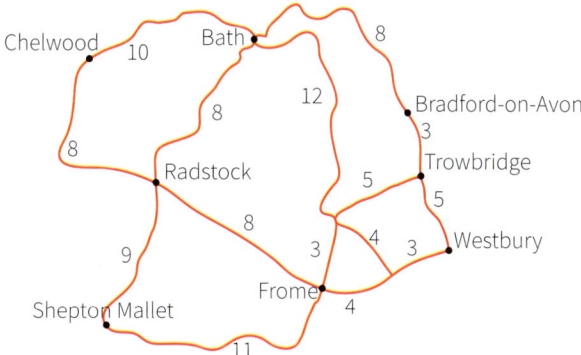

Practice

1. Find the shortest distance by road in miles between:
   a. Radstock and Bath
   b. Bradford-on-Avon and Bath
   c. Chelwood and Radstock
   d. Shepton Mallet and Bath
   e. Chelwood and Frome
   f. Westbury and Shepton Mallet
   g. Trowbridge and Bath
   h. Frome and Bath.

2. A taxi driver starts from Shepton Mallet. He travels to Frome, then Westbury and then Trowbridge by the most direct route. How far does he travel altogether?

3. A delivery van driver starts from Westbury and travels to Trowbridge. He then goes via Bradford-on-Avon to Bath and finally to Chelwood. How far does he travel altogether?

Measures, Shape and Space

B. Use a mile or kilometre chart

Distances in miles

Aberdeen						
216	Carlisle					
129	92	Edinburgh				
146	95	43	Glasgow			
261	45	137	140	Kendal		
84	132	45	62	177	Perth	
227	371	284	296	416	239	Thurso

To find the distance from Carlisle to Perth:

Look down from Carlisle.
Look across from Perth.

Distance = **132 miles**

Practice

1. Use the chart above. Find the distance between:
   a. Aberdeen and Kendal
   b. Edinburgh and Thurso
   c. Carlisle and Glasgow
   d. Thurso and Perth
   e. Perth and Aberdeen
   f. Thurso and Kendal.

Some charts show both kilometres and miles, like the chart below.
Check which side of the chart you need to look at.

2. Use the chart on the previous page to answer the following questions.
   a. What is the distance in kilometres from Birmingham to Oxford?
   b. What is the mileage between Gloucester and Nottingham?
   c. How many miles are there between Coventry and Derby?
   d. How many kilometres are there between Leicester and Stoke-on-Trent?
   e. What is the mileage from Coventry to Nottingham?
   f. How much longer, in miles, is the journey from Birmingham to Nottingham than the journey from Birmingham to Derby?
   g. How many more kilometres do you travel to get from Oxford to Derby than you travel to get from Oxford to Coventry?
   h. You travel from Birmingham to Oxford and then to Nottingham.
      How many kilometres do you travel altogether?

> **Activity**
> Use a road atlas to find the distance in miles from your home town to other towns by road. List the towns in order of distance from your home town.

Measure length in metric units

Specification reference **EL3.M14, EL3.M15, L1.M20**

A. Measure in millimetres and centimetres

A **millimetre** is about the width of this dot •
It is the smallest measurement most people use.

The width of your little finger is probably about a **centimetre**.

> **Key point**
> 10 mm = 1 cm

This ruler measures centimetres (cm) and millimetres (mm).

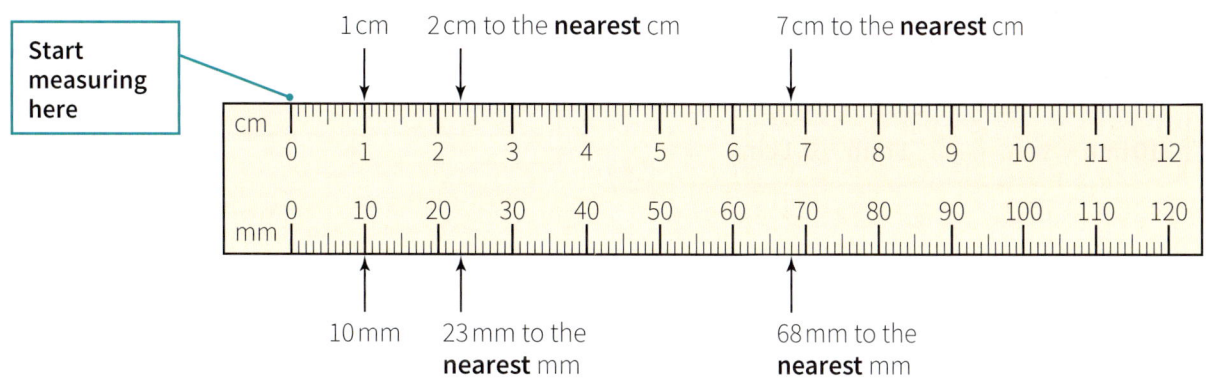

Measures, Shape and Space

Which is the correct way to measure the length of the needle?

A
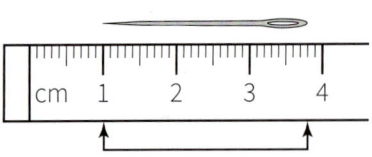

B
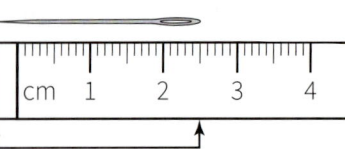

C
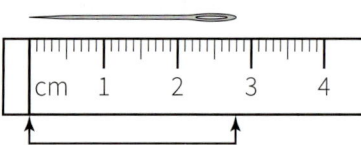

C is the correct way.

> The needle is **3 cm** long to the **nearest cm**.
> More accurately, it is **28 mm** long.

Practice

On the ruler below, the measurement marked by **a** is **1 cm to the nearest cm** and **13 mm to the nearest mm**.

> **Key point**
> Use the **numbered marks** for **the nearest cm**.
> Use the **other marks** for the **nearest mm**.

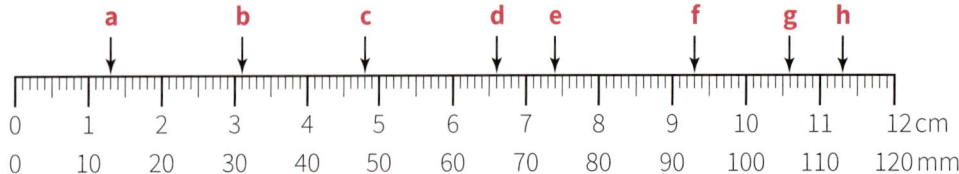

1. Write down the measurements marked by each of the other letters above the ruler.

   Give each answer:
   i. to the nearest cm
   ii. to the nearest mm.

   > **Key point**
   > The ruler shows that 10 mm = 1 cm so to change mm to cm, divide by 10. to change cm to mm, multiply by 10

2. Copy and complete these.

   a. 20 mm = ____ cm
   b. 3 cm = _____ mm
   c. 50 mm = ____ cm
   d. 7 cm = _____ mm
   e. 60 mm = ____ cm
   f. 8 cm = _____ mm
   g. 40 mm = ____ cm
   h. 9 cm = _____ mm
   i. 120 mm = ____ cm

> **Key point**
> You can write lengths using decimals.
> 10 mm = 1 cm means 1 mm = 0.1 cm

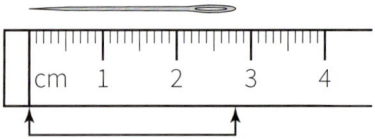

The needle's length = 28 mm or 2 cm 8 mm

This is the same as 2.8 cm

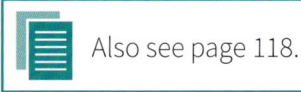
Also see page 118.

Examples: 42 mm = **4.2 cm**   1.7 cm = **17 mm**

3. Copy and complete these.

   a. 15 mm = ___ cm
   b. 1.2 cm = ____ mm
   c. 26 mm = ___ cm
   d. 1.3 cm = ____ mm
   e. 14 mm = ___ cm
   f. 2.1 cm = ____ mm
   g. 84 mm = ___ cm
   h. 3.9 cm = ____ mm
   i. 125 mm = ___ cm

Check that the length of this line is 57 mm

This is the same as 5 cm 7 mm

or 5.7 cm

The first decimal place gives mm.

4. Measure each line. Give each measurement in three different ways.

   a. _____
   b. _____
   c. _____
   d. _____
   e. _____
   f. _____
   g. _____
   h. _____

5. List the lines in question **4** in order of size, **longest** first.

Example

The distance between the rods is **36 mm** or **3 cm 6 mm** or **3.6 cm**.

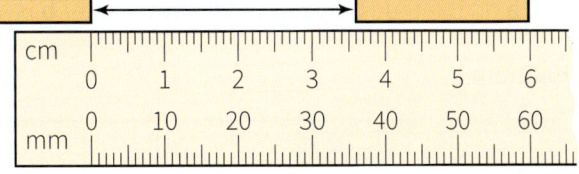

6. Measure the distance between each pair of rods. Write each distance in three ways.

   a.
   b.
   c.

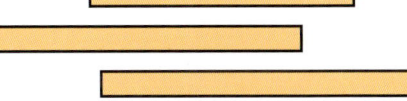

7. Measure the length of each item to the nearest mm. Write each answer in three ways.

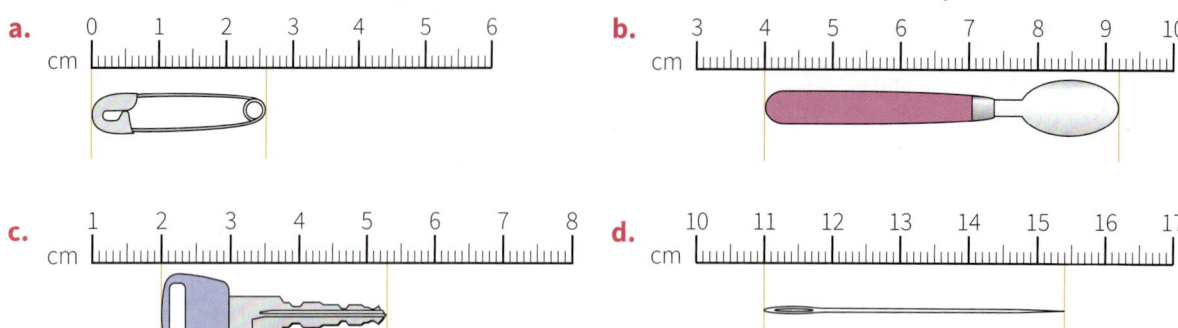

e. Which item was the easiest to measure? Why?

B. Measure in metres, centimetres and millimetres

Long tape measures are used to measure distances like the length of a room. They are labelled in a variety of ways. This tape measure is labelled in centimetres and millimetres.

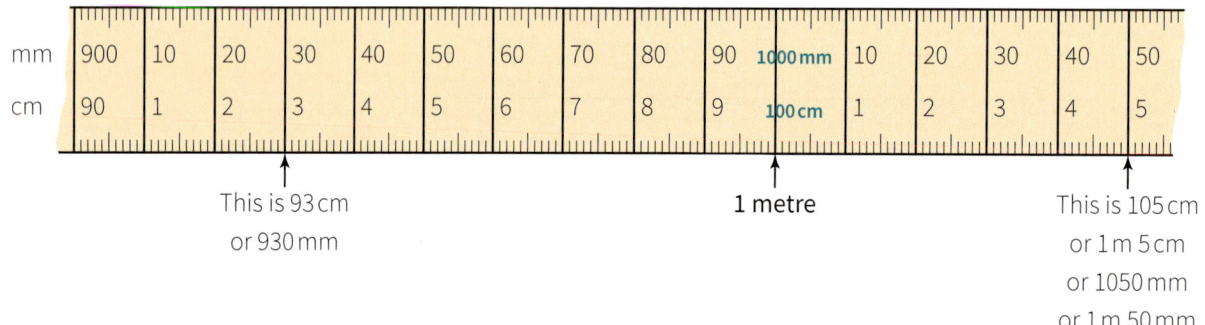

> **Key point**
> 1 m = 100 cm = 1000 mm

The tape measure shows that

Here is part of another tape measure near 1 m. It is labelled in a different way.

The measurement at **a** on the tape is **98 cm** or **980 mm**. Letter **b** is at **111 cm** or **1110 mm**.

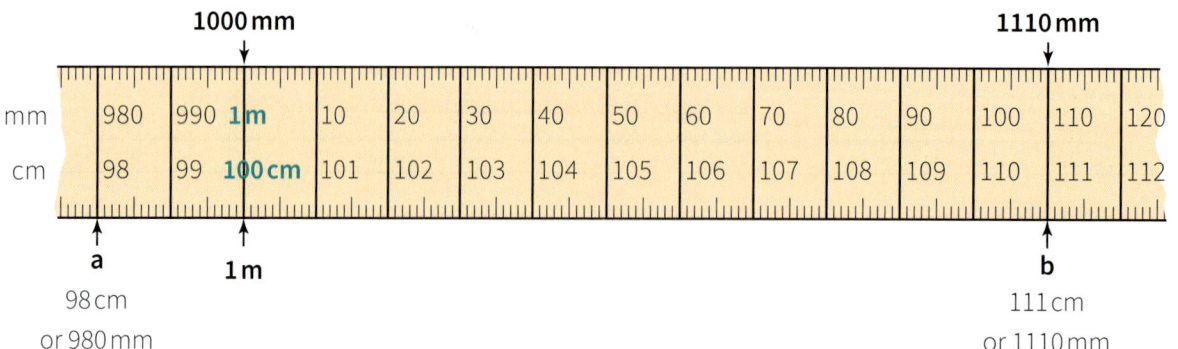

Length

The measurement at **a** is **98 cm** which is the same as **0.98 m**

The measurement at **b** can also be written as **1 m 11 cm** or **1.11 m**

Key point

Remember **1 cm = 10 mm**

The first 2 decimal places are cm.

Practice

For questions **1** and **2** use the ruler at the bottom of page 212.

1. Write the measurement at each of the other letters in cm then in mm.

2. Write the measurement at each of the other letters in metres using decimals.

3. The diagram below shows part of a tape measure labelled in centimetres.

   To the **nearest cm:**   **a** is at **365 cm** or **3.65 m**   and   **b** is at **367 cm** or **3.67 m**.

   i. Give the measurement at each of the other letters to the nearest cm.
   ii. Write each measurement in m using decimals.

4. You can use the small divisions on the tape measure to give lengths more accurately.
   On the tape measure in question **3**, **a** is at **364.8 cm**. In millimetres this is **3648 mm** (multiplying by 10).
   You can write this using metres as **3 m 648 mm** or **3.648 m**.
   b is at **367.4 cm** or **3674 mm** or **3 m 674 mm** or **3.674 m**.

   The first 3 decimal places are mm.

   Write the measurement at each of the other letters in these four different ways.

Activities

1. Copy the table. Use a tape measure, rule and/or trundle wheel to complete it.

Name	Length (m)	Length (cm)	Length (mm)	Width (m)	Width (cm)	Width (mm)
Room						
Window						
Table						

Measures, Shape and Space

Activities

2. Measure your height in metres, then centimetres to the nearest centimetre. Copy and extend the table. Fill it in for yourself and other members of the group.

Name	Height (m)	Height (cm)	Height (mm)

3. List everyone in your group in height order, starting with the tallest.

Estimate and measure lengths
Specification reference EL3.M14, EL3.M18, L1.M20

Sometimes you need to measure very accurately to make sure something will fit. For example, when checking to see whether a kitchen unit will fit into a space, you need to measure the space accurately.

The table suggests the most appropriate units and equipment to use when measuring something accurately.

People don't always use the suggested units. For example, builders usually use metres or millimetres, but not centimetres.

Length	Most appropriate units	Equipment
Short e.g. insect	millimetres (mm)	ruler micrometer
Medium e.g. book	centimetres (cm)	ruler tape measure
Long e.g. room	metres (m)	tape measure trundle wheel
Very long e.g. journey	kilometres (km)	trundle wheel pedometer mileometer

Sometimes you might round up your measurement to the next full unit. For example, when buying carpet you might round the length of the room up to the next full metre to make sure you have enough.

Sometimes you may just need a rough idea of the length; for example, when estimating the size of a lawn to work out how much lawn food you need.

Practice

1. In the following situations, do you need to measure accurately, or round up? Write **accurate** or **round up**.
   a. Measuring the gap for your new sink unit.
   b. Buying worktops that are sold in whole metres for your new kitchen.
   c. Measuring a space to fit a new piece of furniture.
   d. Measuring the height of your windows for new ready-made curtains.
   e. Buying a pane of glass to replace a broken one.

2. Match each item with a likely measurement.
   a. Width of a coffee table
   b. Length of a marathon
   c. Height of a door
   d. Length of a nail
   e. Length of a book
   f. Length of a pencil
   g. Length of a computer mouse
   h. Width of a nail head
   i. Width of a pencil lead

   30 cm   3 cm   14 cm   2 m   1 m   3 mm   40 km   1 mm   11 cm

Some rulers are marked only in centimetres. You have to estimate the number of millimetres.

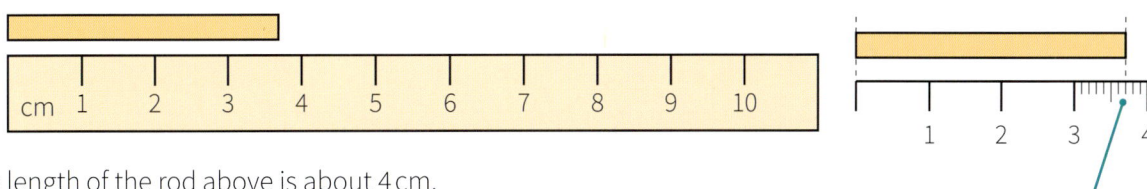

The length of the rod above is about 4 cm.

A more accurate estimate is 3 cm 7 mm or 3.7 cm.

Imagine the millimetres between 3 and 4.

3. a. Estimate the length of each rod below: i. to the nearest cm   ii. to the nearest mm
   b. Measure the lengths accurately.

A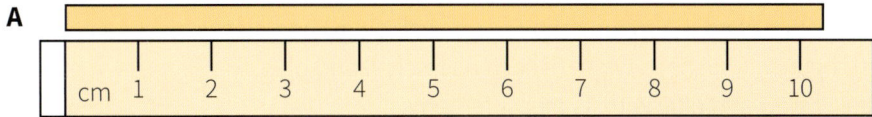

B, C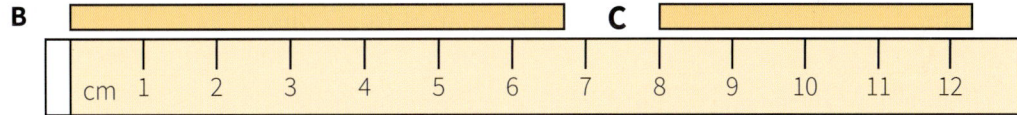

D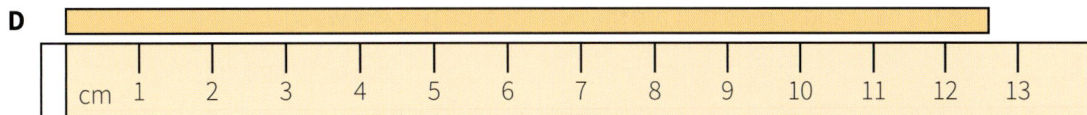

E, F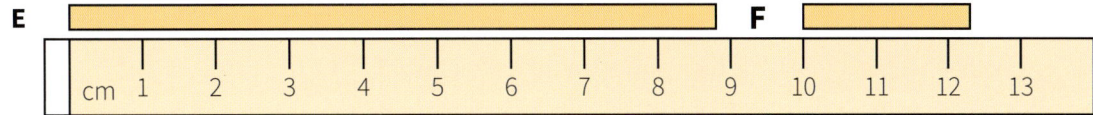

G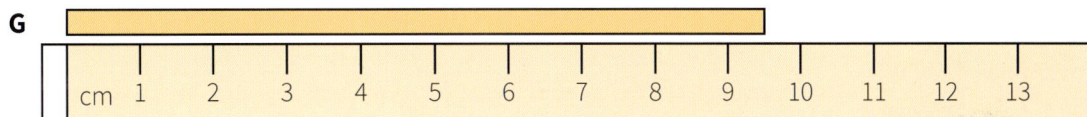

Activities

1. Copy and complete this table. Estimate, then measure, each length.

Length to be measured	Estimate to nearest cm	Accurate measurement
Width of your little finger		
Your handspan (across open hand)		
Length of your foot		
Length of your arm		
Length of a stride		

2. Copy and complete the following table.
   Estimate, then measure, each object to the nearest centimetre.

   Measure the items more accurately in millimetres.

Item	Estimate to nearest cm	Measurement to the nearest cm	Measurement in mm
Length of this book			
Length of a piece of paper			
Width of a piece of paper			
Length of your pencil			
Length of an eraser			

3. You will need a collection of nails, screws, screw plugs (wall plugs) and pieces of wood.
   a. Measure the length and pin head width of each nail, screw and plug.
      Label each nail, screw and plug with its measurements.
   b. Sort the nails and screws in order of length, starting with the shortest.
   c. Sort the nails and screws again, this time in order of pin head width.
   d. Match each screw with a plug.
   e. Sort the screws depending on the width of screwdriver they need.
   f. Measure the thickness of each piece of wood. Label them.
   g. Find the nails and screws that are the best for each piece of wood.

4. Without using a ruler, draw lines that you think are 1 cm, 2 cm, 3 cm, 4 cm and 5 cm long.
   Measure your lines with a ruler to see how accurate they are.

5. Measure the length of your arm span from fingertip to fingertip.
   Measure your height.
   Ask other people to measure their arm spans and their heights.
   Is it possible to estimate someone's height using their arm span?

Length

Convert between metric lengths

Specification reference **EL3.M15, L1.M20**

Key point

1 m = 100 cm = 1000 mm and 1 km = 1000 m

To convert lengths between units, you must multiply or divide by 10, 100 or 1000.

Examples

Convert:

600 mm to cm	120 cm to m	2 km to m	1.3 m to cm
600 ÷ 10 = **60 cm**	120 ÷ 100 = **1.2 m**	2 × 1000 = **2000 m**	1.3 × 100 = **130 cm**
3400 m to km	250 mm to m	0.5 cm to mm	0.04 m to mm
3400 ÷ 1000 = **3.4 km**	250 ÷ 1000 = **0.25 m**	0.5 × 10 = **5 mm**	0.04 × 1000 = **40 mm**

Practice

1. How many mm?
   a. 2.3 cm   b. 4.3 cm   c. 43.5 m   d. 4.5 m   e. 12.45 m   f. 2 km

2. How many cm?
   a. 13 m   b. 40 m   c. 9.6 m   d. 13.7 m   e. 65 mm   f. 2.5 km

3. How many m?
   a. 4000 mm   b. 5 km   c. 2400 cm   d. 5.84 km
   e. 0.74 km   f. 3534 mm   g. 530 cm   h. 680 mm
   i. 96 cm   j. 13.75 km   k. 0.659 km   l. 0.05 km

4. How many km?
   a. 7000 m   b. 9400 m   c. 450 000 cm
   d. 95 000 m   e. 2 500 000 mm

Measures, Shape and Space

5. Copy and complete these.

   a. 4 km = ____ m
   b. 5 m = ____ cm
   c. 45 cm = ____ mm
   d. 5000 m = ____ km
   e. 250 mm = ____ cm
   f. 360 cm = ____ m
   g. 275 cm = ____ m
   h. 275 m = ____ km
   i. 3.6 km = ____ m
   j. 2.7 m = ____ cm
   k. 12.2 cm = ____ mm
   l. 7563 m = ____ km

6. Put these in order of size. Start with the **smallest**.

   150 cm   650 mm   2 m   0.5 m   6 mm   2.6 cm   200 mm

7. A fence panel is 250 centimetres long. What is this in metres?

8. A race is 10 000 metres long. What is this in kilometres?

9. A worktop is 600 millimetres wide. Convert this to: a. centimetres   b. metres.

10. A door is 0.75 metres wide. What is this in: a. centimetres   b. millimetres?

Lengths can also be given using fractions.

 Also see page 90.

> **Examples**
>
> $\frac{1}{5}$ m = 1000 mm ÷ 5 = **200 mm**
>
> 75 cm = $\frac{75}{100}$ = $\frac{3}{4}$ m   (dividing top and bottom by 25)

---

11. Copy and complete these.

    a. $\frac{1}{2}$ m = ____ cm
    b. $\frac{1}{4}$ m = ____ cm
    c. $\frac{1}{2}$ m = ____ mm
    d. $\frac{1}{4}$ m = ____ mm
    e. 400 mm = ____ m
    f. 30 cm = ____ m
    g. 70 cm = ____ m
    h. 600 mm = ____ m

12. a. $1\frac{3}{4}$ m = ____ cm
    b. $3\frac{1}{2}$ m = ____ mm
    c. $3\frac{1}{4}$ m = ____ cm
    d. $3\frac{1}{5}$ m = ____ mm
    e. $5\frac{2}{5}$ m = ____ mm
    f. $3\frac{4}{5}$ m = ____ cm

Calculate with metric lengths

Specification reference **L1.M20**

A. Metres and centimetres

Units	.	Tenths	Hundredths
metres	.	$\frac{1}{10}$ metre	$\frac{1}{100}$ metre
100 cm	.	10 cm	1 cm

decimal point

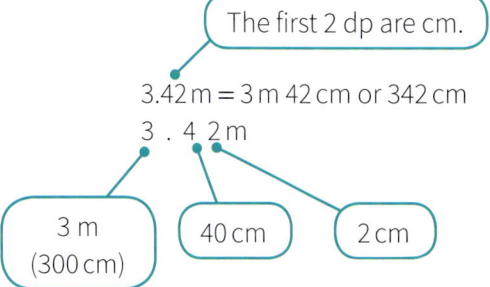

The first 2 dp are cm.

3.42 m = 3 m 42 cm or 342 cm

3 . 4 2 m

3 m (300 cm) 40 cm 2 cm

Example

1.5 m + 50 cm + 5 cm

Either **work in centimetres**:

1.5 m + 50 cm + 5 cm = 150 + 50 + 5 = **205 cm** or **2.05 m**

× 100 = 150 cm   Remember the units.

See page 131–132 to revise decimals.

```
  150
   50
+   5
  205
    1
```

Use a calculator to check.

or **work in metres using decimals**:

1.5 m + 50 cm + 5 cm = 1.5 + 0.5 + 0.05 = **2.05 m**

50 cm   5 cm   Remember the units.

```
  1 . 5
  0 . 5
+ 0 . 05
  2 . 05
    1
```

Keep the decimal points in line.

Key point

To add lengths they must be in the same units.

Practice

1. Work these out. Check your answers using a calculator or another method.

   a. 1.5 m + 75 cm + 5 cm + 3 m
   b. 3 m + 5 cm + 25 cm
   c. 2.5 m + 45 cm + 5 cm + 1.5 m
   d. 5 m − 75 cm
   e. 3.25 m + 90 cm + 5 m + 1.5 m
   f. 4 m + 4 cm − 40 cm
   g. 5 m − 125 cm − 1.5 m
   h. 3 m + 1.25 m − 150 cm
   i. 2.5 m + 1.1 m + 15 cm + 5 cm

See page 94 to revise mixed numbers.

Measures, Shape and Space

2. Work these out in metres.

a. $5m + 2\frac{1}{2}m$
b. $3\frac{1}{2}m - 1\frac{1}{4}m$
c. $2\frac{1}{4}m + 1\frac{1}{2}m$
d. $5\frac{1}{2}m - \frac{3}{4}m$

e. $2\frac{1}{2}m + 1\frac{3}{4}m$
f. $4m - 2\frac{1}{4}m - \frac{1}{2}m$
g. $5m + 3\frac{3}{4}m + 2\frac{3}{4}m$
h. $8m - 3\frac{3}{4}m - 1\frac{3}{4}m$

B. Metres and millimetres

Units	.	Tenths	Hundredths	Thousandths
metres	.	$\frac{1}{10}$ metre	$\frac{1}{100}$ metre	$\frac{1}{1000}$ metre
100 cm	.	100 mm	10 mm	1 mm

decimal point

The first 3 dp are mm.

4.275 m = 4 m 275 mm or 4275 mm

4 . 2 7 5 m

4 m (4000 mm)
200 mm
70 mm
5 mm

Example

3.5 m − 725 mm

Either **work in millimetres**:

3.5 m − 725 mm = 3500 − 725 = **2775 mm** or **2.775 m**

× 1000 = 3500 mm

Remember the units.

```
  3500
−  725
──────
  2775
```
Use a calculator to check.

or **work in metres using decimals**:

3.5 m − 725 mm = 3.5 − 0.725 = **2.775 m**

700 mm   20 mm   5 mm

```
  3.500
− 0.725
───────
  2.775
```
Fill up with zeros

Practice

1. Work these out. Check your answers using a calculator or another method.

a. 2.5 m + 125 mm + 50 mm
b. 3.5 m − 475 mm
c. 520 mm + 95 mm + 1.5 m
d. 1.4 m + 825 mm + 25 mm
e. 1.25 m + 950 mm + 3 m + 2.5 m
f. 2.6 m + 54 mm − 620 mm

C. Mixed calculations

Practice

1. Use metres or centimetres or millimetres. Give your final answer in metres.
   Check each answer using a calculator or another method.

   a. 25 cm + 375 mm + 2 m **b.** 4.36 m + 48.5 cm + 625 mm **c.** 35 cm + 195 mm + 2.5 m

2. A kitchen wall is 3 m long.
   Will a cooker of width 90 cm and units of width 60 cm, 1.2 m and 0.5 m fit along this wall?
   Show your working and explain your answer.

3. A gardener needs 20 m of lawn edging.
   She already has some pieces with lengths 2 m 40 cm, $1\frac{1}{2}$ m, $3\frac{1}{4}$ m, 2 m 80 cm and 4 m 60 cm.
   What extra length does she need?

4. A householder wants to make two new curtains, each 1.3 m long.
   He allows 15 cm extra on each curtain for hems.
   What total length of fabric does he use?

5. **a.** Mick has 5 m of red bunting, 7.5 m of green bunting, $4\frac{1}{2}$ m of white bunting and 520 cm of mixed red and white bunting.
   What length of bunting has he got altogether?

   b. Mick needs 36 m.
   How much more bunting does he need to buy?

6. **a.** An interior designer has $3\frac{1}{2}$ m of fabric for cushions.
   She makes 3 cushions, each using $\frac{3}{4}$ m.
   How much fabric is left?

   b. She also has $7\frac{1}{2}$ m of velvet.
   She makes 2 curtains, using $1\frac{3}{4}$ m each and 4 cushions using $\frac{3}{5}$ m each.

   i. How much velvet does she use?

   ii. How much velvet is left?

7. Wooden edging is put around the roof of a summer house. The length of wood required is $10\frac{1}{2}$ m.
   The builder plans to use the wooden slats from a fence panel.
   There are 18 slats in the fence panel, each with length 1.2 m.
   The builder thinks he will have half of the fence panel left over. Is he right?
   Explain your answer.

Measures, Shape and Space

Use a scale on a plan or map

Specification reference **L1.M21, L2.M18**

Level 1

Plans and maps use **scales**. The scale tells you the relationship between lengths on the plan or map and the real distances.

In this plan of a flat the scale is **1 cm to 2 m**. Each centimetre on the plan represents 2 metres in the actual flat.

Measure the length of the bedroom.
It is 3 cm on the plan.

The actual length = 3 × 2 = 6 m

Measure the width of the kitchen.
It is 1.5 cm on the plan.
The actual width = 1.5 × 2 = 3 m

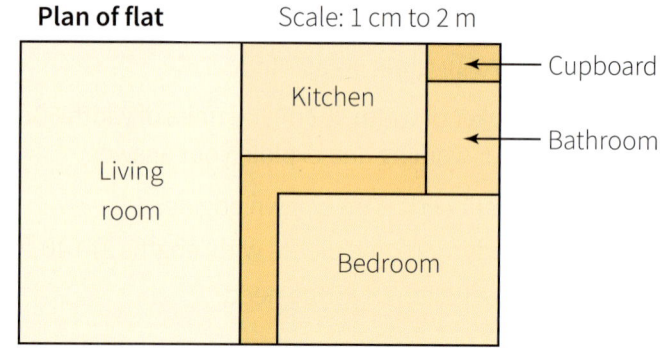

Plan of flat Scale: 1 cm to 2 m

These measurements have been put into the table in question **1** below.

Practice

1. Use the plan above. Copy and complete the table.

Room	Length on plan	Actual length	Width on plan	Actual width
Bedroom	3 cm	3 × 2 = 6 m		
Kitchen			1.5 cm	1.5 × 2 = 3 m
Living room				
Bathroom				
Cupboard				

222 MyMaths 1103, 1117 SEARCH

Length

2. Here is a plan of a group of houses.
Each house has its own plot of land.

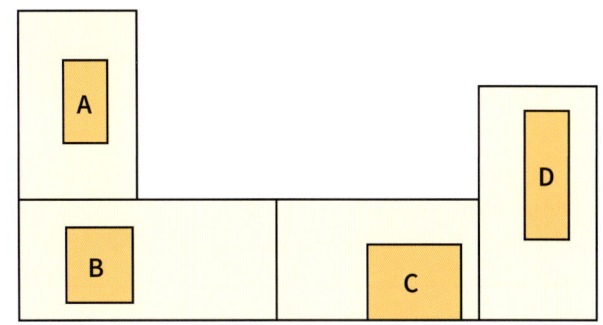

Scale: 1 mm to 1 m

Copy and complete the following table.

House	Measurements on the plan				Actual measurements			
	House length	House width	Plot length	Plot width	House length	House width	Plot length	Plot width
A								
B								
C								
D								

3. This drawing shows the front of a house.
The scale is 10 mm to 1 m.

a. On the drawing, measure in mm the heights of points A, B, C and D above the ground.

b. Use the scale 10 mm to 1 m, to find the actual heights of points A, B, C and D.

c. Copy and complete the table below by measuring from the plan in mm and then working out the actual measurements.

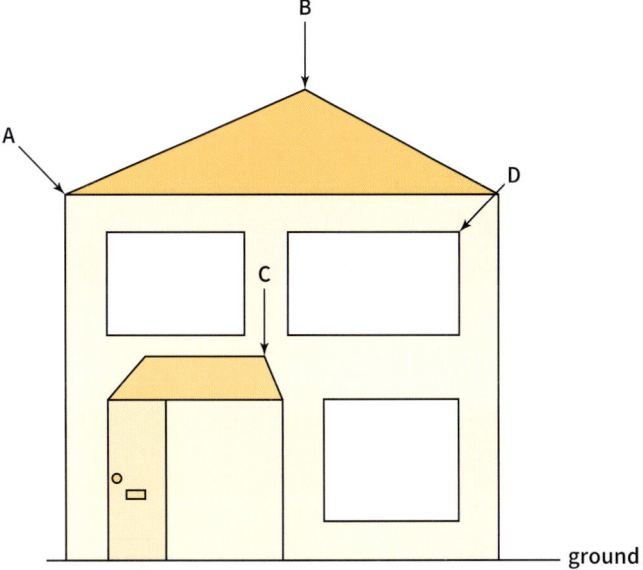

	Measurement on drawing (mm)	Actual measurement
i. The length of the house		
ii. The width of the downstairs window		
iii. The width of the smaller upstairs window		
iv. The width of the larger upstairs window		
v. The height of the downstairs window		
vi. The height of the upstairs windows		
vii. The width of the front porch		

Measures, Shape and Space

Maps often show the scale like this.
Use your ruler to measure the length of the line on this map which represents 10 km.
It is 2 cm long.
This means that on this map the scale is 1 cm to 5 km.
You can use this scale to measure distances on the map.

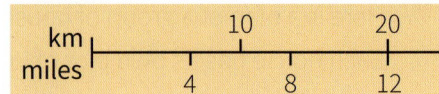

Example

Use a ruler to measure the distance between Harrogate and Otley. It is 2.8 cm.

The **direct** distance between Harrogate and Otley = 2.8 cm × 5 = **14 km**

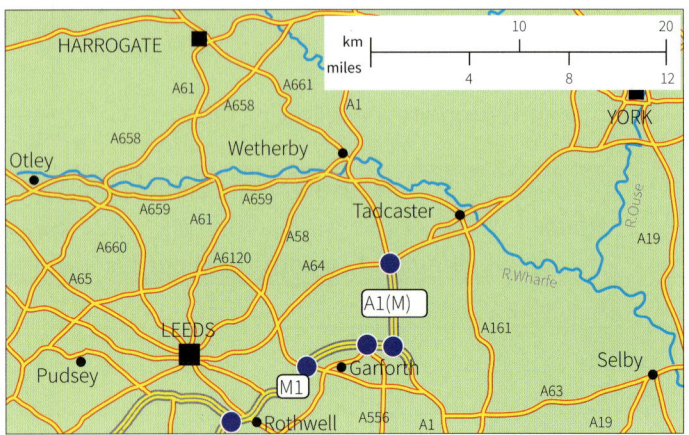

Sometimes you might want to measure distances that are not straight.

Example

To estimate the distance **along the road** from Leeds to Pudsey, lie a piece of cotton (or string) along the road on the map.

Then lie it along the scale.
The actual distance is 11 km or (7 miles).

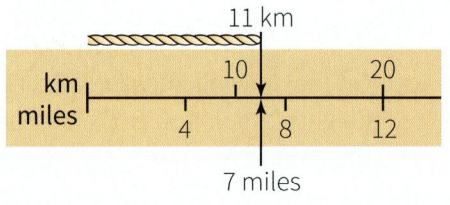

If the distance is too long to lie along the scale, measure the length of the cotton with your ruler. Then use the scale 1 cm to 5 km.

4. a. Use a ruler to find the **direct** distance in kilometres between:
    i. York and Tadcaster
    ii. Leeds and Garforth
    iii. Harrogate and York
    iv. Garforth and Tadcaster.

    b. Find the distance in kilometres **along the road** from:
    i. Leeds to Wetherby
    ii. Tadcaster to York
    iii. Selby to Wetherby
    iv. Wetherby to Harrogate.

5. A tutor uses this map when visiting college sites at A, B, C and D.

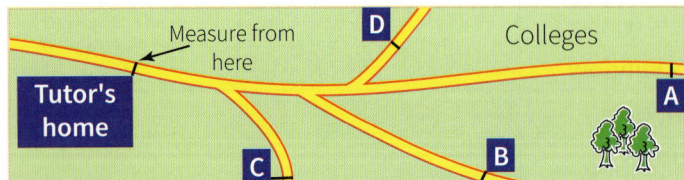

Scale: 1 cm to 500 m

Use the map on the previous page to copy and complete the table:

Journey	Length on map (cm)	Actual distance (km)
Tutor's home to A		
Tutor's home to B		
Tutor's home to C		
Tutor's home to D		

Use ratios on scale drawings

Specification reference L1.M21, L2.M18

A. Use ratio scales

A scale of **1:20** on a plan means **actual measurements are 20 times those on the plan**.
So 5 cm on the plan represents 20 × 5 = 100 cm (= 1 m) in real life.
Another way of giving this scale is **5 cm to 1 m**.

 Example

The plan of a shop has a scale of 1:500. On the plan the shop is 12 cm long and 9 cm wide.
What are its actual dimensions?

Length = 500 × 12 = 6000 cm   Width = 500 × 9 = 4500 cm
       = 60 m   = 45 m

Multiply by 500 to find the real length.

Divide by 100 to change cm to m.

 **Practice**

1. Some of the other measurements from the plan of the shop are given below.
   Use the scale 1:500 to find the actual measurements.
   a. Length of car park 10 cm
   b. Width of car park 6 cm
   c. Length of stockroom 5 cm
   d. Width of stockroom 4 cm
   e. Length of office 2 cm
   f. Width of office 1.2 cm
   g. Length of display area 3.2 cm
   h. Width of display area 2.3 cm

2. The plan of a flat has a scale of 1:200.
   a. Copy and complete the table to give the actual measurements of the rooms.
   b. What does 1 cm on the plan represent?
      Give your answer in metres.

Room	Dimension	Measurement on plan (mm)	Actual measurement
Lounge	length	30	
	width	25	
Kitchen	length	18	
	width	14	
Bathroom	length	15	
	width	12	
Bedroom	length	24	
	width	16	

Measures, Shape and Space

3. Here is a plan of the downstairs layout of a house.
   a. Measure the dimensions (that is, length and width) of Rooms A, B and C and the hallway D on the plan.
   b. Find the actual dimensions.

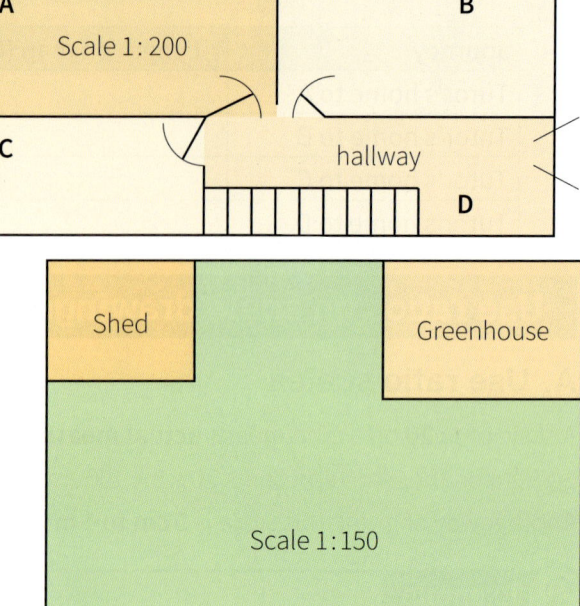

4. This is a plan of a garden.
   Find the **actual**:
   a. length of the patio
   b. width of the patio
   c. length of the shed
   d. width of the shed
   e. length of the greenhouse
   f. width of the greenhouse
   g. length of the whole garden
   h. width of the whole garden.

5. This map has a scale of 1 : 25 000.
   Copy and complete the table below.
   Measure the distances by road on the map as accurately as you can.
   (Places are shown by blue dots.)

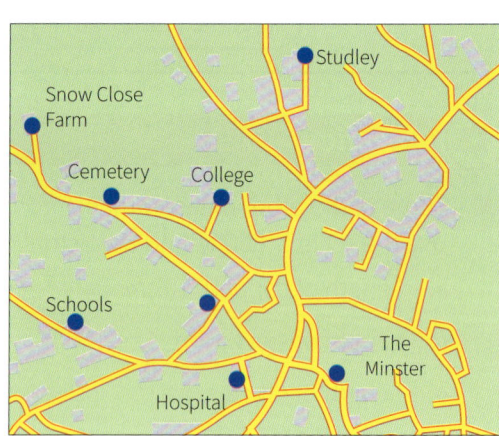

Journey	Distance on map	Actual distance
a. The Minster to the Hospital		
b. The Minster to the Cemetery		
c. Snow Close Farm to the Hospital		
d. College to the Minster		
e. Snow Close Farm to the Minster		
f. Schools to the Hospital		
g. Studley to the Minster		

To write a scale like 4 cm to 1 km as a ratio scale you must make the units the same, then simplify the ratio (if possible).

Example

4 cm : 1 km = 4 cm : 1 × 1000 × 100 cm
 = 4 : 100 000
 = **1 : 25 000**

Key point

1 km = 1000 m
1 m = 100 cm

This is the scale used on some Ordnance Survey maps.

Key point

To calculate a ratio start with the same units, then simplify.

6. Write each of these scales as a ratio.
   a. 1 cm to 1 m
   b. 2 cm to 1 m
   c. 5 cm to 1 m
   d. 1 cm to 20 m
   e. 1 cm to 500 m
   f. 2 cm to 5 km
   g. 5 cm to 8 m
   h. 4 cm to 5 km
   i. 1 mm to 1 m
   j. 5 mm to 1 km
   k. 1 mm to 0.5 cm
   l. 1 mm to 2.5 m

B. Draw scale diagrams

If the scale of a plan or map is 1 : n, then you need to divide actual distances by n to find the corresponding distances on the plan or map.

Example

A drive is 20 m long. How long is it on a plan with a scale of 1 : 500?

Length of drive = 20 m.
In cm this is 20 × 100 = 2000 cm

Key point

It is more convenient to work in cm for lengths on a plan or map.

On a plan with a scale of 1 : 500, the length of the drive = $\frac{2000}{500}$ = **4 cm**

Key point

Find measurements on a plan with scale 1 : n by first measuring with a ruler and then dividing by n.

Measures, Shape and Space

Practice

1. For each part, draw lines to represent the given distances to the given scale.
   a. Using scale 1:10, draw lines to represent   i. 60 cm   ii. 1.3 m
   b. Using scale 1:500, draw lines to represent   i. 16 m   ii. 24 m
   c. Using scale 1:200, draw lines to represent   i. 26 m   ii. 17.4 m
   d. Using scale 1:1000, draw lines to represent   i. 70 m   ii. 43 m
   e. Using scale 1:10 000, draw lines to represent i. 450 m   ii. 360 m
   f. Using scale 1:20 000, draw lines to represent i. 840 m   ii. 1.8 km
   g. Using scale 1:50 000, draw lines to represent i. 3.5 km   ii. 5.7 km

2. The sketch shows the dimensions of an office.
   It contains:

A	a computer desk	1 m by 1.5 m
B	a table	1.2 m by 0.6 m
C	a filing cabinet	60 cm by 50 cm
D	a shelf	40 cm wide.

   Draw a scale diagram using a scale of 1:25.

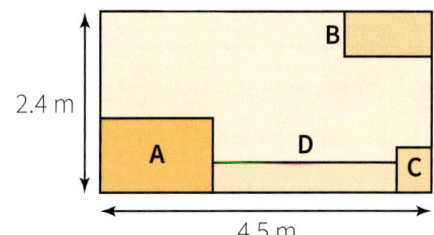

Activities

1. Use Ordnance Survey maps or maps from the internet to work out actual distances.
2. Measure a room and the largest items in it (for example, a classroom, lounge, kitchen or bedroom). Draw a scale diagram of the room.

Measure length in imperial units

Specification reference EL3.M14, EL3.M18

Entry Level 3

The imperial units for measuring lengths are **inches**, **feet**, **yards** and **miles**.

This ruler is marked in inches. Each inch is divided into 16 parts, called $\frac{1}{16}$ ths.

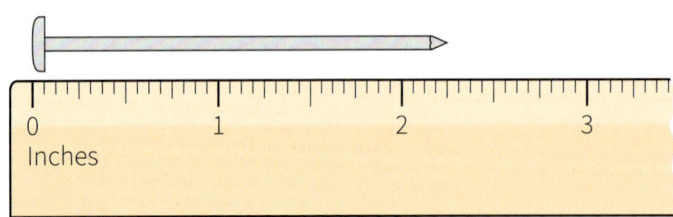

Screws, nails and wood thickness are sometimes measured in inches.

The length of this nail = $2\frac{4}{16}$ inches = $2\frac{1}{4}$ inches.

This can be written as $2\frac{1}{4}$ in or $2\frac{1}{4}"$

See page 87–89 for equivalent fractions.

Length

Practice

1. Measure the length of these screws and nails in inches.

a. b. c.
d. e. f.
g. h. i.
j. k. l.

Longer lengths, such as the length of a room, are measured in feet or yards.

1 foot = 12 inches   3 feet 6 inches can be written as 3 ft 6 in or 3′ 6″

1 yard = 3 feet   4 yards can be written as 4 yd

Activities

1. Estimate your height in feet and inches then measure it to the nearest inch. Estimate, then measure the heights of other students in your group. Put your results in a table.

2. a. Measure the length and width of the room in feet and inches.
   b. Write each measurement in yards, feet and inches.

Convert between imperial lengths

Specification reference **L1.M20**

Level 1

Key point

12 inches = 1 foot   3 feet = 1 yard   1760 yards = 1 mile

÷12   ÷3   ÷1760   ×1760   ×3   ×12
inches → feet → yards → miles   miles → yards → feet → inches

Activities

A shelf is 36 inches long. How many feet is this?

Length of shelf 36 inches   12 inches = 1 foot

36 inches ÷ 12 = 3 feet

The shelf is 3 feet long

Measures, Shape and Space

Examples

Convert:

72 inches to yards
72 inches ÷ 12 = 6 feet
6 feet ÷ 3 = 2 yards
so **72 inches** = **2 yards**

1 mile to inches
1 mile × 1760 = 1760 yards
1760 yards × 3 = 5280 feet
5280 feet × 12 = 63 360 inches
so **1 mile** = **63 360 inches**

4' 6" to inches
4' × 12 = 48 inches
48 + 6 = 54 inches
so **4' 6"** = **54 inches**

> Use a calculator when the arithmetic is very difficult.

Practice

1. How many inches?
   a. 5 yards
   b. 6'
   c. 28 feet
   d. 16 feet
   e. 2 yards
   f. 12 yards
   g. 9 feet 5 inches
   h. $4\frac{1}{2}$ feet

2. How many feet?
   a. 2 yards
   b. 80 yards
   c. 30 inches
   d. 144"
   e. 5 yards
   f. 60"
   g. $1\frac{1}{3}$ yards
   h. 28 inches

3. How many yards?
   a. 72 inches
   b. 15'
   c. 4 miles
   d. 144 inches

4. How many miles?
   a. 5280 yards
   b. 15 840 yards
   c. 17 600 yards
   d. 10 560 yards

5. A room measures 9' 9" by 12' 9". What is the perimeter of the room:
   a. in feet
   b. in yards?

   See page 309 for perimeter.

6. Three children measure their heights in inches:
   Hana 58 inches   Imran 65 inches   Caleb 73 inches.
   Write each height in feet and inches.

7. a. A carpenter has 3 lengths of wood:
      5' 4", 4' 8" and 3' 10"
      What length of wood is this altogether?
   b. The carpenter has a worktop surface of length 8' 4". She uses 3' 6" of the worktop. What length is left?

Length

Convert between metric and imperial lengths
Specification reference **L2.M14**

A. Approximate metric/imperial conversions

> **Key point**
> 1 inch ≈ 2.5 cm   1 foot ≈ 30 cm   1 m is slightly more than 1 yard

cm $\xrightarrow{\div 2.5}$ inches   feet $\xrightarrow{\times 30}$ cm

inches $\xrightarrow{\times 2.5}$ cm   cm $\xrightarrow{\div 30}$ feet

> **Key point**
> ≈ means approximately equal to

Example

This pencil is 4 inches long. How many cm?

1 inch ≈ 2.5 cm   so   4 inches ≈ 4 × 2.5 = 10 cm.   The pencil is **about 10 cm** long.

Practice

1. Copy the tables below, then use approximate conversions to fill the gaps.
   Remember to write the measurement carefully, for example, 3 yd 2 ft, not 3.2 yd.

   0.2 yd is $\frac{2}{10}$ of a yard.
   2 feet = $\frac{2}{3}$ of a yard.

Inches	Centimetres
2	
6	
8	
	7.5
7	
	25
	80
18	
	100

Yards/feet	Centimetres	Metres
2 ft		
$2\frac{1}{2}$ ft		
	90	
	105	
$4\frac{1}{2}$ ft		
	150	
	210	
2 yd 2 ft		
3 yd		

1 km ≈ $\frac{5}{8}$ mile or 0.6 miles   1 mile ≈ $\frac{8}{5}$ km or 1.6 km

km $\longrightarrow$ miles   miles $\longrightarrow$ km
÷ 8, then × 5   ÷ 5, then × 8

> **Key point**
> 5 miles ≈ 8 km

Examples

Convert:

40 km to miles	30 miles to km
40 km ÷ 8 = 5 then 5 × 5 = **25 miles**	30 miles ÷ 5 = 6 then 6 × 8 = **48 km**

Alternative method:

1 km ≈ 0.6 miles	**1 mile ≈ 1.6 km**
40 km ≈ 40 × 0.6 = **24 miles**	30 miles ≈ 30 × 1.6 = **48 km**

Not quite the same as before, but both 24 miles and 25 miles are good **estimates**.

2. **a.** Convert these distances to miles. **i.** 80 km **ii.** 208 km **iii.** 30 km
   b. Convert these distances to kilometres. **i.** 60 miles **ii.** 240 miles **iii.** 30 miles

3. The table below gives the distances between pairs of European cities.
   Copy the table, then use approximate conversions to fill the gaps.
   Use a calculator if you wish.

Journey	Miles	Kilometres
a. Paris to Boulogne	159	
b. Brussels to Calais		216
c. Berlin to Cherbourg	847	
d. Brussels to Dieppe		310
e. Paris to Dunkerque	174	
f. Frankfurt to Amsterdam	283	
g. Munich to Boulogne		944
h. Turin to Ostend		967
i. Zurich to Calais	476	
j. Warsaw to Dieppe		1675

Give answers to the nearest whole number.

B. More accurate conversions

Some more accurate conversion factors are given below.

Key point

1 inch = 2.54 cm   1 yard = 0.914 m   1 mile = 1.61 km

To convert, either multiply or divide by the conversion factor.

Look carefully at the examples on the next page. Use your calculator to check the answers.

Length

 Examples

Convert:

6 inches to cm
6 inches × 2.54 = **15.24 cm**

5 yards to metres
5 yards × 0.914 = **4.57 m**

4 miles to km
4 × 1.61 = **6.44 km**

15 cm to inches
15 cm ÷ 2.54 = **5.91 inches**

5 m to yards
5 m ÷ 0.914 = **5.47 yards**

6 km to miles
6 km ÷ 1.61 = **3.73 miles**
(rounded to 2 dp)

 Practice

Use a calculator where necessary.

1. Change these into cm. (First change into inches if necessary.)
   a. 4 inches   b. 9 inches   c. 10.5 inches   d. 1 ft   e. 1 foot 6 inches

2. Change these into metres. Give the answers to 2 decimal places.
   a. 10 yards   b. 6 yards   c. $4\frac{1}{2}$ yards   d. 7 ft   e. 180 inches

3. Change these into inches. Give the answers to 2 decimal places.
   a. 15 cm   b. 45 cm   c. 24.8 cm   d. 2.5 m   e. 3 m

4. Change these distances to miles. Give the answers to 1 decimal place.
   a. 48 km   b. 16 km   c. 40 km   d. 30 km   e. 23.5 km

5. Change these distances to km. Give the answers to 1 decimal place.
   a. 15 miles   b. 25 miles   c. 42 miles   d. 30 miles   e. $9\frac{1}{2}$ miles

6. a. A map says it is 640 miles from Berlin to Calais. How many kilometres is this?
   b. Rome to Cherbourg is 1090 miles. How many kilometres is this (to the nearest km)?

7. How many miles is this (to the nearest mile)?

8. The maximum speed limits on different roads in Europe are 120 km per hour and 100 km per hour. What are these speeds in miles per hour? Give answers to the nearest mile per hour.

 Lengths can also be converted using a conversion graph — see page 378–379.

Chapter Summary
13 Length

- To measure long distances, Britain uses miles and the rest of Europe uses kilometres (km).
- 1 km is about $\frac{2}{3}$ mile so 1 mile is longer than 1 km.
- It takes about 20 minutes to walk 1 mile and about 15 minutes to walk 1 kilometre.
- Metric units of length include: **millimetres** (**mm**), **centimetres** (**cm**), **metres** (**m**) and **kilometres** (**km**).
- Metric conversions include: 10 mm = 1 cm, 100 cm = 1 m and 1000 m = 1 km
- Rulers can be used to measure cm or mm (remember to start measuring from the zero, 0, mark).
- Depending on what is being measured, you can choose which measuring tool will be most appropriate: micrometer, ruler, tape measure, trundle wheel, pedometer or mileometer.
- If you don't need to be accurate then you can estimate a length by rounding up a measurement.
- Read unlabelled divisions on scales by finding the difference between marked values and dividing by the number of divisions.
- Imperial units of length include: **inches** (**in** or "), **feet** (**ft** or '), **yards** (**yd**) and **miles** (**m**) where 12 inches = 1 foot, 3 feet = 1 yard and 1760 yards = 1 mile
- An **inch** is divided into 16 parts, called $\frac{1}{16}$ ths (sixteenths).

- For metric units, multiply or divide by 10, 100 or 1000 to convert between different units of length using 1 mm = $\frac{1}{10}$ cm = 0.1 cm, 1 cm = $\frac{1}{100}$ m = 0.01 m and 1 m = $\frac{1}{1000}$ km = 0.001 km
- Plans and maps use **scales**, which give the relationship between lengths on the plan/map and the real dimensions/distances.
- Scales can be written as ratios of 1 : n where multiplying the measurements given on the plan/map by n will give the measurements in reality.
- Ratios have to be written in the same units before you can simplify the ratio.
- Multiply and divide using imperial conversions to convert between imperial measurements.
- To add or subtract lengths, the units must be the same.
- Take care with mixed imperial units, e.g. in and ft, they cannot be written easily as a decimal.
- Remember to write the units in the answer.

- A piece of cotton/string can be used to measure distances that are not straight on a plan/map.
- For scale ratios 1 : n, dividing real measurements by n gives the measurements of the plan/map.
- Approximate metric/imperial conversions are: 1 inch ≈ 2.5 cm, 1 foot ≈ 30 cm, 1 metre is slightly more than 1 yd, 1 km ≈ $\frac{5}{8}$ mile or 0.6 miles, 1 mile ≈ $\frac{8}{5}$ km or 1.6 km
- More accurate metric/imperial conversions are: 1 inch = 2.54 cm, 1 yard = 0.915 m, 1 mile = 1.61 km
- Lengths can also be converted using a **conversion graph**.

Measures, Shape and Space

14 Weight

Measure weight in metric units

Specification reference: EL3.M14, EL3.M16, L1.M20

A. Know metric units of weight

The common metric units for weight are **grams (g)** and **kilograms (kg)**.

1 g is about the weight of 10 matchsticks.

A bag of sugar weighs 1 kg.

Key point
1 kg = 1000 g

The weight of very small items like tablets is measured in **milligrams (mg)**.

Key point
1 g = 1000 mg

Practice

1. Which unit would you use to measure the weight of:

   a. a packet of tea
   b. a bag of flour
   c. a small tin of tuna
   d. a packet of crisps
   e. a frozen chicken
   f. a pill?

2. Each bag of satsumas should weigh 1 kg.
   Some bags are only partly filled. Their weights are given below.
   What weight of satsumas must be added to each bag to make 1 kg?

   a. 500 g
   b. 300 g
   c. 470 g
   d. 780 g
   e. 250 g
   f. 970 g
   g. 840 g
   h. 580 g
   i. 360 g
   j. $\frac{1}{4}$ kg
   k. $\frac{1}{2}$ kg
   l. $\frac{3}{4}$ kg

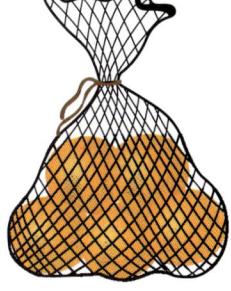

You can write weights in g, kg or a mixture of these units.

Examples

5000 g = 5 kg   5200 g = 5 kg 200 g

1000 g = 1 kg so
5000 g = 5 kg

 1105 SEARCH

Measures, Shape and Space

3. Write each of these weights in kilograms or a mixture of kilograms and grams.

   a. 7000 g   b. 4000 g   c. 2000 g   d. 8000 g
   e. 4200 g   f. 7300 g   g. 2600 g   h. 2870 g
   i. 5080 g   j. 5389 g   k. 5020 g   l. 1005 g

4. Write each of these weights in grams.

   a. 4 kg   b. 2 kg   c. 3 kg   d. 1 kg
   e. $1\frac{1}{2}$ kg   f. $1\frac{1}{4}$ kg   g. $2\frac{1}{2}$ kg   h. $3\frac{3}{4}$ kg

B. Measure in grams and kilograms

Practice

1. The spring balance on the right weighs up to 10 kg.

   a. How many parts is each kilogram divided into?
   b. How many grams does each small division represent?
   c. Write down in kg and g the weight shown by each arrow: **i, ii, iii, iv, v, vi**.

2. a. What is the maximum number of kilograms that you can weigh on these scales?
   b. How many parts is each kilogram divided into?
   c. How many grams are represented by each small division?
   d. Write down in kg and g the weight shown by each arrow: **i, ii, iii, iv, v**.

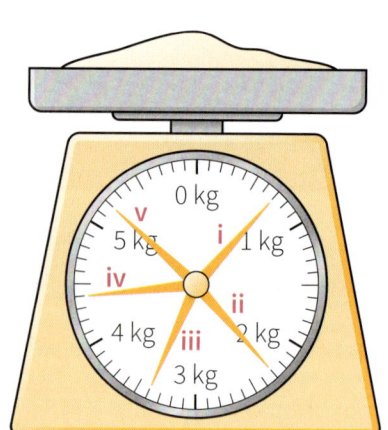
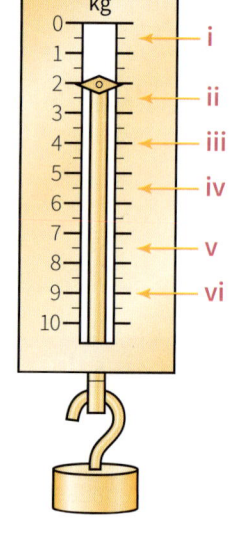

> Each kg on the scale is divided into 10 parts.
> Each part represents $\frac{1}{10}$ kg = 0.1 kg (= 100 g).
> So the weight shown by arrow **v** can be written as 5.2 kg.

   e. Write the weight shown by arrows **i–iv** in kg using decimals.

3. Some scales weigh only light objects.

   a. What is the maximum weight these scales can measure?

   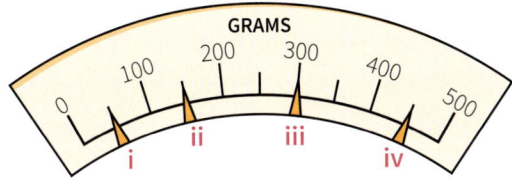

   b. What weight is shown by each arrow?

Look at the scale below. The first arrow is nearer 1 kg than 2 kg.

This means the first reading is 1 kg to the nearest kilogram.

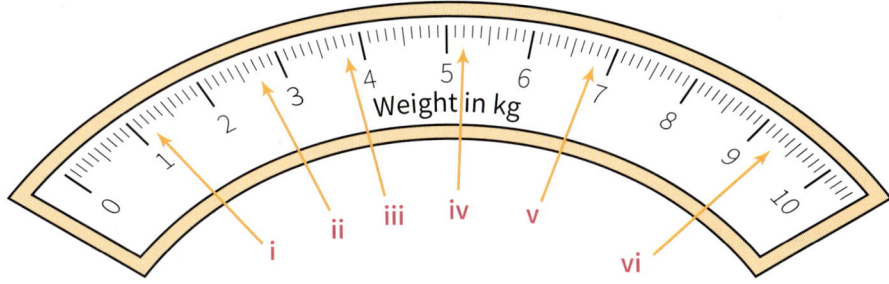

The second arrow is nearer 3 kg than 2 kg.

The second reading is 3 kg **to the nearest kilogram**.

---

4. Write down the rest of the readings on the scale above, giving each reading to the nearest kilogram.

5. Write the weight shown by each of the other arrows on the scale above:

   a. in kg and g   b. in kg using decimals.

   > Each small division on the scale represents $100\,g = \frac{1}{10}\,kg = 0.1\,kg$.
   > So the weight shown by arrow **vi** can be written as 9 kg 400 g or 9.4 kg.

6. Look carefully at this scale.

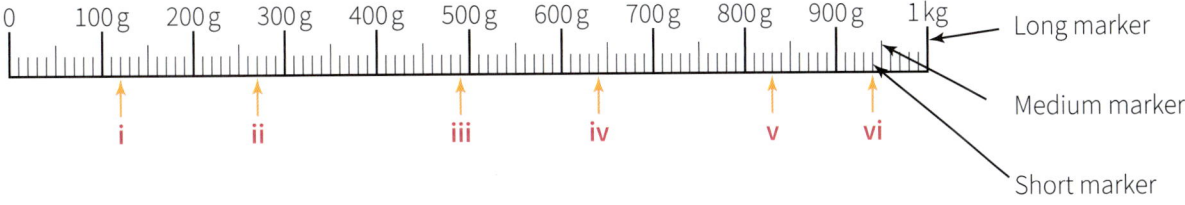

There is 100 g between each long marker and the next.

Measures, Shape and Space

a. What weight is between a long marker and the next medium marker?

b. What weight is between each short marker and the next short marker?

c. What is the weight shown by each arrow?

7. a. Write down, in kilograms, the weights shown by each arrow on this scale.

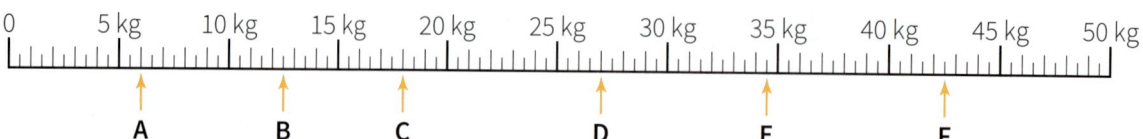

b. What is the difference in weight between:

   i. **A** and **B**   ii. **C** and **D**   iii. **E** and **F**?

8.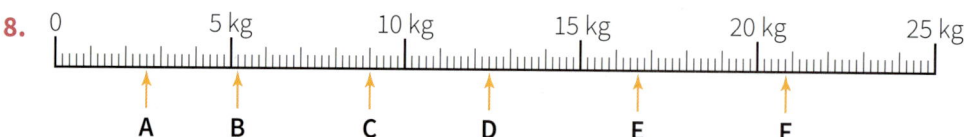

a. What do the medium markers show on this scale?

b. How many grams do the smallest divisions represent?

c. Write down the weights at **A**, **B**, **C**, **D**, **E** and **F**.
   Give your answers in kilograms and grams.

d. What is the difference in weight between:

   i. **A** and **B**   ii. **C** and **D**   iii. **E** and **F**?

C. Estimate weights between marked divisions

Some scales look like this.
You have to estimate between the labelled divisions.

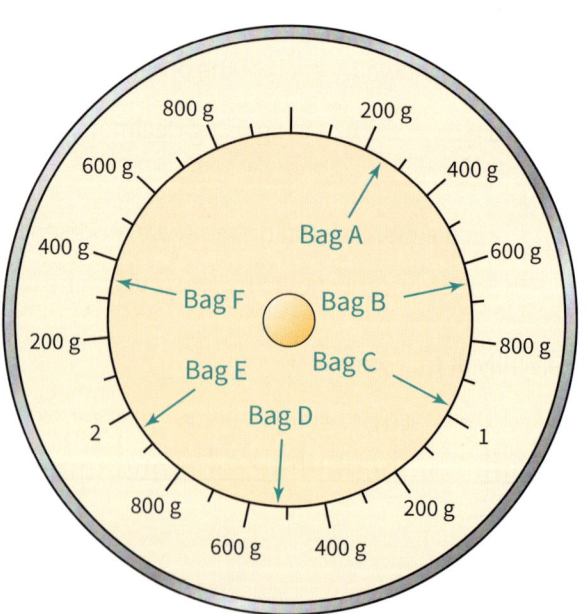

Practice

1. Look at the scale shown on the previous page.

    a. Estimate the weight of each bag as accurately as you can.
    b. Estimate the difference in weight between:
        i. bags **A** and **B**
        ii. bags **C** and **D**
        iii. bags **E** and **F**
        iv. bags **A** and **F**
        v. bags **C** and **E**
        vi. bags **B** and **D**.
    c. How much needs to be added to bags **A**, **B** and **C** if they should each weigh $1\frac{1}{4}$ kg?
    d. How much needs to be added to bags **D**, **E** and **F** if they should each weigh $2\frac{1}{2}$ kg?
    e. There is also a bag **G**. The total weight of the seven bags is 10 kg. What is the weight of bag **G**?

Activities

1. Write down an estimate of the weight of 10 items in grams or kilograms.
   Use a table like this.

Item	Estimated weight	Measured weight

   Use scales or a spring balance to weigh each item accurately.

2. Estimate your own weight in kg. Weigh yourself. How accurate was your estimate?
   Ask other people you know if you can weigh them.
   (Remember that people are often sensitive about their weight.)
   Put your results in a table.

3. Use a set of kitchen scales to weigh 100 g of sugar. Put it in a bag.
   Weigh 100 g of paper.
   Find a book that you think weighs about 100 g. Weigh the book as accurately as you can.
   How close was it to 100 g?

4. Choose 10 objects that you have not weighed before.
   (For example, you could use things like a bunch of 5 pens.)
   Estimate the weight of each object to the nearest 50 g.
   Weigh the objects. Record your results in a table.
   Now list the objects in order of their weights, starting with the **lightest**.

Measures, Shape and Space

Choose units and instruments
Specification reference EL3.M18, L1.M20

Practice

1. For each item choose a likely weight.

   a. Medium tin of beans
   b. Packet of crisps
   c. Bag of potatoes
   d. Packet of crackers
   e. Bag of flour
   f. Egg
   g. Packet of butter
   h. Box of 160 tea bags
   i. Bag of sugar
   j. Adult's weight

   25 g   250 g   410 g   5 kg   50 g   70 kg   125 g   500 g   1.5 kg   1 kg

2. Items are often weighed to the nearest **gram**, **10 grams**, **100 grams** or **kilogram**. How accurately would you weigh these items?

   a. A bag of concrete mix
   b. Airmail letters
   c. Sugar for a cake recipe
   d. Carrots for a large batch of soup

3. a. Which of these scales would be the best to weigh each of these parcels?

   P — 9 kg   Q — 4 kg 400 g   R — 8.5 kg   S — 5.4 kg

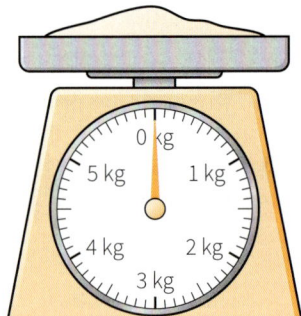

Scale A   Scale B

   b. Put the parcels in order of weight, **lightest** first.
   c. A postman weighs a parcel on scale **A** and says it weighs 3 kg 500 g.

   He then measures it on scale **B** and says it weighs 3 kg 600 g. Which answer do you think is likely to be more accurate? Why?

Convert between metric weights
Specification reference L1.M20

Key point
1000 mg = 1 g   1000 g = 1 kg   1000 kg = 1 tonne

To convert between these units you need to multiply or divide by 1000

from **mg** →÷1000→ **g** →÷1000→ **kg** →÷1000→ **tonnes**   from **tonnes** →×1000→ **kg** →×1000→ **g** →×1000→ **mg**

240

Weight

Examples

Convert:

5000 mg to g
5000 ÷ 1000 = **5 g**

6700 g to kg
6700 ÷ 1000 = **6.7 kg**

200 kg to tonnes
200 ÷ 1000 = **0.2 tonnes**

1.5 g to mg
1.5 × 1000 = **1500 mg**

0.625 kg to g
0.625 × 1000 = **625 g**

0.08 tonnes to kg
0.08 × 1000 = **80 kg**

The first 3 figures after the decimal point are grams.

Practice

1. How many kilograms?
   a. 4000 g
   b. 6500 g
   c. 5485 g
   d. 34 500 g
   e. 800 g
   f. 250 g
   g. 300 000 g
   h. 750 000 mg
   i. 4 tonnes
   j. 3.54 tonnes
   k. 0.5 tonnes
   l. 0.25 tonnes

2. How many grams?
   a. 7 kg
   b. 4.5 kg
   c. 8.268 kg
   d. 16.4 kg
   e. 3.05 kg
   f. 0.3 kg
   g. 0.06 kg
   h. 1.025 kg
   i. 2000 mg
   j. 7500 mg
   k. 500 mg
   l. 0.001 tonne

3. How many milligrams?
   a. 44 g
   b. 30.5 g
   c. 3.3 g
   d. 0.83 g
   e. 12.3 g
   f. 0.07 g
   g. 0.05 kg
   h. 3.75 kg

4. How many tonnes?
   a. 503 000 kg
   b. 42 000 kg
   c. 4500 kg
   d. 589 000 g

5. Copy and complete these.
   a. 3 tonnes = _____ kg
   b. 0.5 g = _____ mg
   c. 1.5 kg = _____ g
   d. 0.5 tonnes = _____ kg
   e. 7 tonnes = _____ kg
   f. 0.25 g = _____ mg
   g. 750 kg = _____ tonnes
   h. 5000 kg = _____ tonnes
   i. 10 kg = _____ g

6. Put each group in order of size, starting with the **smallest**.
   a. 450 g   0.4 kg   4 000 000 mg   0.4 tonnes   450 kg
   b. $\frac{1}{2}$ kg   0.25 kg   330 g   25 600 mg   0.45 kg

Measures, Shape and Space

Calculate using metric weights

Specification reference **L1.M20**

Level 1 A. Kilograms and grams

Parts of a kilogram

Units	.	Tenths	Hundredths	Thousandths
kg	.	$\frac{1}{10}$ g	$\frac{1}{100}$ kg	$\frac{1}{1000}$ kg
1000 g	.	100 g	10 g	1 g

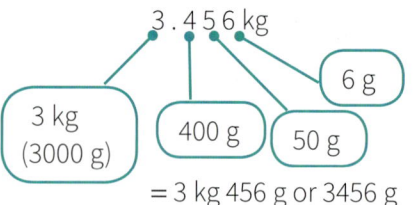

The first 3 dp are grams.

3.456 kg

3 kg (3000 g)   400 g   50 g   6 g

= 3 kg 456 g or 3456 g

Example

1.5 kg + 400 g + 30 g + 5 g

Either **work in grams**:

1.5 kg + 400 g + 30 g + 5 g = 1500 + 400 + 30 + 5 = **1935 g** or **1.935 kg**

× 1000 = 1500 g

Remember the units.

```
  1500
   400
    30
+    5
  1935
```

or **work in kilograms using decimals**:

1.5 kg + 400 g + 30 g + 5 g = 1.5 kg + 0.4 kg + 0.03 kg + 0.005 kg
= **1.935 kg**

Remember the units.   4 × 100 g   3 × 10 g   5 g

Use a calculator to check.

```
   1.5
   0.4
   0.03
+  0.005
   1.935
```

Practice

1. Work these out. Give the answer in kilograms if it is more than 1000 g.
   Check your answers using a calculator or another method.

   a. 3 kg + 500 g + 2 kg + 200 g
   b. 2.5 kg + 500 g + 75 g
   c. 700 g + 2 kg + 400 g + 50 g
   d. 1.5 kg + 500 g + 0.25 kg
   e. 1 kg + 750 g + 20 g + 2 kg
   f. 4 kg + 20 g − 1.75 kg
   g. $5\frac{1}{2}$ kg − 800 g
   h. 2.5 kg − 900 g
   i. 4 kg − 60 g
   j. 2 kg − 400 g + 25 g
   k. 2 kg − 100 g − $\frac{1}{4}$ kg
   l. 4 kg + 40 g + 4 g
   m. 2 kg + 300 g + 40 g + 5 g
   n. 1 kg − 4 g

 See pages 130–131 to revise adding and subtracting decimals.

242   MyMaths 1105 SEARCH

2. Find the difference in weight between:

   a. 1.75 kg and 5 kg
   b. 3.5 kg and 1.75 kg
   c. 475 g and 6.5 kg.

3. Three parcels weigh 2.75 kg, 2.5 kg and 800 g.
   What is their total weight?

4. How much flour must be added to 285 g to make 570 g?

5. A bag of frozen peas holds $2\frac{1}{2}$ kg. A chef uses 700 g.
   What weight is left?

6. A piece of cheese weighs 1.2 kg. Two pieces, each weighing 120 g are used for lunch packs.
   What weight of cheese is left? Give the answer in grams.

7. A woman makes a cake. She uses 150 g flour, 150 g butter, 150 g sugar, 250 g mixed dried fruit, 100 g fruit peel and 50 g chopped cherries.
   What is the total weight of these ingredients?

8. A fruit grower picks 2.4 kg of strawberries and 1.75 kg of raspberries.

   a. How many more grams of strawberries than raspberries does she pick?
   b. She uses 500 g of strawberries and 400 g of raspberries in a fruit pudding.
      What total weight of strawberries and raspberries is left?
      Give your answer in kg.

B. Mixed calculations

Practice

1. A caterer buys 10 kg of potatoes, $1\frac{1}{2}$ kg of tomatoes, $1\frac{1}{4}$ kg of carrots and $1\frac{3}{4}$ kg of apples.
   What is the total weight of the shopping?

2. Small pots hold 50 g of salt. How many pots can be filled from a $\frac{1}{2}$ kg bag?

3. A shopper buys $\frac{1}{2}$ kg of spinach, 2.5 kg of sweet potatoes, $\frac{1}{4}$ kg of onions and a bag of mushrooms weighing 360 g. How heavy is the shopping?

4. A tin of beans weighs 440 g. How much do 6 tins of beans weigh in kilograms?

5. A box weighs 420 g. A second box is 4 times as heavy. What is the total weight of the 2 boxes?
   Give the answer in kilograms.

6. A bag of 12 grapefruit weighs 4.2 kg. Find the average weight per grapefruit.

7. How many 300 g bags of nuts can be made from 4.5 kg of nuts?

Measures, Shape and Space

8. 360 g of cake mix is divided equally between 24 small cake papers.
   How much cake mix is in each cake paper?

9. 2.5 kg of yeast is put into 50 g packets. How many packets are there?

10. A crate holds 17 kg biscuits. The biscuits are in packets each holding 340 g.
    How many packets are there in the crate?

C. Kilograms and tonnes

Practice

1. A hospital uses 125 kg potatoes each day.
   How long will a 2 tonne delivery of potatoes last?

   Key point
   Remember 1000 kg = 1 tonne

2. A tonne of grain is divided into 2.5 kg bags.
   How many bags are there?

3. A diesel locomotive weighs 100 tonnes.
   A car transporter truck weighs 20 tonnes and carries 4 cars. Each car weighs 800 kg.
   There are 15 full transporter trucks.

   a. Find the total weight of the cars on the trucks in tonnes.

   b. i. Which is the greater weight: the cars or the diesel locomotive?

      ii. Work out the difference in weight in tonnes.

   c. What is the total weight of the car transporter trucks?

   d. What is the total weight of the locomotive, transporter trucks and cars?

Weigh with metric and imperial units

Specification reference EL3.M14, EL3.M18

Grams (g) and **kilograms (kg)** are **metric** units.
Ounces (oz), **pounds (lb)** and **stones (st)** are **imperial** units.
Many scales show both metric and imperial units.

Key point
1000 g = 1 kg

Key point
16 oz = 1 lb   14 lbs = 1 st

Activities

1. Use grams, then ounces, to weigh some items,
   for example, a book, a dictionary, a pencil case or a bag.

2. Use kilograms, then pounds, to weigh some items,
   for example, a rubbish bin, 5 books, a chair, yourself.

Weight

Convert between imperial weights

Specification reference **L1.M20**

Level

💡 Key point

16 oz = 1 lb   14 lb = 1 st   2240 lb = 1 ton

Note: A ton is different from the metric tonne.

```
      ÷16      ÷14                          ×14      ×16
ounces   pounds   stones   tons    tons   stones   pounds   ounces
                   ÷2240                    ×2240
```

🔍 Examples

Convert:

3 st to lb	2 lb 4 oz to oz	64 oz to lb	$\frac{1}{2}$ ton to lb.
3 × 14 = **42 lb**	2 × 16 = 32 oz	64 ÷ 16 = **4 lb**	2240 ÷ 2 = **1120 lb**
	32 + 4 = **36 oz**		

⚙ Practice

Use a calculator where necessary.

1. Convert these to ounces (oz).

   a. 2 lb
   b. 4 lb 6 oz
   c. 6 lb 4 oz
   d. 12 lb
   e. 4 lb 8 oz
   f. 3 lb 7 oz
   g. $\frac{1}{4}$ lb
   h. $\frac{1}{2}$ lb
   i. $\frac{3}{4}$ lb
   j. $2\frac{1}{2}$ lb

2. How many pounds (lb) are there in each of these?

   a. 16 oz
   b. 96 oz
   c. 48 oz
   d. 128 oz
   e. 80 oz
   f. 2 st
   g. 4 st
   h. $2\frac{1}{2}$ st
   i. 2 tons
   j. $1\frac{1}{2}$ tons

Take care with mixed imperial weights.

🔍 Example

To convert 72 oz to lb and oz:

Find how many whole pounds first   72 ÷ 16 = 4 whole lbs
Find how many ounces are used   4 × 16 = 64 oz
Find how many ounces are left   72 oz
                                           − 64 oz
                                           8 oz

so 72 oz = **4 lb 8 oz**

You can do this by long division, but take care if you use a calculator. This gives 4.5 lb. The 0.5 is half of a pound, **not** 5 ounces.

💡 Key point

When calculating a value in pounds, the decimal digits give fractions of a pound, **not** ounces.

Measures, Shape and Space

3. How may lb and oz are there in each of these?

   a. 56 oz
   b. 82 oz
   c. 38 oz
   d. 73 oz
   e. 44 oz
   f. 20 oz
   g. 55 oz
   h. 81 oz

Calculate using imperial weights

Specification reference L1.M20

Level 1 — Practice

Use a calculator where necessary.

1. Jacob weighs 183 lb. What is this in stones and pounds?

2. Amir weighs 115 lb. What is this in stones and pounds?

3. How much lighter is Amir than Jacob:

   a. in pounds
   b. in stones and pounds?

4. Paul's weight is halfway between Jacob and Amir. How much does Paul weigh:

   a. in pounds
   b. in stones and pounds?

5. What is the average weight of Jacob, Amir and Paul?

6. a. Jacob decides to lose weight. He starts at 183 lb and loses 4 lbs in the first week of his diet. Copy and complete his weight chart.

	Week 1	Week 2	Week 3	Week 4	Week 5	Week 6
Weight lost	4 lb	4 lb		3 lb		2 lb
New weight in stones and pounds					11 st 11 lb	
New weight in pounds	179 lb		171 lb			

   b. How much did Jacob lose altogether during these six weeks?
   c. How much more weight must he lose to reach his target of 10 st 7 lb?

7. Paul makes a cake using the following ingredients:

   4 oz butter
   4 oz flour
   3 oz sugar
   1 oz cherries
   3 oz mixed sultanas, raisins and mixed peel
   6 oz ready-made icing

   a. What is the weight of the cake?
   b. The cake is used for a competition 'Guess the weight of the cake'. Amir guesses that the weight is $2\frac{1}{2}$ lb.
   How many oz over or under the real weight is this guess?

Convert between metric and imperial weights

Specification reference: **L2.M14**

A. Approximate metric/imperial conversions

Level 2

Activity

Weigh some items in ounces and then the same items in grams.
Some suggestions are given in the table.

Item	Weight (oz)	Weight (g)
Calculator		
5 pens		
A pad of paper		
Pencil case		

Key point

1 oz ≈ 25 g   1 lb ≈ 450 g

Remember this sign means 'approximately equal to'.

An ounce is about the same as 25 grams.
If your pencil case weighs 4 oz, it should weigh about 100 g (4 × 25 = 100).
Check your measurements in the table in the same way.

Key point

Approximate conversion factors between metric and imperial units of weight are:

1 lb is just under $\frac{1}{2}$ kg (about 450 g)   1 kg is just over 2 lb   1 oz ≈ 25 g

Examples

$4\frac{1}{2}$ kg ≈ $4\frac{1}{2}$ × 2 = **9 lb**   360 g ≈ 360 ÷ 25 = **14 oz** (nearest oz)

Practice

Use the approximate conversion factors above to answer these questions.

1. Which is the correct answer?

   a. 4 oz is approximately _____.   5 g   2 kg   100 g   50 g
   b. 1 kg is _____ than 2 lb?   more   less

2. A recipe has the following ingredients.
   Convert each weight into ounces (to the nearest ounce).

   a. 375 g margarine   b. 250 g currants   c. 560 g raisins
   d. 280 g peel   e. 480 g breadcrumbs   f. 720 g flour

Measures, Shape and Space

3. Pineapple cake has the following ingredients.
   Give approximate conversions into grams (to the nearest 5 grams).

   a. 14 oz pineapple rings in juice
   b. 1 oz coconut
   c. 5 oz chopped butter
   d. 8 oz self-raising flour
   e. 4 oz brown sugar
   f. $3\frac{1}{2}$ oz melted butter
   g. $2\frac{1}{2}$ oz plain flour
   h. $7\frac{1}{2}$ oz caster sugar

B. More accurate conversions

Key point

1 kg = 2.2 lb   1 oz = 28 g

To convert, multiply or divide by the conversion factor.

Examples

Convert 5 kg to lb.

5 kg = 5 × 2.2 = **11 lb**

You can check using inverse calculations:
   11 ÷ 2.2 = 5

Convert 6 lb to kg.

6 lb = 6 ÷ 2.2 = **2.73 kg** (to 2 dp)
(using a calculator)

2.73 × 2.2 = 6.006
(near 6, the difference caused by rounding)

Practice

1. Use the conversion 1 kg = 2.2 lb to find the missing values.

   a. 4 kg = _____ lb   b. 22 lb = _____ kg   c. 9 kg = _____ lb   d. 12 lb = _____ kg

2. Use the conversion 1 oz = 28 g to find these missing values.

   a. 4 oz = _____ g   b. 140 g = _____ oz   c. 15 oz = _____ g   d. 70 g = _____ oz

Activity
Use conversions to check weights in recipe books.

See pages 378–379 for another method of converting units using conversion graphs.

Chapter Summary
14 Weight

- The common metric units of weight are: **grams (g)** and **kilograms (kg)**.
- 1 g is about the weight of 10 matchsticks, 1 kg is the weight of a bag of sugar.
- **Milligrams** (**mg**) are used to weigh very small items, such as tablets.
- **Metric tonnes** are used to weigh heavy objects.
- Metric conversions are: 1000 mg = 1 g, 1000 g = 1 kg or 100 g = 0.1 kg
- Read scales to the labelled divisions, or find the value of unlabelled divisions by dividing the difference in value between marked divisions.
- Imperial units of weight are: **ounces (oz)**, **pounds (lb)**, **stones (st)** where 16 oz = 1 lb, 14 lbs = 1 st

- The **metric tonne** weighs 1000 kg.
- For metric units, multiply or divide by 10, 100 or 1000 to convert between different units of weight using 100 g = $\frac{1}{10}$ kg = 0.1 kg, 10 g = $\frac{1}{100}$ kg = 0.01 kg and 1 g = $\frac{1}{1000}$ kg = 0.001 kg and 100 kg = $\frac{1}{10}$ tonne = 0.1 tonne, 10 kg = $\frac{1}{100}$ tonne = 0.01 tonne, 1 kg = $\frac{1}{1000}$ tonne = 0.001 tonne.
- Multiply and divide using imperial conversions to convert between imperial measurements.
- The **imperial ton** is different to the metric tonne, and weighs 2240 lbs.
- To add or subtract weights, the units must be the same.
- Take care with mixed imperial units, for example, lb and oz. They cannot be written easily as a decimal, you need to convert them into one unit.
- Remember to write the units in the answer.

- An imperial ton is smaller than a metric tonne.
- To convert between metric and imperial measurements, multiply or divide using approximate or accurate conversions.
- Approximate metric/imperial conversions include: 1 oz ≈ 25 g, 1 lb ≈ 450 g, 1 kg is just over 2 lbs
- More accurate metric/imperial conversions include: 1 kg = 2.2 lb, 1 oz = 28 g
- Weights can also be converted using a **conversion graph**.

Measures, Shape and Space

15 Capacity

Measure capacity and volume
Specification reference: EL3.M14, EL3.M17

A. Know metric measures

The amount of liquid that a container holds when full is its **capacity**.
Volume is the amount of space something takes up.
The metric unit we use for capacity and volume of liquids is a **litre (ℓ)**.

Many fruit juice drinks and squashes are sold in bottles that hold 1 litre.
Even large volumes, like the amount of water in a swimming pool, are measured in litres.

Activities

1. You need:
   - a 5 litre plastic bottle (the sort used by campers)
   - a $\frac{1}{2}$ litre measuring jug.

   Measure $\frac{1}{2}$ litre water and pour it into the bottle.

   Mark the $\frac{1}{2}$ litre level on the bottle.

   Measure another $\frac{1}{2}$ litre water and pour it into the bottle.

   Mark and label this level as 1 litre.

   Repeat this until you have the bottle marked every $\frac{1}{2}$ litre up to 5 litres.

2. Collect together some large containers, for example, bowls, saucepans, tins.

   Estimate, then measure, how much each container holds.

   Put your results in a table with the headings shown below.

Container	Estimate capacity to nearest $\frac{1}{2}$ litre	Measure capacity to nearest $\frac{1}{2}$ litre

We measure small amounts of liquid in **millilitres (mℓ)**.

1 mℓ is just a few drops.

5 mℓ is the capacity of a medicine spoon/teaspoon.

Measuring jugs are often labelled in millilitres.

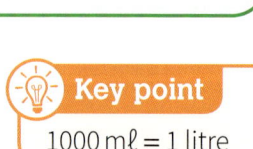

Key point

1000 mℓ = 1 litre

5 mℓ

250

Capacity

Practice

1.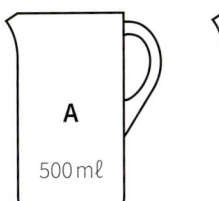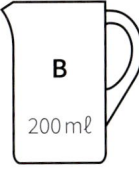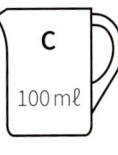

   a. How many jugs **A** are needed to fill this 1 litre jug?
   b. How many jugs **B** are needed to fill this 1 litre jug?
   c. How many jugs **C** are needed to fill this 1 litre jug?

2. How many millilitres are there in:

   a. 1 litre   b. $\frac{1}{2}$ litre   c. $\frac{1}{4}$ litre   d. $\frac{3}{4}$ litre   e. 1.5 litres?

3. How many litres are equal to:

   a. 3000 mℓ   b. 5000 mℓ   c. 9000 mℓ   d. 12 000 mℓ   e. 4500 mℓ?

B. Measure in litres and millilitres

Practice

1. This jug measures 2 litres.
   Each division represents 200 mℓ.

   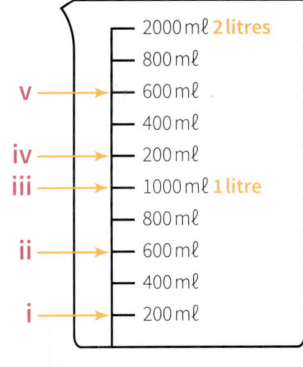

   a. Write the amount shown by each arrow.
      Give your answers in mℓ.

   > 200 mℓ is the same as 0.2 litres, so each division on the scale measures 0.2 litres.
   >
   > The volume shown by arrow **v** can be written as 1.6 litres.

   b. Write the amount shown by each of the other arrows in litres using decimals.

2.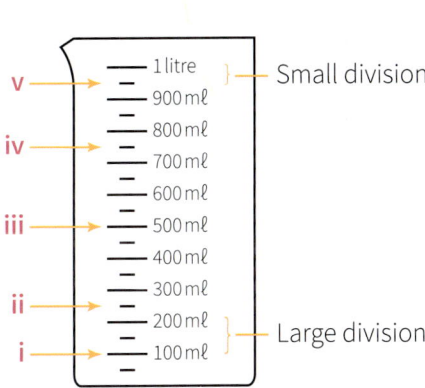

   a. What is the maximum volume this jug can measure?
   b. How many millilitres are represented by the large labelled divisions?
   c. How many millilitres are represented by the small unlabelled divisions?
   d. Write the measurements shown by each arrow.
   e. How many millilitres are there in $\frac{1}{2}$ litre?

251

3. a. What is the greatest volume this cylinder can measure?
    b. How many large divisions are there between 100 mℓ and 200 mℓ?
    c. How many mℓ does each large division represent?
    d. How many mℓ does each small division represent?
    e. Write the measures shown by the arrows.

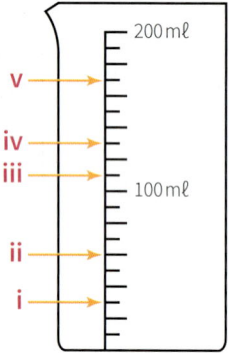

C. Estimate between marked divisions

Sometimes you need to estimate between the divisions on a scale.
Arrow **i** is about halfway between 350 mℓ and 400 mℓ.
An estimate of this reading is **375 mℓ**.

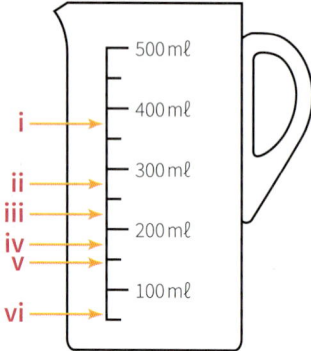

Practice

1. Estimate the readings shown by the other arrows on the jug above, as accurately as you can.
2. Here is another measuring jug.
    a. What is the greatest volume this jug measures?
    b. Write the measures shown by the arrows as accurately as you can.

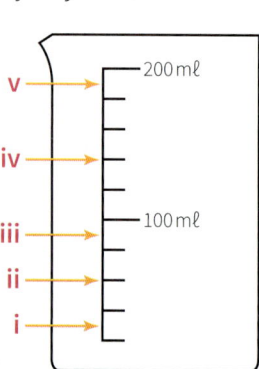

Activities

1. You will need a measuring jug marked in hundreds of millilitres to 1 litre.
   You also need a cup and some water.

   a. How many cupfuls of water do you need to fill the jug to the 1 litre mark?

   b. How many cupfuls do you need to fill to the $\frac{1}{2}$ litre level?

2. Collect some bottles, jars and pots.
   Estimate then measure how much each container holds.
   Put your results in a table.

3. Pour 300 mℓ water into a measuring jug.
   Put a stone in the jug.
   Make sure it is covered with water.
   Measure the level of the water again as accurately as you can.
   The difference between the two measurements is the volume of the stone.

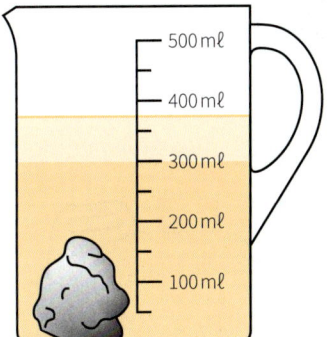

 Example

The 1st water level was 300 mℓ.

The 2nd water level is 375 mℓ. The difference is 75 mℓ.

This is the same as **75 cm³**.

(The volume of solid objects is usually measured in cm³.)

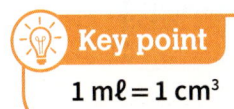

Key point

$1\ m\ell = 1\ cm^3$

Find a selection of small objects or stones.
Find the volume of each.

4. **a.** Find the capacity of:

   i. a teaspoon   **ii.** a dessertspoon   **iii.** a tablespoon.

   b. i. How many teaspoons of water are needed to make $\frac{1}{2}$ litre?

   ii. How many dessertspoons of water are needed to make $\frac{1}{2}$ litre?

   iii. How many tablespoons of water are needed to make $\frac{1}{2}$ litre?

5. Weigh an empty measuring jug. Pour in 1 litre of water then weigh it again.
   If you have measured and weighed accurately, you will have found that
   1 litre of water weighs 1 kg.

   How much does 1 mℓ weigh?

Measures, Shape and Space

Choose units and instruments

Specification reference **EL3.M17**

Practice

1. Which unit, litres or millilitres, would you use to measure these?

    a. The volume of water in a bath
    b. The capacity of a baby's bottle
    c. The capacity of a wine glass
    d. The volume of water used to wash a car
    e. The capacity of a water butt
    f. The water a hamster drinks in a day

2. Which measuring container is most suitable to measure each amount?

    A    B 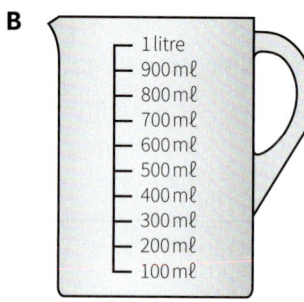   C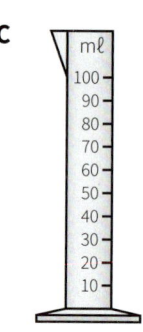

    a. The volume of car shampoo to wash a car
    b. The volume of lemon juice in a cocktail
    c. The capacity of a jam jar
    d. The volume of paint to decorate a bedroom
    e. The capacity of a casserole dish

3. Which measuring container would you use to measure each volume?

    A    B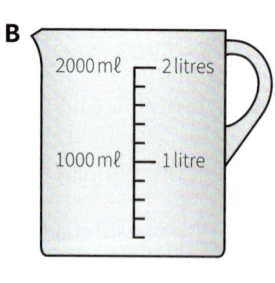

    a. 1.8 litres   b. 300 mℓ   c. 600 mℓ   d. 1500 mℓ
    e. $3\frac{1}{2}$ litres   f. 2.5 litres   g. 1400 mℓ   h. 500 mℓ

4. Which level of accuracy would you use to measure the volume of each item?
   Choose from the **nearest 1 mℓ, 10 mℓ, 100 mℓ** or **1 litre**.
   a. Kettle
   b. Indoor watering can
   c. Medicine
   d. Sauce bottle
   e. Fish tank
   f. Saucepan
   g. Concentrated plant food to mix with 1 litre of water

Convert between millilitres, litres and centilitres

Specification reference **L1.M20**

Litres and millilitres are the most common metric units for capacity.

To convert between litres and millilitres, multiply or divide by 1000.

Key point
1 litre = 1000 mℓ

You can use millilitres, litres or a mixture of these.
For example, 1400 mℓ is the same as 1.4 litres or 1 litre 400 mℓ.

Examples
Convert: **4 litres to mℓ**   **2.5 litres to mℓ**   **4875 mℓ to litres**
$4 \times 1000 =$ **4000 mℓ** $2.5 \times 1000 =$ **2500 mℓ** $4875 \div 1000 = 4.875$ litres

or 4 litres and 875 millilitres (the first 3 dp are mℓ)

Practice

1. Write these in millilitres.
   a. 5 ℓ
   b. 2.6 ℓ
   c. 12.5 ℓ
   d. 3.625 ℓ
   e. 0.682 ℓ
   f. 1.85 ℓ
   g. 5.063 ℓ
   h. 0.75 ℓ
   i. 0.083 ℓ
   j. 0.04 ℓ

2. Write these in litres, using a decimal point where necessary.
   a. 6000 mℓ
   b. 3500 mℓ
   c. 11 000 mℓ
   d. 1100 mℓ
   e. 65 400 mℓ
   f. 330 mℓ
   g. 250 mℓ
   h. 425 mℓ
   i. 7300 mℓ
   j. 5320 mℓ

3. Write these in millilitres.
   a. 3 litres 400 mℓ
   b. 6 litres 250 mℓ
   c. 3 litres 630 mℓ
   d. 8 litres 760 mℓ

Measures, Shape and Space

4. Write these as: **i.** litres and millilitres **ii.** litres using a decimal point.
   a. 1200 mℓ
   b. 3830 mℓ
   c. 4935 mℓ
   d. 5769 mℓ
   e. 15 800 mℓ
   f. 5098 mℓ

5. Find the matching volumes.
A	100 mℓ	**B**	10 mℓ	**C**	250 mℓ	**D**	50 mℓ
E	2550 mℓ	**F**	500 mℓ	**G**	0.1 litre	**H**	0.05 litre
I	0.5 litre	**J**	2.55 litres	**K**	0.01 litre	**L**	0.25 litre

6. Put the bottles in order of size, starting with the **greatest** capacity.

   A  1.1 litres
   B  94 mℓ
   C  1.650 ℓ
   D  875 mℓ

Another unit that is used for measuring small quantities of liquid, such as alcoholic drinks, is the **centilitre (cℓ)**.

> **Key point**
> **1 cℓ = 10 mℓ** (like cm and mm)   **1 litre = 100 cℓ** (like m and cm)

To convert between these metric units you need to multiply or divide by 10, 100 or 1000.

from mℓ cℓ ℓ   ÷10 ÷100   ÷1000

from litre ×100 cℓ ×10 mℓ   ×1000

Examples
Convert:

320 mℓ to cℓ   45 cℓ to litres   3.45 litres to cℓ
320 ÷ 10 = **32 cℓ**   45 ÷ 100 = **0.45 litres**   3.45 × 100 = **345 cℓ**

7. How many litres are the same as:
   a. 300 cℓ
   b. 250 cℓ
   c. 3050 cℓ
   d. 740 cℓ
   e. 50 cℓ
   f. 33 cℓ
   g. 75 cℓ
   h. 3210 cℓ?

8. How many centilitres are the same as:
   a. 30 mℓ
   b. 500 mℓ
   c. 250 mℓ
   d. 85 mℓ
   e. 3.5 litres
   f. 1.75 litres
   g. $\frac{1}{2}$ litre
   h. 0.46 litres?

Capacity

Calculate using metric units of capacity

Specification reference **L1.M20**

A. Litres and millilitres

Parts of a litre

Units	.	Tenths	Hundredths	Thousandths
litres	.	$\frac{1}{10}$ litre	$\frac{1}{100}$ litre	$\frac{1}{1000}$ litre
1000 mℓ	.	100 mℓ	10 mℓ	1 mℓ

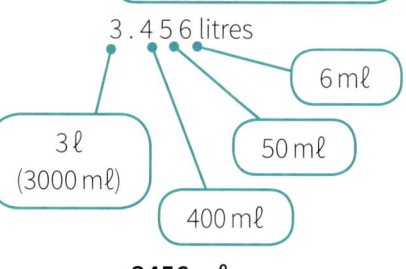

Example

Either **work in millilitres**:

2.4 ℓ + 200 mℓ + 15 mℓ = 2400 + 200 + 15 = **2615 mℓ** or **2.615 ℓ**

× 1000 = 2400 mℓ   Remember the units.

```
  2400
   200
+   15
------
  2615
```

or **work in litres using decimals**:

2.4 ℓ + 200 mℓ + 15 mℓ = 2.4 ℓ + 0.2 ℓ + 0.015 ℓ = **2.615 ℓ**

2 × 100 mℓ   10 mℓ   5 mℓ

```
    2.4
    0.2
+ 0.015
-------
  2.615
```

Use a calculator to check.

Practice

1. Work these out. Give the answer in litres if it is more than 1000 mℓ.
   Check your answers with a calculator.

   a. 3 litres + 650 mℓ + 50 mℓ
   b. 1 litre + 2 litres + 400 mℓ + 25 mℓ
   c. 7 litres + 2 litres + 75 mℓ
   d. 3.6 litres + 850 mℓ + 80 mℓ
   e. 400 mℓ + 1.64 litres + 40 mℓ
   f. 4.7 litres + 2 litres + 50 mℓ
   g. 150 mℓ + 5 mℓ + 50 mℓ
   h. 10 litres − 4 litres − 40 mℓ
   i. 5 litres − 2 litres − 340 mℓ
   j. $7\frac{1}{2}$ litres − 3.2 litres + 75 mℓ

2. A caterer mixes together 2.5 litres lemonade, 2 litres orange juice, 1.25 litres apple juice and 750 mℓ pineapple juice. How much liquid is this altogether?

3. A student buys 2 litres of milk. He drinks 350 mℓ then gives 30 mℓ to the cat. How much milk is left?

4. Give the answers to these in litres. Check with a calculator.
   a. 6.2 litres + 600 mℓ + 3 cℓ
   b. 50 mℓ + 43 cℓ + 0.6 litre
   c. 5 litres − 43 cℓ
   d. 10 litres − 1 litre − 1 cℓ

5. For each part assume you start with 1 litre of fruit juice.
   How much is left after pouring out the drinks described?
   a. 2 cups holding 250 mℓ each
   b. 3 glasses holding 200 mℓ each
   c. 4 glasses holding 150 mℓ each
   d. 2 tumblers holding 420 mℓ each

6.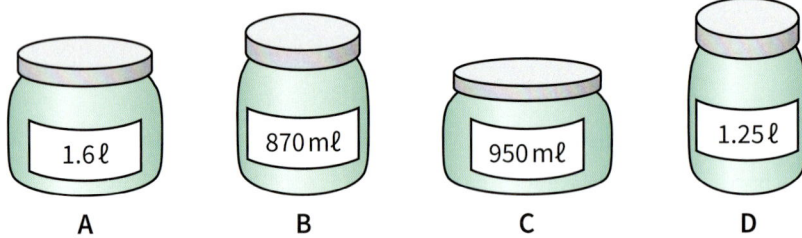

   A: 1.6 ℓ   B: 870 mℓ   C: 950 mℓ   D: 1.25 ℓ

   a. What is the total capacity of the 4 jars?
   b. What is the difference in capacity between the largest and the smallest jars?
   c. Which 2 jars have a total capacity of 2.12 ℓ?
   d. A new jar has half the capacity of **A**. How much does it hold?
   e. Another jar holds 4 times as much as **D**. What is its capacity?

B. Mixed calculations

Practice

1. a. A 5 mℓ dose of medicine is taken 4 times a day. What is the total dose per day?
   b. The medicine bottle holds 140 mℓ. How many days will the medicine last?

2. A water butt holds 100 litres of water. A watering can holds 5 litres.
   How many times can you fill the can from the water butt?

3. Water drips from a tap at a rate of 400 mℓ every 5 minutes.
   How much water drips from the tap in an hour?

4. a. 24 children go to a party. Each child drinks two 200 mℓ glasses of cola.
      How much cola do they drink altogether?
   b. A bottle holds 1.5 litres. How many bottles are used at the party?

Capacity

5. A recipe needs 3 tablespoons of oil. The cook doesn't have a tablespoon, but she does have a teaspoon. She knows a tablespoon holds 15 ml and a teaspoon holds 5 ml.
How many teaspoons of oil does she need to use?

6. a. Each packet of choc whip needs 300 ml milk.
How much milk is needed for 6 packets?

   b. The whip is divided between 24 children.
How much milk does each child get in their whip?

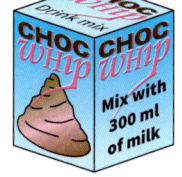

7. Each jelly dish holds 850 ml. How much will 5 jelly dishes hold?

8. A children's party game uses a large bucket of water. A 750 ml jug is used to fill the bucket. The jug is filled 8 times. How much water is in the bucket?

9. A cocktail recipe for 4 glasses needs
60 ml orange juice,   80 ml lemonade,   30 ml rum   and   20 ml tequila.

   a. For 10 glasses of the cocktail, how much of each ingredient is needed?

   b. How much cocktail is made altogether?

10. a. How many people are in your maths group?

    b. If everyone is to have a 200 ml drink, how much liquid is needed altogether?

    c. A drink recipe is: $\frac{1}{3}$ lemonade, $\frac{1}{4}$ orange juice, $\frac{1}{6}$ apple juice
    $\frac{1}{6}$ grapefruit juice and $\frac{1}{12}$ lemon juice
    How much of each ingredient do you need to make the drink for your group?

Measure with metric and imperial units of capacity

Specification reference EL3.M14, L1.M20

 Entry Level 3

Many measuring jugs and other containers show both metric and imperial measures.

The common metric units are millilitres and litres.

> **Key point**
> 1000 ml = 1 litre

The common imperial units are fluid ounces (fl oz), pints (pt) and gallons (gal).

> **Key point**
> 1 pt = 20 fl oz   1 gal = 8 pt

Measures, Shape and Space

 Activities

1. Fill a pint milk bottle with water.

   Pour the water into a measuring jug similar to the one shown on the previous page.

   Does the milk bottle hold: a. more or less than 1 litre

   b. more or less than $\frac{1}{2}$ litre?

2. Collect some containers that hold less than 1 pint, for example, cup, mug, small jug, egg cup. Estimate, then measure, the capacity of each container in appropriate metric and imperial units. Record your results in a table like this:

Container	Imperial		Metric	
	Estimate	Measurement	Estimate	Measurement

3. Collect some containers that hold more than 1 pint, for example, tin, bowl, saucepan. Add these to your table and compare the imperial and metric measurements.

   Can you see that a litre is a little less than 2 pints?

Convert between imperial units of capacity

Specification reference **L1.M20**

 Level 1

 **Key point**

1 pint = 20 fluid ounces   1 gallon = 8 pints

To convert between units multiply or divide by the conversion factor.

fl oz $\xrightarrow{\div 20}$ pt $\xrightarrow{\div 8}$ gal   gal $\xrightarrow{\times 8}$ pt $\xrightarrow{\times 20}$ fl oz

 Examples

Convert:

80 fl oz to pints   **2.5 gallons to pints**

80 ÷ 20 = **4 pints**   2.5 × 8 = **20 pints**

260

Capacity

Practice

1. Convert these to pints.
   - a. 60 fl oz
   - b. 40 fl oz
   - c. 70 fl oz
   - d. 150 fl oz
   - e. 4 gallons
   - f. 1.5 gallons
   - g. $\frac{1}{2}$ gallon
   - h. $\frac{1}{4}$ gallon

2. Convert these to gallons.
   - a. 24 pints
   - b. 2 pints
   - c. 60 pints
   - d. 140 pints

3. Convert these to fluid ounces.
   - a. 2 pints
   - b. 0.1 pint
   - c. $\frac{1}{2}$ pt
   - d. $\frac{1}{4}$ pt

Calculate capacity and volume using imperial units
Specification reference L1.M20

Level 1 Practice

1. A mocktail recipe needs the following ingredients:

   1 pt lemonade, $\frac{1}{2}$ pt orange juice, $\frac{1}{4}$ pt apple juice,

   $\frac{1}{8}$ pt mango pulp, $\frac{1}{10}$ pt lemon juice.

   a. Write each volume in fluid ounces.
   b. What is the total volume in fluid ounces?

2. Sixty guests have $\frac{3}{10}$ pint of mocktail each. How many gallons is this?

3. a. Five gallons of milk are poured into pint bottles. How many bottles are filled?

   b. Pints of milk are sold for 64p each. At the end of the day only 6 pints remain unsold. How much money is taken?

4. A bottle of concentrated disinfectant holds $1\frac{1}{5}$ pints.
   The disinfectant is diluted by mixing 4 fluid ounces with 1 gallon of water.
   How many gallons of water are mixed with the concentrated disinfectant?

5. A day centre orders milk. There are 5 groups in the centre with 16 people in each group. Each person drinks 1 pint of milk per day.

   a. How many pints of milk are needed:
      i. each day   ii. each week   iii. each year?   (Assume 365 days in 1 year.)
   b. Convert each of your answers to part **a** into gallons.

Measures, Shape and Space

Convert between metric and imperial measures

Specification reference **L2.M14**

A. Approximate metric/imperial conversions

There's a rhyme about the approximate conversion between litres and pints:

'A litre of water's a pint and three quarters.'

This means:

> **Key point**
> 1 litre ≈ $1\frac{3}{4}$ pints

Other useful approximations are:

> **Key point**
> 1 fl oz ≈ 30 mℓ   1 pint ≈ $\frac{2}{3}$ litre   1 gallon ≈ $4\frac{1}{2}$ litres

Practice

1. Which is larger: **a.** a pint or a litre   **b.** $\frac{1}{2}$ litre or 1 pint?

2. Copy and complete these.
   - **a.** 2 litres ≈ _____ pt
   - **b.** 3 pt ≈ _____ litres
   - **c.** 120 mℓ ≈ _____ fl oz
   - **d.** 45 ℓ ≈ _____ gal
   - **e.** 4 gal ≈ _____ litres
   - **f.** 8 fl oz ≈ _____ mℓ

3. $\frac{1}{2}$ pint is poured out of a 1 litre bottle. How much is left?

4. **a.** Which petrol can holds more: 2 gallon   or   10 litre?
   b. Which yoghurt pot holds more: 6 fl oz   or   120 mℓ?

B. More accurate conversions

> **Key point**
> 1 fl oz = 28.4 mℓ   1 pt = 568 mℓ   1 gallon = 4.55 litres   1 litre = 0.22 gallons

To convert units, multiply and/or divide by the conversion factor(s). Use a calculator when necessary.

Capacity

Examples

Convert: 5 fl oz to mℓ.

5 fl oz = 5 × 28.4 = **142 mℓ**

Check: 142 ÷ 28.4 = 5

Convert 330 mℓ to fl oz.

330 mℓ = 330 ÷ 28.4 = **11.6 fl oz** (to 1 dp)

Check: 11.6 × 28.4 = 329.44
(nearly 330 – the difference is due to rounding)

Example

A water tank holds 500 litres of water. Use the conversion 10 litres = 2.2 gallons to find its capacity in gallons.

Capacity = 500 ÷ 10 × 2.2 = 50 × 2.2 = **110 litres**

Practice

Use a calculator when the calculations are very difficult.

1. Use the conversion 1 pint = 0.57 litres to find the missing values.
   a. 2 pt = _____ litres
   b. 2.85 litres = _____ pt
   c. 8 pt = _____ litres
   d. 4 litres = _____ pt

2. Use the conversion 1 gallon = 4.55 litres to find the missing values.
   a. 5 gal = _____ litres
   b. 500 litres = _____ gal
   c. 9 gal = _____ litres
   d. 36 litres = _____ gal

3. Use 2.2 gallons = 10 litres for each part.
   a. A water container holds 20 litres. How many gallons is this?
   b. How many litres does a 12 gallon petrol tank hold?

4. A medicine bottle holds 3 fl oz. How many mℓ is this? (1 fl oz = 28.4 mℓ)

5. a. A pond holds 80 gallons water. How many litres is this? (1 gallon = 4.55 litres)
   b. The pond loses 2.5 litres each day from a leak at the bottom. How many gallons of water are lost each week?
   c. How long will it take for the pond to be empty? Give your answer to the nearest week.

You can also use a conversion graph to convert between metric and imperial units of capacity. See page 362.

Chapter Summary
15 Capacity

- The amount of liquid that a container holds when full is its **capacity**.
- **Volume** is the amount of space something takes up.
- The metric units we use for capacity and volume of liquids are: **litres (ℓ)** and **millilitres (mℓ)**.
- 1 mℓ is a few drops, 5 mℓ is the capacity of a teaspoon.
- Measuring jugs are often labelled with mℓ, fruit juices and squashes are often sold in bottles that hold 1 litre.
- Metric conversions include: 1000 mℓ = 1 litre
- Read scales to the labelled divisions, or find the value of unlabelled divisions by dividing the difference in value between marked divisions.
- Imperial units of capacity include: **fluid ounces (fl oz), pints (pt), gallons (gal)** where 20 fl oz = 1 pint, 8 pt = 1 gallon
- The volume of solid objects is usually measured in cm³. 1 cm³ = 1 mℓ

- **Centilitres (cℓ)** are also used to measure small quantities of liquids where 1 cℓ = 10 mℓ and 100 cℓ = 1 ℓ
- **For metric units,** multiply or divide by 10, 100 or 1000 to convert between different units of capacity using 100 mℓ = $\frac{1}{10}$ litre = 0.1 ℓ, 10 mℓ = $\frac{1}{100}$ litre = 0.01 ℓ, 1 mℓ = $\frac{1}{1000}$ litre = 0.001 ℓ
- Multiply and divide using imperial conversions to convert between imperial measurements.
- To add or subtract capacities, the units must be the same.
- Take care with mixed imperial units, for example fl oz and pts. They cannot be written easily as a decimal, you need to convert them into one unit.
- Remember to write the units in the answer.

- To convert between metric and imperial measurements, multiply or divide using approximate or accurate conversions.
- Approximate metric/imperial conversions include: 1 litre ≈ $1\frac{3}{4}$ pints, 1 fl oz ≈ 30 ml, 1 pint ≈ $\frac{2}{3}$ litre, 1 gallon ≈ $4\frac{1}{2}$ litres
- More accurate metric/imperial conversions include:
  1 fl oz = 28.4 mℓ, 1 pt = 568 mℓ, 1 gal = 4.55 litres, 1 litre = 0.22 gal
- Capacities can also be converted using a **conversion graph**.

Measures, Shape and Space

16 Temperature

Measure temperature on the Celsius scale

Specification reference: EL3.M14

Temperature is measured using a thermometer.

There are many different types of thermometer.

The diagram shows part of a medical thermometer. It is placed under a patient's arm or tongue.

The level of the liquid in the tube shows the patient's temperature.

The large divisions on the thermometer scale go up in full degrees Celsius.

The enlarged section of the scale shows each degree is divided into 10 small divisions.

After 35 °C, the markers show 35.1°, 35.2°, 35.3°, …, up to 35.9° (just before 36 °C).

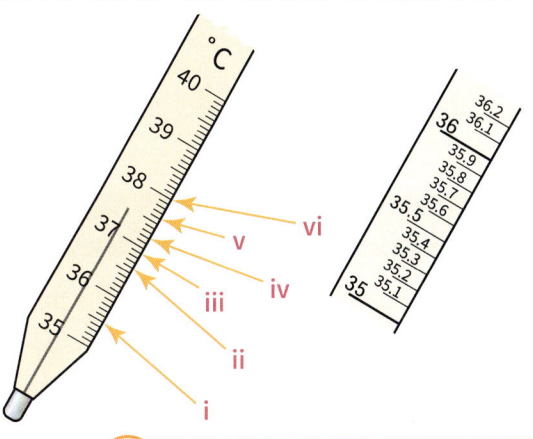

> **Key point**
> Temperature is usually measured in **degrees Celsius (°C)**.

Practice

1. **a.** What is the highest temperature the medical thermometer above can measure?
   b. What is the lowest temperature it can measure?
   c. Write down the temperatures shown by each arrow on the medical thermometer above.

2. Room thermometers often look like this.
   a. What is the highest temperature that it can show?
   b. What is the lowest temperature it can show?
   c. Write down the temperatures shown by each arrow.

3. **a.** What is the highest temperature that this thermometer measures?
   b. What is the lowest temperature that it measures?
   c. What does each small division on the scale show?
   d. Write down the temperature shown by each arrow.

4. For each part, find the number of degrees the temperature **rises**.

   a. 15 °C → 24 °C
   b. 25 °C → 32 °C
   c. 3 °C → 11 °C
   d. 5 °C → 21 °C
   e. 9 °C → 33 °C
   f. 12 °C → 39 °C

Measures, Shape and Space

5. For each part, find the number of degrees the temperature **falls**.

   a. 21 °C → 12 °C
   b. 27 °C → 9 °C
   c. 34 °C → 27 °C

6. For each part, choose a likely temperature from the list below.

   a. sauna
   b. cool workroom
   c. the surface of the sun
   d. hotel room
   e. ice cube
   f. sunny summer day

   0 °C,   11 °C,   20 °C,   28 °C,   54 °C,   6000 °C

Temperatures below freezing point
Specification reference L1.N2, L2.N1

Level 1

The Celsius scale has **negative** numbers **below the freezing point of water**.

−1 °C = getting colder   −2 °C = colder still   −3 °C = even colder

See also pages 6–7.

Key point
0 °C = freezing point

Practice

1. a. What is the highest temperature this thermometer measures?
   b. What is the lowest temperature it measures?
   c. Write down the temperature shown by each arrow.
   d. From your answers to part **c** write:
      i. the warmest temperature
      ii. the coldest temperature.

2. The cool fridge in the supermarket should be at −4 °C. Which phrase describes the cool fridge with the temperature shown?

   A too cold
   B the right temperature
   C too warm

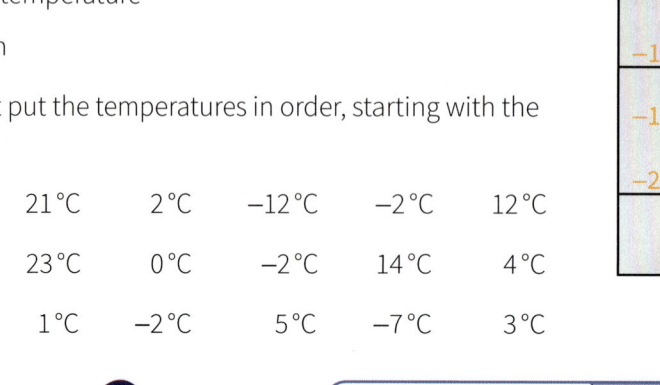

Level 2

3. For each part put the temperatures in order, starting with the **warmest**.

   a. −21 °C   21 °C   2 °C   −12 °C   −2 °C   12 °C
   b. −4 °C   23 °C   0 °C   −2 °C   14 °C   4 °C
   c. 7 °C   1 °C   −2 °C   5 °C   −7 °C   3 °C

MyMaths 1776 SEARCH

4. For each part, find the number of degrees the temperature **rises**.

   a. −5°C to 4°C
   b. −2°C to 12°C
   c. −3°C to 11°C
   d. −6°C to 10°C
   e. −9°C to 13°C
   f. −12°C to 29°C
   g. −7°C to −2°C
   h. −20°C to −3°C

5. For each part, find the number of degrees the temperature **falls**.

   a. 21°C to −2°C
   b. 17°C to −9°C
   c. 14°C to −7°C
   d. 15°C to −3°C
   e. 22°C to −4°C
   f. 18°C to −1°C
   g. −1°C to −10°C
   h. −4°C to −18°C

6. This chart shows the temperature over a period of 10 days.

   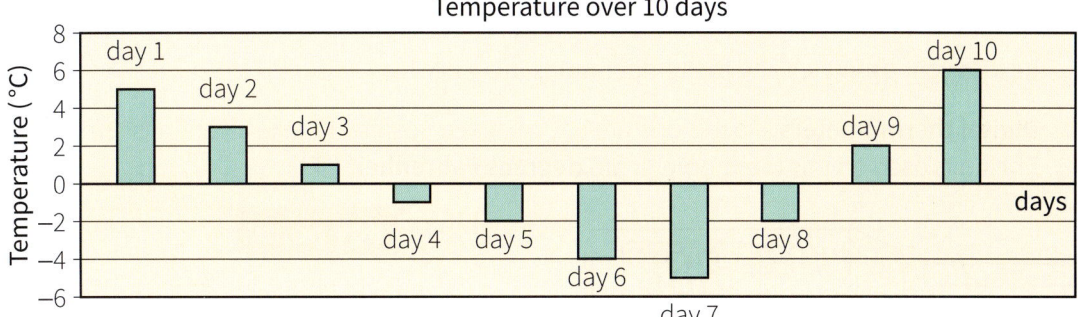

   a. What was: i. the highest temperature   ii. the lowest temperature?
   b. On which days was the temperature below freezing point?
   c. What was the range of the temperatures over the 10 days?

   For range see page 393.

7. The table below shows the central heating settings in a house.

   The differences between the inside temperatures and those outside the house are missing.

   Copy the table and fill in these missing values. The sitting room has been done for you.

Central heating settings		Difference between the inside and outside temperature when the outside temperature is:		
Room	Temperature	11°C	6°C	−3°C
Sitting room	21°C	10°C	15°C	24°C
Dining room	20°C			
Kitchen	16°C			
Bedroom 1	19°C			
Bedroom 2	16°C			
Bedroom 3	13°C			

   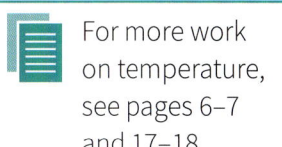

   For more work on temperature, see pages 6–7 and 17–18.

Measures, Shape and Space

Activities

1. **a.** Use a medical thermometer to take your temperature.
   b. Take the temperature of some other people. Make sure you wash the thermometer after each person has used it. Record your results in a table.

2. Draw a diagram of a thermometer.
   Mark and label the scale to show the following descriptions that weather forecasters use: Very hot 30 °C, Warm 20 °C, Mild 15 °C, Cold 5 °C.

3. Estimate the temperature for different places, for example, room, corridor, outside, window sill or the top of a heater.
   Place a room thermometer in each place for 2 minutes.
   Record your estimates and the temperatures in a table.

4. **Digital thermometers** like this one are often used in hospital to take a patient's temperature. The units used on this thermometer are **degrees Fahrenheit (°F)**.

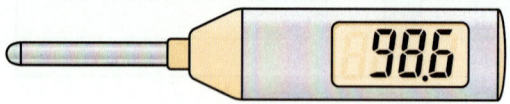

> **Key point**
> Temperature can also be measured in degrees Fahrenheit (°F)

Generally only the numbers are shown, not the °C or °F sign.

Use a digital thermometer to find temperatures, for example a warm drink, your body temperature, the room or outside. Record your results in a table.

Celsius and Fahrenheit

Specification reference **EL3.M14**

Ovens measure temperatures in Celsius, Fahrenheit or gas marks.
This table gives equivalent temperatures and a description for cooking.

°C	°F	Gas mark	Description
110	225	$\frac{1}{4}$	cool
120/130	250	$\frac{1}{2}$	
140	275	1	very low
150	300	2	
160/170	325	3	low/moderate
180	350	4	moderate/warm
190	375	5	moderately hot
200	400	6	hot
210/220	425	7	
230	450	8	
240	475	9	very hot

Temperature

Practice

1. Look at the table at the bottom of page 268.

   a. Which °C settings should you use for:

      i. a hot oven   ii. a warm oven   iii. a cool oven?

   b. Repeat part **a** for °F.

2. a. A roasting temperature for meat is 180 °C. What is this in °F?

   b. The roasting temperature for poultry is 50 °F higher than for other meats. What is the temperature in °F for roasting poultry?

   c. Draw dials like those shown below.

   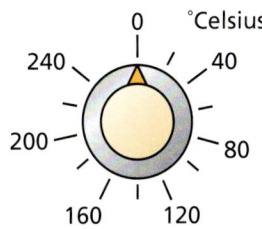
   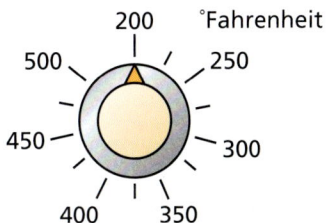

   On each dial mark the temperature for cooking: i. meat   ii. poultry.

Use formulae to convert temperatures

Specification reference **L2.N3**

This rhyme might help you remember how to convert between Celsius and Fahrenheit:

'If C to F confuses you, $\frac{9C}{5} + 32$ is all you have to do.'

For work on formulae, see pages 69–72.

Example

Convert: 40 °C to °F

$$F = \frac{9C}{5} + 32 = \frac{9 \times 40}{5} + 32 = \frac{360}{5} + 32 = 72 + 32 = \mathbf{104\,°F}$$

Key point

$F = \frac{9C}{5} + 32$

Practice

1. Below are some of the temperatures taken in places around the world.
   Convert each temperature to °F.

   a. Alexandria   20 °C   b. Barbados   30 °C   c. Toronto   5 °C

   d. Belgrade   15 °C   e. Berlin   10 °C   f. Algiers   25 °C

   g. London   12 °C   h. New York   14 °C

To convert from °F to °C use:

> **Example**
> Convert: 86°F to °C
> $$C = \frac{5(86-32)}{9} = \frac{5 \times 54}{9} = \frac{270}{9} = \mathbf{30\,°C}$$

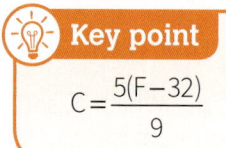

Key point
$$C = \frac{5(F-32)}{9}$$

2. Here are some more temperatures from cities.
   Convert these temperatures into Celsius. (Round to the nearest degree.)

   a. Amsterdam 52°F b. Athens 66°F c. Bahrain 93°F
   d. Belfast 48°F   e. Hong Kong 81°F f. Moscow 55°F
   g. Paris 59°F

Chapter Summary
16 Temperature

- Temperature can be measured in degrees **Celsius (°C)** or **degrees Fahrenheit (°F)**.
- Oven temperatures may be given as °C, °F, or as gas mark figures.
- Cool oven temperature: 110°C = 225°F = gas mark $\frac{1}{4}$
- Moderate/warm oven temperature: 180°C = 350°F = gas mark 4
- Very hot oven temperature: 240°C = 475°F = gas mark 9
- 0°C = **freezing point of water**

- The freezing point on the Celsius scale is 0°C, so temperatures below freezing are negative numbers.

- To convert from Celsius to Fahrenheit:
  $F = \frac{9C}{5} + 32$ ("If C to F confuses you, $\frac{9C}{5} + 32$ is all you have to do.")
- To convert from Fahrenheit to Celsius: $C = \frac{5(F-32)}{9}$

Measures, Shape and Space

17 Shape

Angles

Specification reference: EL3.M19, L1.M24, L1.M26

A **polygon** is a shape with straight **sides**.

Where two sides meet, an **angle** is formed.

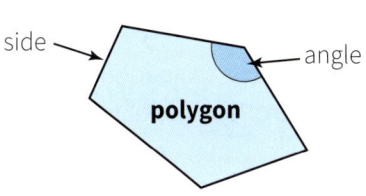

Get a sheet of paper.

Fit a corner into this drawing of a **right angle**.

Does it fit exactly?

If so, the corner is a right angle.

Try the other corners.

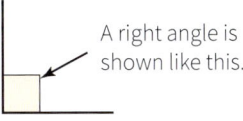

A right angle is shown like this.

> **Key point**
> A right angle is a $\frac{1}{4}$ **turn**. **Two right angles** make a **straight line**. This is also a $\frac{1}{2}$ **turn**.

Practice

1. These letters all have right angles. How many right angles are there in each?

   a. L   b. T   c. F   d. U   e. E   f. H

2. Write down 10 objects in the room that have right angles.

Angles are measured in **degrees (°)** using a **protractor**.

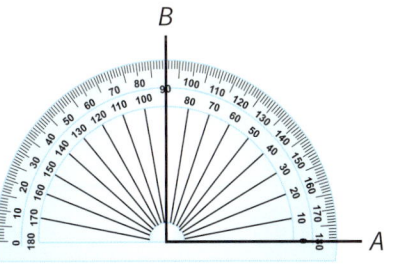

Line B meets line A at 90°
Line B is perpendicular to line A.

> **Key point**
> A right angle = 90°
> 2 right angles = 180°

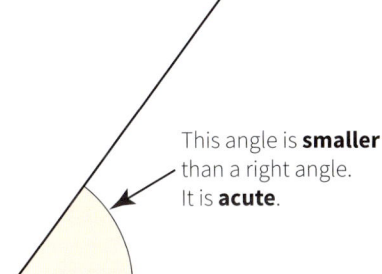

This angle is **smaller** than a right angle. It is **acute**.

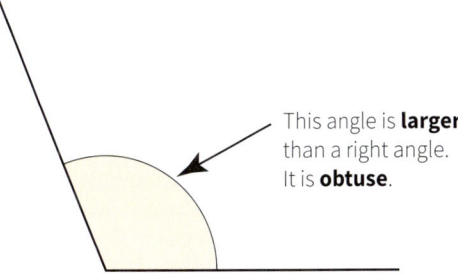

This angle is **larger** than a right angle. It is **obtuse**.

Measures, Shape and Space

To measure an angle:

1. Put the centre of your protractor on the point of the angle.
2. Lie the zero line of the protractor over one side of the angle.
3. Follow the scale round the edge of the protractor to the other side of the angle.
4. Read the size of the angle.

Take care to use the correct scale!

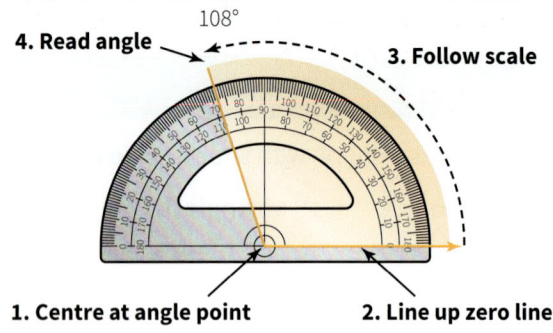

---

3. Measure each angle.

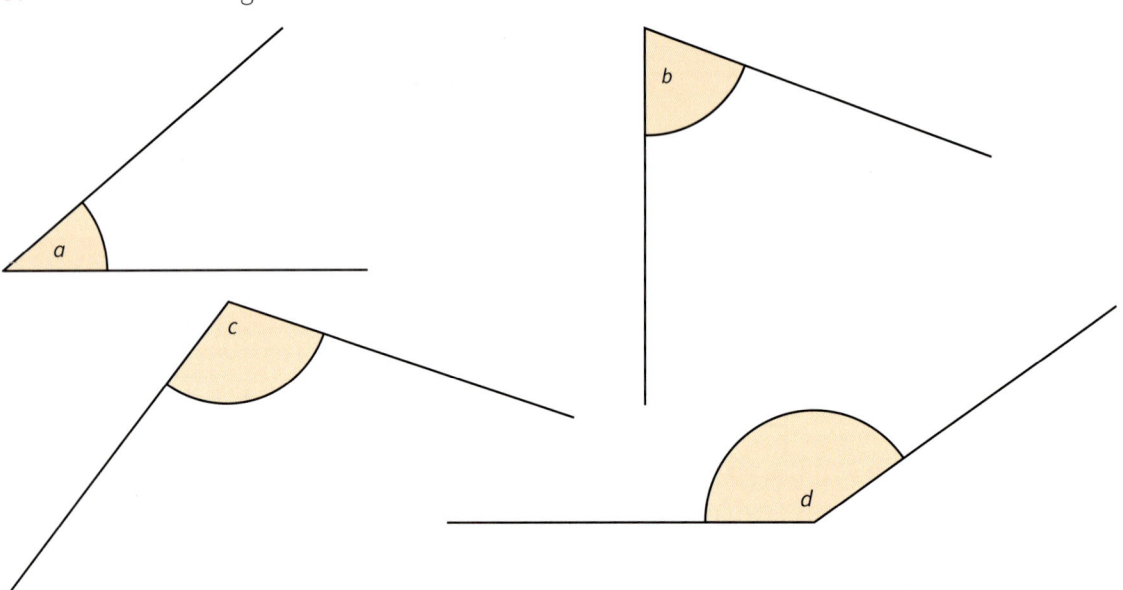

4. **a.** Estimate the size of each angle in the triangles.

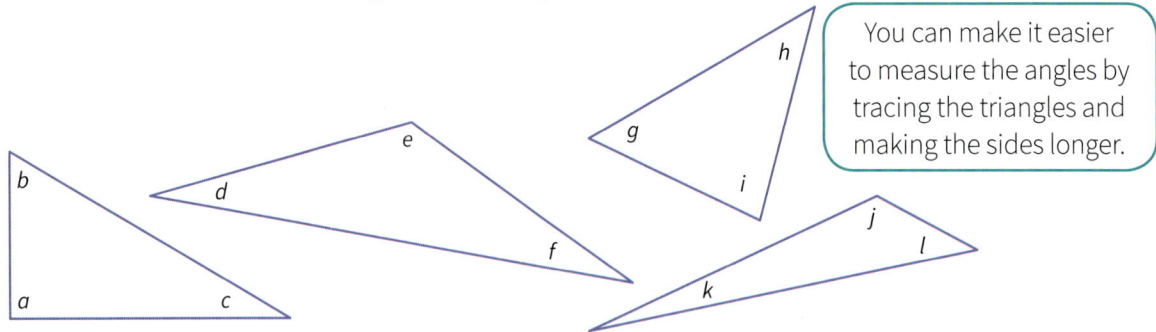

You can make it easier to measure the angles by tracing the triangles and making the sides longer.

b. i. Measure each angle *a* to *l*.

   ii. Compare your answers with your answers to part **a**.

c. For each angle *a* to *l*, say if it is an acute angle, an obtuse angle, or a right angle.

5. Each week a physiotherapist checks how far a patient can raise his arm. She estimates the angle between the patient's body and his raised arm (as shown for week 1).

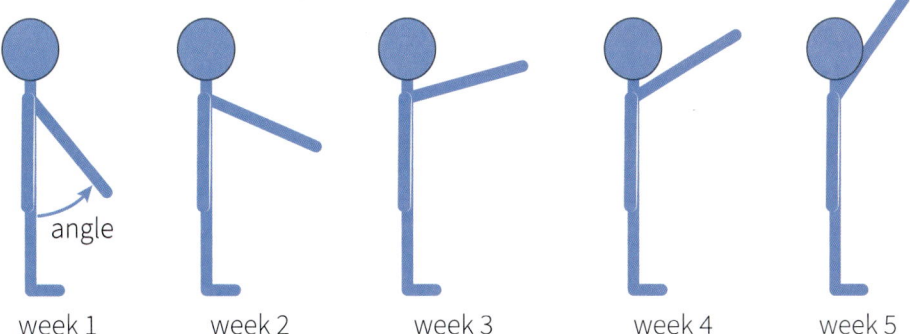

week 1 week 2 week 3 week 4 week 5

a. Estimate the angle for each week.

b. Measure each angle and compare with your answers to part **a**.

Horizontal, vertical and parallel lines
Specification reference EL3.M20, L2.M22

A. Horizontal and vertical lines

Horizontal lines go straight across, from left to right.

Vertical lines go straight up and down.

Practice

1 a. Which lines are vertical?
   b. Which lines are horizontal?

2 a. List examples of vertical lines in everyday life.
   b. List examples of horizontal lines in everyday life.

3 Rebecca uses 4 vertical pieces of wood and 2 horizontal pieces of wood to make a fence.

   Draw a rough sketch of her fence.

Measures, Shape and Space

B. Parallel lines

Parallel lines are always the same distance apart, like railway tracks or the sides of a door.

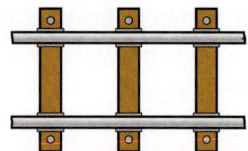

Practice

1. At different points, measure the distance between each of these pairs of lines.

   Which pairs of lines are parallel?

   A 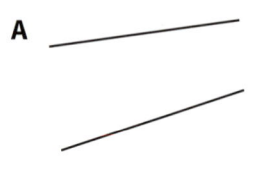 B 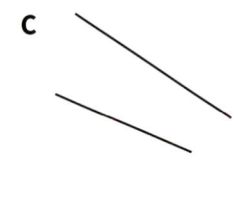 C D E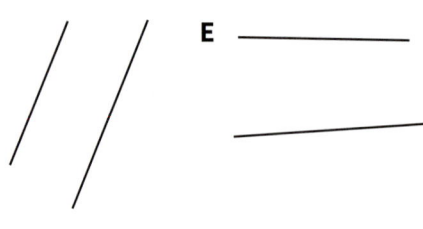

2. List examples of parallel lines from everyday life.

 Level 2

A line which intersects parallel lines is called an intersecting transversal.

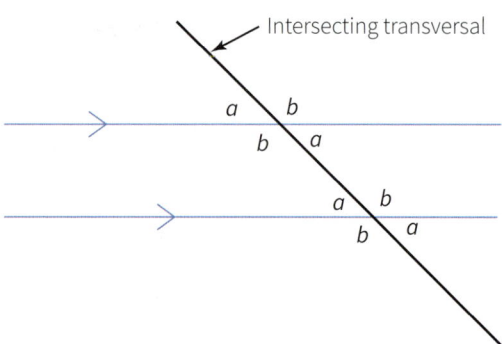

Because the lines being intersected (crossed) are parallel, all the angles marked 'a' are the same, and all the angles marked 'b' are the same.

Angles a + b together make a straight line (or half-turn) so add up to 180°.

Key point
Arrowheads indicate that lines are parallel.

Example

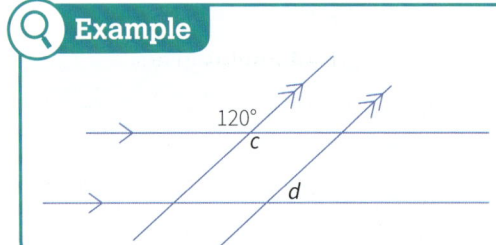

Angle c is opposite the 120° angle, so it will also be 120°.
Using the diagram above, angle d will be equal to the angle which makes a straight line with 120°.
180° − 120° = 60°
Angle d is therefore 60°

Key point
Opposite angles on an intersecting transversal are equal.

274

Shape

Practice

3. Without using a protractor, find the values of:
   a. angle e
   b. angle f.

4. A designer uses this pattern for curtain fabric. Without using a protractor, find the values of:
   a. angle g
   b. angle h
   c. angle i
   d. angle j.

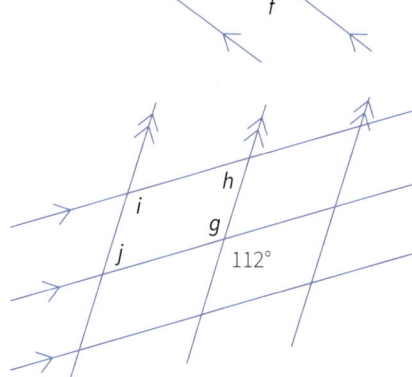

Two-dimensional (2-D) shapes

Specification reference EL3.M19, L1.M24

Apart from the circle, all the following shapes are **polygons**.

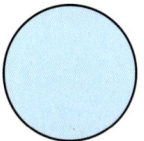

Circle

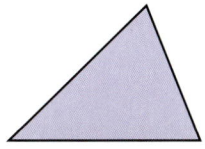

Triangle
3 sides
3 angles

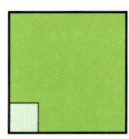

Square
4 equal sides
4 right angles
2 pairs of parallel sides

Rectangle
2 equal long sides
2 equal short sides
4 right angles
2 pairs of parallel sides

Parallelogram
2 equal long sides
2 equal short sides
2 pairs of equal angles
2 pairs of parallel sides

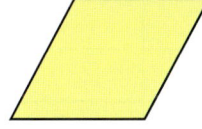

Rhombus
4 equal sides
2 pairs of equal angles
2 pairs of parallel sides

Trapezium
4 sides
1 pair of parallel sides

Key point

The **4 right angles** in a square or rectangle add up to **360°**

The **4 angles** in any **quadrilateral** (four-sided shape) add up to **360°**

Any polygon with **5 sides** is a **pentagon**.

Any polygon with **6 sides** is a **hexagon**, etc.

Regular means the sides are all the same length and the angles are all the same size.

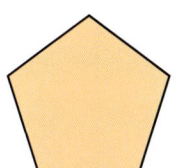

Regular pentagon
5 equal sides
5 equal angles

Regular hexagon
6 equal sides
6 equal angles

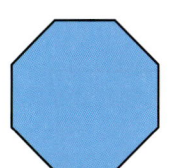

Regular octagon
8 equal sides
8 equal angles

Measures, Shape and Space

 Practice

1. Look at the polygons on the previous page. Compare each angle with a right angle. Copy and complete the following table.

Shape	Number of angles that are:		
	Right angles	Smaller than a right angle	Larger than a right angle
Square			
Rectangle			
Regular hexagon			
Regular octagon			
Regular pentagon			
Parallelogram			
Rhombus			
Trapezium			

2. Look at the polygons on the previous page. Many have four sides.
   Some of the shapes have parallel sides.
   Copy the following table. Tick where appropriate.

Shape	4 sides equal	4 right angles	Opposite sides equal	Opposite angles equal	No parallel sides	1 pair of parallel sides	2 pairs of parallel sides
Square							
Rectangle							
Parallelogram							
Rhombus							
Trapezium							

3. Use a protractor to measure the angles in these shapes on the previous page.
   a. Regular pentagon
   b. Regular hexagon
   c. Regular octagon

4. For each quadrilateral
   a. measure the sides
   b. measure the angles
   c. give the name.

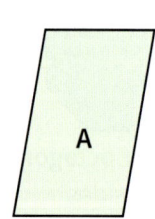
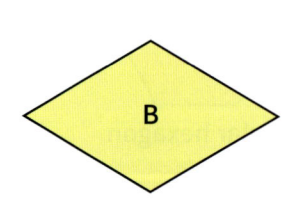
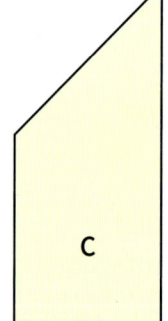

A   B   C

Triangles

Specification reference EL3.M19, L1.M24, L1.M26, L2.22

There are different types of triangle.

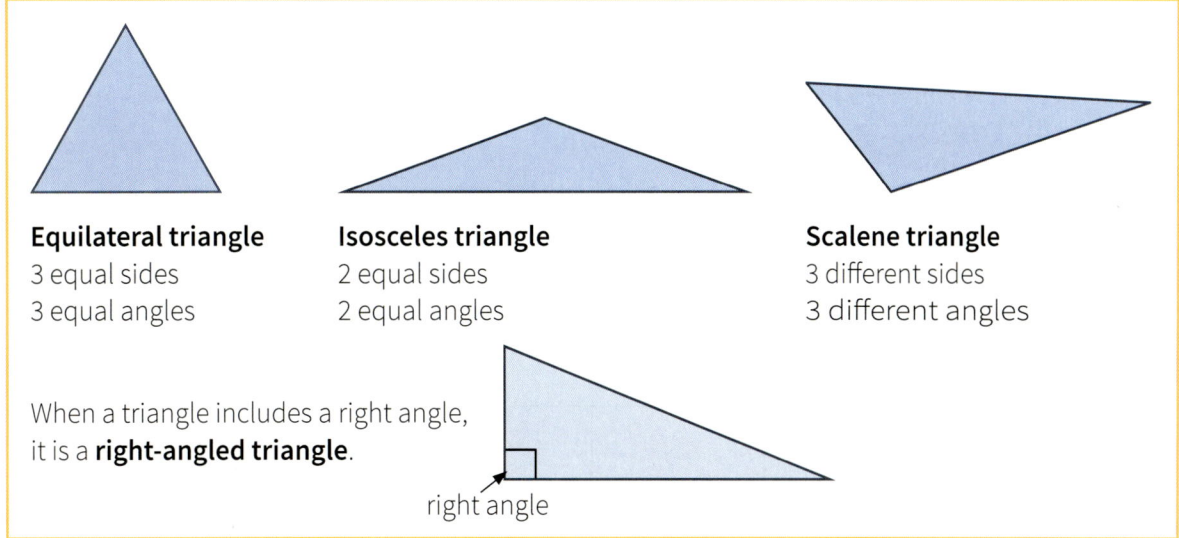

Equilateral triangle
3 equal sides
3 equal angles

Isosceles triangle
2 equal sides
2 equal angles

Scalene triangle
3 different sides
3 different angles

When a triangle includes a right angle, it is a **right-angled triangle**.

right angle

Practice

1. Copy the table. Tick the boxes that apply.

Shape	3 equal sides	3 equal angles	2 equal sides	2 equal angles	no equal sides	no equal angles
Equilateral triangle						
Scalene triangle						
Isosceles triangle						

2. List the triangles that are
   a. equilateral
   b. isosceles
   c. scalene.

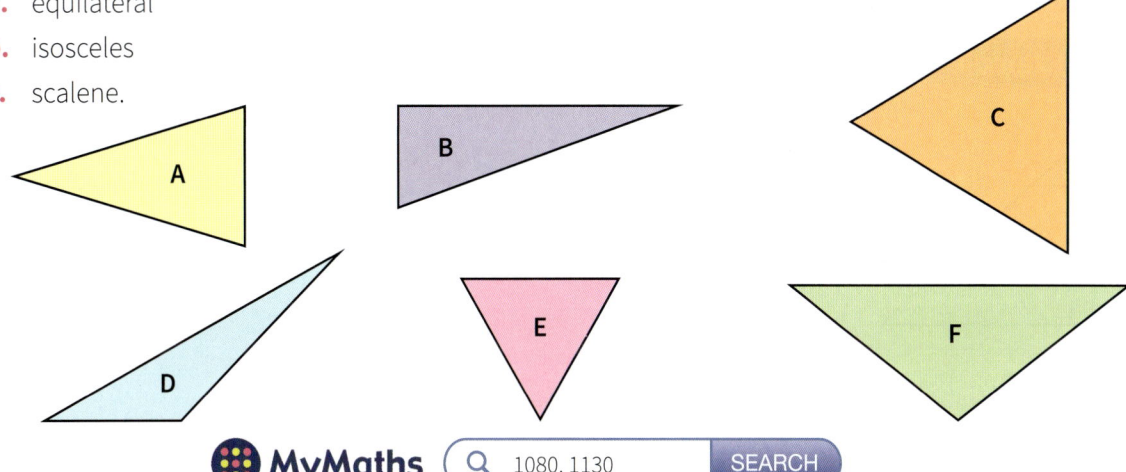

Measures, Shape and Space

Activities

Level 1

1. Draw triangles to investigate the following:
   a. Can a scalene triangle also be a right-angled triangle? Explain your answer.
   b. Can an isosceles triangle also be a right-angled triangle? Explain your answer.
   c. Can an equilateral triangle also be a right-angled triangle? Explain your answer.
   d. Draw 3 different scalene triangles.

2. a. Copy the table below and add extra rows for the triangles you have drawn for part **1d**.

Shape	Angle 1	Angle 2	Angle 3	Total number of degrees in the triangle
Equilateral triangle				
Scalene triangle				
Isosceles triangle				
Right- angled triangle				

Measure all the angles and complete your table.

> **Key point**
> The total number of degrees in a triangle is always 180°.

   b. If any of your answers do not agree with the statement in the key point box, measure the angles again.

See pages 275–276 for more practice with shapes.

Level 2

Sometimes it is possible to calculate an angle from the information given.

Example

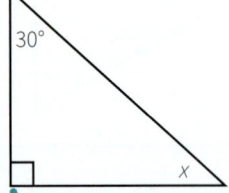

Calculate the angle marked x

The angles in a triangle add up to 180°

$90 + 30 + x = 180$

$x = 180 - 90 - 30$

$x = \mathbf{60°}$

Remember: a right angle = 90°

Example

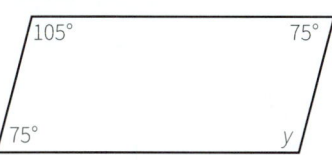

Calculate the angle marked y

The angles in a quadrilateral add up to 360°

$75 + 75 + 105 + y = 360$

$y = 360 - 75 - 75 - 105$

$y = \mathbf{105°}$

3. Calculate the angles marked by letters in these shapes

a. 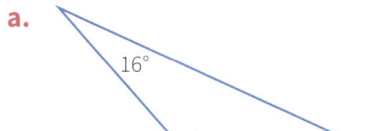   b.   c.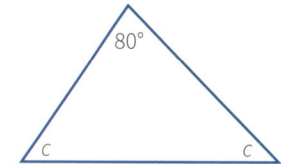

4. The diagram below shows the side of a shed.

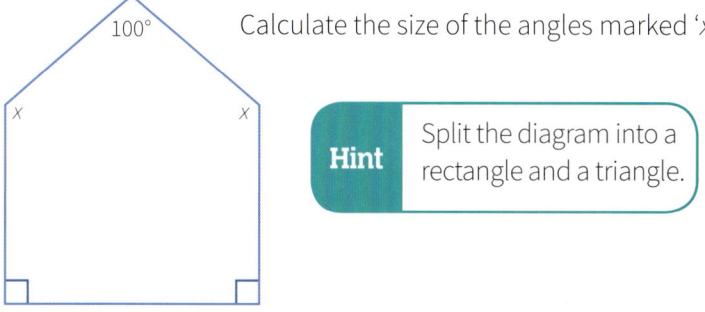

Calculate the size of the angles marked 'x'.

Hint Split the diagram into a rectangle and a triangle.

5. A pattern is created with square and triangular floor tiles.

Hint Think about angles on a straight line.

a. What sort of triangles are used?
b. Calculate the angles in the triangles.

6. a. In this rectangle, what sort of triangles are shaded

   i. green   ii. yellow.

  b. Calculate the angles marked by letters.

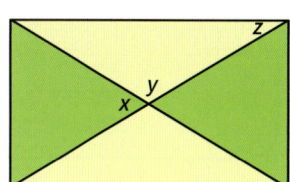

Measures, Shape and Space

Symmetry

Specification reference EL3.M19, L1.M24

When a shape can be folded in half so that the halves match, it has **line symmetry**.

The fold line is a **line of symmetry**. Sometimes it is called a **mirror line** because each side is like the **reflection** of the other side in a mirror.

Butterflies are symmetrical.

Line of symmetry

Some shapes have more than one line of symmetry.

This triangle has 3 lines of symmetry.

Example

Complete this shape so that the dotted line is a line of symmetry.

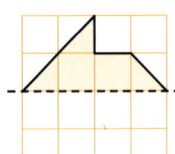

Drawing the reflection in the dotted line completes the shape.

(Use tracing paper to check this matches when you fold it.)

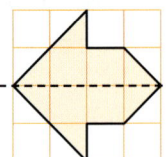

Key point

A shape has line symmetry if it can be folded in half so that one half fits exactly over the other.

When a shape **looks exactly the same** when it is **rotated** by less than a full turn to a **new** position, then the shape has **rotational symmetry**.

The shape's **order** of rotational symmetry is the number of different positions in which it looks the same during a complete turn.

The triangle above has **rotational symmetry of order 3**

The butterfly does not have rotational symmetry.

Key point

You can use tracing paper to check line symmetry and rotational symmetry.

Example

Shade two more squares so that the result has rotational symmetry of order 2

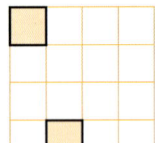

Two more squares have been shaded so that the pattern looks the same in two different positions during a turn.

(Use tracing paper to check this.)

Key point

A shape has rotational symmetry if it looks exactly the same when rotated less than a full turn.

Practice

1. How many lines of symmetry does each of these letters have?

   a. T b. H c. E d. A
   e. D f. O g. B h. Z
   i. M j. S k. X l. V

2. Which letters in question **1** have rotational symmetry?

   Write down the order of rotational symmetry for each of these letters.

3. Draw each of the following shapes on squared or isometric paper: square, rectangle, rhombus, regular hexagon, parallelogram, equilateral triangle, isosceles triangle, scalene triangle.

   Cut out each shape.

   By folding, find which of the shapes have:

   a. no lines of symmetry
   b. one line of symmetry
   c. two lines of symmetry
   d. more than two lines of symmetry.

4. Use tracing paper to copy each of the following shapes from pages 275 and 277: square, rectangle, parallelogram, rhombus, regular pentagon, regular octagon, equilateral triangle, isosceles triangle. Rotate the tracing paper to find the order of rotational symmetry of each shape.

5. Copy and complete each shape. The dotted line is a line of symmetry.

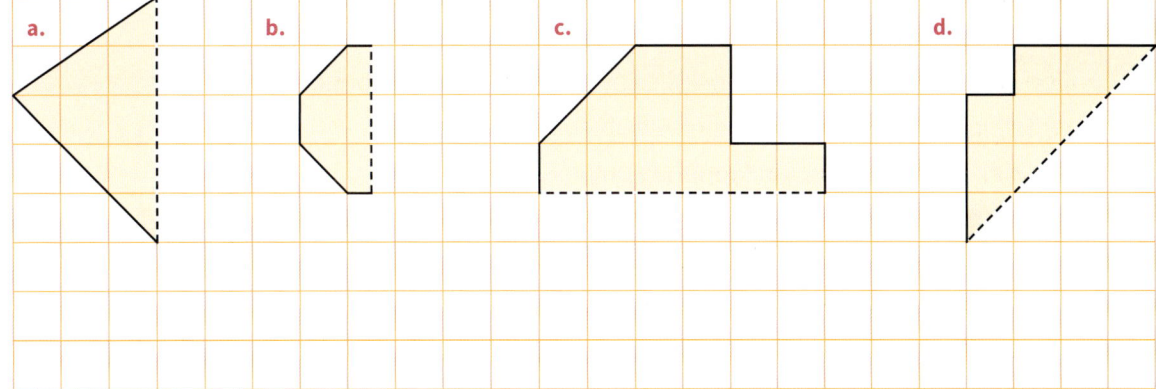

6. Copy each grid onto squared paper. Shade more squares so that the results have rotational symmetry of order 2

   a. 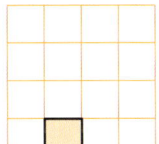   b. 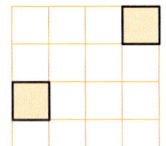   c.

7. Copy and complete each shape. Each dotted line is a line of symmetry.

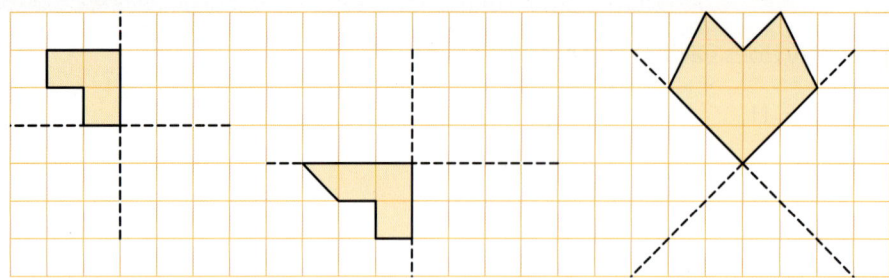

8. On squared paper draw some shapes that have:
   a. 1 line of symmetry
   b. 2 lines of symmetry
   c. 4 lines of symmetry.

9. 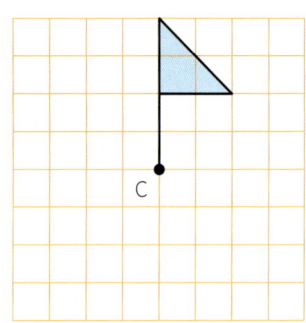 When the flag is rotated clockwise through 90°, 180° and 270° about the point C, the result is this pattern.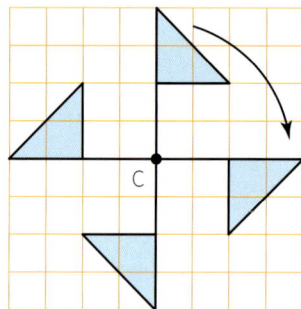

   For this pattern, write down:
   i. the order of rotational symmetry
   ii. the number of lines of symmetry.

10. For each shape below:
    i. Copy the shape and rotate it clockwise by the given angle(s) about point C.
    ii. Write the order of rotational symmetry of the resulting pattern.
    iii. Write the number of lines of symmetry of the resulting pattern.

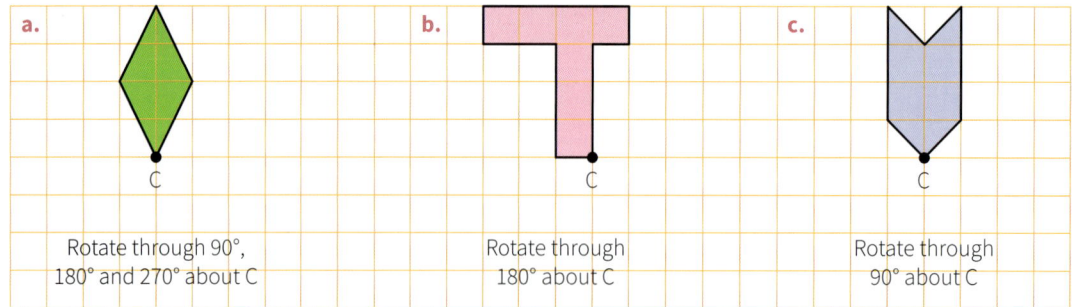

a. Rotate through 90°, 180° and 270° about C

b. Rotate through 180° about C

c. Rotate through 90° about C

11. On squared paper draw some patterns that have:
    a. rotational symmetry of order 2
    b. rotational symmetry of order 4

Shape

Tessellations

Specification reference **L1.M24**

Shapes **tessellate** if they fit together leaving no gaps.

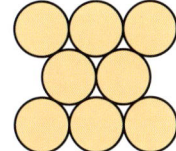
Circles do not tessellate. They leave gaps.

Hexagonal cells tessellate in a honeycomb.

Practice

1. How many triangles fit together to make each rectangle?

   a.    b. 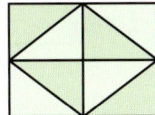   c.    d.

2. Name the shapes in these tessellations.

   a.    b.

Activities

1. Cut out 10 crosses like the one labelled **a** (below) from squared paper.

   Fit them together to form a tessellation. Repeat this with shapes **b**, **c** and **d**.

   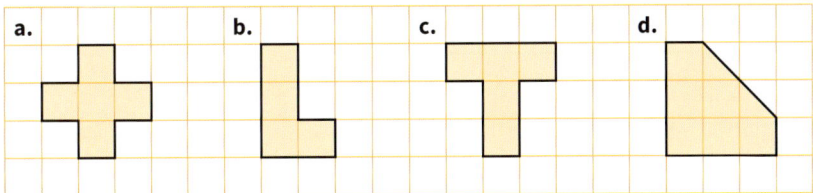

2. Use tracing paper to copy a hexagon, an octagon, a pentagon and a parallelogram. Cut out several of each shape.

   a. Which shapes tessellate by themselves?
   b. Which shapes leave triangles or squares when you try to tessellate them?

3. Many houses and other buildings have walls and floors covered with tiles. Find and draw some interesting tiling patterns. Name the shapes used.

Measures, Shape and Space

Three-dimensional (3-D) shapes

Specification reference EL3.M19

3-D (3-dimensional) shapes have: **edges**, **vertices** (that is, corners) and **faces**.

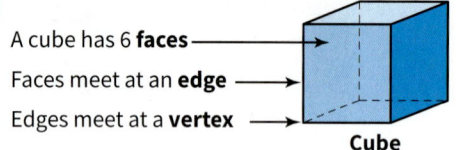

A cube has 6 **faces**
Faces meet at an **edge**
Edges meet at a **vertex**

Cube

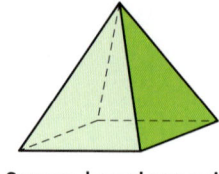

Square-based pyramid

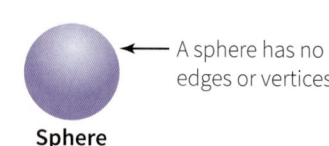

A sphere has no edges or vertices

Sphere

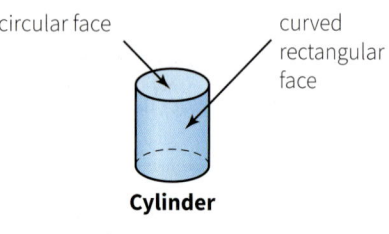

circular face
curved rectangular face

Cylinder

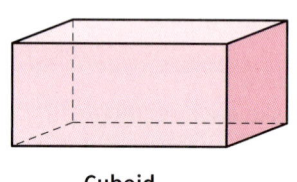

Cuboid

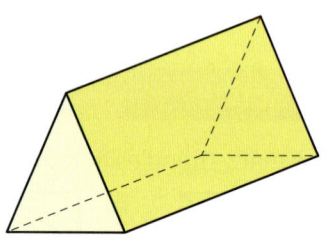

Triangular prism

Practice

1. Copy and complete the following table.

Shape	Shape of faces	Number of faces	Number of edges	Number of vertices
Cube				
Cuboid				
Cylinder				
Square-based pyramid				
Triangular prism				

 Activity

Collect together some examples of each of the 3-D shapes.

1. Which shapes stack together easily on a shelf?
2. Which shapes are difficult to stack? Why?

Shape

Plans and elevations Specification reference L1.M25, L2.M18, L2.M20, L2.M21

A. Interpret plans and elevations

Architects and engineers draw buildings and other objects in a variety of ways.

This diagram shows a **plan**, a **front elevation** and a **side elevation** of a van.

The plan shows what you see looking straight down on the van from above.

The front elevation shows what you see looking straight at the van from the front.

The side elevation shows what you see looking straight at the van from the side.

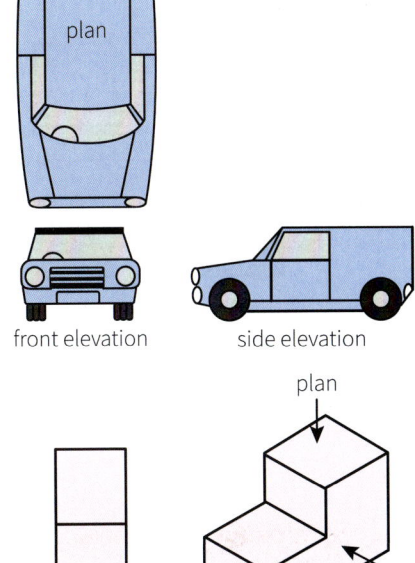

Here is a 3-D drawing of a pair of steps and its plan, front elevation and side elevation.

When you look straight down on the steps from above you just see the tops. You don't see the side or front.

When you look straight at the steps from the side or front, you don't see the tops.

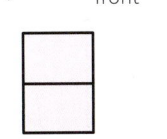
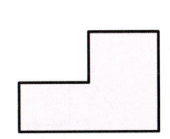

> **Key point**
>
> A plan shows the view of an object looking down from above.
> A side elevation shows the view of an object from the side.
> A front elevation shows the view of an object from the front.

Practice

1. For each part say which shape, **A**, **B** or **C**, is shown by the plan and elevations.

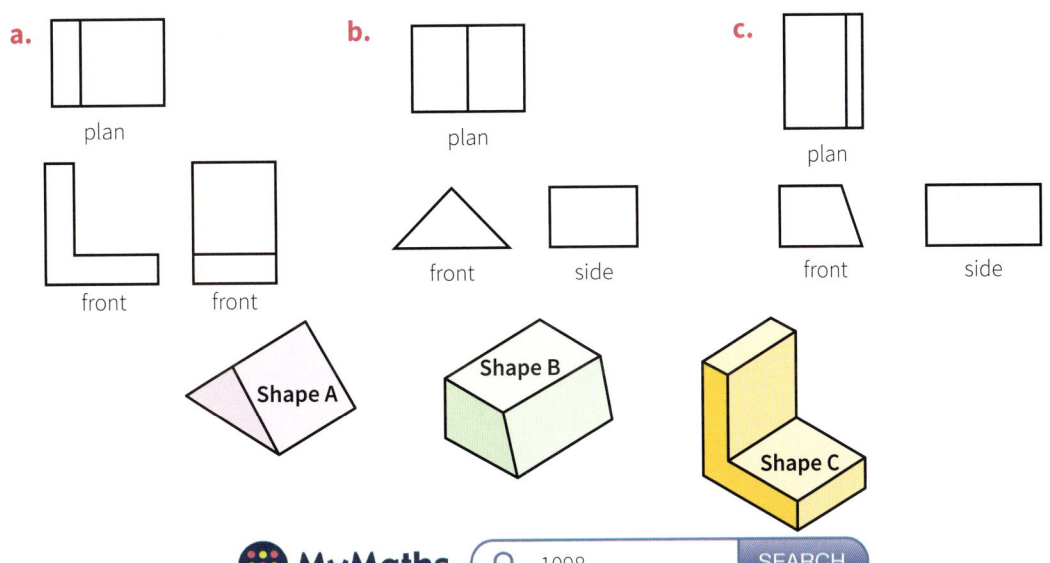

MyMaths 1098 SEARCH

2. The table shows the plan and elevations of some 3-D shapes.

   Name each shape.

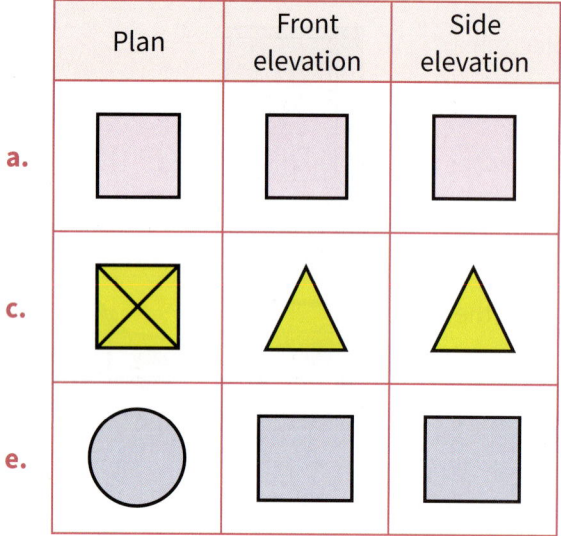

3. For each part say which object is shown by the plan and elevations.

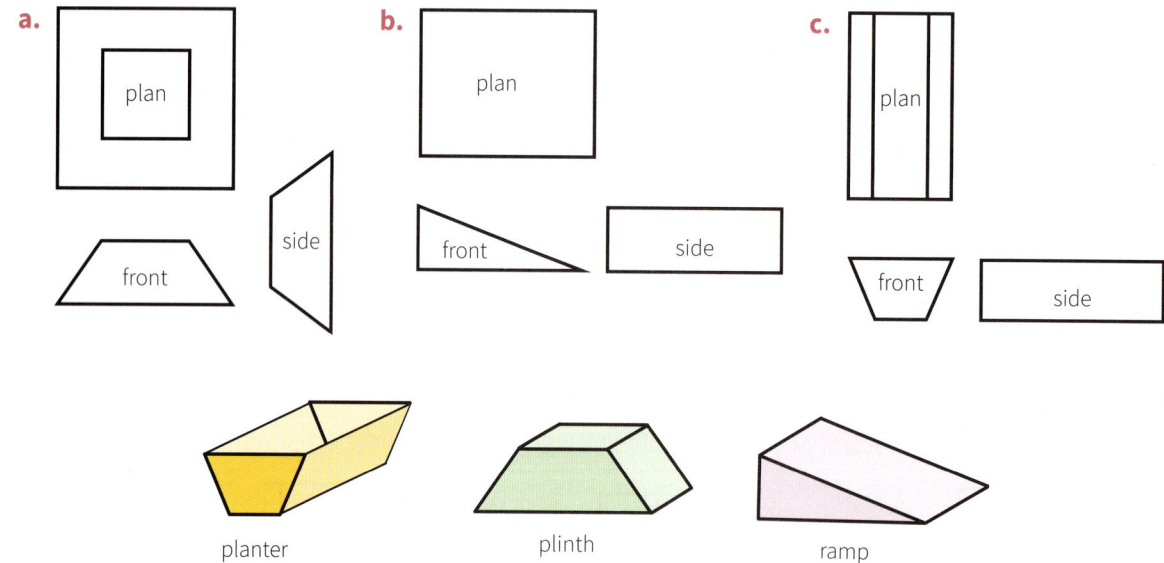

4. Describe three objects for which the plan, front elevation and side elevation are identical circles as shown.

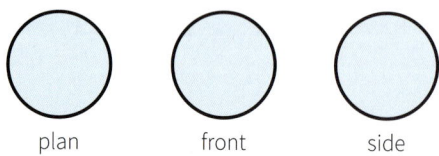

Level 2 The diagrams below show a block of wood with a triangular hole going through it. Dotted lines show the hidden edges of the block and the hole.

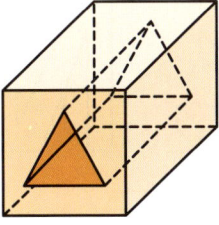

3-D diagram

front elevation

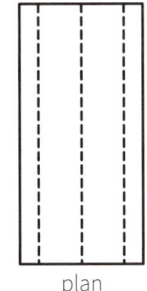

plan

side elevation

For a circular hole the dotted lines on the plan and side elevation show the hole's diameter.

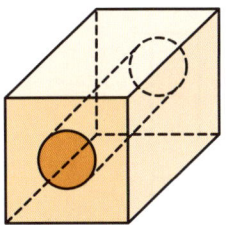

3-D diagram

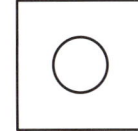

front elevation

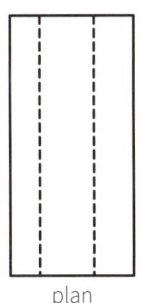

plan

side elevation

Key point

Dotted lines on plans and elevations show hidden edges.

5. For each part say which shape is shown by the plan and elevations.

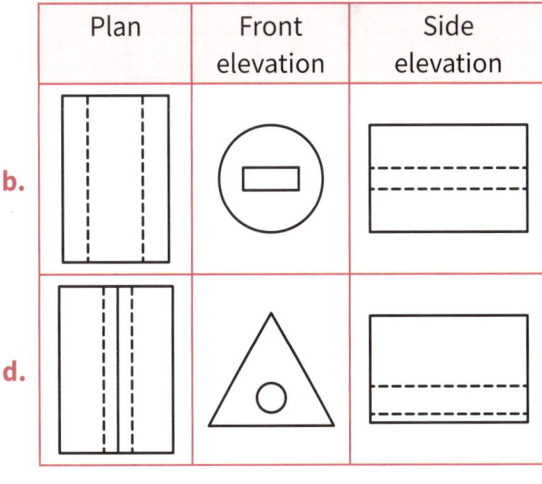

A 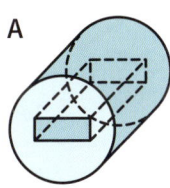   B 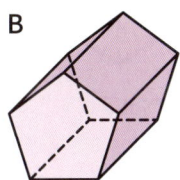   C 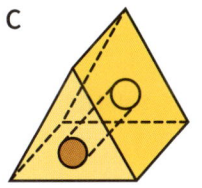   D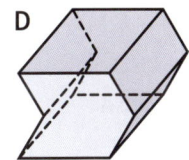

6. For each 3-D letter shape:

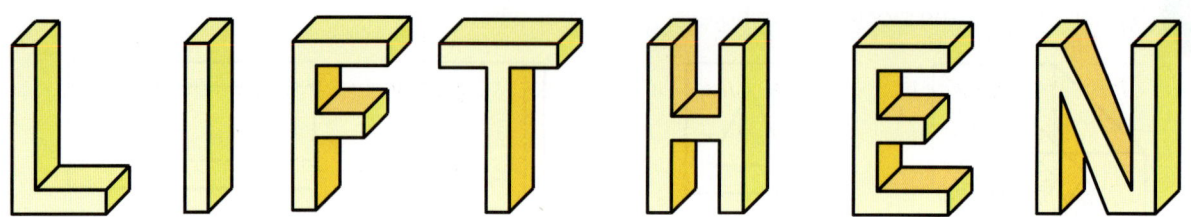

   a. state which diagram below is the correct plan.

   b. state which diagram below is the correct side elevation from the right.

   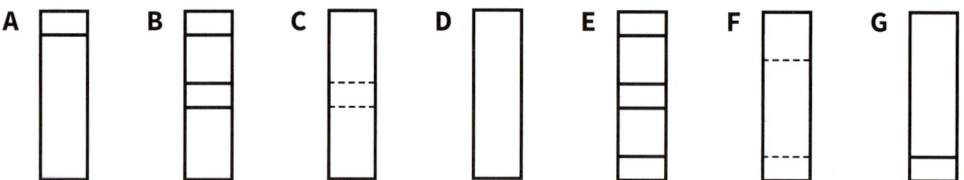

7. Each of these diagrams is a plan or elevation of one of the solids below. For each diagram say which solid it represents and whether it is a plan, a front elevation or a side elevation.

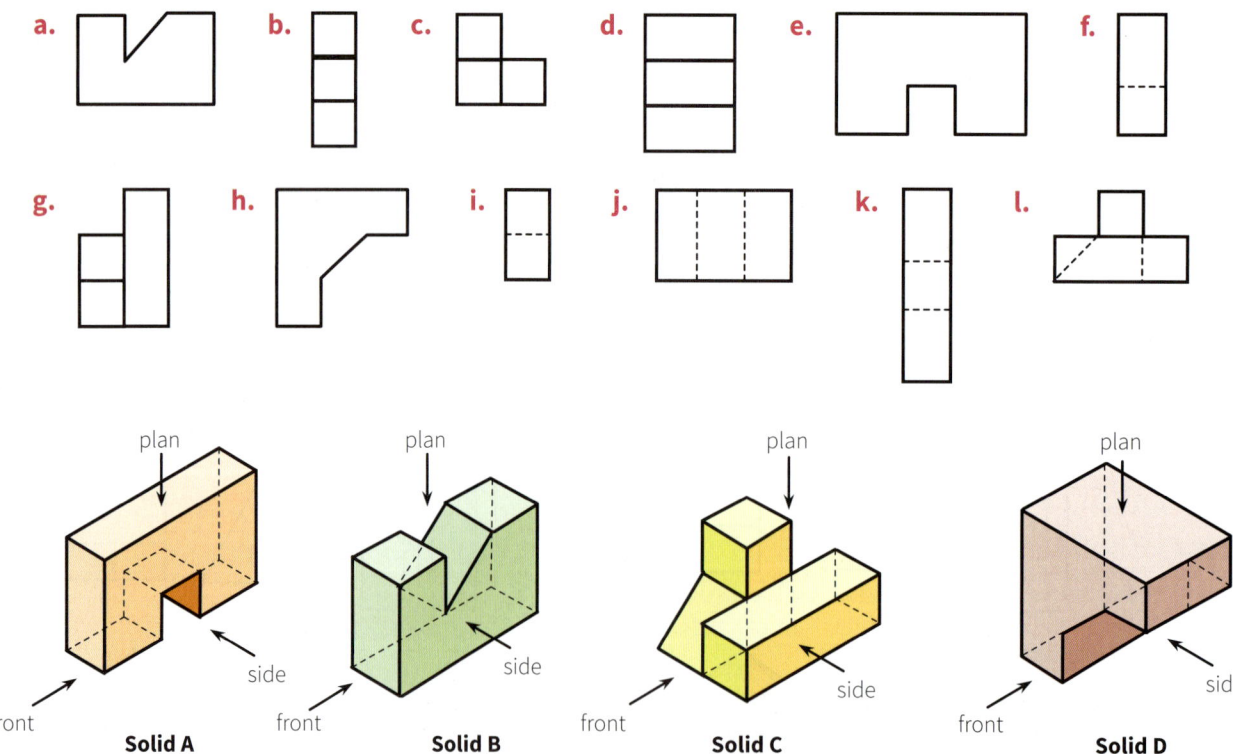

Shape

B. Draw plans and elevations

When a sketch of a 3-D object is given, you can draw a plan and elevations.

When the sketch of the object has dimensions, you can draw an accurate plan and accurate elevations to scale. You can use graph or square paper if you wish.

Example

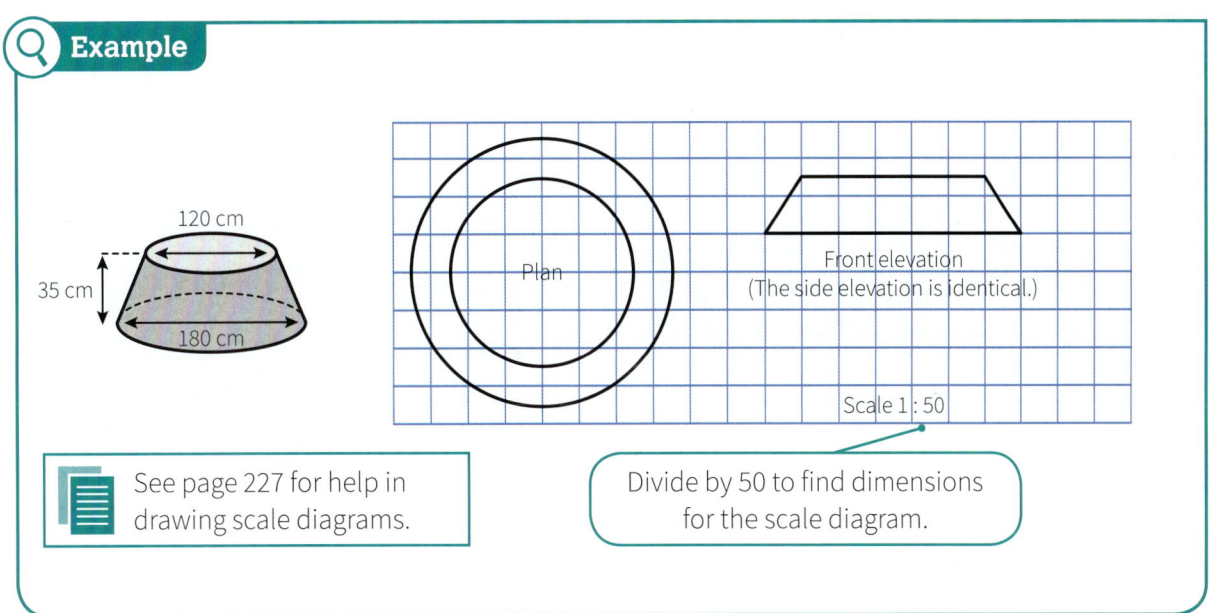

See page 227 for help in drawing scale diagrams.

Divide by 50 to find dimensions for the scale diagram.

Practice

1. Draw a plan, front elevation and side elevation (from the right) of each seat.

2. Draw a plan and front elevation of each 3-D shape.

   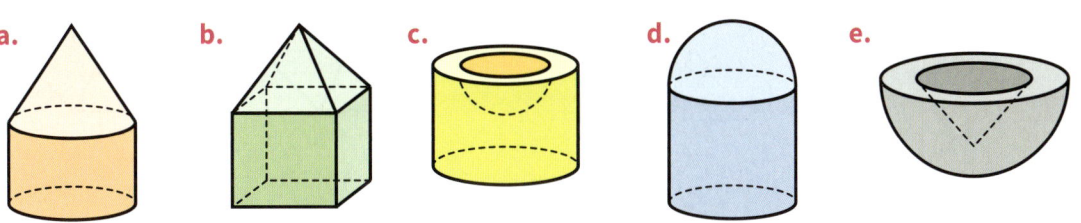

Measures, Shape and Space

3. Draw an accurate plan and accurate front and side elevations of each object.

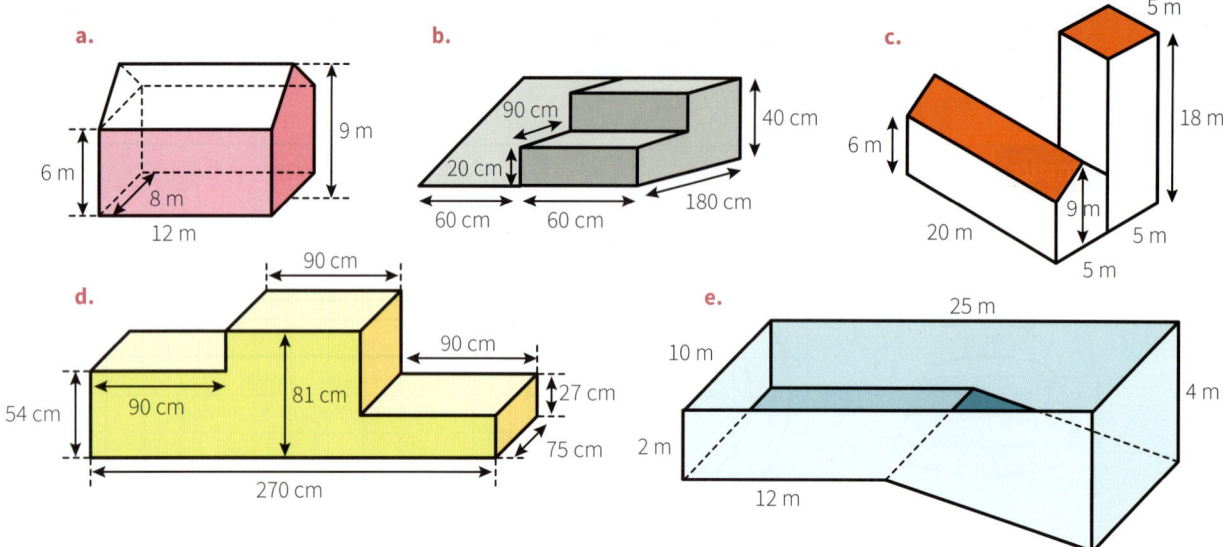

 C. Draw 3-D shapes

Level 2

You can use a grid of lines or dots to help you draw **oblique** and **isometric** diagrams of 3-D objects such as a triangular prism or a cuboid.

To draw an oblique diagram

- Use a square grid or square dotted paper.
- Draw the front face, using units on the grid to represent vertical and horizontal lengths. (Use a scale if you wish.)
- Draw the edges that are perpendicular to the front. Draw these at an angle of 45°. These edges are drawn shorter than their actual length in the scale. (often half the actual length). Include hidden edges if you wish.
- Edges that are parallel are drawn parallel on the diagram.

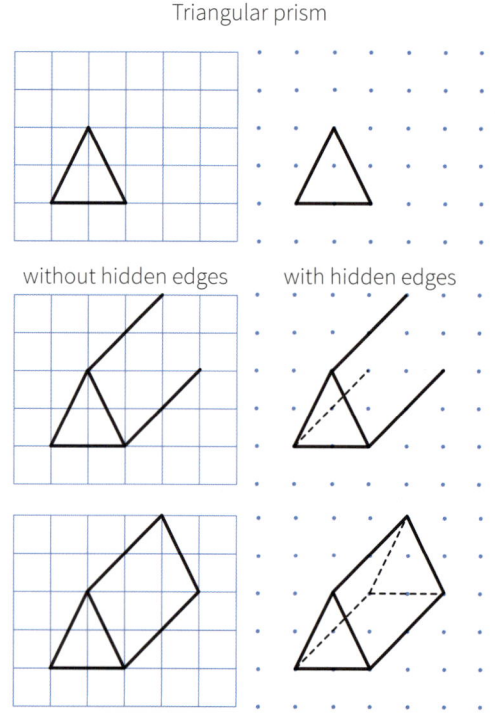

Triangular prism

Shape

Practice

1. Draw an oblique diagram of each shape. Use dotted lines for hidden edges.

   a. Cube   b. Cuboid   c. Cylinder   d. Square-based pyramid

2. These plans and elevations represent symmetrical solids. Draw an oblique diagram of each solid. Use dotted lines for hidden edges.

   a.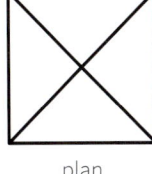
   plan

   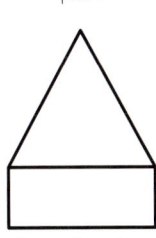
   front elevation
   (and side elevation)

   b.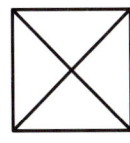
   plan

   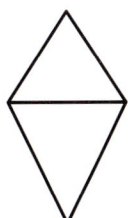
   front elevation
   (and side elevation)

   c.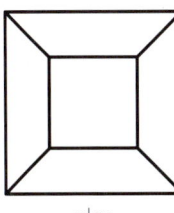
   plan

   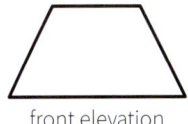
   front elevation
   (and side elevation)

3. Draw an oblique diagram of each object. Do not include hidden edges.

   a. A signpost
   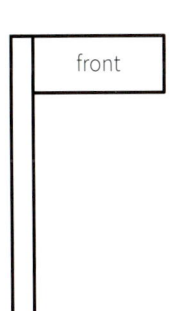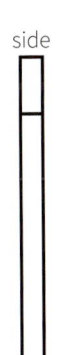

   b. A seat
   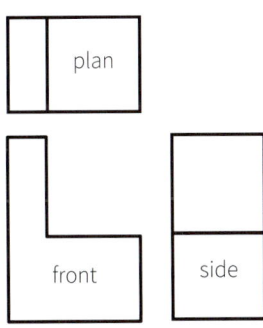

   c. A bracket
   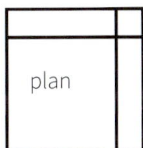
   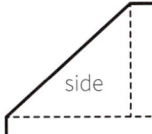

4. The diagram shows the plan and elevations of a waste skip.

   The scale used is 1 : 100.

   Draw an oblique diagram of the skip and label its dimensions. Include hidden edges.

     side

Measures, Shape and Space

5. This plan and these elevations represent a tunnel.
   Draw an oblique diagram of the tunnel. Label its dimensions.

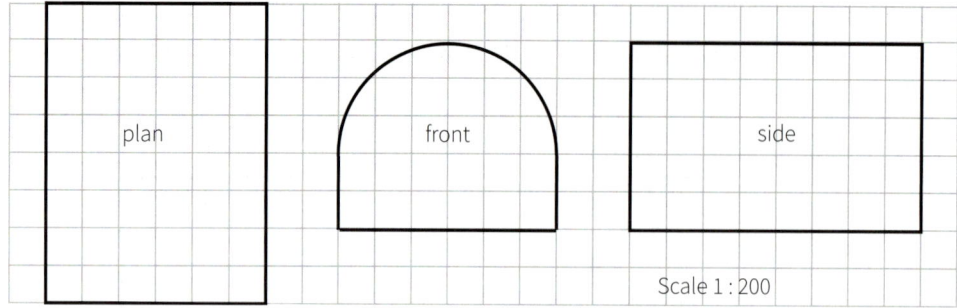

6. The diagram shows the plan and elevations of a water trough. The scale used is 1 : 20. Draw an oblique diagram of the water trough and label its dimensions.

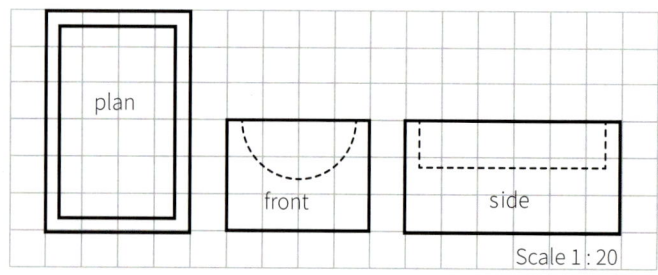

To draw an isometric diagram

- Use an isometric grid or isometric dotted paper.

> **Key point**
>
> 'Isometric' means 'of equal measure' and the units on the grid represent equal lengths.

- Use the vertical gridlines or dots to draw the vertical edges of the shape.

- Use the other gridlines or dots to show the horizontal edges of the shape. (They are at 30° to the horizontal on the diagram.) Parallel edges that are equal on the shape are parallel and equal on the diagram.

- Use the gridlines or dots to complete the diagram. Show hidden edges if you wish.

Cuboid

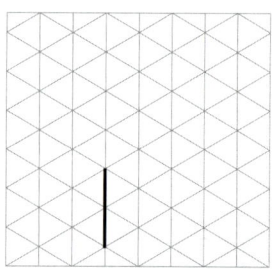
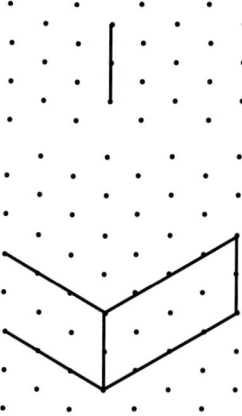

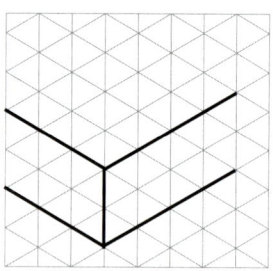

without hidden edges   with hidden edges

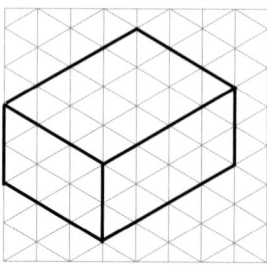
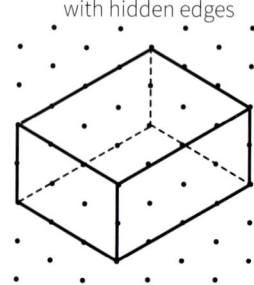

7. Draw an isometric diagram of each of these shapes.

   a. Cube
   b. Triangular prism
   c. Square-based pyramid

8. For each part draw an isometric diagram of the object shown by the plan and elevations. Show hidden edges if you wish.

   a. A roof
   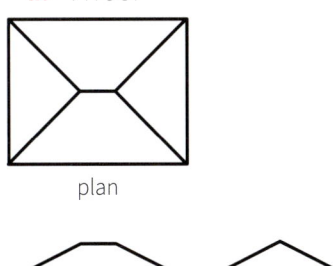

   b. A garage
   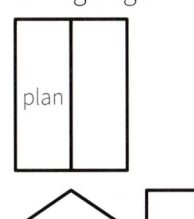

   c. A carport

9. Draw an isometric diagram of each 3-D solid represented below. In each case use dotted lines to show unseen edges.

   a.
   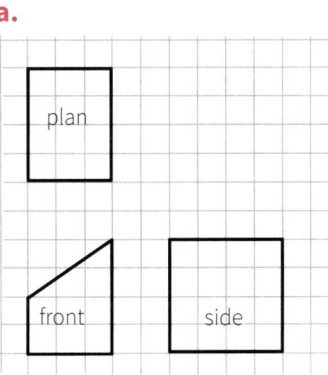

   b.
   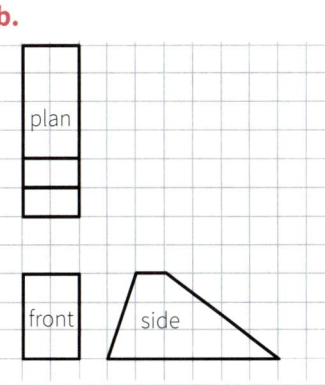

   c.
   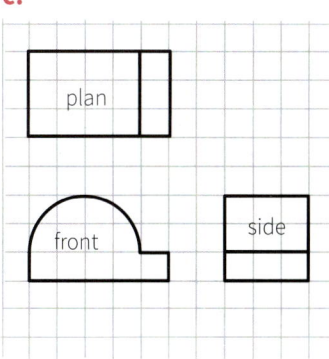

10. Draw an isometric diagram of each 3-D solid represented below. Do not show unseen edges.

    a.
    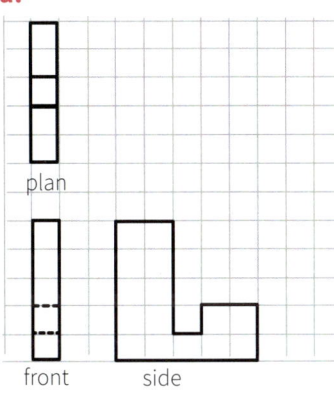

    b.
    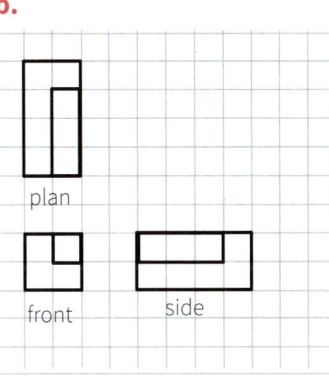

    c.
    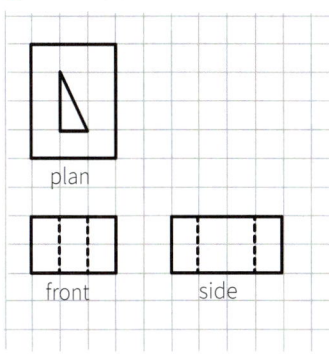

Chapter Summary
17 Shape

- A **right angle** is $\frac{1}{4}$ turn or 90°
- **Horizontal** lines go straight across from left to right, **vertical** lines go straight up and down.
- **Parallel** lines are always the same distance apart. They are shown using arrows.
- A **polygon** is a 2-D shape with straight sides. A **pentagon** has 5 sides. A **hexagon** has 6 sides.
- A **regular** polygon has equal sides and equal angles.

		Sides	Angles
Triangle	Equilateral triangle	3 equal sides	3 equal angles
	Isosceles triangle	2 equal sides	2 equal angles
	Scalene triangle	0 equal sides	0 equal angles
Quadrilateral	Square	4 equal sides 2 pairs of parallel sides	4 right angles
	Rectangle	2 pairs of equal sides 2 pairs of parallel sides	4 right angles
	Parallelogram	2 pairs of equal sides 2 pairs of parallel sides	2 pairs of equal angles
	Rhombus	4 equal sides 2 pairs of parallel sides	2 pairs of equal angles
	Trapezium	May or may not have a pair of equal sides 1 pair of parallel sides	May or may not have pairs of equal angles

- 3-D shapes have edges, vertices (corners), and faces (sides).
- A shape has **line symmetry** if it can be folded exactly in half. The fold line is the **line of symmetry**, or the **mirror line**. Each side of the mirror line is a **reflection**.

- An **acute** angle is less than 90°. An **obtuse** angle is between 90° and 180°
- **Perpendicular** lines meet at 90°
- A shape has **rotational symmetry** if it looks the same after rotating less than a full turn.
- The **order of rotational symmetry** is the number of different positions in which a shape looks the same during a complete turn.
- Shapes **tessellate** if they fit together with no gaps.
- A **plan** is the view of an object from above, **a side elevation** is the view of an object from the side and a **front elevation** is the view of an object from the front.

- The 4 angles in any quadrilateral (4-sided shape) add up to 360°
- The angles in a triangle always add up to 180°

Measures, Shape and Space

18 Position and Direction

Compass points

Specification reference **EL3.M20, L1.M26**

The points of a compass are: N (north), NE (north-east), E (east), SE (south-east), S (south), SW (south-west), W (west) and NW (north-west).

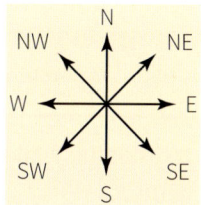

Practice

1. Solar panels are most effective if they face south, south-west or south-east.
   The diagram shows the roof tops of five houses. Each roof slope is numbered.
   Which roof slope faces:
   a. south
   b. south-west
   c. south-east?

2. a. Pat faces north and makes a $\frac{1}{2}$ turn. Which way is she facing now?
   b. Liu faces south and makes a $\frac{1}{4}$ turn clockwise. Which way is she facing now?
   c. Saj faces east and makes a $\frac{1}{4}$ turn anticlockwise. Which way is he facing now?
   d. Hannah was facing west, but is now facing south. What turn did she make?
   e. Lloyd faces north-east and makes a half turn. Which way is he facing now?
   f. Sam faces north-west and makes a $\frac{1}{4}$ turn clockwise. Which way is he facing now?
   g. Micah faces south-west and makes a $\frac{1}{4}$ turn anticlockwise. Which way is he facing now?

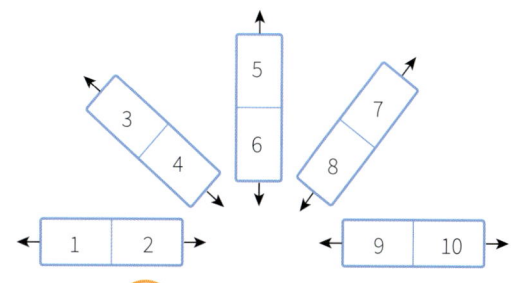

clockwise turn right · anticlockwise turn left

 For $\frac{1}{2}$ and $\frac{1}{4}$ turns see p277.

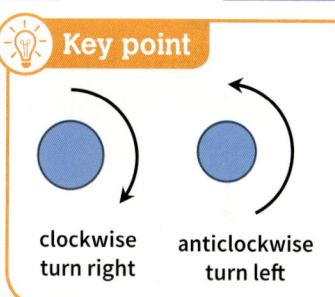

$\frac{1}{4}$ turn = a right angle = 90°
$\frac{1}{2}$ turn = 180°

3. How many degrees are there between:
   a. N and S
   b. N and E
   c. N and NE
   d. S and W
   e. S and SW
   f. N and SE
   g. E and W
   h. W and NW
   i. E and SW?

Measures, Shape and Space

Describe positions and give directions

Specification reference: **EL3.M20, L1.M25**

Here is a sketch map of a town centre.

You can use the sketch to describe where things are.

To give directions, you need to imagine walking along the route.

Sometimes you can use the compass points: north (N), south (S), east (E), west (W).

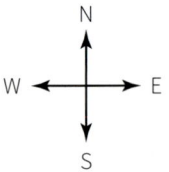

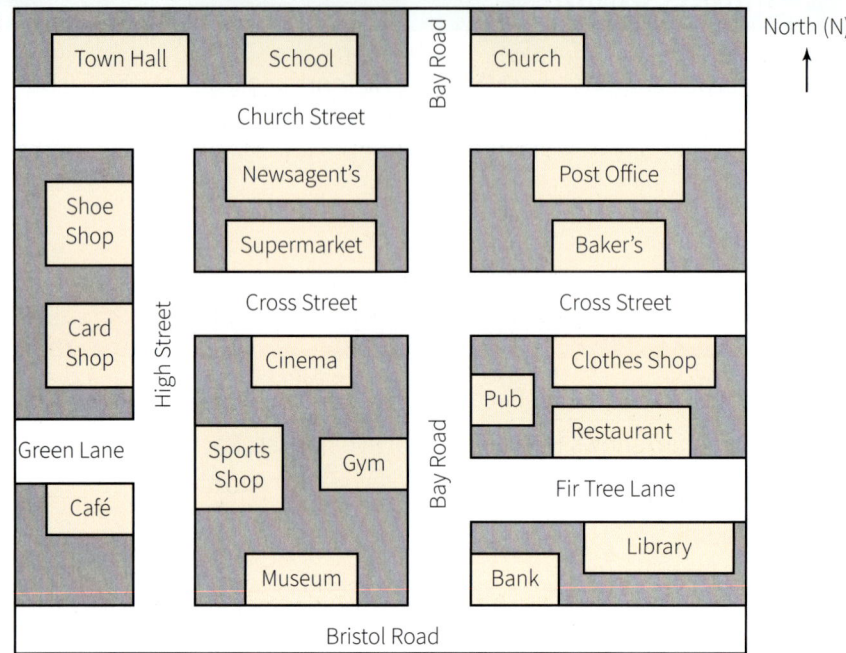

Example

- The cinema is on Cross Street opposite the supermarket.
- To go from the post office to the café, walk west along Church Street to High Street. Turn left (south) and walk down High Street past Cross Street. The café is on the right on the corner where High Street meets Green Lane.

Practice

1. Use the map to answer the questions.
   a. What is on the corner where Bay Road meets Bristol Road?
   b. I start from the café and walk north up High Street.
      i. What is the first shop I pass on my left?
      ii. Which way must I turn to go to the cinema?
   c. From the baker's, I walk west along Cross Street to Bay Road.
      Which way must I turn to go to the bank?
   d. Copy and fill in the gaps to give directions from the school to the library.

      Walk .... along Church Street to Bay Road and turn ....

      Walk .... down Bay Road, cross over .... and turn ....

      into .... The library is on the ....

296 MyMaths 1231 SEARCH

Position and Direction

2. Work in pairs. Use the sketch map to make up more questions.
   Ask your partner to answer them, then check the answers they give.

Here is a sketch map of another town centre.

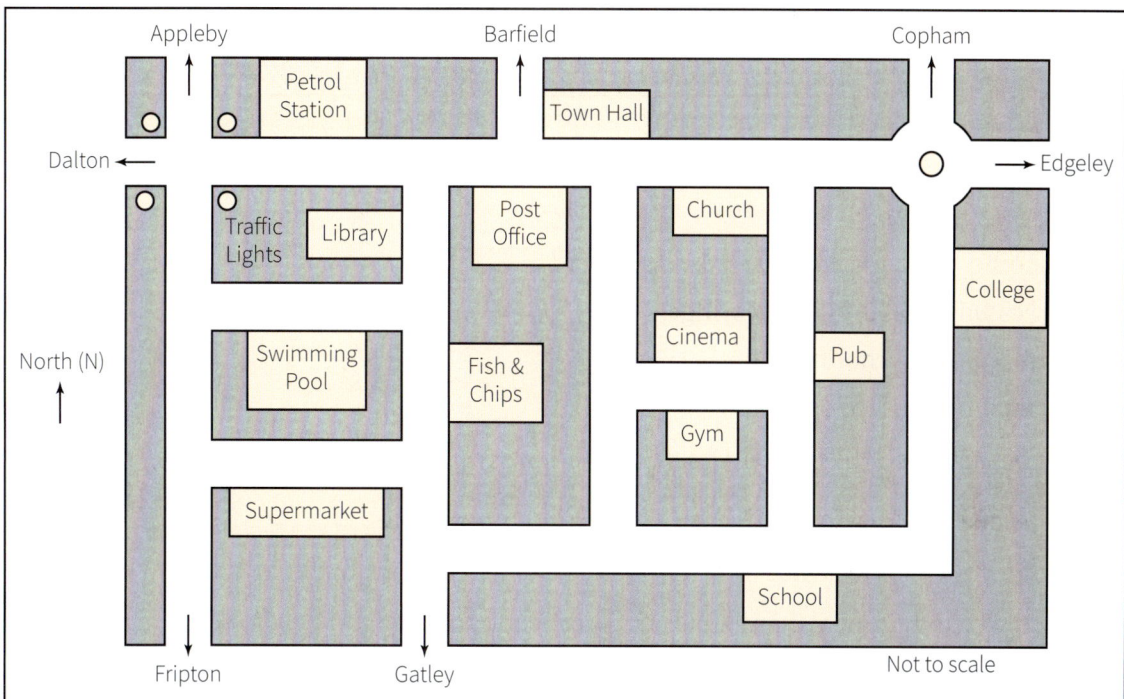

> **Example**
>
> A student from Fripton asks for directions to the college.
> One possible route is:
> Coming into town from Fripton, turn right (east) after the supermarket, turn right again (south) at the T-junction (taking the road to Gatley), then first left.
> Follow this road past the school and round a left-hand bend.
> The college is further along on the right.

3. Write down directions to the college for a student from:
   a. Copham   b. Edgeley   c. Dalton
   d. Gatley   e. Barfield   f. Appleby.

4. Write down directions to go from:
   a. the college to the post office   b. the school to the petrol station
   c. the gym to the fish and chip shop   d. the cinema to the supermarket
   e. the swimming pool to the pub   f. the cinema to the swimming pool.

Measures, Shape and Space

5. There is more than one way to go from the college to the swimming pool.
   a. Give the directions for two different routes.
   b. Which route do you think is best? Why?
6. Work in pairs. Use the sketch to make up more questions.
   Ask your partner to answer them, then check the answers they give.

Bearings

Specification reference L1.M26

The points on a compass are not always accurate enough for describing positions or giving directions. For greater accuracy we use angles written as **3-figure bearings**. The diagram shows how north, south, east and west are written as bearings.

N 000°
W 270°
E 090°
S 180°

To find the bearing of an object from a point:

- draw a north line from the point
- measure the angle **clockwise** from the north line to the direction of the object.
- When the bearing is more than 180° you may need to add (or subtract) angles.

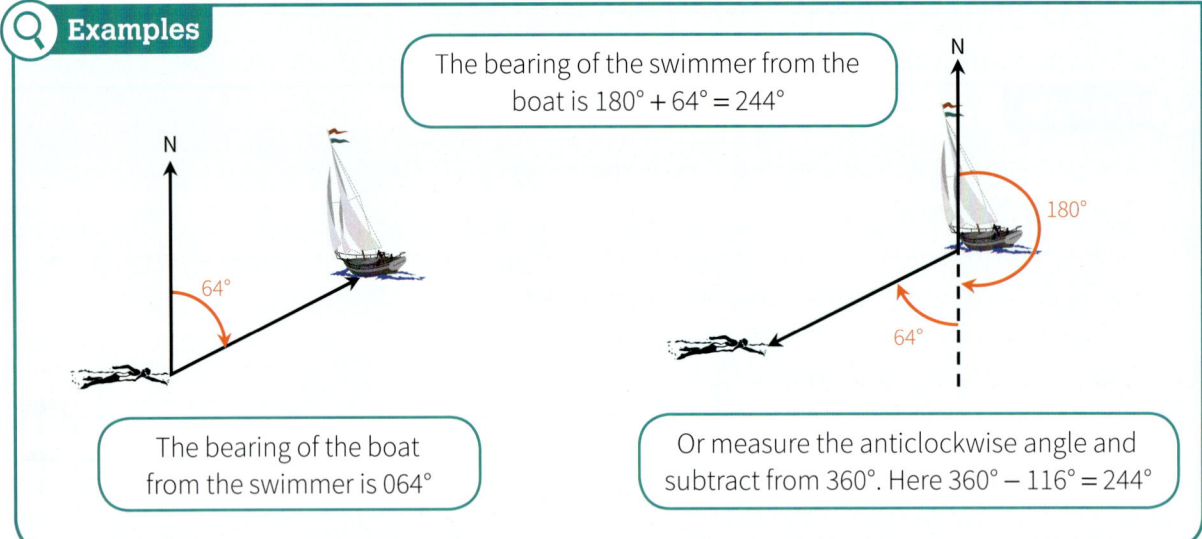

Examples

The bearing of the swimmer from the boat is 180° + 64° = 244°

The bearing of the boat from the swimmer is 064°

Or measure the anticlockwise angle and subtract from 360°. Here 360° − 116° = 244°

Key point

To find a bearing, draw a north line first.
Measure the angle clockwise from the north line.
Or measure the anticlockwise angle and subtract from 360°

 1086 SEARCH

Position and Direction

 Key point

A bearing is always written using three figures. If the angle is less than 100°, a leading zero must be added to provide 3 figures for example 064°

 Practice

1. Measure the bearing of each boat from the lighthouse.
   Use the dots to represent the position of the lighthouse and the boat.

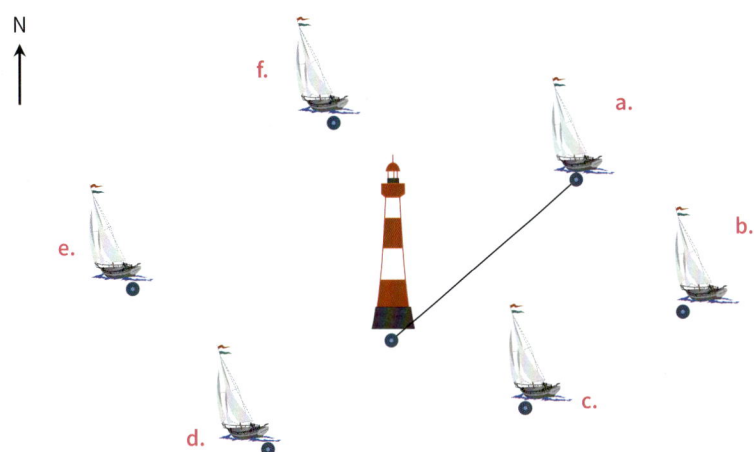

2. a. What direction must the shark take to reach the boat?
    b. What direction must the boat take to reach the shark?

3. Jane and Wadhah walk across a field during a search and rescue exercise.
   Use tracing paper to trace the dots that give the starting positions for Jane and Wadhah.

Wadhah

Jane

Jane walks on bearing 245°
Wadhah walks on bearing 100°
   a. Who walks further before they meet?
   b. Draw a diagram to illustrate your answer.

Measures, Shape and Space

Positions on maps

Specification reference EL3.M20

Maps often use a grid of squares to give locations of places of interest.
This map of Kensington Gardens in London has squares labelled by letters and numbers.
The museum, **M**, is in the **D2** square.

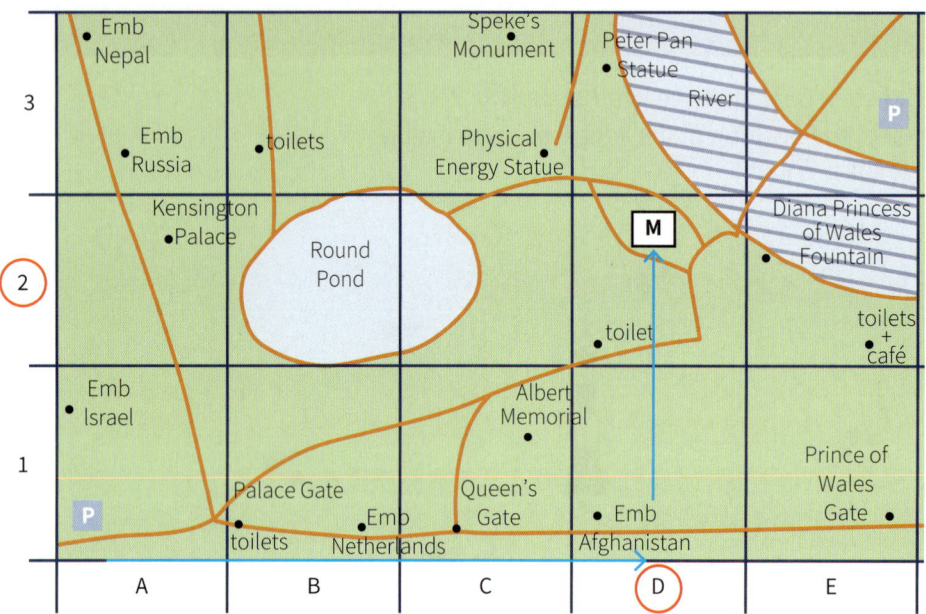

Go across, then up.
A useful reminder is:
'Along the hall before the stairs'.

Practice

1. A charity event is to be held in Kensington Gardens.
   a. A treasure hunt says an item is in the embassy in square **B1**. Which embassy is this?
   b. Another item is at a statue in square **D3**. Which statue is this?
   c. During the event three parachutists aim to land at the following sites. Name the squares in which they lie.
      i. Princess of Wales Fountain
      ii. Albert Memorial
      iii. Speke's Monument
2. List all the squares that contain:
   a. embassies,
   b. toilets.
3. The orange lines on the map are paths.
   a. From Queen's Gate you can walk along paths to the Round Pond. List the squares you walk through.
   b. You can walk along paths from the embassy of Nepal to the car park on the opposite side of the river. List the squares you walk through.

Position and Direction

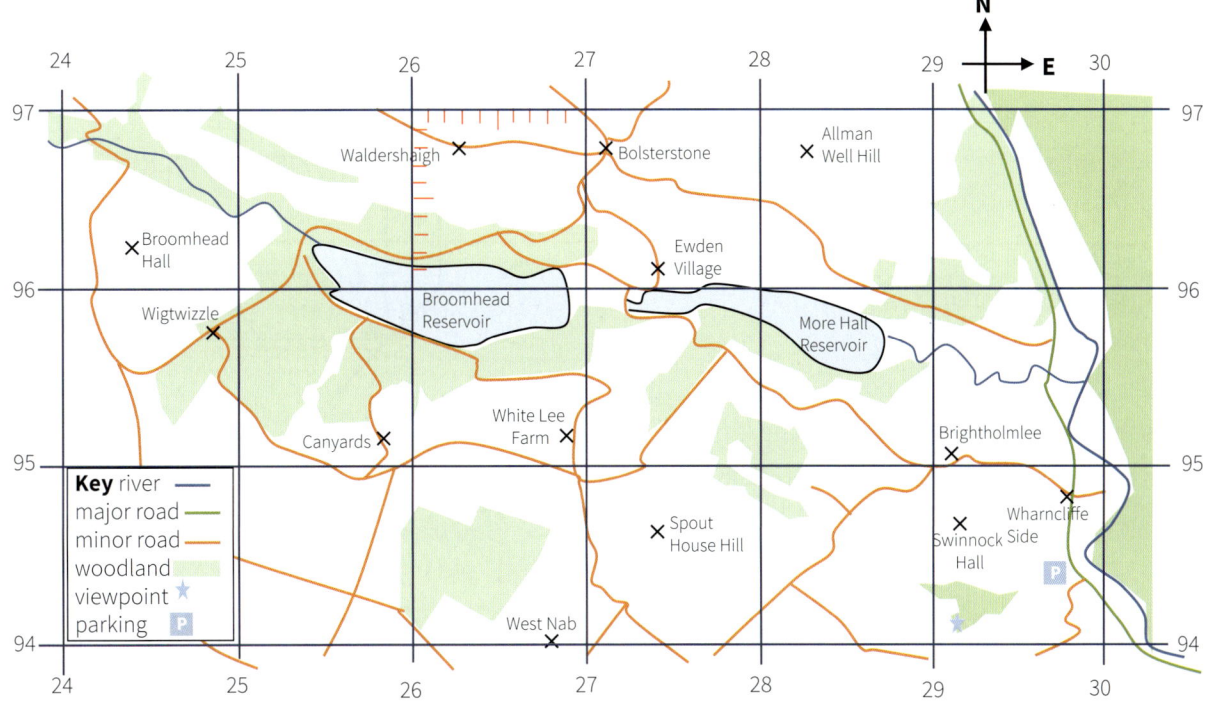

Practice

1. Write down 6-figure grid references for these places on the map:
   a. West Nab
   b. Brightholmlee
   c. Broomhead Hall
   d. Canyards
   e. Swinnock Hall
   f. Wigtwizzle
   g. Bolsterstone
   h. Wharncliffe Side.

2. Describe what lies at the following grid references:
   a. 269 952
   b. 283 967
   c. 274 961
   d. 274 946
   e. 297 944
   f. 253 955
   g. 292 942
   h. 260 960

Activity

Use an Ordnance Survey map of your local area to plan a day out visiting a variety of places of interest. Give grid references for the places you will visit.

3-D coordinates

Specification reference L2.M22

In a rectangular room you can use 2-D coordinates (x, y) to give the position of something on the floor. To give the position of something that is not on the floor, you also need a third coordinate to give its height above the floor. This is called the z-coordinate.

The set of coordinates that locates a point in space is (x, y, z).

The x, y and z axes are all at right angles to each other.

Measures, Shape and Space

Example

The diagram shows a cuboid with
OA = 3 units, OB = 5 units and
OC = 4 units.
Starting from O and moving
3 squares in the *x*-direction,
5 squares in the *y*-direction and
4 squares in the *z*-direction
takes you to E, so E is the point (3, 5, 4).
D is the point (3, 5, 0). Its *z*-coordinate is 0.
C is the point (0, 0, 4). Its *x* and *y* coordinates are both 0.

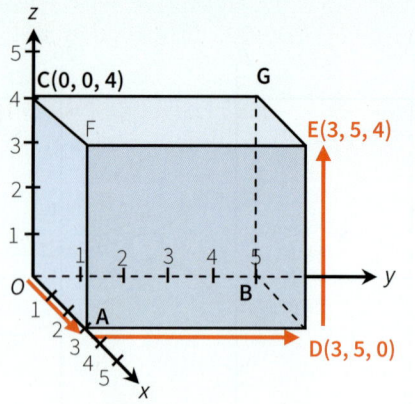

Key point
Always write coordinates in the order (*x*, *y*, *z*).

Practice

1. Write the coordinates of the points O, A, B, F and G in the Example above.

2. In this diagram of a cuboid,
   vertex P is the point (10, 8, 6).

   Write the coordinates of Q, R, S, T, U and V.

   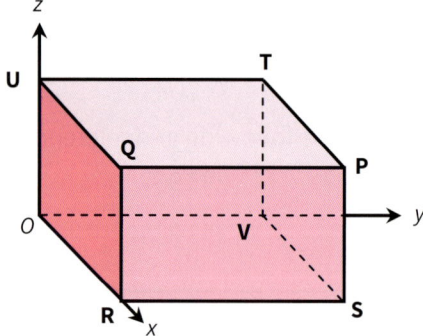

3. The diagram shows a cube with vertices ABCDEFGH and edges of length 3 units.

   The coordinates of vertex A are (0, 1, 2).
   Write the coordinates of the other vertices.

   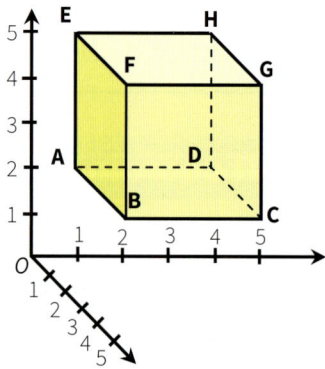

Position and Direction

4. Five unit cubes are arranged as shown.
   Write the coordinates of A, B, C, D, E and F.

   > All edges of a **unit cube** are 1 unit long.

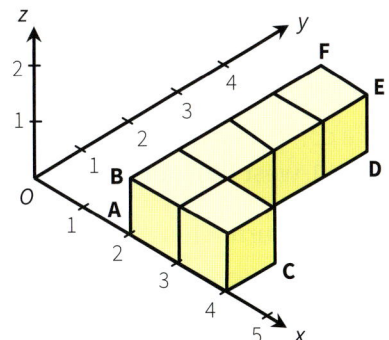

5.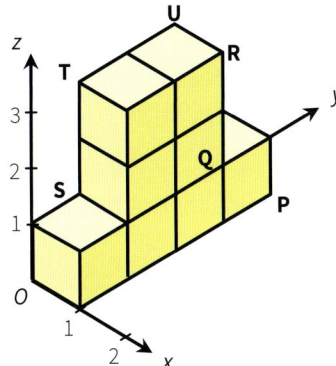

   Eight unit cubes are arranged as shown.

   Write the coordinates of P, Q, R, S, T and U.

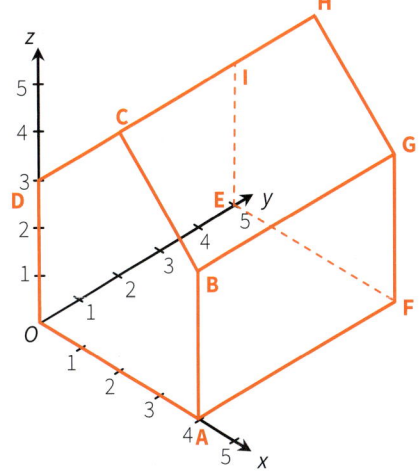

6. The diagram shows a building.
   Each unit represents 1 metre.
   a. Write down the length, width and height of the building.
   b. Write the coordinates of O, A, B, C, D, E, F, G, H and I.

7. On this plan and elevation of a row of buildings, the scale of the *x, y* and *z* axes is in metres.

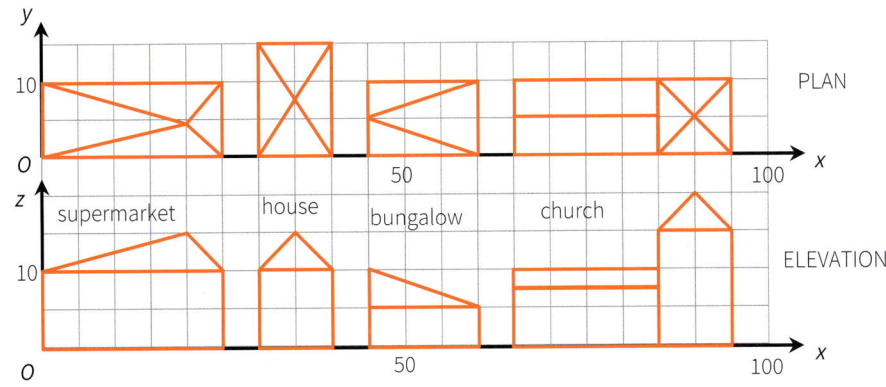

   Write the 3-D coordinates of the highest point on each building.

   > For a reminder of plans and elevations of 3-D shapes see page 285.

8. A square-based pyramid is 6 units high.
   Three of the base vertices are at (0, 0, 0), (8, 8, 0) and (0, 8, 0).
   Find the coordinates of:
   a. the other base vertex
   b. the top of the pyramid.

Chapter Summary
18 Position and Direction

- The points of a compass are **north (N)**, **north-east (NE)**, **east (E)**, **south-east (SE)**, **south (S)**, **south-west (SW)**, **west (W)**, **north-west (NW)**.
- A **full turn** = 360°, $\frac{1}{2}$ **turn** = 180°, $\frac{1}{4}$ **turn** = 90° = **a right angle**
- Maps use squares on a grid to give locations, for example to find square D2: go across to D, then up to 2 (along the hall before the stairs).

- **Bearings** are 3-figure angles that give directions from north.
- To find the bearing of an object from a point, draw a north line at the point. Measure the angle clockwise from the north line to the direction of the object. Bearings are always written using 3 digits (so 65° is written as 065°).
- When a bearing is more than 180°, measure anticlockwise from the north line then subtract from 360° or measure the angle from the south line and then add 180°

- **2-D coordinates** give the position of a point on a graph (or any flat surface). They are written as (*x*, *y*) where *x* and *y* may be positive or negative numbers. The **origin**, **O**, is the point (0, 0).
- 6-figure **grid references** use **eastings** (horizontal grid references) and **northings** (vertical grid references) to give accurate locations on maps.
- **3-D coordinates** give the position of a point in space (3-D). They are written as (*x*, *y*, *z*).
- The *x*, *y* and *z* axis are all at right angles to each other.

Measures, Shape and Space

19 Perimeter, Area and Volume

Perimeter

Specification reference **L1.M22, L2.N3, L2.M16**

The **perimeter** of a shape is the distance all the way round it.

Measuring the sides of this shape gives the lengths shown.

Perimeter of the shape = 2.5 + 5 + 6.5 + 3

= **17 cm**

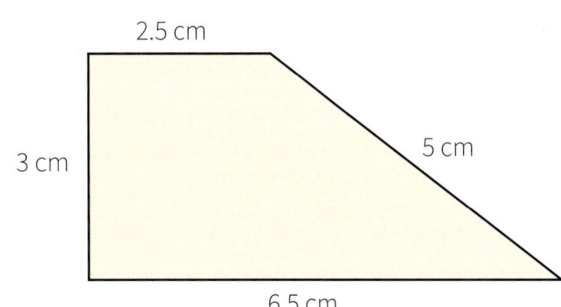

Key point
The perimeter is the total length of its sides.

Practice

1. For each shape: **i.** use a ruler to measure each side   **ii.** work out the perimeter.

   a.    b. 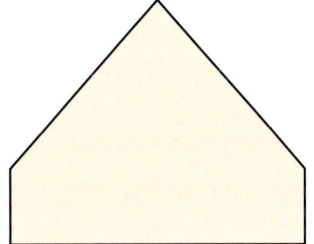   c.

   d. 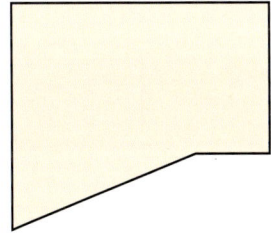   e.    f.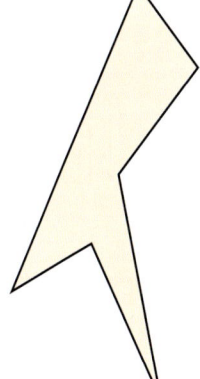

2. **a.** What is the perimeter of this shape?
   b. Did you need to measure all the sides to find the perimeter?

   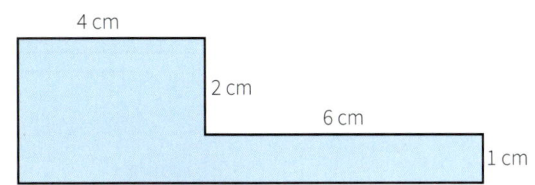

Measures, Shape and Space

Example

A gardener wants to put lawn edging around the perimeter of this lawn.

Work out the total length he needs.

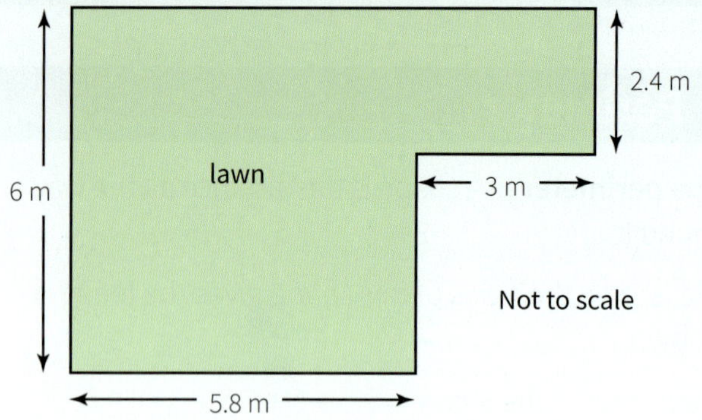

The lengths of two sides are not given on the diagram. These must be worked out first.

Length needed (perimeter)

$= 8.8 + 2.4 + 3 + 3.6 + 5.8 + 6$

$= \mathbf{29.6\ m}$

Check by rounding:
$9 + 2 + 3 + 4 + 6 + 6 = 30$

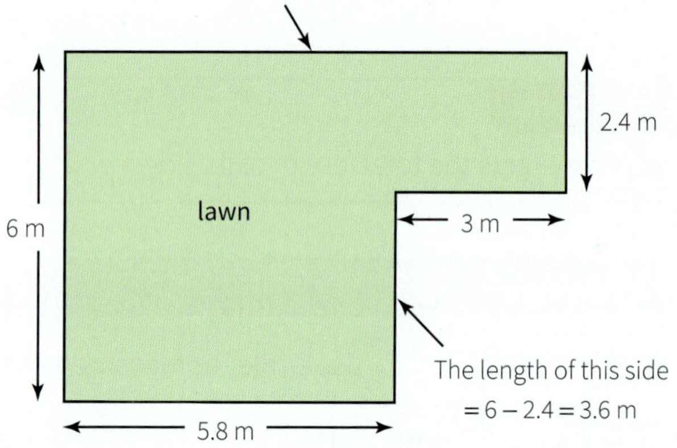

The length of this side
$= 5.8 + 3 = 8.8\ m$

The length of this side
$= 6 - 2.4 = 3.6\ m$

Not to scale

3. A decorator needs coving to go round these ceilings. Work out the total length she needs for each ceiling.

Diagrams not to scale

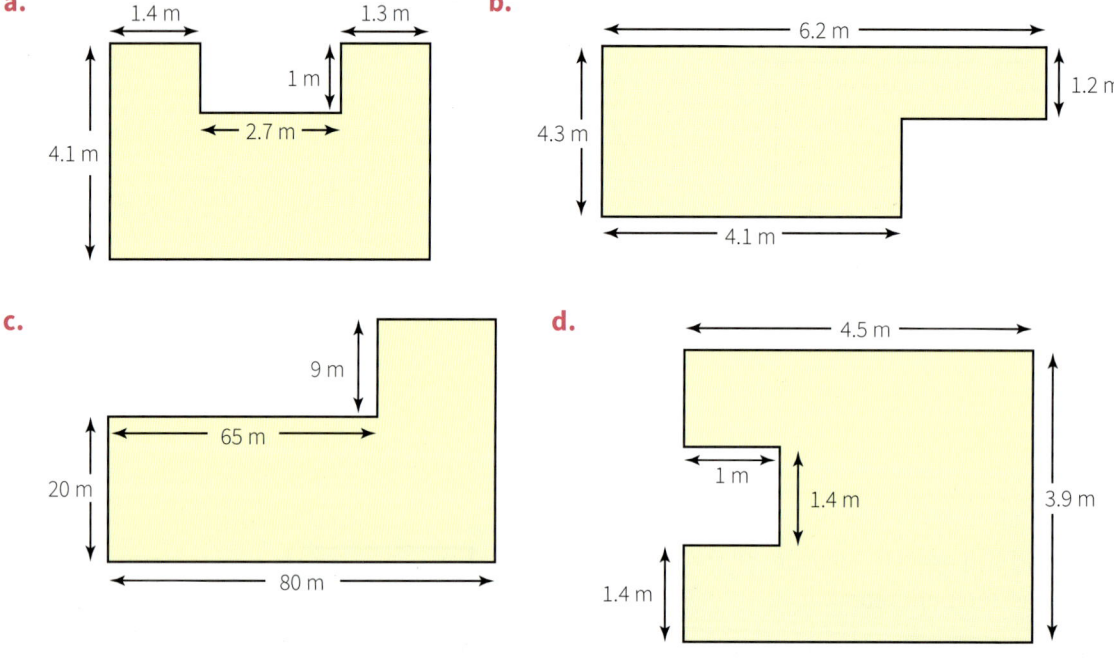

Perimeter, Area and Volume

4. Find the length of sealant needed to go round the base of the shower shown in the diagram.

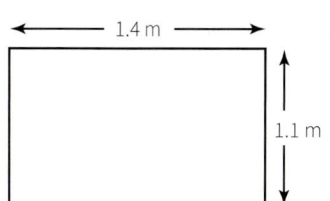

5. The sketch shows a loft hatch.
   Find the length of draft excluder needed to go round it.

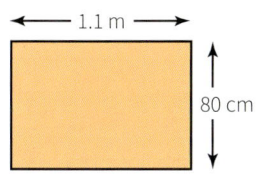

> **Key point**
> You must use the same units for each side.

6. The table gives the lengths and widths of some rectangles. Copy and complete the table.

7. Copy and complete the table below.
   Give the length and width of two possible rectangles for each perimeter.

Length	Width	Perimeter
6 cm	2 cm	
10 mm	6 mm	
20 cm	6.2 cm	
4.5 m	3 m	
20 mm	15 mm	
2.7 m	2.25 m	

Perimeter	Rectangle 1		Rectangle 2	
	length	width	length	width
a. 14 cm				
b. 20 cm				
c. 18 cm				
d. 28 cm				
e. 32 cm				

8. A rectangular field is 400 m long and 250 m wide. What is its perimeter?

9. Lace is needed to go round the perimeter of a 80 cm square tablecloth. What length of lace is needed?

10. A rectangular rabbit run is 2 m 40 cm long and $1\frac{1}{2}$ m wide. What is its perimeter?

To find the perimeter of the rectangular shapes in questions **3** and **4** you have added together 2 lengths and 2 widths. This can be written as a formula:

> **Key point**
> Perimeter of rectangle = 2 × (length + width)

Note that length and width are sometimes called **dimensions**.

In letters the perimeter formula is:

> **Key point**
> $P = 2(l + w)$

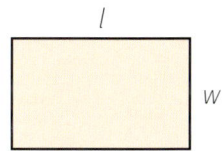

Use this formula to check your answers to the previous questions.

> For more on formulae, see pages 69–72.

Measures, Shape and Space

Area

Specification reference L1.M22, L2.N3, L2.M16

A. Measuring in square units

Area is the amount of surface inside a 2-D shape (flat shape).

We measure area in **square units**, e.g. **square centimetres (cm²)** or **square metres (m²)**.

Example

This is 1 cm².

The area of this shape is **4 cm²**.

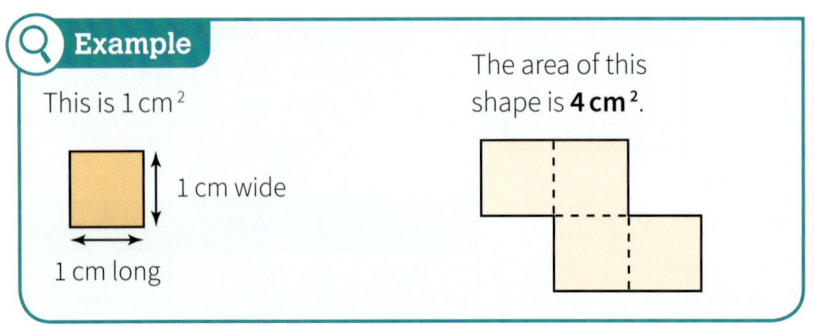

Key point

Area is measured in square units for example. cm² or m²

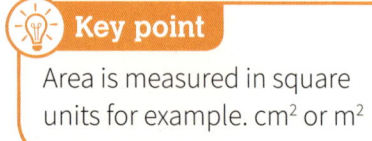

Practice

1. Write the area of each of these shapes, where one small square represents 1 cm².

    a.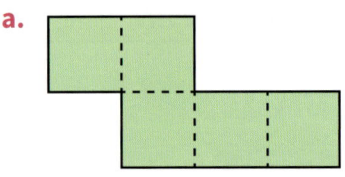
    b.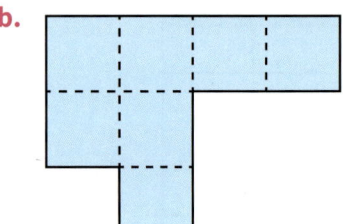
    c.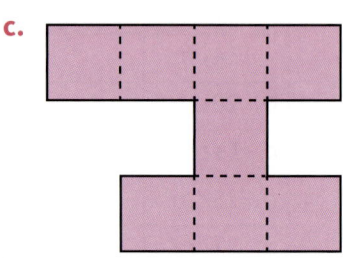

2. On cm squared paper, draw 4 different shapes, each with an area of 12 cm².

B. Area of a rectangle

Example

Find the area of a rectangular room that is 6m long and 3m wide.

You can sketch a rectangle and count the squares.
The area of the room is **18 m²**.

You can also find the area without drawing the squares.
The area of the room is 6 × 3 = **18 m²**.

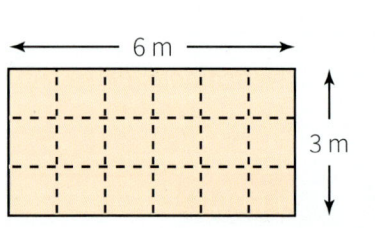

Key point

You need to learn:

Area of a rectangle = length × width

Use the same units for both sides.

Perimeter, Area and Volume

Practice

1. Find the area of these rectangles.

a. 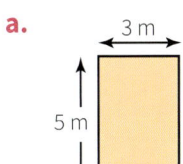   b. 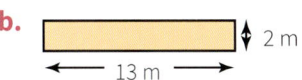   c.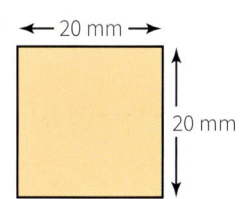

d. 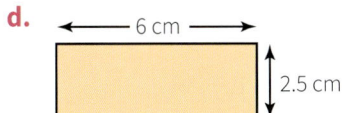   e. 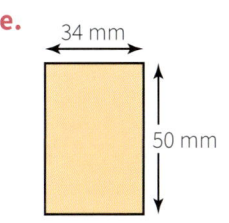   f.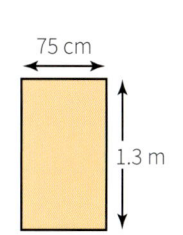

2. Give possible dimensions for rectangles with these areas.

a. $24\,cm^2$ b. $18\,m^2$ c. $35\,cm^2$ d. $80\,mm^2$ e. $75\,m^2$ f. $320\,cm^2$

> **Key point**
>
> Area = length × width
> This formula in letters is: $A = l \times w$ or $A = lw$
> You need to learn this.

 Level 2

3. A rectangular lawn has dimensions $l = 9$ metres and $w = 6$ metres.
   a. What is the area of the lawn?
   b. A gardener spreads fertiliser on the lawn. She uses 20 grams per square metre. How much fertiliser does she use?

 Level 1

C. Areas of shapes made from rectangles

Sometimes the area of a shape can be found by splitting it into parts.

> **Example**
>
>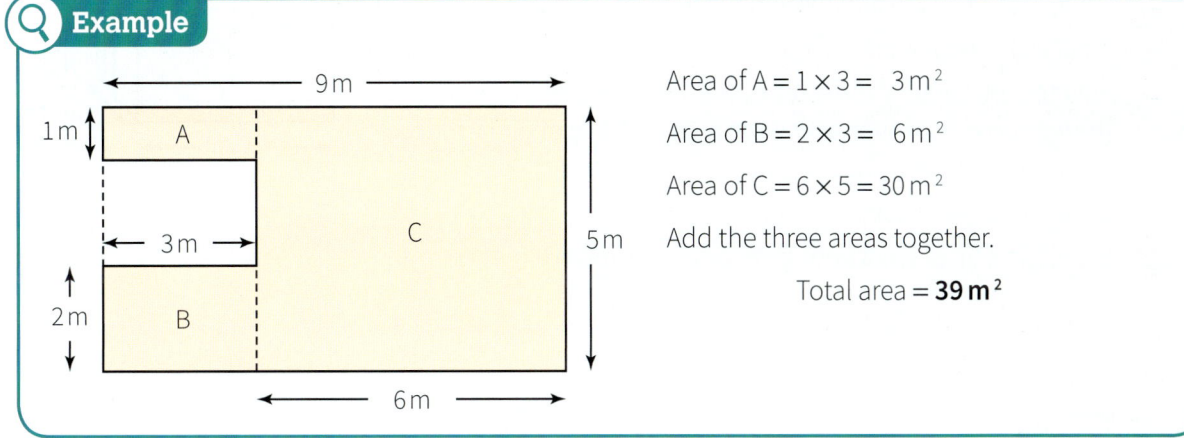
>
> Area of A = 1 × 3 = $3\,m^2$
> Area of B = 2 × 3 = $6\,m^2$
> Area of C = 6 × 5 = $30\,m^2$
> Add the three areas together.
> Total area = **$39\,m^2$**

Measures, Shape and Space

Sometimes you can make a rectangle around the shape and subtract part of it.

🔍 Example

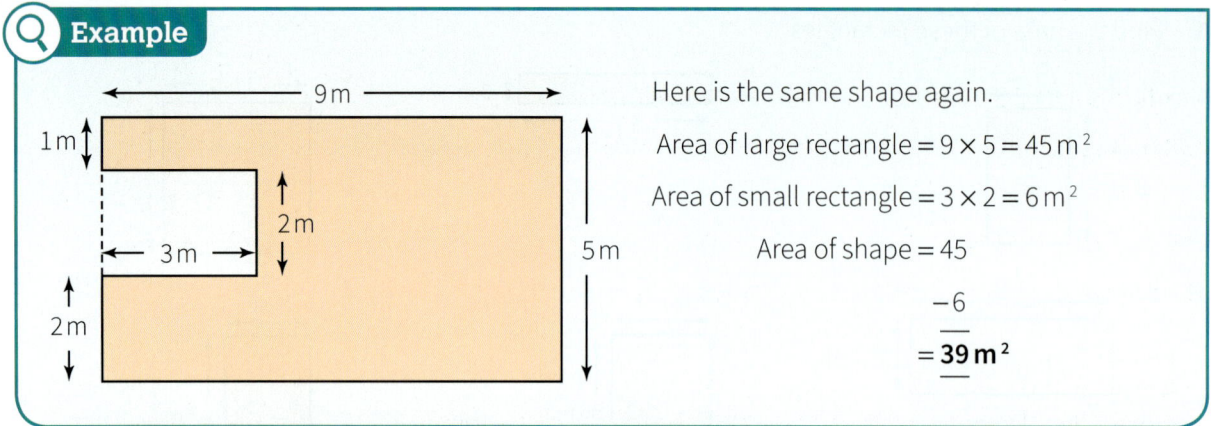

Here is the same shape again.

Area of large rectangle = 9 × 5 = 45 m²

Area of small rectangle = 3 × 2 = 6 m²

Area of shape = 45
                −6
             = 39 m²

⚙ Practice

1. Find the area of each room.

   a., b., c.

   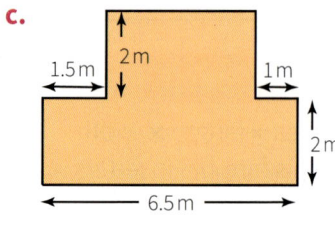

   d.

   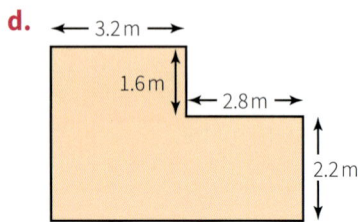

   e.

   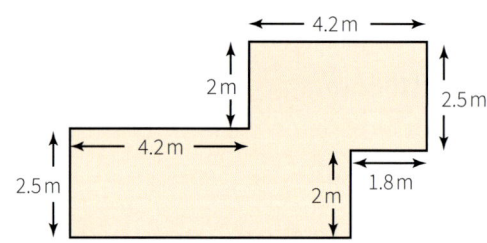

2. A room is 3.6 m long and 3 m wide. The walls are 2.2 m high.
   The door is 0.8 m by 2 m and the window is 1.5 m by 1.2 m.

   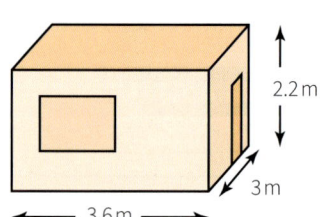

   a. What is the area of the ceiling?
   b. Find the total area of the walls by adding together the areas of the walls and then subtracting the area of the door and window.
   c. The walls and ceiling need painting.
      Each litre of paint covers 12 m².
      Is a 2.5 litre tin of paint enough to paint this room?

Circles

Specification reference **L2.M16**

A. Circumference

A **radius** is a straight line from the centre of a circle to the edge.

A **diameter** is a straight line from one side of the circle to the other that passes through its centre.

The diameter is twice the length of the radius.

The perimeter of a circle is called its **circumference**.

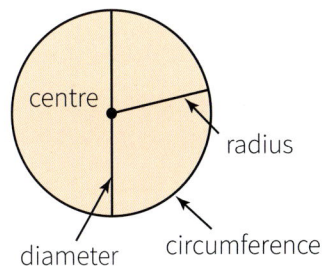

Activity

You can find the circumference of a coin by rolling it along a ruler.

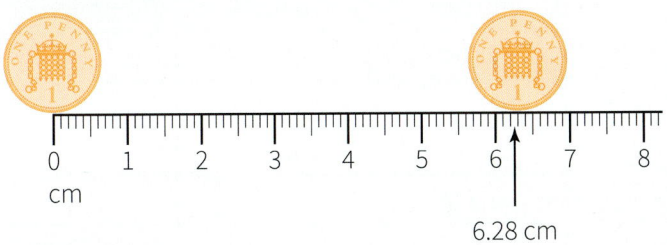

Coin	Diameter	Circumference
1p	2 cm	6.3 cm
2p	2.5 cm	7.9 cm
5p	1.7 cm	5.3 cm

Do this with the coins listed in the table. Check all the measurements given.

Divide the circumference of each coin by its diameter. What do you find?

You should find that circumference ÷ diameter is always a little greater than 3

A more accurate result is 3.14 (to 2 decimal places) or 3.142 (to 3 decimal places).

The exact answer is a never-ending decimal called **pi**, which is usually written as π.

Your calculator might have a key for π. If so, press it and you should get the number 3.14159265…

The relationship between the diameter and the circumference gives these formulae:

Key point

You need to learn:

Circumference = π × diameter $C = \pi d$

Circumference = 2 × π × radius $C = 2\pi r$

Example

Find the circumference of a circular pond with a radius of 3 m.

$C = 2\pi r = 2 \times \pi \times 3 = 18.84955… =$ **18.8 m** (using the π key on a calculator)

or $2 \times 3.14 \times 3 = 3.14 \times 6 = 18.84 =$ **18.8 m** (without a calculator) (rounded to 1 decimal place)

Measures, Shape and Space

Practice

In questions **1** to **3** give your answers to 1 decimal place.

1. **a.** Measure the diameter of these coins (in centimetres). **i.** 10p **ii.** £2
   b. Multiply the diameter by π to find the circumference of each coin.
   c. Check your answers to **b** by measuring.

2. Find the circumference of each circle. Use 3.14 for π.
   a. diameter 10 cm
   b. radius 7 cm
   c. diameter 1.5 m
   d. radius 0.8 m
   e. diameter 45 m
   f. diameter 30 m
   Check using your calculator key for π.

3. Copy and complete the table.
   Use your calculator key or 3.14 for π.

Radius	Diameter	Circumference
2 cm		
	30 mm	
	6 m	
1.2 m		
		15.7 cm
		75.4 mm

4. A wheel has a radius of 24 cm.
   How far does the wheel travel in one full turn (to the nearest cm)?

5. A circular window needs insulating.
   The diameter of the window is 80 cm.
   What length of insulation tape is needed to go around the window (to the nearest cm)?

6. A figure of eight is made from two circles.
   The diameter of the small circle is 12 mm
   The diameter of the large circle is 15 mm.

   Find the total length of the lines that make the figure of eight.
   Give your answer, correct to 1 decimal place, in
   a. millimetres,
   b. centimetres.

B. Area of a circle

The formula for the area of a circle in letters is $A = \pi r^2$

In words this means: **Area of a circle = π × radius × radius**

> **Key point**
> You need to learn:
> $A = \pi r^2$ (r^2 means $r \times r$)

Example

Find the area of a circular pond with a radius of 3 m.

$A = \pi \times 3^2 = \pi \times 3 \times 3 = 28.2743... = \mathbf{28.3 \text{ m}^2}$ (using the π key on a calculator)

or $3.14 \times 9 = 28.26 = \mathbf{28.3 \text{ m}^2}$ (without a calculator)

(rounded to 1 decimal place)

Perimeter, Area and Volume

Practice

In each question use your calculator key or 3.14 for π.

In questions **1** to **3** round answers to 1 decimal place.

1. Find the area of each circle.

   a. 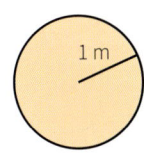 b. 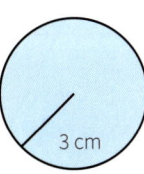 c. 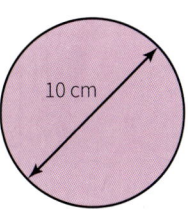 d.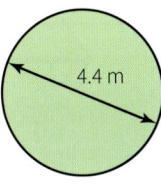

2. Find the area of a circle with a radius of:

   a. 7 cm b. 2 m c. 8 mm d. 12 mm e. 15 cm f. 1.4 m.

3. Find the area of a circle with a diameter of:

   a. 8 cm b. 20 mm c. 11 cm d. 2.5 m e. 14 mm f. 80 cm.

4. A circular flower bed has a diameter of 0.75 m.
   Find the area in cm² to the nearest 10 cm².

5. a. What is the diameter of this mirror including the frame?
   b. Find the area of the mirror including the frame.
   c. Find the area of the glass.
   d. What is the area of the frame to the nearest cm²?

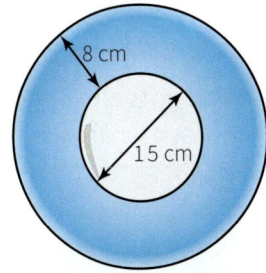

Use formulae to find areas of triangles and other shapes

Specification reference **L2.M16**

Level 2

The formula for the area of a triangle is $A = \dfrac{bh}{2}$

b is the base of the triangle and h is its perpendicular height.

> **Key point**
>
> You need to learn this.
>
> Area of a triangle = $A = \dfrac{bh}{2}$

Example

The base of this triangle is 5 cm and its height is 3.6 cm.

The area of the triangle is $A = \dfrac{5 \times 3.6}{2} = \dfrac{18}{2} = \mathbf{9\ cm^2}$

There must be a right angle between the base and the height.

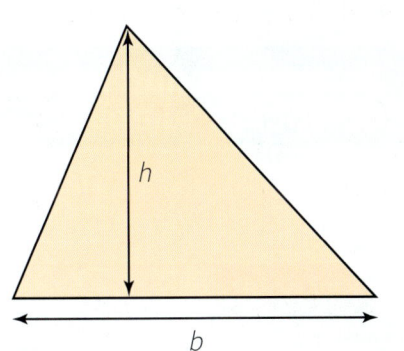

MyMaths 1108, 1128, 1129 SEARCH

Measures, Shape and Space

Practice

1. Use the formula given on the previous page to find the area of these triangles.

   a.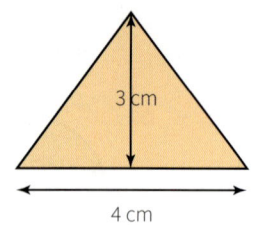
   b.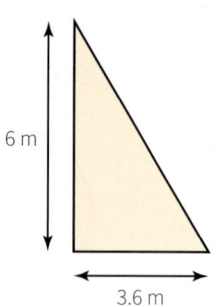
   c.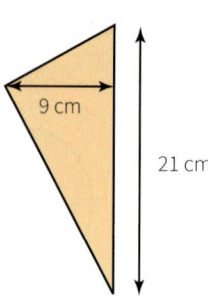

   For part **c**, use 21 as the base and 9 as the height.

2. A triangular sign has a base 1.5 m long and its height is 1.4 m. What is the area of the sign?

3. The formula for the area of a kite is $A = 0.5\,wl$ where w is the width and l is the length.
   A kite is 80 cm wide and 1.2 m long.
   What is its area? (Remember to use the same units for each length.)

   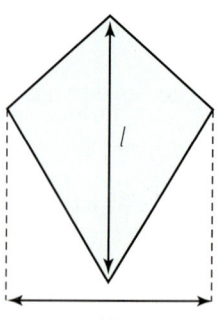

4. This shape is called a trapezium.
   The formula for its area is $A = \dfrac{h(a+b)}{2}$
   Find the area when $h = 12$, $a = 11$ and $b = 19$ (all in cm).

   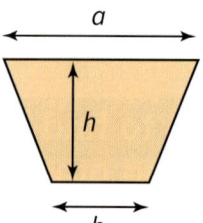

5. The formula for the area of this shape is $A = \dfrac{\pi ab}{4}$
   A pond of this shape is 2.2 m long and 1.3 m wide.
   Use your calculator to find the area of the pond.
   (Use 3.14 or the special key on your calculator for π.)
   Give your answer to 1 decimal place.

   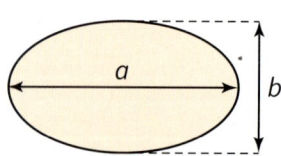

Perimeters and areas of composite shapes

Specification reference **L2.M16**

The table on the following page gives formulae for the perimeters and areas of some of the most common shapes. Many 2-D shapes in real life are combinations of these common shapes.

Key point

Learn the formulae for rectangles, triangles and circles.

Perimeter, Area and Volume

Rectangle	Triangle	Circle	Parallelogram	Trapezium
Perimeter $= 2l + 2b$	Perimeter $= a + b + c$	Perimeter (circumference) $= \pi d$ or $2\pi r$	Perimeter $= 2a + 2b$	Perimeter $= a + b + c + d$
Area $= lb$	Area $= \dfrac{bh}{2}$	Area $= \pi r^2$	Area $= bh$	Area $= \dfrac{h(a+b)}{2}$

Example

The diagram shows a symmetrical lawn in the shape of a semi-circle combined with a trapezium.

A semi-circle is half of a circle.

Find the perimeter and the area of the lawn.

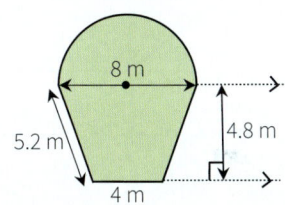

Perimeter

half of $2\pi r$

Length of semi-circle $= \pi r = \pi \times 4 = 4\pi = 12.566\ldots$

Total perimeter $= 12.566\ldots + 5.2 + 4 + 5.2$

Where possible continue the working rather than re-entering figures on your calculator.

$= 26.966\ldots = $ **27 m** (nearest metre)

Area

Area of semi-circle $= \dfrac{\pi r^2}{2} = \dfrac{\pi \times 4^2}{2} = \dfrac{\pi \times 16}{2} = 8\pi$

Area of trapezium $= \dfrac{h(a+b)}{2} = \dfrac{4.8(8+4)}{2} = \dfrac{4.8 \times 12}{2}$
$= 4.8 \times 6$

You can simplify each part before adding them on a calculator or calculate each part separately and use calculator memories to store the results before adding.

Total area $= 8\pi + 4.8 \times 6$

$= 53.93\ldots = $ **54 m²** (nearest m²)

Practice

1. Calculate the perimeter of these shapes.

   a.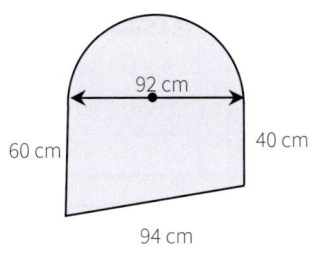

   b.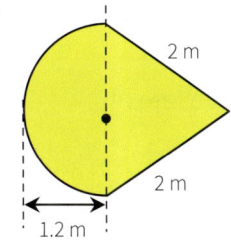

   c.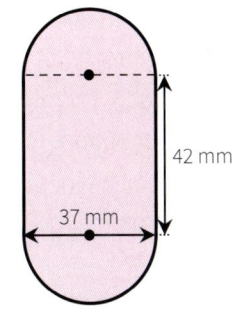

2. Calculate the area of these shapes.

   a.

   b.

   c.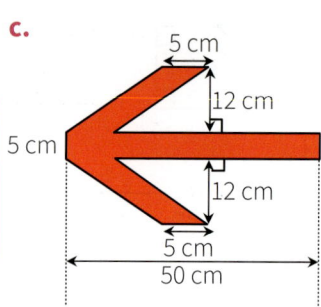

3. Calculate the perimeter and area of these shapes.

   a.

   b.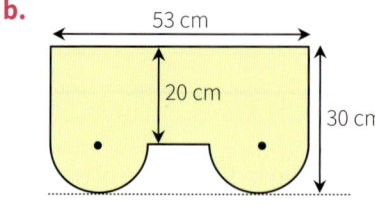

   c.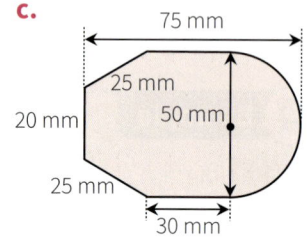

4. The diagrams show the walls needed for a clubhouse.
   Each window is 2 m wide and 1.2 m high.
   The door is 0.8 m wide and 2 m high.

   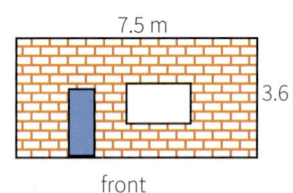 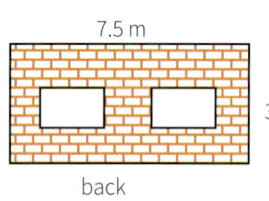 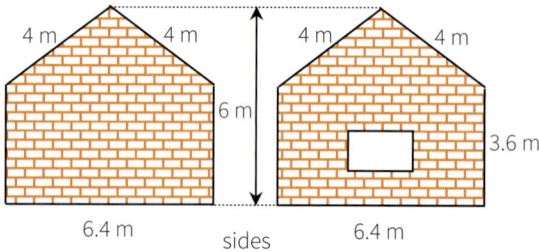

   front   back   sides

   The builder says he needs 60 bricks per m² of wall.
   How many bricks do you think he should order for the walls? Explain your answer.

5. The sketch shows the layout of a garden.

   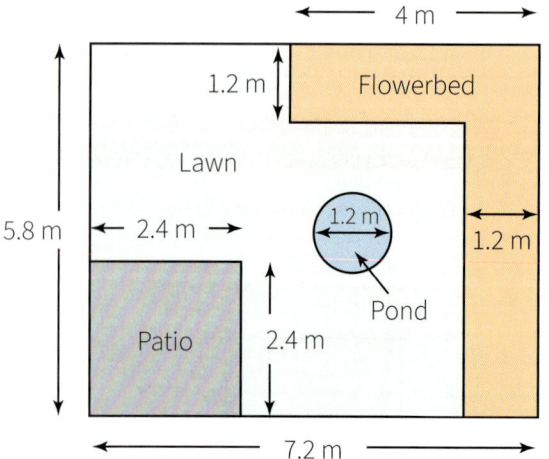

   a. Find the area of:
      i.   the patio   iii. the pond (to 2 dp)
      ii. the flowerbed   iv. the lawn.

   b. Fertiliser is spread onto the flowerbed
      at a rate of 20 g per square metre.
      How much fertiliser is used to the nearest
      10 grams?

   c. Weedkiller is spread onto the lawn at a rate of
      50 g per square metre.
      How much weedkiller is used to the nearest
      10 grams?

6. **a.** An athlete says that running round this track 25 times gives a distance of 10 km.
   Is the athlete correct? Explain your answer.

   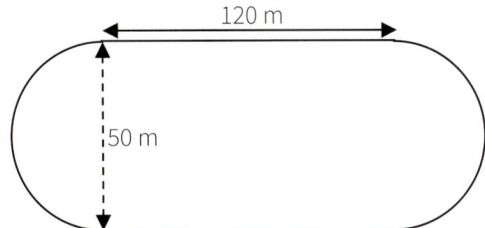

   b. A groundsman plans to sow grass seed inside the track.
   The groundsman says that he has ordered 50 packs of this grass seed.
   Is this sensible? Explain your answer.

7. The shape of a window is the combination of a rectangle and semi-circle.

   a. Using the approximation π ≈ 3, show that:

   i. an approximate formula for the perimeter of the window is:
   $P = 2h + 2.5d$

   ii. an approximate formula for the area of the window is:
   $A = hd + \dfrac{3d^2}{8}$

   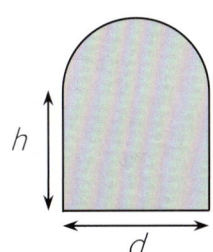

   b. Estimate the perimeter and area of a window with this shape that is 2 metres wide and 2.6 metres tall.

Nets

Specification reference **L1.M25**

Folding these 2-D patterns gives the 3-D shapes beside them. The patterns are called nets.

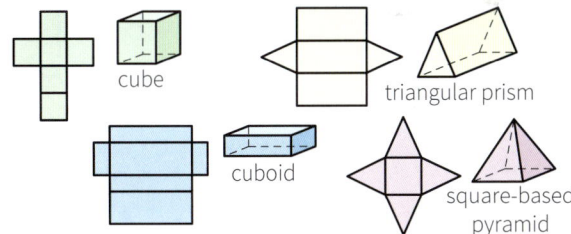

cube, cuboid, triangular prism, square-based pyramid

Practice

1. Name the 3-D shape that can be made from each net.

   a.

   b.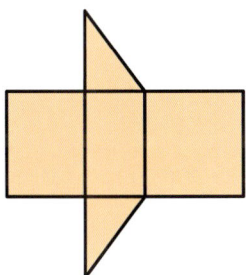

   c.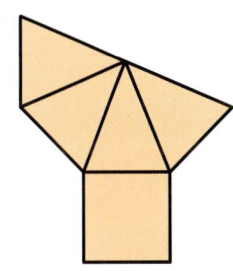

Measures, Shape and Space

2. Which of these are nets of a cube?

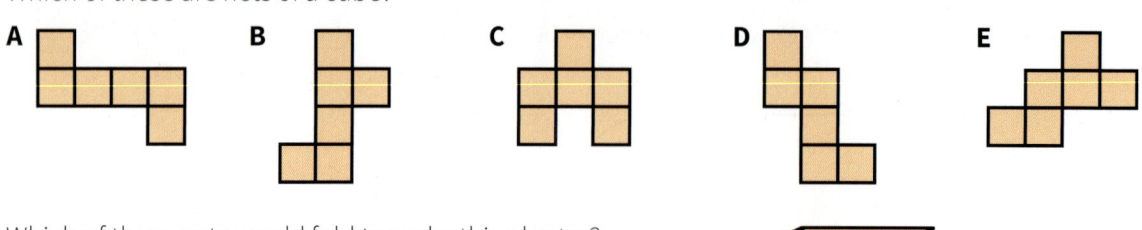

3. Which of these nets would fold to make this planter?

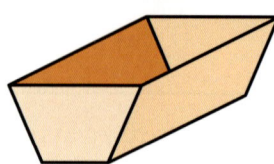

A
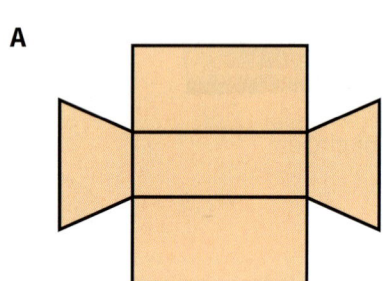

B
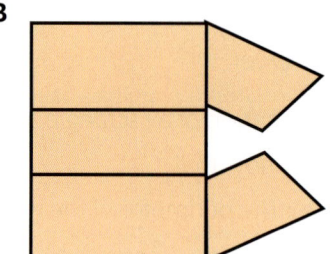

C
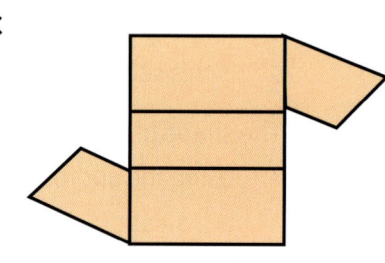

D
E
F
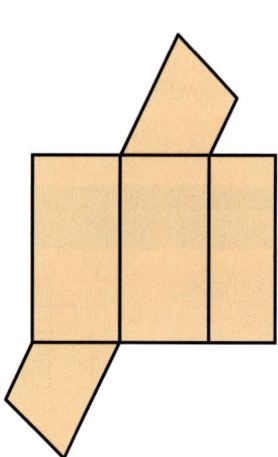
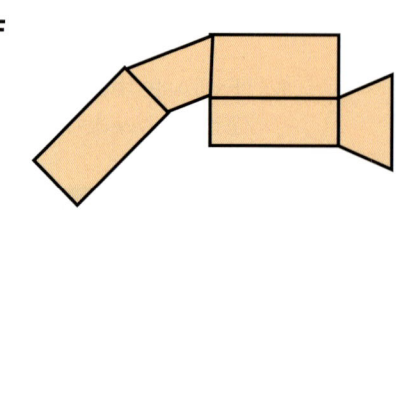

Activities

Use graph paper.

1. Draw four different nets for a cube.
2. Draw three different nets for a triangular prism.
3. Draw three different nets for a cuboid.
4. Make a net for:
    a. a pyramid with a 5 cm square base and triangular faces of height 7 cm
    b. prism of length 12 cm, with triangular ends of width 6 cm and height 5 cm.
5. Make a net for a cube with a pyramid on top.

Surface area

Specification reference L2.M17

 Level 2

Sometimes it is important to work out the total area of the surfaces of a 3-D shape. For example, manufacturers often want to know how much material will be needed to make a container or how much paint it will take to cover it.

Example

The amount of heat lost from a hot water tank depends on its surface area.

Calculate the surface area of this cylindrical hot water tank.

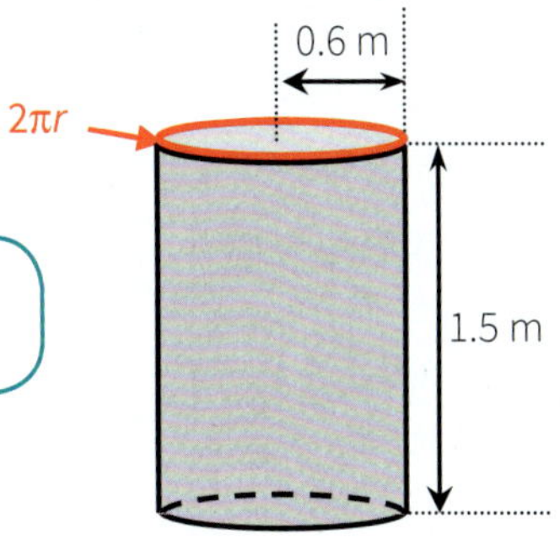

The diagram below shows a net of the tank.
It consists of two circles and a rectangle.

A net can be useful, but is not essential.

The length of the top edge of the rectangle is equal to the circumference of the circles.

Area of each circular face
$= \pi r^2 = \pi \times 0.6^2 = 1.13097\ldots \text{ m}^2$

Use a calculator memory to store this for use later.

Area of rectangular face
$= 2\pi rh = 2 \times \pi \times 0.6 \times 1.5 = 5.65486\ldots \text{ m}^2$

Total surface area $= 5.65486\ldots + 2 \times 1.13097\ldots$
$= \mathbf{7.9 \text{ m}^2}$ (to 1 dp)

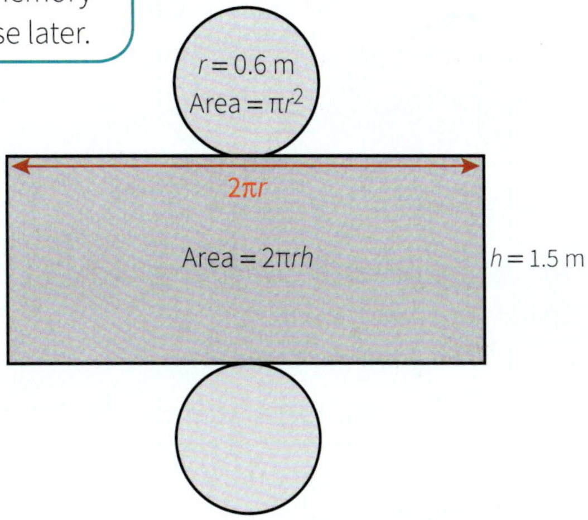

Key point

Surface area of a cylinder $= 2\pi r^2 + 2\pi rh$

You must learn this or be able to work it out.

Practice

1. Calculate the surface area of each 3-D shape.

   a.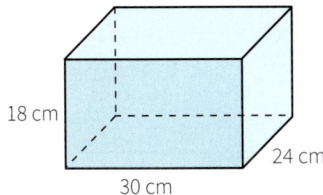

   b.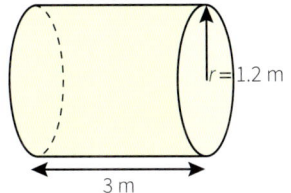

   c.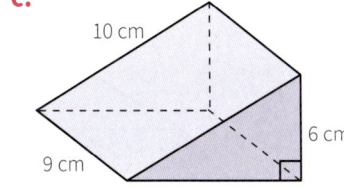

MyMaths 1107 SEARCH

2. Calculate the surface area of each object.
   a. water tank
   b. cola can
   c. metal bar

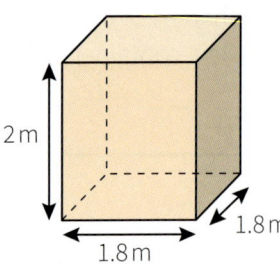
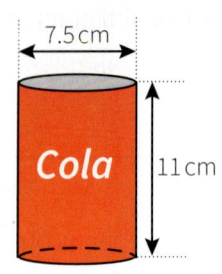
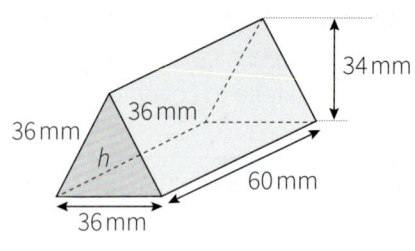

3. a. Sketch a net of this square-based pyramid.
   b. Work out the surface area of the pyramid.

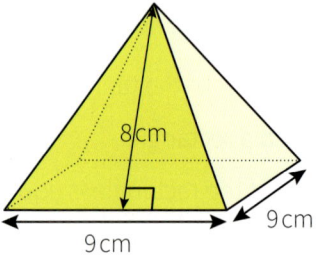

4. The formula for the area of the **curved surface** of a cone is $A = \pi r l$
   Calculate the total surface area of a cone with $r = 5$ cm and $l = 10$ cm

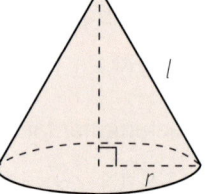

5. The diagram gives the dimensions of an open-topped waste skip.
   a. Draw a net of the waste skip.
   b. Find the area of metal used to make the waste skip.

   > Area of a trapezium with parallel sides a and b and height $h = \dfrac{h(a+b)}{2}$

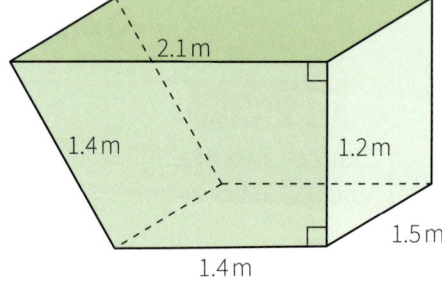

6. The diagram shows a plinth in the shape of a prism with a trapezium cross-section.
   Calculate the surface area of the plinth.
   Give your answer in square metres.

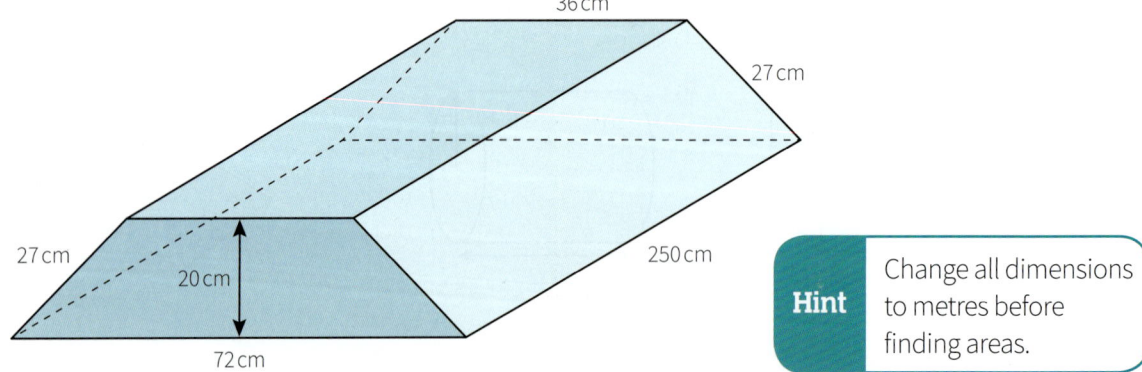

Hint Change all dimensions to metres before finding areas.

Perimeter, Area and Volume

Volume of a cuboid
Specification reference L1.M23

Volume is the space taken up by a 3-D shape (a solid) or liquid.

We measure volume in **cubic units**. This is 1 cubic centimetre.

To find the volume of a shape, you need to find the number of unit cubes that fill it.

The shape of a box is called a **cuboid**.

The volume of this cuboid is 3 cm³.

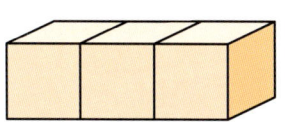

> **Key point**
> Volume is measured in units cubed, for example, cm³

Practice

1. Write down the volume of each cuboid. Assume each of the small cubes is 1 cm³.

   a. 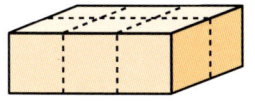 b. 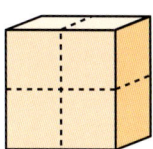 c. 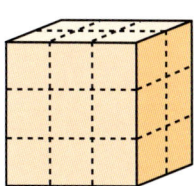 d.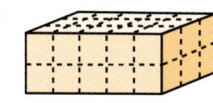

You can find the volume of a cuboid without drawing and counting the cubes.

Look at the cuboid in question **1d** again. It is 5 cm long, 3 cm wide and 2 cm high.

Its volume is $5 \times 3 \times 2 = 30$ cm³

> **Key point**
> You need to learn:
> Volume of a cuboid = length × width × height

---

2. Find the volume of each cuboid.

   a. 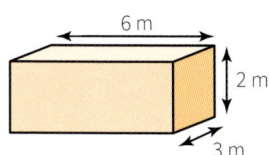   b.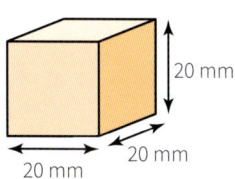

   c. 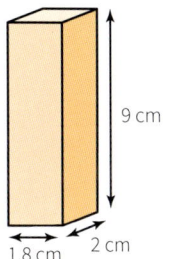   d.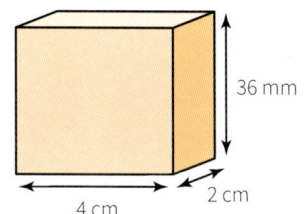

> **Key point**
> Use the same units for all the sides.

3. Copy and complete this table:

Length	Width	Height	Volume
2 cm	4 cm	5 cm	
3 m	3.4 m	3.5 m	
4 mm	2.5 mm	6 mm	
9 cm	6.2 cm	8 cm	

4. A box has a 1 m square base and it is $\frac{1}{2}$ m high. What is the volume of the box?

5. What is the volume of a box that is 50 cm long, 10 cm wide and 8 cm high?

6. A carton of fruit juice has a volume of 1 litre (that is, 1000 cm³).
   Find possible dimensions for the length, width and height of the carton.

7. A sand pit is 100 cm long, 75 cm wide and 15 cm high.
   What is the volume of sand it holds when full?

8. Each side of a dice is 25 mm long. What is its volume?

9. The diagram shows a cube with edges of length 1 metre.
   a. What is the length of each edge in cm?
   b. What is the area of each face in cm²?
   c. What is the volume of the cube in cm³?

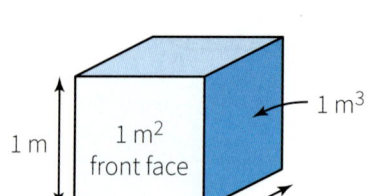

Key point

You need to learn these:

The formula for the volume of a cuboid is $V = l \times w \times h = lwh$

The formula for the volume of a cube is $V = l \times l \times l = l^3$ (say this as 'l cubed')

10. The diagram shows a podium made from three cuboids. Each cuboid is 40 cm wide.
    a. Find the volume of each cuboid in m³.
    b. What is the total volume of the podium?

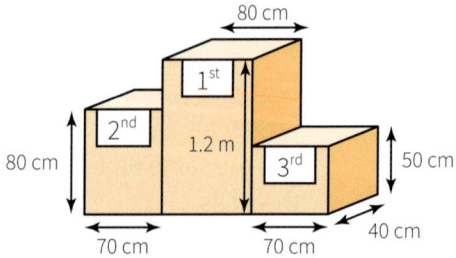

To find one dimension, divide the volume by the product of the others.

> **Example** If a cuboid has length 5 cm, width 4 cm and volume 120 cm³, its height is:
>
> $120 \div (5 \times 4) = 120 \div 20 =$ **6 cm**

11. Copy and complete this table showing the dimensions and volume of cuboids.

Length	Width	Height	Volume
4 m	2 m		24 m³
3 cm		8 cm	48 cm³
	3 m	9 m	54 m³
4 cm	4 cm		64 cm³

Volume of a cylinder

Specification reference **L2.M17**

Level 2

The formula for the volume of a cylinder is $V = \pi r^2 h$

This means $V = \pi \times r \times r \times h$

When finding volumes remember:

- The same units must be used for each measurement.
- The volume units are cubed, for example, 4 **cm³** or 35.6 **m³**
- You can convert volume to litres using **1 litre = 1000 cm³**

> **Key point**
>
> You need to learn this.
> **Volume of a cylinder $V = \pi r^2 h$**

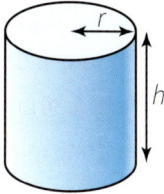

> **Example**
>
> This pipe is 0.8 m long and has a diameter of 40 mm.
>
> To find the volume we need r and h in the same units.
>
> Here it is sensible to use cm:
>
> $r = 20$ mm $= 2$ cm
>
> $h = 0.8$ m $= 80$ cm
>
> The volume is $V = \pi \times r \times r \times h$
> $= \pi \times 2 \times 2 \times 80$
> $=$ **1005 cm³** (to the nearest cm³, using a calculator).
>
> If the pipe is filled with water it will hold just over 1 litre.

Measures, Shape and Space

Practice

In each question use the π key on your calculator or π = 3.14
In questions 1 and 2 give the answers to 1 dp.

> **Key point**
> Use the same units for r and h.

1. Find the volume of each cuboid.

   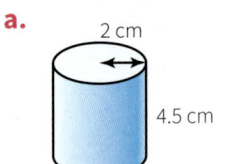
   a. 2 cm, 4.5 cm
   b. 1 m, 25 m
   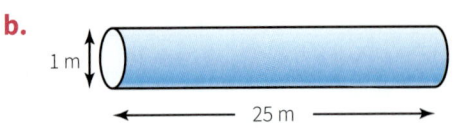
   e. 12 mm, 6 cm — Give the answer in cm^3.
   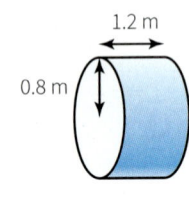
   c. 1.2 m, 0.8 m
   d. 3 m, 60 cm — Give the answer in m^3.

2. Calculate the volume of a cylinder with:
   a. radius 1.2 m and height 2 m
   b. radius 6 cm and height 9 cm
   c. radius 3 m and height 2.2 m
   d. radius 3 m and height 1.6 m
   e. diameter 12 cm and height 2.5 cm
   f. diameter 1 m and height 0.5 m.

3. Find the volume of each cylinder.
   (Give your answers to **b** and **c** in cm^3 and the rest in m^3 to 2 decimal places.)
   a. diameter 4 m and height 30 cm
   b. diameter 2.5 cm and height 16 mm
   c. radius 1.2 cm and height 6 mm
   d. radius 70 cm and height 0.6 m
   e. radius 0.3 m and height 40 cm
   f. diameter 1.2 m and height 50 cm

4. A paddling pool has a radius of 60 cm and a depth of 30 cm.
   How much water does it hold when full? Give your answer in m^3.

Use other formulae to find volumes

Specification reference L2.M17

Level 2

The volume formulae for a cuboid and a cylinder are similar. In both formulae the volume is the area of the base multiplied by the height.

> **Key point**
> Volume of a prism = area of base × height

Shapes like these are called **prisms**.

Some of the shapes in the following questions are also prisms.

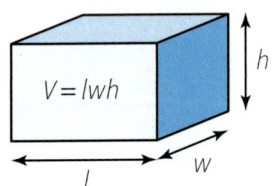
$V = lwh$

Area of rectangular base = lw

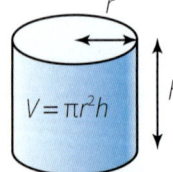
$V = \pi r^2 h$

Area of circular base = πr^2

Perimeter, Area and Volume

Practice

1. The sketch shows a triangular prism.
   The formula $V = \dfrac{bhl}{2}$ gives its volume.
   Find the volume when $b = 10$, $h = 8$ and $l = 30$ (all measured in cm).

   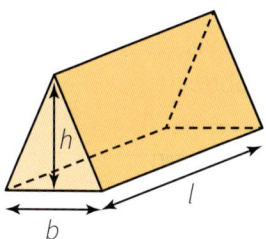

2. The diagram shows the shape of a plant trough.
   The formula $V = \dfrac{hl(a+b)}{2}$ gives its volume.

   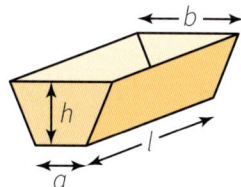

   > **Key point**
   > 1 litre = 1000 cm^3

   a. Find V if $h = 25$ cm, $l = 120$ cm, $a = 20$ cm and $b = 30$ cm.
   b. A gardener buys compost in 40 litre bags.
      How many bags does she need to fill the trough?

3. This shape is called a square-based pyramid.
   Its volume formula is $V = \dfrac{x^2 h}{3}$.
   a. What is the volume of a pyramid with $x = 6$ cm and $h = 5$ cm?
   b. How many paperweights of this shape can be made from 25 litres of molten metal?

   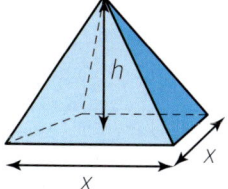

4. The formula that estimates the volume of this section of gutter is $V = \dfrac{3d^2 l}{8}$
   How many litres of water will it hold if $d = 12$ cm and $l = 5$ m?

   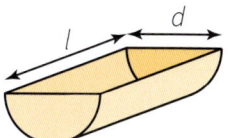

5. The formula for the volume of a sphere is $V = \dfrac{4}{3}\pi r^3$

   The formula for the volume of a cone is $V = \dfrac{1}{3}\pi r^2 h$
   where h is the height of the cone.
   Show that the volume of this sphere is equal to the volume of this cone.

   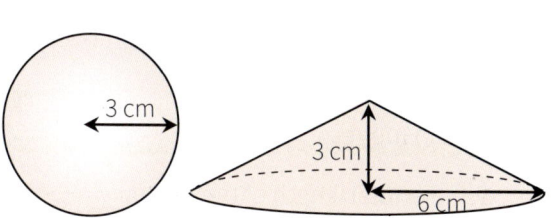

6. This is part of a toy which consists of a cylinder joined to a hemisphere.
   Its volume is given by $V = \dfrac{\pi d^2 (3h + d)}{12}$
   Calculate the volume when $d = 6$ cm and $h = 5$ cm

   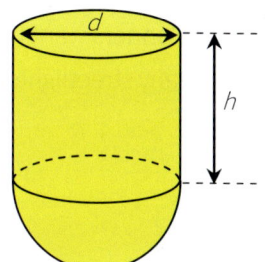

Measures, Shape and Space

Solve problems involving 2-D and 3-D shapes

Specification reference: L1.M20, L1.M25, L2.M16, L2.M17, L2.M20

Level 1

When some dimensions of an item are given on a diagram, you can often work out other dimensions by adding, subtracting, multiplying or dividing the given lengths.

Example

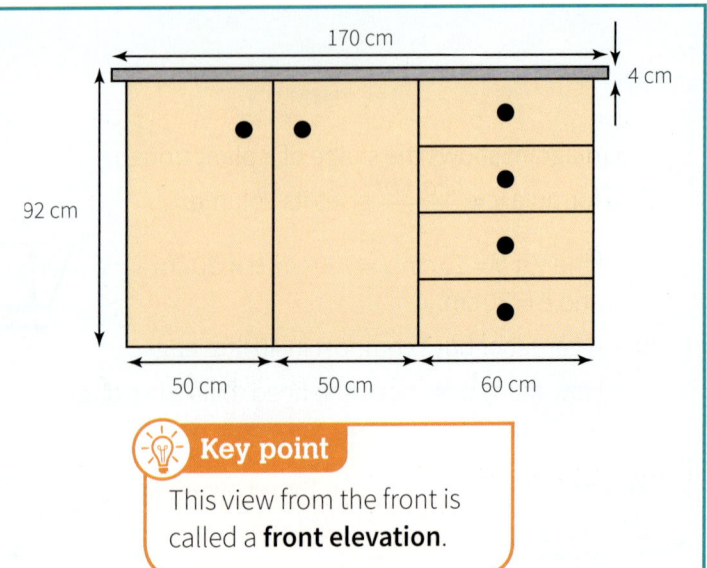

From this diagram of storage units we can work out that the total width of the cupboards and drawers = 50 + 50 + 60

= 160 cm = **1.6 m**

This means the top is 10 cm wider than the units. Assuming the top overhangs the units equally at each side, the overhang at each side is 10 ÷ 2 = **5 cm**

> **Key point**
> This view from the front is called a **front elevation**.

Practice

1. For the storage units shown above, calculate:

   a. the height of the cupboards

   b. the height of each drawer (assuming they are identical).

2. Here is a bedroom unit.
   Find in metres:

   a. the total length of the unit

   b. the total height of the unit.

3. A road is 2 kilometres long.
   Town planners want to put streetlights at intervals of 50 metres along this road.
   How many streetlights will they need?

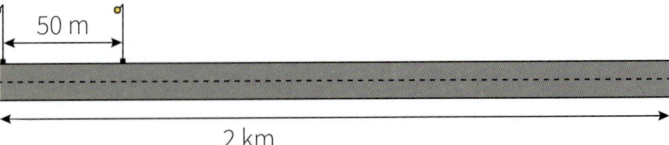

330

Level 2

Some problems may involve other topics such as costs, nets, areas, volumes and densities.

Example

Plan means view from above.

This is the plan of a kitchen.
The work surface is 2.75 m long and 60 cm wide.
Square tiles with sides 20 cm long are used to cover the work surface.
They cost £28.99 per pack of 25. How much will it cost?

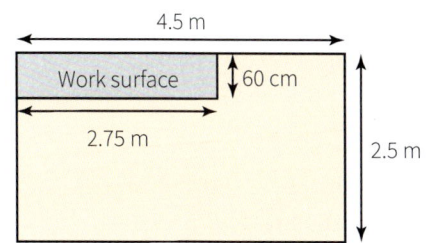

To find out how many tiles are needed look at the length then the width.

Length = 2.75 m = 275 cm.
Number of tiles = 275 ÷ 20 = 14 tiles (rounded up)
Width = 60 cm
Number of tiles = 60 ÷ 20 = 3 tiles

Always round up. It is sensible to have spare tiles to allow for breakages.

Total number of tiles = number along length × number along width
= 14 × 3 = 42 tiles
Number of packs needed = 2
Cost = 2 × £28.99 = **£57.98**

---

4. a. Square tiles with sides 50 cm long are used to cover the ceiling of the kitchen in the example. How many packs of 4 tiles are needed?

b. Square tiles with sides 25 cm long are used to cover the whole floor of the kitchen (including under the worktop). How many packs of 16 tiles are needed?

5. The walls of the kitchen are tiled above where the worksurface meets them with square tiles whose sides are 20 cm long. The height of these parts of the walls is 1.6 m.

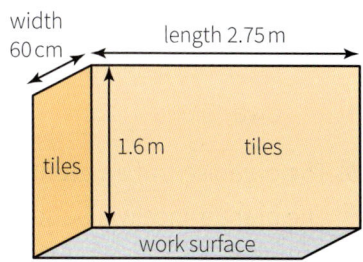

a. How many tiles are needed altogether for this part of the walls?

b. The tiles cost £24.99 per pack of 25. How much will it cost?

6. A rectangular bathroom is being decorated. It is 2.2 m long and 2 m wide.

a. A piece of lino 2 m wide and 2.2 m long is bought for the floor at a price of £9.99 per square metre. What is the cost of the lino?

b. The wall is re-tiled along the length and width of the bath.
The length of the bath is 1.7 m.
The width of the bath is 0.7 m.
The height of the wall above the bath is 1.8 m.
What is the area that is re-tiled?

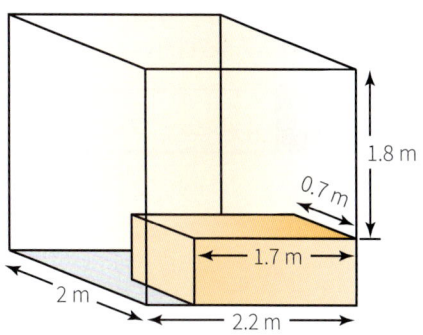

Measures, Shape and Space

7. Cans of soup have diameter 7.5 cm and height 10 cm.

   a. What is the **maximum** number of cans that you could pack upright in a box that is 90 cm long, 75 cm wide and 30 cm high?

   b. How many whole cans of soup can be poured into this pan?

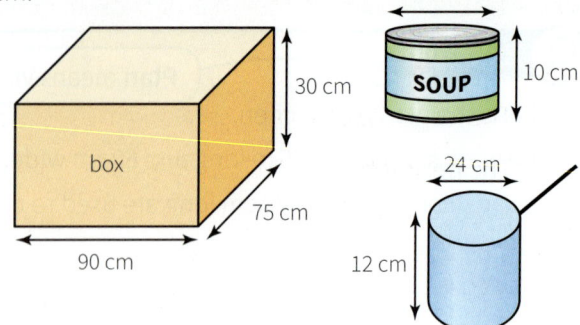
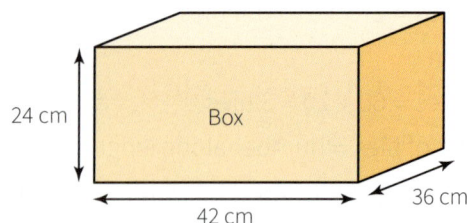

8. a. What is the greatest number of packs of butter that will fit inside the box?.

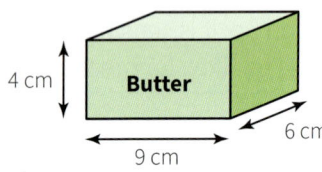
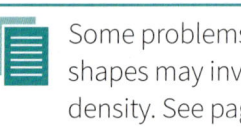

   b. Draw a net of the box (which has a lid) and give its dimensions.

   > Some problems on 3-D shapes may involve density. See page 336–337.

9. The surface area of a dice is 13.5 cm².

   a. Find:
      i. the length of each edge of the dice
      ii. the volume of the dice.

   b. Draw a diagram of a box that will hold 160 dice. Give its dimensions.

10. The organisers of an event want to offer each of the guests a glass of orange juice.
    The orange juice will be served in cylindrical glasses as shown in the diagram.
    The organisers expect 120 people to attend.
    They want to buy enough cartons of orange juice.
    Each carton holds 1 litre and costs 79 pence.
    Suggest how many cartons the organisers should buy, and how much it will cost.

    Hint 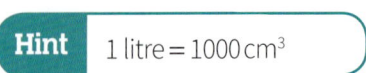 1 litre = 1000 cm³

Chapter Summary
19 Perimeter, Area and Volume

- The length, width and height of a shape are sometimes called its **dimensions**.
- The **perimeter** of a 2-D shape is the total length of its sides.
- **Area** is the amount of space inside a 2-D shape (flat shape). It is measured in square units, for example, cm² and m². Remember to write the units with the answer.
- It is sometimes possible to find the area of a shape by splitting it into rectangles or surrounding it by a rectangle.
- **Volume** is the space taken up by a 3-D shape (a solid) or liquid. It is measured in cubic units, for example, cm³ and m³. Remember to write the units with the answer.
- The **perimeter of a rectangle** = 2 × length + 2 × width, or 2 × (length + width)
- The **area of a rectangle** = length × width
- The **volume of a cuboid** = length × width × height
- If you know the volume and two dimensions of a 3-D shape, you can find the other dimension by dividing the volume by the product (multiplication) of the dimensions you know.
- When adding, subtracting or multiplying lengths, the units must be the same.
- The **net** of a 3-D shape is a 2-D pattern that can be folded to make the shape.

- The **radius** is a straight line from the centre of a circle to the edge.
- The **diameter** is a straight line from one side of a circle to the other, passing through the centre.
- **pi (π)** is the ratio of the circumference (perimeter) of a circle to its diameter.
  π = circumference ÷ diameter = 3.14 (to 2 dp)
- The **circumference of a circle** = π × diameter = πd or 2 × π × radius = 2πr
- The area of a circle = π × radius × radius = πr^2
- The area of a triangle = $\dfrac{\text{base} \times \text{perpendicular height}}{2} = \dfrac{bh}{2}$ or $\dfrac{1}{2}$ × base × height = $\dfrac{1}{2}bh$
  (there must be a right angle between the base and height).
- **Surface area** is the total area of the faces of a 3-D shape. Drawing a net can help you to find the surface area.
- **Surface area of a cylinder** = 2πr^2 + 2πrh
- **Volume of a cylinder** = πr^2h
- A **prism** is a 3-D shape with two identical parallel faces.
- **Volume of a prism** = area of base × height
- If a question requires you to calculate a value and then use it in another calculation, continue your working on a calculator or use its memories rather than re-entering digits. Round the final answer to a sensible degree of accuracy.

Measures, Shape and Space

20 Compound Measures

Calculate using compound measures

Specification reference L2.M15

Level 2

A. Calculate speed, distance and time

Speed measures how fast something moves. You can find the **average speed** of an object if you know the **distance travelled** and the **time taken**. Use this triangle to help you to remember.

Speed = $\frac{\text{Distance}}{\text{Time}}$

Distance = Speed × Time

Time = $\frac{\text{Distance}}{\text{Speed}}$

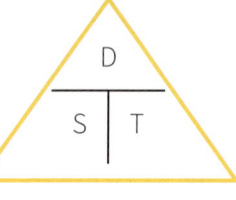

Cover the letter you want to find.

The position of the other 2 letters tells you to multiply or divide.

The units used for distance and time tell you the units for speed.

The units are usually kilometres per hour (km/h), metres per second (m/s) or miles per hour (mph).

Examples

1. A car travels 90 miles in 2 hours. What is the average speed?

   Speed = $\frac{\text{Distance}}{\text{Speed}}$ = 90 ÷ 2 = **45 mph**

   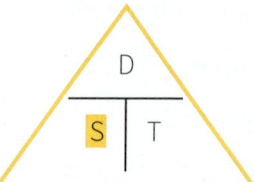

   Remember the units:

   Distance in miles and time in hours gives speed in miles per hour.

2. A tortoise walks at an average speed of 0.015 m/s for 60 seconds.

   How far does it walk?

   Distance = Speed × Time
   = 0.015 × 60 = **0.9 m**

   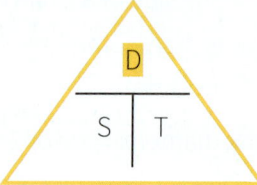

   Remember the units:

   Speed in metres per second and time in seconds gives distance in metres.

Practice

1. Calculate the average speed for each journey.
   a. A car travels 120 miles in 3 hours.
   b. A marathon runner runs 10 miles in 2 hours.
   c. A train travels 170 km in 4 hours.
   d. A plane flies 2900 km in 5 hours.
   e. An athlete runs 200 m in 40 seconds.
   f. A cyclist travels 20 miles in $2\frac{1}{2}$ hours.
   g. A swimmer takes 40 seconds to swim 50 m.
   h. A skier takes 2.5 hours to ski 1.5 km.

See page 136 for dividing by a decimal.

2. Find the distance travelled for each journey.
   a. A car travels at an average speed of 30 mph for 3 hours.
   b. A plane flies at an average speed of 650 km/h for 5 hours.
   c. An athlete runs at an average speed of 6 m/s for 10 seconds.
   d. A bird flies for $\frac{1}{2}$ hour at an average speed of 8 mph.

3. Calculate the time taken for each journey.
   a. A car travels 68 miles at an average speed of 34 mph.
   b. Adam walks 10 miles at an average speed of $2\frac{1}{2}$ mph.
   c. A feather falls 6 metres at a speed of 1.5 m/s.
   d. A can moves 1.6 metres along a conveyor belt at a constant speed of 0.2 m/s.

4. Joel drives 145 miles in $2\frac{1}{2}$ hours. He then stops for $\frac{3}{4}$ hour before driving a further 35 miles in 45 minutes. Calculate the average speed for the whole journey.

   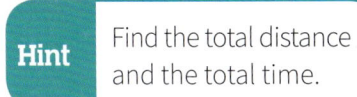
   Hint Find the total distance and the total time.

5. Amira swims 2 km in 50 minutes. She then rests for 40 minutes before swimming a further 1.5 km in an hour. Calculate her average speed for the whole journey. Give your answer in km/h.

Activity

Plan a journey by car from your home to a theme park or other place of interest.

Use maps to estimate the distance you will travel on minor roads and motorways.

Estimate how fast you will be able to go on these roads and work out how long your journey is likely to take. (For example, you could assume an average speed of 25 mph on minor roads and an average speed of 60 mph on motorways.)

Use an internet website such as AA Route Planner to plan the same journey and compare your estimates with the values it gives.

B. Convert speeds

The diagram shows how to convert between kilometres per hour and metres per second.

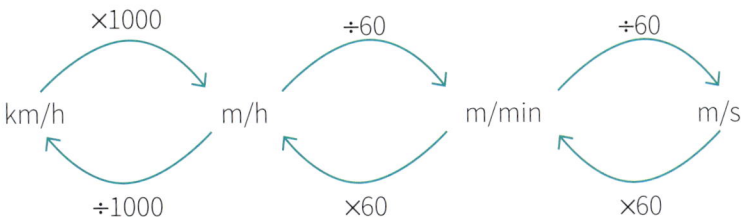

Examples

Convert   1. 36 km/h into m/s   2. 1.5 m/s into km/h.

1. 36 km/h × **1000** =   36 000 m/h ÷ **60**   =   600 m/min ÷ **60**   =   **10 m/s**
2. 1.5 m/s × **60**   =   90 m/min × **60**   =   5400 m/h ÷ **1000** =   **5.4 km/h**

For approximate conversions between kilometres per hour and miles per hour, use the conversion factor 1 mph ≈ 1.6 km/h.

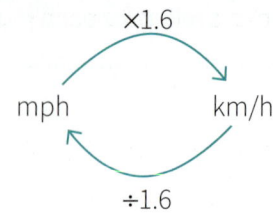

Example

Convert **1.** 50 mph to km/h **2.** 20 km/h to mph.

1. 50 mph ≈ 50 × 1.6 = **80 km/h**
2. 20 km/h ≈ 20 ÷ 1.6 = **12.5 mph**

Practice

1. Convert the following.

   a. 72 km/h into m/s   b. 18 km/h into m/s   c. 108 km/h into m/s
   d. 25 m/s into km/h   e. 12 m/s into km/h   f. 8 m/s into km/h

2. A sky diver falls from a height of 4500 metres to the ground in 2 minutes. Find the average speed

   a. in m/s   b. in km/h.

3. The table gives the usual speed limits in France. Copy and complete the table to give the speeds in mph to the nearest mph.

4. Draw a table similar to that in question **3**. List typical speed limits for roads in the UK in mph and what they would be in km/h.

Speed limits in France		
	km/h	mph
2-lane roads	80	
3-lane roads	90	
4-lane expressways	110	
motorways	130	

C. Density, mass and volume

Mass is the amount of substance within a volume.
Density is the **mass per unit volume** of the substance.

Density is usually measured in grams per cubic centimetre (g/cm^3) or kilograms per cubic metre (kg/m^3).

To find the density of something, divide its mass by its volume.

Use this triangle to help you to remember:

Density = $\dfrac{\text{Mass}}{\text{Volume}}$

Mass = Density × Volume

Volume = $\dfrac{\text{Mass}}{\text{Density}}$

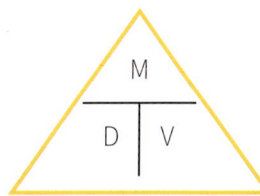

> Mass is different from weight. Weight measures how heavy a substance is and depends on the pull of gravity. So the mass of an astronaut is the same on the Moon as it is on Earth, but his weight is different.

> Cover the letter you want to find.
> The position of the other 2 letters tells you to multiply or divide.

The units used for mass and volume tell you the units for density.

Example

An object has a mass of 125 g. The volume is 6 cm³.

What is the density of the object?

Density = $\dfrac{\text{Mass}}{\text{Volume}}$ = 125 ÷ 6 = 20.83… = **20.8 g/cm³** (to 1 dp)

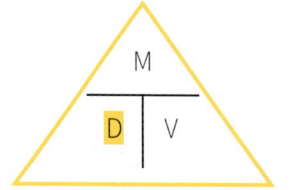

Remember the units:

Mass in grams and volume in cm³ gives density in g/cm³.

Practice

1. This table gives the mass and volume of some pieces of metal. Find the density of each type of metal.

   Write your answers in g/cm³ to 1 decimal place.

Metal	Mass (g)	Volume (cm³)
Copper	54	6
Lead	56.5	5
Steel	98	12.5
Iron	150	19

2. Use this table to find the mass of:

   a. 5 cm³ of platinum

   b. 45 cm³ of brass

   c. 4.4 cm³ of gold

   d. 18 cm³ of aluminium.

Metal	Density (g/cm³)
Platinum	21.4
Brass	8.5
Tin	7.3
Gold	19.3
Bronze	8.8
Aluminium	2.8

3. Use the table in question **2** to find the volume of:

   a. 146 g of tin

   b. 171 g of platinum

   c. 141 g of brass

   d. 28 g of bronze

   e. 1 kg of gold

   f. 1 kg of aluminium.

4. A necklace is made from 1.6 cm³ of silver. The density of silver is 10.4 g/cm³.

   The necklace is priced at £1.40 per gram.

   What is the price of the necklace?

5. A bottle holds 330 cm³ of water. When full the bottle has a mass of 380 g.

   The density of water is 1 g/cm³.

   What is the mass of the empty bottle?

6. This steel beam has a mass of 81 kg.

   What is the density of the steel? Give your answer in kg/m³.

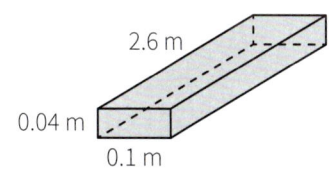

Measures, Shape and Space

7. The mass of this candle is 80 grams. Find, to 1 decimal place:
   a. the volume of the candle wax
   b. the density of the candle wax.

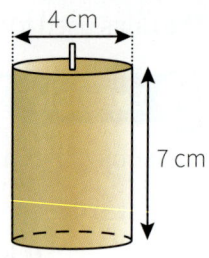

8. The diagrams show the shape of a planned road tunnel. The soil that must be removed has a density of 2000 kg/m³. Find the mass of this soil. Give your answer to the nearest 10 tonnes.

   Volume = area of front × length
   1 tonne = 1000 kg

    For a reminder of how to calculate the area of a composite 2-D shape, see pages 318–319.

   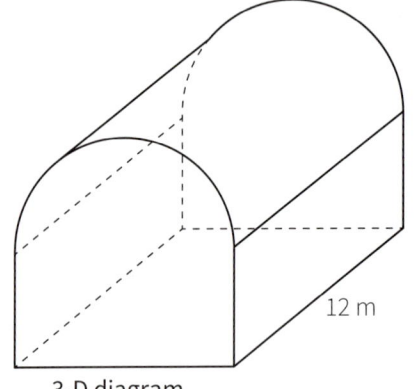

   3-D diagram

   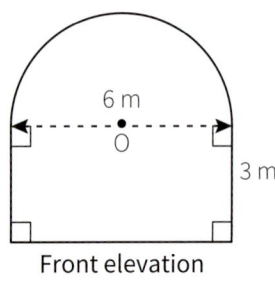

   Front elevation

9. A candle maker wants to make 300 candles to sell at a craft market.

   The diagram shows the dimensions of a candle.

   The table lists prices of the items she needs to make the candles. Items can be bought in any quantity, the table shows the price per amount.

   The prices will have VAT of 20% added.

   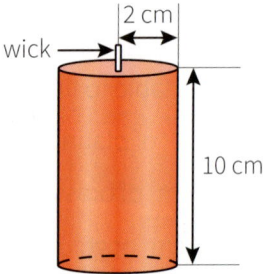

Item	Amount	Price (excluding VAT)
Wax	800 g	£3
	5 kg	£14
	10 kg	£25
Fragrance oil	500 mℓ	£22.99
Dye	10 mℓ	£1.70
Wicks	50	£3

   1 cm³ = 1 mℓ
   When working out the volume of wax, ignore the volume of the wick, oil and dye.

   a. The density of the wax is 0.9 g/cm³. How much wax is needed to make
      i. 1 candle
      ii. 300 candles.
   b. What is the price of the wax needed to make 300 candles before VAT?
   c. The candle maker needs to mix 50 mℓ of fragrance oil and 4 mℓ of dye to every kilogram of wax. What will it cost to add fragrance oil and dye to the batch of 300 candles before VAT?
   d. What is the total cost of materials to produce 300 candles including VAT?

D. Population density

Population density is a measure of how populated an area is.

To find population density, divide the population by the area.

Use this triangle to help you to remember:

Population Density = $\dfrac{\text{Population}}{\text{Area}}$

Population = Population Density × Area

Area = $\dfrac{\text{Population}}{\text{Population Density}}$

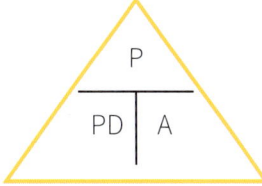

Cover the letter you want to find. The position of the other letters tells you to multiply or divide.

Example

The UK has a land area of 243 thousand square kilometres.

The population is 65.6 million.

What is the population density?

Population density = $\dfrac{\text{Population}}{\text{Area}}$

= 65 600 000 ÷ 243 000

= **270 people per km²**

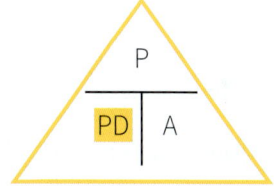

Remember the units:

Population is a number of people, area is in km² so population density is in people/km².

Practice

1. England has a land area of 130 thousand square kilometres. The population is 55 million.
   Find the population density of England.

2. Scotland has a land area of 79 thousand square kilometres. The population density is 68 people per km².
   What is the population of Scotland?

3. Wales has a population of 3.1 million. The population density is 150 people per km².
   Find the land area of Wales.

4. Northern Ireland has a land area of 14.1 thousand km². The population is 1.8 million.
   a. Find the population density of Northern Ireland.
   b. Compare the population densities of England, Scotland, Wales and Northern Ireland. (Use information from questions **1** to **3**.)

Measures, Shape and Space

5. **a.** Copy and complete this table.
   b. Write a paragraph explaining what the data in the table shows.

Country	Area (km²)	Population	Population density
Spain	500 000		92 people/km²
Germany		82 million	230 people/km²
Iceland	100 000	330 thousand	

Activity

Research populations and land areas for other countries to find the most densely and least densely populated countries.

Chapter Summary
20 Compound Measures

Level 2

- **Speed** is a measure of how fast something moves.
- Average speed = $\dfrac{\text{Distance}}{\text{Time}}$ Distance = Average speed × Time   Time = $\dfrac{\text{Distance}}{\text{Average speed}}$
  (Use the Distance-Speed-Time triangle to help.) Always write the units with the answer.
- The units of speed are given by the units of distance and the units of time: km/h, m/s, mph
- To convert between seconds and minutes, or minutes and hours, multiply or divide by 60
- To convert between miles and kilometres, multiply or divide by 1000
- For an approximate conversion between km/h and mph use 1 mph ≈ 1.6 km/h
- **Mass** is the amount of substance within a volume. It is not the same as **weight** because weight depends on the pull of gravity.
- **Density** is the mass per unit volume of a substance.
- Density = $\dfrac{\text{Mass}}{\text{Volume}}$ Mass = Density × Volume   Volume = $\dfrac{\text{Mass}}{\text{Density}}$
  (Use the Mass-Density-Volume triangle to help.) Always write the units with the answer.
- The units of density are given by the units of mass and the units of volume: g/cm³, kg/m³.
- **Population density** is a measure of how populated an area is.
- Population density = $\dfrac{\text{Population}}{\text{Area}}$ Population = Population density × Area   Area = $\dfrac{\text{Population}}{\text{Population density}}$
  (Use the Population-Population density-Area triangle to help.) Always write the units with the answer.
- The units of population density are given by the units population and the area. Population units are people so: people/km².

Handling Information and Data

21 Extracting and Interpreting Information

Information from lists, tables and pictograms
Specification reference EL3.H21

A. Find information from lists

Lists are often used to give information. Examples can be found in books, catalogues, newspapers, magazines, maps and websites.

Lists can be arranged:

- in alphabetical order — as in an index
- numerically — a list of instructions is often numbered
- using dates — as in bank statements
- in categories, that is, grouped by type — as in sales catalogues
- randomly — some shopping lists are written this way.

Practice

1. Look at this list.
   a. How is the list ordered?
   b. Why do you think it is ordered like this?
   c. Write down the school's phone number.
   d. Write down the dentist's phone number.
   e. Whose phone number is 778887?

Phone Numbers	
After school club	453521
Child minder	797654
Dentist	787652
Doctor	778887
Fire station	773774
Police station	776431
Railway station	768998
School	791455
Work	798976

2. Here is a list of important events.

School play	17/03
Party	11/04
Joe's birthday	13/04
Dental appointment	15/04
Dinner date	17/04
Wedding anniversary	20/04

   a. How is this list ordered?
   b. What is happening on 17th April?
   c. On what date is the wedding anniversary?
   d. When is the school play?
   e. Parents' evening is on 19th April. Where would this go in the list?

3. a. How are words in a dictionary arranged?
   b. How are events ordered in a diary?
   c. How are items ordered on a credit card or bank statement?
   d. How are items ordered in an index?
   e. How are items ordered in a directory of local services?

Lists on the internet

A **search engine** looks for information on the internet. When you type in a subject the search engine gives you a list of websites in order of relevance. **Relevant** means closely linked to your search word or words. The list you get depends on the words you use.

Suppose you wanted to find some information about Kirk Michael in the Isle of Man.

Typing Kirk Michael into a search engine gave the website list shown here.

Which of these websites do you think are relevant?
Which are not relevant? Why?

Typing in 'Kirk Michael Isle of Man' gives more relevant results. Try this if you can.

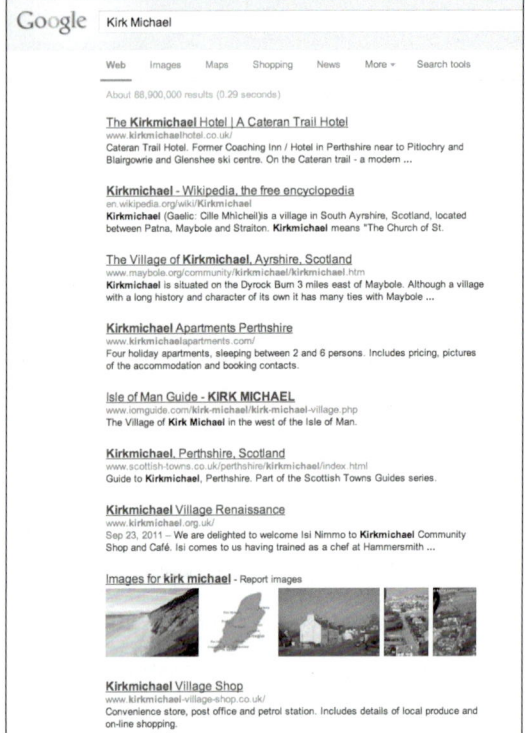

Source: Google search engine

Activities

(If necessary ask your tutor or teacher for help.)

1. Use a dictionary to find the following words.

   evaluate   proportion   integer   frequency

2. Use a local directory of services to find the address and phone number of a plumber, a gardener, a taxi and a vet.

3. Use a search engine to find a list of websites that have information on a subject you find interesting. Type in just one word and look at the list of the first 10 websites the search engine finds.

   Are all these websites relevant?

   Carry out another search using more than one word.

   Do you get more relevant results?

   Investigate further, using different combinations of words.

   Find out how to use quotation marks ("…").

B. Find information from tables

This table shows the number of men and women in some college evening classes.

This table has a **title** at the top to tell us what the table is about.

Each column has a **heading**. The first column's heading tells us that this column gives the evening classes. The other column headings show that these columns give the number of women and men in each class. Without the title and headings we would not understand what the table is about.

Number of students in evening classes

Evening class	Number of women	Number of men
Local History	10	7
Horticulture	11	5
Italian	8	9
Carpentry	4	15

Practice

1. Use the table above to answer these questions.
   a. How many women are there in the Horticulture class?
   b. How many men are there in the Local History class?
   c. How many more men than women are there in the Carpentry class?
   d. Altogether, how many students are in the Italian class?
   e. Which class has the most students?

2. Use the Book Prices table to answer these questions.
   a. How much is 'Mystery Man' from the internet?
   b. How much is 'Desert Love' from the shop?
   c. Is 'Get It?' cheaper from the internet or shop?
   d. Which is more expensive from the shop — 'The Invasion' or 'Get It?'
   e. How much more is 'Cygnus-B51' from the shop than from the internet?

Book Prices

Book	Internet price	Shop price
Pursuit	£12.00	£15.99
Cygnus-B51	£10.99	£14.00
Mystery Man	£11.00	£13.99
Get It?	£9.00	£12.00
The Invasion	£11.99	£15.00
Desert Love	£9.00	£11.99

3. Use the information in the Car Hire table to answer the questions.

   Car Hire

Vehicle type	Hire period		
	1 day	3 days	7 days
Compact	£43	£75	£129
Economy	£40	£84	£114
Intermediate	£62	£95	£150
People Carrier	£84	£145	£179
Luxury	£95	£200	£325
Standard	£68	£105	£165

   a. How much does it cost to hire:
      i. a Compact car for 3 days
      ii. a People Carrier for 7 days?
   b. What is the cheapest type of car you can hire for a week?
   c. How much more does it cost to hire a Luxury car for 7 days than for 3 days?
   d. How much more does it cost to hire a Standard car than an Economy car for:
      i. 3 days   ii. 7 days?
   e. An Intermediate car is hired for 7 days. How much does this cost per day, to the nearest pound?

4. **Flight Information**

Route	Flight number	Departure – Return Days	Outward times		Return times	
			Depart	Arrive	Depart	Arrive
Heathrow – Split	453/65S	Sat – Sat	16:50	21:00	14:30	17:40
Gatwick – Split	789/45S	Fri – Fri	10:00	13:50	21:00	23:50
Manchester – Split	791/75S	Sat – Sat	19:00	22:50	18:10	21:00
Heathrow – Pula	465/71P	Thurs – Thurs	11:30	15:20	12:20	15:30
Gatwick – Pula	781/31P	Fri – Fri	07:00	11:10	06:30	09:20
Manchester – Pula	867/91P	Sat – Sat	18:00	21:50	17:10	20:00

   a. What is the flight number of the flight from Manchester to Split?
   b. What time is the flight from Gatwick to Pula due to arrive?
   c. What time does the return flight for flight number 781/31P leave?
   d. Which route does flight number 781/31P fly?
   e. On what day of the week does the flight from Manchester to Pula fly?

5. a. What is missing from the table below?

Altea	H/Esplendia	7	HB	750	FB	1010	14	HB	1076	FB	1568
Benidorm	H/Fantastica	7	HB	600	FB	950	14	HB	989	FB	1300
Malaga	H/Luxuriosa	7	HB	570	FB	900	14	HB	976	FB	1286
Salou	H/Fabulosa	7	HB	500	FB	845	14	HB	855	FB	1015

   HB = Half Board, FB = Full Board

   b. Redraw the table. Put in the missing items.

c. How much does it cost to stay in Hotel Luxuriosa for 14 nights full board?

d. How much does it cost to stay in Hotel Fabulosa for 7 nights half board?

e. Your hotel costs £1010.

　　i. Where are you staying?

　　ii. Is it half board or full board?

　　iii. How many nights are you staying there?

f. How much more does it cost to stay full board for 7 nights in Hotel Fantastica in Benidorm than in Hotel Fabulosa in Salou?

6. The table below gives the cost for winter sport travel insurance.

   Children under 2 years old are covered for free.

Age	2 – 15 years		16 – 64		65 or over	
Number of nights	Europe	Outside Europe	Europe	Outside Europe	Europe	Outside Europe
6 – 9	£26	£72	£29	£83	£57	£166
10 – 17	£31	£82	£35	£94	£66	£196
18 – 23	£40	£92	£45	£105	£82	£226

Use the table to find the total cost for each of these families who are going on a skiing holiday.

a. 14 nights in Europe

　Mr Bell　　Age 28

　Mrs Bell　 Age 26

　Ben　　　Age 4

　Julie　　　Age 1

b. 21 nights outside Europe

　Mr Khan　　　　　Age 38

　Mrs Khan　　　　 Age 39

　Imran　　　　　　Age 14

　Mr Khan (senior)　Age 67

Activities

1. Choose a holiday from a brochure or website.

   Use information from the brochure to find out the total cost and the flight times.

2. Look up prices in tables in catalogues.

3. Find the distance between cities from a road atlas table. (See pages 208–209.)

4. Many internet websites show comparisons by giving information in tables, for example, to compare different savings accounts, insurance offers or cars for sale.

   Find a table on a comparison website for something you are interested in and write a short report on what you find.

C. Find information from pictograms

A **pictogram** uses pictures or symbols to represent data.

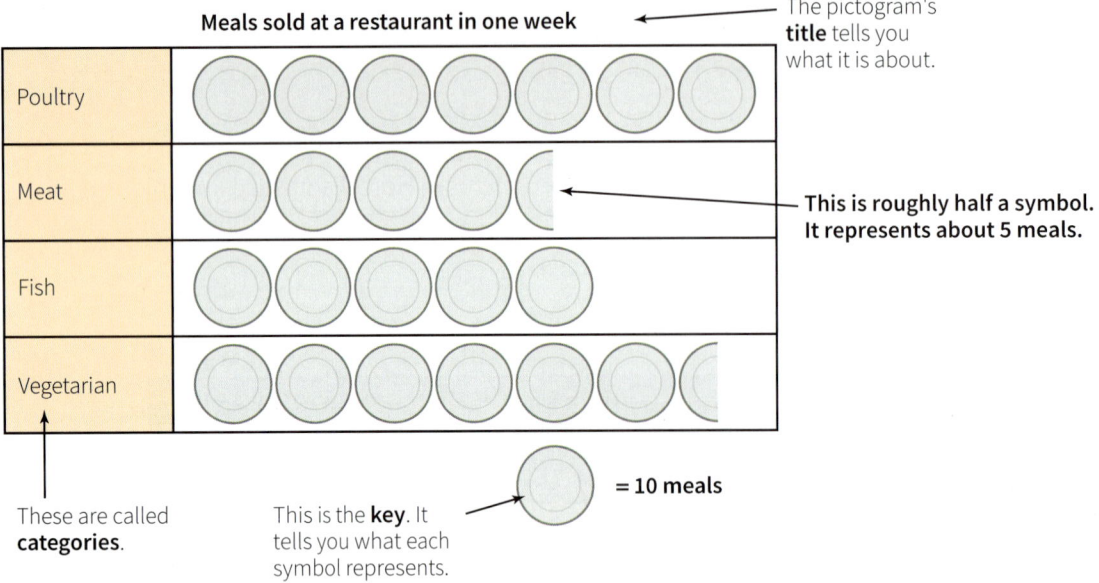

When each symbol represents a number of items, you can only estimate how many are in each category when parts of symbols are used.

Practice

1. Use the pictogram above to answer these questions.
   a. How many meat meals were sold?
   b. Which type of meal was: i. the most popular   ii. the least popular?
   c. How many more vegetarian meals were sold than fish meals?
   d. How many meals were sold altogether?

2. The pictogram below shows how much a householder spends on renovating his bedroom.

   a. Which category of goods cost: i. the most   ii. the least?
   b. Estimate how much he spends: i. on each category   ii. altogether.

Extracting and Interpreting Information

Information from bar charts and line graphs

Specification reference **EL3.H21, EL3.H22, L1.H27**

A. Find information from bar charts

Bar charts use vertical or horizontal bars to give data.

The bar chart below shows the type of morning drinks chosen by the workers in a large open-plan office. The main features are labelled.

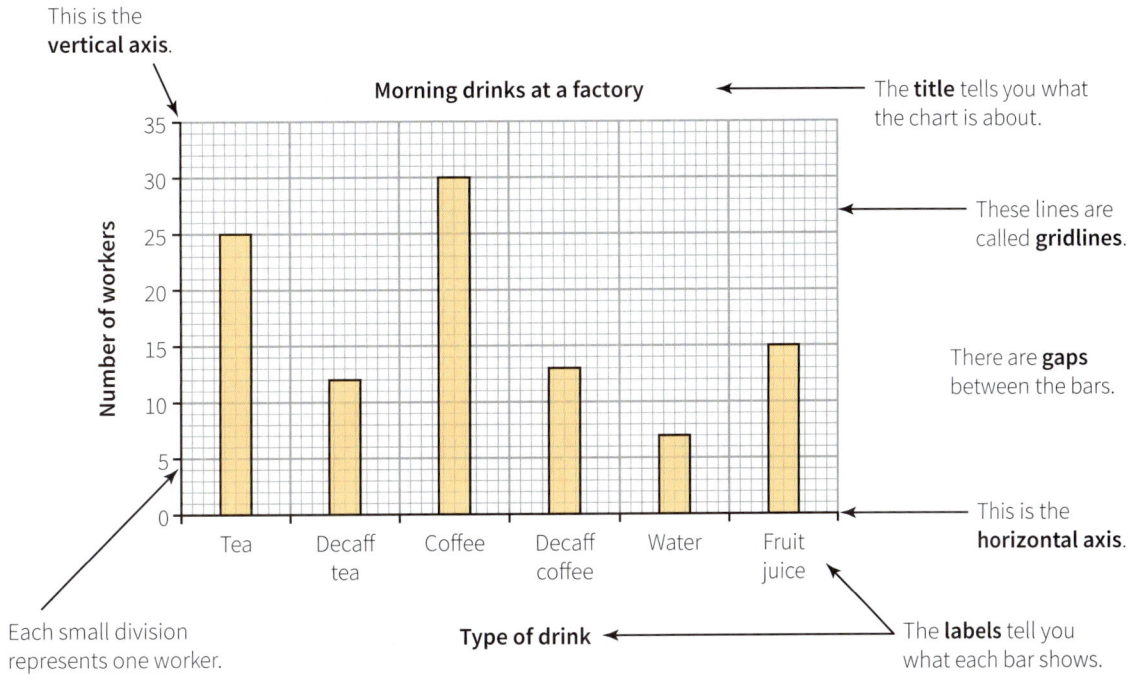

The **scale** on the vertical axis tells you how many workers had each type of drink. The first bar shows 25 workers had tea. The second bar shows 12 workers had decaffeinated (decaff) tea.

Practice

1. a. Copy this table. Use the bar chart above to fill in the missing numbers.

    Use the table to answer these questions then use the bar chart to check.

    b. How many more workers had tea than decaffeinated tea?

    c. How many more workers had fruit juice than water?

    d. Altogether how many workers had decaffeinated drinks?

    e. How many workers were there altogether?

Type of drink	Number of workers
Tea	25
Decaff tea	12
Coffee	
Decaff coffee	
Water	
Fruit Juice	

 1193, 6018

347

Handling Information and Data

In a survey people are asked which type of TV programmes they like best. The bar chart below shows the results. The label on the vertical axis shows that the number of people is also called the **frequency**. Frequency means how often something happens – in this case how often people chose each type of TV programme.

Can you see what each division on the vertical axis represents this time?

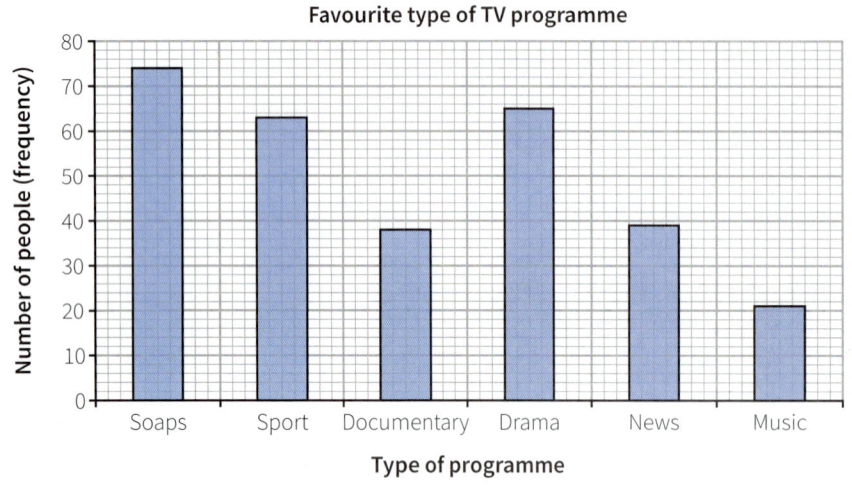

 **Key point**

Make sure you understand the scale before you read values from a chart or graph.

Each division represents 2 people.

The number of people who like soaps best is 74

The top of the bar for sport lies between 62 and 64. This means the number of people who like sport best is 63

---

2. Use the bar chart above to answer these questions.
   a. How many people chose:
      i. documentaries   **ii.** drama   **iii.** news   **iv.** music?
   b. Which is:
      i. the most popular type of programme   **ii.** the least popular type?
   c. How many more people chose documentaries than music?
   d. How many more people chose soaps than drama?
   e. Altogether, how many people chose soaps or drama?
   f. In total, how many people chose sport, documentary or news?
   g. Altogether, how many people took part in the survey?

This bar chart shows the population of the UK and some countries in Europe.

Can you see what each division on the horizontal axis represents?

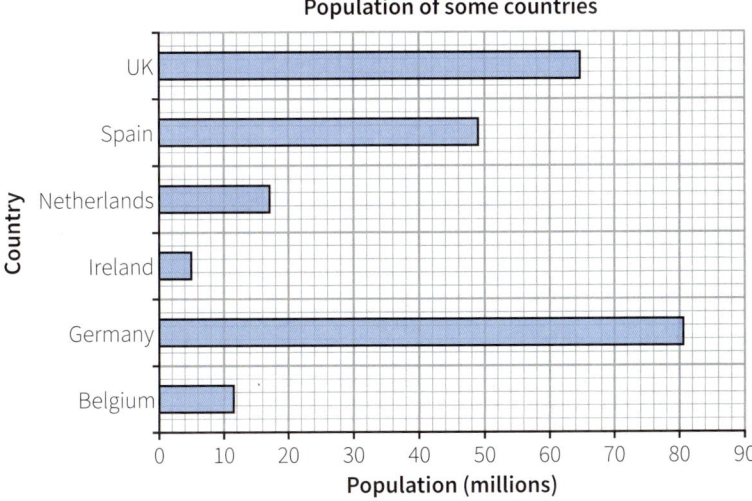

Data source: www.oecd.org

Each division represents **2 million** people. It is not possible to read the populations accurately, but you can estimate them to the nearest million.

---

3. Use the bar chart above to answer these questions.
   a. Which of the countries has:
      i. the largest population
      ii. the smallest population?
   b. Write down the population of each country. Give your answers to the nearest million.
   c. i. How many more people live in Germany than in the UK?
      ii. How many more people live in the UK than in the Netherlands?
   d. What is the total population of the UK and Ireland?

4. The bar chart shows the average prices of different types of monthly magazines.
   a. Which is the most expensive type of magazine?
   b. Which is the cheapest type of magazine?
   c. What is the average price of:
      i. a monthly current affairs magazine
      ii. a monthly gardening magazine?
   d. How much cheaper, on average, is a monthly motoring magazine than a monthly music magazine?

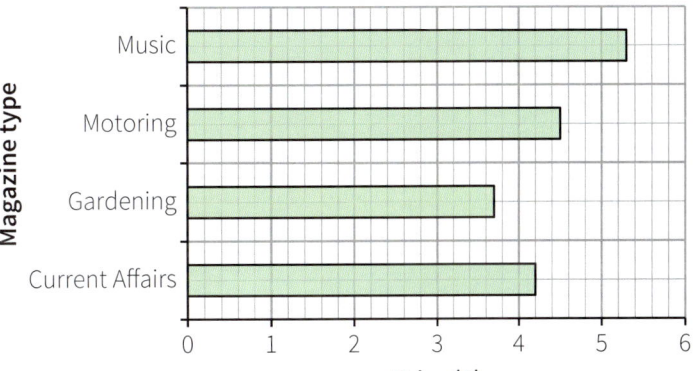

The bar chart below shows the height of each student in a class.
Their names are given in a **key** because it is difficult to fit them along the horizontal axis.
What does each division on the vertical axis represent?

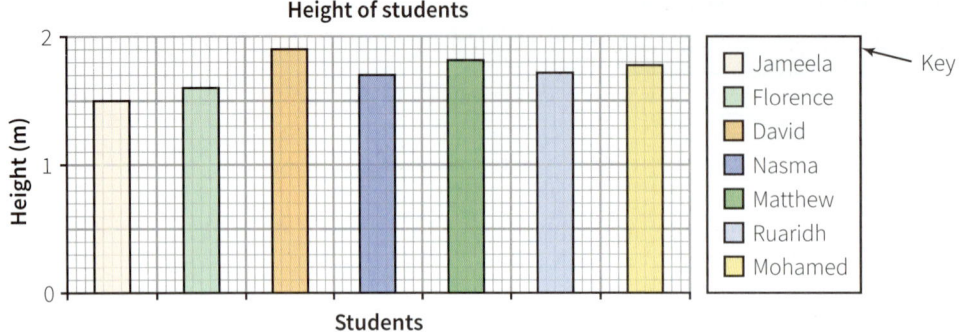

Each division represents 0.1 metres (or 10 cm).
Some of the tops of the bars lie between two gridlines.
Using the **nearest gridline** gives the height to the **nearest 0.1 m**.
For example, Mohamed's height is 1.8 m to the nearest 0.1 m.

---

5. Look at the bar chart above.

   a. Copy this table.

      Use the bar chart to fill in the missing heights, correct to the nearest 0.1 m.

   b. Who is the **shortest** student?

   c. Who is the **tallest** student?

   d. Who is **taller**: Nasma or Ruaridh?

   e. Who is **shorter**: Matthew or Mohamed?

Student	Height (m)
Jameela	
Florence	
David	
Nasma	
Matthew	
Ruaridh	
Mohamed	1.8

6. A café sells baked potatoes with a choice of fillings.
   The bar chart shows the number of each type of filling bought in one day.

a. What is missing from the bar chart?
b. Which was the **most** popular filling?
c. Which was the **least** popular filling?
d. Draw a table giving the frequency for each type of filling.
   Give your answers as accurately as you can.
e. How many baked potatoes were sold altogether?
f. How many more potatoes were filled with cheese than were filled with tuna?

These two charts both show the same information.

Chart A

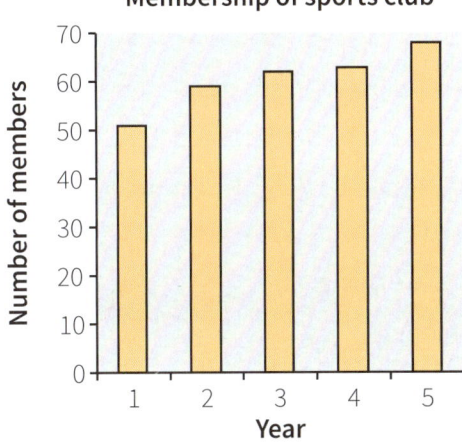

Chart B

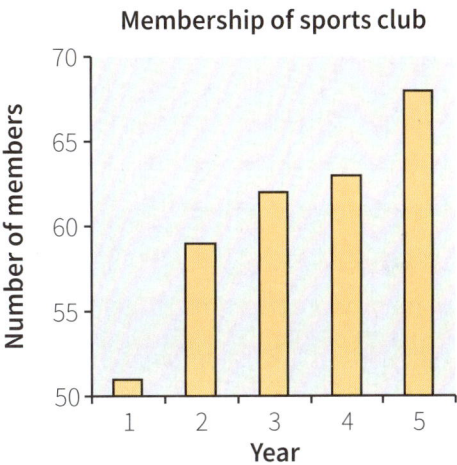

Changing the scale on an axis changes the impression a chart gives.
Starting at a non-zero value also makes it look different.

7. a. Look at the charts above. Which chart makes the increase in the number of members look more dramatic?
   b. The charts do not have any gridlines, but you can estimate the number of members.

   Look at Chart A. The number of members in Year 1 is just above 50. A reasonable estimate is 51. This has been entered into the table.

   i. Copy the table and use Chart A to complete the second column.
   ii. Use Chart B to complete the last column of your table.
   iii. Which chart was easier to use when estimating the number of members?

Year	Chart A	Chart B
1	51	
2		
3		
4		
5		

To emphasise that an axis has a non-zero starting value, you can start the axis with a zigzag line like this:

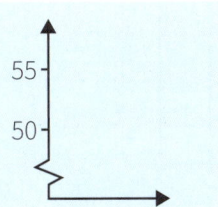

351

The chart below is a **comparative** bar chart. It gives a comparison between the number of full-time and part-time students on vocational courses at a college.

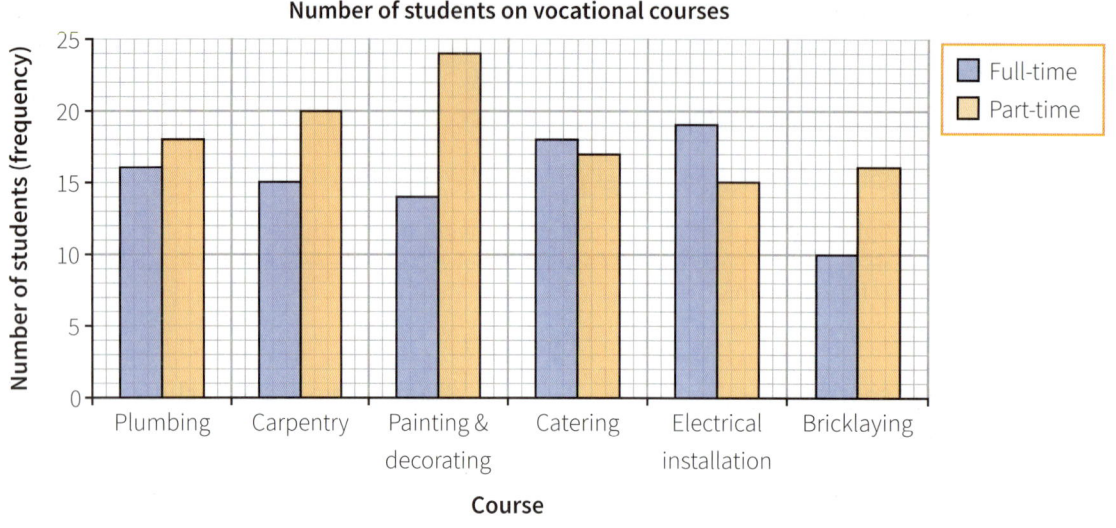

8. Use the chart above to answer these questions.
   a. On which courses are there more full-time than part-time students?
   b. How many more part-time students than full-time students are doing:
      i. carpentry   ii. plumbing   iii. painting and decorating?
   c. Find the total number of students who are doing:
      i. bricklaying   ii. catering   iii. electrical installation.
   d. Find the total number of:
      i. full-time students   ii. part-time students.

The chart below is a **component** bar chart. It shows the amounts earned in one week by the people who work in a car showroom. The amount earned is the total of basic pay and commission.

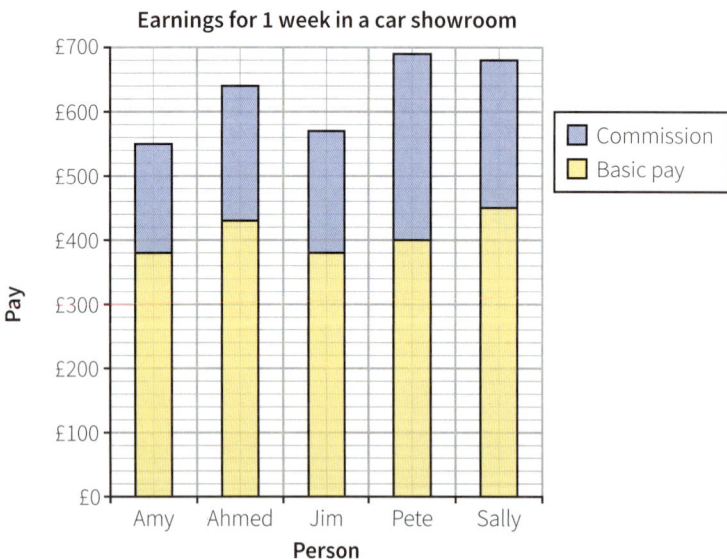

Extracting and Interpreting Information

9. Use the bar chart at the bottom of page 352 to answer these questions.
   a. i. Who earned the **most**? ii. How much was this?
   b. i. Who earned the **least**? ii. How much was this?
   c. Write down the amount earned by each of the other people.
   d. i. Who has the highest basic pay? ii. How much is this?
   e. i. Which people have the same basic pay? ii. How much is it?
   f. i. Find the commission earned by each person.
      ii. List the people in order of their commission, starting with the person who earned the **most** commission.

You have met many different types of data in this chapter.
Qualitative data is not numerical. Examples include colours, types of drink.
Quantitative (numerical) data can be discrete or continuous.
Discrete data takes only particular values, for example shoe sizes or number of children in families.
Continuous data can take any value in a given range, for example, heights, weights, time to complete a task and other things that you measure.

---

10. Give three examples of each of:
    a. qualitative data   b. discrete data   c. continuous data.

11. The chart shows the grades achieved by the candidates in some A level exams one year.
    a. Which subject had the biggest percentage of candidates achieving grade A*?
    b. Every grade except U is a pass grade.
       Which subject had the best pass rate?
    c. Draw up a table to give the percentage of candidates getting each grade for each subject.

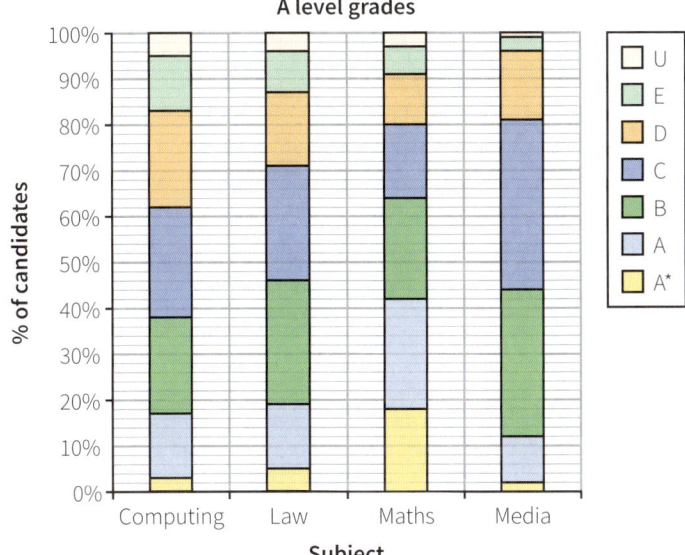

Data source: www.qca.org.uk

12. The National Readership Survey estimates the number of adults who read magazines. The chart shows the results for some weekly magazines.

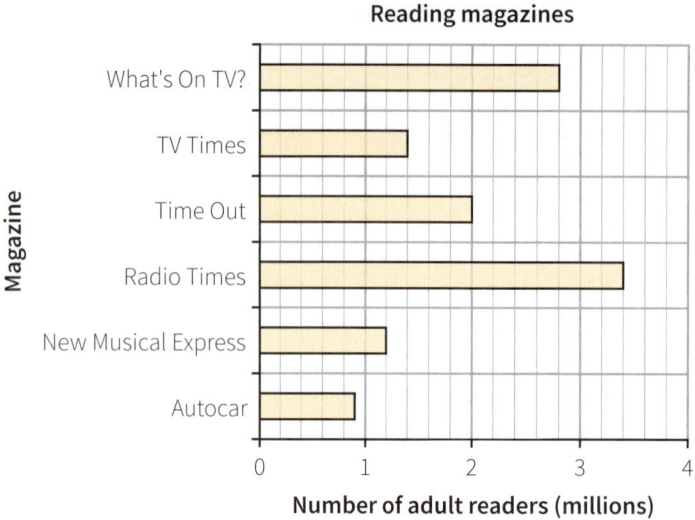

Data source: The Publishers Audience Measurement Company (pamco.co.uk)

Estimate the number of adult readers of each magazine.
Give each answer:

a. to the nearest million

b. to the nearest 100 000

B. Find information from line graphs

Line graphs are often used to show how something changes as time goes by.

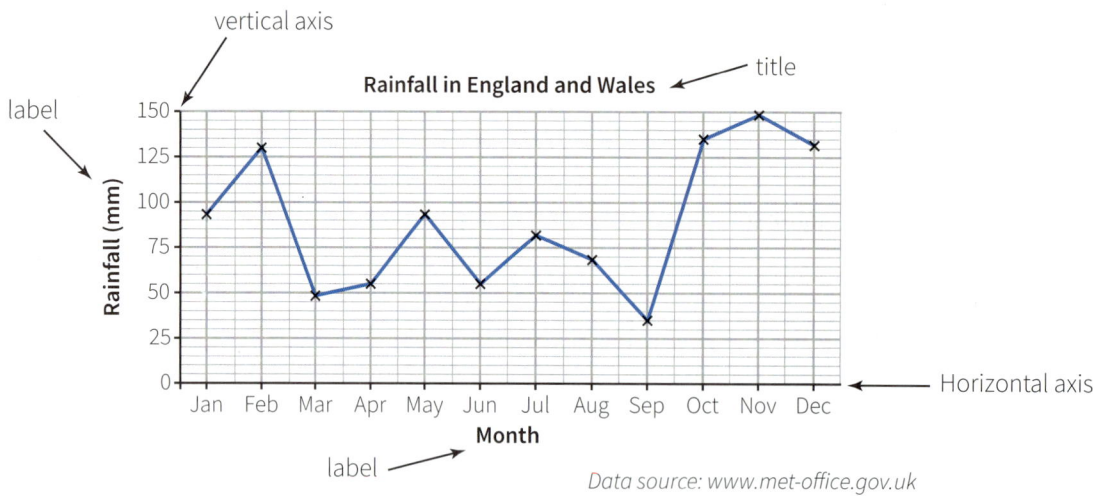

Data source: www.met-office.gov.uk

The **title** and **labels** on this line graph show that it is about the rainfall in England and Wales.
The **crosses** show the rainfall that was recorded.
The **lines** that join them show how the rainfall went up and down during the year.

Extracting and Interpreting Information

Practice

1. Use the line graph on the previous page to answer these questions.
   a. What does each small division represent on the vertical axis?
   b. i. In which month did the **most** rain fall?   ii. Estimate how much rain fell in this month.
   c. i. In which month did the **least** rain fall?   ii. Estimate how much rain fell in this month.
   d. How much more rain fell in December than in June?
   e. Estimate the total rainfall for the year.

2. The graph shows the number of children who attended a nursery between 2014 and 2019.

   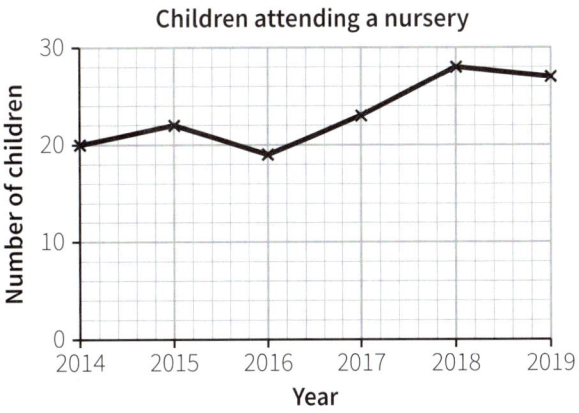

   a How many children attended in
      i. 2015   ii. 2017?
   b i. Which year had the highest number of children?
      ii. What was this number?
   c i. Which year had the lowest number of children?
      ii. What was this number?
   d The manager says that 7 more children attended in 2019 than in 2014. Is the manager correct? Explain your answer.

Level 1

3. Use this line graph to answer the questions that follow.

   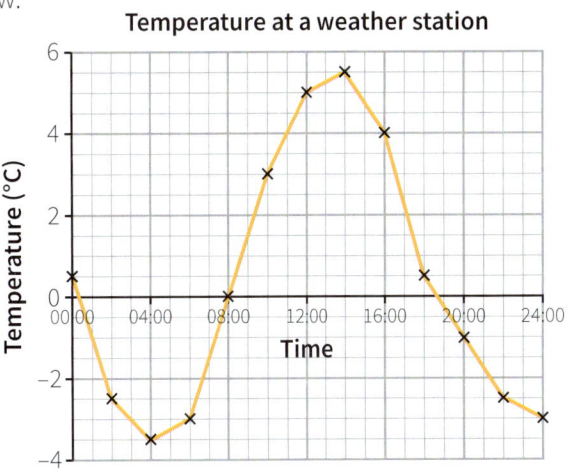

   a. What does each small square represent on:
      i. the horizontal axis
      ii. the vertical axis?
   b. How often was the temperature measured?
   c. i. What was the **highest** temperature measured?
      ii. When was this reading taken?
   d. i. What was the **lowest** temperature measured?
      ii. When was this reading taken?
   e. i. When was the temperature **measured** as 0 °C?
      ii. **Estimate** the other times when the temperature was 0 °C.
   f. Between what times was the temperature:
      i. rising   ii. falling?
   g. When was the temperature rising most quickly?

4. These graphs both show the profit made by a company over a 5-year period.

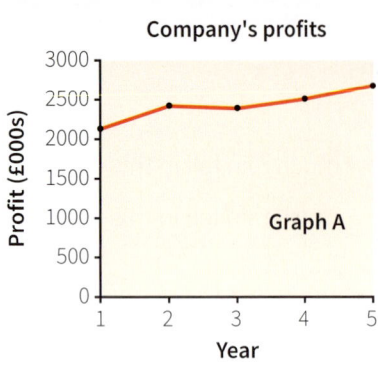
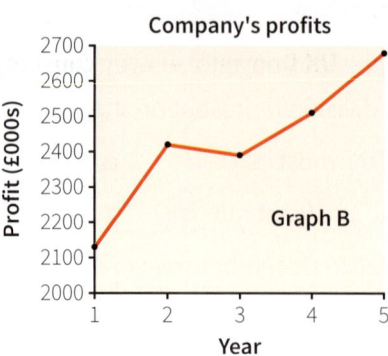

a. i. Which graph gives the best estimates of the yearly profits?
    ii. Use this graph to estimate the profit each year.
b. Explain why graph B may be misleading.

> **Key point**
> Line graphs can be used to show **more than one set of data**.

5. This graph shows the average number of hours of sunshine per day over the course of a year in Scotland and in England.

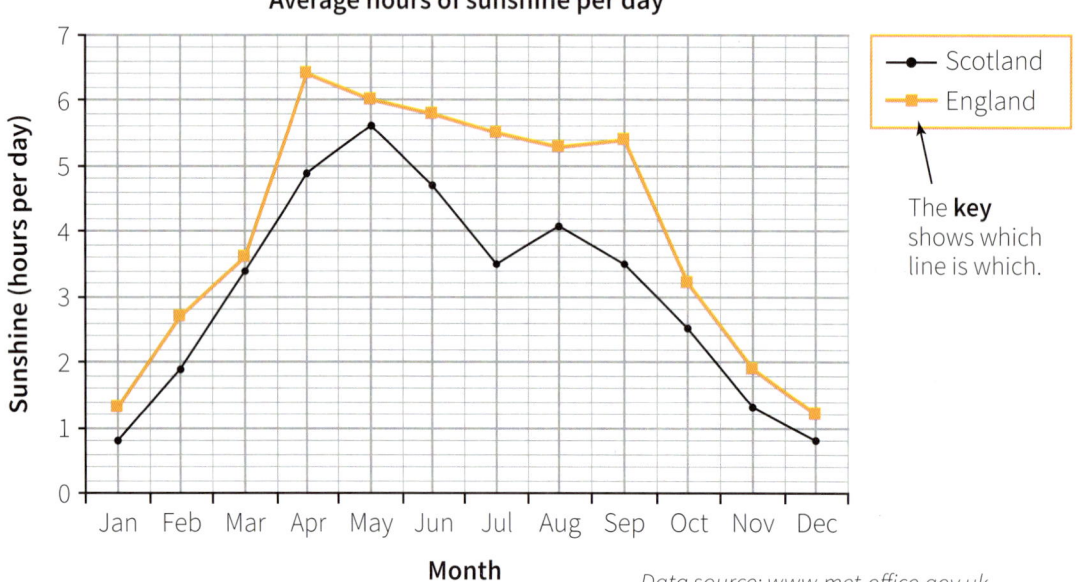

The **key** shows which line is which.

a. Which month had the **most** sunshine in:
   i. England   ii. Scotland?
b. Which month(s) had the **least** sunshine in:
   i. England   ii. Scotland?
c. How much more sunshine was there in England than in Scotland in:
   i. January   ii. July?
d. How much more sunshine was there in August than November in:
   i. England   ii. Scotland?
e. Write a paragraph to explain what the graph shows.

Extracting and Interpreting Information

6. The graph shows the amount of solid fuel, petroleum and gas consumed by households in the UK during the years 1970–2015.

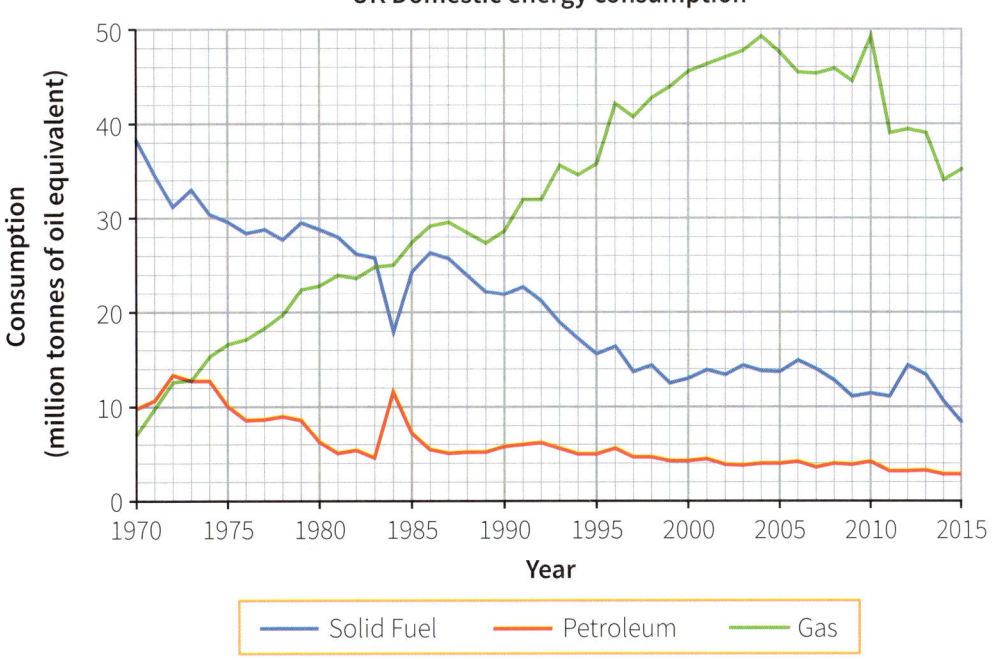

Data source: www.gov.uk

a. In which year was the consumption of solid fuel the **lowest**?

b. In which year was the consumption of petroleum the **highest**?

c. Estimate the **increase** in gas consumption between 1970 and 2010.

d. Estimate the **decrease** in the consumption of solid fuel between 1980 and 2000.

e. Estimate the total consumption of solid fuel, petroleum and gas in 1990.

f. Describe what happened to solid fuel and petroleum consumption in 1984.

g. Describe the way in which the consumption of each type of fuel changed between 1970 and 2015.

Activities

1. Look for examples of charts, graphs and diagrams in newspapers and magazines and on websites. Explain what they show.

2. Look at the government's statistics website at www.gov.uk/government/statistics and find reports on topics that interest you.
Print some of the information given in charts and graphs and discuss what they show.
Find other information including charts and graphs on the internet.

Handling Information and Data

Information from pie charts

Specification reference **L1.H27**

Level 1

Pie charts show how something is divided into parts.

The pie chart below shows how a student spends a typical day.

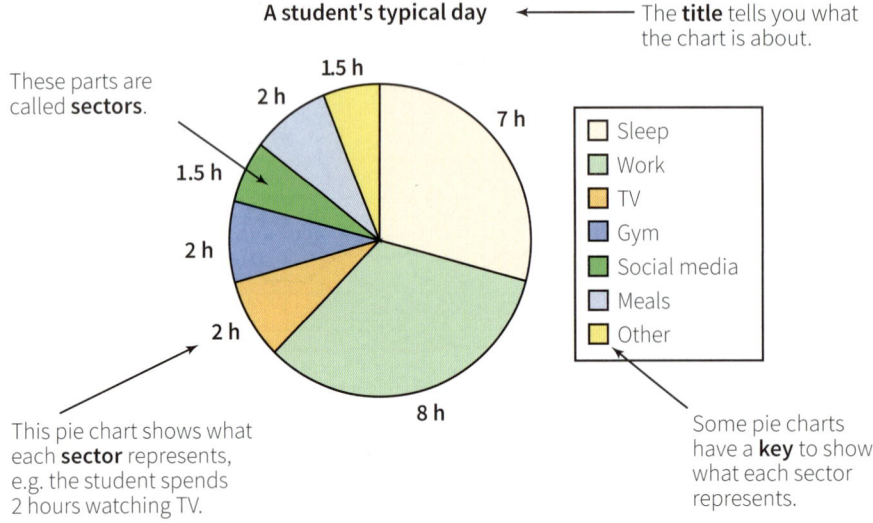

The **title** tells you what the chart is about.

These parts are called **sectors**.

Some pie charts have a **key** to show what each sector represents.

This pie chart shows what each **sector** represents, e.g. the student spends 2 hours watching TV.

Practice

1. Use the pie chart above to answer these questions.
   a. Which activity took the **most** time?
   b. How much longer did the student spend at the gym than on social media?
   c. What is the total time shown on the pie chart? Why?

2. This pie chart shows the results of a survey about how people travel to work.
   a. Which is:
      i. the **most** popular way of getting to work
      ii. the **least** popular way of getting to work?
   b. What fraction of the people:
      i. travel to work by bus
      ii. walk to work
      iii. travel to work by train
      iv. drive to work
      v. cycle to work?
   c. Altogether, 400 people took part in the survey.
      Find how many travelled by each method.

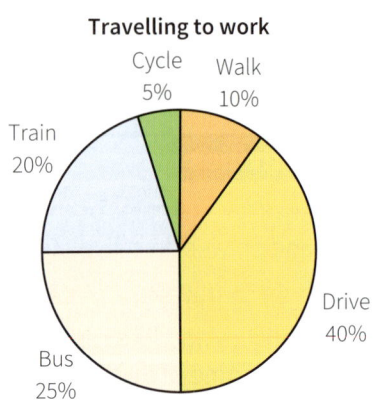

358 MyMaths 1206 SEARCH

Extracting and Interpreting Information

Sometimes pie charts do not give the number or the percentage of items in each sector.
You can **estimate** the fraction or percentage from the size of the sector.

If you are told the total number of items you can estimate how many are in each category.
For example, if a pie chart represents altogether 100 people, then half of the circle represents 50 people.

3. This pie chart shows the grades given to students for an exam.
   a. Estimate the fraction of the students who got each grade.
   b. Altogether, 48 students took the exam.
      Estimate how many got each grade.

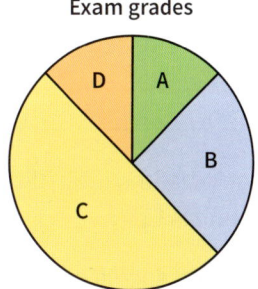

Exam grades

4. The pie chart shows the proportion of each type of property a developer builds on a new estate.
   a. Say which of the following statements are true and which are false.
      i. More than a quarter of the properties are flats.
      ii. There are more bungalows than flats.
      iii. There are approximately the same number of bungalows as detached houses.
      iv. There are more terraced properties than any other type.
   b. Put the types of property in order of the numbers built by the developer, starting with the **largest**.

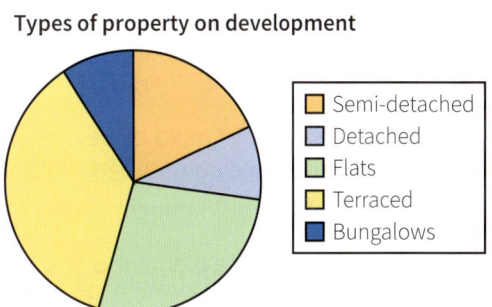

Types of property on development

- Semi-detached
- Detached
- Flats
- Terraced
- Bungalows

For more accurate values you need to measure the angles of the pie chart with a **protractor**.

See page 272 for help with measuring an angle.

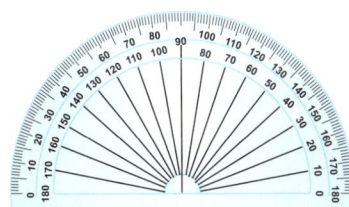

There are 360° in a circle. To find accurate information from a pie chart you must find the connection between the angles and the data.

For example, the pie chart on the following page shows how a telephone bill of £180 is shared between five flatmates.

360° represents £180   so   1° represents $\frac{£180}{360}$ = £0.50 (that is, 50p)

Measure the angle that shows Bev's share.

The angle is 120°. So Bev's share of the bill = 120 × £0.50 = £60

5. **a.** Copy and complete this table.

Flatmate	Angle	Amount to pay
Bev	120°	120 × £0.50 = £60
Mia		
Jess		
Oliver		
Matt		

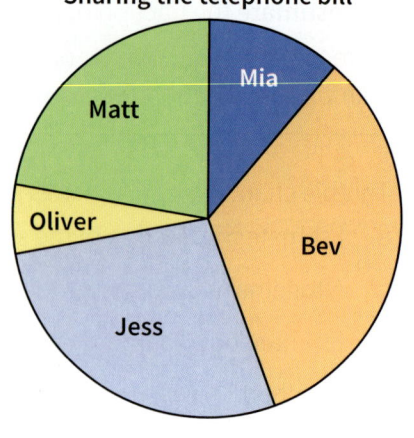

Sharing the telephone bill

  b. Check that the total of the amounts in the last column is £180

6. This pie chart shows how a day's takings were divided between different types of goods at a DIY store.

    a. On which type of goods did customers spend the **most**?

    b. Did customers spend more or less on gardening tools than decorating equipment?

    c. The manager says that more than half of the takings were from goods for decorating. Is this true or false?

    d. The total amount taken in the day was £8100

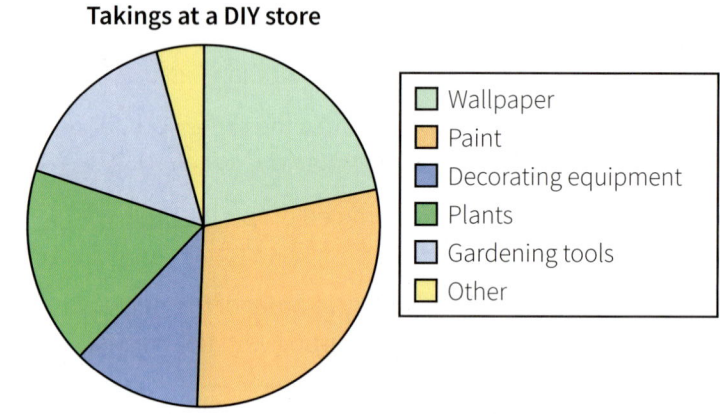

    Measure the angles and calculate how much was spent on each type of goods.

7. This pie chart shows the employees in each department of a company. There are 90 **office workers**.

    a. Work out what 1° represents.

    b. Find the number of employees in each of the other departments.

    c. How many employees are there altogether?

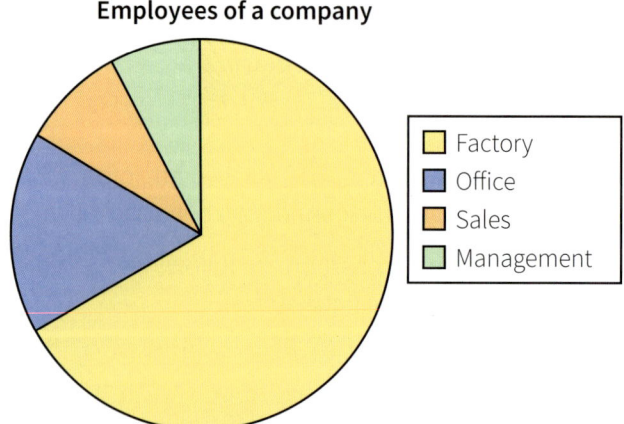

8. The pie charts show the people who visit a leisure centre on two days.

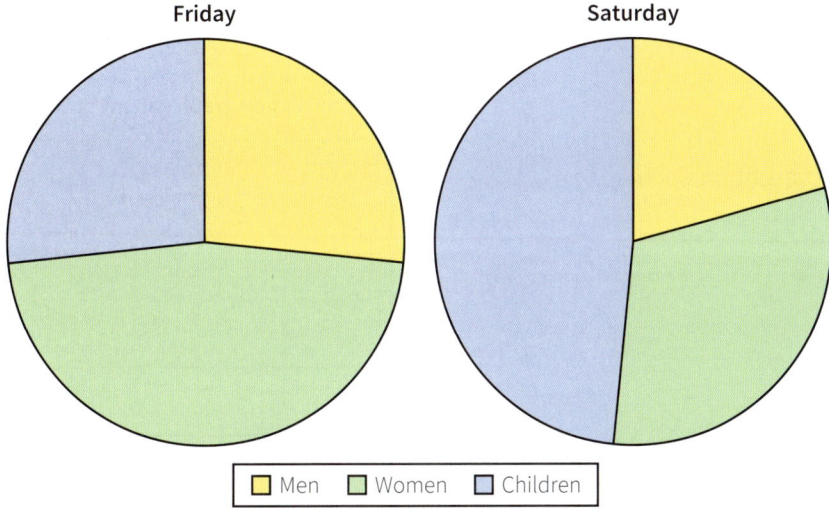

☐ Men   ☐ Women   ☐ Children

a. Which of the statements given below **must** be true?

   A More women than men visited the leisure centre on Friday.

   B The number of men who visited the leisure centre on Friday was the same as the number of children.

   C More than half of the people who visited the leisure centre on Friday were women.

   D More than a quarter of the people who visited the leisure centre on Saturday were women.

   E More men visited the leisure centre on Friday than on Saturday.

   F More than twice as many children as men visited the leisure centre on Saturday.

b. In fact, 240 children visited the leisure centre on Friday.

   i. Measure the angle of the children sector on the Friday pie chart.

   ii. Work out how many people are represented by each degree on the Friday pie chart.

   iii. Copy the table and complete the column for Friday.

	Fri	Sat
Men		
Women		
Children		
Total		

c. The total number of visitors to the leisure centre on Saturday was 1200

   i. Complete the Saturday column in your table.

   ii. Answer the questions in part **a** from your table.

   Do all of your answers agree with your answers for part **a**?

Handling Information and Data

Information from conversion graphs

Specification reference L2.M14

This line graph is a **conversion graph**. You can use it to convert gallons to litres and vice versa.

Look at the scales.
What does a small square represent on each axis?

The arrows show that:

14 gallons ≈ 64 litres

16 litres ≈ 3.5 gallons.

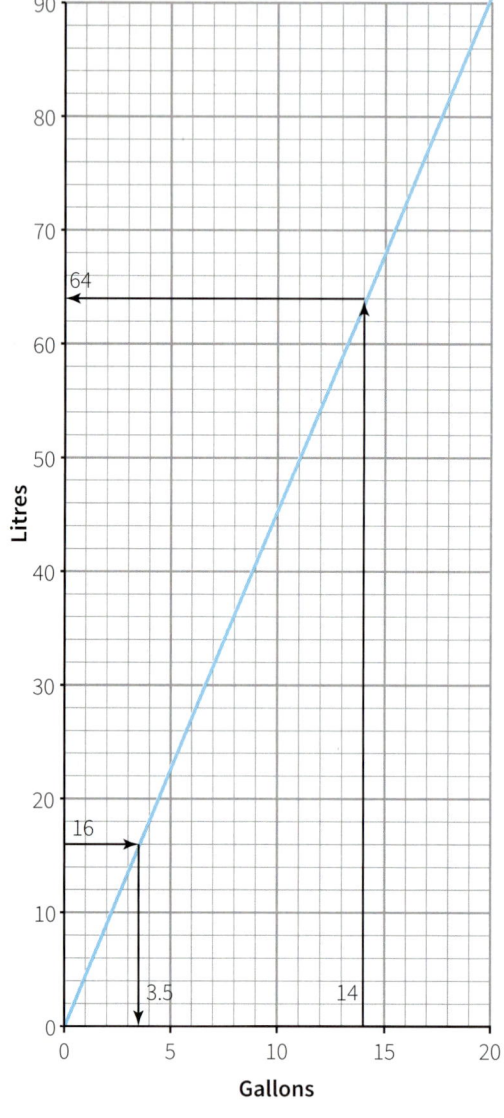

> **Key point**
>
> Remember: ≈ means 'approximately equal to'.

 Practice

1. **a.** Copy and complete each part, giving each answer to the nearest litre.

    i. 10 gallons ≈ ___ litres

    ii. 5 gallons ≈ ___ litres

    iii. 18 gallons ≈ ___ litres

    iv. 7.5 gallons ≈ ___ litres

   b. Copy and complete each part, giving each answer to the nearest 0.5 gallon.

    i. 40 litres ≈ ___ gallons

    ii. 72 litres ≈ ___ gallons

    iii. 24 litres ≈ ___ gallons

    iv. 67 litres ≈ ___ gallons

   c. The petrol tank of a car holds 15 gallons. How many litres is this?

   d. There are 82 litres of water left in a tank. How many gallons is this?

   e. A large bottle holds 6 pints of milk.

    How many litres of milk are needed to fill 20 bottles?

    (1 gallon = 8 pints)

 Also see page 262 for an alternative method using a conversion factor.

MyMaths 1059 SEARCH

2. The graph below converts temperatures from Celsius to Fahrenheit and vice versa.
   a. What does each small square represent on:
      i. the horizontal axis   ii. the vertical axis?

Temperature conversion graph

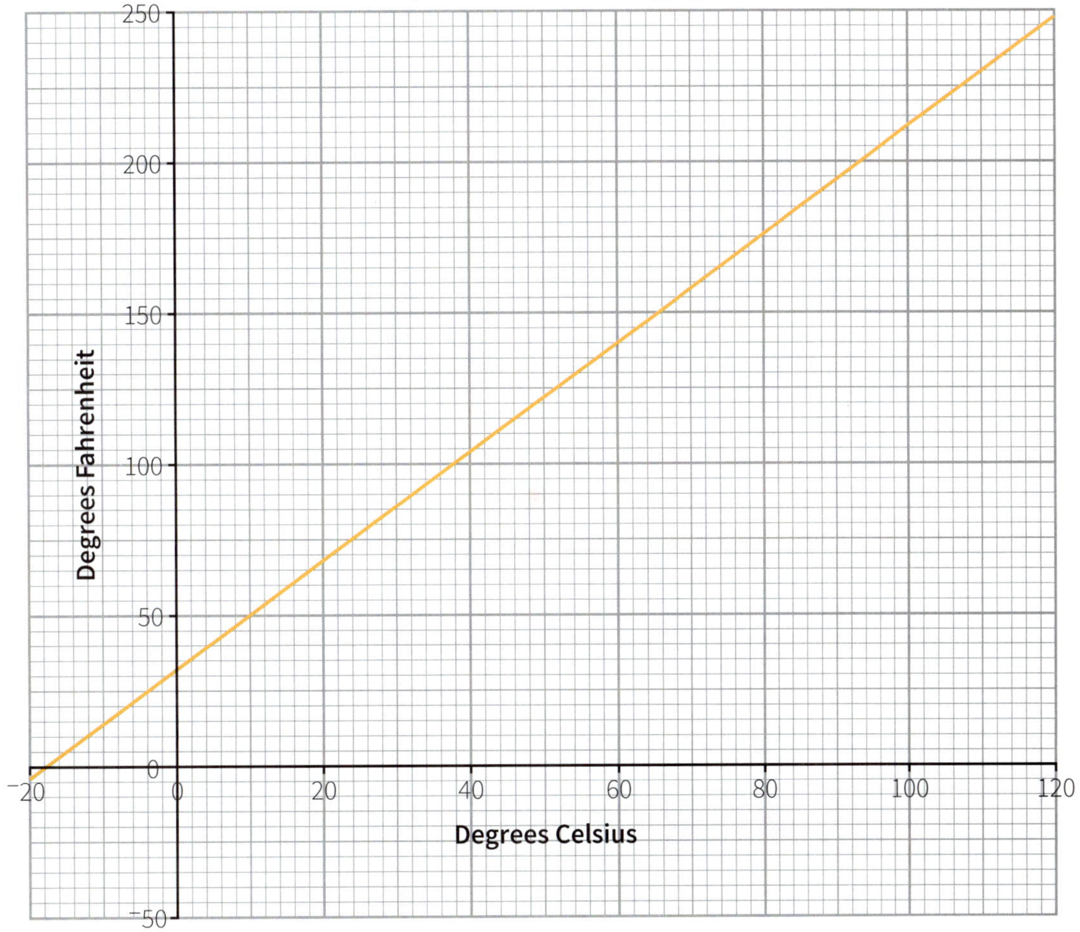

Degrees Fahrenheit vs *Degrees Celsius*

Copy and complete these. Estimate each answer as accurately as you can.

b. i. 20 °C ≈ ___ °F   ii. 48 °C ≈ ___ °F   iii. 75 °C ≈ ___ °F
   iv. 27 °C ≈ ___ °F   v. −10 °C ≈ ___ °F   vi. −7 °C ≈ ___ °F

c. i. 50 °F ≈ ___ °C   ii. 140 °F ≈ ___ °C   iii. 75 °F ≈ ___ °C
   iv. 205 °F ≈ ___ °C   v. 184 °F ≈ ___ °C   vi. 28 °F ≈ ___ °C

d. Water freezes at 0 °C and boils at 100 °C.
   What are these temperatures in Fahrenheit?

 Also see page 269 for an alternative method using a formula.

e. In England, the average temperature in July 1910 was 57 °F.
   Compare this with the average temperature in July 2010 which was 17 °C.

Chapter Summary
21 Extracting and Interpreting Information

- Use the **title** and **headings** of columns or rows to find information from a table.
- A **key** tells you what a symbol or colour represents in a graph or chart.
- A **pictogram** uses a symbol or picture to represent data. The key tells you what the symbol or picture represents. Each row of the pictogram represents a different **category**.
- **Bar charts** use horizontal or vertical bars to represent data. The title and labels on the axes tell you what the chart is about.
- The **frequency** tells you how many times something occurs.
- **Line graphs** often show how something varies over time.
- Make sure that you understand the scale of a chart or graph before reading off values.

- The vertical axis may not start at zero. This is sometimes emphasised by a zigzag line at the start of the axis.
- Changing the scale on an axis changes the impression given by a chart or graph.
- **Qualitative data** is not numerical.
- **Quantitative data** is numerical and can be **discrete** (data only takes specific values) or **continuous** (data can take any value in a given range).
- A **comparative** bar chart uses adjacent bars to show more than one data set.
- A **component** bar chart shows the data from more than one data set in each bar.
- Line graphs can have more than one line, to enable sets of data to be compared.
- **Pie charts** show how something is divided into **sectors** (parts).
  They often have a key to show what each sector represents.
- Sometimes you need to use a protractor to measure the angles on a pie chart.
  The sum of the angles should be 360°
- Pie charts sometimes give information as percentages.
  The percentages in the chart should add up to 100%

- You can use a **conversion graph** to convert between different units. To convert a quantity, find it on one axis. Then draw a line up (or across) to a point on the conversion line then across (or down) to the other axis.
- ≈ means 'approximately equal to'.

Handling Information and Data

22 Collecting and Illustrating Data

Create frequency tables

Specification reference EL3.H21, L1.H28

How could you find out which type of pet is most popular?

One way is to carry out a survey asking people which pets they have.

The more people you ask, the more representative the results.

Before starting the survey you need to think of the possible answers and how to organise them.

The best way of organising the information you collect is in a **tally chart**.

Here is a tally chart from a survey about pets.

The question asked was: **Which types of pet do you own?**

Type of pet	Tally	Frequency
Dog	ʜʜʜ ʜʜʜ ʜʜʜ I	16
Cat	ʜʜʜ ʜʜʜ IIII	
Rabbit	ʜʜʜ	
Bird	II	
Fish	III	
Reptile	I	
Other	ʜʜʜ I	
None	ʜʜʜ ʜʜʜ III	

A **tally mark** I is put into the table whenever a person says they have a particular type of pet.

The fifth tally mark is drawn across the first four as a slash / to make a group of five. This makes it easier to count the total.

The total number of people owning each type of pet is the **frequency**.

Practice

1. **a.** The frequency for dogs in the table above is 16

   Write down the frequency for each other type of pet.

   b. Which is the most popular type of pet?

   c. List some types of pet that could be in the 'Other' category.

2. The pet survey also asked people how many pets they had. The answers were:

   0, 1, 3, 1, 2, 1, 0, 6, 4, 3, 1, 1, 0, 1, 3, 1, 1, 0, 1, 6,
   1, 2, 1, 3, 1, 0, 0, 1, 2, 1, 1, 2, 4, 1, 0, 3, 2, 1, 1, 0,
   3, 1, 0, 2, 5, 1, 1, 2, 1, 3, 1, 0, 0, 1, 2, 1, 0, 1, 2, 0

   a. This tally chart has been started to show the results. It shows the first four answers.

   Copy and complete the tallies and the frequencies.

   Check that the total frequency is the same as the number of items in the list.

Number of pets	Tally	Frequency
0	I	
1	II	
2		
3	I	
4		
5		
6		

365

Handling Information and Data

   b. How many people had:
      i. no pets   ii. 3 pets   iii. more than 3 pets?
   c. How many people took part in the survey?

A table that gives just the categories and the frequencies is called a **frequency table**.

3. The tally chart below shows the grades awarded to students on a course.
   a. Create a frequency table to show this data.
   b. How many students were on the course?
   c. What fraction of the students got:
      i. a distinction   ii. a merit?
   d. What percentage of the students failed the course?

Grade	Tally
Distinction	ЖН II
Merit	ЖН ЖН IIII
Pass	ЖН ЖН ЖН IIII
Fail	ЖН ЖН

4. A college library's records show the number of books taken by each student who borrowed books during one lunch hour. This data is given below:

   1 3 4 1 2 5 4 1 3 1 2 5 1 3 1 2 2 4 1 1 4
   2 1 1 6 3 6 1 5 2 1 3 1 2 1 1 4 1 3 1 5 2
   1 4 3 3 1 1 2 1 6 4 1 3 4 2 5 6 3 2 3 1 1
   5 2 1 3 4 1 5 1 1 2 3 2 1 4 1 5 3 2 1 4 2

   a. Create a frequency table to show these results.
   b. What was the most common number of books borrowed?
   c. How many students borrowed books during this lunch hour?
   d. What % of students borrowed more than 4 books?

It is often useful to group data. For marks in a test out of 60 the tally chart below shows possible groups of marks. It also shows how the gender of each candidate could be recorded.

The frequency table for this data is shown alongside. This is called a **grouped frequency table**.

Tally chart

Mark	Female	Male
1–10	I	
11–20	II	III
21–30	IIII	II
31–40	ЖН	ЖН II
41–50	II	III

Frequency table

Mark	Frequency Female	Frequency Male
1–10	1	0
11–20	2	3
21–30	4	2
31–40	5	7
41–50	2	3

5. A garage records the time taken (to the nearest minute) for car mechanics to find the cause of a particular engine problem.

   The results are:

11	23	30	22	9	25	14	19	23	18	12
25	10	29	21	16	18	8	13	21	24	28
13	18	26	20	13	19	15	21	27	17	22

   a. Copy the table and complete the tallies and frequencies.
   b. What was the **most common** time group?
   c. How many times were recorded?
   d. What fraction of the recorded times were less than 11 minutes?
   e. What % of the recorded times were more than 20 minutes?

Time (minutes)	Tally	Frequency
6–10		
11–15		
16–20		
21–25		
26–30		

6. The ages of people taking a driving test at a centre during one day are listed below with their results: pass (P) or fail (F).

   Create a grouped frequency table of this data.

18P	22F	19F	27P	34F	25P	17P	21F	18F	41P
27F	19P	51F	47P	31P	18F	27P	25P	42P	17F
20P	17F	21P	24F	19P	22P	18P	28F	35P	18P

Represent data in pictograms

Specification reference EL3.H23, L1.H27

A **pictogram** uses simple pictures or symbols to illustrate data.

When drawing a pictogram you should:

- Choose a **simple symbol** that is easy to draw.
- Decide how many items each symbol stands for.
- Work out how many symbols you need for each category.
- Draw the pictogram. Use squared paper. This makes it easier to line up the symbols. Try to keep the symbols the same size (except when only part of a symbol is needed).
- Give the pictogram a **title** saying what it is about.
- Include a **key** showing what each symbol stands for.

Handling Information and Data

Practice

1. The table shows the number of hours of sunshine at a seaside resort each day during a week in August.
   Draw a pictogram to show this data.

   Use to represent 2 hours of sunshine.

   Use  to represent 1 hour of sunshine.

Day	Hours of sunshine
Monday	6
Tuesday	4
Wednesday	3
Thursday	5
Friday	8
Saturday	10
Sunday	9

2. The table shows the number of houses sold by an estate agent in the first six months of a year.
   Draw a pictogram to show this information.

   Use ▭ to represent 10 houses.

   You will have to decide how much of the symbol to use when you need to show less than 10 houses.

Month	Number of houses
January	25
February	30
March	45
April	52
May	60
June	57

3. A car manufacturer keeps records of the colours of the cars sold. The table gives the results for one model.
   Choose a symbol to represent 100 cars and draw a pictogram.

Colour	Number of cars sold
Red	650
Black	425
White	386
Blue	541
Green	150

Activity

Create a frequency table to record the colours, ages or types of vehicles in a car park or travelling along a road, then use a pictogram to illustrate your results.

Represent data in bar charts and line graphs

Specification reference EL3.H23, L1.H27, L1.H28

A. Draw a bar chart

A **bar chart** uses vertical or horizontal bars to illustrate data.

When drawing a bar chart you should:

- Use **squared** or **graph** paper.
- Use an **easy scale**, that is, make each small square an easy value to use.
  (for example, 1, 2, 5, 10, 20, 50, 100, 200, 500 are easier than 3, 4, 7, 8, 9, 30, 40, ...)

See pages 347–351 for examples of bar charts.

Collecting and Illustrating Data

- Aim for a large chart that is easy to read.
- Before drawing the chart, make sure you choose scales that will fit all of the given data.
- Use a ruler and sharp pencil to draw the chart. Leave gaps between the bars.
- Give the bar chart a **title** saying what it is about.
- **Label** the axes (give **units** if necessary). Use a pen to do this if you wish.

Practice

1. The pizza toppings ordered in a snack bar during one day are shown in the table.
    a. Draw a bar chart to show this information. Use vertical bars.
    b. Use your chart to answer these questions.
        i. Which topping is **most** popular?
        ii. Which topping is **least** popular?

Topping	Number of pizzas
Cheese & tomato	15
Seafood	8
Ham & mushroom	12
Pepperoni	18
Roasted vegetable	11

2. The table gives the type and number of fruit trees in an orchard.
    a. Draw a bar chart to show this information. Use horizontal bars.
    b. Use your chart to answer these questions.
        i. Which is the **most common** type of fruit tree?
        ii. How many more plum trees than pear trees are there?

Type of tree	Number of trees
Apple	36
Cherry	12
Pear	18
Plum	25

3. A company offers holiday homes for rent in some European countries.
   The table shows the number of properties it has in each country.
    a. Draw a bar chart to show this data.
    b. In which country does the company have the **most** properties?
    c. How many more properties does the company have
        i. in France than in Belgium
        ii. in France than in Spain?

Country	Number of properties
Belgium	15
France	63
Germany	42
Greece	27
Italy	36
Spain	54

> Also draw bar charts of the data given in the Practice questions for frequency tables and pictograms on pages 365–368.

Handling Information and Data

4. A cinema complex records the number of tickets sold for films of different categories in one month.

   The table shows the results for one week.

   a. Draw a bar chart to show this data.
   b. Which category was **most** popular?
   c. Which category was **least** popular?
   d. List the categories in order of popularity, starting with the **most popular**.

Film type	Number of tickets (thousands)
Adventure	340
Children's	276
Comedy	125
Horror	205
Musical	83
Sci-fi	107
Thriller	194

5. A newsagent records the number of newspapers delivered to the houses he supplies. The results for one day are given in the table.

   a. Draw a bar chart to show this data.
   b. Describe briefly what the chart shows.

Number of newspapers	Number of houses
1	324
2	191
3	54
4	27
5	8

Level 1

6. The table shows estimates of the number of adults who read some daily newspapers.

   a. Draw a bar chart to show this data.
   b. Which of these newspapers is:
      i. most popular
      ii. least popular?
   c. List the newspapers in order of popularity, starting with the **most popular**.

Newspaper	Number of readers (thousands)
Daily Express	1833
Daily Mail	7034
Daily Star	1055
Daily Telegraph	3519
Guardian	4714
Mirror	3831
Sun	6178
Times	1389

   Data source: The Publishers Audience Measurement Company (pamco.co.uk)

7. The table gives the life expectancy of men and women in eight countries.

   a. Draw a comparative bar chart to illustrate this data.
   b. In which of these countries is:
      i. male life expectancy **greatest**
      ii. female life expectancy **lowest**?
   c. i. Briefly compare male and female life expectancy.
      ii. In which country is the difference between male and female life expectancy greatest?
   d. Compare life expectancy in the eight countries.

Country	Life expectancy (years)	
	Male	Female
Angola	51	54
Brazil	71	79
China	75	78
India	67	70
Malawi	57	60
Russia	65	76
UK	79	83
USA	77	82

   Data source: World Health Statistics 2016 (www.who.int)

   See page 352 for an example of a comparative bar chart.

8. The table shows the number of men and women employed in UK industries.

    a. Copy and complete the table by filling in the totals.
    b. Draw a component bar chart to show the data.
    c. Which industry has:
        i. the greatest total number of employees
        ii. the greatest number of male employees
        iii. the greatest number of female employees?
    d. Briefly compare the number of men and women employed in each industry.

Number of employees (thousands)			
Industry	Male	Female	Total
Construction	2034	296	
Education	912	2324	
Health and social work	906	3356	
Manufacturing	2194	724	
Wholesale and retail	2277	1981	

Data source: Labour Force Survey May 2018

 See page 352 for an example of a component bar chart.

Bar charts can also be used to illustrate grouped discrete data.

> **Example**
>
> The table gives the class sizes in a college.
>
> | Number of students | 1–5 | 6–10 | 11–15 | 16–20 | 21–25 |
> |---|---|---|---|---|---|
> | Number of classes | 1 | 4 | 15 | 34 | 26 |
>
> Draw and interpret a bar chart of the data.
>
> The bar chart is shown here
>
>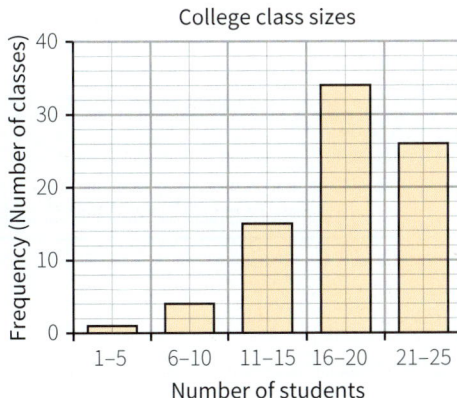
>
> The number of classes is the frequency. The vertical axis needs to show up to 34 (the highest frequency).
>
> The bar chart shows that the majority of the classes have between 16 and 25 students. There are very few small classes with 10 or fewer students.

9. A company records how many days each employee is absent from work.

   The table gives the results for one month.

Number of days of absence	0–4	5–9	10–14	15–19	20–24	25–29
Number of employees	36	14	7	2	0	1

   Draw and interpret a bar chart of the data.

10. A call centre (open 8 hours a day) records the number of calls it receives during each hour over a 30-day period.

Number of calls	0–9	10–19	20–29	30–39	40–49	50–59
Number of hours	18	32	78	65	42	5

    Draw and interpret a bar chart of the data.

11. The % marks scored by students in an exam are listed below:

68%	52%	74%	61%	53%	25%	64%	62%	58%	64%
57%	61%	51%	48%	69%	68%	57%	93%	42%	55%
65%	27%	54%	58%	12%	49%	62%	71%	35%	67%

    Draw and interpret a bar chart of these results.

    > **Hint** First, create a table for the results. Choose an appropriate group size (make them equal, for example, groups of 10 or 5). Find the frequency for each group, then draw the bar chart.

12. The list below gives the weekly wages of a company's employees.

£364	£587	£280	£380	£419	£320	£427	£342
£420	£485	£341	£475	£525	£457	£354	£410
£215	£575	£422	£347	£476	£376	£262	£476
£364	£587	£467	£419	£290	£429	£464	£269
£448	£414	£471	£432	£682	£584	£438	£327
£359	£258	£412	£318	£480	£270	£362	£454

    Draw and interpret a bar chart of this information.

Activity

Collect some data and draw a bar chart to illustrate it. Here are some suggestions:

- Keep a record of how long you spend on different activities (for example, watching TV, browsing the internet, shopping, doing housework, studying) during a week.
- Carry out a survey, asking students questions such as 'What is your favourite sport?', 'What type of films do you like best?'.

Use a comparative or component bar chart to compare the results of your survey for male and female students.

Collecting and Illustrating Data

B. Draw a line graph

A **line graph** is often used to show how something changes as time goes by.

To draw a line graph:

- Use **squared** or **graph** paper.
- Use an **easy scale**, that is, make each small square an easy value to use (for example, 1, 2, 5, 10, 20, 50, 100, 200, 500 are easier than 3, 4, 7, 8, 9, 30, 40, ...).

See pages 354–357 for examples of line graphs.

- Aim for a **large graph** that fills most of the page.
- Before drawing the graph, make sure you choose scales that will fit all of the given data.
- Use a ruler and sharp pencil to draw the graph.
- Give the graph a **title** saying what it is about.
- **Label** the axes (give **units** if necessary). Use a pen to do this if you wish.
- If your graph has more than one line, label each line or use a key to show what each line represents. (**Level 1 only.**)

Practice

1. Students on a college course can attend an extra drop-in class for help.
   The number of students who go to this class each week is shown in the table.

Week	1	2	3	4	5	6	7	8	9	10
Number of students	1	0	6	9	5	8	12	15	10	7

   a. Draw a line graph to illustrate this data. Put the week number on the horizontal axis and the number of students on the vertical axis.

   b. Use your graph to answer these questions.
      i. In which week did the **greatest** number of students attend the class?
      ii. In which week did the **least** number of students attend the class?
      iii. Describe how the attendance varied over the weeks shown.

2. The table shows how the number of computers owned by a school varied between 1985 and 2015.

Year	1985	1990	1995	2000	2005	2010	2015
Number of computers	12	30	60	120	170	200	380

   a. Draw a line graph to illustrate this data.
   b. Estimate how many computers the school had in: i. 1994 ii. 2007 iii. 2013.
   c. Estimate the year when the school had:
      i. 100 computers   ii. 150 computers   iii. 350 computers.

Handling Information and Data

3. The table below shows the number of lawnmowers sold at a UK garden centre last year.

Month	Jan	Feb	Mar	Apr	May	June	July	Aug	Sept	Oct	Nov	Dec
Number of lawnmowers	0	2	48	59	27	25	30	24	15	24	0	0

   a. Draw a line graph to show these results.
   b. Describe how the sales of lawnmowers varied during the year and suggest reasons.

4. Jack measures the temperature of a mug of coffee every 10 minutes after making it.
   The table gives his results.

Time (minutes)	0	10	20	30	40	50	60	70	80
Temperature (°C)	86	74	64	56	49	43	38	34	31

   a. Use the results to draw a line graph.
   b. Estimate the temperature after:
      i. 5 minutes
      ii. quarter of an hour
      iii. three quarters of an hour.
   c. Estimate how long it took for the temperature to fall to:
      i. 60 °C
      ii. 50 °C
      iii. 40 °C.
   d. i. When did the temperature fall most **quickly**?
      ii. When did it fall most **slowly**?
      iii. What do you think will happen after that?

5. A health and safety officer records the noise level in a factory in decibels (dB) every hour.
   The results are given in the table below.

Time	8 am	9 am	10 am	11 am	noon	1 pm	2 pm	3 pm	4 pm	5 pm
Noise (dB)	40	65	85	89	82	74	84	83	72	54

   a. Use these results to draw a line graph.
   b. Use your graph to estimate the times when the noise level is exactly 80 decibels.
   c. Estimate the total time when the noise level is over 70 decibels.
   d. Describe briefly how the noise level varies during the day.
      Suggest reasons for high and low values.

6. A clothing company has shops in London and Manchester.
   The table below gives the value of sales at these shops during the months of a year.

Month		Jan	Feb	Mar	Apr	May	Jun	Jul	Aug	Sep	Oct	Nov	Dec
Sales (£000s)	Lon	385	143	162	189	221	254	207	198	240	262	376	437
	Man	258	124	138	142	196	205	212	186	193	187	256	328

   a. Draw a graph with two lines showing the sales in London and Manchester.
   b. For each shop write:
      i. the month when sales were **highest**
      ii. the month when sales were **lowest**
      iii. the months in which sales were above £300 000

c. In which month was the difference between the London and Manchester sales:

   i. the **greatest**   ii. the **least**?

d. Briefly describe how sales varied in each shop over the course of the year. Describe any similarities and differences in the sales patterns.

7. The table below gives the average temperature in England and Wales, Scotland and Northern Ireland during each month of a year.

Month		Jan	Feb	Mar	Apr	May	Jun	Jul	Aug	Sep	Oct	Nov	Dec
Average temp (°C)	E & W	5.3	6.6	7.2	8.8	11.4	13.9	15.4	16.5	13.9	9.8	8.2	5.4
	Scot	4.2	3.6	5.0	7.0	9.5	11.8	12.5	14.0	11.8	6.8	6.2	3.5
	NI	6.1	5.6	6.8	8.3	10.6	12.9	13.6	15.0	13.0	8.6	7.8	4.9

Data source: www.met-office.gov.uk

a. Draw a graph with a line for each set of data.

b. For each set of data write down the months when the average temperature was below 6 °C.

c. Describe how the temperature varied in these countries over the course of the year. Describe any similarities and differences.

8. A nurse measures the temperature of a patient every three hours.

   The results are given in the table below.

Time	7 am	10 am	1 pm	4 pm	7 pm	10 pm	1 am	4 am
Temp (°F)	99.8	101.2	102.9	103.7	103.6	102.9	101.1	99.3

a. Draw a line graph to illustrate these results. Show times from 7 am to 4 am on the horizontal axis and temperatures from 98 °F to 104 °F on the vertical axis.

b. A patient has a fever when their temperature is 100 °F or more. Use your graph to estimate how long this patient's fever lasted.

c. This patient has a normal temperature of 98.5 °F. Use your graph to estimate the time when this patient's temperature returns to normal.

9. The table gives the number of speeding offences detected in three police force areas for 2011 to 2016.

   a. Draw a line graph to show the data.

   b. Compare the results for the three areas.

   c. What else should be considered in a comparison of speeding offences in the three areas?

Year	Number of speeding offences		
	Essex	Surrey	Sussex
2011	25 980	49 904	80 422
2012	28 823	51 086	68 030
2013	45 706	54 310	56 974
2014	73 170	51 745	58 975
2015	79 049	72 218	63 651
2016	98 545	47 732	68 541

Data source: 'A preliminary analysis of the latest statistics on speed limit enforcement' by Dr Adam Snow (RAC)

Handling Information and Data

> **Activities**
>
> 1. Record the outside temperature over the course of a day. Use your results to draw a line graph.
> 2. Use the internet to find out how currency exchange rates or share prices vary over a period of time. Draw a line graph to show the changes.

Illustrate data using a pie chart   Specification reference L1.H27

Pie charts show how something is divided into parts.

A pie chart is the best way to show the **proportion** (or fraction) of the data that is in each category.

To draw a pie chart:

- Find the **total** of the data (unless it has been given).
- **Divide 360° by the total** to find how many degrees represent each item.

 See pages 358–361 for examples of pie charts.

- **Multiply this by the number of items** in each category to find the **angle** for each category. **Check** the total angle is 360°.
- Write a **title** to say what information the pie chart gives.
- Use a **compass** to draw a circle and a **protractor** to measure the angles needed.
- **Label** each sector of the pie chart or give a **key** to show what each sector represents.

Example

The table shows the percentage of students on a course who got each grade.

Grade	% of students
Distinction	13
Merit	31
Pass	45
Fail	11

As the data are percentages, the total must be 100% (but check to make sure).

Each % will be represented by:

$$\frac{360°}{100} = 3.6°$$

The table shows how the angle is worked out for each grade.

Use your calculator to check the working in the table.

Grade	% of students	Angle (nearest °)
Distinction	13	13 × 3.6 = 47
Merit	31	31 × 3.6 = 112
Pass	45	45 × 3.6 = 162
Fail	11	11 × 3.6 = 40
Total	100	361

Here the total angle is 361°

The rounding has given an extra degree. When this happens, take 1° away from the largest angle, here the angle for the Pass grade should be changed to 161°

Collecting and Illustrating Data

Practice

1. **a.** Use the information from the Example on the previous page.
   Draw a pie chart to show the proportion of students who got each grade.

   b. According to your chart, which grade had:

   i. the **smallest** proportion of students   **ii.** the **largest** proportion?

2. A group of students has lunch at a snack bar
   The table shows what the students eat.

   a. How many students are there altogether?

   b. In a pie chart how many degrees represent each student?

   c. Copy the table and add an extra column to show how you work out the angles.

   d. Draw a pie chart to illustrate the data.

Lunch	Number of students
Sandwich	6
Pasta	5
Baked potato	8
Salad	4
Pizza	1
Total	

3. The table shows the number of cars owned by households in the UK.

   a. Draw a pie chart to illustrate this.

   b. What is the most common number of cars owned by households?

   c. What fraction of households has no car?

Number of cars	% of households
0	25
1	43
2 or more	32

   Data source: National Travel Survey

4. The table gives estimates of the number of vehicles produced in each region during a year.

   a. Use the data to draw a pie chart.

   b. Which region produces the greatest proportion of vehicles?

Region	Number of vehicles (millions)
Europe	21.7
North America	18.2
South America	2.7
Asia	51.8
Other	0.9

   Data source: www.oica.net

5. The total amount spent on different types of advertising is given in the table.

   a. Draw a pie chart to illustrate this data.

   b. Use your chart to answer these questions.

   i. What type of advertising takes the **greatest** share of the money?

   ii. Does advertising on television earn more or less than advertising in the press (newspapers and magazines)?

   iii. Is it true that more than half of the total amount spent on advertising is spent on the internet?

Type of advertising	Amount (£billions)
Internet	10.3
Cinema	0.3
Radio	0.6
Television	5.3
Press	3.0

   Data source: www.thedrum.com

Handling Information and Data

6. The table gives the population and area of each country in the UK.
   a. Draw a pie chart for each set of data.
   b. Write a paragraph explaining what your charts show.

Country	Population (millions)	Area (000 km²)
England	55.3	130.4
N. Ireland	1.9	13.6
Scotland	5.4	78.1
Wales	3.1	20.8

Data source: Office for National Statistics

Activities

1. Draw a pie chart to show how you spent your time during one day.
2. Collect information from your class, for example, hair colour, eye colour, method of travel to college, and use pie charts to illustrate the results.
3. Plan a budget to show what you intend to spend money on next week. Use a pie chart to illustrate your plan. (**Level 2 only**)

 See pages 173–176 for help with planning a budget.

Draw and use conversion graphs

Specification reference **L2.M14**

 A **conversion graph** is used to convert units from one system to another.

When drawing a conversion graph you should use graph paper, choose scales and label in the same way as for other line graphs. But before you can do this you need to work out values for some points on the graph.

 See pages 362–363 for a reminder of conversion graphs.

Example

Using 1 inch = 2.54 cm gives this table:

Note: only 3 points have been found — 2 points are enough to give the line; the 3rd point acts as a check.

In this case it has been assumed that lengths up to 10 inches will need to be converted. If you wished to convert lengths up to 30 inches, then it would be sensible to use 0, 15 and 30 in the table rather than 0, 5 and 10.

Now a sensible scale is needed on both axes.
One possible graph is shown in Practice question **1** on the following page.

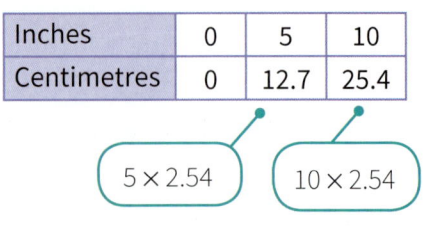

 See page 373 for help with drawing a line graph.

378

Practice

1. a. Write down what a small square represents on each of the axes on this graph.

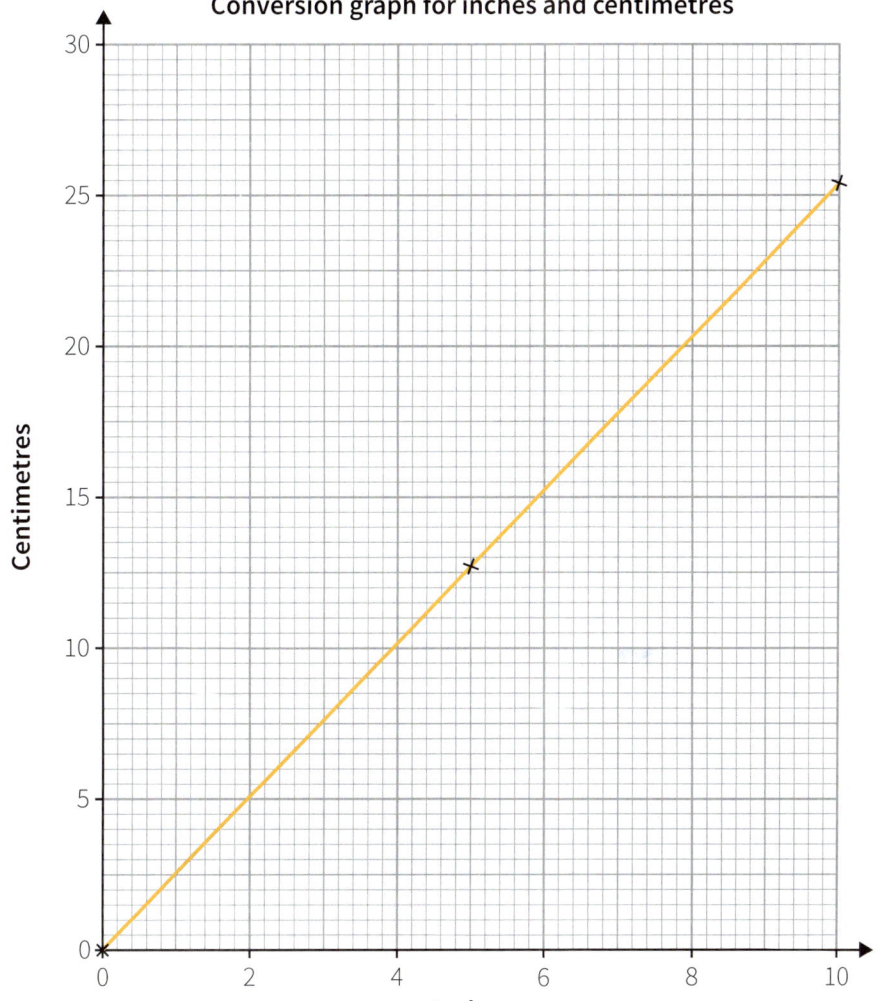

Conversion graph for inches and centimetres

b. Check that the points shown on the graph agree with the values given in the table on the previous page.

c. Use the graph to complete these. Remember that ≈ means 'approximately equal to'.

- **i.** 6 in ≈ _____ cm
- **ii.** 9 in ≈ _____ cm
- **iii.** 2.6 in ≈ _____ cm
- **iv.** 4.3 in ≈ _____ cm
- **v.** 10 cm ≈ _____ in
- **vi.** 25 cm ≈ _____ in
- **vii.** 18 cm ≈ _____ in
- **viii.** 12.5 cm ≈ _____ in

Check your answers by calculation.

 See page 231 for an alternative method using a conversion factor.

Handling Information and Data

2. **a.** Use the approximation 1 kg ≈ 2.2 lb to draw a conversion graph for kilograms and pounds up to 20 kg.
   b. Use your graph to complete the following, then check by calculation.

   i.   15 kg ≈ _____ lb
   ii. 9 kg ≈ _____ lb
   iii. 12.5 kg ≈ _____ lb
   iv. 30 lb ≈ _____ kg
   v.   14 lb ≈ _____ kg
   vi. 38.5 lb ≈ _____ kg

3. **a.** Use the conversion factor 1 gallon ≈ 4.5 litres to draw a conversion graph for capacities up to 10 gallons.
   b. **i.** A fish tank holds 25 litres of water. How many gallons does it hold?
         ii. Petrol costs £1.35 per litre. How much does it cost to fill an 8 gallon tank?

> ### Activities
> 1. Draw a conversion graph for miles and kilometres. Find the distance between your home town and major cities such as Birmingham and Manchester from a road atlas.
>   Use your conversion graph to convert the distances to kilometres.
> 2. Draw a conversion graph for grams and ounces and/or pints and litres.
>   Use your graph(s) to convert the amounts given in recipes.
> 3. Use a spreadsheet to draw charts and graphs. Use the data given in the questions or that you find on the internet. Much of the data from government websites is available in spreadsheet form.

Choosing a statistical diagram
Specification reference L1.H27, L1.H28

The choice of statistical diagram depends on what you want to show.

For example:

- If you want to show how something is divided into parts, a pie chart is probably the best.
- If you want to show how something varies over time, then a line graph is likely to be the most appropriate.
  You can draw two or more lines on the graph to compare how different things vary over time.
- A bar chart can be used in many different situations, particularly when you want to compare two sets of data.
  A comparative bar chart emphasises the difference between the data sets, whereas a component bar chart emphasises the total for each category or group while also showing how this total is made up.

Often you can illustrate data in a variety of effective ways.

Collecting and Illustrating Data

Practice

For each question below:
- Choose the diagram that you think will illustrate the data best.
  Choose from bar chart, pie chart or line graph.
- Draw the diagram.
- Describe briefly what your diagram shows.

1. Cinema attendances in the months of a year:

Month	Jan	Feb	Mar	Apr	May	Jun	Jul	Aug	Sep	Oct	Nov	Dec
Attendance (millions)	15.2	17.2	11.1	11.2	13.3	12.7	17.8	21.4	11.5	13.6	12.9	13.6

Data source: British Film Institute, www.bfi.org.uk

2. The percentage of last month's earnings that Tracy spent on different things:

	Food	Rent	Transport	Clothes	Entertainment	Other
Percentage of earnings	29%	32%	9%	14%	10%	6%

3. The numbers of men and women who read different magazines:

Magazine:	Car Buyer	Country Life	Gardener's World	Hello!
Number of men (thousands)	1136	220	449	665
Number of women (thousands)	529	261	830	3677

4. The number of drink–drive accidents reported in one year at different times of day:

Time of day	12 am	1 am	2 am	3 am	4 am	5 am	6 am	7 am	8 am	9 am	10 am	11 am
Number of accidents	854	804	700	582	412	296	238	230	178	176	158	150

Time of day	12 pm	1 pm	2 pm	3 pm	4 pm	5 pm	6 pm	7 pm	8 pm	9 pm	10 pm	11 pm
Number of accidents	180	186	200	274	374	520	538	592	596	672	756	822

Data source: Department for Transport, www.dft.gov.uk

5. Age of people employed by a bakery company.

Age	Sales	Office	Deliveries
16–19	4	1	0
20–39	19	9	10
40–59	16	12	7
60 and over	10	6	1

6. A survey asks people who are moving house to give the main reason.
   The table shows the results.

Reason	Number of people
Need different size of house	90
Personal (e.g. marriage, divorce)	63
To move to a better area	30
Job-related reason	96
Other	21

7. This table shows the number of students in a class who achieved each grade in the two papers of an exam.

Grade	Paper 1	Paper 2
A	2	1
B	5	5
C	8	5
D	6	6
E	7	9
F	2	4

8. Population of continents in 2017:

Region	Population (millions)
Asia	4504
Africa	1256
Europe	742
North America	361
South America	646
Oceania	41

Data source: www.worldometers.info

9. Medals won by four different countries in the 2016 Olympics:

Country	Gold	Silver	Bronze
United States of America (USA)	46	37	38
China	26	18	26
Great Britain (GB)	27	23	17
Russia	19	18	19

Data source: www.bbc.co.uk

Activity

Use internet searches or visit useful government websites (for example, www.gov.uk, www.ons.gov.uk) to find data on something you are interested in (for example, sport, the film industry, population, employment, tourism, crime, transport, education, housing).
Write a report on your findings. Include statistical diagrams to illustrate the data.

Chapter Summary
22 Collecting and Illustrating Data

- Use a tally chart to organise data and count how many items are in each category. One tally mark is used to represent one piece of data. Tally marks are grouped in fives with the fifth tally mark drawn as a slash across the previous four tally marks.
- The total number of items in each category is called the **frequency**.
- A frequency table lists each category and the number of times it occurs in a data set.
- For pictograms, use a simple symbol (which you can redraw easily) to represent a number of items. Use squared paper. Always include a title and key.
- Draw bar charts and line graphs on graph paper. Choose a scale that is easy to use: it must show all the values and give a reasonably large bar chart or graph. Use a pencil for drawing — this makes it easy to correct any errors. Remember to include a title and label the axes (including units).

- A **grouped frequency table** has more than one group of data for each category.
- Bar charts can be used to illustrate grouped discrete data.
- Use a **comparative bar chart** (with bars next to each other) when you want to compare two or more data sets. Use a **component bar chart** (with bars on top of each other) when totals from two or more data sets are important. Each chart needs a key.
- When you use a line graph to show more than one data set, label each line carefully or include a key.
- To draw a pie chart, divide 360° by the total number of items to find how many degrees represent each item. Multiplying this by the number of items in a category then gives the angle of the sector that represents that category. Check that the total of the angles is 360°.
- Use a compass and protractor to draw a pie chart. Remember to include a title and use labels or a key.
- Choose which statistical diagram to use depending on what you want to show: **pie charts** show something divided into parts, a **line graph** can show how something varies over time, a **bar chart** can be used to show data grouped into categories in a wide variety of contexts.

- To draw a conversion graph use the conversion factor to work out at least 3 points. Then draw the graph as you would other line graphs.

Handling Information and Data

23 Averages and Range

Find the mean

Specification reference L1.H29, L2.H24, L2.H25

An **average** is a representative or 'typical' value. There is more than one type of average.

The **mean** is the **arithmetical average**.

To find the mean, add all the values together, then divide by how many there are.

> **Key point**
>
> $$\text{Mean} = \frac{\text{sum of data values}}{\text{number of values}}$$

Sum means total (add up the values).

Example

The number of goals scored by a footballer in the games he played this season were:

2   0   1   1   0   3   1   2   3   1

Sum of data values = 2 + 0 + 1 + 1 + 0 + 3 + 1 + 2 + 3 + 1 = 14

Number of values = 10   Mean score = $\frac{14}{10}$ = **1.4** goals per match

Check by reverse calculation: mean × no. of items should equal the total
1.4 × 10 = 14

Practice

1. Find the mean of each set of data. Check each answer.

   a. The number of students absent from a class each week of a term:

      0   1   2   2   1   4   3   0   2   3

   b. The number of calls a student makes on her mobile phone each day in a week:

      5   2   4   0   8   12   11

   c. The ages of the children in a family: 12   10   6   4   1

   d. The number of letters delivered to each house in a street:

      4   5   2   0   4   5   8   6

   e. The weights of puppies in a litter:

      0.41 kg   0.36 kg   0.32 kg   0.36 kg   0.41 kg   0.39 kg

   f. Prizes in a lottery:

      £10   £10   £10   £250   £10   £10   £10   £10

Note: in part **f** the mean is **distorted** by the large win of £250

It is not a good representative value.

2. The table shows the scores of five batsmen in four cricket matches.

Player	1	2	3	4
Andy	112	16	3	49
Imran	0	–	68	43
Mark	–	11	–	37
Stuart	40	33	17	25
Tim	35	27	54	43

   Note: – means 'did not play'.

   a. Find the mean score for each batsman. Check each answer.
   b. Which batsman has:
      i. the **best** mean score
      ii. the **worst** mean score?

3. Four assistants in an office each earn £12 per hour.

   Their manager earns £45 per hour.

   a. Find the mean wage.
   b. Is this mean a good representative value for the wages in the office?

4. The table below shows the number of tickets sold for a concert.

Day	Mon	Tues	Wed	Thurs	Fri	Sat	Sun
Ticket sales	126	205	167	152	298	324	282

   Find the mean number of tickets sold:

   a. per day at the weekend (Sat and Sun)
   b. per weekday (Mon to Fri).

5. The chart shows the rates of pay of six part-time workers.
   a. Write down the rate of pay for each worker.
   b. Calculate the mean rate of pay.
   c. Which workers get more than the mean rate of pay?

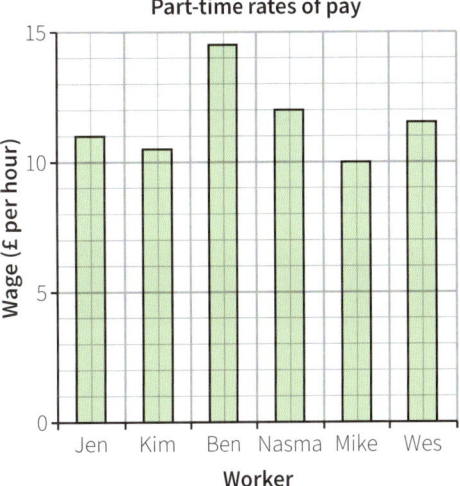

For extra practice, find the mean of each set of data in these questions:

Represent data in pictograms, pages 367–368, questions 1, 2

Draw a bar chart, pages 368–370, questions 1, 2, 3, 4

Draw a line graph, pages 373–374, questions 1, 3, 5

Handling Information and Data

When data is given in a frequency table it is more difficult to find the mean.

Example

A survey investigates the number of occupants in a block of flats.
The table gives the results.

Number of occupants	Number of flats
0	1
1	6
2	12
3	7
4	3
5	0
6	1

The mean number of occupants per flat

$$= \frac{\text{total number of occupants}}{\text{total number of flats}}$$

The total number of flats is the sum of the 2nd column:
$1 + 6 + 12 + 7 + 3 + 0 + 1 = 30$

Take care with the number of occupants, the total is **not** just $0 + 1 + 2 + \ldots$
Think about what each row in the table means:

    No occupants in 1 flat   = 0 occupants
    1 occupant in each of 6 flats   = 6 occupants
    2 occupants in each of 12 flats = 24 occupants
    3 occupants in each of 7 flats = 21 occupants   and so on.

Total number of occupants $= 0 \times 1 + 1 \times 6 + 2 \times 12 + 3 \times 7 + 4 \times 3 + 5 \times 0 + 6 \times 1$
                                  $= 0 + 6 + 24 + 21 + 12 + 0 + 6 = 69$

A table can be used to show this working neatly.

x	f	Multiply	xf
0	1	0×1	0
1	6	1×6	6
2	12	2×12	24
3	7	3×7	21
4	3	4×3	12
5	0	5×0	0
6	1	6×1	6
Total	30		69

Here, x represents the number of occupants and f, the frequency, is the number of flats.

Mean number of occupants per flat $= \frac{69}{30} = \mathbf{2.3}$

(Total number of flats — 30)
(Total number of occupants — 69)

The method can be written as a formula:

Key point

Mean from a frequency table $= \dfrac{\text{sum of (value} \times \text{frequency)}}{\text{sum of frequencies}}$

    or in letters: **mean** $= \dfrac{\Sigma xf}{\Sigma f}$ where Σ means 'add up'.

6. A trainee proofreader has her work checked to see how many errors she misses. The table shows the results for one document she reads.
   a. How many pages are in the document?
   b. Find the mean number of errors missed per page.

Number of errors missed	Number of pages
0	9
1	8
2	0
3	2
4	1

7. A health visitor notes the number of children in each of the families she visits.

   The table shows her results.
   a. Find the mean number of children.
   b. How many families had more than the mean number of children?

Number of children	Number of families
1	2
2	8
3	4
4	4
5	1
6	1

8. A rail company records the number of trains on a particular route that arrive late each day.

   The table gives the results for June.
   a. Find the mean number of late trains per day.
   b. Five trains travel on this route per day. What % of the trains were late in June?

Number of late trains	Number of days
0	8
1	11
2	9
3	1
4	1

9. The table gives the ages of students on a carpentry course.
   a. How many students are over 20 years old?
   b. Find the mean age.

Age (years)	Number of students
16	5
17	7
18	3
19	4
20	3
21	2
22	1

10. The table gives the number of goals scored by a football team in home and away matches.

Number of goals		0	1	2	3	4	5	6
Number of games	Home	2	4	3	0	2	0	1
	Away	4	6	0	1	1	0	0

a. Find the mean number of goals scored per match: i. at home   ii. away.

b. Is the team better at scoring goals at home or away?

Example

The table gives the class sizes in a college.

Number of students	1–5	6–10	11–15	16–20	21–25
Number of classes	1	4	15	34	26

Estimate the mean number of students per class. Use the mid-value in each group.

If the mid-value of a group is not obvious, find it by dividing the sum of the end-values by 2

e.g. Mid-value of first group = $\frac{1+5}{2} = 3$

Mid-value of the last group = $\frac{21+25}{2} = 23$

Mid-value x	Frequency f	xf
3	1	3
8	4	32
13	15	195
18	34	612
23	26	598
Total	80	1440

Total number of classes   Total number of students

Mean number of students per class = $\frac{1440}{80} = 18$

Note that this gives an estimate of the mean, rather than an accurate value. This is because the mid-value of each group was used rather than the accurate number of students in each class.

Key point

To find an estimate of the mean when data is grouped, use the mid-value in each group.

11. Estimate the mean of each set of data.

a.
Number of errors	0–4	5–9	10–14	15–19	20–24
Number of pages in a report	12	8	3	0	1

b.

Marks in a test	1–10	11–20	21–30	31–40	41–50
Number of students	0	5	16	25	14

c.

Amount a student spent on food (nearest £)	10–19	20–29	30–39	40–49
Number of weeks at university	2	14	19	1

12. The points scored by teams in the UK Premier League in the 2017–18 season were:

100 81 77 72 70 63 54 49 47 44
44   44 42 41 40 37 36 33 33 31

Data source: www.worldfootball.net

a. Find the mean:
   i. using all the values in the list
   ii. using a frequency table with groups 31–40, 41–50, etc.
b. Which of your answers in part **a** is more accurate? Explain why.

13. A market gardener buys 60 packs of seeds. Each pack contains 50 seeds.

The packs claim that the average germination rate is 80%.

The market gardener keeps a record of the number of seeds that germinate.
The table gives her results.

Number of seeds that germinate	1–10	11–20	21–30	31–40	41–50
Number of packs	0	5	16	26	13

a. Estimate the mean number of seeds that germinate per pack.
b. Comment on the claim made on the packs.

For extra practice, find the mean of each set of data given in these questions:

Draw a bar chart, page 372, questions 9, 10

Find the mode and the median

Specification reference: L2.H23, L2.H25

The mean is not the only type of average. There are two others.

> **Key point**
> The **mode** is the **most common value** in a data set.

Sometimes there is more than one mode (when two or more values are equally common).
Sometimes there is no mode (when all values occur just once).

> **Key point**
> The **median** is the **middle value** in an ordered list.

If there are two middle values, add them together and divide by 2
This gives the value halfway between them.

Handling Information and Data

> **Example**
>
> The numbers of tracks on a band's CDs are:
> 15   12   14   12   12   14   10   13
>
> Putting these in order gives:
> 10   12   12   **[12   13]** ← middle values   14   14   15
>
> The modal number of tracks is **12**. This is the value that occurs most often.
> There are 2 middle values, 12 and 13. The median number of tracks is **12.5**
> Also, the mean = $\dfrac{15 + 12 + 14 + 12 + 12 + 14 + 10 + 13}{8} = \dfrac{102}{8} =$ **12.75** tracks

Often one of the averages is a better representative of the data than the others.

In the Example above, the mode is the only average that gives a number of tracks that is possible, so you could argue that the mode is the best average to use.

> **Example**
>
> An estate agent sold six properties in one week. The property prices are listed below.
> £199 000   £249 950   £1.5 million   £365 000   £199 000   £299 000
> Which average is the best representative value of this data set? Explain your choice.
>
> Putting the amounts in order gives:
> £199 000   £199 000   **[£249 950   £299 000]** ← middle values   £365 000   £1.5 million
>
> Median = $\dfrac{£249\,950 + £299\,000}{2} =$ £274 475
>
> Mode = £199 000
>
> Mean = $\dfrac{£199\,000 + £249\,950 + £1\,500\,000 + £365\,000 + £199\,000 + £299\,000}{6} =$ £468 658 (nearest £)
>
> The median is the most representative value (even though it is not any of the values in the list) because it is in the centre of the data set. The mode only occurs twice and is actually the smallest amount. The mean is higher than nearly all of the amounts because it is skewed by the untypically high value of £1.5 million.
>
> The estate agent wants property owners to use his agency, so he may prefer to use the mean because it is higher than the other averages.

Some of the advantages and disadvantages of each average are given below.

- The **mean** has the advantage of **using all the data values**. A disadvantage is that **abnormally high or low data values can make it 'distorted'**. The mean is **not usually one of the values in the data set**.
- The **mode** is **always one of the values in the data set**. It is **useful to manufacturers** who want to know the most common size. However, sometimes there is **no mode** or **a lot of modes**. The mode **may be at one end of the distribution**.

- Being in the middle means the **median** is **not affected by abnormal values**. However, if there are two middle values, the median **may not be one of the values in the data set**.

Which average you choose to use will depend on which of these characteristics you think are most important. Opinions may differ about this.

Practice

1. Find the mode, median and mean of each set of data.
   Decide which is the best representative value: the mean, the mode or the median.
   In each case explain your choice.

   a. The number of pints of milk delivered to a house each day in a week:

       2   1   1   0   1   6   0

   b. The number of students attending a class each week during a term:

       18   17   17   17   18   16   16   15   12   16

   c. The ages of the players on a football team:

       19   18   18   20   29   34   18   18   18   21   19

   d. The time taken in minutes by students to complete a test:

       32   28   28   30   27   25   36   27   31   33   30   28

   e. Heights of a group of children:

       1.24 m   1.26 m   1.18 m   1.21 m   1.17 m   1.19 m

> Find the mode and median for each set of data given in this question:
>
> **Find the mean, page 384, question 1**
>
> Look back at the scores given for the batsmen in:
>
> **Find the mean, page 385, question 2**
>
> What happens if you try to find the mode for each batsman?
>
> Find the median for each batsman.
>
> Why do you think the mean is usually used to compare batsmen rather than the median or mode?

Key point

To find the mode from a frequency table, look for the value with the highest frequency.

Handling Information and Data

Example

The results of the survey done in a block of flats are shown again in the first two columns of the table below. The **highest frequency** (number of flats) is 12
This means that the **modal number of occupants per flat** is **2**
(More flats had 2 occupants than any other number of occupants.)

It is more difficult to find the **median**. It helps if you add another column to the table to show **cumulative frequency**, i.e. a 'running total' of the frequencies.

Number of occupants	Number of flats	Cumulative frequency
0	1	1
1	6	7
2	12	19
3	7	26
4	3	29
5	0	29
6	1	30

$1 + 6 = 7$
$7 + 12 = 19$
$19 + 7 = 26$
Total number of flats

There are 30 flats altogether. If the numbers of occupants for all of these flats were written in a line, there would be two middle values — the 15th and 16th:

```
                              15th 16th
0 1 1 1 1 1 2 2 2 2 2 2 ②  ② 2 2 2 3 3 3 3 3 3 4 4 4 6
                              Middle
```

(Whenever there is an even number of data values, there are two middle values.)

Look at the cumulative frequency column in the table. The 15th and 16th values are both after the 7th value, but before the 19th. This means the 15th and 16th values are both 2
The median is **2 occupants**.

---

2. The table shows the ages of the children in a creche one morning.

   a. Find:

      i. the mode

      ii. the median

      iii. the mean.

   b. Which value from part **a** do you think is the best representative value?

Age	Number of children
1	1
2	5
3	6
4	8

3. A clothes shop keeps records of the sizes of dresses it sells. The table shows the results for one style of dress.
   a. Find:
      i. the mode
      ii. the median
      iii. the mean.
   b. Which of these averages do you think is most useful to the shop manager?

Size	Number sold
8	2
10	8
12	10
14	13
16	5
20	2

Find the mode and median for each set of data given in these questions:
Find the mean, pages 385–388, questions 3, 6, 7, 8, 9, 10
Compare your answers with the means you found for these questions.
In each question say which average you think is most appropriate and why.

4. In a survey, new drivers are asked how many attempts they needed to pass their driving test. The table gives the results for new drivers aged under 20, and those aged 20 or over.
   a. What is the mode for:
      i. those under 20
      ii. those 20 or over?
   b. What is the median for:
      i. those under 20
      ii. those 20 or over?
   c. Calculate the mean for:
      i. those under 20
      ii. those 20 or over?
   d. Were those aged under 20 or those aged 20 and over the better learners in this group of people? Why do you think this?

Number of attempts	Number of drivers aged:	
	under 20	20 or over
1	7	9
2	8	7
3	2	3
4	2	0
5	1	1

Find the mean, mode and median for the data given in this question:
Draw a bar chart, page 370, question 5
Which of the averages do you think is the best representative? Why?

Find the range

Specification reference L1.H29, L2.H25

The range gives a measure of how spread out the values are in a set of data.

Key point

Range = highest value − lowest value

Handling Information and Data

 Example

The table gives the marks achieved by two students in assignments.

Assignment	1	2	3	4
Ethan	76%	65%	54%	69%
Matt	71%	58%	45%	75%

The range of Ethan's marks = 76% − 54% = 22%

The range of Matt's marks = 75% − 45% = 30%

Matt's marks are more spread out than Ethan's.

Ethan is the more **consistent** student and Matt is the more **variable**.

 Practice

1. The table gives the prices of tins of fruit in a number of supermarkets.

Fruit	Penny-Saver	Sam's Store	Low-Price	Super-Food
Apricots	78p	82p	75p	93p
Grapefruit	71p	77p	69p	81p
Peaches	72p	80p	72p	£1.05
Pineapple	85p	94p	90p	89p

   a. Find the price range for each type of fruit.
   b. Which type of fruit has:
      i. the most consistent price   ii. the most variable price?

2. This table gives the scores of six snooker players in the last 10 games they have played.

Player	Scores in the last 10 games									
Alex	38	0	56	83	12	64	21	34	54	71
Chloe	34	56	27	39	42	35	50	76	57	29
Khadijah	63	19	27	32	60	55	48	85	94	87
Paul	76	58	32	103	67	82	59	147	96	49
Rhona	25	92	147	120	45	62	0	76	15	83
Saif	93	21	47	56	109	74	23	37	88	43

   a. Find the mean and range for each player.
   b. Who do you think is the best player and why?
   c. Who do you think is the most consistent player and why?

> Find the range for each set of data given in these questions:
>
> *Find the mean, pages 384–385, questions 1, 2, 3, 4, 5*
>
> *Find the mode and the median, page 391, question 1*

3. A student has drawn this bar chart to show how long she spent on her laptop last week. Each time is shown to the nearest 5 minutes.

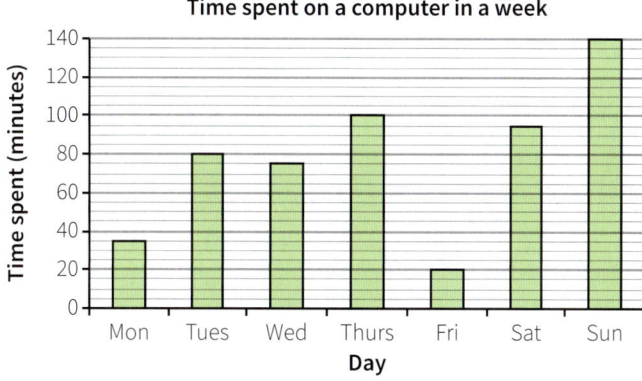

a. Find the mean time per day.
b. Find the range of the times.

You can also find the range from a frequency table, but **take care to use the correct values**.

Example

The results of the survey carried out in a block of flats are shown again in the table.

The highest number of occupants is 6 and the lowest number is 0

The range = 6 − 0 = **6**

Note: When the data is given in a frequency table, **watch out for zero values** in the frequency column. If the last two values in the second column had been the other way round, the highest number of occupants would have been 5 rather than 6

Number of occupants	Number of flats
0	1
1	6
2	12
3	7
4	3
5	0
6	1

---

4. A social worker records the number of home visits she makes to patients each day. The results are given in the table.
   a. What is the range of the number of visits?
   b. What is the modal number of visits?

Number of visits	Number of days
0	0
1	4
2	6
3	10
4	7
5	2
6	1

Handling Information and Data

5. Twenty students enrol on a college course. The number of students who attend the class is recorded each week. The table gives the results for a year's classes (36 weeks).

Number of students attending	Number of weeks (frequency)
15	2
16	4
17	6
18	8
19	9
20	7

   a. Write down the modal number of students who attend the class per week.
   b. Find the range of the number of students attending.

6. The students in a class are asked to estimate the width of the classroom door, giving their answers to the nearest tenth of a metre. The results are given in the table.

Estimate of height of door (m)	0.5	0.6	0.7	0.8	0.9	1.0	1.1	1.2
Number of students	0	3	4	8	7	6	2	0

   a. Find the range of the estimates.
   b. What is the modal estimate?

7. The table shows the ages of the children on a summer camp.

Age (years)	Number of: boys	Number of: girls
8	3	0
9	5	2
10	12	5
11	6	8
12	5	6
13	2	2
14	0	2
15	1	0

   a. What is the range of ages for:
      i. boys   ii. girls?
   b. What is the modal age for:
      i. boys   ii. girls?
   c. Use your answers to **a** and **b** to compare the age distribution of the girls and boys.

   > Find the range for each set of data given in these questions:
   >
   > *Find the mean, pages 387–388, questions 6, 7, 8, 9, 10*
   >
   > *Find the mode and the median, pages 392–393, questions 2, 3, 4*

8. The chart shows the number of licence penalty points awarded by a court to drivers convicted of driving offences.

   a. For the data for men find:
      i. the mode
      ii. the median
      iii. the mean
      iv. the range.
   b. Repeat part **a** for the women.
   c. Compare your results for parts **a** and **b**.

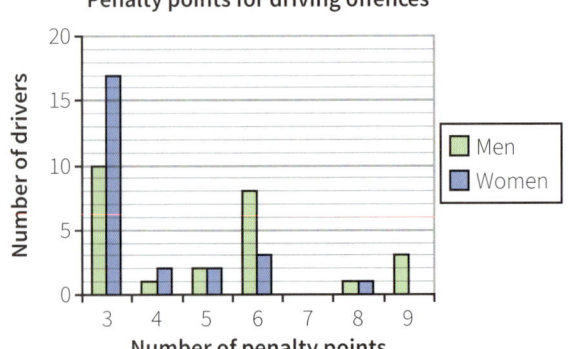

Penalty points for driving offences

Averages and Range

Compare data sets

Specification reference L2.H25

When comparing two sets of data it is usual to compare the most appropriate average and also to compare the range. The average gives a representative value for the data set and the range indicates its spread.

Example

A driving test centre records the number of attempts needed by men and women to pass a practical driving test. The table gives the results for those who pass in one week.

Number of attempts	1	2	3	4	5	6
Number of men	23	12	5	3	2	0
Number of women	20	16	5	4	0	1

Compare the number of attempts needed by men and women.

Mode:

The mode is **1 attempt** for both men and women.

Median:

The cumulative frequency table shows that 45 men and 46 women were tested.

The median for men is the 23rd value (22 values at each side of the median) which is **1 attempt**.

There are two middle values for women, the 23rd and 24th values. Both of these are 2 attempts so the median for women is **2 attempts**.

Number of attempts x	Cumulative frequency — men	Cumulative frequency — women
1	23	20
2	35	36
3	40	41
4	43	45
5	45	45
6	45	46

Mean:

From a frequency table, mean $= \dfrac{\sum xf}{\sum f}$. The table for men and women is below.

Number of attempts x	Number of men f_m	xf_m	Number of women f_w	xf_w
1	23	23	20	20
2	12	24	16	32
3	5	15	5	15
4	3	12	4	16
5	2	10	0	0
6	0	0	1	6
Total	45	84	46	89

> You can use separate tables for men and women if you prefer.

Handling Information and Data

Mean for men = $\dfrac{\sum xf_m}{\sum f_m} = \dfrac{84}{45} = 1.87$ attempts (to 2 dp)

Mean for women = $\dfrac{\sum xf_w}{\sum xf_w} = \dfrac{89}{46} = 1.93$ attempts (to 2 dp)

Range:

The range for men = $5 - 1 =$ **4 attempts**

The range for women = $6 - 1 =$ **5 attempts**

Comparison:

The averages and ranges for men and women are shown in the table below.

	Mode	Median	Mean	Range
Men	1 attempt	1 attempt	1.87 attempts	4 attempts
Women	1 attempt	2 attempts	1.93 attempts	5 attempts

In this case the mode suggests no difference between the performance by the men and women, but the median and the mean both indicate that **on average the women took more attempts than the men to pass the test**.

The mean is the most appropriate average to use for comparison here, because it combines all of the data. It shows that the performance by the women was only slightly worse than that by the men.

The range shows that **success for the women was more variable than that for the men**.

Practice

1. The table gives the number of assignments completed by some students on a course.
   Compare the work completed by the students in Class A and Class B.

Number of completed assignments		0	1	2	3	4	5
Number of students	Class A	1	0	3	4	8	1
	Class B	0	2	1	3	7	3

2. The numbers of runs scored by two batsmen in the last 10 games they have played are listed below.

   | Ahmed | 27 | 40 | 12 | 35 | 19 | 56 | 74 | 26 | 54 | 83 |
   | Mark | 15 | 32 | 76 | 0 | 92 | 26 | 89 | 3 | 13 | 41 |

   a. Compare the results for the two batsmen.

   b. A coach needs to pick one of these batsmen for the team.
      Who would you pick and why?

3. The table gives the number of goals a team scored in home and away matches last season.
   Compare the team's results in home and away matches.

Number of goals		0	1	2	3	4	5	6
Number of matches	Home	1	5	7	2	3	0	1
	Away	5	6	5	2	1	0	0

4. The pupils in a class are asked how much pocket money they get per week.

   The results are listed below:

Girls	£6	£8	£5	£7	£5	£7	£6.50
	£5	£6	£7.50	£8	£6	£9	£5
Boys	£5	£9	£8	£7.50	£4	£9	£8
	£8	£7.50	£6	£9	£5	£8	£7.50

   Compare the amounts given to the girls and the boys.

5. A student is comparing the readability of two books for children. She counts the number of letters per word on one page of each book with these results.

Number of letters per word		1	2	3	4	5	6	7	8	9	10
Number of words	Book A	5	7	10	12	8	2	0	1	0	0
	Book B	4	8	7	9	8	5	1	3	0	1

   a. Compare the two data sets.
   b. Which book do you think may be harder to read? Explain your answer.

> ### Activity
>
> Collect data from your class or from the internet, newspapers, etc.
>
> Find and compare averages and ranges. Some suggestions are given below:
>
> From your group: ages, number of pets, heights, time spent on homework, etc.
>
> From other sources: temperature or rainfall at two or more places
>
> prices of cars of different makes and/or ages
>
> prices of houses, electrical equipment, length of films or music tracks etc.
>
> season's results for two sports teams
>
> Use a spreadsheet to work out the MODE, MEDIAN, AVERAGE (mean), MAX – MIN (range).

Chapter Summary
23 Averages and Range

- An **average** is a representative value. There are several types of average.
- The arithmetical average is the **mean** of a data set = $\dfrac{\text{sum of data values}}{\text{number of values}}$
- The mean value can be distorted by a very high or very low value in the data set.
- From a frequency table, Mean = $\dfrac{\text{sum of (value} \times \text{frequency)}}{\text{sum of frequency}} = \dfrac{\sum xf}{\sum f}$
- The **range** of a data set gives a measure of how spread out values are in a data set.
  range = highest value − lowest value

- To **estimate the mean** from a grouped frequency table, use the mid-value of each group as *x*.
- There are three types of average: the **mean**, **median** and **mode**.
- The **mode** is the most common value in a data set. In a frequency table, the mode is the value with the highest frequency.
- The **median** is the middle value in a data set. If there are two middle values, add them together then divide by 2
- Adding a column for cumulative frequency to a frequency table can help you to find the median.
- Each type of average has advantages and disadvantages so one average may be more representative of the data than the others.
- The mean uses all the data values, but it can be distorted by an abnormally high or low value and it is usually not a value in the data set.
- When it exists, the mode is a value in the data set, but it may be a very low or high value. Sometimes there is more than one mode.
- The median is often, but not always, a value in the dataset. The median is a central value not affected by abnormal values.
- To compare data sets, compare the most appropriate average (the most representative value) and the range (indicating the spread).

Handling Information and Data

24 Scatter Diagrams

Scatter diagrams and correlation

Specification reference **L2.H28**

A. Draw and interpret scatter diagrams

Researchers, scientists and some organisations measure variables. For example, car manufacturers test vehicles to measure fuel efficiency and harmful emissions. The table below gives the results for small cars made by one company.

Model	Engine size (cm^3)	Fuel efficiency (miles per gallon)	Carbon dioxide (CO_2) (grams per kilometre)	Nitrous oxide (NOx) (milligrams per kilometre)
A	998	66.5	95	13
B	999	65.7	99	25
C	1084	64.2	101	23
D	1242	54.3	122	28
E	1198	56.5	114	36
F	1388	47.1	139	50
G	1596	44.1	149	51
H	1498	44.8	149	20

A **scatter diagram** is a graph used to investigate whether there is a relationship between two variables. For example, the data for engine size and fuel efficiency gives this scatter diagram.

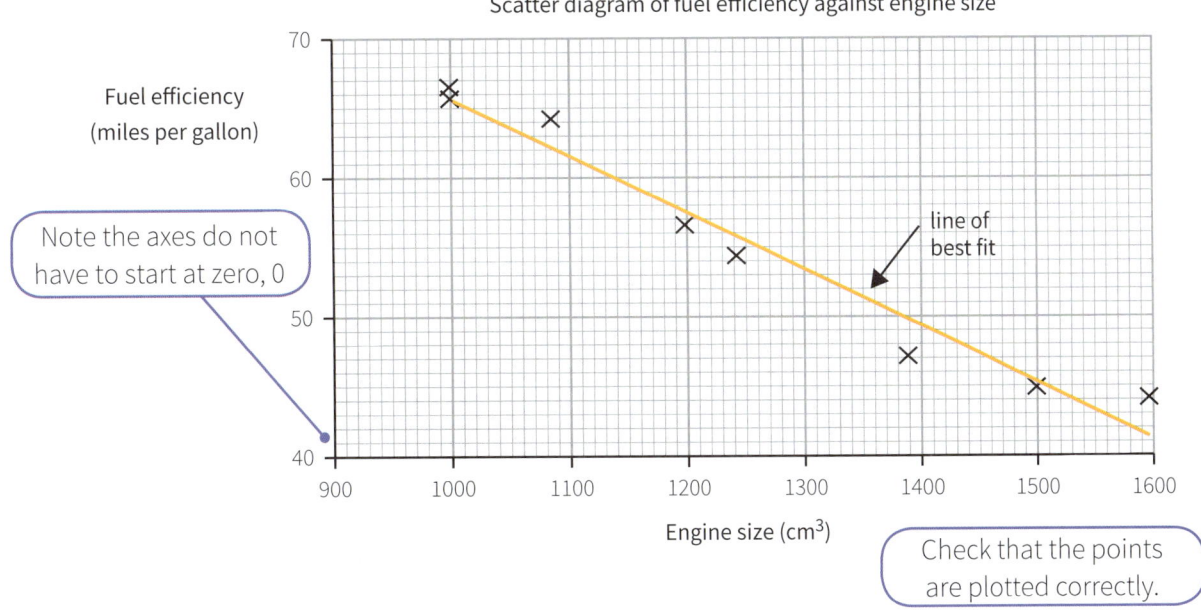

The graph shows that the bigger the engine, the lower the number of miles per gallon. The points on the graph lie near a straight line called the **line of best fit**. This means that there is a strong relationship between engine size and the number of miles per gallon. As the engine size increases, the number of miles per gallon decreases. This is called negative **correlation**.

To draw and interpret a scatter diagram:

- Look for the highest and lowest value of each variable.
- Decide on a scale for each axis. Remember to aim for a reasonably large graph with a scale that is easy to use.

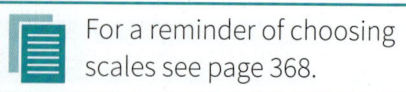
For a reminder of choosing scales see page 368.

- Use a ruler and sharp pencil to draw the axes. Remember to label them (including the units).
- Use each pair of values to plot a point on the graph.
- Do the points lie near a straight line? If so, say there is **strong correlation**.

  If the points lie in a broad band, say there is **weak correlation**.

  If the points lie all over the place, say there is **no correlation**.

- Do the points go up across the page (left to right)? This is **positive correlation**.

  Do the points go down across the page? This is **negative correlation**.

- Explain what the graph shows about the relationship between the variables.

Here are some examples of different kinds of correlation and what they show.

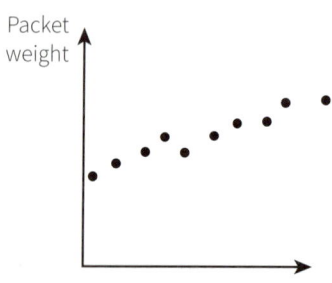

The more sweets there are, the heavier the packet is.

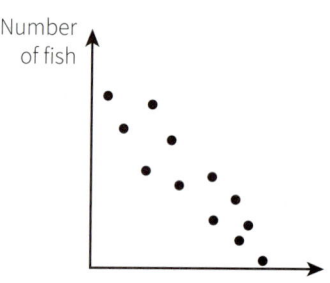

The more pollution there is, the fewer fish there are.

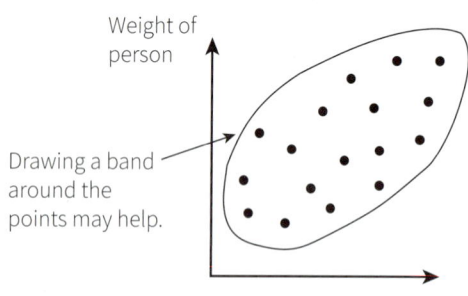

Taller people tend to weigh more, but the relationship between height and weight is not very strong.

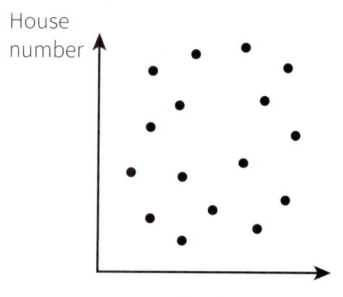

There is no connection between the height of a person and the number of their house.

Scatter Diagrams

Example

A researcher investigates the relationship between the price of houses and rents in regions of England.

The table gives data she finds on the internet. Use a scatter graph to investigate the relationship between house prices and rents.

Region	Average house price (£thousands)	Average rent (£/month)
North East	131	495
North West	158	550
Yorkshire & the Humber	157	525
East Midlands	186	550
West Midlands	191	595
East	290	750
London	484	1433
South East	322	875
South West	254	695

Data source: UK House Price Index summary: December 2017 (www.gov.uk)

Average house prices range from £131 thousand to £484 thousand and average rents range from £495 per month to £1433 per month. Plotting points on reasonable axes gives this graph.

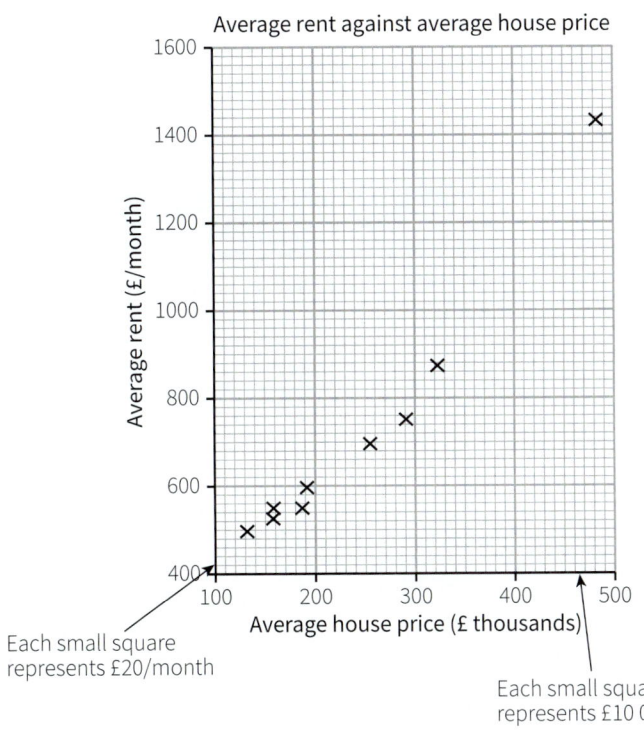

Each small square represents £20/month

Each small square represents £10 000

A larger graph with intervals of £50 thousand on the horizontal axis and £100/month on the vertical axis would be better, but too big for the available space here.

The points are near to a straight line going up across the page. This is strong positive correlation. The higher the average house price, the higher the average rent.

Note:
London is so expensive that the point that represents it is a long way from the other points. The researcher may decide to ignore this outlier because it is a special case. The other points would still lie close to a straight line.

Handling Information and Data

Practice

Draw scatter graphs with sensible scales and as large as your graph paper allows.

1. The table gives the percentage marks scored by students on two test papers.

Paper 1	76	54	90	48	29	62	37	86	17	54	72	49	97	58
Paper 2	68	62	67	53	41	55	43	91	24	58	80	57	82	63

Draw a scatter graph and describe the correlation.

2. The table shows the number of sunhats and the number of umbrellas that a market trader sells during the summer weeks.

Week	1	2	3	4	5	6	7	8	9	10
Number of sunhats	32	22	3	9	37	16	11	14	28	27
Number of umbrellas	3	14	29	26	1	14	20	19	16	11

Draw a scatter graph and describe the correlation.

3. The table gives average petrol and diesel prices over a 10 year period.

Year	2008	2009	2010	2011	2012	2013	2014	2015	2016	2017
Petrol price (p/litre)	108	94	120	135	142	137	129	113	106	117
Diesel price (p/litre)	117	102	121	141	148	141	136	119	107	120

Data source: Energy and environment: data tables (ENV) (www.gov.uk)

Draw a scatter graph and describe the relationship between the prices.

4. Ellie carries out a survey to find out how much time students in her class spent watching TV and on social media during one week.

   The table gives Ellie's data.

   Draw a scatter graph and describe the correlation.

Learner	Hours spent on watching TV	Hours spent on social media
Ahmed	9.4	11.0
Becky	10.8	4.8
Carol	15.2	2.2
Dan	13.4	5.6
Ellie	9.4	5.7
Farid	5.6	10.8
George	3.8	5.0
Hannah	2.7	13.9
Imran	10.3	8.8
Jen	3.4	12.1
Kyle	7.4	9.1
Louise	14.1	2.2
Maisy	6.6	6.4
Nick	5.2	14.6

5. Use the emissions data in the table on page 401 to investigate the relationship between:
   a. carbon dioxide emissions and engine size
   b. nitrous oxide emissions and engine size.
   c. Compare the results and state your interpretation clearly.

> It is not essential to draw a line of best fit unless it is requested, but sometimes it helps to illustrate an answer.

Scatter Diagrams

6. A travel agent uses the internet to find the distances from Leeds to a number of resorts and the time that it takes to travel to them. The table gives her results.

   Draw a scatter graph and describe the correlation.

From Leeds to	Distance (miles)	Time
Bamburgh	148	2h 43min
Blackpool	86	1h 36min
Bognor Regis	272	4h 43min
Eastbourne	278	4h 53min
Great Yarmouth	194	3h 56min
Newquay	363	5h 50min
Scarborough	67	1h 33min
Skegness	114	2h 21min
Torquay	300	5h 4min
Whitby	73	1h 41min

7. Rowan says that the price of a car depends on its mileage. Seth says that the age of a car is more important than its mileage. Rowan and Seth use the internet to find the price, age and mileage of a number of cars of the same type.

Age (years)	0	0.5	1	1.5	2	2.5	3	3.5	4
Mileage (miles)	250	745	2048	14 032	35 022	14 896	25 864	14 829	9000
Price (£)	12 500	11 990	10 995	9275	8750	8995	7990	7995	7940

   a. Use a scatter diagram to investigate the relationship between:

   i. age and price ii. mileage and price.

   b. Comment on what Rowan and Seth said.

Activities

1. List pairs of the following body measurements that you think are related:

   height, armspan, handspan, foot length, head circumference, wrist circumference length from knee to foot, length from elbow to wrist.

2. To check whether you are correct:
   - Ask the students in your class to provide the data you need.
   - Draw a scatter diagram for each pair of measurements.
   - Describe the correlation.
   - Write a report of your findings.

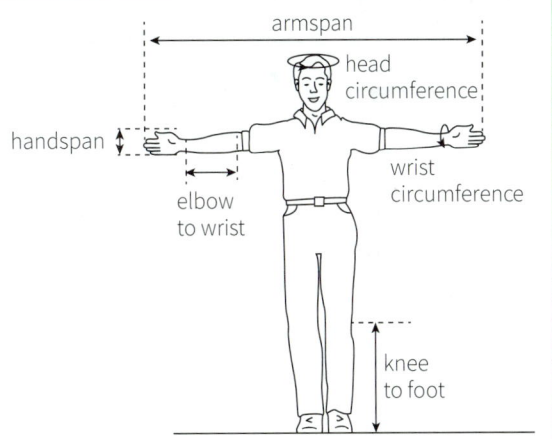

B. Draw and use lines of best fit

If a line of best fit can be drawn and there is a strong correlation, you can estimate the value of one quantity where the other value is known.

Example

This scatter diagram shows the results students gained in two maths papers.

The line of best fit shows a strong correlation between the marks. Students who did well in paper 1, also did well in paper 2.

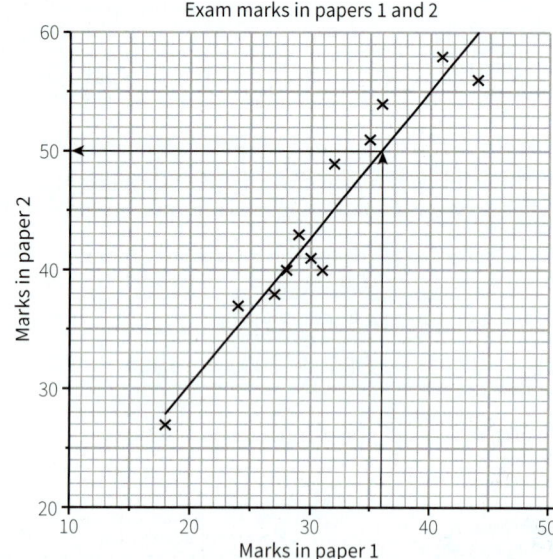

When drawing the line of best fit, try to follow the direction of the points with the same number of points either side of the line.

The line of best fit can be used to estimate a mark, when the other mark is known.

Saima scored 36 in paper 1.

An estimate of Saima's mark in paper 2 is **50**

Practice

1. Look at the scatter diagram in the Example above.
   a. Estimate the mark in paper 1 for a student who scored 32 in paper 2.
   b. Estimate the mark in paper 2 for a student who scored 39 in paper 1.

2. Add a line of best fit to the scatter diagram you drew in question **6** of 'Draw and interpret scatter diagrams' (page 405), showing the distance and journey times from Leeds to holiday resorts.
   a. Estimate the average time to travel 190 miles.
   b. Estimate the average distance travelled in 330 minutes.

3. Add a line of best fit to the scatter diagram you drew in question **5a** of 'Draw and interpret scatter diagrams' (page 404), showing carbon dioxide emissions against engine size.
   a. Estimate the engine size where the CO_2 emissions are 130 g per km.
   b. Estimate the CO_2 emissions when the engine size is 1215 cm^3.

4. The table gives the length and wingspan in centimetres of some garden birds.

	Blackbird	Blue tit	Crow	Magpie	Pigeon	Robin	Sparrow	Starling	Wren
Length	25	12	46	45	33	14	15	22	10
Wingspan	36	19	99	56	67	21	23	40	15

   a. i. Draw a scatter graph to show this data, including the line of best fit.
      ii. Describe the correlation.
   b. i. A song thrush is 23 cm long. Use the scatter graph to predict its wingspan.
      ii. The wingspan of a house martin is 27 cm. Use the scatter graph to predict its length.

5. The table gives the average temperature (in °C) and the consumption of coal and gas (in million tonnes of oil equivalent) in each month of a year.

	Jan	Feb	Mar	Apr	May	Jun	Jul	Aug	Sep	Oct	Nov	Dec
Temperature	7.2	7.6	9.4	11.8	14.3	15.9	17.0	14.5	10.3	8.8	6.0	9.3
Coal	4.1	3.4	3.6	2.4	2.8	2.7	2.9	2.2	2.8	3.5	4.0	4.2
Gas	10.9	9.5	9.6	7.9	7.1	5.6	5.5	5.2	5.8	8.2	9.0	10.6

Data source: Energy Consumption in the UK (www.gov.uk) and UK climate maps and data (www.metoffice.gov.uk)

   a. Draw a scatter graph of:
      i. coal consumption against average temperature
      ii. gas consumption against average temperature.
   b. Compare the correlation of coal consumption and gas consumption with temperature.
   c. Estimate the consumption of gas and coal in a month with an average temperature of 12 °C.

Chapter Summary
24 Scatter Diagrams

- A **scatter diagram** is used to investigate whether there is a relationship between two variables.
- To draw a scatter diagram look for the highest and lowest value of each variable, then decide on a scale that is easy to use. You do not need to start at zero. Plot a point on the graph to represent each pair of values.
- The **line of best fit** is a straight line that lies as close as possible to the points and shows the trend of the data. When drawing the line of best fit, try to get the same number of points either side of the line.
- If the points lie near the line of best fit, there is **strong correlation**. This suggests that there is a strong relationship between the variables.
- If the points lie in a broad band around the line of best fit, there is **weak correlation**.
- If the points lie all over the graph then there is **no correlation**.
- If the points go up across the page (from left to right), there is **positive correlation**. If the points go down across the page, there is **negative correlation**.
- When the correlation is strong, you can use the line of best fit to estimate the value of one variable from the value of the other.

Handling Information and Data

25 Probability

Compare the likelihood of events
Specification reference L1.H30, L1.H31

Level 1

Some things are **certain** to happen, e.g. 10 am is certain to come after 9 am.
Some things are **impossible**, for example, if you empty a bucket the water won't flow uphill.
Other things may or may not happen – these **'events'** may be **likely** or **unlikely**.

There are six different possibilities when a dice is thrown: 1, 2, 3, 4, 5, 6
Assuming the dice is **not biased**, the possibilities are all **equally likely**.
One of the six numbers is a 5. We say there is a **1 in 6 chance** of getting a 5
Three of the numbers are even numbers, so there is a **3 in 6 chance** of getting an even number.
There is no 8, so there is a **0 in 6 chance** of getting an 8. It is **impossible**.
All of the numbers are less than 7, so there is a **6 in 6 chance** of getting a number less than 7
This event is **certain**.
When something is equally likely to happen or not happen this is sometimes called an **even chance**. There is an even chance of getting a number less than 4 on a dice because three numbers are less than 4, but the other three numbers are not less than 4.

Practice

1. Say whether each of these **events** is **impossible, unlikely, likely** or **certain**.
   a. You will watch television tonight.
   b. You will win a prize with the next raffle ticket you buy.
   c. You will meet a dinosaur on your way home.
   d. It will get dark tonight.
   e. A relative will visit you next week.

2. a. How many possibilities are there when a coin is tossed?
   b. What is the chance of getting a head when you toss a coin?

3. A spinner is numbered 1 to 5 as shown.
   a. When it is spun, what is the chance of getting:
      i. 4
      ii. an even number
      iii. an odd number?
   b. Which is more likely: an even number or an odd number?

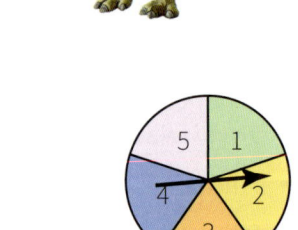

4. A pack of 52 playing cards is shuffled, then one is picked out at random.
   a. How many possibilities are there?
   b. What is the chance of getting:
      i. an ace
      ii. a diamond
      iii. the ace of diamonds?

5. The letters of the alphabet are written on pieces of paper and put into a hat.
   A letter is taken out at random.
   a. How many possibilities are there?
   b. What is the chance of getting:
      i. Z
      ii. a vowel (a, e, i, o or u)
      iii. a consonant (a letter that is not a vowel)?

Activity

1. What is the chance of getting a head when a coin is tossed?
2. Toss a coin 10 times.
   Record your results in a table like that shown here.

Toss number	1	2	3	4	5	6	7	8	9	10
Result										

   Do your results support your answer to part **1**?
3. Compare your results with those of other students in your group.
4. Add the number of heads for all the students in your group together.
   Does the total support your answer to part **1**?

Use fractions to measure probability

Specification reference L1.H30, L1.H31, L2.H27

Level 1

Probability is a measure of how likely something is to happen.
If an event is **impossible**, we say the probability is **0**
If an event is **certain**, we say the probability is **1**
Other events have probabilities between 0 and 1
The probabilities of different outcomes can be written as fractions.
To find the fraction when all outcomes are equally likely use:

Key point

Probability of an event = $\dfrac{\text{number of ways the event can happen}}{\text{total number of possibilities}}$

Example

When a coin is tossed, the probability of a head is $\dfrac{1}{2}$

You should get a head for about half of the tosses.

> Head is 1 out of 2 equally likely possibilities.

Look back at your results from the Activity above. Were half of the tosses heads?

Handling Information and Data

Example

A set of 20 number cards is numbered from 1 to 20. If you take a card at random:

1. the probability of getting 5 is:
   1 in 20   or $\frac{1}{20}$ as a fraction

2. the probability of getting an odd number (1, 3, 5, 7, 9, 11, 13, 15, 17, 19) is:
   10 in 20   or $\frac{10}{20} = \frac{1}{2}$ as a fraction

3. the probability of getting a number less than 6 (1, 2, 3, 4 or 5) is:
   5 in 20   or $\frac{5}{20} = \frac{1}{4}$ as a fraction

4. the probability of getting 7 or more
   (7, 8, 9, 10, 11, 12, 13, 14, 15, 16, 17, 18, 19 or 20) is:
   14 in 20   or $\frac{14}{20} = \frac{7}{10}$ as a fraction

These probabilities can be shown and compared on a **probability line**:

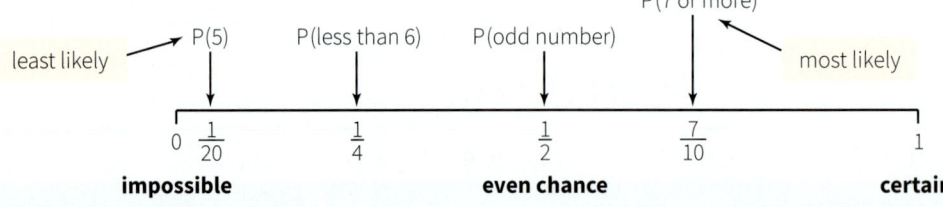

Practice

In these questions give probabilities between 0 and 1 as fractions.

1. A set of 10 number cards is numbered from 1 to 10. Suppose you take a card at random.
   a. Find the probability of each event.
      i. getting a 3
      ii. getting an odd number
      iii. getting less than 7
      iv. getting 8 or more
   b. Show the results on a probability line.

2. A dice is thrown. What is the probability of getting:
   a. 5   b. an even number   c. 8   d. a number less than 7?

3. This spinner is numbered 1 to 5
   a. When it is spun, what is the probability of getting:
      i. 4   ii. an even number   iii. an odd number?
   b. Show the results on a probability line.

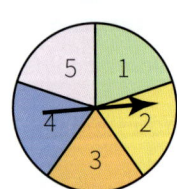

4. A pack of playing cards is shuffled, then one is picked out at random.
   a. Find, as fractions in their simplest form, the probability of getting:
      i. a king
      ii. a club
      iii. the king of clubs
      iv. a red card
      v. a red king
      vi. a jack or queen.
   b. List the events in order of their probabilities, starting with the least likely.

5. Five 2p coins, two 10p coins and a £1 coin are put into a bag.
   A coin is taken out at random.

   a. Find the probability that it is:
      i. 2p
      ii. 10p
      iii. £1.
   b. Show the results on a probability line.

6. A set of 40 number cards is numbered 1 to 40
   a. A card is taken at random. Write down the probability of it being:
      i. more than 35
      ii. an even number greater than 10
      iii. less than 15
      iv. an odd number less than 20
   b. List the events in order of their probabilities, starting with the most likely.

Write probabilities as decimals and percentages

Specification reference **L2.H27**

Probabilities can be written as decimals or percentages.

To write fractions as decimals and percentages see page 145.

Example

A set of 50 number cards is numbered 1 to 50. If you take a card at random:

1. the probability that it is more than 45 is
   $$\frac{5}{50} = \frac{1}{10} = 10\% \text{ or } 0.1$$

   There are 5 possible numbers: 46, 47, 48, 49 and 50

2. the probability of getting a square number is
   $$\frac{7}{50} = \frac{14}{100} = 14\% \text{ or } 0.14$$

   There are 7 possible numbers: 1, 4, 9, 16, 25, 36 and 49

Handling Information and Data

Practice

1. A set of 100 number cards is numbered 1 to 100. A card is taken at random.
   Find the probability of each event as a percentage and as a decimal.

   a. getting a number higher than 90
   b. getting a number lower than 5
   c. getting an odd number
   d. getting a multiple of 6

2. A bag contains four 10p coins, three 2p coins and one £1 coin. A coin is taken out at random.

   a. Find, as a percentage, the probability that it is:
      i. 10p   ii. £1   iii. 2p   iv. worth more than 5p.
   b. Show the results on a probability line.

3. In a raffle the tickets are numbered from 1 to 1000
   All the tickets ending in 0 or 5 win a prize. If you buy a ticket, what is the probability that you will get a prize? Give your answer as a decimal and as a percentage.

4. A person says he was born in a leap year. Find, as a fraction, the probability that he was born:

   a. on Christmas Day
   b. in January
   c. in June
   d. in February
   e. before May 1st?

5. The table shows the number of part-time and full-time students in a college maths class and whether they are male or female.

   a. A student is chosen from the class at random. Find the probability that the student is:
      i. a male full-time student

	Part-time	Full-time
Male	5	7
Female	9	4

   ii. a female part-time student.

   b. One student is to be chosen at random to represent the class. Sally says there is a higher chance of a woman being chosen than a man. Is Sally correct? Use probabilities to explain your answer.

In some situations the possibilities are not equally likely.

On this spinner there are 3 numbers, but the probability of getting 1 is not $\frac{1}{3}$.
It is $\frac{1}{4}$ because the sector for 1 covers a quarter of the spinner.
If the spinner is spun 40 times, about 10 results should be 1s.
Sometimes you need to use data, rather than logic, to find probabilities.

Activity

Toss a drawing pin 10 times. Use a table to record whether it lands point up or point down.

Work out the percentage of times it lands point up.

Compare your results with those of other students.

Combine your results and find, for the whole group, the percentage of tosses that landed point up.

Probability

> **Example**
>
> In one year, 304 635 boys and 289 999 girls were born in the UK (www.ons.gov.uk).
>
> The total number of babies was 594 634
>
> This suggests that: the probability that a baby is a boy = $\dfrac{304\,635}{594\,634}$
>
> and: the probability that a baby is a girl = $\dfrac{289\,999}{594\,634}$
>
> Use your calculator to write these fractions as percentages.
>
> You should find that the probability of a boy is **51%** and for a girl **49%** (nearest %).
>
> These are typical values — usually near 50%, with slightly more boys than girls.

6. Look at the spinner shown on the previous page.
   a. What is the probability of getting: i. 2   ii. 3?
   b. Out of 40 spins, how many would you expect to be i. 2   ii. 3?

7. a. If this spinner is spun, what is the probability of getting:
      i. A   ii. B   iii. C?
   b. Out of 60 spins, how many would you expect to be:
      i. A   ii. B   iii. C?

8. The table shows the number of sports accidents that needed hospital treatment during one year.
   a. Find the probability that a sports injury needing hospital treatment is from each category of sport. Give your answers as a % to 1 dp.
   b. Interpret your answers to part **a**.

Sport	No. of accidents
Ball sports	562 656
Combat sports	24 197
Wheel sports	38 757
Winter sports	23 410
Animal sports	22 625
Water sports	25 404
Other	43 020
Total	740 069

Combined events

Specification reference **L2.H26**

A. Identify possible outcomes of combined events

Two events are **independent** if the outcome of one has no effect on the probability of the other.

For example, when a couple have two children, the gender of the first child has no effect on the gender of the second.

Using B to mean boy and G to mean girl, all the possibilities can be shown in a table like this — 2nd child

		1st child	
		B	G
2nd child	B	BB	GB
	G	BG	GG

They can also be shown in a tree diagram like this.
Both show that there are 4 possibilities:

BB   boy then another boy
BG   boy then a girl
GB   girl then a boy
GG   girl then another girl.

If the probability of a boy is about the same as a girl (see page 413), the 4 possibilities for 2 children are also approximately equally likely.

So about a quarter (1 out of 4) of all couples who have 2 children will have 2 boys, about a quarter will have 2 girls, and about a half (2 out of 4) will have one of each.

Follow the branches across the tree to find the possibilities.

Practice

1. The table shows all the possibilities when two dice are thrown. The centre of the table shows some of the total scores:

   $1 + 1 = 2$ $2 + 1 = 3$ $3 + 6 = 9$ $6 + 2 = 8$

   a. Copy and complete the table.
   b. How many totals are there in the centre of the table?
   c. Write down the probability of each possible total, giving your answers as fractions.
   d. Which total is most likely?

   Score on 1st dice

	1	2	3	4	5	6
1	2	3				
2						8
3						
4						
5						
6			9			

   Score on 2nd dice

2. Draw up another table like the one in question **1**. This time multiply the two scores together, instead of adding them. (Multiplying gives the **product** of the scores.)
   What is the probability that the product is: a. odd   b. even?

3. a. Draw a table to show all the possibilities when two coins are tossed.
   b. Draw a tree diagram to show all the possibilities when two coins are tossed.
   c. What is the probability of getting: i. 2 heads   ii. the same on each coin?

4. A tree diagram showing the possible genders of a set of triplets has been started here.
   Copy and complete it to show all the possible combinations of genders.

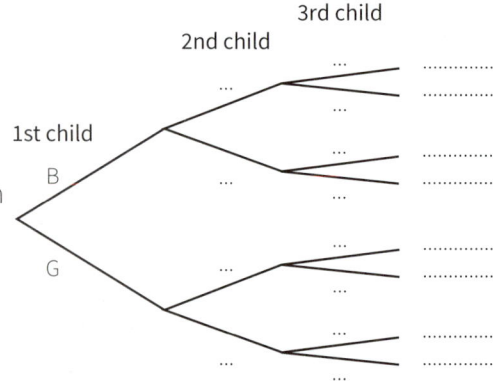

5. a. Draw a tree diagram to show all the possibilities when three coins are tossed.
   b. What is the probability of getting:
      i. 3 tails   ii. 2 tails and 1 head (in any order)?

B. Calculate combined probability

You can show probabilities of the outcomes of two events on a tree diagram and use them to calculate combined probabilities.

Example

A dice is biased so that 20% of the throws give a 6. The dice is thrown twice.
Find the probability of getting at least one 6.

On each throw P(6) = 20% = 0.2
P(not 6) = 1 − 0.2 = 0.8

For combined events, **multiply** the probabilities.
P(double 6) = 0.2 × 0.2 = 0.04
P(6, then not 6) = 0.2 × 0.8 = 0.16
P(not 6, then 6) = 0.8 × 0.2 = 0.16
Then **add** the probabilities.
P(at least one 6) = 0.04 + 0.16 + 0.16 = **0.36**

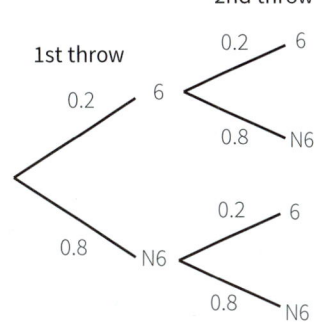

Alternative method
P(not 6 on both throws) = 0.8 × 0.8 = 0.64
P(at least one 6) = 1 − 0.64 = 0.36

> Use one method to find the answer and the other to check.

Example

Sonja and Aiman often play tennis.
The probability that Sonja wins the first set is $\frac{1}{3}$. When Sonja wins the first set, the probability that she also wins the second set is $\frac{3}{4}$. If she loses the first set, the probability of her winning the second set is just $\frac{1}{6}$.
Find the probability that in one match Sonja loses the first two sets.

In each set Sonja wins (W) or loses (L).

In the 1st set P(W) = $\frac{1}{3}$ and P(L) = 1 − $\frac{1}{3}$ = $\frac{2}{3}$

If Sonja wins the 1st set, then in the 2nd set P(W) = $\frac{3}{4}$ and P(L) = 1 − $\frac{3}{4}$ = $\frac{1}{4}$

If Sonja loses the 1st set, then in the 2nd set P(W) = $\frac{1}{6}$ and P(L) = 1 − $\frac{1}{6}$ = $\frac{5}{6}$

The probability that Sonja loses both sets is
P(L L) = $\frac{2}{3} \times \frac{5}{6} = \frac{10}{18} = \frac{5}{9}$

> Multiply fractions by multiplying the numerators, then the denominators.

Check
Check that the total is 1:
P(W W) = $\frac{1}{3} \times \frac{3}{4} = \frac{1}{12}$ P(W L) = $\frac{1}{3} \times \frac{1}{4} = \frac{1}{12}$
P(L W) = $\frac{2}{3} \times \frac{1}{6} = \frac{2}{18}$ P(L L) = $\frac{2}{3} \times \frac{5}{6} = \frac{10}{18}$
Check total = $\frac{1}{12} + \frac{1}{12} + \frac{2}{18} + \frac{10}{18} = \frac{9}{36} + \frac{3}{36} + \frac{4}{36} + \frac{20}{36}$
= $\frac{36}{36}$ = **1** (or use a calculator)

Practice

1. An article in a car magazine says that 60% of learner drivers pass the theory test and 50% of learner drivers pass the practical test.

   a. Copy and complete the tree diagram to show the probabilities of a learner driver passing (P) and failing (F) each test.

   b. Use the tree diagram to find the probability that a learner driver:

      i. passes both tests   ii. passes at least one of the tests.

2. A factory employs 100 workers. Of these, 20 workers are skilled and the rest are unskilled.
   Five skilled workers and ten unskilled workers work part-time and the others work full-time.
   One worker is chosen at random to represent the company.

   a. Copy and complete the tree diagram to show the probabilities of the worker being skilled (S), unskilled (U), part-time (PT) or full-time (FT).

   b. Work out the probability that the worker is:

      i. unskilled and part-time   ii. full time.

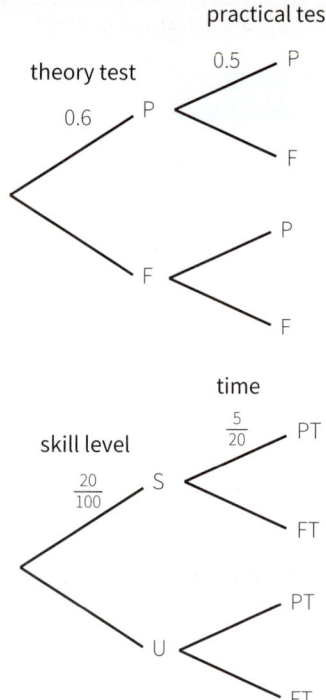

3. Delivery Plus claims that it delivers 90% of parcels within 24 hours.
   Tina sends two parcels by Delivery Plus.
   Use a tree diagram to find the probability that:

   a. they both arrive within 24 hours   b. neither parcel arrives within 24 hours.

4. When a company prints invitation cards in blue and gold, one or both colours may fail to print.
   The probability that the blue fails to print is 0.2
   The probability that the gold fails to print is 0.15
   Use a tree diagram to work out the probability that:

   a. both colours print   b. only one of the colours prints.

5. A pack of 52 playing cards has an equal number of black and red cards.
   A card is taken and its colour noted.
   After replacing the card and shuffling the pack, another card is taken.

   a. Find the probability that:

      i. both cards are black   ii. the cards are different colours.

   b. Repeat part **a** assuming that the first card is **not** replaced.

6. A gardener has a mixed bag of 10 crocus bulbs. Three bulbs give yellow flowers, 5 give purple flowers and the rest give white flowers. The gardener plants 2 bulbs in a pot.

   a. Copy and complete the tree diagram to show the possible combinations of colours and their probabilities when the bulbs flower.

   b. Find the probability that the flowers are:
      i. both yellow   ii. the same colour   iii. different colours.

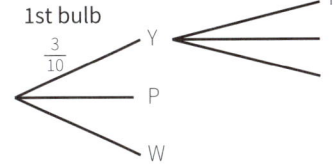

7. A coin is biased so that the probability of a head is $\frac{2}{3}$
   The coin is tossed three times.
   Draw a tree diagram and find the probability of getting more heads than tails.

8. Athletes are tested for a performance-improving drug. 40 out of the 200 athletes in one event are taking the drug. The test is not perfect. It gives a positive result for 90% of the athletes who are taking the drug. But it also gives a positive result for 5% of athletes who are not taking the drug.
   Find the probability that the test gives an accurate result for a randomly chosen athlete at this event.

Chapter Summary
25 Probability

Level 1
- Events can be **impossible, unlikely, likely** or **certain**.
- A dice is **not biased** if it is equally likely to land on any of its faces.
- **Probability** is a measure of how likely something is to happen.
- If an event is **impossible**, its probability is 0. If an event is **certain**, its probability is 1.
  You can use a probability line from 0 to 1 to illustrate probabilities.
- The **total probability** of all possible outcomes is 1
- For **equally likely possibilities**, the probability of an event can be found as a fraction.

  $$\text{Probability of an event} = \frac{\text{number of ways the event can happen}}{\text{total number of possibilities}}$$

Level 2
- Probabilities can be written as decimals or percentages.
- When the possibilities are not all equally likely, you can find probabilities from an experiment or data that has been collected by someone else.
- To show all the possibilities for combined events, you can use a **table** or **tree diagram**. (Follow the branches to find the possibilities.)
- Events are **independent** if they have no effect on each other.
- A tree diagram can show probabilities of the outcomes of two or more events to calculate combined probabilities.
- Multiply probabilities to find the probability of **a combined event.** You can check results by adding the probabilities of all the possible combined events, the total should be 1

Answers

Number

1 Number Value

Numbers up to 1000

A. Place value (p 1)

1. a. 165   b. 53   c. 212
   d. 403   e. 990   f. 68
   g. 820   h. 7   i. 217
   j. 902

2. a. Two hundred and thirty-six;
      2 hundreds, 3 tens, 6 units
   b. One hundred and five; 1 hundred, 5 units
   c. Six hundred and seventeen;
      6 hundreds, 1 ten, 7 units
   d. Eighty-two; 8 tens, 2 units
   e. Seven hundred and fifty;
      7 hundreds, 5 tens
   f. Five hundred; 5 hundreds
   g. One hundred and twenty-three;
      1 hundred, 2 tens, 3 units
   h. Ninety; 9 tens
   i. Nine hundred and thirty-eight;
      9 hundreds, 3 tens, 8 units
   j. Three hundred and forty-four;
      3 hundreds, 4 tens, 4 units

3.
Planet	Number of days	Planet	Approx number of years
Earth	365	Jupiter	12
Mercury	88	Neptune	165
Mars	687	Saturn	30
Venus	225	Uranus	84

4. Mercury, Venus, Earth, Mars, Jupiter, Saturn, Uranus, Neptune

5. Ceres: five, Eris: five hundred and fifty-seven, Haumea: two hundred and eighty-five, Makemake: three hundred and ten, Pluto: two hundred and forty-eight.

B. Count in 10s (p 3)

1. a. 41   91   121
   b. 461   501   531   571
   c. 403   443   483   513

2. a. 165   125   85
   b. 576   546   506   466
   c. 119   99   49   9

C. Count in 100s (p 3)

1. a. 225   525   725   925
   b. 163   363   663   863

2. a. 782   582   282
   b. 807   607   307   7

Large numbers

A. Place value (p 4)

1.
			Thousands			
	M	H	T	U	H	T	U
a.				2	0	0	0
b.			3	2	0	0	0
c.		1	6	5	2	0	0
d.		1	0	9	8	7	0
e.	4	2	0	0	0	0	0
f.			9	0	7	5	0
g.				8	0	2	5
h.		1	1	9	0	0	0
i.	6	2	9	9	0	0	0
j.	9	0	0	0	3	0	6

2. a. Forty-five thousand
   b. Three hundred and seventy-five thousand
   c. Six million, seven hundred thousand
   d. Two hundred and five thousand
   e. Seventy thousand, seven hundred and fifty
   f. One million, two hundred thousand
   g. Five thousand and sixty-five
   h. Twenty thousand, three hundred and six
   i. Forty thousand, three hundred and fifty-two
   j. Nine million, six hundred and seventy thousand and eighty
   k. Five million, ninety thousand and four hundred
   l. Three million, five hundred and three thousand, two hundred and forty-one.

3. 5 065, 20 306, 40 352, 45 000, 70 750, 205 000, 375 000
   1 200 000, 3 503 241, 5 090 400, 6 700 000, 9 670 080

4. a. b.
Year	Estimated population
1100	25 000
1300	100 000
1500	50 000
1600	200 000
1801	1 117 000
1851	2 685 000
1939	8 700 000
2000	7 640 000

Answers

c. i. 1300 and 1500, 1939 and 2000
   ii. 1939

B. Greater than > and less than < (p 6)
1. a. 1 < 3   b. 7 > 5   c. 9 > 4
   d. 0 < 1
2. a. 2 < 8   b. 6 > 1   c. 18 > 13
   d. 19 < 23   e. 99 < 101   f. 170 > 159
3. a. 269 < 270   b. 15 000 > 2500
   c. 9900 > 7500   d. 50 000 < 75 000
   e. 9 < 900   f. 10 500 > 10 499
   g. 99 900 < 100 000   h. 4 010 000 > 4 009 999

Positive and negative numbers in practical contexts (p 7)
1. a. −5 °C, −2 °C, 0 °C, 1 °C, 4 °C, 8 °C
   b. −10 °C, −8 °C, −7 °C, 6 °C, 9 °C, 10 °C
   c. −18 °C, −15 °C, −10 °C, 0 °C, 12 °C, 20 °C
2. a. 9 °C, −1 °C
   b. −16 °C, −17 °C, −14 °C
   c. −18 °C, −19 °C, −17 °C
3. a. M Patel   b. J Robinson
4. Yes because the account will be £225 overdrawn, £25 more than the agreed overdraft.

Compare numbers of any size (p 8)
1. a. 2 500 000   b. 2 560 000
   c. 1 700 000 000   d. 1 850 000 000
   e. 30 000 000   f. 300 000 000
   g. 1 300 000 000   h. 500 000 000
   i. 250 000
2. a. 2.5 million   b. 5.6 million
   c. 4.75 million   d. 3.8 billion
   e. 2.95 billion   f. 1.05 billion
   g. 20 million
   h. 600 million or 0.6 billion
   i. 34.5 million
3. £161 700 000, £148 700 000, £121 300 000, £113 000 000
4. a. i. Company B   ii. Company C
      iii. Company B
   b. i. Companies C, E and G   ii. Company E

2 Addition and Subtraction
Add and subtract 3-digit numbers
A. Add in columns (p 11)
1. a. 379   b. 779   c. 496
   d. 489   e. 780   f. 672
   g. 394   h. 787   i. 500
   j. 318   k. 946   l. 305
   m. 400   n. 931   o. 621
   p. 610
2. a. 989   b. 472   c. 241
3. 341 employees   4. 440 photocopies
5. 350 miles   6. 482 cases
7. £795   8. £926
9. 215 tickets

B. Add in your head (p 12)
1. a. 57   b. 57   c. 69
   d. 43   e. 72   f. 63
   g. 85   h. 98
2. a. 241   b. 181   c. 398
   d. 387   e. 208   f. 185
   g. 406   h. 246   i. 362
   j. 301   k. 568   l. 538
   m. 574   n. 371   o. 501
   p. 493

C. Subtract in columns (p 14)
1. a. 211   b. 321   c. 200
   d. 515   e. 309   f. 227
   g. 70   h. 31   i. 153
   j. 199   k. 179   l. 67
   m. 245   n. 69   o. 299
   p. 501   q. 329   r. 299
2. a. 387   b. 97   c. 698
3. 325 envelopes   4. £324
5. 127 more men   6. £106
7. 163 miles

D. Subtract in your head (p 15)
1. a. 23   b. 16   c. 28
   d. 56   e. 19   f. 42
   g. 37   h. 34
2. a. 149   b. 199   c. 149
   d. 622   e. 401   f. 205
   g. 206   h. 199   i. 326
   j. 490   k. 157   l. 699
   m. 199   n. 299   o. 709
   p. 294

E. Use addition and subtraction (p 15)
1. £94   2. 53p   3. 16
4. 61   5. £741   6. £385
7. 352
8. a. 540   b. 184
9. 682   10. £77

419

Answers

Add and subtract large numbers (p 16)

1. a. 52 359
   b. 39 505
   c. 28 595
   d. 160 499
   e. 3 740 000
   f. 6 527 500
   g. 312 089
   h. 212 475
   i. 1 525 500
   j. 895 276
   k. 363 250
   l. 296 350
2. 23 868 miles
3. £47 762
4. 1 332 000 people
5. 1 734 miles
6. £1 186 400
7. a. £65 150
   b. £934 850
8. a. 1 068 181
   b. 250 235
9. No. £449 500 − £372 900 = £76 600
   or £77 400 + 372 900 = 450 300
10. 375 160

Add and subtract positive and negative numbers (p 18)

1.
Temperature now	Temperature change	New temperature
−3°C	rises by 8°C	5°C
−3°C	falls by 8°C	−11°C
7°C	falls by 10°C	−3°C
−1°C	rises by 6°C	5°C
−2°C	falls by 7°C	−9°C

2. a. −£15 b. £25 c. −£40
3. a. 4.9°C b. 4.7°C
   c. 4.8°C d. 0.7°C
4. England 65°C, Northern Ireland 50°C, Scotland 60°C, Wales 58°C

Add and subtract numbers of any size (p 19)

1. a. 3.5 million
   b. 2.6 million
   c. £1 113 500 million
   d. £6.5 billion
   e. £2.25 billion
   f. £2.41 billion
2. £2.19 million
3. a.
Outlet	Total profit (£ million)
A	4.7
B	−0.8
C	10.7
D	−4.4
Total	10.2

   b. i. £0.4 million   ii. £0.8 million
      iii. £1.2 million iv. £5.5 million
      v. £15.1 million
      vi. £3.6 million (D **lost** £3.6 million more than B.)

3 Multiplication and Division

Multiplication (p 21)

Multiplication Using Times Tables Check: 25, 24, 21, 72, 0, 42, 96, 121

1. a. 60   b. 200   c. 360
   d. 350 e. 270   f. 280
   g. 540 h. 720   i. 640
   j. 630 k. 480   l. 810
   m. 600 n. 400   o. 800
   p. 1000

Multiplication methods

A. Multiply 1-digit with 2-digit numbers (p 22)

1. a. 48   b. 93   c. 88   d. 126
   e. 105 f. 172   g. 260   h. 450
   i. 234 j. 448   k. 304   l. 534
   m. 616 n. 441   o. 485   p. 837
2. 60 rings   3. 75 plates   4. 180 minutes
5. £333   6. 161 rooms   7. 378 pages
8. 425 miles 9. 600 grams

B. Multiply 2-digit with 2-digit numbers (p 24)

1. a. 575   b. 748   c. 874
   d. 990   e. 792   f. 984
   g. 728   h. 957
2. 720   3. 960   4. 270   5. 336
6. £884   7. 750 metres

Division (p 24)

Division Using Times Tables Check:
5, 11, 6, 6, 5 r2, 7 r2, 5 r5, 8 r1

A. Use standard method to divide 2-digit numbers (p 25)

1. a. 24   b. 33   c. 40
   d. 12   e. 15   f. 23
   g. 13   h. 19   i. 29
   j. 29 r 1 k. 18 r 2 l. 12 r 2
   m. 12 r 3 n. 17 r 2 o. 31 r 2
   p. 14 r 5
2. 18 doses   3. £17
4. a. 12 trays   b. 3 plants

B. Divide 3-digit numbers (p 27)

1. a. 128   b. 232   c. 138
   d. 78   e. 64   f. 73 r 1
   g. 99 r 4 h. 49 r 1 i. 41
   j. 102 r 2 k. 302 r 1 l. 99 r 7

2. 30 metres
3. 50 boxes
4. £246
5. a. 29 boxes b. 1 plant left over
6. No, because 7 does not divide exactly into 214.
   214 ÷ 7 = 30 r4
7. £75
8. £32
9. a. 42 b. 52 c. 45
   d. 37 e. 13 f. 25
10. £48
11. 25 boxes

Multiply and divide whole numbers by 10, 100 and 1000

A. Multiply by 10, 100 and 1000 in your head (p 29)

1. a. 130 b. 750 c. 1360
   d. 2020 e. 900 f. 1900
   g. 1200 h. 3700 i. 12 900
   j. 12 000 k. 30 300 l. 23 000
   m. 70 000 n. 904 000 o. 750 000
   p. 3 581 000
2. 500 pence
3. 200 ten-pence coins
4. 660 millimetres
5. 1500 centimetres
6. 2500 envelopes
7. £450
8. 500 cards
9. £2500
10. 12 000 millimetres
11. 250 000 leaflets
12. 78 000 grams
13. £300 000
14. 1 000 000 grams

B. Divide by 10, 100 and 1000 in your head (p 31)

1. a. 46 b. 460 c. 46 d. 46
   e. 53 f. 530 g. 53 h. 530
   i. 990 j. 75 k. 57 l. 38
   m. 64 n. 2.3 o. 96.2 p. 2.75
2. £120
3. 15p
4. 72 centimetres
5. 240 metres
6. 2750 boxes
7. 350 boxes
8. 176 calls
9. 15 people
10. a. 18 kilometres
    b. 3.5 kilometres
    c. 0.675 kilometres
11. £0.15 or 15p
12. £32.50

Use multiplication and division (p 32)

1. a. 28 b. 70 c. 10 d. 6
   e. 40 f. 63 g. 90 h. 6
   i. 8 j. 8 k. 400 l. 20
2. 10 two pence coins
3. 9 boxes
4. £9
5. £63
6. 9 boxes
7. 4 months
8. 200 hours
9. 20 tickets
10. a. 3600 b. 50 c. 70
    d. 900 e. 300 f. 25 000
    g. 24 000 h. 40 i. 120 000
11. £1200
12. 200 tickets
13. 3600 seconds
14. 50 bags

Recognise numerical relationships

A. Number sequences (p 33)

1. a. Add 4; 24, 28, 32 b. Add 4; 25, 29, 33
   c. Subtract 2; 10, 8, 6 d. Add 5; 27, 32, 37
   e. Add 6; 33, 39, 45 f. Subtract 5; 45, 40, 35
   g. Subtract 3; 36, 33, 30 h. Subtract 4; 40, 36, 32
   i. Subtract 10; 47, 37, 27 j. Subtract 20; 40, 20, 0
2. a. 7th April, 11th April
   b. Yes. Reason: 27 is in the sequence 3, 7, 11, 15, 19, 23, 27; or 27th is 24 days after the start and 24 can be divided exactly by 4.
3. 14 tablets. Working: The number of tablets used after each day is Mon 4, Tues 8, Wed 12, Thurs 16, so the number left after Thurs is 30 − 16 = 14; or the number left after each day is Mon 26, Tues 22, Wed 18, Thurs 14.

B. Multiples (p 34)

1. a. 12, 32, 40 b. 21, 42, 70
   c. 12, 24 d. 10, 30
2. a. 6, 12, 18, 24, 30, 36, 42, 48, 54, 60, 66, 72, 78, 84, 90, 96
   b. 8, 16, 24, 32, 40, 48, 56, 64, 72, 80, 88, 96
   c. 9, 18, 27, 36, 45, 54, 63, 72, 81, 90, 99
   d. 11, 22, 33, 44, 55, 66, 77, 88, 99
   e. 20, 40, 60, 80
3. a. 50, 100, 150, 200, 250, 300, 350, 400, 450, 500, 550, 600, 650, 700, 750, 800, 850, 900, 950
   b. 200, 400, 600, 800
   c. 250, 500, 750
4. Any 5 multiples of 1000 (for example, 2000, 3000, 4000, 5000, 6000)

Square numbers and indices

A. Square numbers (p 35)

1. 1, 4, 9, 16, 25, 36, 49, 64, 81, 100, 121, 144
2. a. 900 b. 2500 c. 3600 d. 8100
3. a. 784 b. 1764 c. 3969 d. 9801
4. a. 16 b. 32 c. 120 d. 250

B. Calculating with indices (p 36)

1. a. 512 b. 729 c. 1728 d. 16
   e. 32 f. 1296 g. 1 000 000
2. Students' checks

Answers

3.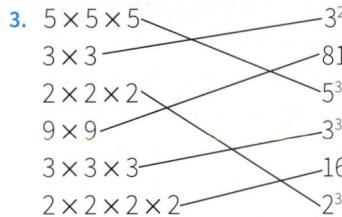
 - 5 × 5 × 5 → 5^3
 - 3 × 3 → 3^2
 - 2 × 2 × 2 → 2^3
 - 9 × 9 → 81
 - 3 × 3 × 3 → 3^3
 - 2 × 2 × 2 × 2 → 16

Multiply and divide large numbers

A. Multiply large numbers (p 37)
1. **a.** 4305 **b.** 29 704 **c.** 12 825
   d. 27 360 **e.** 32 256 **f.** 12 978
   g. 67 968 **h.** 27 504
2. 7000 miles
3. 9125 kilometres
4. 31 025 days old

B. Divide large numbers (p 39)
1. **a.** 985 **b.** 405 **c.** 881
   d. 3652 **e.** 4210 **f.** 6825
   g. 1813 r 4 **h.** 10 416 r 4 **i.** 8375 r 2
   j. 8158 r 2 **k.** 5555 r 5 **l.** 20 056 r 1
2. 250 people
3. £225
4. 3221 tickets
5. 4250 boxes
6. 5200 samples
7. £22 500
8. £62 500
9. **a.** 354 **b.** 524
   c. 512 **d.** 835
10. £450

Efficient methods of calculating with numbers of any size

A. Multiples, factors and prime numbers (p 40)
1. **a.** 98, 364, 720
   b. 165, 720, 945, 25 245
   c. 165, 243, 720, 945, 25 245
   d. 243, 720, 945, 25 245
2. **a.** 15 **b.** 12 **c.** 6 **d.** 7
3. **a.** 3, 6 and 12 **b.** 3 and 9
4. **a.** 5 **b.** 29
5. 3

B. Calculations with numbers of any size (p 41)
1. **a.** £300 **b.** £90 **c.** £36
2. 42 000 statements
3. £150 000
4. 128 000 people
5. £1 500 000
6. £300 000
7. £2 900 000
8. 6.5 million tourists
9. £375 000 or £0.375 million
10. £2.16 million

4 Rounding and Estimation

Approximate and estimate with numbers up to 1000

A. When to estimate (p 44)
1. **a.** Yes **b.** No **c.** Yes **d.** No
   e. No **f.** Yes **g.** Yes **h.** No
   i. Yes **j.** No

B. Round to the nearest 10 and 100 (p 45)
1. **a.** 40 **b.** 20 **c.** 20 **d.** 90
   e. 140 **f.** 220 **g.** 420 **h.** 990
   i. 410 **j.** 100 **k.** 700 **l.** 310
   m. 240 **n.** 180 **o.** 370 **p.** 710
   q. 370 **r.** 810 **s.** 900 **t.** 280
2. **a.** 200 **b.** 400 **c.** 600 **d.** 900
   e. 200 **f.** 400 **g.** 600 **h.** 900
   i. 400 **j.** 200 **k.** 800 **l.** 700
   m. 900 **n.** 1000 **o.** 200 **p.** 400
   q. 900 **r.** 800 **s.** 300 **t.** 100
3. **a.** 450 **b.** 549

C. Use estimates to check calculations (p 47)
1. **a.** £70 + £30 = £100 so answer is probably incorrect
   b. £160 − £70 = £90 so answer is probably correct
   c. £70 + £60 = £130 so answer is probably correct
   d. £90 ÷ £30 = 3 so answer is probably incorrect
   e. £85 − £25 = £60 (or £90 − £30 = £60) so answer is probably correct
   f. 10 × £25 = £250 so answer is probably correct
   g. £160 × 3 = £480 so answer is probably incorrect
   h. £160 − £120 = £40 so answer is probably incorrect
2. **a.** 889 **b.** 126
3. **a.** £338 **b.** £736 **c.** £858
4. Part **b.** too small: 900 − 100 = 800, part **c.** too small: 30 × 7 = 210

Approximate and estimate with large numbers

A. Round to the nearest 1000, 10 000, 100 000, 1 000 000 (p 50)
1. **a.** 5000 **b.** 7000 **c.** 27 000
   d. 31 000 **e.** 256 000 **f.** 105 000
   g. 951 000 **h.** 1 366 000
2. **a.** 30 000 **b.** 50 000 **c.** 150 000
   d. 210 000 **e.** 770 000 **f.** 230 000
   g. 680 000 **h.** 1 910 000
3. **a.** 500 000 **b.** 300 000 **c.** 1 500 000
   d. 4 600 000 **e.** 1 700 000 **f.** 2 800 000
   g. 2 000 000 **h.** 12 800 000

4. a. 3 000 000   b. 3 000 000   c. 7 000 000
    d. 16 000 000 e. 4 000 000   f. 2 000 000
5. a. 3 000 000 unemployed
    b. 7000 job losses
    c. 13 000 (or 12 800) people attend charity event
    d. £2 000 000 lottery win
    e. 4700 (or 5000) new jobs created
    f. 3 000 000 copies of record sold
    g. £21 000 000 profits for company
    h. 280 000 (or 300 000) people to benefit

B. Use estimates to check calculations (p 51)

(Note: there are alternative methods.)

1. a. True 300 000 − 100 000 = 200 000
    b. False 90 000 × 2 doesn't equal 300 000
    c. True 170 000 × 3 = 510 000
    d. False 120 000 × 3 doesn't equal 660 000
    e. False 120 000 + 90 000 doesn't equal 300 000
    f. True
       495 212 is just under 500 000 which is half a million
    g. True 300 000 + 700 000 = 1 000 000
2. a.

Income	Total (£)
2976 tickets @ £25 each	74 400
2204 tickets @ £12 each	26 448
1008 progs. @ £3 each	3024
592 mugs @ £8 each	4736
Total	108 608

Expenditure	Total (£)
Hire of venue and insurance	17 750
Publicity and printing	4899
8 technicians @ £489	3912
50 security staff @ £175 each	8750
Performers	0
Total	35 311

    b. Money raised £73 297

Strategies for checking calculations with numbers of any size

A. Use estimates to check answers are of the correct order (p 53)

1. a. 300 × 80 = 24 000. Answer given is of the wrong order so not correct.
    b. 1 240 000 − 40 000 = 1 200 000. Answer given is of the correct order.
    c. 288 000 ÷ 100 = 2880. Answer given is of the wrong order so not correct.
    d. 400 000 + 400 000 + 1 200 000 = 2 000 000. Answer given is of the correct order.
2. a. Between 1935 and 1945 = 672 700 000 increase
       Between 1945 and 1955 = 403 200 000 decrease
       Between 1955 and 1965 = 855 000 000 decrease
       Between 1965 and 1975 = 210 500 000 decrease
       Between 1975 and 1985 = 44 300 000 decrease
       Between 1985 and 1995 = 42 600 000 increase
       Between 1995 and 2005 = 50 000 000 increase
       Between 2005 and 2015 = 6 900 000 increase
    b. Students' check

B. Use reverse calculations to check answers are accurate (p 53)

1. a. 50 944
       Check: 50 944 ÷ 256 = 199
    b. 819 163
       Check: 819 163 − 188 995 − 32 546 = 597 622
    c. 786
       Check: 786 × 152 = 119 472
    d. 9 778 412
       Check: 9 778 412 + 28 732 + 192 856 = 10 000 000
2. £443 000
    Check: 443 000 × 3 = 1 329 000
3. −£12
    Check: −12 − 41 + 189 + 176 = 312

5 Ratio and Proportion

Work with ratio and proportion

A. Ratios (p 56)

1. a. 200 ml   b. 400 ml   c. 1000 ml = 1 l
2. a. 1500 ml or 1.5 litres
    b. 3000 ml or 3 litres
    c. No. 800 + 4 800 = 5 600 ml
3.

	Cement	Sand
Standard mortar	5 kg	25 kg
	10 kg	50 kg
	15 kg	75 kg
Strong mortar	3 kg	9 kg
	12 kg	36 kg
	20 kg	60 kg

B. Direct proportion (p 57)

1. a. i. 300 ml milk   4 tsp caster sugar
          900 g plain flour   4 tsp dried yeast
          300 ml plain yoghurt 1 tsp salt
          2 eggs   2 tsp baking powder
                               4 tbls veg. oil

Answers

  ii. 75 mℓ milk   1 tsp caster sugar
  225 g plain flour   1 tsp dried yeast
  75 mℓ plain yoghurt $\frac{1}{4}$ tsp salt
  1 small egg $\frac{1}{2}$ tsp baking powder
      1 tbls veg. oil

  b. 50 mℓ milk, 150 g plain flour
  50 mℓ plain yoghurt

2. a. 8 teaspoons   b. 2 teaspoons
   c. 1 teaspoon
3. a. i. 500 mℓ (or 0.5 litres or $\frac{1}{2}$ litre)
      ii. 200 mℓ (or 0.2 litres or $\frac{1}{5}$ litre)
      iii. 100 mℓ (or 0.1 litres or $\frac{1}{10}$ litre)
   b. i. 2 litres water : 5000 g or 5 kg plaster
      ii. 4 litres water : 10 000 g or 10 kg plaster

Calculate with ratios

A. Simplify ratios and find amounts (p 59)

1. a. 2 : 1   b. 1 : 5   c. 14 : 1
   d. 1 : 5   e. 3 : 1
2. a. 1 : 4
   b. i. 12 litres   ii. 100 millilitres
3. a. 5 : 1
   b. i. 250 litres   ii. 60 litres
4. a. 2 : 3   b. 2 : 9   c. 4 : 1 : 6
   d. 2 : 3 : 5   e. 33 : 18 : 10
5. a. i. 1 : 4   ii. 400 mℓ
   b. i. 2 : 3   ii. 600 mℓ
6. a. i. 50 : 450 : 500 = 1 : 9 : 10
      ii. 720 mℓ moss, 800 mℓ leaf green
      iii. 200 mℓ white, 2000 mℓ (2 ℓ) leaf green
   b. i. 200 : 300 : 500 = 2 : 3 : 5
      ii. 120 mℓ beige, 200 mℓ chocolate brown
      iii. 120 mℓ white, 300 mℓ chocolate brown
      iv. 300 mℓ white, 450 mℓ beige
7. a. 1 : 25   b. 4 : 1   c. 1 : 20
   d. 8 : 1   e. 1 : 50   f. 5 : 1
8. a. 1 : 5   b. 1 litre   c. 250 mℓ
9. a. 1 : 2   b. 400 g   c. $1\frac{1}{4}$ kg
10. a. 1 : 50   b. 12 mm
    c. 4500 mm = 4.5 m
11. a. 3 : 100   b. 5 : 4   c. 1 : 14
    d. 13 : 4   e. 1 : 50 000 f. 5 : 1
    g. 1 : 2 : 9 h. 4 : 2 : 2 : 3
12. a. 50 : 4000 = 1 : 80
    b. 3200 mℓ or 3.2 ℓ   c. 30 mℓ
13. a. 1500 g : 400 g : 200 g = 15 : 4 : 2
    b. i. 150 g cereal, 40 g nuts
       ii. 160 g nuts, 80 g seeds
    c. i. 10 cm   ii. 5 cm   iii. 3 cm   iv. 1.5 cm

14. a. 500 m   b. 1 km

B. Make a total amount (p 63)

1. 15 black   30 white
2. a. 300 g oats   100 g fruit
   b. 750 g oats   250 g fruit
3. a. 600 g white   150 g brown
   b. 800 g white   200 g brown
4. a. 200 mℓ orange squash, 800 mℓ water
   b. 300 mℓ orange squash, 1200 mℓ water
5. a. 1 litre tangerine, 1 litre white, 3 litres buttercup
   b. 200 mℓ tangerine, 200 mℓ white, 600 mℓ buttercup
6. a. 12 : 5 : 3
   b. i. 480 g cereal, 200 g fruit, 120 g nuts
      ii. 1080 g cereal, 450 g fruit, 270 g nuts
7. a. 15 000 : 45 000 : 150 000
      1 : 3 : 10
   b. 30 red-haired, 90 blonde-haired and 300 dark-haired
8. a. 4000 : 10 000 : 16 000 = 2 : 5 : 8
   b. A £6000, B £15 000, C £24 000
   c. £75 000
   d. £187 500
   e. A £41 000, B £102 500, C £164 000

C. Use ratios to compare prices (p 65)

1. a. Pack of 9   b. 600 mℓ bottle
   c. 375 g box   d. 100 envelopes
   e. 24 tins
2. a. 0.5 tonne @ £27.50 = £55 per tonne
      1 tonne @ £52.50 = £52.50 per tonne
      5 tonnes @ £240 = £48 per tonne
      25 kg @ £2.75 = £110 per tonne
      40 kg @ £4.50 = £112.50 per tonne
      5 kg @ £5.50 = £500 per tonne
   b. £11   c. 24p

Inverse proportion (p 67)

1. 10 grapes
2. 50 bags
3. a. £40   b. £20
4. a. 20 mins   b. 10 mins
5. a. $1\frac{1}{2}$ hours (90 mins)   b. $\frac{1}{2}$ hour (30 mins)
6. a. $1\frac{1}{2}$ minutes (90 seconds)   b. 45 seconds
7. 140 minutes or 2 hours 20 minutes, assuming identical pumps
8. 12 days, assuming the crop is the same size and all workers pick at the same rate as last year
9. 1 extra labourer, assuming they all work at the same rate
10. £750 more, assuming that the same total investment is needed and they continue to contribute equally
11. 7 meals, assuming that everyone is given the same amount of rice at every meal

Answers

12. $2\frac{1}{2}$ minutes longer, assuming the relationship is inverse proportion

6 Using Algebra

Number patterns and formulae (p 70)

1. a. multiples of 4
   b. Cost = £4 × number of mugs
   c. £24
   d. Continue pattern (+ 4) giving £20, £24

2. a.
Number of hours	2	3	4	5
Cost (£)	40	55	70	85

   b. Total cost = £15 × number of hours + £10 (or Total cost = number of hours × £15 + £10)
   c. £130
   d. Continue sequence in table to give 6 hours £100, 7 hours £115, 8 hours £130

3. a.
Length of fencing (metres)	3	4	5	6
Total cost of the fencing and gate (£)		66	78	90	102

   b. Total cost = £12 × length of fence + £30
   c. £150
   d. Continue pattern (+ 12) giving £114, £126, £138, £150

4. a.
Number of weeks that Ian has been saving	1	2	3	4
Amount still to be saved (£)	240	200	160	120

   b. Each number is 40 less than the previous number.
   c. £0 Ian has now saved what he needs.
   d. Continue pattern (−40) giving £80, £40, £0

5. a.
Number of hours taken	1	2	3	4
Total cost (£)	67	92	117	142

   b. Each number is 25 more than the previous number
   c. Total cost = £42 + £25 × number of hours
   d. £242
   e. Continue pattern (+ 25) giving: £167, £192, £217, £242

Use simple formulae (p 71)

1. a. Number of delegates → Multiply by 15 → Add 75 → Cost in £
   b. i. £225 ii. £375 iii. £825
2. a. Number of kilograms → Multiply by 50 → Add 25 → Cooking time in minutes
   b. i. 125 mins (or 2 hrs 5 mins)
      ii. 150 mins (or $2\frac{1}{2}$ hours)
      iii. 65 mins (or 1 hour 5 mins)
3. a. Number of miles → Multiply by 1.6 → Add 8 → Fare in £
   b. i. £16 ii. £27.20 iii. £36
4. a. Number of customer accounts → Multiply by 7.5 → Add 340 → Weekly earnings in £
   b. i. £370 ii. £415 iii. £452.50
5. a. i. 90 bricks ii. 375 bricks
   b. Yes, because 6 × 0.8 × 60 = 288 bricks

Order of operations (BIDMAS) (p 73)

1. a. 8   b. 6   c. 68   d. 144
   e. 5   f. 27   g. 10   h. 72
   i. 22   j. 52   k. 100 l. −4
   m. 1   n. 21   o. 150
2. a. $(12 − 4) × 2 = 16$ b. $20 ÷ (5 − 3) = 10$
   c. $15 × (8 − 6) = 30$ d. $(6 + 6) ÷ (7 − 3) = 3$
   e. $(4 + 1)^2 = 25$ f. $(2 × 5)^2 = 100$
3. a. 100°C b. 20°C c. 80°C d. 0°C

Evaluate algebraic expressions and make substitutions in formulae (p 74)

1. a. $C = 50n + 25$
   b. i. £125 ii. £225 iii. £325
2. a. $P = 11t + 5n$
   b. i. £103 ii. £190 iii. £500
3. a. 50 metres   b. 27 metres
4. a. £114 000   b. £159 000
   c. £195 000   d. £278 850
5. 120 volts
6. a. 60 miles per hour
   b. 0.4 km per min
      (or 400 m per min or 24 km per hour)
7. a. $C = 28n + En + 10$ or $C = 10 + n(E + 28)$ or $C = n(E + 28) + 10$
   b. i. £109 ii. £185 iii. £298.75
8. a. 18 cm²   b. 68 cm²
   c. 10.5 cm² d. 285 cm²
9. a. 100°C   b. 25°C
10. a. 3 cm²   b. 27 cm²   c. 75 cm²
11. a. 24   b. 25   c. 25

7 Mixed Operations and Calculator Practice

Solve problems (p 78)

1. 576
2. £156
3. a. 786   b. 22
4. a. £468   b. £533
5. a. £895   b. £447.50
6. a. £153   b. £571
7. a. 270   b. 9
8. a. £992   b. £817

Answers

9. **a.** 33 boxes **b.** 5 bulbs
10. **a.** 5 × 5 litre tins and 1 × 2 litre tin
    b. 7 × 5 litre tins and 2 × 2 litre tins
    c. 25 × 5 litre tins, 1 × 2 litre tin and 1 × 1 litre tin
11. **a.** 4 packs of 10
    b. 1 pack of 50 and 1 pack of 25
    c. 5 packs of 50 and 1 pack of 25
    d. 7 packs of 50 and 1 pack of 10
12. **a.** £51 **b.** £175
13. **a.** 3 packs of 2 (one pack is free) £6
    b. 4 packs of 2 (one pack is free) £9
    c. 1 pack of 10 £10
    d. 6 packs of 2 (2 packs are free) £12
14. **a.** £65   2 × £25 and 1 × £15
    b. £100   1 × £25 and 5 × £15
    c. £90   1 × £75 and 1 × £15
    d. £200   8 × £25
    e. £180   2 × £75 and 2 × £15
    f. £190   2 × £75, 1 × £25, 1 × £15

Calculate efficiently (p 82)

1. **a.** Part-time receptionist by £440 a year
   b. Warehouse supervisor by £1080 a year
2. **a.** **i.** £488 **ii.** £1324 **iii.** £1776
   b. £292 **c.** £972
   d. **i.** 12 nights **ii.** 6 nights

Calculate efficiently with numbers of any size (p 83)

1. 55.6°C
2. £0.91 million
3. 25th Feb £582.81 out
   26th Feb £817.11 out
   27th Feb £2778.86 in
   28th Feb £2097.68 out
4. **a.** **i.** in debit   **ii.** £95.10
   b. **i.** in credit **ii.** £74.00
5. **a.**

Year	Profit (£)
2010	1 200 000
2011	700 000
2012	−300 000
2013	−550 000
2014	−100 000
2015	−1 000 000
2016	−500 000
2017	0
2018	500 000

   b. **i.** £2 200 000 **ii.** −£50 000

8 Fractions

Understand fractions

A. Fractions in words, numbers and sketches (p 85)

1. **a.** $\frac{2}{3}$ **b.** $\frac{1}{5}$ **c.** $\frac{3}{8}$ **d.** $\frac{5}{12}$
2. **a.** one half   **b.** one quarter
   c. three fifths   **d.** five sixths
   e. five eighths   **f.** seven ninths
3. **a.** $\frac{1}{4}$, one quarter   **b.** $\frac{1}{5}$, one fifth
   c. $\frac{1}{9}$, one ninth   **d.** $\frac{5}{6}$, five sixths
   e. $\frac{2}{3}$, two thirds   **f.** $\frac{5}{8}$, five eighths
   g. $\frac{4}{7}$, four sevenths **h.** $\frac{7}{12}$, seven twelfths
   i. $\frac{4}{9}$, four ninths

B. Shade fractions (p 86)

1. B, C
2. B, D
3. **a.** 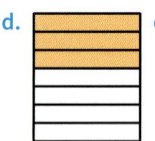 **b.** 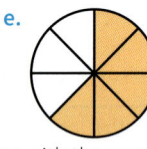 **c.**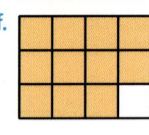
   d. **e.** **f.**

   or alternatives with the same number of sections shaded.
4. Fractions shown on students' own shapes
5. C does not have $\frac{3}{5}$ shaded as the parts are not equal sizes.

C. Read about fractions (p 87)

1. half $\frac{1}{2}$, one third $\frac{1}{3}$
2. quarter $\frac{1}{4}$, three quarters $\frac{3}{4}$, one and a half $1\frac{1}{2}$, half $\frac{1}{2}$
3. two thirds $\frac{2}{3}$, half $\frac{1}{2}$
4. one fifth $\frac{1}{5}$, two thirds $\frac{2}{3}$, three quarters $\frac{3}{4}$

Equivalent fractions

A. Use sketches (p 88)

1. **a.** $\frac{1}{2} = \frac{2}{4} = \frac{3}{6}$ **b.** $\frac{1}{5} = \frac{2}{10}$
   c. $\frac{3}{4} = \frac{6}{8} = \frac{9}{12}$ **d.** $\frac{3}{4} = \frac{12}{20}$
2. Students' own sketches

B. Use numerators and denominators (p 89)

1. **a.** True **b.** True **c.** False **d.** True
   e. True **f.** False **g.** False **h.** True

Answers

2. a. 15   b. 24   c. 4   d. 8
    e. 10   f. 3   g. 2   h. 4
3. a. Yes   b. No, $\frac{1}{5}$
4. Any 6 other fractions equal to $\frac{1}{2}$ (eg $\frac{4}{8}, \frac{5}{10}, \frac{6}{12}, \frac{7}{14}, \frac{8}{16}, \frac{9}{18}$)
5. a. Any 3 other fractions equal to $\frac{2}{8}$ (eg $\frac{1}{4}, \frac{4}{16}, \frac{6}{24}, \frac{8}{32}$)
    b. Any 3 other fractions equal to $\frac{2}{5}$ (eg $\frac{4}{10}, \frac{6}{15}, \frac{8}{20}, \frac{10}{25}$)
    c. Any 3 other fractions equal to $\frac{2}{6}$ (eg $\frac{1}{3}, \frac{4}{12}, \frac{6}{18}, \frac{8}{24}$)
    d. Any 3 other fractions equal to $\frac{4}{10}$ (eg $\frac{2}{5}, \frac{8}{20}, \frac{12}{30}, \frac{16}{40}$)
6. Yes, $\frac{12}{30} = \frac{2}{5}$
7. 2, 4, 5, 7, 11, 15, 20, 100
8. a. $\frac{6}{18}, \frac{4}{12}, \frac{5}{15}, \frac{2}{6}, \frac{3}{9}$ b. $\frac{6}{9}, \frac{8}{12}, \frac{4}{6}, \frac{12}{18}, \frac{10}{15}$
9. No, $\frac{15}{20} = \frac{3}{4}$ not $\frac{3}{5}$
10. a. $\frac{1}{5}$ — $\frac{9}{15}$; $\frac{3}{4}$ — $\frac{15}{18}$; $\frac{2}{5}$ — $\frac{15}{20}$; $\frac{5}{6}$ — $\frac{2}{10}$; $\frac{1}{3}$ — $\frac{5}{15}$; $\frac{3}{5}$ — $\frac{6}{15}$

    b. $\frac{3}{4}$ — $\frac{6}{24}$; $\frac{2}{3}$ — $\frac{4}{24}$; $\frac{1}{3}$ — $\frac{9}{24}$; $\frac{1}{4}$ — $\frac{9}{12}$; $\frac{3}{8}$ — $\frac{8}{12}$; $\frac{1}{6}$ — $\frac{8}{24}$

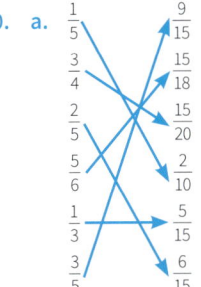

C. Write quantities as fractions (p 90)

1. a. $\frac{1}{2}$ cm   b. $\frac{2}{5}$ cm   c. $\frac{3}{5}$ cm
2. a. $\frac{1}{2}$ kg   b. $\frac{3}{4}$ kg   c. $\frac{1}{10}$ kg
    d. $\frac{1}{5}$ kg   e. $\frac{3}{5}$ kg
3. a. $\frac{1}{200}$ km   b. $\frac{1}{20}$ km   c. $\frac{1}{2}$ km
    d. $\frac{1}{10}$ km   e. $\frac{3}{20}$ km
4. a. $\frac{1}{50} \ell$ b. $\frac{1}{20} \ell$ c. $\frac{1}{5} \ell$
    d. $\frac{1}{2} \ell$ e. $\frac{2}{5} \ell$
5. a. $\frac{1}{5}$ m   b. $\frac{1}{2}$ m   c. $\frac{9}{10}$ m
    d. $\frac{4}{5}$ m   e. $\frac{1}{20}$ m   f. $\frac{1}{10}$ m
    g. $\frac{1}{5}$ m   h. $\frac{2}{5}$ m   i. $\frac{3}{5}$ m
    j. $\frac{1}{50}$ m

Compare fractions

A. Compare unit fractions (p 91)

1. a. $\frac{1}{8}$ b. $\frac{1}{10}$ c. $\frac{1}{20}$ d. $\frac{1}{12}$
2. a. $\frac{1}{20}$ b. $\frac{1}{17}$ c. $\frac{1}{5}$ d. $\frac{1}{11}$
3. $\frac{1}{20}, \frac{1}{15}, \frac{1}{12}, \frac{1}{10}, \frac{1}{6}, \frac{1}{5}, \frac{1}{4}, \frac{1}{3}, \frac{1}{2}$
4. $\frac{1}{7}, \frac{1}{8}, \frac{1}{9}, \frac{1}{11}, \frac{1}{13}, \frac{1}{14}, \frac{1}{16}, \frac{1}{17}, \frac{1}{21}$

B. Use fraction walls (p 92)

1. a. 2   b. 4   c. 8   d. 6
    e. 12   f. 6   g. 10   h. 1

2. a. $\frac{5}{16}, \frac{3}{8}, \frac{7}{16}$ b. $\frac{1}{2}, \frac{9}{16}, \frac{5}{8}$ c. $\frac{3}{4}, \frac{13}{16}, \frac{7}{8}$
3. a. 5, 10   b. 5   c. 2   d. 4
    e. 6   f. 10
4. $\frac{9}{10}, \frac{4}{5}, \frac{7}{10}, \frac{3}{5}, \frac{1}{2}, \frac{2}{5}, \frac{3}{10}, \frac{1}{5}, \frac{1}{10}$
5. a. $\frac{3}{4}$ b. $\frac{1}{2}$ c. $\frac{2}{5}$ (with sketches)
6. a. $\frac{1}{2}$ b. $\frac{3}{5}$ c. $\frac{3}{4}$ (with sketches)
7. Emma is wrong: $\frac{3}{7}$ is less than $\frac{1}{2}$, $\frac{3}{7} = \frac{6}{14}$ and $\frac{1}{2} = \frac{7}{14}$. $\frac{6}{14}$ is less than $\frac{7}{14}$.

C. Put fractions in order using a common denominator (p 93)

1. a. $\frac{2}{3}$ b. $\frac{7}{9}$ c. $\frac{9}{10}$
2. a. $\frac{2}{5}, \frac{3}{5}, \frac{4}{5}$ b. $\frac{1}{7}, \frac{2}{7}, \frac{4}{7}, \frac{5}{7}$ c. $\frac{1}{9}, \frac{2}{9}, \frac{4}{9}, \frac{5}{9}, \frac{8}{9}$
3. a. $\frac{1}{4}$ b. $\frac{3}{5}$ c. $\frac{3}{4}$ d. $\frac{4}{7}$
4. a. $\frac{3}{8}, \frac{1}{2}, \frac{5}{8}$ b. $\frac{1}{4}, \frac{3}{10}, \frac{2}{5}$
    c. $\frac{5}{16}, \frac{1}{2}, \frac{3}{4}, \frac{7}{8}$ d. $\frac{2}{3}, \frac{3}{4}, \frac{5}{6}, \frac{11}{12}$
    e. $\frac{3}{7}, \frac{1}{2}, \frac{5}{7}, \frac{3}{4}$ f. $\frac{1}{4}, \frac{1}{3}, \frac{3}{8}, \frac{5}{12}, \frac{1}{2}$
5. a. $\frac{4}{7}, \frac{1}{2}, \frac{2}{7}$ b. $\frac{5}{6}, \frac{2}{3}, \frac{5}{9}$
    c. $\frac{3}{4}, \frac{2}{3}, \frac{1}{2}, \frac{4}{9}$ d. $\frac{9}{10}, \frac{13}{15}, \frac{4}{5}, \frac{2}{3}$
    e. $\frac{5}{8}, \frac{7}{12}, \frac{5}{9}, \frac{4}{9}$ f. $\frac{13}{15}, \frac{11}{15}, \frac{7}{10}, \frac{2}{3}, \frac{3}{5}, \frac{2}{9}$

Mixed numbers and improper fractions (p 94)

1. a. $1\frac{1}{2} = \frac{3}{2}$ b. $1\frac{4}{5} = \frac{9}{5}$
    c. $2\frac{3}{10} = \frac{23}{10}$ d. $3\frac{5}{6} = \frac{23}{6}$
    e. $1\frac{7}{9} = \frac{16}{9}$ f. $2\frac{3}{8} = \frac{19}{8}$
2. Mixed numbers and improper fractions on students' own shapes
3. a. Mixed numbers and fractions on students' own shapes
    b. $\frac{5}{8}, \frac{3}{4}, \frac{7}{8}, 1\frac{1}{4}, 1\frac{3}{8}, 1\frac{1}{2}, 2\frac{1}{2}$
4. a. $\frac{3}{4}, 1\frac{1}{2}, 1\frac{3}{5}, 2\frac{1}{3}, 2\frac{2}{5}$
    b. $\frac{4}{7}, \frac{5}{8}, 1\frac{7}{12}, 1\frac{3}{4}, 1\frac{5}{6}$
    c. $\frac{4}{9}, \frac{5}{7}, 1\frac{3}{4}, 2\frac{3}{7}, 2\frac{1}{2}, 2\frac{2}{3}$
    d. $\frac{1}{4}, 1\frac{5}{8}, 1\frac{2}{3}, 1\frac{5}{6}, 1\frac{11}{12}, 2\frac{1}{8}$

Find or estimate fractions (p 96)

1. a. i. $\frac{1}{2}$ ii. $\frac{1}{2}$ b. i. $\frac{1}{3}$ ii. $\frac{2}{3}$
    c. i. $\frac{3}{4}$ ii. $\frac{1}{4}$
2. a. $\frac{4}{5}$ full   b. $\frac{3}{5}$ full   c. $\frac{2}{5}$ full
3. a. $\frac{1}{2}$ full   b. $\frac{2}{3}$ full   c. $\frac{3}{4}$ full
4. a. $\frac{3}{5}$ left   b. $\frac{1}{3}$ left   c. $\frac{1}{5}$ left
5. a. i. $\frac{1}{4}$ ii. $\frac{3}{4}$ b. i. $\frac{1}{3}$ ii. $\frac{2}{3}$
    c. i. $\frac{2}{3}$ ii. $\frac{1}{3}$

427

Answers

Calculate a fraction of something

A. By dividing when the numerator is 1 (p 98)
1. a. £28   b. 24 cm   c. £156
   d. £99   e. £204   f. £91
   g. 72 m   h. £47
2. 12
3. a. £15   b. £30
4. a. 14   b. 56
5. 15 litres
6. £85
7. a. 3500   b. 17 500
8. a. 125 g   b. 875 g

B. Find more than one part (p 99)
1. a. £630   b. £104   c. 30 m
   d. 150 g   e. 350 cm   f. £460
   g. £1800   h. 1460 kg
2. 240
3. 18
4. £33 750
5. 31 050
6. 165
7. £5750
8. 360 000

C. Estimate to check answers (p 100)
1. A, B, E, F, H are wrong.
2. A 19   B 76   E 297
   F 450   H 192

D. Other methods (p 100)
1. a. £1140   b. 42 kg   c. 324 m
2. a. Students' own sketches
   b. i. £480   ii. £120   iii. £600
3. a. Students' own sketches
   b. i. 64 m   ii. 32 m   iii. 96 m
4. a. Students' own sketches
   b. i. £3600   ii. £2400   iii. £6000
   c. 1200

E. Scale up and down (p 101)
1. a. 180 g potatoes, 300 g leeks,
      500 mℓ milk, 100 mℓ stock
   b. 360 g potatoes, 600 g leeks,
      1 ℓ or 1000 mℓ milk, 200 mℓ stock
2. a. $\frac{3}{4}$
   b. 300 g nuts, 150 g breadcrumbs, 180 g tomatoes,
      3 onions
3. a. $\frac{4}{5}$
   b. 240 g flour, 128 g sugar, 112 g butter,
      48 g ground almonds
4. a. 3 loaves, 600 g butter, 6 tomatoes,
      $1\frac{1}{2}$ cucumbers, 300 g paté, 225 g chicken,
      375 g cheese, $\frac{3}{4}$ lettuce
   b. 5 loaves, 1 kg or 1000 g butter,
      10 tomatoes, $2\frac{1}{2}$ cucumbers, 500 g paté,
      375 g chicken, 625 g cheese, $1\frac{1}{4}$ lettuce

One number as a fraction of another

A. Simplest form (p 103)
1. $\frac{2}{5}$ 2. $\frac{3}{4}$ 3. $\frac{1}{3}$ 4. $\frac{2}{5}$ 5. $\frac{4}{5}$
6. $\frac{2}{3}$ 7. $\frac{1}{2}$ 8. $\frac{3}{4}$ 9. $\frac{1}{3}$ 10. $\frac{3}{4}$
11. $\frac{1}{5}$ 12. $\frac{3}{10}$ 13. $\frac{2}{3}$ 14. $\frac{3}{7}$ 15. $\frac{3}{5}$

B. Write one quantity as a fraction of another (p 104)
1. a. $\frac{1}{4}$h   b. $\frac{1}{3}$h   c. $\frac{4}{5}$h
2. a. $\frac{1}{10}$kg   b. $\frac{3}{4}$kg   c. $\frac{2}{5}$kg   d. $\frac{16}{25}$kg
3. a. $\frac{3}{10}$cℓ   b. $\frac{1}{2}$cℓ   c. $\frac{1}{5}$cℓ   d. $\frac{2}{5}$cℓ   e. $\frac{3}{5}$cℓ
4. a. $\frac{1}{20}$kg   b. $\frac{1}{2}$g   c. $\frac{1}{4}$kg   d. $\frac{1}{4}$g   e. $\frac{1}{5}$kg
5. a. $\frac{1}{2}$lb   b. $\frac{1}{4}$lb   c. $\frac{3}{4}$lb   d. $\frac{3}{8}$lb
6. $\frac{2}{3}$ 7. $\frac{1}{5}$ 8. $\frac{3}{5}$ 9. $\frac{11}{18}$
10. a.

	Men	Women	Total
Car	240	300	540
Bus	120	270	390
Train	80	100	180
Cycle	15	10	25
Walk	25	40	65
Total	480	720	1200

   b. i. Men: Car $\frac{1}{2}$ Bus $\frac{1}{4}$ Train $\frac{1}{6}$
                 Cycle $\frac{1}{32}$ Walk $\frac{5}{96}$
      ii. Women: Car $\frac{5}{12}$ Bus $\frac{3}{8}$ Train $\frac{5}{36}$
                    Cycle $\frac{1}{72}$ Walk $\frac{1}{18}$
   c. i. $\frac{2}{5}$ ii. $\frac{3}{5}$

C. Estimate one quantity as a fraction of another (p 105)
1. a. $\frac{1}{4}$ b. $\frac{3}{4}$
2. a. i. $\frac{5}{6}$ ii. $\frac{4}{5}$
   b. both are 200, giving 1
3. a. i. $\frac{3}{4}$ ii. $\frac{2}{3}$
   b. aii
4. a. i. $\frac{1}{10}$ ii. $\frac{1}{60}$ iii. $\frac{1}{30}$ iv. $\frac{7}{8}$
   b. i. $\frac{5}{8}$ ii. $\frac{3}{8}$
5. a. ii. $\frac{3}{4}$ b. $\frac{1}{4}$
   Note: Other answers are possible.
6. a. 141 200 000
   b. i. $\frac{2}{7}$ ii. $\frac{3}{14}$ iii. $\frac{3}{7}$ iv. $\frac{1}{14}$
7. Paper and cardboard $\frac{1}{2}$, glass $\frac{1}{4}$, metal $\frac{1}{10}$, plastic $\frac{1}{7}$,
   wood $\frac{1}{20}$

Answers

Add and subtract fractions

A. Add and subtract fractions with the same denominator (p 107)

1. $\frac{4}{5}$
2. $\frac{2}{5}$
3. 1
4. $\frac{2}{3}$
5. $\frac{5}{7}$
6. $\frac{3}{7}$
7. $\frac{1}{2}$
8. $\frac{2}{3}$
9. $\frac{4}{5}$
10. 1
11. $\frac{2}{5}$
12. $\frac{1}{2}$
13. a. $\frac{3}{5}$ b. $\frac{2}{5}$
14. a. $\frac{3}{8}$ b. $\frac{1}{4}$

B. Add and subtract fractions with different denominators (p 109)

1. $\frac{7}{10}$
2. $\frac{1}{2}$
3. $\frac{5}{6}$
4. $\frac{1}{3}$
5. $\frac{11}{12}$
6. $\frac{7}{20}$
7. $\frac{1}{8}$
8. $\frac{8}{9}$
9. $\frac{4}{15}$
10. $\frac{19}{21}$
11. $\frac{11}{15}$
12. $\frac{3}{10}$
13. $\frac{3}{4}$
14. $\frac{9}{40}$
15. $\frac{29}{30}$
16. $\frac{1}{18}$
17. $\frac{17}{36}$
18. $\frac{3}{20}$
19. 0
20. $\frac{7}{8}$
21. a. $\frac{3}{4}$ b. $\frac{1}{4}$

C. Improper fractions and mixed numbers (p 110)

1. $1\frac{4}{5}$
2. $2\frac{3}{5}$
3. $4\frac{1}{3}$
4. $5\frac{2}{3}$
5. $3\frac{3}{4}$
6. $4\frac{1}{2}$
7. $6\frac{1}{2}$
8. $1\frac{3}{7}$
9. $5\frac{1}{4}$
10. $2\frac{5}{6}$
11. $6\frac{1}{3}$
12. $6\frac{3}{5}$
13. $2\frac{7}{8}$
14. $3\frac{7}{10}$
15. $4\frac{4}{9}$
16. $1\frac{1}{3}$
17. $1\frac{1}{7}$
18. $1\frac{5}{8}$
19. $1\frac{1}{6}$
20. $1\frac{1}{2}$
21. $1\frac{9}{28}$
22. $1\frac{1}{5}$
23. $2\frac{5}{24}$

D. Add and subtract mixed numbers (p 111)

1. $\frac{3}{2}$
2. $\frac{5}{2}$
3. $\frac{7}{2}$
4. $\frac{5}{3}$
5. $\frac{8}{3}$
6. $\frac{11}{5}$
7. $\frac{19}{5}$
8. $\frac{13}{6}$
9. $\frac{11}{6}$
10. $\frac{19}{8}$
11. $\frac{17}{7}$
12. $\frac{47}{8}$
13. $\frac{49}{10}$
14. $\frac{31}{9}$
15. $\frac{44}{7}$
16. $2\frac{3}{4}$
17. $\frac{17}{20}$
18. $5\frac{1}{3}$
19. $1\frac{5}{12}$
20. $8\frac{1}{8}$
21. $2\frac{5}{6}$
22. $\frac{19}{20}$
23. $6\frac{1}{10}$
24. $3\frac{13}{15}$
25. $6\frac{1}{14}$
26. $7\frac{1}{4}$
27. $1\frac{1}{8}$
28. 3 hours
29. $4\frac{1}{4}$ pounds
30. a. $15\frac{1}{2}$ hours b. $1\frac{1}{4}$ hours c. $2\frac{3}{4}$ hours

Multiply fractions (p 113)

1. $\frac{1}{10}$
2. $\frac{1}{21}$
3. $\frac{2}{9}$
4. $\frac{4}{7}$
5. $\frac{6}{11}$
6. $\frac{1}{10}$
7. $\frac{1}{2}$
8. $\frac{7}{10}$
9. Yes
10. $\frac{1}{3} \times \frac{1}{4} = \frac{1}{12}$ and $\frac{1}{2} \times \frac{1}{6} = \frac{1}{12}$
11. $1\frac{2}{3}$
12. $1\frac{4}{5}$
13. $1\frac{1}{4}$
14. $\frac{2}{3}$
15. 3
16. $4\frac{1}{2}$
17. $10\frac{1}{2}$
18. $5\frac{5}{7}$
19. $1\frac{2}{3}$ kg
20. a. $2\frac{2}{5}$ m b. $1\frac{3}{5}$ m c. $\frac{4}{5}$ m $\frac{1}{6} \times \frac{24}{5} = \frac{24}{30} = \frac{4}{5}$

Divide fractions (p 115)

1. 3
2. $\frac{1}{2}$
3. 4
4. 2
5. $\frac{3}{4}$
6. $\frac{7}{10}$
7. $\frac{5}{6}$
8. $1\frac{11}{24}$
9. 8
10. $\frac{6}{9} = \frac{2}{3}$ (cancelling by 3) and $\frac{2}{3} \div \frac{1}{9} = \frac{2}{3} \times \frac{9}{1} = \frac{18}{3} = 6$
11. 10
12. $\frac{1}{2}$
13. $3\frac{3}{4}$
14. $\frac{5}{8}$
15. $1\frac{17}{18}$
16. $1\frac{5}{7}$
17. $\frac{2}{3}$
18. $2\frac{19}{28}$
19. 6
20. 8

9 Decimals

Understand decimals in context (up to 2 decimal places) (p 118)

1. a. 0.4 cm b. 2.5 cm c. 4.1 cm
   d. 5.6 cm e. 7.8 cm f. 10.3 cm
   g. 12.5 cm h. 15.2 cm i. 17.9 cm
   j. 20.6 cm k. 21.4 cm l. 23.7 cm
2. a. 2.5 cm, 2.4 cm, 2.1 cm, 1.9 cm, 1.8 cm
   b. 4.5 cm, 4.3 cm, 4.1 cm, 3.9 cm, 3.8 cm, 3.4 cm
   c. 11.1 cm, 10.7 cm, 10.6 cm, 10.5 cm, 9.9 cm, 9.6 cm
   d. 6.4 m, 6.2 m, 6.1 m, 5.8 m, 5.7 m, 5.5 m, 5.3 m, 5.1 m
   e. 2.9 km, 2.3 km, 2.1 km, 1.8 km, 1.7 km, 1.4 km, 1.2 km, 0.9 km
3. a. 100p b. 218p c. 109p
   d. 407p e. 62p f. 824p
   g. 570p h. 904p i. 1017p
   j. 1640p
4. a. £2.13 b. £4.02 c. £0.85
   d. £3.50 e. £1.03 f. £6.00
   g. £7.25 h. £9.37 i. £10.00
   j. £24.09
5. a. £1.02 £1.19 £1.21 £1.37
      £1.46 £1.87 £2.07
   b. £47.20 £56.78 £63.02
      £63.21 £66.18 £74.02
   c. £10.07 £10.08 £10.70
      £11.01 £11.17 £11.91
6. a. 22 cm b. 107 cm c. 173 cm
   d. 74 cm e. 133 cm f. 112 cm
   g. 115 cm h. 67 cm i. 260 cm
   j. 540 cm
7. a. 1.54 m b. 3.15 m c. 0.94 m
   d. 1.2 m e. 7.62 m f. 4.02 m
   g. 0.7 m h. 2.5 m i. 11.34 m
   j. 22.3 m

Answers

8. a. 1.5 m, 1.55 m, 1.63 m, 1.67 m, 1.72 m, 1.74 m, 1.8 m
   b. 1.26 m, 1.28 m, 1.3 m, 1.31 m, 1.32 m, 1.39 m, 1.4 m
   c. 0.72 m, 0.84 m, 0.88 m, 0.99 m, 1.01 m, 1.02 m, 1.03 m
9. a. i. 1.5 m ii. 7.5 m iii. 10.5 m
   b. i. $2\frac{1}{2}$ m ii. $6\frac{1}{2}$ m iii. $15\frac{1}{2}$ m

Write and compare decimals up to 3 decimal places

A. Place value (p 122)

1. a.

Hundreds 100s	Tens 10s	Units 1s	.	Tenths 10ths	Hundredths 100ths	Thousandths 1000ths
	1	6	.	7	4	
	3	7	.	5	4	
	1	2	.	0	6	
		4	.	5	2	
5	3	6	.	0	9	
5	0	6	.	9	2	6
	6	7	.	3	5	4
1	2	7	.	0	6	3
1	0	7	.	4	0	1
2	3	1	.	0	7	9
6	1	9	.	1	0	2
4	2	3	.	0	7	3

b. i. $\frac{7}{10}$ ii. $\frac{4}{100}$ iii. 2
   iv. $\frac{5}{10}$ v. 500 vi. $\frac{6}{1000}$
   vii. $\frac{5}{100}$ viii. $\frac{3}{1000}$ ix. $\frac{4}{10}$
   x. $\frac{9}{1000}$ xi. 600; $\frac{1}{10}$ xii. 20; $\frac{3}{1000}$

2.

Hundreds 100s	Tens 10s	Units 1s	.	Tenths 10ths	Hundredths 100ths	Thousandths 1000ths
	5	7	.	3	2	
		6	.	9		
	1	2	.	4	1	
1	0	0	.	3	5	
	9	6	.	0	7	
	1	2	.	5	0	6
4	9	7	.	6	4	3

3. a. $\frac{7}{10}$ b. $\frac{6}{100}$ c. $\frac{3}{1000}$ d. $\frac{4}{100}$
   e. $3\frac{5}{100}$ f. $6\frac{4}{10}$ g. $15\frac{7}{1000}$ h. $8\frac{2}{100}$
   i. $10\frac{6}{10}$ j. $240\frac{9}{1000}$

4. a. $\frac{1}{10} + \frac{7}{100}, \frac{17}{100}$
   b. $\frac{4}{10} + \frac{9}{100}, \frac{49}{100}$
   c. $\frac{3}{100} + \frac{1}{1000}, \frac{31}{1000}$
   d. $\frac{3}{10} + \frac{5}{100} + \frac{7}{1000}, \frac{357}{1000}$
   e. $6 + \frac{2}{10} + \frac{3}{100}, 6\frac{23}{100}$
   f. $8 + \frac{4}{100} + \frac{3}{1000}, 8\frac{43}{1000}$
   g. $42 + \frac{1}{10} + \frac{7}{1000}, 42\frac{107}{1000}$
   h. $1 + \frac{2}{10} + \frac{4}{100} + \frac{1}{1000}, 1\frac{241}{1000}$
   i. $502 + \frac{6}{10} + \frac{9}{100}, 502\frac{69}{100}$
   j. $17 + \frac{6}{10} + \frac{5}{100} + \frac{3}{1000}, 17\frac{653}{1000}$

B. Write decimals as common fractions (p 123)

1. $\frac{1}{2}$ 2. $\frac{1}{5}$ 3. $\frac{2}{5}$ 4. $\frac{3}{5}$ 5. $\frac{4}{5}$
6. $\frac{3}{20}$ 7. $\frac{7}{20}$ 8. $\frac{11}{20}$ 9. $\frac{1}{4}$ 10. $\frac{9}{20}$

C. Put decimals in order of size (p 124)

1. a. 7.21, 7.11, 6.76, 6.12, 5.98, 5.03, 5.02, 4.68, 4.32
   b. 14.26, 14.21, 13.1, 13.03, 12.97, 12.5, 12.43, 12.07
   c. 26.47, 26.42, 26.11, 25.17, 25.06, 21.8, 21.5, 21.43
   d. 7.84, 7.21, 6.96, 6.48, 5.74, 4.06, 3.5, 3.21, 3.19
2. a. 0.003, 0.23, 0.307, 1.05, 1.075, 1.11, 1.761
   b. 12.005, 12.05, 12.121, 12.429, 12.5, 12.502
   c. 19.006, 19.16, 19.375, 20.095, 21.101, 21.35
   d. 412.438, 428.003, 483.562, 581.098, 581.879, 604.002
3. a. 2.032 kg, 2.009 kg, 1.762 kg, 1.104 kg, 1.045 kg
   b. 1.707 kg, 1.7 kg, 1.077 kg, 1.07 kg, 1.007 kg
   c. 0.405 kg, 0.318 kg, 0.201 kg, 0.058 kg, 0.041 kg
4. a. 11.099, 11.909, 12.009, 12.037, 12.056, 12.201
   b. 18.302, 18.411, 18.567, 18.591, 19.002, 19.041
   c. 25.021, 25.072, 25.503, 25.601, 26.001, 26.057

Use a calculator to solve problems (p 125)

1. a. 14.05 b. £4.76 c. 2 m
   d. 10.7 e. £3.71 f. £8.81
   g. 4.5 m h. 21.86 i. 15.09
   j. £1.53 or £1.54 k. 1 kg l. £28.60
   m. 2.15 (2dp) n. £0.78 (2dp) o. 20
   p. 6.75
2. £11.70 3. £5.37 4. £28
5. a. 5.25 m b. 0.3 m
6. £29.10 7. £8.76 8. £4.26

Multiply and divide decimals by 10, 100 and 1000 (p 127)

1. a. 174 b. 563 c. 17 200
   d. 117.43 e. 16 010 f. 11 220
2. a. 5.622 b. 0.6304 c. 0.0144
   d. 10.201 e. 0.0574 f. 0.106
3. a. 261.1 b. 0.577 c. 104
   d. 1.21 e. 47 200 f. 0.56602

4. a. 300 mm b. 370 cm c. 1.45 m
   d. 4.5 cm e. 345p f. £7.89
   g. 66 cm h. 0.65 litres i. 1.567 kg
   j. 1.8 cm k. 600 m l. 7.58 km
5. a. 7500 g — 2.3 m
      230 cm — 0.75 ℓ
      2300 g — 7.5 kg
      75 cℓ — 1.25 ℓ
      125 cℓ — 2.3 kg
   b. 0.5 m — 750 g
      1.2 ℓ — 5 mℓ
      0.75 kg — 50 cm
      1.2 cm — 120 cℓ
      0.5 cℓ — 12 mm

Round decimal numbers and approximate (p 128)

1. a. 15 b. 13 c. 7 d. 4
   e. 10 f. 6 g. 16 h. 12
   i. 10 j. 12 k. 15 l. 1
   m. 4 n. 6 o. 0 p. 27
   q. 250 r. 100
2. £15 3. 6 m 4. £6 5. 6 kg 6. £14.50
7. a. 5.68 b. 16.59 c. 11.33
   d. 21.90 e. 155.79 f. 16.22
   g. 131.08 h. 6.75 i. 121.90
   j. 1.89 k. 2.40 l. 16.71
   m. 15.92 n. 13.56 o. 1.01
8. a. £1.27 b. 2.73 kg c. £12.16
   d. 17.42 m e. 22.57 km f. 14.73 g
   g. 16.19 cm h. £9.64 i. 0.47 ℓ
   j. 15.10 km
9. a. £15 b. 14 kg c. 5.11 litres
   d. £31.57 e. £7.17 f. 6.60 m
10. a. 9.5 b. 12.4 c. 13.2
    d. 6.7 e. 121.8 f. 5.7
    g. 91.8 h. 151.9 i. 65.1
    j. 73.6
11. a. £7.36 b. 6.2 kg c. 4.75 m
    d. £123.69 e. 9.2 litres
12. a. 5.792 b. 16.938 c. 3.749
    d. 0.974 e. 4.032 f. 16.770
    g. 12.081 h. 27.901 i. 1.550
    j. 17.700
13. 1.609 km 14. 0.568 litres

Add and subtract decimals (p 131)

1. a. 9.1 kg b. 2.8 m c. 23.36 cm
   d. £22.67 e. £7.77 f. £30.54
   g. £127.16 h. 1.35 m i. 163.16 km
   j. £1.05 k. 127.57 kg l. £156.54
2. £136.86 3. £882.81 4. £6.51
5. £86.35 6. 150.25 m 7. £415.41
8. 309 m
9. a. Team A 91.13 seconds, Team B 90.78 seconds
   b. Team B by 0.35 seconds
10. £244.67
11. £1927.61
12. a. 10.491 b. 6.315 c. 4.129
13. 16.116 seconds

Decimal sequences (p 133)

1. a. Add 0.2; 2.2, 2.4, 2.6 b. Add 0.2; 3.7, 3.9, 4.1
   c. Add 0.05; 1.8, 1.85, 1.9 d. Add 1.1; 6.6, 7.7, 8.8
   e. Add 0.3; 1.7, 2, 2.3 f. Add 0.05 0.3, 0.35, 0.4
   g. Subtract 0.5; 7.5, 7, 6.5 h. Subtract 0.2; 3, 2.8, 2.6
   i. Subtract 0.01; 1.91, 1.9, 1.89
   j. Subtract 0.1; 10.1, 10, 9.9
2. a. 0.95 m b. 1.85 m
3. a.

Number of cakes tied with ribbon	Length of remaining ribbon (metres)
0	5
1	4.4
2	3.8
3	3.2
4	2.6
5	2
6	1.4
7	0.8
8	0.2

   b. 8 cakes c. 0.2 m

4. a.

Number of glasses	Amount of remaining lemonade (litres)
0	2
1	1.7
2	1.4
3	1.1
4	0.8
5	0.5
6	0.2

   b. 6 c. 0.2 litres

Multiply decimals (p 134)

1. a. 2.4 b. 0.02 c. 0.35
   d. 0.12 e. 14.6 f. 59.1
   g. 5.61 h. 14.85 i. 32.56
   j. 5.14 (to 2 dp) k. 10.52 (to 2 dp)
   l. 1.24 (to 2 dp) m. 37.89 (to 2 dp)
   n. 8.02 (to 2 dp) o. 66.25 (to 2 dp)
   p. 13.05 (to 2 dp)
2. 15 m 3. 4.5 litres 4. £335.63 (2dp)

answers

5.

Order No	Item description	Price of item	Quantity	Price
PHF/1357	A4 paper	£4.99	5	£24.95
PHF/1359	A3 paper	£8.75	3	£26.25
ZL/129	Box black pens	£3.59	8	£28.72
FL/376	White board pens	£3.02	6	£18.12
GH/76P	Chrome stapler	£6.50	3	£19.50
GH/76L	Staples	£1.49	12	£17.88
		Total cost of all items		£135.42

6. 1238 m²
7. a. 29.8 b. 1.6776 c. 22.3987
8. 107915.2 yen
9. 35.5 m³ (to 1 dp)
10. 10.1 m, 8.0 m²

Divide decimals (p 136)

1. a. 12.3   b. 11.26   c. 15.98
   d. 33.21 e. 15.32   f. 11.18
   g. 141.02 h. 37.6425
2. a. 4   b. 3   c. 20   d. 2
   e. 130 f. 34 g. 26.5 h. 360
   i. 62.5 j. 48.57 (to 2 dp)
   k. 1236 l. 36 m. 18.35 (to 2 dp)
   n. 17 o. 960 p. 140
   q. 5.23 (to 2 dp) r. 15.19 (to 2 dp)
   s. 3.11 (to 2 dp) t. 47
3. 1.2 mm per day 4. £5.50
5. 50 6. 6060
7. a. 1940 b. 31.5 c. 19.2 d. 113.6
8. £15 9. £154
10. a. 32.02 b. 7.20 c. 13.76
    d. 5.68   e. 41.17 f. 12.56
    g. 12.45 h. 3.91   i. 21.62
11. a. £97.84 b. £65.23 12. 9 rolls

10 Percentages
Understand percentages (p 139)

1. black = 19%, orange = 21%,
   grey = 17%, white = 43%
2. a. 34 squares red   16 squares green
      21 squares blue 19 squares black
   b. 10% are not coloured
3. a. 20% b. 45% c. 16% d. 85%
4. a. 17p b. 99p c. 22p d. 51p
5. a. 20p b. 30p c. 50p
   d. £1 (or 100p)
6. a. 40p b. 60p c. £1 or (100p)
   d. £2 (or 200p)

Find percentages of quantities
A. Find 50%, 25% and 75% (p 141)

1. a. 125 g plain flour, 60 g butter, 45 g sugar,
      140 g blackberries, 100 g red currants,
      75 g strawberries
   b. 2 people
2. a. £80   b. 25 m   c. 48 km
   d. £22.50 e. 390 kg f. 450 g
3. £60   4. 45 m
5. a. £15   b. 23 m   c. 3.2 m
   d. £6.20 e. 192 m   f. 49 cm
   g. £37.50 h. £6.85   i. 3.85 kg
   j. 24.75 m k. 11.25 km l. £1.65
6. a. £135   b. 72 m   c. 270°
   d. 390 m e. 132 kg f. £27.30
   g. £9.60 h. 93 cm   i. 3.6 m
   j. 13.86 kg k. 15.45 g l. £55.65
7. Students' checks on 3 parts of question 6
8. 75 tickets   9. 45 seats
10. a. 80   b. 240
11. 360 blue tiles
12. a. £467.50 b. £1402.50
13. £10.74   14. £2.4 million

B. Use 10% (p 143)

1. a. £45   b. 9 m   c. £240
   d. 5.4 cm e. 6.2 kg f. 32.5 m
   g. 42p   h. 80p   i. £2.37
   j. £10.50 k. 0.28 tonnes l. 0.07 km
2. a. £24   b. 51 kg   c. 336 g
   d. 384 m e. 10.8 kg f. £6
   g. £3.60 h. £114.80 i. £44.24
   j. 72.8 m k. 12.78 kg l. 11.1 km
3. a. 4 kg   b. £640   c. £2.25
   d. £3.12 e. 21.8 m f. 3.64 litres
   g. £6.48 h. 0.475 km
4. £32 990   5. £1290
6. £78.75   7. £67.35
8. £206.50   9. 351 rolls   10. £829.60
11. Thea 25% = £160 so $12\frac{1}{2}\% = £160 \div 2 = £80$
    Jack 10% = £64, 5% = £32, $2\frac{1}{2}\% = £16$ so
    $12\frac{1}{2}\% = £64 + £16 = £80$

C. Use 1% (p 145)

1. a. 5   b. 6.3 km   c. 8.94 g
   d. 30p   e. £4.80   f. 26 p
2. a. 12   b. £16.20   c. 2.4 km
   d. £1.50 e. 1.05 kg f. 51 p
3. a. 280   b. 18 m   c. 30 g
   d. 3.8 km e. £14.40   f. £1.28

Answers

4. a. 35 b. 112 kg c. 6.3 litres
   d. £1.75 e. 28.35 cm f. £6.23
5. a. 180 b. £65.70 c. 10.8 m
   d. 6.3 kg e. 6.75 litres f. £5.58

Equivalent fractions, decimals and percentages

A. Convert between percentages and decimals (p 146)

1. a. 0.25 b. 0.35 c. 0.4
   d. 0.3 e. 0.8 f. 0.05
   g. 0.1 h. 0.15 i. 0.04
   j. 0.08 k. 0.55 l. 0.85
2. a. 0.16 b. 0.32 c. 0.49
   d. 0.95 e. 0.64 f. 0.52
   g. 0.175 h. 0.625 i. 0.378
   j. 0.036 k. 0.025 l. 0.0125
3. a. 75% b. 25% c. 65%
   d. 60% e. 6% f. 10%
   g. 1% h. 50% i. 5%
   j. 90% k. 9% l. 99%
4. a. 29% b. 57% c. 43%
   d. 150% e. 250% f. 87.5%
   g. 32.5% h. 6.5% i. 0.5%
   j. 20.5% k. 16.8% l. 245%
5. a. 0.013, 0.045, 12.5%, 15%, 0.9
   b. 0.098, 0.1, 11%, 0.65, 75%
   c. 0.018, 0.202, 22%, 33.3%, 0.4
   d. 0.5%, 0.006, 17%, 0.3, 0.52
   e. 0.2%, 1.2%, 0.017, 16%, 31%

B. Write percentages as fractions (p 147)

1. a. $\frac{1}{10}$ b. $\frac{1}{5}$ c. $\frac{2}{5}$ d. $\frac{4}{5}$
   e. $\frac{7}{10}$ f. $\frac{9}{10}$ g. $\frac{1}{2}$ h. $\frac{1}{4}$
   i. $\frac{1}{20}$ j. $\frac{3}{20}$ k. $\frac{9}{20}$ l. $\frac{3}{100}$
2. a. $\frac{19}{100}$ b. $\frac{16}{25}$ c. $\frac{19}{20}$ d. $\frac{2}{25}$
   e. $\frac{43}{50}$ f. $\frac{18}{25}$ g. $\frac{41}{100}$ h. $\frac{24}{25}$
3. a. $\frac{3}{200}$ b. $\frac{1}{40}$ c. $\frac{8}{125}$ d. $\frac{1}{8}$
   e. $\frac{17}{200}$ f. $\frac{5}{8}$ g. $\frac{3}{8}$ h. $\frac{21}{200}$
   i. $\frac{7}{80}$ j. $\frac{2}{3}$ k. $\frac{16}{125}$ l. $\frac{3}{80}$

C. Write fractions as decimals and percentages (p 149)

1. a. 50% b. 30% c. 25%
   d. 45% e. 80% f. 28%
   g. 34% h. 72%
2. a. 0.1, 10% b. 0.2, 20% c. 0.4, 40%
   d. 0.05, 5% e. 0.06, 6% f. 0.04, 4%
   g. 0.35, 35% h. 0.16, 16%

3.

Fraction	Decimal	%
$\frac{1}{2}$	0.5	50%
$\frac{1}{4}$	0.25	25%
$\frac{3}{4}$	0.75	75%
$\frac{1}{10}$	0.1	10%
$\frac{1}{5}$	0.2	20%
$\frac{1}{3}$	0.333...	$33\frac{1}{3}$%

Fraction	Decimal	%
$\frac{2}{5}$	0.4	40%
$\frac{7}{10}$	0.7	70%
$\frac{7}{20}$	0.35	35%
$\frac{3}{5}$	0.6	60%
$\frac{9}{10}$	0.9	90%
$\frac{3}{20}$	0.15	15%

4. a. 0.55, 55% b. 0.625, 62.5%
   c. 0.875, 87.5% d. 0.28, 28%
   e. 0.675, 67.5% f. 0.667, 66.667% (3dp)
   g. 0.0625, 6.25% h. 0.1333, 13.3333% (4dp)
5. a. $\frac{3}{4}$, 0.76, 78% b. 0.49, $\frac{1}{2}$, 51%
   c. 0.22, 24%, $\frac{1}{4}$ d. 19%, $\frac{1}{5}$, 0.21
   e. 50%, $\frac{5}{9}$, 0.58 f. 88%, $\frac{8}{9}$, 0.9
   g. 0.56, $\frac{7}{12}$, 59% h. $\frac{7}{16}$, 45%, 0.49

Percentage increase and decrease

A. Find the change first (p 150)

1. Breakfast £8.40, Lunch £16.80, Evening Meal £25.20
   Single Room £73.50, Double Room £126
2. a. i. £88 ii. £132 iii. £858
      iv. £70.40 v. £11.77 vi. £70.84
   b. i. £104 ii. £156 iii. £1014
      iv. £83.20 v. £13.91 vi. £83.72
3. £630 4. 27.5 m
5. a. 675 b. 225
6. 72 7. £780 8. £1242
9. Jess £364, Kate £338, Luke £332.80, Wes £306.80
10. £18.20
11. a. £11.16 b. £82.77 c. £550.56
    d. £1357.80 e. £14 229
12. a. £842.40 b. £2073.60 c. £91.26
    d. £22.95 e. £18.09

433

Answers

B. Find the new amount directly (p 152)
1. £10.30
2. choco bar 88p, pastilles 55p, toffee £1.32, chocolate truffles £8.25
3. £39.20
4. £10 800

Use a calculator to find percentages (p 153)
1. a. £3.25   b. £59.50   c. 9.6 m
   d. £442   e. 3.75 kg   f. 414 g
   g. 23.50 euros   h. 13.8 cm   i. 0.8 litre
   j. 92.4 m   k. £504   l. £97.90
   m. 48.1 km   n. £6.75   o. £34
   p. 84 cm
2. dress £43.19   stereo £209.99
   guitar £202.80   crockery £107.99
   TV £299.99
3. Website A: £181.30
   Website B: £186.75
   Website A's offer is best buy.
4. £9620
5.

	Loan	Bayleys	Anchor	Rock Solid	Direct
APR		6.6	6.5	6.3	6.7
a.	£1000	£66	£65	£63	£67
b.	£2500	£165	£162.50	£157.50	£167.50
c.	£1750	£115.50	£113.75	£110.25	£117.25
d.	£3225	£212.85	£209.63	£203.18	£216.08
e.	£12 500	£825	£812.50	£787.50	£837.50
f.	£0.8 million	£52 800	£52 000	£50 400	£53 600

6. a. 4.5 cm × 3 cm
   b. 7.5 cm × 5 cm
   c. 7.98 cm × 5.32 cm
   d. 8.46 cm × 5.64 cm
7. a. £32.76   b. 113.4 g   c. 690 m
   d. 34.02 m   e. 31.68 km   f. 93.28 kg
   g. 65.55 m   h. 16.25 litres   i. £22.40
   j. £11.25
8. £98.29

Write one number as a percentage of another (p 155)
1. a. 60%   b. 40%
2. 40%
3.

Assignment	1	2	3	4
Student's marks	18	56	52	66
Marks available	30	70	80	120
%	60%	80%	65%	55%

4. a. 50%   b. $33\frac{1}{3}$%   c. 5%
   d. 25%   e. 5%   f. 33%
5. 8%   6. 8%
7. a. £1045   b. 4.5%
8. 60%   9. 12.5%   10. 28%
11. a. 32%   b. 14%   c. 57.3%
12. a. i. 66.7%   ii. 33.3%
    b. Students' checks
13. 46.3%
14. a. 28.5%   b. 7.0%
15. 14.2%
16. a. 50%   b. 50%   c. 25%   d. 25%
    (Other estimated percentages are acceptable.)
17. a. i. 20% women   ii. 25% children
       iii. 55% men
18. a. £593.26
    b. i. 20%   ii. 10%   iii. 30%   iv. 40%
    (Other estimated percentages are acceptable.)
    c. Students' checks

Calculate the original value after a percentage change (p 159)
1. £200   2. £210   3. £236
4. 27 300   5. £68   6. 9
7. £486.80
8. a. £400
   b. The shopper has found 40% of the reduced price.
9. 160 ml

Measures, Shape and Space

11 Money

Write in pounds (£) and pence (p 161)
1. a. £30   b. 3p   c. £3   d. 30p
   e. £300
2. a. £90   b. 90p   c. £9   d. 9p
   e. £900
3. a. £110   b. £25.20   c. £12.50
   d. £30.05   e. £230.15   f. £413.25
   g. £303.03   h. £325
4. £731.34, £732.61, £736.02, £741.12
5. a. ten pounds, fifty pence
   b. five pounds, ninety-nine pence
   c. twelve pounds, fifty pence
   d. five hundred and five pounds
   e. two pounds, fifteen pence
   f. four hundred and ten pounds, four pence
   g. forty-five pounds, forty-nine pence
   h. two hundred and nine pounds, nine pence
6. £342.41   £342.14   £324.41   £324.14
   £234.41   £234.14

Answers

Calculate with money
A. Add and subtract money (p 162)
1. a. £6.31   b. £16.80   c. £2.67
    d. £5.40   e. £4.35   f. £3.45
    g. £5.05   h. £2.60   i. £1.01
    j. £3.51   k. £25.56   l. £64.06
2. £8
3. £2.65
4. a. £4.24   b. £15.76

B. Use a calculator to add and subtract money (p 163)
1. a. £2.05   b. £2.50   c. £2.98
    d. £3.02   e. £3.39   f. 97p
    g. £2.83   h. £4.45   i. 59p
    j. £6.25   k. £12.98   l. £12.52

C. Multiply and divide money (p 164)
1. a. £27.80   b. £89.94   c. £4.50
    d. £5.16   e. £116.55 f. £2.10
    g. 83p
2. a. £253.50 b. £282.10
3. £137.20
4. a. £31.98   b. £15.99
5. £42.72

Round money to the nearest 10p or £1
A. Round to the nearest 10p (p 165)
1. a. 10p   b. 30p   c. 30p   d. 40p
    e. 90p   f. 60p   g. 30p   h. 60p
    i. 50p   j. 80p   k. 90p   l. 0p
2. a. £2.10   b. £4.40   c. £5.70
    d. £7.20   e. £6.90   f. £9.10
    g. £5.70   h. £4.20   i. £3.30
    j. £8.90   k. £18.00 l. £28.00
3. a. 40p + 30p + 40p = £1.10
    b. 30p + 30p + 50p = £1.10
    c. 40p + 30p + 50p = £1.20

B. Round to the nearest £1 (p 166)
1. a. £3   b. £3   c. £5   d. £5
    e. £7   f. £7   g. £8   h. £9
    i. £2   j. £1   k. £10   l. £20
2. a. £12   b. £34   c. £16   d. £27
    e. £337   f. £9   g. £26   h. £24
    i. £13   j. £229   k. £77   l. £76
3. a. i. £2 + £2 + £6 = £10
       ii. £2 + £3 + £1 = £6
       iii. £4 + £4 + £5 = £13
    b. i. £10.16   ii. £6.53   iii. £13.09

Discounts in multiples of 5%
A. Find the discount (p 168)
1. a. £3   b. £1.20
    c. £2.80   d. £1.75
    e. 39p   f. 29p (nearest pence)
2. a. trainers £6.30 b. racket £18.75
    c. ball £8.25   d. cricket set £16.98
    e. T-shirt £17.49 f. helmet £17.18
    g. skates £107.24 h. bottle £2.80
3. No. Hotel break discount = £258, river cruise discount = £269.15, so she will save £11.15 more on the river cruise.

B. Find the price after the discount (p 169)
1. a. i. £152   ii. £475   iii. £1425
       iv. £1748 v. £10.07   vi. £847.40
    b. i. £128   ii. £400   iii. £1200
       iv. £1472 v. £8.48   vi. £713.60
    c. i. £120   ii. £375   iii. £1125
       iv. £1380 v. £7.95   vi. £669
    d. i. £136   ii. £425   iii. £1275
       iv. £1564 v. £9.01   vi. £758.20
2. a. £42.25   b. £27.30
3. £855

Simple interest (p 170)
1. a. £20   b. £175   c. £2500
2. £48.29   3. £15
4. a. £45   b. £397.50   c. £4950
5. £9775   6. No. It will be £2000.

Compound interest (p 171)
1. a. £530.45   b. £4455.78 c. £8062.84
2. a. £6998.40 b. £7558.27 (nearest pence)
3. a. £2315.25 b. £2431.01 (nearest pence)
4. a. £562.75   b. £3492.28
    c. £8349.42 (all nearest pence)
5. a. £2382.03 b. £10 617.82
    c. £20 787.88 (all nearest pence)
6. Yes. The total interest is £3077.27. (nearest pence)

Budget with money
A. Simple budgeting (p 173)
1. No, Yasmin can't quite afford it. The total cost comes to £3565 and she has only £3500
2. There is £86 left in Ethan's budget for the weekend. He can afford:
   either 5 km run + 10 km run = £65
   or 5 km run + half marathon = £80
   He cannot afford 10 km run + the half marathon = £89

Answers

3. Cost of flowers = £48.05. Parveen can afford vase A, with £1.45 left over. She needs an extra £1.55 for vase B.
4. **a.** **i.** £275.89 **ii.** £260.89 **iii.** £249.89 **iv.** £234.89
   b. Either **iii** or **iv** with reasons (for example, within budget and **iii** because hens will be safer or **iv** because cheaper).
5. The table gives the total cost of the different options, including the bed and the desk.

Wardrobe	Chair	Total cost	Is this within budget?
medium	swivel	£573.96	no
medium	standard	£569.46	no
small	swivel	£558.46	Yes
small	standard	£553.96	Yes

Either of the last two options are acceptable (with appropriate reasons). The student must buy the small wardrobe with either the swivel chair (more comfortable) or the standard chair (cheaper).

6. Yes. Saving on wages £1 805 500; savings on other items £664 000; total savings £2 469 500
7. **a.** £50.40 **b.** £34

B. Household budgeting (p 175)

1. **a.** £52.93
   b. No, not a good idea as this is not much for petrol and repairs.
2. **a.** **i.** £7.25 **ii.** £15.65
   b. Yes
   £97.90 + £50 saving = £147.90
   £206.20 − £147.90 = £58.30 left over
3. **a.** **i.** £75 **ii.** £21 **iii.** £7
   b. £817.14
   c. Yes, probably. Holidays £125 per month, so she would still have £692.14 a month for other expenses.
4. **a.** £747.24 **b.** £1497.76
   c. Student's budget - appropriate amounts for food, travel, purchases and repairs, leisure and holidays, saving, adding up to £1497.
5. Lesley has £2316.12 after all the bills, but she is unlikely to save £2000 as she has not budgeted for any unexpected bills.

Calculate using rates of pay (p 178)

1. **a.** £290 **b.** £304 **c.** £327 **d.** £352
2. 4 TVs
3. **a.** Poppy **b.** 20p per hour
4. Bees' Academy is better, because the annual salary there of £12 529.44 is £174.44 more than the Alpha College salary.
5. £378
6. **a.** Week beginning 4th March
   b. $\frac{1}{2}$ hour
   c. Week beginning 18th March
   d. £13.86 more than week beginning 11th March, £27.72 more than week beginning 4th March
7. **a.** £380.63 (nearest pence) **b.** £10.28
   c. **i.** £10.22 **ii.** £362.81
   d. Liu
8. **a.** $36\frac{1}{4}$ hours **b.** £406 **c.** 6 weeks

Value Added Tax (VAT)
A. Calculate VAT (p 181)

1. **a.** £180 **b.** £480 **c.** £36
   d. £72 **e.** £19.60 **f.** £9.20
   g. £5.16 **h.** £1.92 **i.** £4.48
   j. £19.36 **k.** £24.16 **l.** £5.50
2. **a.** £20 **b.** £15
   c. £38 **d.** £3.50
   e. £6.40 **f.** £1.22
   g. £1.52 (nearest pence) **h.** 97p (nearest pence)
3. £96
4. £13.74
5. **a.** £196 **b.** £49.80 **c.** £11.98
   d. £13.90 **e.** £2.99 **f.** £12.00

B. Calculate total cost including VAT (p 183)

1. **a.** £144 **b.** £252 **c.** £86.40
   d. £57.60 **e.** £358.80 **f.** £39
2. £8880 3. £160.23 4. £89.25
5. coffee maker £58.32, washing machine £478.80, radio £31.08, camera £203.99 (nearest pence)

C. Calculate original price and VAT (p 184)

1. **a.** £155, £31 **b.** £60, £12 **c.** £20, £4
   d. £10, £2 **e.** £305, £61 **f.** £45, £9
   g. £199, £39.80 **h.** £21.50, £4.30 **i.** £39, £7.80
2. £230
3. **a.** £123.20 **b.** £156.80
   c. £203.20 **d.** £398.60
4. **a.** £4895 **b.** £979

Taxes on income
A. Income tax (p 185)

1. **a.** £1230 **b.** £1550 **c.** £2570 **d.** £3670
   e. £598 **f.** £2910 **g.** £5100 **h.** £6214

B. National Insurance (NI) (p 185)

1. **a.** £4.56 **b.** £22.56
   c. £9.36 **d.** £32.40
   e. £42.96 **f.** £54.78
   g. £67.63 (nearest pence) **h.** £87.39
2. **a.** £1149.12 **b.** £1341.12 **c.** £1953.12
   d. £2613.12 **e.** £769.92 **f.** £2157.12
   g. £3471.12 **h.** £4139.52

Answers

C. Net pay (p 187)

1. a. NI = £2229.12, income tax = £3030, net pay = £21 740.88
    b. NI = £2889.12, income tax = £4130, net pay = £25 480.88
    c. NI = £1203.12, income tax = £1320, net pay = £15 926.88
    d. NI = £1953.12, income tax = £2570, net pay = £20 176.88
    e. NI = £2805.12, income tax = £3990, net pay = £25 004.88
    f. NI = £4026.72, income tax = £6026, net pay = £31 927.28
    g. NI = £1806.12, income tax = £2325, net pay = £19 343.88
    h. NI = £4228.08, income tax = £6361.60, net pay = £33 068.32
2. a. £17 537.68   b. £18 738.48
    c. £21 392.88   d. £15 136.08
    e. £17 221.68   f. £22 631.60
    g. £27 042.96   h. £30 967.68
3. £578
4. a. £22 505.60   b. £49.05 (nearest pence)
5. a.

Payment for week		Deductions for week	
Hours worked	35	National Insurance	£56.16
Wage per hour	£18	Income tax	£80.42
Total pay	£630	Total deductions	£136.58
		Take-home pay	£493.42

b.

Earnings		Monthly deductions	
Annual gross earnings	£28 500	NI	£200.76
Monthly gross earnings	£2375	Pension (6%)	£142.50
		Income tax	£249.00
		Total	£592.26
		Net monthly earnings	£1782.74

Convert between currencies (p 189)

1. Mr Black 1116 US dollars
    Mrs Smith 3502.5 zloty
    Miss Patten 21 384 rand
    Ms Chang 265 920 yen
    Mr Davies 13 128 rupees
    Ms Bailey 96 250 euros
2. a. £245   b. £29   c. £252
    d. £8   e. £108 f. £1538
3. Mr Wragg £554
    Miss Yen £194
    Mr Ennis £24
    Ms Masters £62
    Miss Sharif £1043
    Mr Caine £1837
    Ms Wright £19
4. £704
5. a. 1165 (US dollars)   b. £886   c. £64
6. a. 5874 zloty   b. 106 zloty   c. £133

12 Time

Read, measure and record time

A. am and pm (p 192)

1. a. 7:00 am   b. 4:00 pm   c. 11:30 am
    d. 5:00 pm   e. 1:00 am   f. 8:45 am
2. a. iii   b. i   c. ii
3. Any suitable suggestions
4. a. 12 hours   b. 13 hours   c. 17 hours
    d. $9\frac{1}{2}$ hours   e. 11 hours   f. $11\frac{1}{2}$ hours

B. Read and record time to the nearest 5 minutes (p 193)

1. a. 20 minutes past 2, 2:20
    b. 40 minutes past 1, 1:40
    c. 25 minutes past 11, 11:25
    d. 50 minutes past 1, 1:50
2. a. 35 minutes past 10, 25 minutes to 11, 10:35
    b. 40 minutes past 2, 20 minutes to 3, 2:40
    c. 40 minutes past 12, 20 minutes to 1, 12:40
    d. 45 minutes past 3, 15 minutes to 4, 3:45
    e. 35 minutes past 2, 25 minutes to 3, 2:35
    f. 55 minutes past 7, 5 minutes to 8, 7:55
    g. 50 minutes past 11, 10 minutes to 12, 11:50
    h. 55 minutes past 5, 5 minutes to 6, 5:55

Use the 12 and 24 hour clock

A. 12 and 24 hour clock times (p 195)

1. a. 15:50   b. 07:00   c. 09:15
    d. 22:26   e. 15:42   f. 13:30
    g. 06:45   h. 00:05   i. 19:40
    j. 18:59   k. 06:42   l. 20:25
2. a. 03:15   b. 16:45   c. 07:30
    d. 08:50   e. 23:10   f. 12:00
    g. 15:55   h. 07:45   i. 17:35
    j. 14:50   k. 16:05   l. 11:10
3. a. 16:06   b. 15:15   c. 08:11
    d. 09:45   e. 18:50   f. 23:35
    g. 10:55   h. 12:12   i. 21:20
    j. 18:30
4. a. 11:30 pm   b. 6:45 am   c. 7:12 am
    d. 4:45 pm   e. 12:10 pm   f. 1:10 am
    g. 12:16 pm   h. 2:10 pm   i. 12 am
    j. 6:05 am   k. 1:46 pm   l. 9:15 am

437

Answers

5. a. 15:52, 8 minutes to 4 in the afternoon, 3:52 pm
   b. 03:46, 14 minutes to 4 in the morning, 3:46 am
   c. 17:05, 5 minutes past 5 in the afternoon, 5:05 pm
   d. 23:54, 6 minutes to midnight, 11:54 pm
   e. 19:09, 9 minutes past 7 in the evening, 7:09 pm
   f. 16:32, 28 minutes to 5 in the afternoon, 4:32 pm

B. Use timetables (p 197)

1. a. i. 0628   ii. 0703
   b. 0702
   c. i. 0620   ii. 0633
   d. 0640
   e. 0707
   f. i. 0637   ii. 0648
2. a. 8:45 am   b. 12:20 pm
   c. i. 2:10 pm   ii. 3 pm
   d. 8:53 am   e. 12:45 pm
   f. i. 9:15 am   ii. 12:30 pm   iii. 12:55 pm
   g. 2:03 pm

Units of time (p 198)

1. a. 30   b. 3   c. 30   d. 200
   e. 15   f. 1000   g. 6   h. 104
   i. 14   j. 26
2. a. i. 30   ii. 30   iii. 29
   b. i. 62   ii. 61
3. a. minutes   b. seconds
   c. days   d. days or weeks
   e. hours   f. weeks or months
   g. years or centuries
4. a. 210   b. 3   c. 270   d. 5
   e. 36   f. $2\frac{1}{2}$ g. 49   h. 5
   i. 450   j. 5   k. 3000   l. 10
5. £1250
6. 4 weeks
7. 150 seconds
8. 105 min
9. 13 weeks
10. a. £78   b. £312
11. a. August 4th   b. 14 nights

Calculate time

A. Add and subtract time in hours, minutes and seconds (p 200)

1. a. 5 hours 20 minutes
   b. 8 minutes 57 seconds
   c. 3 minutes 35 seconds
   d. 6 minutes 15 seconds
   e. 9 hours 45 minutes
   f. 4 hours 5 minutes
2. a. 2 hours 20 minutes
   b. 1 hour 40 minutes
   c. 1 minute 20 seconds
   d. 52 seconds
   e. 3 hours 35 minutes
   f. 1 minute 21 seconds

3. a. 11 minutes   b. 7 minutes 15 seconds
4. 55 minutes
5. $4\frac{3}{4}$ hours or 4 hours 45 minutes

B. Find the difference between times by adding on (p 201)

1. a. 2 hours 41 min   b. 2 hours 42 min
   c. 2 hours 45 min   d. 1 hour 33 min
   e. 3 hours 48 min   f. 3 hours 50 min
   g. 3 hours 11 min   h. 3 hours 21 min
   i. 4 hours 15 min   j. 8 hours 36 min
   k. 3 hours 41 min   l. 5 hours 50 min
   m. 5 hours 6 min   n. 7 hours 30 min
   o. 9 hours 45 min   p. 21 hours 45 min
2. a. 3 hours 30 min   b. 6 hours 15 min
   c. 5 hours 30 min   d. 4 hours 15 min
   e. 5 hours 30 min   f. 7 hours 45 min
3. a. 5 hours 21 min   b. 4 hours 18 min
   c. 4 hours 6 min   d. 4 hours 12 min
   e. 4 hours 35 min   f. 2 hours 13 min
   g. 2 hours 32 min   h. 2 hours 24 min
   i. 3 hours 25 min   j. 3 hours 9 min
   k. 4 hours 14 min   l. 2 hours 12 min
4. 7 hours 59 min

C. Find the difference between times by subtracting (p 202)

1. a. 2 hours 27 min   b. 2 hours 29 min
   c. 1 hour 13 min   d. 1 hour 33 min
   e. 7 hours 26 min   f. 6 hours 11 min
   g. 1 hour 49 min   h. 3 hours 45 min
   i. 1 hour 27 min   j. 4 hours 17 min
   k. 1 hour 40 min   l. 10 hours 29 min
2. a. i. 3 hours 48 minutes
      ii. 3 hours 43 minutes
      iii. 2 hours 38 minutes
      iv. 4 hours 7 minutes
   b. 5 minutes

Use timers (p 204)

1. Analogue and digital clocks (as in question) showing:
   a. 10:30 pm   b. 6 am
   c. 11:15 pm   d. 8:30 am
2. a. Start cooking 17:30   b. Start cooking 15:15
      Cooking time 1:30   Cooking time 2:15
   c. Start cooking 18:35   d. Start cooking 17:15
      Cooking time 1:40   Cooking time 1:45
3. a. 1 minute, 16 seconds and 47 hundredths of a second, 1 min 16.47 s
   b. 1 minute, 21 seconds and 5 hundredths of a second, 1 min 21.05 s

Answers

   c. 1 minute, 16 seconds and 59 hundredths of a second, 1 min 16.59 s
   d. 1 minute, 22 seconds and 2 tenths of a second, 1 min 22.20 s
   e. 1 minute, 17 seconds and 8 hundredths of a second, 1 min 17.08 s
   f. 1 minute, 22 seconds and 4 tenths of a second, 1 min 22.40 s

4. a. 2.21 s   b. 0.56 s   c. 2.15 s
   d. 10.68 s   e. 13.52 s   f. 25.02 s
5. 02:16.43, 02:34.05, 02:44.51, 02:49.30, 03:00.24, 03:01.09
   Difference: 17.62 s, 10.46 s, 4.79 s, 10.94 s, 0.85 s

13 Length

Understand distance: miles and kilometres

A. Use distances marked on a map (p 207)

1. a. 8 miles   b. 8 miles
   c. 8 miles   d. 17 miles
   e. 16 miles   f. 18 miles
   g. 11 miles   h. 15 miles
2. 23 miles   3. 26 miles

B. Use a mile or kilometre chart (p 208)

1. a. 261 miles   b. 284 miles   c. 95 miles
   d. 239 miles   e. 84 miles   f. 416 miles
2. a. 98 km   b. 106 miles   c. 45 miles
   d. 82 km   e. 48 miles   f. 11 miles
   g. 72 km   h. 255 km

Measure length in metric units

A. Measure in millimetres and centimetres (p 210)

1. b. i. 3 cm   ii. 31 mm
   c. i. 5 cm   ii. 48 mm
   d. i. 7 cm   ii. 66 mm
   e. i. 7 cm   ii. 74 mm
   f. i. 9 cm   ii. 93 mm
   g. i. 11 cm   ii. 106 mm
   h. i. 11 cm   ii. 113 mm
2. a. 2 cm   b. 30 mm   c. 5 cm
   d. 70 mm   e. 6 cm   f. 80 mm
   g. 4 cm   h. 90 mm   i. 12 cm
3. a. 1.5 cm   b. 12 mm   c. 2.6 cm
   d. 13 mm   e. 1.4 cm   f. 21 mm
   g. 8.4 cm   h. 39 mm   i. 12.5 cm
4. a. 32 mm, 3 cm 2 mm, 3.2 cm
   b. 67 mm, 6 cm 7 mm, 6.7 cm
   c. 31 mm, 3 cm 1 mm, 3.1 cm
   d. 54 mm, 5 cm 4 mm, 5.4 cm
   e. 90 mm, 9 cm 0 mm, 9 cm
   f. 59 mm, 5 cm 9 mm, 5.9 cm
   g. 22 mm, 2 cm 2 mm, 2.2 cm
   h. 45 mm, 4 cm 5 mm, 4.5 cm
5. e b f d h a c g
6. a. 74 mm, 7 cm 4 mm, 7.4 cm
   b. 46 mm, 4 cm 6 mm, 4.6 cm
   c. 67 mm, 6 cm 7 mm, 6.7 cm
7. a. 26 mm, 2 cm 6 mm, 2.6 cm
   b. 52 mm, 5 cm 2 mm, 5.2 cm
   c. 33 mm, 3 cm 3 mm, 3.3 cm
   d. 44 mm, 4 cm 4 mm, 4.4 cm
   e. The safety pin (a) is easiest because it starts at the 0 mark.

B. Measure in metres, centimetres and millimetres (p 213)

1. c. 99 cm, 990 mm   d. 102 cm, 1020 mm
   e. 104 cm, 1040 mm   f. 107 cm, 1070 mm
   g. 110 cm, 1100 mm   h. 112 cm, 1120 mm
2. c. 0.99 m   d. 1.02 m   e. 1.04 m
   f. 1.07 m   g. 1.1 m   h. 1.12 m
3. c. i. 361 cm   ii. 3.61 m
   d. i. 370 cm   ii. 3.7 m
   e. i. 361 cm   ii. 3.61 m
   f. i. 363 cm   ii. 3.63 m
   g. i. 369 cm   ii. 3.69 m
   h. i. 367 cm   ii. 3.67 m
4. c. 360.7 cm, 3607 mm, 3 m 607 mm, 3.607 m
   d. 370.3 cm, 3703 mm, 3 m 703 mm, 3.703 m
   e. 361.3 cm, 3613 mm, 3 m 613 mm, 3.613 m
   f. 363.1 cm, 3631 mm, 3 m 631 mm, 3.631 m
   g. 369.3 cm, 3693 mm, 3 m 693 mm, 3.693 m
   h. 366.6 cm, 3666 mm, 3 m 666 mm, 3.666 m

Estimate and measure lengths (p 214)

1. a. accurate   b. round up   c. accurate
   d. round up   e. accurate
2. a. 1 m   b. 40 km   c. 2 m
   d. 3 cm   e. 30 cm   f. 14 cm
   g. 11 cm   h. 3 mm   i. 1 mm
   (Alternative answers are possible for some parts.)
3. a. A i. 10 cm   ii. 10.3 cm
      B i. 7 cm   ii. 6.7 cm
      C i. 4 cm   ii. 4.3 cm
      D i. 13 cm   ii. 12.6 cm
      E i. 9 cm   ii. 8.8 cm
      F i. 2 cm   ii. 2.3 cm
      G i. 10 cm   ii. 9.5 cm
   b. as **aii**

Convert between metric lengths (p 217)

1. a. 23 mm   b. 43 mm
   c. 43 500 mm   d. 4500 mm
   e. 12 450 mm   f. 2 000 000 mm

Answers

2. a. 1300 cm   b. 4000 cm   c. 960 cm
    d. 1370 cm   e. 6.5 cm   f. 250 000 cm
3. a. 4 m   b. 5000 m   c. 24 m
    d. 5840 m   e. 740 m   f. 3.534 m
    g. 5.3 m   h. 0.68 m   i. 0.96 m
    j. 13 750 m k. 659 m   l. 50 m
4. a. 7 km   b. 9.4 km   c. 4.5 km
    d. 95 km   e. 2.5 km
5. a. 4000 m   b. 500 cm   c. 450 mm
    d. 5 km   e. 25 cm   f. 3.6 m
    g. 2.75 m   h. 0.275 km i. 3600 m
    j. 270 cm   k. 122 mm   l. 7.563 km
6. 6 mm, 2.6 cm, 200 mm, 0.5 m, 650 mm, 150 cm, 2 m
7. 2.5 m   8. 10 km
9. a. 60 cm   b. 0.6 m
10. a. 75 cm   b. 750 mm
11. a. 50 cm   b. 25 cm   c. 500 mm
    d. 250 mm   e. $\frac{2}{5}$ m   f. $\frac{3}{10}$ m
    g. $\frac{7}{10}$ h. $\frac{6}{10}$
12. a. 175 cm   b. 3500 mm   c. 325 cm
    d. 3200 mm   e. 5400 mm   f. 380 cm

Calculate with metric lengths
A. Metres and centimetres (p 219)
1. a. 5.3 m   b. 3.3 m   c. 4.5 m
    d. 4.25 m   e. 10.65 m   f. 3.64 m
    g. 2.25 m   h. 2.75 m   i. 3.8 m
2. a. $7\frac{1}{2}$ m b. $2\frac{1}{4}$ m c. $3\frac{3}{4}$ m d. $4\frac{3}{4}$ m
    e. $4\frac{1}{4}$ m f. $1\frac{1}{4}$ m g. $11\frac{1}{2}$ m h. $2\frac{1}{2}$ m

B. Metres and millimetres (p 220)
1. a. 2.675 m   b. 3.025 m   c. 2.115 m
    d. 2.25 m   e. 7.7 m   f. 2.034 m

C. Mixed calculations (p 221)
1. a. 2.625 m   b. 5.47 m   c. 3.045 m
2. No, the items won't fit because their total width is 3.2 m.
3. 5.45 m   4. 2.9 m
5. a. 22.2 m   b. 13.8 m
6. a. $1\frac{1}{4}$ m
    b. i. $5\frac{9}{10}$ m or 5.9 m   ii. $1\frac{3}{5}$ m or 1.6 m
7. Yes. The builder uses 10.5 ÷ 1.2 = 8.75 or $8\frac{3}{4}$ pieces of fence panel. 9 pieces are left

Use a scale on a plan or map (p 222)

1.

Room	Length on plan	Actual length	Width on plan	Actual width
Bedroom	3 cm	3 × 2 = 6 m	2 cm	2 × 2 = 4 m
Kitchen	2.5 cm	2.5 × 2 = 5 m	1.5 cm	1.5 × 2 = 3 m
Living room	4 cm	4 × 2 = 8 m	3 cm	3 × 2 = 6 m
Bathroom	1.5 cm	1.5 × 2 = 3 m	1 cm	1 × 2 = 2 m
Cupboard	1 cm	1 × 2 = 2 m	0.5 cm	0.5 × 2 = 1 m

2.

House	Measurements on the plan				Actual measurements			
	House length	House width	Plot length	Plot width	House length	House width	Plot length	Plot width
A	11 mm	6 mm	25 mm	16 mm	11 m	6 m	25 m	16 m
B	10 mm	9 mm	35 mm	16 mm	10 m	9 m	35 m	16 m
C	13 mm	10 mm	28 mm	16 mm	13 m	10 m	28 m	13 m
D	17 mm	6 mm	31 mm	16 mm	17 m	6 m	31 m	16 m

3. a. A 48 mm   B 62 mm   C 27 mm   D 43 mm
    b. A .8 m   B 6.2 m   C 2.7 m   D 4.3 m
    c.

	Measurement on drawing in mm	Actual measurement
i. The length of the house	59 mm	5.9 m
ii. The width of the downstairs window	18 mm	1.8 m
iii. The width of the smaller upstairs window	18 mm	1.8 m
iv. The width of the larger upstairs window	23 mm	2.3 m
v. The height of the downstairs window	16 mm	1.6 m
vi. The height of the upstairs windows	13 mm	1.3 m
viii. The width of the front porch	23 mm	2.3 m

4. a. i. approx 14 km   ii. approx 10 km
       iii. approx 29 km   iv. approx 12.5 km
    b. i. approx 17 km   ii. approx 15 km
       iii. approx 34 km   iv. approx 12.5 km

5.

Journey	Length on map	Actual distance
Tutor's home to A	7.4 cm	3.7 km
Tutor's home to B	5 cm	2.5 km
Tutor's home to C	2.4 cm	1.2 km
Tutor's home to D	3.6 cm	1.8 km

(Allow ±0.2 km)

Answers

Use ratios on scale drawings
A. Use ratio scales (p 225)

1. a. 50 m b. 30 m c. 25 m
   d. 20 m e. 10 m f. 6 m
   g. 16 m h. 11.5 m

2. a.

Room	Dimension	On plan	Actual distance
Lounge	length	30 mm	6 m
	width	25 mm	5 m
Kitchen	length	18 mm	3.6 m
	width	14 mm	2.8 m
Bathroom	length	15 mm	3 m
	width	12 mm	2.4 m
Bedroom	length	24 mm	4.8 m
	width	16 mm	3.2 m

   b. 2 m

3. a. A 41 mm × 19 mm   B 37 mm × 19 mm
      C 31 mm × 15 mm   D 47 mm × 15 mm
   b. A 8.2 m × 3.8 m   B 7.4 m × 3.8 m
      C 6.2 m × 3 m   D 9.4 m × 3 m

4. a. 6.6 m b. 3.15 m c. 3 m
   d. 2.4 m e. 4.05 m f. 2.7 m
   g. 11.25 m h. 10.8 m

5.

Distance	On map	Actual
a. The Minster – Hospital	1.8 cm	0.45 km
b. The Minster – Cemetery	4.2 cm	1.05 km
c. Snow Close Farm – Hospital	5.1 cm	1.275 km
d. College – The Minster	3.5 cm	0.875 km
e. Snow Close Farm – The Minster	5.6 cm	1.4 km
f. Schools – Hospital	2.7 cm	0.675 km
g. Studley – The Minster	5.2 cm	1.3 km

6. a. 1 : 100   b. 1 : 50
   c. 1 : 20   d. 1 : 2000
   e. 1 : 50 000 f. 1 : 250 000
   g. 1 : 160   h. 1 : 125 000
   i. 1 : 1000   j. 1 : 200 000
   k. 1 : 5   l. 1 : 2500

B. Draw scale diagrams (p 228)

1. Lines of length:
   a. i. 6 cm   ii. 13 cm
   b. i. 3.2 cm ii. 4.8 cm
   c. i. 13 cm   ii. 8.7 cm
   d. i. 7 cm   ii. 4.3 cm
   e. i. 4.5 cm ii. 3.6 cm
   f. i. 4.2 cm ii. 9 cm
   g. i. 7 cm   ii. 11.4 cm

2. Scale drawing should have the dimensions shown below:

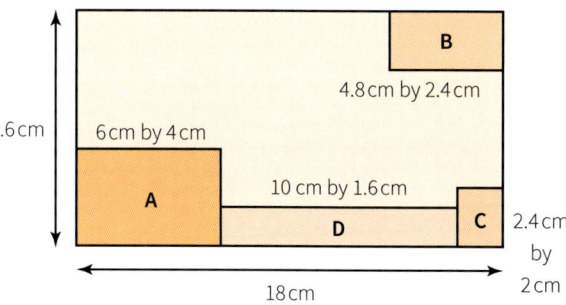

Measure lengths in imperial units (p 229)

1. a. $1\frac{1}{8}''$ b. $1\frac{11}{16}''$ c. $1\frac{3}{16}''$
   d. $1\frac{1}{4}''$ e. $\frac{3}{4}''$ f. $1\frac{5}{8}''$
   g. $1\frac{3}{8}''$ h. $1\frac{9}{16}''$ i. $\frac{11}{16}''$
   j. $1\frac{15}{16}''$ k. $1\frac{5}{8}''$ l. $\frac{3}{4}''$

Convert between imperial lengths (p 230)

1. a. 180 in b. 72 in   c. 336 in
   d. 192 in e. 72 in   f. 432 in
   g. 113 in h. 54 in
2. a. 6 ft   b. 240 ft c. $2\frac{1}{2}$ ft
   d. 12 ft   e. 15 ft   f. 5 ft
   g. 4 ft   h. $2\frac{1}{3}$ ft
3. a. 2 yd   b. 5 yd
   c. 7040 yd d. 4 yd
4. a. 3 miles b. 9 miles
   c. 10 miles d. 6 miles
5. a. 45 ft   b. 15 yd
6. Hana 4 ft 10 inches   Imran 5 ft 5 inches
   Caleb 6 ft 1 inch
7. a. 13' 10" b. 4' 10"

Convert between metric and imperial lengths

A. Approximate metric/imperial conversions (p 231)

1.

Inches	Centimetres
2 in	5 cm
6 in	15 cm
8 in	20 cm
3 in	7.5 cm
7 in	17.5 cm
10 in	25 cm
32 in	80 cm
18 in	45 cm
40 in	100 cm

441

Answers

Yards/feet	Centimetres	Metres
2 ft	60 cm	0.6 m
2½ ft	75 cm	0.75 m
1 yd or 3 ft	90 cm	0.9 m
3½ ft or 1 yd ½ ft	105 cm	1.05 m
4½ ft	135 cm	1.35 m
5 ft or 1 yd 2 ft	150 cm	1.5 m
7 ft or 2 yd 1 ft	210 cm	2.1 m
2 yd 2 ft	240 cm	2.4 m
3 yd	270 cm	2.7 m

2. a. i. 50 miles   ii. 130 miles   iii. 18.75 miles
    b. i. 96 km   ii. 384 km   iii. 48 km

3.
Journey		miles	km
a.	Paris to Boulogne	159	254
b.	Brussels to Calais	135	216
c.	Berlin to Cherbourg	847	1355
d.	Brussels to Dieppe	194	310
e.	Paris to Dunkerque	174	278
f.	Frankfurt to Amsterdam	283	453
g.	Munich to Boulogne	590	944
h.	Turin to Ostend	604	967
i.	Zurich to Calais	476	762
j.	Warsaw to Dieppe	1047	1675

B. *More accurate conversions (p 233)*

1. a. 10.16 cm   b. 22.86 cm   c. 26.67 cm
   d. 30.48 cm   e. 45.72 cm
2. a. 9.14 m   b. 5.48 m   c. 4.11 m
   d. 2.13 m   e. 4.57 m
3. a. 5.91 in   b. 17.72 in   c. 9.76 in
   d. 98.43 in   e. 118.11 in
4. a. 29.8 miles b. 9.9 miles c. 24.8 miles
   d. 18.6 miles e. 14.6 miles
5. a. 24.2 km   b. 40.3 km   c. 67.6 km
   d. 48.3 km   e. 15.3 km
6. a. 1030 km   b. 1755 km
7. 99 miles
8. 75 mph and 62 mph

14 Weight

Measure weight in metric units

A. *Know metric units of weight (p 235)*

1. a. g   b. kg   c. g
   d. g   e. kg   f. mg

2. a. 500 g   b. 700 g   c. 530 g
   d. 220 g   e. 750 g   f. 30 g
   g. 160 g   h. 420 g   i. 640 g
   j. 750 g or ¾ kg   k. 500 g or ½ kg   l. 250 g or ¼ kg
3. a. 7 kg   b. 4 kg
   c. 2 kg   d. 8 kg
   e. 4 kg 200 g f. 7 kg 300 g
   g. 2 kg 600 g h. 2 kg 870 g
   i. 5 kg 80 g   j. 5 kg 389 g
   k. 5 kg 20 g   l. 1 kg 5 g
4. a. 4000 g   b. 2000 g   c. 3000 g
   d. 1000 g   e. 1500 g   f. 1250 g
   g. 2500 g   h. 3750 g

B. *Measure in grams and kilograms (p 236)*

1. a. 2   b. 500 g
   c. i. 500 g   ii. 2 kg 500 g   iii. 4 kg
      iv. 5 kg 500 g v. 7 kg 500 g   vi. 9 kg
2. a. 6 kg   b. 10   c. 100 g
   d. i. 700 g   ii. 2 kg 300 g
      iii. 3 kg 400 g iv. 4 kg 400 g   v. 5.2 kg
      v. 5 kg 200 g
   e. i. 0.7 kg   ii. 2.3 kg   iii. 3.4 kg
      iv. 4.4 kg   v. 5.2 kg
3. a. 500 g
   b. i. 50 g   ii. 150 g
      iii. 300 g   iv. 450 g
4. iii. 4 kg   iv. 5 kg   v. 7 kg   vi. 9 kg
5. a. i. 1 kg 200 g   ii. 2 kg 700 g
      iii. 3 kg 800 g iv. 5 kg 200 g
      v. 6 kg 800 g   vi. 9 kg 300 g
   b. i. 1.2 kg   ii. 2.7 kg
      iii. 3.8 kg iv. 5.2 kg
      v. 6.8 kg   vi. 9.3 kg
6. a. 50 g   b. 10 g
   c. i. 120 g   ii. 270 g
      iii. 490 g   iv. 640 g
      v. 830 g   vi. 940 g
7. a. A 6 kg   B 12.5 kg   C 18 kg
      D 27 kg   E 34.5 kg   F 42.5 kg
   b. i. 6.5 kg   ii. 9 kg   iii. 8 kg
8. a. 1 kg   b. 200 g
   c. A 2 kg 600 g   B 5 kg 200 g
      C 9 kg   D 12 kg 400 g
      E 16 kg 600 g   F 20 kg 800 g
   d. i. 2 kg 600 g   ii. 3 kg 400 g
      iii. 4 kg 200 g

Answers

C. **Estimate weights between marked divisions (p 239)**

(Allow any equivalent weights and some leeway.)

1. a. A 250 g   B 650 g   C 975 g
   D 1525 g   E 1950 g   F 2350 g
   b. i. 400 g   ii. 550 g   iii. 400 g
   iv. 2100 g   v. 975 g   vi. 875 g
   c. A 1 kg   B 600 g   C 275 g
   d. D 975 g   E 550 g   F 150 g
   e. 2300 g

Choose units and instruments (p 240)

1. a. 410 g   b. 25 g   c. 5 kg
   d. 125 g   e. 1.5 kg   f. 50 g
   g. 250 g   h. 500 g   i. 1 kg
   j. 70 kg

   (Allow reasonable alternatives.)
2. a. kg   b. g   c. 10 g   d. 100 g
3. a. P A   Q B   R A   S B   b. Q, S, R, P
   c. Scale B: there are extra divisions allowing you to weigh more accurately.

Convert between metric weights (p 241)

1. a. 4 kg   b. 6.5 kg   c. 5.485 kg
   d. 34.5 kg   e. 0.8 kg   f. 0.25 kg
   g. 300 kg   h. 0.75 kg   i. 4000 kg
   j. 3540 kg   k. 500 kg   l. 250 kg
2. a. 7000 g   b. 4500 g   c. 8268 g
   d. 16 400 g   e. 3050 g   f. 300 g
   g. 60 g   h. 1025 g   i. 2 g
   j. 7.5 g   k. 0.5 g   l. 1000 g
3. a. 44 000 mg   b. 30 500 mg
   c. 3300 mg   d. 830 mg
   e. 12 300 mg   f. 70 mg
   g. 50 000 mg   h. 3 750 000 mg
4. a. 503 tonnes   b. 42 tonnes
   c. 4.5 tonnes   d. 0.589 tonnes
5. a. 3000 kg   b. 500 mg
   c. 1500 g   d. 500 kg
   e. 7000 kg   f. 250 mg
   g. 0.75 tonnes   h. 5 tonnes
   i. 10 000 g
6. a. 0.4 kg   450 g   4 000 000 mg
      0.4 tonnes   450 kg
   b. 25 600 mg   0.25 kg   330 g   0.45 kg $\frac{1}{2}$ kg

Calculate using metric weights

A. Kilograms and grams (p 242)

1. a. 5.7 kg   b. 3.075 kg   c. 3.15 kg
   d. 2.25 kg   e. 3.77 kg   f. 2.27 kg
   g. 4.7 kg   h. 1.6 kg   i. 3.94 kg
   j. 1.625 kg   k. 1.65 kg   l. 4.044 kg
   m. 2.345 kg   n. 0.996 kg or 996 g
2. a. 3.25 kg   b. 1.75 kg   c. 6.025 kg
3. 6.05 kg   4. 285 g   5. 1.8 kg
6. 960 g   7. 850 g
8. a. 650 g   b. 3.25 kg

B. Mixed calculations (p 243)

1. 14.5 kg   2. 10   3. 3.61 kg
4. 2.64 kg   5. 2.1 kg   6. 350 g
7. 15   8. 15 g   9. 50
10. 50

C. Kilograms and tonnes (p 244)

1. 16 days   2. 400
3. a. 48 tonnes
   b. i. locomotive
      ii. 52 tonnes more than the cars
   c. 300 tonnes   d. 448 tonnes

Convert between imperial weights (p 245)

1. a. 32 oz   b. 70 oz   c. 100 oz
   d. 192 oz   e. 72 oz   f. 55 oz
   g. 4 oz   h. 8 oz   i. 12 oz
   j. 40 oz
2. a. 1 lb   b. 6 lb   c. 3 lb
   d. 8 lb   e. 5 lb   f. 28 lb
   g. 56 lb   h. 35 lb   i. 4480 lb
   j. 3360 lb
3. a. 3 lb 8 oz   b. 5 lb 2 oz
   c. 2 lb 6 oz   d. 4 lb 9 oz
   e. 2 lb 12 oz   f. 1 lb 4 oz
   g. 3 lb 7 oz   h. 5 lb 1 oz

Calculate using imperial weights (p 246)

1. 13 st 1 lb   2. 8 st 3 lb
3. a. 68 lb   b. 4 st 12 lb
4. a. 149 lb   b. 10 st 9 lb
5. 149 lb or 10 st 9 lb
6. a. See the chart below.
   b. 20 lb or 1 st 6 lb
   c. 1 st 2 lb or 16 lb

Week 1	Week 2	Week 3	Week 4	Week 5	Week 6
4 lb	4 lb	4 lb	3 lb	3 lb	2 lb
12 st 11 lb	12 st 7 lb	12 st 3 lb	12 st	11 st 11 lb	11 st 9 lb
179 lb	175 lb	171 lb	168 lb	165 lb	163 lb

7. a. 21 oz or 1 lb 5 oz   b. 19 oz over

Answers

Convert between metric and imperial weights

A. Approximate metric/imperial conversions (p 247)
1. a. 100 g b. more
2. a. 15 oz b. 10 oz c. 22 oz
   d. 11 oz e. 19 oz f. 29 oz
3. a. 350 g b. 25 g c. 125 g
   d. 200 g e. 100 g f. 90 g
   g. 65 g h. 190 g

B. More accurate conversions (p 248)
1. a. 8.8 lb b. 10 kg c. 19.8 lb d. 5.45 kg
2. a. 112 g b. 5 oz c. 420 g d. 2.5 oz

15 Capacity

Measure capacity and volume

A. Know metric measures (p 251)
1. a. 2 b. 5 c. 10
2. a. 1000 mℓ b. 500 mℓ c. 250 mℓ
   d. 750 mℓ e. 1500 mℓ
3. a. 3 ℓ b. 5 ℓ c. 9 ℓ
   d. 12 ℓ e. $4\frac{1}{2}$ ℓ

B. Measure in litres and millilitres (p 251)
1. a. i. 200 mℓ ii. 600 mℓ
      iii. 1000 mℓ iv. 1200 mℓ
      v. 1600 mℓ
   b. i. 0.2 litres ii. 0.6 litres
      iii. 1 litre iv. 1.2 litres v. 1.6 litres
2. a. 1 litre b. 100 mℓ c. 50 mℓ
   d. i. 100 mℓ ii. 250 mℓ
      iii. 500 mℓ iv. 750 mℓ
      v. 950 mℓ
   e. 500 mℓ
3. a. 200 mℓ b. 5 c. 20 mℓ
   d. 10 mℓ
   e. i. 30 mℓ ii. 60 mℓ
      iii. 110 mℓ iv. 130 mℓ
      v. 170 mℓ

C. Estimate between marked divisions (p 252)
1. i. 375 mℓ ii. 275 mℓ iii. 225 mℓ
   iv. 175 mℓ v. 145 mℓ vi. 60 mℓ
2. a. 200 mℓ
   b. i. 30 mℓ ii. 60 mℓ iii. 90 mℓ
      iv. 140 mℓ v. 190 mℓ

Choose units and instruments (p 254)
1. a. litres b. mℓ c. mℓ
   d. litres e. litres f. mℓ
2. a. C b. C c. B d. A e. A
3. a. B b. B c. B d. A or B
   e. A f. A g. B h. A or B
4. a. 100 mℓ or 1 litre b. 100 mℓ c. 1 mℓ
   d. 100 mℓ e. 1 litre
   f. 1 litre or 100 mℓ g. 1 mℓ

Convert between millilitres, litres and centilitres (p 255)
1. a. 5000 mℓ b. 2600 mℓ c. 12 500 mℓ
   d. 3625 mℓ e. 682 mℓ f. 1850 mℓ
   g. 5063 mℓ h. 750 mℓ i. 83 mℓ
   j. 40 mℓ
2. a. 6 ℓ b. 3.5 ℓ c. 11 ℓ
   d. 1.1 ℓ e. 65.4 ℓ f. 0.33 ℓ
   g. 0.25 ℓ h. 0.425 ℓ i. 7.3 ℓ
   j. 5.32 ℓ
3. a. 3400 mℓ b. 6250 mℓ
   c. 3630 mℓ d. 8760 mℓ
4. a. i. 1 ℓ 200 mℓ ii. 1.2 ℓ
   b. i. 3 ℓ 830 mℓ ii. 3.83 ℓ
   c. i. 4 ℓ 935 mℓ ii. 4.935 ℓ
   d. i. 5 ℓ 769 mℓ ii. 5.769 ℓ
   e. i. 15 ℓ 800 mℓ ii. 15.8 ℓ
   f. i. 5 ℓ 98 mℓ ii. 5.098 ℓ
5. A and G B and K C and L
   D and H E and J F and I
6. C A D B
7. a. 3 ℓ b. 2.5 ℓ c. 30.5 ℓ
   d. 7.4 ℓ e. 0.5 ℓ f. 0.33 ℓ
   g. 0.75 ℓ h. 32.1 ℓ
8. a. 3 cℓ b. 50 cℓ c. 25 cℓ
   d. 8.5 cℓ e. 350 cℓ f. 175 cℓ
   g. 50 cℓ h. 46 cℓ

Calculate using metric units of capacity

A. Litres and millilitres (p 257)
1. a. 3.7 ℓ b. 3.425 ℓ c. 9.075 ℓ
   d. 4.53 ℓ e. 2.08 ℓ f. 6.75 ℓ
   g. 205 mℓ h. 5.96 ℓ i. 2.66 ℓ
   j. 4.375 ℓ
2. 6.5 ℓ 3. 1.62 ℓ
4. a. 6.83 ℓ b. 1.08 ℓ
   c. 4.57 ℓ d. 8.99 ℓ
5. a. 500 mℓ b. 400 mℓ c. 400 mℓ
   d. 160 mℓ

Answers

6. a. 4.67 ℓ b. 730 mℓ or 0.73 ℓ
    c. B and D d. 800 mℓ e. 5 ℓ

B. Mixed calculations (p 258)

1. a. 20 mℓ b. 7   2. 20
3. 4.8 ℓ
4. a. 9.6 ℓ b. 7   5. 9
6. a. 1.8 ℓ b. 75 mℓ
7. 4.25 ℓ   8. 6 ℓ
9. a. 150 mℓ orange, 200 mℓ lemonade, 75 mℓ rum, 50 mℓ tequila
    b. 475 mℓ
10. Answers depend on the number in the group.

Convert between imperial units of capacity (p 261)

1. a. 3 pints   b. 2 pints
    c. 3.5 pints   d. 7.5 pints
    e. 32 pints   f. 12 pints
    g. 4 pints   h. 2 pints
2. a. 3 gallons   b. $\frac{1}{4}$ gallon
    c. 7.5 gallons d. 17.5 gallons
3. a. 40 fl oz   b. 2 fl oz
    c. 10 fl oz   d. 5 fl oz

Calculate capacity and volume using imperial units (p 261)

1. a. 20 fl oz lemonade 10 fl oz orange juice
       5 fl oz apple juice $2\frac{1}{2}$ fl oz mango pulp
       2 fl oz lemon juice
    b. $39\frac{1}{2}$ fl oz
2. $2\frac{1}{4}$ gal   3. a. 40   b. £21.76
4. 6 gallons
5. a. i. 80 pints ii. 560 pints iii. 29 200 pints
    b. i. 10 gallons ii. 70 gallons iii. 3650 gallons

Convert between metric and imperial measures

A. Approximate metric/imperial conversions (p 262)

1. a. a litre   b. 1 pint
2. a. $3\frac{1}{2}$ pt   b. 2 ℓ   c. 4 fl oz
    d. 10 gal   e. 18 ℓ   f. 240 mℓ
3. ≈ $\frac{2}{3}$ litre   4. a. 10 ℓ   b. 6 fl oz

B. More accurate conversions (p 263)

1. a. 1.14 ℓ   b. 5 pt   c. 4.56 ℓ
    d. 7.02 pt (to 2 dp)
2. a. 22.75 ℓ   b. 110 gal (nearest gal)
    c. 40.95 ℓ   d. 7.91 gal (to 2 dp)

3. a. 4.4 gallons b. 54.5 litres (to 1 dp)
4. 85.2 mℓ
5. a. 364 litres
    b. 3.85 gal (2dp) c. 21 weeks

16 Temperature

Measure temperature on the Celsius scale (p 265)

1. a. 40 °C   b. 35 °C
    c. i. 35.5 °C   ii. 36.6 °C   iii. 36.9 °C
       iv. 37.2 °C v. 37.6 °C   vi. 38 °C
2. a. 50 °C   b. 0 °C
    c. i. 12 °C   ii. 23 °C   iii 26 °C
       iv. 35 °C   v. 44 °C
3. a. 50 °C   b. 0 °C   c. 2 °C
    d. i. 3 °C   ii. 16 °C   iii. 27 °C
       iv. 36 °C   v. 44 °C
4. a. 9 °C   b. 7 °C   c. 8 °C
    d. 16 °C   e. 24 °C   f. 27 °C
5. a. 9 °C   b. 18 °C   c. 7 °C
6. a. 54 °C   b. 11 °C   c. 6 000 °C
    d. 20 °C   e. 0 °C   f. 28 °C

Temperatures below freezing point (p 266)

1. a. 50 °C   b. −20 °C
    c. i. 22 °C   ii. 13 °C   iii. 8 °C
       iv. 2 °C   v. −2 °C   vi. −6 °C
       vii. −12 °C viii. −17 °C
    d. i. 22 °C   ii. −17 °C
2. A too cold
3. a. 21 °C 12 °C   2 °C   −2 °C −12 °C −21 °C
    b. 23 °C 14 °C   4 °C   0 °C   −2 °C   −4 °C
    c. 7 °C   5 °C   3 °C   1 °C   −2 °C   −7 °C
4. a. 9 °C   b. 14 °C   c. 14 °C
    d. 16 °C   e. 22 °C   f. 41 °C
    g. 5 °C   h. 17 °C
5. a. 23 °C   b. 26 °C   c. 21 °C
    d. 18 °C   e. 26 °C   f. 19 °C
    g. 9 °C   h. 14 °C
6. a. i. 6 °C   ii. −5 °C
    b. days 4, 5, 6, 7, 8   c. 11 °C

7.

Sitting room	21 °C	10 °C	15 °C	24 °C
Dining room	20 °C	9 °C	14 °C	23 °C
Kitchen	16 °C	5 °C	10 °C	19 °C
Bedroom 1	19 °C	8 °C	13 °C	22 °C
Bedroom 2	16 °C	5 °C	10 °C	19 °C
Bedroom 3	13 °C	2 °C	7 °C	16 °C

445

Answers

Celsius and Fahrenheit (p 269)
1. a. i. 200 °C ii. 180 °C iii. 110 °C
   b. i. 400 °F ii. 350 °F iii. 225 °F
2. a. 350 °F b. 400 °F
   c. dials showing:
      i. 180 °C (meat), 350 °F (meat)
      ii. 200 °C (poultry), 400 °F (poultry)

Use formulae to convert temperatures (p 269)
1. a. 68 °F b. 86 °F c. 41 °F
   d. 59 °F e. 50 °F f. 77 °F
   g. 53.6 °F h. 57.2 °F
2. a. 11 °C b. 19 °C c. 34 °C
   d. 9 °C e. 27 °C f. 13 °C
   g. 15 °C

17 Shape
Angles (p 271)
1. a. 1 b. 2 c. 3
   d. 2 e. 4 f. 4
2. Any 10 objects with right angles
3. a. 40°, b. 70°, c. 110°, d. 145°
4. a. Students' own estimates
   b. i. a. 90° b. 60° c. 30° d. 25°
         e. 130° f. 25° g. 55° h. 45°
         i. 80° j. 127° k. 13° l. 40°
      ii. Student's comparisons between answers to **b** i and **a**
   c. a right angle, b acute, c acute, d acute, e obtuse, f acute, g acute, h acute, i acute, j obtuse, k acute, l acute
5. a. Students' own estimates
   b. Week 1 40°, week 2 68°, week 3 107°, week 4 122°, week 5 148°; and comparisons with **a**.

Horizontal, vertical and parallel lines
A. Horizontal and vertical lines (p 273)
1. a. D, H b. C, F
2. a. Students' own examples of vertical lines
   b. Students' own examples of horizontal lines
3. See below, or similar with 4 verticals and 2 horizontals.

B. Parallel lines (p 274)
1. B, D
2. Any examples of parallel lines
3. a. 55° b. 125°
4. a. 112° b. 68°
   c. 112° d. 68°

Two-dimensional (2-D) shapes (p 275)
1.

Shape	Number of angles that are:		
	Right angles	Smaller	Larger
Square	4		
Rectangle	4		
Regular hexagon			6
Regular octagon			8
Regular pentagon			5
Parallelogram		2	2
Rhombus		2	2
Trapezium		2	2

2.

Shape	4 sides equal	4 right angles	Opposite sides equal	Opposite angles equal	No parallel lines	1 pair of parallel lines	2 pairs of parallel lines
Square	✓	✓	✓	✓			✓
Rectangle		✓	✓	✓			✓
Parallelogram			✓	✓			✓
Rhombus	✓		✓	✓			✓
Trapezium						✓	

3. a. all 108°
   b. all 120°
   c. all 135°
4. a. A: 2.5 cm, 1.5 cm, 2.5 cm, 1.5 cm
      B: All sides 2 cm
      C: 2.5 cm, 2.8 cm, 4.5 cm, 2 cm
   b. A: 80°, 100°, 80°, 100°
      B: 60°, 120°, 60°, 120°
      C: 90°, 135°, 45°, 90°
   c. A: Parallelogram
      B: Rhombus
      C: Trapezium

Triangles (p 277)
1.

Shape	3 equal sides	3 equal angles	2 equal sides	2 equal angles	no equal sides	no equal angles
Equilateral triangle	✓	✓				
Scalene triangle					✓	✓
Isosceles triangle			✓	✓		

2. a. C, E b. A, F c. B, D
3. a. 140° b. 65° c. 50°
4. 130° each
5. a. Isosceles triangles b. 45°, 45°, 90°
6. a. i. Equilateral
      ii. Isosceles
   b. $x = 60°, y = 120°, z = 30°$

Answers

Symmetry (p 281)

1. a. 1 b. 2 c. 1
   d. 1 e. 1 f. 2
   g. 1 h. 0 i. 1
   j. 0 k. 2 l. 1
2. H order 2, O order 2, Z order 2, S order 2, X order 2
3. a. parallelogram, scalene triangle
   b. isosceles triangle
   c. rectangle, rhombus
   d. square, regular hexagon, equilateral triangle
4. square order 4, rectangle order 2, parallelogram order 2, rhombus order 2, regular pentagon order 5, regular octagon order 8, equilateral triangle order 3, isosceles triangle order 1
5.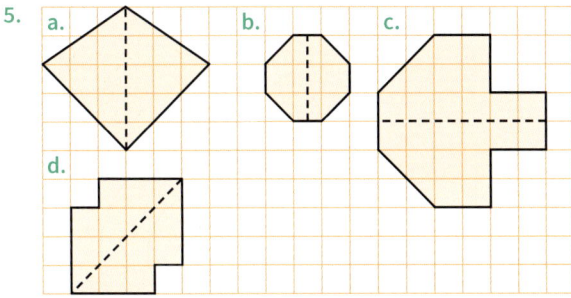
6. a. 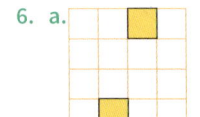 b. 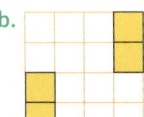 c.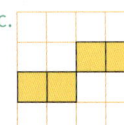
7.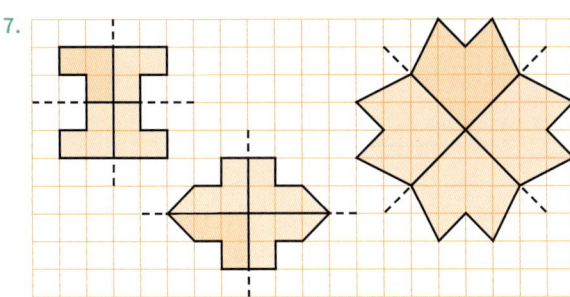
8. Students' diagrams
9. i. 4 ii. 0
10.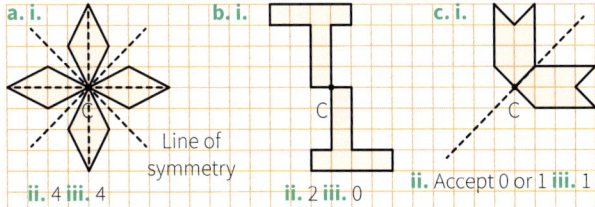
11. Students' diagrams

Tessellations (p 283)

1. a. 8 b. 8 c. 28 d. 8
2. a. hexagon, triangle
   b. square, rhombus, triangle

Three-dimensional (3-D) shapes (p 284)

1.

Shape	Shape of faces	Number of faces	Number of edges	Number of vertices
Cube	Squares	6	12	8
Cuboid	Rectangles	6	12	8
Cylinder	Circles and curved rectangles	3	2	0
Square-based pyramid	Square and triangle	5	8	5
Triangular prism	Triangles and rectangles	5	9	6

Plans and elevations

A. Interpret plans and elevations (p 285)

1. a. Shape C b. Shape A c. Shape B
2. a. cube b. cuboid c. square-based pyramid
   d. cone e. cylinder f. triangular prism
3. a. plinth b. ramp c. planter
4. Any spherical objects, e.g. ball, ball bearing, marble
5. a. B b. A c. D d. C
6. a. L (F) I (A) F (B) T (E) H (C) E (B) N (D)
   b. L (G) I (D) F (B) T (A) H (C) E (E) N (F)
7. a. Solid B, side b. Solid B, plan c. Solid C, front
   d. Solid D, side e. Solid A, side f. Solid A, front
   g. Solid C, plan h. Solid D, front i. Solid B, front
   j. Solid D, plan k. Solid A, plan l. Solid C, side

Answers

B. Draw plans and elevations (p 289)

1. a., b., 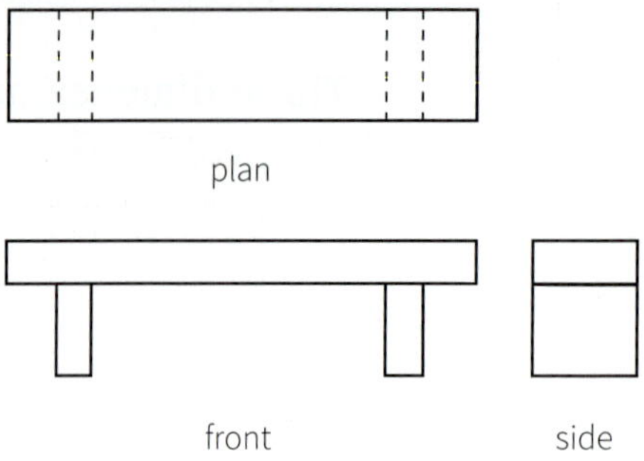 c.

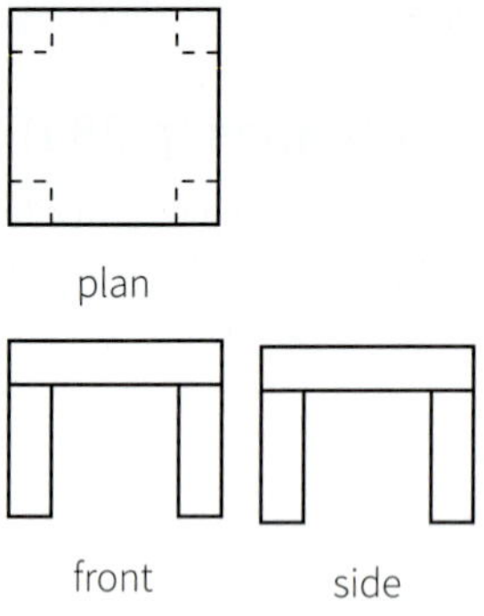

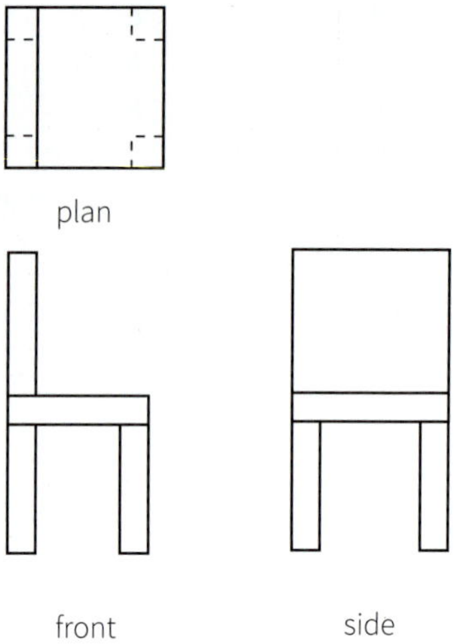

2. a., b.,  c., 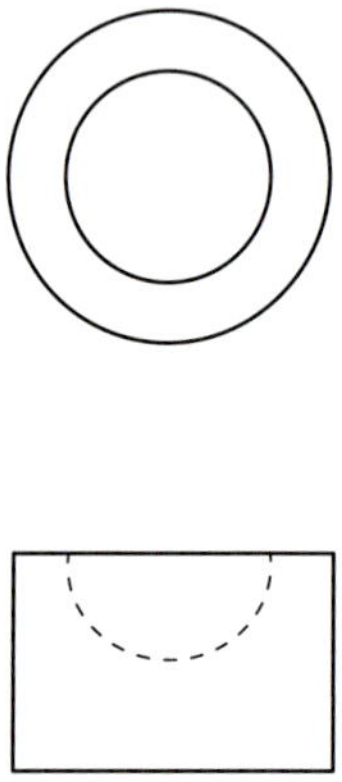 d., 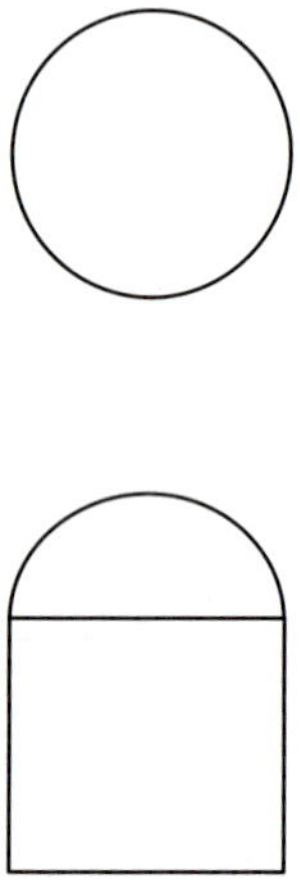 e.

Plan

Front elevation

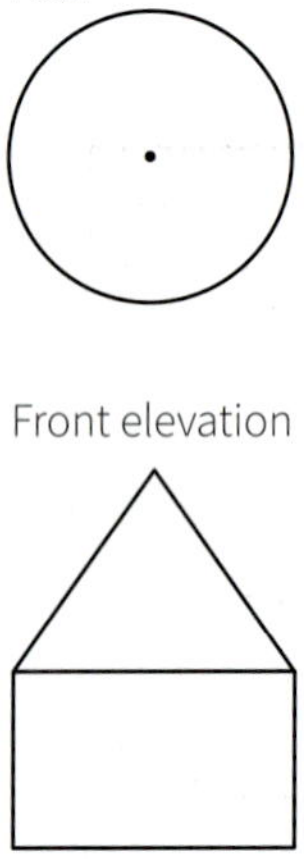

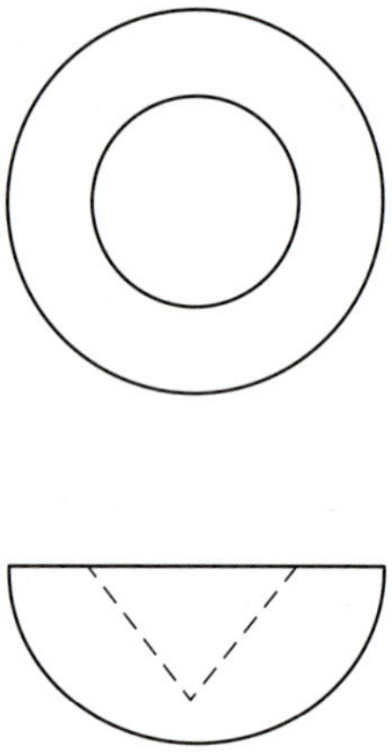

3. a. Scale 1 : 500 (1 cm represents 5 m). Other scales are also acceptable.

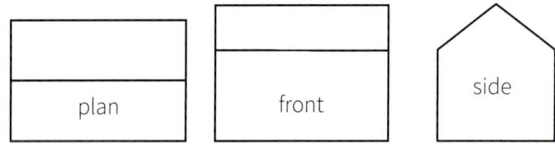

b. In **b** to **e**, side elevations from other sides also acceptable.

Scale 1 : 50 (1 cm represents 0.5 m)

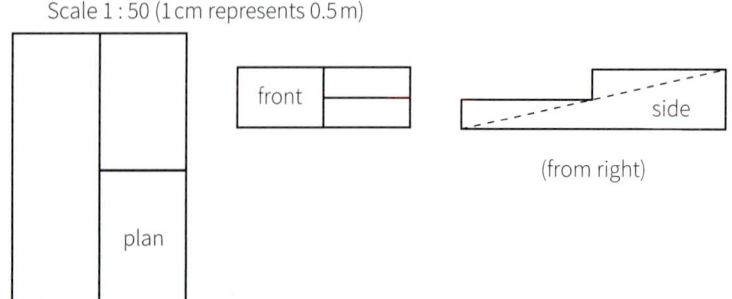

(from right)

Answers

c. Scale 1 cm represents 5 m

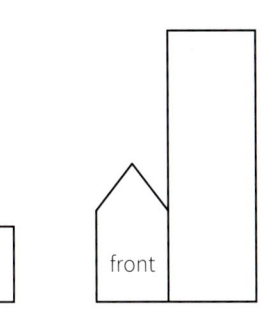 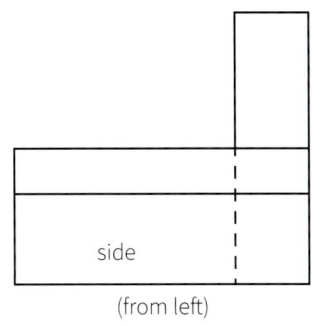

plan front side

(from left)

d. Scale 1 : 50 (1 cm represents 0.5 m)

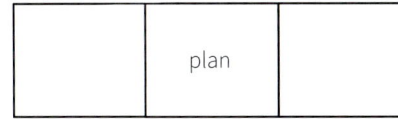 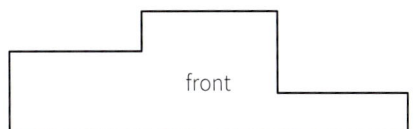 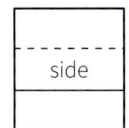

plan front side

(from right)

e. Scale 1 : 500 (1 cm represents 5 m)

  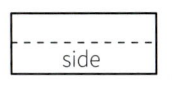

plan front side

(from right)

C. Draw 3-D shapes (p 291)

1. a. 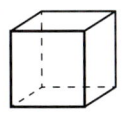 b. 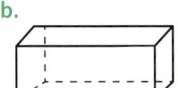 c. 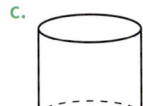 d.

2. a. 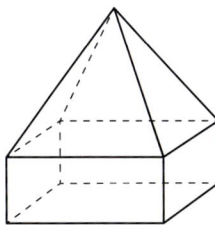 b. 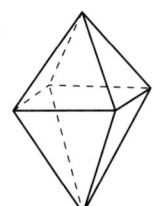 c.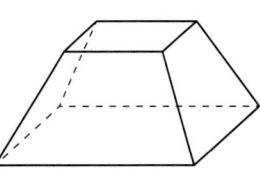

3. a. 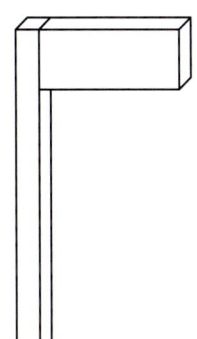 b. 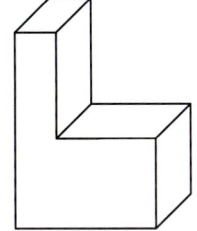 c.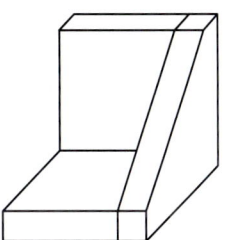

Answers

4.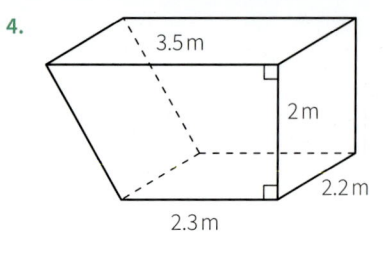

5.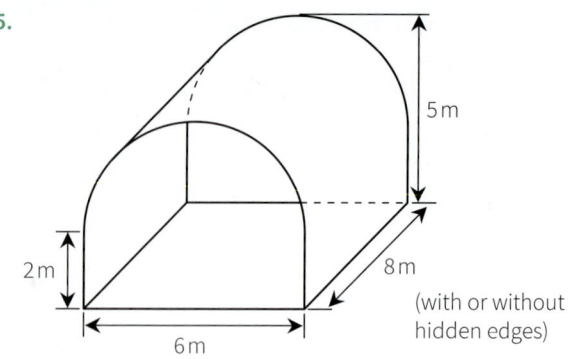
(with or without hidden edges)

6.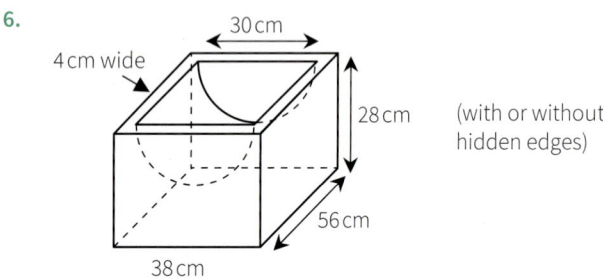
(with or without hidden edges)

7. a. 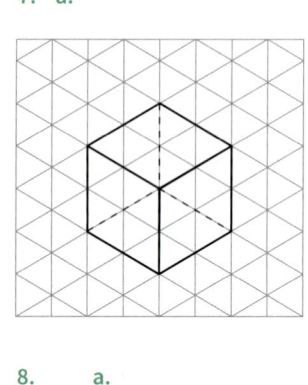   b. 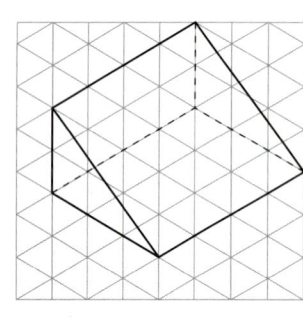   c.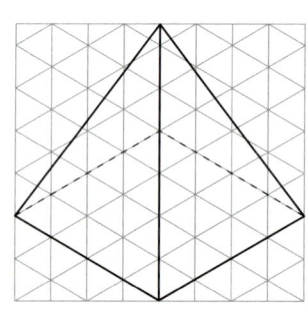
(with or without hidden edges)

8. a.   b.   c.
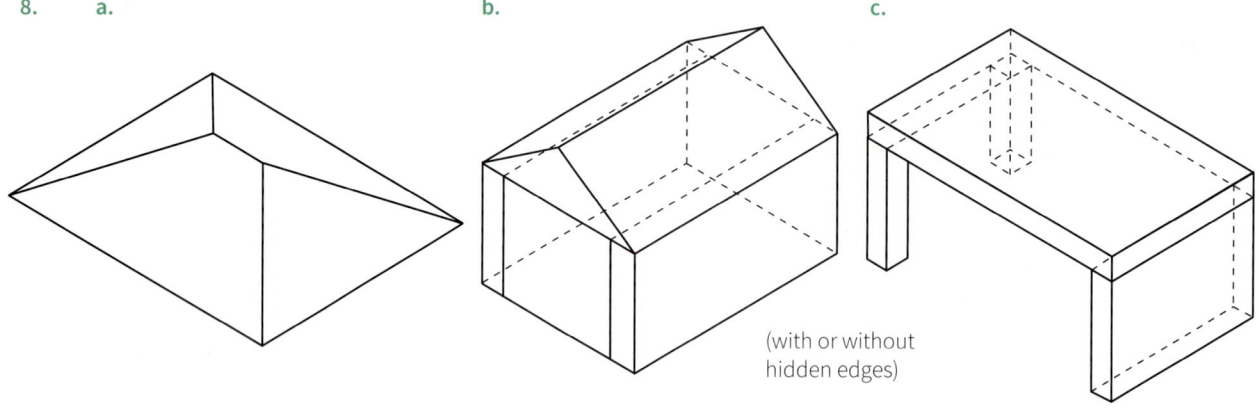
(with or without hidden edges)

9. a. 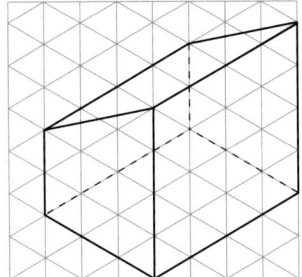   b. 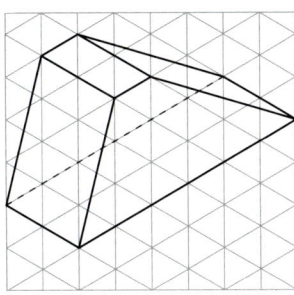   c.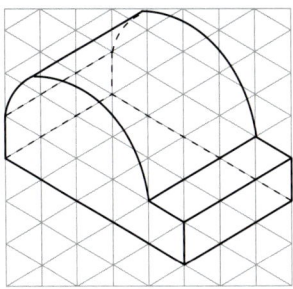

10. a. 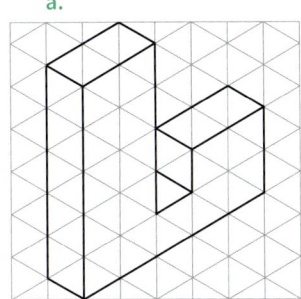   b. 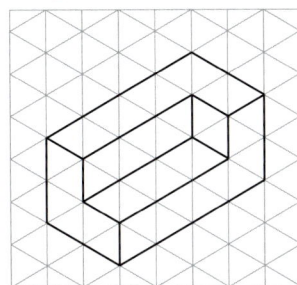   c.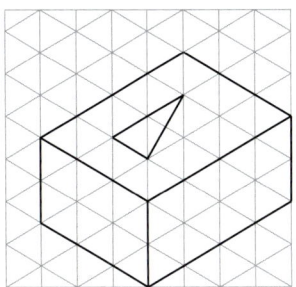

18 Position and Direction

Compass points (p 295)

1. a. 6   b. 8   c. 4
2. a. south   b. west   c. north
   d. $\frac{1}{4}$ turn anticlockwise   e. south-west
   f. north-east   g. south-east
3. a. 180°   b. 90°   c. 45°
   d. 90°   e. 45°   f. 135°
   g. 180°   h. 45°   i. 135°

Describe positions and give directions (p 296)

1. a. bank
   b. i. card shop   ii. right (east)
   c. left (south)
   d. east, right, south, Cross Street, left (east), Fir Tree Lane, right
2. Students' own questions and answers
3. (Other routes are possible.)
   a. Go straight on at the roundabout. The college is on the left.
   b. Turn left (south) at the roundabout. The college is on the left.
   c. Go straight on until the roundabout. Turn right (south) and the college is on the left.
   d. Turn right (east) at the first junction, follow the road past the school and round the left-hand bend. The college is on the right.
   e. Turn left (east) at the Town Hall then right (south) at the roundabout. The college is on the left.
   f. Turn left (east) at the traffic lights then right (south) at the roundabout. The college is on the left.
4. (Accept alternative routes.)
   a. Turn right (north) from the college, then left (west) at the roundabout. The post office is on the left.
   b. Turn left (west) out of the school. Turn right (north) at the 1st T-junction and left (west) at the 2nd T-junction. The petrol station is on the right.
   c. Turn left (west) out of the gym. Turn left (south) at the 1st T-junction and right (west) at the 2nd T-junction and right (north) at the 3rd T-junction. The fish and chip shop is on the right.
   d. Turn right (west) out of the cinema. Turn left (south) at the 1st T-junction, right (west) at the 2nd T-junction and right (north) at the 3rd T-junction, then first left. The supermarket is on the left.
   e., f. There is more than one good answer.
5. (Accept alternative answers.)
   a. **First route**
   On leaving the college, turn left (south). Follow the road round a right-hand bend and straight on to the T-junction.
   Turn right (north) at the T-junction, then take the second left turn.
   The swimming pool is on the left.

451

Answers

Second route
On leaving the college, turn right (north), then go left (west) at the roundabout (1st exit).
Take the third left turn, then first right.
The swimming pool is on the left.
b. Either route with a valid reason, for example, the first route because it has fewer road junctions.
6. Students' own questions and answers

Bearings (p 299)
1. a. 050° b. 084° c. 116° d. 230° e. 281° f. 345°
2. a. 256°   b. 076°
3. a. Jane
   b. Student's diagram

Positions on maps (p 300)
1. a. Netherlands   b. Peter Pan
   c. i. E2   ii. C1   iii. C3
2. a. A1, A3, B1, D1
   b. B1, B3, D2, E2
3. a. C1, D2, D3, C3, C2
   b. A3, A2, A1, B1, C1, D2, E2, E3

Coordinates
A. Positive coordinates (p 301)
1. a. A(2, 8) B(7, 7) C(0, 7) D(5, 7) E(1, 3) F(4, 5)
      G(6, 2) H(8, 7) I(1, 0) J(4, 1) K(8, 5) L(8, 1)
   b. P(2, 4) Q(3, 7) R(5, 6) S(7, 8) T(8, 4) U(7, 0)
      V(5, 2) W(3, 1)
2. a. (15, 6) (17, 4)
   b. Move right 3 and up 3, then move right 2 and down 2.
      (Or move right 5 and up 1 in two separate rows of trees.)
3. a.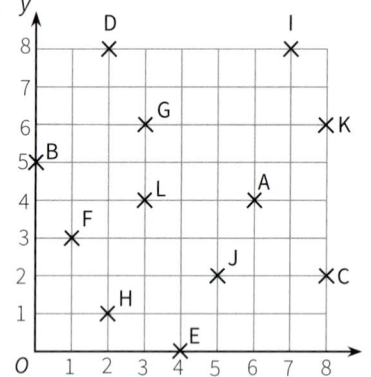

b.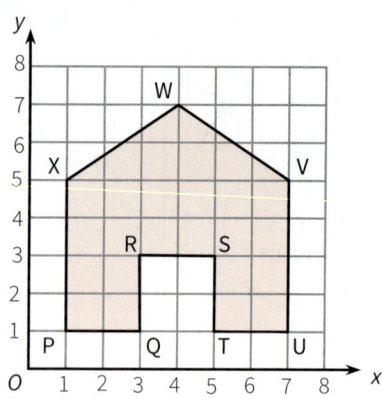

The front of a house (or an archway)

4. a. i., ii.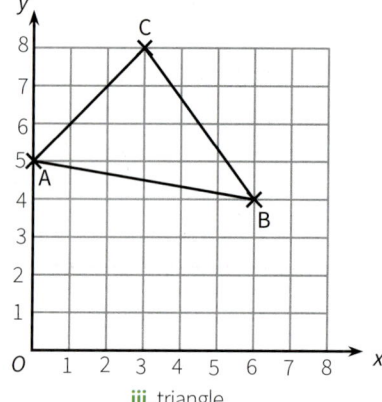

iii. triangle

b. i., ii.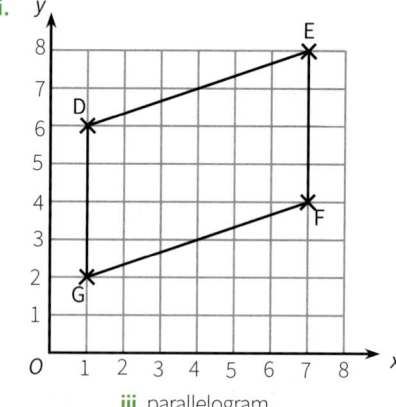

iii. parallelogram

c. i., ii.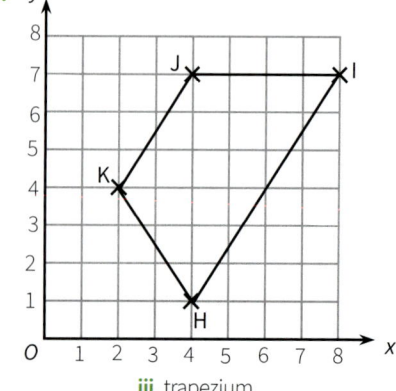

iii. trapezium

452

Answers

d. i., ii.

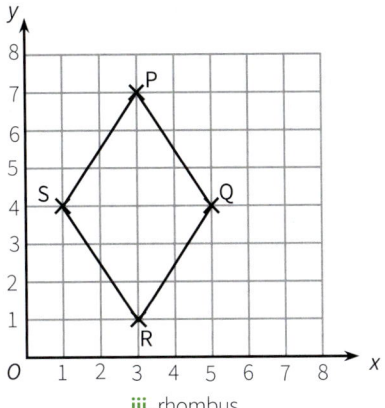

iii. rhombus

5. a, b, c i, d i

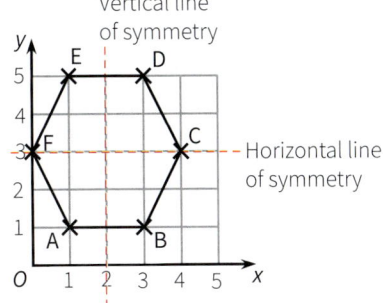

c ii (2, 1), (2, 2), (2, 3), (2, 4), (2,5) or any others with x coordinate 2. All points have x-coordinate 2.

d ii (0, 3), (1, 3), (2, 3), (3, 3), (4, 3) or any others with y coordinate 3. All points have y-coordinate 3.

6. a. i., ii.

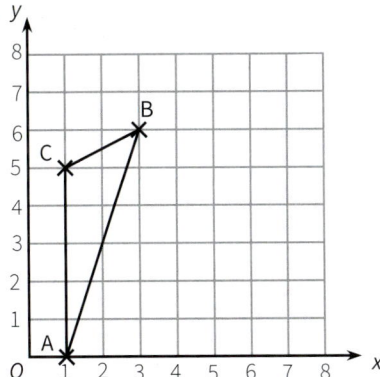

iii. scalene – sides and angles all different

b. i., ii.

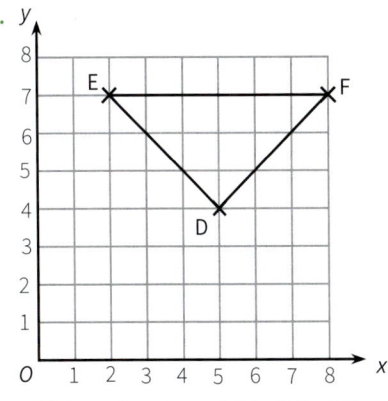

iii. isosceles – 2 equal sides (DE = DF) and 2 equal angles (angle E = angle F)

7. a., b. Three of many possible triangles:

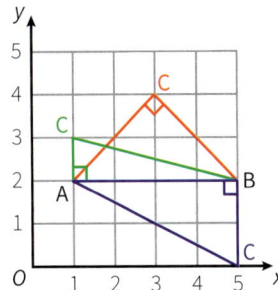

c. Coordinates of students' point C

B. Negative coordinates (p 303)

1. a. A(5, 7) B(7, 3) C(1, 4) D(2, −3) E(7, −4) F(−8, −6)
   G(−5, 6) H(−6, 3) I(4, −6) J(−4, −6) K(−2, 2) L(−5, −2)
   b. A, B, E, I
   c. F, G, H, J, L
   d. B, C, D, E, F, H, I, J, K, L
   e. A, B, C, D, E, G, H, K, L

2.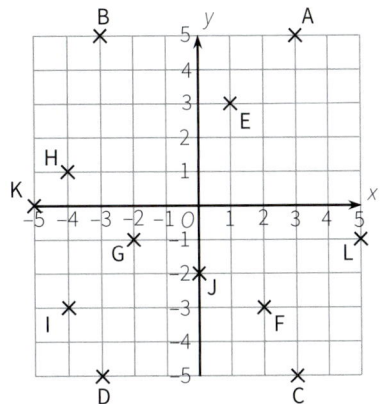

453

Answers

3.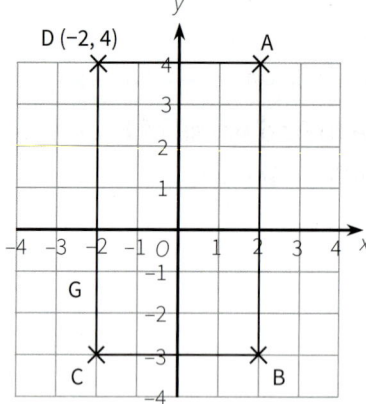

4.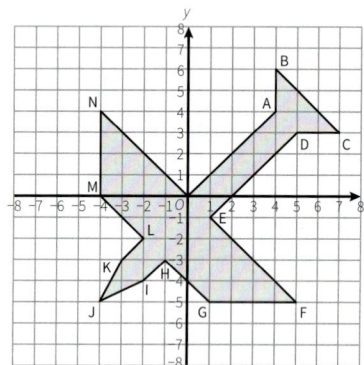

5. a.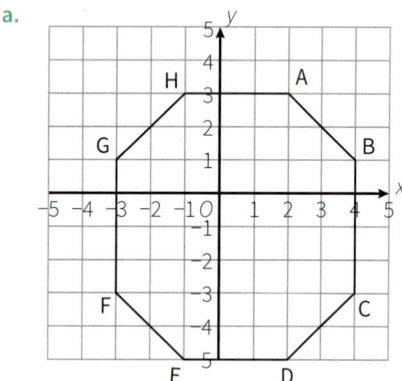

   b. octagon
   c. 135°
   d. No – the sides are not equal.

6. a.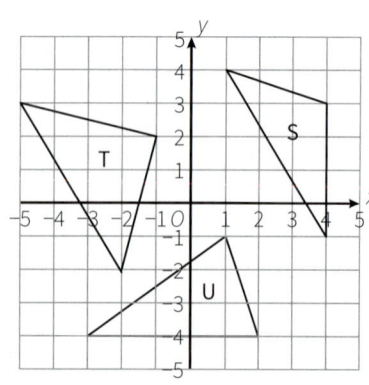

b. i. T is isosceles — it has 2 equal sides and 2 equal angles.
    ii. None of the triangles is equilateral — none has 3 equal sides and 3 equal angles.
c. i. T   ii. S

Grid references (p 305)

1. a. 268 940   b. 291 951   c. 244 962
   d. 258 952   e. 292 947   f. 248 957
   g. 272 968   h. 298 948
2. a. White Lee Farm   b. Allman Well Hill
   c. Ewden Village   d. Spout House Hill
   e. parking   f. woodland
   g. viewpoint   h. Broomhead Reservoir

3-D coordinates (p 306)

1. O(0, 0, 0), A(3, 0, 0), B(0, 5, 0), F(3, 0, 4), G(0, 5, 4)
2. Q(10, 0, 6), R(10, 0, 0), S(10, 8, 0), T(0, 8, 6), U(0, 0, 6), V(0, 8, 0)
3. B(3, 1, 2), C(3, 4, 2), D(0, 4, 2), E(0, 1, 5), F(3, 1, 5), G(3, 4, 5), H(0, 4, 5)
4. A(2, 0, 0), B(2, 0, 1), C(4, 1, 0), D(3, 4, 0), E(3, 4, 1), F(2, 4, 1)
5. P(1, 4, 0), Q(1, 3, 1), R(1, 3, 3), S(0, 1, 1), T(0, 1, 3), U(0, 3, 3)
6. a. length 5 m, width 4 m, height 5 m
   b. O(0, 0, 0), A(4, 0, 0), B(4, 0, 3), C(2, 0, 5), D(0, 0, 3), E(0, 5, 0), F(4, 5, 0), G(4, 5, 3), H(2, 5, 5), I(0, 5, 3)
7. Supermarket (20, 5, 15), house (35, 7.5, 15), bungalow (45, 5, 10), church (90, 5, 20)
8. a. (8, 0, 0)   b. (4, 4, 6)

19 Perimeter, Area and Volume

Perimeter (p 309)

1. i. Students' measurements
   ii. a. 10 cm   b. 12 cm   c. 10 cm
       d. 12.2 cm   e. 13.4 cm   f. 14.2 cm
2. a. 26 cm
   b. No, the bottom is equal to 4 + 6 = 10 cm and the right-hand side is equal to 2 + 1 = 3 cm
3. a. 21 m   b. 21 m   c. 218 m   d. 18.8 m
4. 5 m   5. 3.8 m
6.

Length	Width	Perimeter
6 cm	2 cm	16 cm
10 mm	6 mm	32 mm
20 cm	6.2 cm	52.4 cm
4.5 m	3 m	15 m
20 mm	15 mm	70 mm
2.7 m	2.25 m	9.9 m

7. Any dimensions which fit the given perimeters
8. 1300 m   9. 320 cm   10. 7.8 m

Answers

Area

A. Measuring in square units (p 312)
1. a. $5\,cm^2$ b. $7\,cm^2$ c. $8\,cm^2$
2. Any 4 shapes with an area of $12\,cm^2$

B. Area of a rectangle (p 313)
1. a. $15\,m^2$ b. $26\,m^2$ c. $400\,mm^2$
   d. $15\,cm^2$ e. $1700\,mm^2$
   f. $9750\,cm^2$ or $0.975\,m^2$
2. Any dimensions which match the given areas
3. a. $54\,m^2$ b. $1080\,g$

C. Areas of shapes made from rectangles (p 314)
1. a. $21\,m^2$ b. $13\,m^2$ c. $21\,m^2$
   d. $18.32\,m^2$ e. $25.8\,m^2$
2. a. $10.8\,m^2$ b. $25.64\,m^2$
   c. Yes since 2.5 litres covers $30\,m^2$.

Circles

A. Circumference (p 316)
1. a. 10p diameter = 2.4 cm   £2 = 2.8 cm
   b. 10p circumference = 7.5 cm   £2 = 8.8 cm
   c. Students' check
2. a. 31.4 cm   b. 44.0 cm (1dp)
   c. 4.7 m (1dp)   d. 5.0 m (1dp)
   e. 141.3 m; 141.4 m (1dp) using π   f. 94.2 m

3.

Radius	Diameter	Circumference
2 cm	4 cm	12.6 cm
15 mm	30 mm	94.2 mm
3 m	6 m	18.8 m
1.2 m	2.4 m	7.5 m
2.5 cm	5 cm or 5.0 cm	15.7 cm
12.0 mm	24.0 mm	75.4 mm

4. 151 cm
5. 251 cm
6. a. 84.8 mm   b. 8.5 cm

B. Area of a circle (p 317)
1. a. $3.1\,m^2$ b. $28.3\,cm^2$
   c. $78.5\,cm^2$ d. $15.2\,m^2$
2. a. $153.9\,cm^2$ b. $12.6\,m^2$
   c. $201.0\,mm^2$ or $201.1\,mm^2$
   d. $452.2\,mm^2$ or $452.4\,mm^2$
   e. $706.5\,cm^2$ or $706.9\,cm^2$
   f. $6.2\,m^2$
3. a. $50.2\,cm^2$ or $50.3\,cm^2$
   b. $314\,mm^2$ or $314.2\,mm^2$ c. $95.0\,cm^2$
   d. $4.9\,m^2$ e. $153.9\,mm^2$
   f. $5024\,cm^2$ or $5026.5\,cm^2$

4. $4420\,cm^2$
5. a. 31 cm   b. $754.4\,cm^2$ or $754.8\,cm^2$
   c. $176.6\,cm^2$ or $176.7\,cm^2$ d. $578\,cm^2$

Use formulae to find areas of triangles and other shapes (p 318)
1. a. $6\,cm^2$ b. $10.8\,m^2$ c. $94.5\,cm^2$
2. $1.05\,m^2$
3. $4800\,cm^2$ or $0.48\,m^2$
4. $180\,cm^2$
5. $2.2\,m^2$

Perimeters and areas of composite shapes (p 319)
1. a. 339 cm (nearest cm)   b. 7.8 m (to 1 dp)
   c. 200 mm (nearest mm)
2. a. $610\,m^2$
   b. $820\,cm^2$ (nearest cm^2)   c. $370\,cm^2$
3. a. perimeter = 12.6 m, area = $9.12\,m^2$
   b. perimeter = 169 cm (nearest cm),
      area = $1370\,cm^2$ (nearest $10\,cm^2$)
   c. perimeter = 209 mm (nearest mm),
      area = $3180\,mm^2$ (nearest $10\,mm^2$)
4. Total area = $104.24\,m^2$
   Number of bricks = 6254.4 so 6255
   It would be sensible for the builder to order about 6500 or 7000 bricks, to allow for some breakages.
5. a. i. $5.76\,m^2$ ii. $10.32\,m^2$ iii. $1.13\,m^2$ iv. $24.55\,m^2$ (2dp)
   b. 210 g   c. 1.23 kg or 1230 g
6. a. 25 times round track = $397.0796\ldots \times 25 = 9927\,m$
      This is a little less than 10 km, so what the athlete says is not accurate, though 10 km is a reasonable estimate.
   b. Area = $7963.495\ldots\,m^2$
      Amount of grass seed needed = 238.9 kg
      Number of packs needed = 238.9 ÷ 5 = 47.78
      50 packs is sensible as it allows some spare in case of spillages or in case some of the seeds do not germinate.
7. a. i., ii. Students' own explanations
   b. Perimeter ≈ 8.2 m, area ≈ $4.7\,m^2$

Nets (p 321)
1. a. cuboid   b. triangular prism
   c. square-based pyramid
2. A, B, D, E
3. A, C, D, F

Surface area (p 323)
1. a. $3384\,cm^2$ b. $31.7\,m^2$ (to 1 dp)
   c. $264\,cm^2$
2. a. $20.88\,m^2$ b. $348\,cm^2$ (nearest cm^2)
   c. $7704\,mm^2$

Answers

3. a.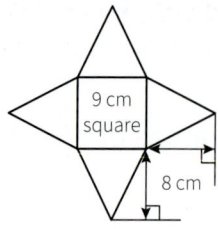

   b. 225 cm²
4. 236 cm² (nearest cm²)
5. a.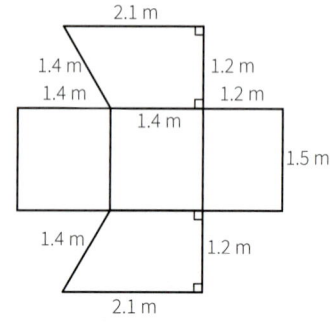

   b. 10.2 m²
6. 4.3 m² (to 1 dp)

Volume of a cuboid (p 325)

1. a. 6 cm³ b. 4 cm³ c. 18 cm³
   d. 30 cm³
2. a. 36 m³ b. 8000 mm³
   c. 32.4 cm³ d. 28.8 cm³
3.
Length	Width	Height	Volume
2 cm	4 cm	5 cm	**40 cm³**
3 m	3.4 m	3.5 m	**35.7 m³**
4 mm	2.5 mm	6 mm	**60 mm³**
9 cm	6.2 cm	8 cm	**446.4 cm³**

4. 0.5 m³
5. 4000 cm³
6. Any 3 dimensions which multiply to make a volume of 1000 cm³
7. 112 500 cm³
8. 15 625 mm³
9. a. 100 cm b. 10 000 cm²
   c. 1 000 000 cm³
10. 1st 0.384 m³   2nd 0.224 m³   3rd 0.14 m³
    b. 0.748 m³
11.
Length	Width	Height	Volume
4 m	2 m	**3 m**	24 m³
3 cm	**2 cm**	8 cm	48 cm³
2 m	3 m	9 m	54 m³
4 cm	4 cm	**4 cm**	64 cm³

Volume of a cylinder (p 327)

1. a. 56.5 cm³ b. 19.6 m³
   c. 2.4 m³ d. 17.0 m³
   e. 6.8 cm³
2. a. 9.0 m³
   b. 1017.4 cm³ or 1017.9 cm³
   c. 62.2 m³ d. 45.2 m³
   e. 282.6 cm³ or 282.7 cm³
   f. 0.4 m³
3. a. 3.77 m³ b. 7.85 cm³
   c. 2.71 cm³ d. 0.92 m³
   e. 0.11 m³ f. 0.57 m³
4. 0.34 m³ (2dp)

Use other formulae to find volumes (p 329)

1. 1200 cm³
2. a. 75 000 cm³ b. 2 bags
3. a. 60 cm³ b. 416
4. 27 litres
5. Volume of sphere = 36π cm³ (or 113 cm³ to nearest cm³)
   Volume of cone = 36π cm³ (or 113 cm³ to nearest cm³)
6. 198 cm³ (to nearest cm³)

Solve problems involving 2-D and 3-D shapes (p 330)

1. a. 88 cm b. 22 cm
2. a. 1.6 m b. 1.15 m
3. 41 streetlights
4. a. 12 packs b. 12 packs
5. a. 136 tiles b. £149.94
6. a. £43.96 b. 4.32 m²
7. a. 360 cans b. 12 cans
8. a. 168
   b. As below. Or other net that gives the box, with correct dimensions

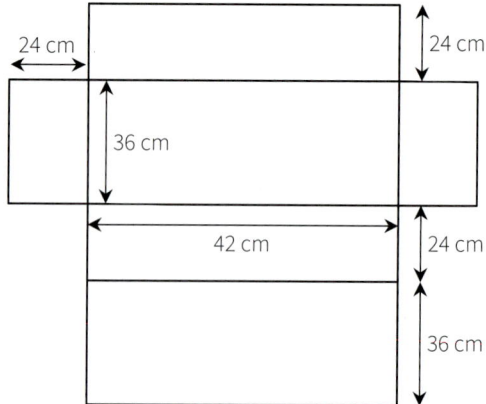

9. a i. 1.5 cm ii. 3.375 cm³
   b There are variety of possible answers.
      For example, the dice could be arranged in 5 layers, each with 4 rows of 8 dice.
      This would lead to a box with dimensions 7.5 cm by 6 cm by 12 cm.

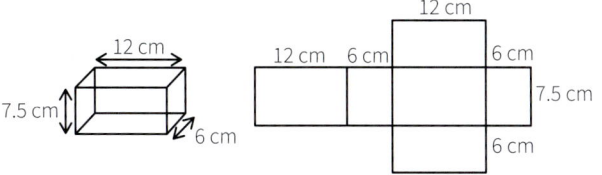

10. For 120 glasses as shown they need 27.7 litres of juice. As a minimum they should buy 28 cartons costing £22.12. It would be sensible to buy 30 litres costing £23.70 to allow extra in case of spills.

20 Compound Measures
Calculate using compound measures
A. Calculate speed, distance and time (p 334)
1. a. 40 mph   b. 5 mph   c. 42.5 km/h
   d. 580 km/h   e. 5 m/s   f. 8 mph
   g. 1.25 m/s   h. 0.6 km/h
2. a. 90 miles   b. 3250 km
   c. 60 metres   d. 4 miles
3. a. 2 hours   b. 4 hours
   c. 4 seconds   d. 8 seconds
4. 45 mph
5. 1.4 km/h

B. Convert speeds (p 336)
1. a. 20 m/s   b. 5 m/s   c. 30 m/s
   d. 90 km/h   e. 43.2 km/h f. 28.8 km/h
2. a. 37.5 m/s   b. 135 km/h
3.

Speed limits in France		
	km/h	mph
2-lane roads	80	50
3-lane roads	90	56
4-lane expressways	110	69
motorways	130	81

4. Student's table, for example

Speed limits in the UK		
	mph	km/h
urban areas	30	48
single carriageways	60	96
dual carriageways	70	112
motorways	70	112

C. Density, mass and volume (p 337)
1. Copper 9.0 g/cm³, lead 11.3 g/cm³, steel 7.8 g/cm³, iron 7.9 g/cm³
2. a. 107 g   b. 382.5 g   c. 84.9 g (1 dp)   d. 50.4 g
3. a. 20 cm³   b. 8.0 cm³ (1 dp)
   c. 16.6 cm³ (1 dp)   d. 3.2 cm³ (1 dp)
   e. 51.8 cm³ (1 dp)   f. 357 cm³ (nearest cm³)
4. £23.30   5. 50 g
6. 7788 kg/m³ (nearest kg/m³)
7. a. 88.0 cm³ (1 dp)   b. 0.9 g/cm³ (1 dp)
8. 770 tonnes (nearest 10 tonnes)
9. a. i. 113 g (nearest gram) ii. 33929 g or 33.929 kg
   b. £127.23   c. £101.07   d. £295.56

D. Population density (p 339)
1. 423 people/km² (to nearest whole number)
2. 5.4 million people (to 1 dp)
3. 20 700 km² (to nearest hundred km²)
4. a. 128 people/km² (to nearest whole number)
   b. The population density of England is the highest, followed by Wales, then Northern Ireland, then Scotland.
5. a.

Country	Area (km²)	Population	Population density
Spain	500 000	46 million	92 people/km²
Germany	357 000	82 million	230 people/km²
Iceland	100 000	330 thousand	3 people/km²

   b. Spain has the greatest area, followed by Germany, then Iceland which is only one fifth the area of Spain. Germany has the greatest population, with Spain having just over half as many people. Iceland has by far the smallest population (Germany has about 250 times as many people and Spain about 140 times as many). Germany is the most densely populated with, on average, over twice as many people per square kilometre than Spain and nearly 80 times as many as Iceland.

Handling Information and Data
21 Extracting and Interpreting Information
Information from lists, tables and pictograms
A. Find information from lists (p 341)
1. a. alphabetically   b. easy to find items
   c. 791455   d. 787652
   e. Doctor's
2. a. by date   b. Dinner date
   c. 20th April   d. 17th March
   e. Between dinner date and wedding anniversary

answers

3. a. alphabetically b. by date
   c. by date d. alphabetically
   e. alphabetically in categories

B. Find information from tables (p 343)

1. a. 11 b. 7 c. 11 d. 17
   e. Carpentry (19 students)
2. a. £11.00 b. £11.99 c. internet
   d. The Invasion e. £3.01
3. a. i. £75 ii. £179
   b. Economy
   c. £125
   d. i. £21 ii. £51
   e. £21
4. a. 791/75S b. 11:10 c. 06:30
   d. Gatwick–Pula e. Saturday
5. a. Title and column headings
   b. Redrawn table with suitable title (for example, Hotel Prices) and column headings (for example, Resort, Hotel, Length of stay and price for HB/FB)
   c. £1286 d. £500
   e. i. Altea Hotel Esplendia ii. full board
      iii. 7 nights
   f. £105
6. a. £101 b. £528

C. Find information from pictograms (p 346)

1. a. 45
   b. i. Poultry ii. Meat
   c. 15 d. 230
2. a. i. carpet ii. decorating
   b. i. curtains £80 bed linen £70 ii. £465
      carpet £155 furniture £104
      decorating £56 (allow ± £3)

Information from bar charts and line graphs

A. Find information from bar charts (p 347)

1. a.

Type of drink	Number of workers
Tea	25
Decaff tea	12
Coffee	30
Decaff coffee	13
Water	7
Fruit juice	15

   b. 13 c. 8 d. 25 e. 102
2. a. i. 38 ii. 65 iii. 39 iv. 21
   b. i. Soaps ii. Music
   c. 17
   d. 9 people

   e. 139 people
   f. 140 people
   g. 300
3. a. i. Germany ii. Ireland
   b. UK 65 million, Spain 49 million, Netherlands 17 million, Ireland 5 million, Germany 81 million, Belgium 12 million
   c. i. 16 million ii. 48 million
   d. 70 million
4. a. Music b. Gardening
   c. i. £4.20 ii. £3.70
   d. £0.80 or 80 pence
5. a.

Student	Height (m)
Jameela	1.5
Florence	1.6
David	1.9
Nasma	1.7
Matthew	1.8
Ruaridh	1.7
Mohamed	1.8

   b. Jameela c. David
   d. Ruaridh e. Mohamed
6. a. Title, vertical axis label, (gridlines)
   b. Cheese c. Baked beans
   d.

Filling	Number bought
Baked beans	16
Cheese	37
Chicken tikka	28
Coleslaw	19
Tuna	18

   e. 118 f. 19
7. a. Chart B
   b. i., ii. Students' own estimates
      (Exact values given below:)

Year	Chart A	Chart B
1	51	51
2	59	59
3	62	62
4	63	63
5	68	68

   iii. Chart B

8. a. Catering, Electrical installation
   b. i. 5 ii. 2 iii. 10
   c. i. 26 ii. 35 iii. 34
   d. i. 92 ii. 110

Answers

9. a. i. Pete ii. £690
   b. i. Amy ii. £550
   c. Ahmed £640, Jim £570, Sally £680
   d. i. Sally ii. £450
   e. i. Amy and Jim ii. £380
   f. i. Amy £170, Ahmed £210, Jim £190, Pete £290, Sally £230
      ii. Pete, Sally, Ahmed, Jim, Amy
10. Any 3 examples of each type of data
11. a. Maths b. Media
    c.

Grades	Percentage of candidates			
	Computing	Law	Maths	Media
A*	3	5	18	2
A	14	14	24	10
B	21	27	22	32
C	24	25	16	37
D	21	16	11	15
E	12	9	6	3
U	5	4	3	1

(allow ±2%)

12.

Magazine	Number of readers	
	a. to nearest million	b. to nearest 100 000
Autocar	1 million	900 000
New Musical Express	1 million	1 200 000
Radio Times	3 million	3 400 000
Time Out	2 million	2 000 000
TV Times	1 million	1 400 000
What's On TV?	3 million	2 800 000

B. Find information from line graphs (p 355)

(Allow approximate answers.)

1. a. 5 mm
   b. i. November ii. 150 mm
   c. i. September ii. 35 mm
   d. 76 mm ± 5 mm e. 1072 mm ± 20 mm
2. a i. 22 ii. 23
   b i. 2018 ii. 28
   c i. 2016 ii. 19
   d Yes. 20 children attended in 2014 and 27 children attended in 2019. 27 − 20 = 7
3. a. i. 1 hour ii. 0.5 °C
   b. every 2 hours
   c. i. 5.5 °C ii. 14:00
   d. i. −3.5 °C ii. 04:00
   e. i. 08:00 ii. 00:20, 18:40 (±10 min)
   f. i. 04:00 to 14:00
      ii. 00:00 to 04:00 and 14:00 to 24:00
   g. 06:00 to 10:00
4. a. i. Graph B
      ii.

Year	Profits (£000s)
1	2130
2	2420
3	2390
4	2510
5	2680

(allow ±10)

   b. Axis does not start at zero.
5. a. i. April ii. May
   b. i. December ii. January and December
   c. i. 0.5 hour (or 30 minutes) per day
      ii. 2 hours per day
   d. i. 3.4 hours (or 3 hours 24 minutes) per day
      ii. 2.7 hours (or 2 hours 42 minutes) per day
   e. More sunshine in England than in Scotland. Least sunshine in winter, but more in spring than in summer.
6. a. 2015 b. 1972
   c. 42 million tonnes (of oil equivalent)
   d. 16 million tonnes
   e. 56 or 57 million tonnes
   f. Solid fuel consumption fell sharply by about 8 million tonnes.
      Petroleum consumption rose sharply by about 8 million tonnes.
   g. Solid fuel consumption fell to just under a quarter of the original amount. Gas consumption rose to about 7 times as much then started to fall. Overall petroleum consumption fell by about half, then remained fairly steady until 2010 when it started to fall again gradually. (Other wording and details are acceptable.)

Information from pie charts (p 358)

1. a. work b. 0.5 hour
   c. 24 hours — total time in a day
2. a. i. drive ii. cycle
   b. i. $\frac{1}{4}$ ii. $\frac{1}{10}$ iii. $\frac{1}{5}$ iv. $\frac{2}{5}$ v. $\frac{1}{20}$
   c. walk 40, drive 160, bus 100, train 80, cycle 20
3. a. Grade A: $\frac{1}{8}$ Grade B: $\frac{1}{4}$
      Grade C: $\frac{1}{2}$ Grade D: $\frac{1}{8}$
   b. Grade A: 6 Grade B: 12
      Grade C: 24 Grade D: 6
4. a. i. T ii. F iii. T iv. T
   b. Terraced, Flats, Semi-detached, Detached and Bungalows (approx. equal)

5. a., b.

Flatmate	Angle	Amount to pay
Bev	120°	120 × £0.50 = £60
Mia	40°	40 × £0.50 = £20
Jess	100°	100 × £0.50 = £50
Oliver	20°	20 × £0.50 = £10
Matt	80°	80 × £0.50 = £40
	Total	£180

6. a. Paint b. more c. true
   d. Wallpaper £1755, Paint £2340
      Decorating equipment £945,
      Plants £1440, Gardening tools £1260,
      Other £360 (Allow ±£22.50)
7. a. 1.5 workers
   b. 360 factory workers, 48 sales workers,
      42 managers
   c. 540
8. a. A, B, D, F
   b. i. 96° ii. 2.5 people
      iii. and c. i. see table
   c. Yes

	Fri	Sat
Men	240	250
Women	420	370
Children	240	580
Total	900	1200

Information from conversion graphs (p 362)

1. a. i. 10 gallons ≈ 45 litres
      ii. 5 gallons ≈ 23 litres
      iii. 18 gallons ≈ 82 litres
      iv. 7.5 gallons ≈ 34 litres
   b. i. 40 litres ≈ 9 gallons
      ii. 72 litres ≈ 16 gallons
      iii. 24 litres ≈ 5.5 gallons
      iv. 67 litres ≈ 14.5 gallons
   c. 68 litres d. 18 gallons e. 68 litres
2. a. i. 2 °C ii. 5 °F
   b. i. 20 °C ≈ 68 °F   ii. 48 °C ≈ 118 °F
      iii. 75 °C ≈ 167 °F iv. 27 °C ≈ 81 °F
      v. −10 °C ≈ 14 °F   vi. −7 °C ≈ 19 °F
   c. i. 50 °F ≈ 10 °C   ii. 140 °F ≈ 60 °C
      iii. 75 °F ≈ 24 °C iv. 205 °F ≈ 96 °C
      v. 184 °F ≈ 84 °C   vi. 28 °F ≈ −2 °C
   d. Freezes at 32 °F, boils at 212 °F.
   e. 57 °F is approximately 14 °C so it was approximately
      3 °C warmer in July 2010.

22 Collecting and Illustrating Data

Create frequency tables (p 365)

1. a. Cat 14, Rabbit 5, Bird 2, Fish 3,
      Reptile 1, Other 6, None 13
   b. Dog
   c. Any type of pet not in the table, e.g. hamster
2. a.

Number of pets	Tally	Frequency
0	ЖЖ III	13
1	ЖЖЖЖЖ I	26
2	Ж IIII	9
3	Ж II	7
4	II	2
5	I	1
6	II	2

   b. i. 13 ii. 7 iii. 5
   c. 60
3. a.

Grade	Frequency
Distinction	7
Merit	14
Pass	19
Fail	10

   b. 50 c. i. $\frac{7}{50}$ ii. $\frac{7}{25}$ d. 20%
4. a.

Number of books	Frequency
1	31
2	16
3	14
4	11
5	8
6	4

   b. 1 c. 84 d. 14% (nearest %)
5. a.

Time (minutes)	Tally	Frequency
6–10	III	3
11–15	Ж II	7
16–20	Ж III	8
21–25	Ж Ж	10
26–30	Ж	5

   b. 21–25 minutes
   c. 33
   d. $\frac{1}{11}$
   e. 45% (to nearest %)

6.

Age	Frequency	
	Pass	Fail
17–20	7	5
21–30	6	5
31–40	2	1
41–50	3	0
51–60	0	1

(other age groupings possible)

Represent data in pictograms (p 368)

1. Sunshine at a seaside resort in a week in August

Monday	☀ ☀ ☀
Tuesday	☀ ☀
Wednesday	☀ ☼
Thursday	☀ ☀ ☼
Friday	☀ ☀ ☀ ☀
Saturday	☀ ☀ ☀ ☀ ☀
Sunday	☀ ☀ ☀ ☀ ☼

Key: ☀ = 2 hours   ☼ = 1 hour

2. Number of houses sold by estate agent

Key: 🏠 = 10 houses

3. Students' own design of pictogram

Represent data in bar charts and line graphs

A. Draw a bar chart (p 369)

Bar charts may have either vertical or horizontal bars, and a variety of scales may be used. Refer to the fully worked solutions for examples.

1. a. Students' own charts
   b. i. pepperoni   ii. seafood
2. a. Students' own charts
   b. i. apple   ii. 7
3. a. Students' own charts
   b. France   c. i. 48   ii. 9

4. a. Students' own charts
   b. Adventure   c. Musical
   d. Adventure, Children's, Horror, Thriller, Comedy, Sci-fi, Musical
5. a. Students' own charts
   b. Most houses he supplies get 1 paper.
      As the number of papers increases, the number of houses decreases.
6. a. Students' own charts
   b. i. Daily Mail   ii. Daily Star
   c. Daily Mail, Sun, Guardian, Daily Mirror, Daily Telegraph, Daily Express, Times, Daily Star
7. a. Students' own charts
   b. i. UK   ii. Angola
   c. i. Life expectancy is greater for females than males in all countries.
      ii. Russia
   d. The UK, closely followed by the USA, have the best life expectancy for both males and females.
      Life expectancy is also reasonably good for both genders in China and Brazil.
      Life expectancy in Russia is reasonably good for females but poorer for males.
      Life expectancy for males is slightly better in India than Russia, but about 6 years worse for females.
      Life expectancy is poor for both males and females in Malawi and even worse in Angola, especially for males.
8. a.

Industry	Number of employees (thousands)		
	Male	Female	Total
Construction	2034	296	2330
Education	912	2324	3236
Health and social work	906	3356	4262
Manufacturing	2194	724	2918
Wholesale and retail	2277	1981	4258

   b. Students' own charts
   c. i. Health and social work (accept both Health and social work and Wholesale and retail).
      ii. Wholesale and retail
      iii. Health and social work
   d. Many more men than women are employed in Construction and Manufacturing.
      Many more women than men are employed in Education and Health and social work.
      Roughly the same number of men and women are employed in Wholesale and retail.

Answers

9.

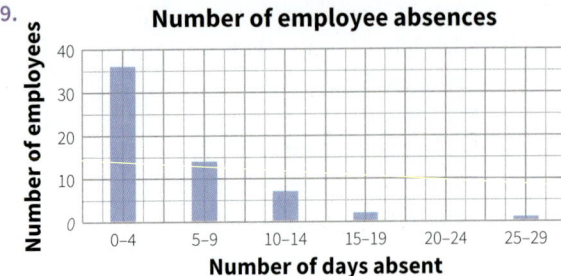

The bar chart shows the majority of employees had between 0 and 4 days of absence. Very few employees had more than 14 days of absence.

10.

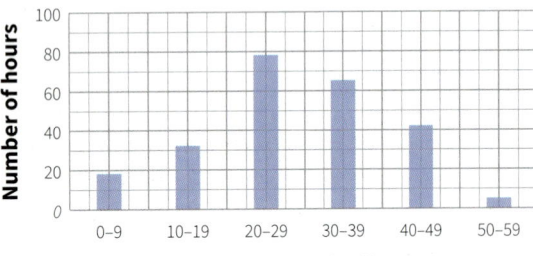

The bar chart shows that there are a few hours with only a few calls, also only very few hours with the largest number of calls. The majority of hours have between 20 and 39 calls.

11.

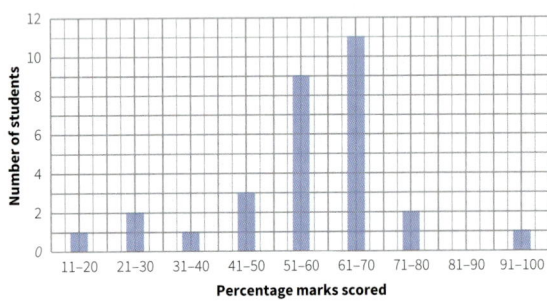

The bar chart shows that the majority of students scored between 51% and 70%.

12.

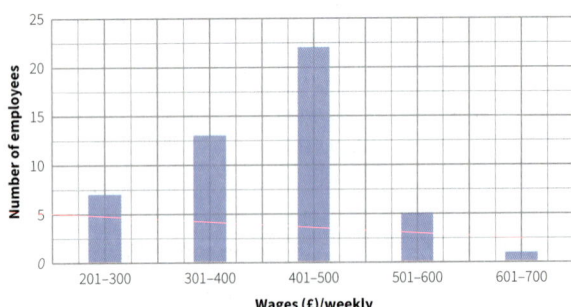

The bar chart shows that the majority of employees earn between £401 and £500 per week. A few employees earn the lowest wages (between £201 and £300 per week) and one employee earns over £600 per week.

B. Draw a line graph (p 373)

Line graphs may use a variety of scales. Refer to the fully worked solutions for examples.

1. a. Students' own graphs
   b. i. Week 8   ii. Week 2
      iii. Low at first, but increasing to 15 after 8 weeks. Decreased at the end.

2. a. Students' own graphs
   b. i. 50   ii. 180   iii. 300 (approx)
   c. i. 1998   ii. 2003   iii. 2014

3. a. Students' own graphs
   b. There were no lawnmowers sold in November, December and January, and few in February, because in the UK this is winter and the grass does not grow in winter temperatures. Sales showed a sharp peak in March and April, which is when grass starts to grow rapidly. Sales were medium in the summer months, when probably lower rainfall meant little growth, and possibly most people had already bought a lawnmower. Then sales showed a small peak in October which was possibly wet but still fairly warm (or there may have been discounted prices).

4. a. Students' own graphs
   b. i. 80 °C   ii. 69 °C   iii. 46 °C
   c. i. 25 min   ii. 39 min   iii. 56 min
   d. i. In the first 10 min   ii. Between 70 and 80 min
      iii. It will drop about 2 °C in the next 10 min and continue to fall gradually, eventually reach a constant temperature of about 25 °C (room temperature).

5. a. Students' own graphs
   b. 9:45 am, 12:15 pm, 1:35 pm, 3:15 pm
   c. 6 hours 50 minutes (allow ±10 min)
   d. Starts low at 8 am (before most of work begins), builds to peak of almost 90 dB at 11 am (peak time for morning work), then falls to 74 dB at 1 pm (lunchtime — less work going on) before rising again to about 84 dB between 2 pm and 3 pm (peak period for afternoon work). Finally falls to 54 dB at 5 pm (most of work finished for day).

6. a. Students' own graphs
   b. i. London Dec, Manchester Dec
      ii. London Feb, Manchester Feb
      iii. London — Jan, Nov, Dec
           Manchester — Dec
   c. i. Jan   ii. Jul
   d. Both sold a lot in January (sales) and in December (before Christmas). Both sold less in February (after the sales), but then sales rose during the spring with

London reaching a peak in June and Manchester in July. Sales at both shops dipped slightly in August. From September onwards the sales in London increased, whereas in Manchester sales didn't rise significantly until after October.

7. a. Students' own graphs
   b. E&W Jan, Dec
      Scot Jan, Feb, Mar, Dec
      NI Feb, Dec
   c. All low in winter months and high in summer, reaching a peak in August. Generally E&W has higher temperatures than NI, with Scotland the coolest. The only exception was in January when NI was warmer than E&W.
8. a. Students' own graphs
   b. approx $19\frac{1}{2}$ hours
   c. 5:20 am (approx)
9. a. Students' own graphs
   b. The number of speeding offences in Surrey and Sussex fluctuate, mostly between 50 000 and 70 000. But the number in Essex rises sharply from 30 000 to almost 100 000 in this period.
   c. The total volume of traffic in the areas should be considered. Other possible considerations include the number of speed cameras or mobile speed traps, areas with substantial roadworks, general congestion on roads.

Illustrate data using a pie chart (p 377)

Pie charts may arrange sections in a variety of different orders. Refer to the fully worked solutions for examples.

1. a. Students' own charts
   b. i. Fail   ii. Pass
2. a. 24   b. 15°
   c.

Lunch	Number of students	Angle
Sandwich	6	6 × 15 = 90°
Pasta	5	5 × 15 = 75°
Baked potato	8	8 × 15 = 120°
Salad	4	4 × 15 = 60°
Pizza	1	1 × 15 = 15°
Total	24	360°

   d. Students' own charts
3. a. Angles: 0 cars 90°, 1 car 155°, 2 or more cars 115°
      Students' own charts
   b. 1.   c. $\frac{1}{4}$
4. a. Angles: Europe 82°, N America 69°, S America 10°, Asia 196°, Other 3°
      Students' own charts
   b. Asia
5. a. Angles: Internet 190°, Cinema 6°, Radio 11°, TV 98°, Press 55°
      Students' own charts
   b. i. Internet   ii. more
      iii. Yes
6. a. Pop. angles   England 303°, NI 10°, Scotland 30°, Wales 17°
      Area angles   England 193°, NI 20°, Scotland 116°, Wales 31°
      Students' own charts
   b. England has over $\frac{3}{4}$ of the population but just over $\frac{1}{2}$ of the land area. Scotland has over $\frac{1}{4}$ of the land area but a much smaller proportion of the population. Wales and Northern Ireland also have a greater proportion of the land area than their population would suggest. This means that the population density in England is greater than in any of the other countries. Scotland is more sparsely populated than the other countries.

Draw and use conversion graphs (p 379)

1. a. Horizontal 0.2 inches, Vertical 0.5 cm
   b. Student's checks
   c. i. 6 in ≈ 15.2 cm
      ii. 9 in ≈ 22.9 cm
      iii. 2.6 in ≈ 6.6 cm
      iv. 4.3 in ≈ 10.9 cm
      v. 10 cm ≈ 3.9 in
      vi. 25 cm ≈ 9.8 in
      vii. 18 cm ≈ 7.1 in
      viii. 12.5 cm ≈ 4.9 in
      Allow ±0.5 cm and ±0.2 in
2. a. Students' own graphs
   b. i. 15 kg ≈ 33 lb   ii. 9 kg ≈ 19.8 lb
      iii. 12.5 kg ≈ 27.5 lb   iv. 30 lb ≈ 13.6 kg
      v. 14 lb ≈ 6.4 kg   vi. 38.5 lb ≈ 17.5 kg
      Allow ±1 lb and ±0.5 kg
3. a. Students' own graphs
   b. i. 5.5 or 5.6 gallons   ii. £48.60

Choosing a statistical diagram (p 381)

A variety of statistical diagrams could be used.
The best types for each question are given below.

1. Line graph (or bar chart)
   Students' own diagrams

Answers

The graph shows that the highest attendance was in August (perhaps because children were taken to the cinema in the school holidays).

The attendance was also quite high in July and February. The attendance was low in the spring (March and April) and also September.

2. Pie chart (or bar chart)
   Students' own diagrams
   Angles: Food 105°, Rent 115°, Transport 32°, Clothes 50°, Entertainment 36°, Other 22°
   Tracy spent over a quarter of her earnings on rent (the largest amount) and over a quarter on food.
   This left less than a half to be spent on transport, clothes, entertainment and other things.

3. Comparative bar chart (or component bar chart)
   Students' own diagrams
   Most of the readers of Car Buyer are men. Most of the readers of Gardeners' World are women. Hello! is by far the most popular magazine and vastly more women than men read it. Few people, both men and women, read Country Life.

4. Line graph (or bar chart)
   Students' own diagrams
   Many drink–drive accidents occur at night between 5 pm and 3 am, with the largest number occurring around midnight.
   Few drink–drive accidents occur between 7 am and 3 pm, with the lowest number occurring around 11 am.

5. Comparative bar chart or component bar chart.
   Students' own diagrams
   The biggest age group is 20–39 but almost as many employees are in the 40–59 age group. Very few of the employees are in the smallest age group which is 16–19. None of the 16–19 year-olds work in Deliveries. The number of employees aged 60 or over is about half as many as the number who are between 20 and 39 years old.
   More people work in Sales than in the Office or Deliveries. The biggest age group in both Sales and Deliveries is 20–39 but the biggest in the Office is 40–59. The smallest age group in all departments is 16–19.

6. Pie chart
   Angles: Need different size of house 108°, Personal 76°, To move to a better area 36°, Job-related reason 115°, Other 25°
   Students' own diagrams

7. Comparative bar chart
   Students' own diagrams
   The students had better results on Paper 1. The most common grade on Paper 1 was C, whilst on Paper 2 it was E. Also more students achieved grades A and C on Paper 1 whilst more got the low grades E and F on Paper 2. The same number of students achieved grade B and grade D on both papers.

8. Pie chart (or bar chart)
   Students' own diagrams
   Angles: Asia 215°, Africa 60°, Europe 35°, North America 17°, South America 31°, Oceania 2°
   Well over half of the world's population live in Asia. Only a very small number live in Oceania.

9. Component bar chart (or comparative bar chart)
   Students' own diagrams
   This shows clearly that the USA won more medals of each type than other countries, that China and GB were roughly on a par and Russia came fourth. The number of silver and bronze medals cannot be compared easily on this chart.
   A comparative bar chart with separate bars for gold, silver and bronze would also be suitable but it would not be so easy to compare total numbers of medals.

23 Averages and Range

Find the mean (p 384)

1. a. 1.8   b. 6   c. 6.6
   d. 4.25   e. 0.375 kg   f. £40
2. a. Andy 45, Imran 37, Mark 24, Stuart 28.75, Tim 39.75
   b. i. Andy   ii. Mark
3. a. £18.60
   b. No — nobody gets £18.60 per hour and it is distorted by the high wage of the manager.
4. a. 303   b. 189.6
5. a. Jen £11.00, Kim £10.50, Ben £14.50, Nasma £12.00, Mike £10.00, Wes £11.50
   b. £11.58   c. Ben, Nasma

(*Represent data in pictograms data*): (p 385)
1. 6.4 hours per day (1 dp)
2. 45 houses (nearest whole number)

(*Draw a bar chart data*): (p 385)
1. 12.8 pizzas (1 dp)   2. 22.8 trees (1 dp)
3. 39.5 properties   4. 190 films

(*Draw a line graph data*): (p 385)
1. 7.3 students
3. 21.2 (1 dp)
5. 72.8 dB

---

6. a. 20   b. 0.9 errors per page
7. a. 2.85 children per family   b. 10
8. a. 1.2 trains per day   b. 24%

9. **a.** 3 **b.** 18.1 years (1 dp)
10. **a.** **i.** 2 goals per match
    ii. 1.1 goals per match (1 dp)
    b. at home
11. **a.** 5.75 **b.** 33.5 **c.** £29.78
12. **a.** **i.** 51.9 **ii.** 52.5
    b. part **i.** is more accurate because the actual values are used to calculate the mean rather than the mid-points of a data set as in part **ii.**
13. **a.** 33.3 (1dp)
    b. 80% of 50 seeds = 40, so the claim is not true for those 60 packs.

(*Draw a bar chart data*): (p 389)
9. 5 days (nearest day)
10. 28 (or 29) calls (nearest whole number)

Find the mode and the median (p 391)

1. 'Best' average underlined (matter of opinion)
   Mean given to 1 dp when not exact
   a. mode = 1, median = 1, mean = 1.6 (pints)
   b. modes = 16, 17, median = 16.5, mean = 16.2
   c. mode = 18 years, median = 19 years, mean = 21.1 years
   d. mode = 28 minutes, median = 29 minutes, mean = 29.6 minutes
   e. no mode, median = 1.2 m, mean = 1.21 m

(*Find the mean data*): (p 391)
1. **a.** mode = 2, median = 2
   b. no mode, median = 5
   c. no mode, median = 6 years
   d. modes = 4, 5, median = 4.5
   e. modes = 0.36 kg, 0.41 kg, median = 0.375 kg
   f. mode £10, median £10
2. No modes as all the scores are different.
   Medians: Andy 32.5, Imran 43, Mark 24, Stuart 29, Tim 39
   The mean uses all the scores.

2. **a.** **i.** 4 years **ii.** 3 years **iii.** 3.05 years
   b. Median
3. **a.** **i.** 14 **ii.** 13 **iii.** 12.95
   b. Mode

(*Find the mean data*): (p 393)
Most appropriate averages given in brackets
3. mode, median both £12 per hour (mode, median)
6. mode = 0 errors, median = 1 error (median)
7. mode = 2 children, median = 2.5 children (mode)
8. mode = 1 train, median = 1 train (mode, median)
9. mode = 17 years, median = 18 years (mode, median)
10. home mode = 1 goal, median = 1.5 goals (mode)
    away   mode = 1 goal, median = 1 goal (mode, median)

4. **a.** **i.** 2 attempts **ii.** 1 attempt
   b. **i.** 2 attempts **ii.** 2 attempts
   c. **i.** 2.1 attempts **ii.** 1.85 attempts
   d. Those aged 20 or over — lower mean and mode

(*Draw a bar chart data*): (p 393)
5. mean = 1.7 (to 1 dp), mode = 1, median = 1
   mode and median – possible number of newspapers

Find the range (p 394)

1. **a.** apricots 18p, grapefruit 12p, peaches 33p, pineapple 9p
   b. **i.** Pineapple **ii.** Peaches
2. **a.** Alex   mean = 43.3   range = 83
       Chloe   mean = 44.5   range = 49
       Khadijah mean = 57   range = 75
       Paul   mean = 76.9   range = 115
       Rhona   mean = 66.5   range = 147
       Saif   mean = 59.1   range = 88
   b. Paul, highest mean
   c. Chloe, lowest range

(*Find the mean data*): (p 394)
1. **a.** 4 students **b.** 12 calls
   c. 11 years   **d.** 8 letters
   e. 0.09 kg   **f.** £240
2. Andy 109 runs, Imran 68 runs, Mark 26 runs, Stuart 23 runs, Tim 27 runs
3. £33 per hour
4. 198 tickets
5. £4.50 per hour

(*Find the mode and median data*): (p 394)
1. **a.** 6 pints   **b.** 6 students
   c. 16 years   **d.** 11 minutes
   e. 0.09 m

Answers

3. a. 77.9 minutes (1 dp) b. 120 minutes
4. a. 5 visits b. 3 visits
5. a. 19 students b. 5 students
6. a. 0.5 m b. 0.8 m
7. a. i. 7 years ii. 5 years
   b. i. 10 years ii. 11 years
   c. The boys' ages are more spread out than the girls' ages. On average the girls are older.

> (*Find the mean data*): (p 396)
> 6. 4 errors
> 7. 5 children
> 8. 4 late trains
> 9. 6 years
> 10. Home 6 goals, Away 4 goals
>
> (*Find the mode and median data*): (p 396)
> 2. 3 years
> 3. 12
> 4. 4 attempts for both age groups

8. a. i. 3 points ii. 5 points
      iii. 5.1 points (1 dp) iv. 6 points
   b. i. 3 points ii. 3 points
      iii. 3.8 points (1 dp) iv. 5 points
   c. On average the women were awarded fewer points and the points awarded to women were less variable.

Compare data sets (p 398)

1. Class A: Mode 4 Median 4 Mean 3.2(1dp) Range 5
   Class B: Mode 4 Median 4 Mean 3.5 Range 4
   The mode and the median are the same; the mean is slightly higher for Class B showing that on average they completed more assignments. The mean is the most appropriate average to use. Class B was also more consistent than Class A.
2. a. Ahmed: Mode none Median 37.5 Mean 42.6 Range 71
      Mark: Mode none Median 29   Mean 38.7 Range 92
   b. Ahmed, because both his median and mean average are higher and the range is lower, showing he scores more on average and his score is less variable.
3. Home: Mode 2 Median 2 Mean 2.3 Range 6
   Away: Mode 1 Median 1 Mean 1.4 Range 4
   All 3 averages show a higher average score for home matches. The number of goals scored was more variable in home matches.
4. Girls: Mode £5 Median £6.25 Mean £6.50 Range £4
   Boys: Mode £8 Median £7.75 Mean £7.25 Range £5
   All 3 averages are higher for boys, although the range shows there is a greater variation in the amount of pocket money they get.
5. a. Book A: Mode 4 Median 4 Mean 3.5 Range 7
      Book B: Mode 4 Median 4 Mean 4.1 Range 9
   b. Books A and B have the same mode and median, but the mean and range are higher for book B. It may therefore be harder to read because the words are on average longer and more variable.

24 Scatter diagrams

Scatter diagrams and correlation

A. Draw and interpret scatter diagrams (p 404)

Scatter graphs may use a variety of scales. Refer to the fully worked solutions for examples.

1. Students' own graphs.
   Fairly strong positive correlation — students who don't do very well on the first paper also get a poor mark on the second paper, and students who do well on the first paper also tend to get a good mark on the second paper.
2. Students' own graphs.
   Strong negative correlation — the larger the number of sunhats that are sold, the fewer the number of umbrellas that are sold and vice versa.
3. Students' own graphs.
   Strong positive correlation — when the petrol price is high, so is the diesel price and when the petrol price is low, so is the diesel price.
4. Students' own graphs.
   Weak negative correlation — the more time students spend watching TV, the less time they spend on social media, but the relationship is not very strong.
5. a. Students' own graphs.
      Strong, positive correlation — the bigger the engine size, the higher the carbon dioxide emissions.
   b. Students' own graphs.
      Weak positive correlation — the bigger the engine size, the higher the nitrous oxide emissions.
   c. Both carbon dioxide and nitrous oxide emissions increase with engine size, but the relationship is less strong for nitrous oxide than for carbon dioxide.
6. Students' own graphs.
   Strong positive correlation — the longer the distance the longer it takes to reach the resort.
7. a. i. Students' own graphs.
         Strong negative correlation — the greater the car's age, the lower the price.
      ii. Students' own graphs.
         Weak negative correlation — the greater the car mileage, the lower the price.
   b. The graphs suggest that Seth is correct — the car's age has more effect on the car's price than the mileage.

B. Draw and use lines of best fit (p 406)

1. **a.** 21 **b.** 54
2. Students' line of best fit
   a. 210 min (3 hours 30 mins) ± 10 mins
   b. 320 miles ± 10 miles
3. Students' line of best fit
   a. 1340 cm^3 ± 10 cm^3 **b.** 116 g per km ± 1 g per km
4. **a. i.** Students' own graphs
   ii. Fairly strong positive correlation.
   b. i. 39 cm (or close answer)
   ii. 16 or 17 cm (or close answer)
5. **a. i, ii** Students' own graphs
   b. In both cases there is negative correlation. This means that as the temperature increases the consumption of coal and gas decreases. The correlation of coal consumption with temperature is stronger than that of gas consumption with temperature, meaning that the relationship between coal consumption and temperature is stronger than that between gas consumption and temperature.
   c. Coal 3.1 million tonnes of oil equivalent
   Gas 7.5 million tonnes of oil equivalent

25 Probability

Compare the likelihood of events (p 408)

1. **a., e.** Students' own answers
   b. unlikely **c.** impossible **d.** certain
2. **a.** 2 **b.** 1 in 2
3. **a. i.** 1 in 5 **ii.** 2 in 5 **iii.** 3 in 5
   b. odd number
4. **a.** 52
   b. i. 4 in 52 (or 1 in 13)
   ii. 13 in 52 (or 1 in 4) **iii.** 1 in 52
5. **a.** 26
   b. i. 1 in 26 **ii.** 5 in 26 **iii.** 21 in 26

Use fractions to measure probability (p 410)

1. **a. i.** $\frac{1}{10}$ **ii.** $\frac{1}{2}$
   iii. $\frac{3}{5}$ **iv.** $\frac{3}{10}$
   b.

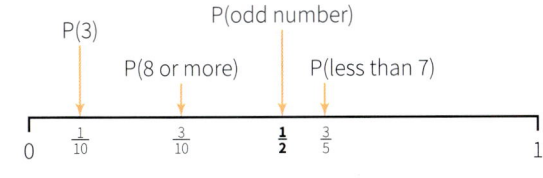

2. **a.** $\frac{1}{6}$ **b.** $\frac{1}{2}$ **c.** 0
   d. 1

3. **a. i.** $\frac{1}{5}$ **ii.** $\frac{2}{5}$ **iii.** $\frac{3}{5}$
   b.

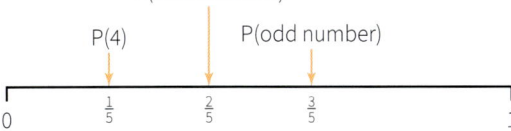

4. **a. i.** $\frac{1}{13}$ **ii.** $\frac{1}{4}$ **iii.** $\frac{1}{52}$ **iv.** $\frac{1}{2}$ **v.** $\frac{1}{26}$ **vi.** $\frac{2}{13}$
   b. the king of clubs, a red king, a king, a jack or queen, a club, a red card
5. **a. i.** $\frac{5}{8}$ **ii.** $\frac{1}{4}$ **iii.** $\frac{1}{8}$
   b.

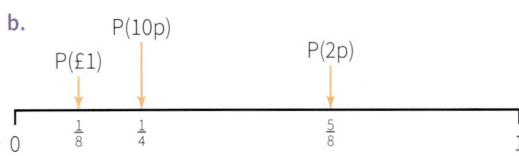

6. **a. i.** $\frac{1}{8}$ **ii.** $\frac{3}{8}$ **iii.** $\frac{7}{20}$ **iv.** $\frac{1}{4}$
   b. ii iii iv i

Write probabilities as decimals and percentages (p 412)

1. **a.** 10%, 0.1 **b.** 4%, 0.04 **c.** 50%, 0.5 **d.** 16%, 0.16
2. **a. i.** 50% **ii.** 12.5% **iii.** 37.5% **iv.** 62.5%
   b.

3. 0.2, 20%
4. **a.** $\frac{1}{366}$ **b.** $\frac{31}{366}$ **c.** $\frac{5}{61}$ **d.** $\frac{29}{366}$ **e.** $\frac{121}{366}$
5. **a. i.** $\frac{7}{25}$ or 0.28 or 28% **ii.** $\frac{9}{25}$ or 0.36 or 36%
   b. Sally is correct because there are 12 men and 13 women so P(man) = $\frac{12}{25}$ or 0.48 or 48% and P(woman) = $\frac{13}{25}$ or 0.52 or 52%. The probability of a woman being chosen is higher than that of a man being chosen.
6. **a. i.** $\frac{1}{4}$ **ii.** $\frac{1}{2}$
   b. i. 10 **ii.** 20
7. **a. i.** $\frac{1}{6}$ **ii.** $\frac{1}{2}$ **iii.** $\frac{1}{3}$
   b. i. 10 **ii** 30 **iii.** 20

Answers

8. a. Ball sports 76.0%, Combat sports 3.3%, Wheel sports 5.2%, Winter sports 3.2%, Animal sports 3.1%, Water sports 3.4%, Other 5.8%
   b. Far more hospital treatments are for injuries from ball sports than from any other type of sport.

Combined events
A. Identify possible outcomes of combined events (p 414)

1. a. Score on 1st dice

	1	2	3	4	5	6
1	2	3	4	5	6	7
2	3	4	5	6	7	8
3	4	5	6	7	8	9
4	5	6	7	8	9	10
5	6	7	8	9	10	11
6	7	8	9	10	11	12

    (Score on 2nd dice)

    b. 36
    c. $P(2) = \frac{1}{36}$, $P(3) = \frac{1}{18}$, $P(4) = \frac{1}{12}$, $P(5) = \frac{1}{9}$, $P(6) = \frac{5}{36}$, $P(7) = \frac{1}{6}$, $P(8) = \frac{5}{36}$, $P(9) = \frac{1}{9}$, $P(10) = \frac{1}{12}$, $P(11) = \frac{1}{18}$, $P(12) = \frac{1}{36}$
    d. 7

2. Score on 1st dice

	1	2	3	4	5	6
1	1	2	3	4	5	6
2	2	4	6	8	10	12
3	3	6	9	12	15	18
4	4	8	12	16	20	24
5	5	10	15	20	25	30
6	6	12	18	24	30	36

    (Score on 2nd dice)

    a. $\frac{1}{4}$ b. $\frac{3}{4}$

3. a.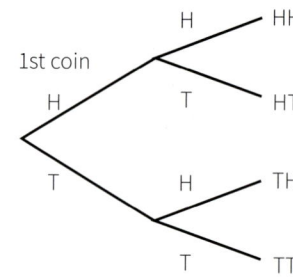

   b.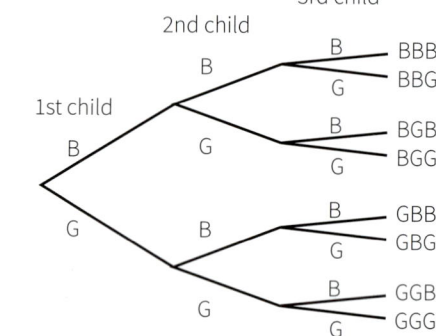

   c. i. $\frac{1}{4}$ ii. $\frac{1}{2}$

4.
   (tree diagram: 1st child, 2nd child, 3rd child → BBB, BBG, BGB, BGG, GBB, GBG, GGB, GGG)

5. a.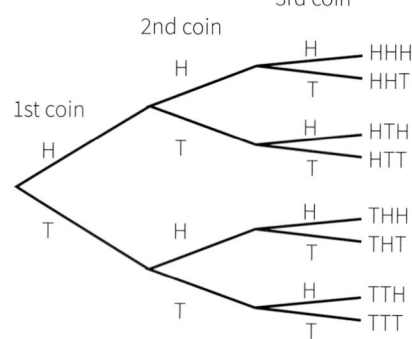

   b. i. $\frac{1}{8}$ ii. $\frac{3}{8}$

Answers

B. Calculate combined probability (p 416)

1. a.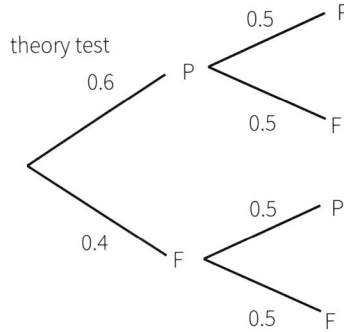

   b. i. 0.3 ii. 0.8

2. a.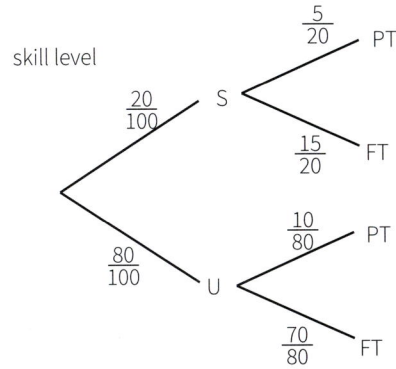

   b. i. $\frac{1}{10}$ (or 0.1 or 10%) ii. $\frac{17}{20}$ (or 0.85 or 85%)

3. a. 0.81 b. 0.01
4. a. 0.68 b. 0.29
5. a. i. $\frac{1}{4}$ ii. $\frac{1}{2}$
   b. i. $\frac{25}{102}$ ii. $\frac{26}{51}$

6. a.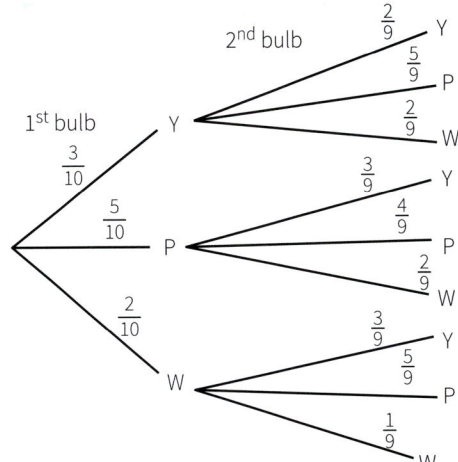

   b. i. $\frac{1}{15}$ ii. $\frac{14}{45}$ iii. $\frac{31}{45}$

7.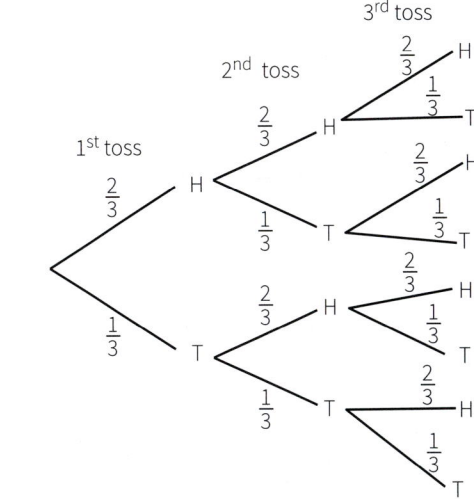

   P(more H than T) = $\frac{20}{27}$

8. P(test correct) = 0.94

Index

acceleration 74
acute angles 271, 272
addition 10–20
    column methods 10–12
    counting in 10s and 100s 2–3
    deciding whether to add or subtract 15–16
    decimals 131–2
    fractions 107–12
    in your head 12
    inverse of subtraction 14, 16
    large numbers 16–17
    time 198–202
    words for 10, 15
algebra 69–76
am/pm (time) 192
analogue/digital clocks 193–4, 203
angles 271–3, 274–5, 278–9
approximately equal sign 247, 362
approximations 43–54
    see also rounding
area
    of circles 316–17
    of composite shapes 318–21
    population density relationship 339–40
    of squares and rectangles 312–14
    surface area of solid shapes 323–4
    of triangles 317–18
arithmetical average see mean
averages 383–400
    advantages and disadvantages 390–1
    comparing data sets 395–9
    from frequency tables 386–9, 391–3
    mean 384–90, 397–9
    median 389–94
    mode 389–91
axes
    bar charts 347–8, 351, 368
    coordinates 301, 303–4, 305–6
    line graphs 354–7, 362

balance of bank accounts 6, 7, 53, 169, 171
bar charts 347–54, 368–72, 380
bearings 298–9
bias affecting probability 408, 415
billions 7–8
brackets in formulae 72
budgeting 173–6

calculators 77–84
    checking answers 16
    decimals 124–5
    fractions 115–16
    making errors 77

    memory 81, 82, 323
    money 163
    percentages 151–4
    scientific 35, 36, 73
cancelling to simplify fractions 102–3, 105, 107
capacity 250–64
    estimation 252
    imperial units 259–63
    metric/imperial conversion 262–3, 362
    metric units 250–9
Celsius 265–70
centilitres 256
centimetres
    calculating with 219–21
    converting 127, 217
    cubic 325, 336
    decimals 118, 120
    measuring with 209–15
    'of the correct order' 50, 52
    square 312
certain events 408, 409
chance see probability
checking answers
    are sensible 43, 47, 77, 81, 125
    estimation 47–8, 50–3
    reverse calculations 14, 16, 25–6, 53
circles 275, 315–17, 319
circumference of a circle 315–16, 319
clocks 193–7, 203
    see also time; timers
clockwise and anticlockwise 295, 298
column methods for calculations 10–12, 13–14, 22, 23, 37, 131
combined events, probability 413–17
commission on currency conversion 190
common denominators 92–3, 108
comparative bar charts 352–3, 380
compass points 295–8
component bar charts 352–3, 380
compound measures 334–40
cones 324, 329
continuous data 353
conversion graphs 362–3, 378–9
coordinates 301–7
correlation, scatter diagrams 401–7
costs see prices
counting in 10s and 100s 2–3
credit 83
cubes and cuboids 284, 325–7
cubes/cube roots of numbers 35–6
cumulative frequency 397
currency conversion 188–90
cylinders 284, 323, 327–8

Index

data handling
    averages and range 383–400
    collecting and illustrating 365–83
    comparing data sets 395–9
    extracting and interpreting information 341–64, 401–7
    frequency tables 386–9, 391–3
    probability 408–17
    representation 346–64, 367–83
    types 353
data tables 340, 343–5, 409, 412, 413
debit 83
deciding digit when rounding 48, 49, 128
decimal places 119, 121
decimals 118–38
    adding and subtracting 131–2
    decimal point 118
    division 126–7, 135–7
    estimation 128–30
    fraction conversion 121, 122, 123, 148–9
    measurement 118–19, 120–1
    money 119–20, 121, 161
    multiplication 126–7, 134–5
    percentage conversion 146, 148, 155
    probability 411–13
    sequences 132–3
degrees
    angles 271–2
    bearings 298–9
    temperature 265–70
denominators of fractions 85, 88, 91, 92–3
density of objects 336–7
density of populations 338–40
difference *see* subtraction
digits 1, 2
dimensions of shapes 225, 311, 327, 330
directions *see* positions and directions
direct proportion 56–7
discounts, percentage change in cost 150–2, 158, 167–9
discrete data 353, 371
distance
    measurement 207–8
    speed and time relationships 74, 334–6
    see also length
division
    by 10s 30–1
    decimals 126–7, 135–7
    fractions 113–15
    inverse of multiplication 24, 25
    in your head 30–1
    large numbers 30–1, 38, 41
    methods 24–8
    money 164
    words for 24
divisor lines 74, 76

earnings
    budgeting 175–6
    calculating pay rates 177–80
    pension contributions 185, 186–7
    percentage changes 150, 151, 177–80, 184
    taxes 184–8
elevations and plans 285–93
equilateral triangles 277, 278
equivalent fractions 88–90
estimation 43–54
    angles 272, 273
    capacity 252
    checking answers 47–8, 50–3
    decimals 128–30
    fractions 96–7, 99–100, 105–6
    from bar charts 349
    from line graphs 355
    from pie charts 359
    large numbers 48–53
    length 214–16
    mean of grouped frequency tables 388–9
    percentages 157–8
    rounding 44–6, 48–50, 128–30, 165–6
    uses 43–4
    weight 238–9

factors 39–40
Fahrenheit 268–70
feet (imperial) 228–33
flow charts 71, 72, 73
fluid ounces 259–63
foreign currency 188–90
formulae 69–76
fractions 85–117
    adding and subtracting 107–12
    calculators 115–16
    comparing 91–4
    decimal conversion 121, 122, 123, 148–9
    dividing 113–15
    equivalent 88–90
    estimating 96–7, 99–100, 105–6
    finding 96–7, 98–100
    improper 94–5, 109–12
    mixed numbers 94–5, 109–12
    multiplying 112–13
    of numbers 97–100
    percentage conversion 140, 147–9, 155
    probability 409–11
    quantities 103–4
    scaling 101–2
    simplest form 102–3, 105, 107
    time 199
    unit fractions 85, 91
fraction walls 91–2

Index

freezing point of water 266
frequency on bar charts 348, 352, 371
frequency tables 365–8, 386–9, 391–3, 395, 397

gallons 259–63
gas mark temperatures 268
grams 127, 235–44
graphs
    conversion graphs 362–3, 378–9
    coordinates 301–4
    line graphs 354–7, 373–5
    scatter diagrams 401, 403, 406
'greater than' symbol 6
grid method of multiplication 37
grid references 300, 304–5
gross pay 184, 185–8
grouped discrete data 371
grouped frequency tables 366–7, 388–9

hexagons 275
horizontal lines 273
household budgeting 175–6
hundreds 1, 2, 3, 10, 13
hundredths 119–20
    see also percentages

imperial units
    capacity 259–63, 362
    length 207, 228–33, 379
    speed 336
    weight 244–8
impossible events 408, 409
improper fractions 94–5, 109–12
inches 228–33, 379
income tax 184–5, 186, 187
independent events 413–14
indices (powers) 34–6, 72
information
    collecting and using data 365–83
    data analysis 383–417
    extracting and interpreting 341–64
    lists 341–2
    representation 346–64, 367–83
    tables 340, 343–5
interest 169–72
internet use 188, 342, 345, 380, 382
inverse operations 14, 16, 24, 25
inverse proportion 65–6
isometric diagrams 292
isosceles triangles 277, 278

keys, data representation 346, 350, 356, 358, 367
kilograms 127, 235–44, 253
kilometres 130, 207, 208, 217, 231–3

large numbers 4–8
    adding and subtracting 16–17, 19–20
    comparing 7–8
    dividing 30–1, 38, 41
    estimation 48–53
    multiplying 38, 41
    negative 8
    place value 4–5
length 207–34
    calculations 219–21
    estimation 214–16
    imperial/metric conversion 231–3, 379
    imperial units 207–8, 228–33
    measuring methods 214
    metric units 209–14
    perimeters 309–11, 315–16, 319
    scale plans and maps 222–8
'less than' symbol 6
likelihood of events 408
line graphs 354–7, 373–5
lines of best fit 401, 404, 406
lines of symmetry 280–2
lists 341–2
litres 55, 61, 79, 250–9

maps
    distances on 207, 224–5
    giving directions 296–8
    grid references 304–5
    location squares 300
    scales 61, 62, 224–5
mass
    volume and density relationship 336–7
    see also weight
mean 384–90, 397–9
measurement 118
    capacity 250–64
    distances 207, 224–5
    length 118–19, 207–34
    temperature 265–70
    weight 235–49
median 389–94
memory on calculators 81, 82, 323
mental arithmetic (in your head) 12, 15, 28–9, 30, 32, 41
metres 120, 127, 212–14, 217, 219–21
miles 207–8, 229–30, 231–3
milligrams 235, 401
millilitres 55, 61, 250–9
millimetres 209–12, 214, 219–20
millions 4–5, 7–8
mirror line see symmetry
mixed numbers 94–5, 109–12
mode 389–91

472

Index

money 161–91
    adding and subtracting 162–3
    budgeting 173–6
    calculators 163
    currency conversion 188–90
    decimals 119–20, 161
    interest 169–72
    multiplying and dividing 164
    percentage changes 150–4, 158–9, 167–9
    rates of pay 150, 151, 177–80, 184
    rounding 165–6
    taxes on income 184–8
    VAT 143, 153, 154, 159, 180–4
multiples 34, 39–40, 69
multiplication 21–42
    by 10s 21, 28–9, 32
    column methods 22, 23, 37
    decimals 126–7, 134–5
    fractions 112–13
    as inverse of division 24, 25
    in your head 28–9
    large numbers 38, 41
    methods 21–4, 37
    money 164
    times tables 21, 24, 31
    words for 21

National Insurance 185, 186, 187
negative coordinates 303–4
negative correlation 401, 402
negative numbers 6–7, 8, 17–18, 19–20, 82–3
net pay (take home pay) 184, 185–8
nets of three-dimensional shapes 321–2
non-zero starting point on axes 531
number patterns/relationships 33–4, 69, 132–3
number values 1–9
numerators of fractions 85, 88, 91

obtuse angles 271, 272
octagons 275
ordering fractions 92–3, 95
ordering numbers 2, 5, 7, 8, 123–4
order of operations (BIDMAS) 72–3
origin of graphs 301
ounces 244–8
    see also fluid ounces
outcomes, probability 409, 413, 415
oven temperatures 268–9
overtime payments 177, 180

parallel lines 274–5, 290
parallelograms 275–6, 319
pay see earnings
pension contributions 185, 186–7
pentagons 275

per annum (finance) 169–71, 184–6, 199
percentages 139–60
    calculators 151–4
    decimal conversion 146, 148, 155
    discounts 150–2, 158, 167–9
    estimation 157–8
    fraction conversion 140, 147–9, 155
    increase and decrease 150–2, 156, 158–9, 167–9
    interest 169–72
    one number as percentage of another 155–8
    probability 411–13
    of quantities 140–1
    reverse percentages 158–9
    taxes on income 184–8
    using 1% 144–5
    using 10% 142–4
    VAT charges 143, 153, 154, 159, 180–4
perimeters of shapes 309–11, 315–16, 318–21
perpendicular lines 271, 290
personal allowances for tax 184, 185, 186
pi (π) 315–16, 323, 327–8, 329
pictograms 346, 367–8
pie charts 358–61, 376–7, 380
pints 259–63
place value 1–2, 4–5, 122, 164
plans drawn to scale 222–8
plans and elevations 285–93
polygons 271, 275–9
population density 338–40
positions and directions 295–308
    bearings 298–9
    compass points 295–8
    coordinates 301–4
    grid references 304–5
    maps 296–8, 300, 304–5
    three-dimensional coordinates 305–7
    turning 271, 280, 295
positive coordinates 301–3
positive and negative numbers 6–7, 8, 17–18, 19–20
possible outcomes, probability 408–9, 413–14, 415
pounds (money) see money
pounds (weight) 244–8
powers (indices) 34–6, 72
prices
    comparisons 64–5, 79–81, 120
    percentage increase/decrease 150–4, 156, 158–9
    see also money; VAT
prime numbers 39
prisms 284, 290, 321, 328
probability 408–17
    bias affecting 408, 415
    combined events 413–17
    decimals/percentages 411–13
    fractions 409–11
    possible outcomes 408–9, 413–14, 415

473

Index

product *see* multiplication
profit and loss 8, 19–20
proportion 56–7, 65–6, 376–7
protractors 271–2, 359
pyramids 284, 321, 329

quadrilaterals 275
qualitative/quantitative data 353

radius of circles 315–17
ranges of data sets 393–9
ratios 55–68, 225–8
rectangles 275, 311–14
reflection *see* symmetry
regular shapes 275
remainders of division 24, 25, 26, 38, 79, 84
reverse calculations 14, 16, 25–6
reverse percentages 158–9
rhombus 275
right-angled triangles 277, 278
right angles 271, 275
roots of numbers 35, 36
rotational symmetry 280–2
rounding
    deciding digit 48, 49, 128
    decimals 128–30
    money 165–6
    numbers 44–6, 48–50

scalene triangles 277, 278
scales
    bar charts 347, 348, 351, 368–9, 373, 378
    graphs 362, 373, 378, 401, 402
    maps and drawings 61–2, 222–8, 289–92
    weighing 236–40
scaling up and down, fractions 101–2
scatter diagrams 401–7
scientific calculators 35, 36, 73
sequences 33–4, 69, 132–3
shapes 271–94
    angles 271–5
    areas 312–14, 316–21, 323–4
    circles 275, 315–17
    coordinates 301
    perimeters 309–11, 315–16, 319
    plans and elevations 285–93
    rectangles 275, 311–14
    tessellation 283
    three-dimensional shapes 283–92
    triangles 275, 277–8, 317–18
    two-dimensional shapes 275–83
    volumes 325–9
shares *see* division
simplest form of fractions 102–3, 105, 107
simplification of ratios 58–60

speed 334–6
spheres 284, 329
square-based pyramids 284, 321, 329
square numbers and square roots 34–5
squares (shape) 275
square units of measurement 312
statistical diagrams 346–64, 367–83
stones (weight) 244–8
subtraction 10, 13–20
    column methods 13–14
    counting in 10s 2–3
    counting in 100s 2–3
    deciding whether to add or subtract 15–16
    decimals 131–2
    fractions 107–12
    inverse of addition 14, 16
    in your head 15
    large numbers 16–17
    time 200, 202–3
    words for 13, 15
sum *see* addition
surface area of shapes 323–4
symmetry 280–2

tables
    frequency 365–8, 386–9, 391–3, 395, 397
    information/data 340, 343–5
    multiplication 21, 24, 31
take away *see* subtraction
take-home pay (net pay) 175–6, 184, 185–8
tally charts 365, 366
taxes 143, 153, 154, 159, 180–8
telling the time 192–4
temperature 6–7, 17–18, 265–70, 362
tens 1, 2–3, 10, 13
tenths 85, 92, 118–19, 121, 142–4
tessellation 283
thermometers 265–6, 268
thousands 4–5
three-dimensional shapes 283–92
    nets 321–2
    surface area 323–4
    volumes 325–9
time 192–206
    12 hour/24 hour clock 194–7
    calculations 198–203
    read/measure/record 192–4
    speed and distance relationship 334–6
    units 198–9
timers 203–5
times *see* multiplication
timetables 194, 196–7
tonnes (metric) 240, 244, 245
tons (imperial) 245
trapezium 275, 318, 319

Index

tree diagrams, probability 414–17
triangles 275, 277–8, 317–18
turning 271, 280, 295
two-dimensional shapes 275–83
    area 312–14, 316–21
    perimeters 309–11, 315–16, 318–9

unitary method for proportion 66
unit conversion
    graphs 362–3, 378–80
    imperial 207, 229–30, 244–6, 260–1
    metric 61, 217–18, 240–1, 247–8, 255–6
    metric/imperial 262–3, 362, 379
unit fractions 85, 91
units (number) 1, 10, 13

value for money 64–5
value (place values) 1–2, 4–5, 122, 164
VAT (Value Added Tax) 143, 153, 154, 159, 180–4
vertical lines 273

volume 250–64
    cuboids 325–7
    cylinders 327–8
    mass and density relationship 336–7
    three-dimensional shapes 325–9
    see also capacity

weight
    calculations 242–4
    estimation 238–9
    imperial units 244–8
    instruments 240
    mass relationship 336
    metric/imperial conversion 247–8
    metric units 235–9

x and y axes of graphs 301, 303, 305–6

yards 228–33

z axis of 3D graphs 305–6